THESE UNITED STATES

A NATION IN THE MAKING

1945 TO THE PRESENT

PHYSICAL/POLITICAL MAP
OF THE
UNITED STATES

THESE

A NATION IN THE MAKING

UNITED

1945 TO THE PRESENT

STATES

GLENDA ELIZABETH GILMORE
THOMAS J. SUGRUE

W. W. Norton & Company
New York • London

W. W. NORTON & COMPANY has been independent since its founding in 1923, when William Warder Norton and Mary D. Herter Norton first published lectures delivered at the People's Institute, the adult education division of New York City's Cooper Union. The firm soon expanded its program beyond the Institute, publishing books by celebrated academics from America and abroad. By midcentury, the two major pillars of Norton's publishing program—trade books and college texts—were firmly established. In the 1950s, the Norton family transferred control of the company to its employees, and today—with a staff of four hundred and a comparable number of trade, college, and professional titles published each year—W. W. Norton & Company stands as the largest and oldest publishing house owned wholly by its employees.

Editor: Steve Forman
Associate Editors: Justin Cahill and Scott Sugarman
Editorial Assistant: Travis Carr
Manuscript Editor: Janet Biehl
Managing Editor, College: Marian Johnson
Managing Editor, College Digital Media: Kim Yi
Production Manager: Ashley Horna
Media Editor: Laura Wilk
Media Project Editor: Penelope Lin
Marketing Manager: Sarah England
Design Director: Jillian Burr
Photo Editor: Stephanie Romeo

Frontispiece image: On the march for voting rights from Selma to Montgomery, March 23, 1965, Lowndes County, Alabama.

The Library of Congress has cataloged the earlier edition as follows:
Gilmore, Glenda Elizabeth, author.
These United States : a nation in the making, 1890 to the present /
Glenda Elizabeth Gilmore, Thomas J. Sugrue. — First edition.
        pages cm
Includes bibliographical references and index.
ISBN 978-0-393-23952-2 (hardcover)
1. United States—History—20th century. 2. United States—History—1865–1898.
I. Sugrue, Thomas J., 1962– author. II. Title.
E741.G56 2015
973.9—dc23

                                                      2015019091

This edition: ISBN 978-0-393-28307-5

W. W. Norton & Company, Inc., 500 Fifth Avenue, New York, NY 10110
wwnorton.com

W. W. Norton & Company Ltd., Castle House, 75/76 Wells Street, London W1T 3QT

For Ben, my *anam cara*

For Brittany

ABOUT THE AUTHORS

 **Glenda Elizabeth Gilmore** is the Peter V. and C. Vann Woodward Professor of History at Yale University. She focuses on the American South, specializing in African American and women's history and twentieth-century U.S. politics. She earned her Ph.D. at the University of North Carolina at Chapel Hill in 1992. Her most recent book, *Defying Dixie: The Radical Roots of Civil Rights, 1919–1950*, was one of the American Library Association's Notable Books of 2008 and one of the *Washington Post*'s Best Books of 2008. She is the editor of *Who Were the Progressives?* (2002) and co-editor of *Jumpin' Jim Crow: Southern Politics from Civil War to Civil Rights* (2000). Her first book, *Gender and Jim Crow: Women and the Politics of White Supremacy in North Carolina, 1896–1920* (1996), won the Organization of American Historians' Frederick Jackson Turner Award, the OAH's James A. Rawley Prize, and the Southern Association for Women Historians' Julia Cherry Spruill Prize.

 **Thomas J. Sugrue** is Professor of History and Social and Cultural Analysis at New York University. A specialist in twentieth-century U.S. politics, urban history, civil rights, and race, Sugrue was educated at Columbia University, King's College, Cambridge, and Harvard University, where he earned his Ph.D. in 1992. He is author of *Not Even Past: Barack Obama and the Burden of Race* (2010) and *Sweet Land of Liberty: The Forgotten Struggle for Civil Rights in the North*, a finalist for the 2008 *Los Angeles Times* Book Prize. His first book, *The Origins of the Urban Crisis* (1996), won the Bancroft Prize in American History, the Philip Taft Prize in Labor History, the President's Book Award of the Social Science History Association, and the Urban History Association Award for Best Book in North American Urban History.

"I do not look upon these United States
as a finished product. We are still in the making."

————

FRANKLIN DELANO ROOSEVELT, 1936

CONTENTS

Chapter 1
A Rising Superpower, 1944–1954   1

MAPS AND FIGURES

PREFACE

"WE ARE STILL IN THE MAKING"

The thirty-second president of the United States, Franklin Delano Roosevelt, spoke on the radio from his childhood home at Hyde Park, New York, on February 23, 1936. It was Brotherhood Day, an event sponsored by the National Conference of Christians and Jews as a time for Americans to honor their common interests and values. "I am happy to speak to you from my own home on the evening of a Sabbath Day," the president told a nation shivering in single-digit temperatures over much of its expanse. His voice warmed them. "I like to think of our country as one home in which the interests of each member are bound up with the happiness of all." He assured his listeners, who had endured years of economic hardship, that they would not be abandoned: "the welfare of your family or mine cannot be bought at the sacrifice of our neighbor's family . . . our wellbeing depends, in the long run, upon the wellbeing of our neighbors." With public confidence at a low ebb, FDR promised that the government would act to restore prosperity. "I do not look upon these United States as a finished product," he told his audience. "We are still in the making."[1]

It is safe to say that most of the nation was listening that night, since Roosevelt regularly captured an audience of up to 70 percent of Americans when he spoke in his intimate fashion to them. Saul Bellow, the novelist, recalled an occasion when he was "walking eastward on the Chicago Midway on a summer evening. . . . drivers had pulled over, parking bumper to bumper, and turned on their radios to hear Roosevelt. They had rolled down the windows and opened the car doors. Everywhere the same voice, its odd Eastern accent. . . . You could follow without missing a single word as you strolled by."[2]

✳

From the depths of the Depression, Roosevelt and his listeners could see that the American dream of expanding opportunity was not the inevitable result of markets and elections. It took work, legislation, organization, and planning to build a strong democracy. The twentieth century as a whole, however, permits different perspectives on the dynamics of American democracy. From the Progressive era to the Great Society, with the exception of the Great Depression, the United States established a solid, prosperous middle class that perpetuated its ability to make life better for each succeeding generation. By the 1950s, many observers considered it inevitable that this achievable dream would extend to almost all Americans. Poverty would diminish, affordable educational institutions would flourish, and social conflict would become a vestige of the past.

But this was not to be. *These United States* starts and ends in periods of massive inequality. Experts conclude that the arc of inequality in the United States over the long twentieth century resembles an upside-down bell curve: the maldistribution of income starts out high in the 1890s, dips in the midcentury, and begins rising again in the 1970s.[3] In 1900, the top 10 percent of earners took home about 41 percent of the nation's income. The figure rose to a high of 45 percent in 1930, but the Great Depression, New Deal measures, and the economic leveling of World War II reduced the top decile's share to 33 percent in 1950, where it stayed for the next twenty years.[4]

Contemporary economists predicted that this equalization of income would continue. They attributed the maldistribution of income and wealth at the beginning of the century to the shock of rapid industrialization in the United States. In the 1950s and 1960s, they reasoned, the mature industrial economy would deliver consistent growth, which would in turn ameliorate income disparities and expand the middle class. The American dream would inexorably unfold.[5] In the immediate post–World War II decades, the country seemed on track to fulfill their rosy predictions.

Instead, income inequality began to grow after 1970. The top 10 percent, who took home 34 percent of the wages in 1970, collected almost 48 percent in 2010, a higher share than at any time in the twentieth century. The strong middle class built during the midcentury period began to weaken after 1970, as the percentage of wages claimed by the top 10 percent rose by a steady 5 percent per year through the end of the century.[6] The share of wages claimed by the top 1 percent of earners is even more striking: 18 percent in 1910, 8 percent in 1970, and 18 percent in 2010.[7]

Many of those who listened to FDR over the radio in February 1936 had lost their homes; others had saved them through New Deal programs such as the Home Owners' Loan Corporation or the Emergency Farm Mortgage Act. Their children would purchase homes through Veterans Administration loans or with help from the Federal Housing Administration. Some of their great-grandchildren would lose their homes in the 14 million foreclosures that took place during the Great Recession of 2007–2009.[8] The twentieth-century history of the United States raises the question of whether the American dream of an expanding middle class was a historical accident, the contingent result of an industrial nation coming of age, the growth of a federal social safety net, and the spending on the military-industrial complex that began in World War II.

Roughly one out of every ten people who listened to Roosevelt that night was African American. Since they occupied the lowest-paying jobs, the Great Depression hit black Americans harder overall than white Americans. Seven months after FDR's speech, they would abandon the Republican Party en masse to vote for the Democrats' New Deal. *These United States* opens in the 1890s as African Americans mount a vigorous movement to fight Jim Crow segregation and the loss of the voting rights that Reconstruction had guaranteed them. The book ends with an African American in his second term as president. During his first run for the presidency in 2008, on the anniversary of Martin Luther King, Jr.'s, death, Senator Barack Obama quoted King, himself paraphrasing a white abolitionist in 1853: "the

arc of the moral universe is long, but it bends towards justice." Obama added, in an echo of FDR, "But here is the thing; it does not bend on its own. It bends because each of us in our own ways put our hand on the arc and we bend it in the direction of justice."[9]

From Jim Crow to Ferguson, *These United States* chronicles African Americans with their "hand[s] on the arc." A long civil rights movement spans our pages. We meet a young black woman, Ida B. Wells, handing out brochures in protest of African Americans' exclusion from the nation's 1893 World's Columbian Exposition; a young couple, William and Daisy Myers, facing jeering white protesters as they integrated Levittown, Pennsylvania, in 1957; and John Lewis, the son of sharecroppers, in a Nashville jail cell in 1960, speaking from the rostrum at the presidential inauguration in 2009. Like an expanding middle class, the drive for racial equality gives us another measure of America's success in developing a strong democracy across the twentieth century. In *These United States*, we present African American history not as a separate story but as American history itself.

The long twentieth century was also pivotal for this nation of immigrants. Debates over immigration policy consumed voters and elected officials repeatedly over the century. Politics, prejudice, and labor demands usually drove these debates, which often flared into violence. Anti-Chinese actions in the West culminated in exclusion laws once the foundation for the nation's railroads had been laid. And when fears of immigrant radicalism outweighed the need for unskilled labor, Congress adopted laws to curb immigration from southern and eastern Europe in 1924. During the 1930s, the government limited Mexican immigration, but when it needed workers during World War II and into the 1960s, authorities brought them into the country through the bracero program. In 1965 immigration reform lifted the 1924 quotas and led to a strong increase in newcomers from Latin America, the Caribbean, and Asia. By 1990, 20 million legal immigrants lived in the United States. Millions more came without documentation. In 1990 the United States removed 30,039 "inadmissible or deported aliens" from the country. By 2000, that number had grown to 188,467; by 2010, it reached 383,031.[10] In a rapidly globalizing world, citizenship issues and immigration policies continue to divide communities and political parties.

By the time FDR spoke on Brotherhood Day, Eleanor Roosevelt was the "foremost political woman in the United States."[11] Twenty-five years earlier, her husband's endorsement of woman suffrage had surprised her. She believed that women could implement social change without the ballot. After women won the right to vote in 1920, she became a politician in her own right. By 1980, women who reported voting outnumbered men by 6.4 million. By 2012, that gap had grown to 10.3 million.[12] Through traditional party politics and social movements, women expanded American democracy over the long twentieth century.

The patterns of women's work also changed over the period. When *These United States* opens, most Americans, including many women, thought that working women took jobs away from men who needed to support entire families. This idea of the "family wage" and the lone male breadwinner eroded over the century. The female component of the labor force, 17 percent in 1890, grew to 47 percent in 2010.[13] During World War II and afterward, women organized to improve working conditions, increase their wages, and get the support that they needed to raise families while bringing home paychecks. In the 1940s a young labor journalist, Betty Friedan, argued that unionization would provide economic security for women workers, and in the 1960s she helped found the National Organization for Women to push for equal pay for equal work and to prevent discrimination by sex in the workplace. There has been progress on this front, though a gap remains still to close: in 1979 women working full time earned 62 percent of men's earnings; in 2012 they earned 81 percent.[14]

Other women activists called for a stronger safety net to help young mothers stay at home and raise their children, and they fought against stereotypes, proffered by the New Right, that they were nothing but "welfare queens." Beginning in the 1970s, feminist activists calling for women's reproductive freedom faced a formidable challenge from other women who argued for the preservation of the "traditional family." The struggle over family, morality, and sexuality shaped everyday life and national politics in the last quarter of the twentieth century and beyond.

Most of Roosevelt's 1936 listeners looked to the New Deal—and hence to the federal government—for access to their country's political, economic, and social promise. They grappled, as we do, with the responsibility of the government to its people. In 1890 the federal government was small, with unenforceable antitrust regulations. The Progressive era and the New Deal expanded the role of the federal government, which now acted to regulate commerce, support decent working conditions and workers' rights, and build programs such as Social Security to protect people from hardship. By midcentury, the federal government had the tools to manage the economy and regulate financial institutions.

During the post–World War II years, as federal regulation and the sheer size of government grew, a well-funded and well-organized conservative insurgency rose to challenge the New Deal state and liberalism. Business leaders like General Electric's Lemuel Boulware and his spokesman, actor Ronald Reagan, celebrated free enterprise and argued that social welfare sapped Americans' work ethic, while regulation and taxation endangered individual liberty. They were joined by a growing group of religious conservatives who saw godliness as the antidote to Communism. Opponents of civil rights joined the cause, on the grounds that antidiscrimination laws represented government intrusion into individual rights to freedom of association.

By the 1960s, that New Right had become a major insurgent movement within the Republican Party. Fueled by opposition to urban riots and black power in the

1960s and by growing unease at new norms regarding personal sexuality unleashed by the liberation movements of the period, the New Right gained adherents. By the late 1970s and 1980s, those insurgents pushed aside moderate Republicans, turning the GOP rightward and leading many Democrats to reinvent liberalism. Democratic and Republican presidents embraced deregulation, arguing that government rules on food production, air traffic control, banking, and home mortgage lending impeded competition and growth. Ronald Reagan promoted supply-side economics on the theory that cutting taxes and regulatory controls would increase corporate profits, which would "trickle down" to poor and middle-class Americans. By the end of the century, the mainstream of the Democratic Party had accepted much of the conservative critique of the New Deal and called for less government and lower taxes, although they held their ground on the questions of reproductive rights and individual liberties. Ideological arguments hardened, producing a weaker state, less effective commercial regulation, a frayed social safety net, and deeper inequality.

Less than two weeks after FDR's Brotherhood Day address, Adolf Hitler ordered German troops into the Rhineland, violating the terms of the Versailles Treaty that had ended World War I. The U.S. Congress, dominated by isolationist sentiment, passed a series of neutrality acts designed to keep the nation out of developing conflicts. Differences over the nation's interests abroad have buffeted American foreign policy since 1898, when the Spanish-American War raised issues of interventions in foreign conflicts. Indeed, after 1914, as war spread through Europe, many Americans opposed U.S. intervention for the sake of markets or empire. President Woodrow Wilson changed the tenor of that debate by asserting the U.S. responsibility to "make the world safe for democracy." In 1917 he used this sense of mission to persuade a reluctant public to enter the war. After the Central Powers' defeat, the isolationists in Congress refused to accept Wilson's global mission and declined to join the League of Nations. Isolationism kept the country from intervening against Nazi aggression until the Japanese attack at Pearl Harbor in 1941. The last war's lessons often overshadow the realities of later confrontations.

The American troops who achieved victory in World War II believed that they were indeed making the world safe for democracy. After the "good war," the founding of the United Nations, the successful occupation of Japan, and the rebuilding of Europe, most Americans believed that they had a duty actively to export democracy, in part to ensure national security. This belief in triumphant democracy infused Americans with the will to challenge the USSR throughout the Cold War. The Korean conflict and the Vietnam War represented tangible commitments to that belief: U.S. security depended, many thought, upon stopping Communism in far-flung nations. During the Vietnam War, massive resistance at home grew and even spread to the military itself, forcing President Richard Nixon to announce a program of Vietnamization of the war and simultaneously a pullout of American troops. The loss in Vietnam brought to the forefront questions not only about the country's purpose but also about its ability to perpetuate its global power. Conversely, the 1991 fall of the Soviet Union inspired new hope that the United States could proceed to democratize the world.

Our current debates are driven by the legacies of decades of intervention in the Middle East. From Eisenhower's decision to back a coup in Iran in 1953 to the oil crises after the Yom Kippur War of 1973, the United States has been diplomatically, militarily, and economically entangled with the region. In the 1980s the United States intervened in the Iraq-Iran War, empowering Saddam Hussein, and provided military and economic aid to Afghan rebels fighting the Soviet Union. Many of them were Islamic fundamentalists who later became active in the terrorist group Al Qaeda. For twenty-five years, beginning in 1991, the United States paid the price of those interventions in two wars against Iraq (1991 and 2003–11), a war in Afghanistan (2001–14), and struggles against extremist organizations throughout the region.

The attacks on the United States on September 11, 2001, and the Bush administration's war on terror, raised questions of intervention, human rights, and national security to high relief. In a moment of intense fear and moral outrage, the United States created clandestine prisons, tortured suspected terrorists, and rejected many of the conventional laws of war in the name of a national emergency. But the targets of the war on terror proved to be elusive, and the costs considerable. Many Americans now argue that, with limited resources and growing problems of domestic inequality, military intervention endangers the country as never before. Economic globalization, with its attendant costs to the domestic prosperity, threatens the United States' ability to sustain itself as a global power.

Throughout *These United States*, we track the connections between grassroots actions and elite power. Woman suffragists confronted President Woodrow Wilson through mass demonstrations in the streets of the capital. Their promise to help mobilize for the Great War secured his commitment to support a national suffrage amendment. Civil rights demonstrators produced clashes across the South that helped persuade President Lyndon Johnson to sponsor the Civil Rights Act of 1964. The electoral victories of activists on the right helped shape the agenda of Congress and presidents from Nixon to Obama. Rights and access won by one movement laid legal, structural, and aspirational foundations for the next. The debates of the twentieth century remain the debates of the twenty-first.

Finally, in the spirit of FDR's observation, we share a commitment to the individual lives, well known and unknown, who join together to make history. You will meet some unforgettable characters in the pages that follow. William Frank Fonvielle, a hopeful African American college student, sets off on a trip through the South in 1893 to report on the strange new phenomenon of segregation. Lew Sanders, in 1936 a bored radio salesman, learns to fly and leads a heroic band of college-age men through every major air battle of the Pacific theater during World War II. Lawrence James Merschel, the all-American son of a World War II veteran, lands in Vietnam twenty days after the Tet Offensive and a month before Lyndon Johnson decides to pull back his commitment to the war. Betty Dukes, a black California woman, discovers the limits of race and gender equality when she tries to advance in Wal-Mart, the world's largest corporation. Through these and many more twentieth-century lives, we root the broad history of the United States in the intimacy of personal experience. Here we find a nation in the making.

FOR THE STUDENT EDITION

We wrote *These United States* primarily for students taking courses in the twentieth-century history of the United States. The full version of our book begins in 1890 to set a baseline for the history that follows, and extends to the present with a chapter on the years since 2000. The post-1945 version begins with a chapter on Truman and the postwar period and comes up to the present. Apart from this later starting point, the books are the same. *These United States* assumes no prior preparation in American history. It can be used with students in a U.S. survey course that focuses on the twentieth century.

The **student edition** of *These United States* includes a number of special features:

Each chapter begins with a narrative vignette that puts students in direct touch with people, many ordinary Americans, who experienced the history in the chapter. Often we use these lives as a narrative thread through a chapter.

To engage students in the critical use of primary sources, each chapter includes the "Making a Nation" feature, which pairs documents that take different perspectives on a major issue. The accompanying headnotes and questions prepare students to understand the documents and compare their points of view.

To strengthen the geographical skills of students, the book includes twenty full-color maps. Each chapter also includes a chronology of major events and developments.

At the end of each chapter, we include an annotated list of Suggested Reading that represents the best and most recent scholarship on the chapter subjects. We have also created review pages with study questions and key terms. The key terms are defined in the glossary at the back of the book.

The Appendix includes core documents in American history as well as reference tables on presidential elections and broad subject areas such as population.

For **instructors**, we offer a digital test bank of over 400 multiple-choice and short-essay questions, and PowerPoint slides of the illustrations, maps, and tables in the text.

Glenda Elizabeth Gilmore

Thomas J. Sugrue

ACKNOWLEDGMENTS

The authors are grateful to Steve Forman, our editor at Norton, who brought us together, and who encouraged us, cajoled us, edited us, and enabled us to see this project through. Steve's colleagues Justin Cahill and Scott Sugarman masterfully shepherded us through crunch time.

Our readers saved us from embarrassing errors, gave us tips, pointed out gaping holes, and forced us to reevaluate our emphasis and approach in each chapter. The book is more correct, balanced, and comprehensive thanks to them. Some read more chapters than others, but everyone's reading proved invaluable. We are proud to be their colleagues.

James Anderson, Michigan State University
Kathryn Brownell, Purdue University–West Lafayette
Cindy Hahamovitch, The College of William & Mary
Shane Hamilton, University of Georgia
Michael Marino, The College of New Jersey
Norman Markowitz, Rutgers University
Craig Pascoe, Georgia College
Allison Perlman, University of California, Irvine
Kim Philips-Fein, New York University
Jonathan Rees, Colorado State University
Paul Rubinson, Bridgewater State University
Mark Sample, Monroe Community College
Matthew Sutton, Washington State University, Pullman
Gregory Wood, Frostburg State University

• • •

Glenda Gilmore is indebted to Lauren Pearlman, Sam Schaffer, Ashley Tallevi, Stephon Richardson, and Emily Yankowitz for their invaluable research assistance. Since I began this book, Lauren and Sam earned Ph.D.'s, and Ashley is in graduate school. Emily is a Yale undergraduate history major. Stephon began working on this book when he was in high school; he is now writing his senior thesis at Clark University. All of them showed great patience while chasing down facts, verifying figures, finding quotes, and powering through my repeated (and sometimes repetitious) queries. Eric Rutkow and Christopher McKnight Nichols provided sobering readings at a time when I sorely needed them. My Yale students in American Politics and Society, 1900–1945, and generations of graduate students in Readings in U.S. History in the Twentieth Century proved Jacquelyn Hall's observation when I accepted the job at Yale: "You will learn so much from your students!"

My teachers at the University of North Carolina at Chapel Hill taught me the interconnectedness of American history at a time when the profession sorted it into competitive subfields. William E. Leuchtenberg taught me the importance of political history, the significance of the New Deal, and the joy of birdwatching. William Barney's undergraduate survey represented the consummate lecture course. Jacquelyn Hall's women's history courses for undergraduates and graduates made the field central to American history. Nell Painter patiently showed me that African American history is American history.

Mia-lia, Derry, and Miles grew up and Ben wrote two books while I worked on *These United States*. Now that it's over, I promise them more bacon, more hikes, more Ireland, and one day soon, more Crete.

Glenda Elizabeth Gilmore

To an outside observer, writing seems a lonely occupation. I have spent many hours alone surrounded by books and papers, filling a blank screen with words. But for me, this book has been a collective project. Jessica Bird, Colin McGrath, and Kristian Taketomo provided timely research assistance. I have been very lucky to spend the first twenty-four years of my career at the University of Pennsylvania, where I tried out many of the ideas in these pages on enthusiastic and hardworking undergraduates in my courses on the New Deal, postwar politics and culture, civil rights, liberalism and conservatism, urban inequality, and America in the 1960s. I continue to learn from my dissertation advisees, a remarkably talented group, whose work has reshaped the field. Of my many talented Penn colleagues, let me single out a few who guided me on new paths through the twentieth century. Bruce Kuklick steered me toward power and ideas; Sally Gordon toward religion and law; Amy Offner toward economics and empire; and Michael Katz (may his memory be a blessing) toward education and welfare.

I have the world's best friends and family. Thanks to Peter Siskind for walks in the Wissahickon; Warren Breckman, Cordula Grewe, John Skrentny, Minh Phan-Ho, Greg Goldman, and Liz Hersh for standing by me in good times and bad, and especially for hosting a lot of good parties along the way; and Andrew Diamond and Caroline Rolland-Diamond for great conversation and food on both sides of the Atlantic. For all of you who have schmoozed with me over a cup of coffee, a lunch or dinner, or a late night drink, cheers. Finally, Brittany, Anna, and Jack: how can a line in my acknowledgments possibly capture all you have meant to me?

Thomas J. Sugrue

THESE
UNITED
STATES

A NATION IN THE MAKING

1945 TO THE PRESENT

A Rising
Superpower

✳

1944–1954

who matter more than most. For
s Dean Acheson, the leading archi-
tect of America's post–World War II foreign policy. Acheson started
his career as a protégé of the brilliant legal scholar and future Supreme Court
justice Felix Frankfurter and, like many bright and well-credentialed young
men, was tapped by Franklin Roosevelt to serve in his administration. As an
undersecretary of the treasury, Acheson oversaw the Lend-Lease program
during World War II and, always a quick study, became expert on finance and
international relations. In 1944 he stood in for the ailing secretary of state,
Edward Stettinius, at the Bretton Woods conference. He spent the first half of
the Truman years as undersecretary of state, better qualified for the position
than his boss, James F. Byrnes, the former South Carolina senator and Supreme Court justice whose term in office was marred by hostility and rivalry
with the president. Acheson then served as a key aide to George C. Marshall,
the general turned statesman who relied on his blunt advice.

Born in Middletown, Connecticut, the son of an Episcopal bishop, Acheson grew up in the heart of the New England establishment. A man whose brilliance was nearly as great as his self-assurance, he sailed through Groton, Yale University, and Harvard Law School. He would spend most of his career within a few blocks of the White House, shuttling back and forth between the law and government service.

Acheson was a man of words, eloquent words, from his carefully crafted speeches all the way to his Pulitzer Prize–winning memoir, published less than two years before his death in 1972. The quintessential polymath, one of the "wise men"—a bipartisan group of highly regarded foreign policy experts who advised presidents, diplomats, and pundits from World War II through the 1960s—he was as comfortable on Wall Street as he was in the Oval Office, as happy to spar with his fellow Yale trustees as with truculent members in Congress.

Truman and the Postwar World Order

Acheson's rise coincided with the unlikely ascent of Harry S. Truman to the White House. The president responsible for wrapping up World War II had little foreign policy experience. Other than spending part of 1918 serving in the military in Europe and later taking a short trip to Latin America, Truman lacked the worldly disposition of his predecessor. The only twentieth-century U.S. president without a college degree, Truman was a self-taught intellectual. "Mr. Truman read, I sometimes think, more than any of the rest of us," recalled Acheson.[1]

It would be left to Truman and his aides to figure out what role America would play in a radically altered world order. Before the war, the United States had been second to Great Britain in manufacturing might. It lacked the far-flung imperial holdings that symbolized "great power" status in the nineteenth and early twentieth centuries. Americans became bitterly divided over what role their country should play in the postwar world. But the United States emerged in 1945 as the world's leading industrial and financial power, a position that was the result, in part, of the devastation that Europe had suffered through two wars. America's postwar rise was an act of will, the result of economic policies that elevated the dollar, expanded America's markets across the world, built a massive military, and justified it with an unstable mix of international humanitarianism, militant anti-Communism, and missionary capitalism.

< Senator Joseph McCarthy, standing, and army attorney Joseph Welch, seated on left, head in hand, at the 1954 Army-McCarthy hearings (*previous page*).

Chronology

1938	House Un-American Activities Committee (HUAC) created
1940	Smith Act
1944	Bretton Woods Conference
	Servicemen's Readjustment Act (GI Bill)
	World Bank founded
1945	Harry S. Truman (Democrat) becomes president
	United Nations chartered
	V-J Day
	General Motors strike begins
1946	Fair Employment Practices Committee dissolved
	The "long telegram"
	CIO launches Operation Dixie
	Strikes by electrical, meatpacking, coal mining, and steel workers
	President Truman nationalizes railroads
	The Best Years of Our Lives released
	Republicans win control of U.S. House and Senate
1947	Truman Doctrine
	Taft-Hartley Act
	National Security Act
	Central Intelligence Agency created
	National Security Council created
	Executive Order 9835 creates loyalty review boards
	HUAC investigates Hollywood
1948	Marshall Plan
	United Nations Universal Declaration of Human Rights
	Executive Order 9981 desegregates U.S. military
	Harry S. Truman elected president
1949	People's Republic of China founded
1950	Senator Joseph McCarthy (R-WI) speech in Wheeling, West Virginia
	Korean War begins
	Battle of Inchon
	Treaty of Detroit
1951	Truman removes General Douglas MacArthur
1952	Dwight D. Eisenhower (Republican) elected president
1953	Korean War ends
1954	Army-McCarthy hearings

and nullifies domestic law." The UN, he warned, had created "the machinery for extraditing Americans charged with genocide and for shipping them overseas to be tried for acts committed in their hometowns," perhaps "for as little as having been charged with inflicting 'mental harm' on a 'national, ethnical, racial, or religious group.'"[8] The U.S. Senate feared that the UN would investigate civil rights abuses, a justifiable concern, given America's long history of mistreating African Americans and Native Americans. It refused to ratify the genocide convention.

REDEPLOYING THE MILITARY: OCCUPATION At the end of World War II, few envisioned that the United States would soon find itself once again on a war footing. The country never had much of a tradition of standing armies, at least not large ones. Although the Democrats and Republicans jostled for power in Congress, they shared a bipartisan conventional wisdom after the war ended that emphasized the necessity of huge troop reductions and drastic cuts in military spending. Budgetary constraints weighed heavily. The federal debt reached an all-time record, nearly $242 billion in 1945, greater than America's entire gross domestic product that year. Both parties demanded deficit reduction measures. The small but vocal band of isolationists in Congress called for a policy of noninterventionism. New Dealers hoped to trade guns for butter. And ordinary Americans were just plain exhausted.

In the two years following the end of World War II, the American defense budget plummeted from $81 billion to $13 billion. The army reduced its ranks by some 7 million troops, the Navy by 2.5 million. Demobilization and budget cuts required shuttering hundreds of shipyards and selling, scrapping, or retiring about six thousand ships. The U.S. Army Air Force, with two hundred combat units on call at the end of the war, cut the number to fifty. The American military nevertheless remained a mighty force in late 1947, with a little more than a million and a half troops serving worldwide.

The main task of the remaining American troops overseas was the occupation and reconstruction of former enemy nations. Occupation was a process that began piecemeal, first in Italy. Immediately after the fall of Mussolini in July 1943 and the victory over the Axis in Sicily in August, the United States and its allies began rebuilding Italy. Newsreels conveyed images of a benign takeover: Italians mobbing and hugging American soldiers, who were depicted as liberators. In a frenzied three weeks of intense writing, author John Hersey captured the vision of America as the great liberator, penning *A Bell for Adano*, a novel published in 1944. Hersey portrayed the occupation of Sicily as a humanitarian venture, embodied in the protagonist, Major Victor Joppolo, a Bronx-bred, Italian-speaking officer. Joppolo takes over a fascist-led town, falls in love with an Italian girl, restores the local fishing industry, and in the novel's culmination replaces the church bell that had been melted down to arm Mussolini's troops. The book would soon be turned into a wildly popular film.[9]

The occupation of Nazi Germany and Austria was to take a more aggressive form than Joppolo's benign mayoralty. In 1945 the Joint Chiefs of Staff issued a directive

Japan Surrenders In a ceremony on the deck of the *USS Missouri* in Tokyo Bay on September 2, 1945, the Japanese government formally surrendered to the Allies.

that Germany was "not to be occupied for the purpose of liberation but as a defeated enemy nation."[10] The victorious allies—Britain, France, the Soviet Union, and the United States—each controlled a quadrant of Germany and also divided the capital, Berlin, which was in the Soviet quadrant, into four parts. Together the allies agreed on a strict agenda of "de-Nazification" that included war crimes trials for Nazi military and political leaders.

Japan's surrender was even more abject. Hiroshima and Nagasaki had been leveled by the atomic bomb, and sixty-six Japanese cities had been mostly reduced to rubble during sustained air raids. About 2.7 million Japanese, between 3 and 4 percent of the country's population, had died in the war, and millions more were injured. At war's end, only a handful of Japanese ships remained afloat; nearly the entire air force had been destroyed. On September 2, 1945, Japanese officials gathered on the

USS Missouri to surrender officially, dwarfed by the boat's massive artillery. Less than two weeks later, General Douglas MacArthur, who oversaw the occupation, declared Japan to be a "fourth rate nation," a deliberate effort to humiliate the former empire.

The U.S. charge was to pacify the country, to create enduring democratic institutions, to decentralize Japan's *zaibatsu* system (an economy directed by large industrial conglomerates), and prevent the rise of another militant Japanese empire. To that end, the United States convened war crimes trials, forbade prominent military and political leaders to take positions of authority, drafted a new constitution that created a parliamentary democracy and reduced the emperor to a symbolic role, and instituted land reforms to diminish the power of wealthy rural landowners who had supported the war. To Americans who had spent the wartime years hearing the Japanese denounced as subhuman and vicious "monkey-men," the prospect of democratization required draconian measures.

In many respects, the United States was ill prepared to impose military rule in Germany and Japan. When the fleeting thrill of liberation wore off, the military needed to provide special incentives, including hardship pay and the promise of cars and well-appointed apartments, to encourage war-weary soldiers to reenlist in the occupation forces. Wherever possible, the United States relied on native language speakers, whether wartime refugees who had volunteered to serve in the U.S. military, like the young Henry Kissinger, whose family had fled Nazi Germany in 1938, or the children of Americanized immigrants, who were often distant from their parents' language and culture. Likewise the military recruited Japanese Americans—many of them nisei or sansei, some of them held in internment camps during the war—to support the American occupation of Japan, assuming, quite dubiously in many cases, that they had the language skills and cultural competencies to understand postwar Japan. To prepare carefully selected officers to oversee the occupation, the military supported training programs on American college campuses, immersing future occupiers in the language, geography, and history of their countries.

The early days of occupation hardly resembled Joppolo's humanitarian ventures: they were chaotic and often exploitative. Troops used their access to goods and power, not to mention the desperate circumstances of widows, single women, and war orphans, to get sex. Prostitution was rife. To maintain morale and discourage illicit activity, occupation officials tried to create licit spaces—on-base dances and social clubs—where troops could meet local women, rather than procure their favors. By the late 1940s, the military allowed officers and then enlisted men to move their families overseas.

The Origins of the Cold War

The occupations of Japan and Germany, which lasted until 1952, entailed everything from finding housing for refugees and providing them basic food and supplies to rounding up suspected collaborators and war criminals. Occupying forces reorganized local and regional governments, ousting fascists. But escalating tensions between the

Soviet Union and the United States changed the nature of occupation in Germany. For the United States, exporting the Four Freedoms receded in importance in favor of neutralizing Communism.

Although the United States and the Soviet Union had been allied in the struggle against Nazi Germany between 1941 and 1945, the relationship had been one of convenience that quickly frayed at war's end. On February 9, 1946, Stalin stunned the United States and its allies with a speech that seemed to signal a new Soviet belligerence. While Stalin praised the Allies for their collaboration in defeating fascism, he denounced both world wars as the consequence of capitalist greed, and in words that American observers found particularly threatening, he called for a five-year plan to rebuild the Soviet economy. *The New York Times* ran a banner headline that sounded the alarm: "STALIN SETS A HUGE OUTPUT NEAR OURS IN 5-YEAR PLAN: EXPECTS TO LEAD IN SCIENCE."[11] Supreme Court justice William Douglas hyperbolically called it "the declaration of World War III."[12]

For all of Stalin's grand promises, the Soviets were hardly a military or economic threat to the United States. Much of his rhetoric was meant for Russian ears, to restore morale in a country that had suffered more than others during the war. The Soviet Union had a weak air force and navy. Its army had been decimated on the Eastern Front. It lacked nuclear weapons and had no effective air defense system to repel a missile attack. With at least twenty million of its people dead, vast agricultural regions laid waste, and tens of thousands of factories destroyed, its economy was crippled.

World War III was a long way off. American intelligence experts believed that it would take a decade or two for the USSR to rebuild its industrial and military capacity. In 1946 the Joint Intelligence Staff in the War Department noted that "the offensive capabilities of the United States are manifestly superior to those of the U.S.S.R. and any war between the U.S. and the U.S.S.R. would be far more costly to the Soviet Union than to the United States."[13]

But to many American politicians and opinion leaders, Stalin's were fighting words. In the month following his speech, U.S.-Soviet relations chilled. President Truman lashed out at those who called for the "appeasement" of the Soviets, drawing a comparison with the British decision to allow Hitler to annex the Sudetenland in 1938. Truman's Republican opponents accused him of inaction. Anything short of an aggressive policy to thwart Stalin would lead to "another Munich." Influential columnist Walter Lippmann argued that the United States needed "to reinforce, rebuild and modernize the industrial power of Western Europe, and to take a leading part in the development of . . . Asia."[14] That effort would require more than just dollars and American know-how: the United States would need to muster the "moral energy" to face the Soviet threat.

KENNAN AND THE LONG TELEGRAM On February 22, less than two weeks after Stalin's speech, George Kennan, the U.S. *chargé d'affaires* in Moscow, dispatched a "long telegram," warning of the Soviet Union's imperial ambitions. Kennan,

who ha
and join
Profoun
At a mor
the Sovie
burly, ove
over the b
after the w

Kennar
always more
nan, by cont
came to facin
that former C
telegram ham
force committ
dus vivendi, th
be disrupted, o
state be broken,
this force is und
bly [the] greatest
to solve—and th
torical exclamatic
Churchill used th
an "iron curtain" r

GREAT POWE

World War II hac
and military trou
States, as a world
influence in Europe la
"great powers" mo
frail economies, anyhor

Their far-flung
stages of resistance
rebellions in Mada
dochina under siege
and the empire's in
ularly Turkey and C

Truman faced
United States turn
gap left by the deci
nial struggles world

M "a wage-price spiral" and blamed the "labor monopoly" for
"r things you need."[19]

vas the prospect of mass unemployment. Would the United
St other depression? Union leaders, like Walter Reuther, head
of tomobile Workers (UAW), demanded that the federal gov-
er yment policy, including public works programs to build
h or the jobless. "We have but to mobilize for peace the re-
s know-how which put the B-29 into the skies over Tokyo
rashing into Hiroshima," stated Reuther optimistically,
ns and sub-standard housing, both rural and urban."[20] At
Americans surveyed believed that "it should be up to the
yment "for everyone who wants to work." Congressional
port, began drafting "full employment" legislation, tak-
jobs."[21]

AVE The postwar tension over wages and security
of labor unrest in American history. As soon as the
nists took to the picket lines. In the year following
toppages involving over five million workers affected
nomy. In late 1945, 200,000 General Motors workers
to work for 113 days.[22] In early 1946, some 93,000
orkers went on strike; 180,000 electrical workers
d General Electric plant in the United States and
er plants," lamented Charles E. Wilson, GE's chief
f people, actually joining hands and going around
that nobody could get through."[23] GE executives
fact that the public seemed to be on the workers'
ed picket lines. Police officers often showed more
bosses. Ministers and priests blessed the protest-
least for the moment, to be on the wrong side of

h the spring, leaving few sectors of the economy
ners in Pennsylvania, West Virginia, Kentucky,
ork for forty days. And in May, 300,000 railway
vast transportation system.[24] Tens of thousands
rs, printers, lumberjacks, and clerical workers,
walked out of their jobs, demanding better

ral labor laws prevented employers from bru-
ad in the labor upheavals of the 1890s or the
ecourse to "scabs," the slang for replacement
fears of joblessness, no huge reserve army of

Soviet Union and the United States changed the nature of occupation in Germany. For the United States, exporting the Four Freedoms receded in importance in favor of neutralizing Communism.

Although the United States and the Soviet Union had been allied in the struggle against Nazi Germany between 1941 and 1945, the relationship had been one of convenience that quickly frayed at war's end. On February 9, 1946, Stalin stunned the United States and its allies with a speech that seemed to signal a new Soviet belligerence. While Stalin praised the Allies for their collaboration in defeating fascism, he denounced both world wars as the consequence of capitalist greed, and in words that American observers found particularly threatening, he called for a five-year plan to rebuild the Soviet economy. *The New York Times* ran a banner headline that sounded the alarm: "STALIN SETS A HUGE OUTPUT NEAR OURS IN 5-YEAR PLAN: EXPECTS TO LEAD IN SCIENCE."[11] Supreme Court justice William Douglas hyperbolically called it "the declaration of World War III."[12]

For all of Stalin's grand promises, the Soviets were hardly a military or economic threat to the United States. Much of his rhetoric was meant for Russian ears, to restore morale in a country that had suffered more than others during the war. The Soviet Union had a weak air force and navy. Its army had been decimated on the Eastern Front. It lacked nuclear weapons and had no effective air defense system to repel a missile attack. With at least twenty million of its people dead, vast agricultural regions laid waste, and tens of thousands of factories destroyed, its economy was crippled.

World War III was a long way off. American intelligence experts believed that it would take a decade or two for the USSR to rebuild its industrial and military capacity. In 1946 the Joint Intelligence Staff in the War Department noted that "the offensive capabilities of the United States are manifestly superior to those of the U.S.S.R. and any war between the U.S. and the U.S.S.R. would be far more costly to the Soviet Union than to the United States."[13]

But to many American politicians and opinion leaders, Stalin's were fighting words. In the month following his speech, U.S.-Soviet relations chilled. President Truman lashed out at those who called for the "appeasement" of the Soviets, drawing a comparison with the British decision to allow Hitler to annex the Sudetenland in 1938. Truman's Republican opponents accused him of inaction. Anything short of an aggressive policy to thwart Stalin would lead to "another Munich." Influential columnist Walter Lippmann argued that the United States needed "to reinforce, rebuild and modernize the industrial power of Western Europe, and to take a leading part in the development of . . . Asia."[14] That effort would require more than just dollars and American know-how: the United States would need to muster the "moral energy" to face the Soviet threat.

KENNAN AND THE LONG TELEGRAM On February 22, less than two weeks after Stalin's speech, George Kennan, the U.S. *chargé d'affaires* in Moscow, dispatched a "long telegram," warning of the Soviet Union's imperial ambitions. Kennan, who had joined the Foreign Service after graduating from Princeton, learned Russian and joined the staff of the U.S. embassy to the Soviet Union when it opened in 1933. Profoundly pessimistic, Kennan found himself the resident contrarian in Moscow. At a moment when many Western politicians and intellectuals were enraptured with the Soviet experiment, Kennan was hardheaded and skeptical. "Will the pathos of the burly, over-alled worker, with his sleeves rolled up, brandishing a red flag and striding over the bodies of top-hatted capitalists, ever grasp the hearts of people as it did just after the war?" he asked in 1935. "I doubt it."[15]

Kennan and Acheson got along, despite their very different styles. Acheson was always more of an empiricist, someone who gathered data to make his opinion. Kennan, by contrast, was more ideological, trusting his gut instincts, particularly when it came to facing down the Soviets. Kennan had opposed de-Nazification on the grounds that former German leaders could be mobilized in the anti-Communist cause. His telegram hammered home the anti-Soviet point, arguing that "we have here a political force committed fanatically to the belief that with US there can be no permanent *modus vivendi*, that it is desirable and necessary that the internal harmony of our society be disrupted, our traditional way of life be destroyed, the international authority of our state be broken, if Soviet power is to be secure." He concluded that "how to cope with this force is undoubtedly [the] greatest task our diplomacy has ever faced and probably [the] greatest it will ever have to face," but that "the problem is within our power to solve—and that without recourse to any general military conflict."[16] Putting a rhetorical exclamation point on the anti-Soviet message, British prime minister Winston Churchill used the occasion of a March 3 address at a small Missouri college to warn of an "iron curtain" separating the Soviet Union from Western Europe.

GREAT POWER POLITICS By 1946, hyperbolic rhetoric aside, it was clear that World War II had changed the international balance of power. For all its economic and military troubles, the Soviet Union had risen to second place, after the United States, as a world power, victorious against the Nazis and eager to expand its sphere of influence in Europe and Asia. Britain, France, and of course Germany and Japan were "great powers" mostly in the past tense, with decimated militaries, bombed-out cities, frail economies, and thin public support for military engagement.

Their far-flung empires, churning with anti-imperial insurgencies, were in various stages of resistance and rebellion. In the years following World War II, France faced rebellions in Madagascar, Tunisia, and Algeria, and it found its imperial hold in Indochina under siege by a growing revolutionary movement. India rose against Britain, and the empire's influence in Egypt, Palestine, and the eastern Mediterranean, particularly Turkey and Greece, was on the wane.

Truman faced three foreign policy challenges in 1946 and beyond. Should the United States turn its arsenal toward the Soviets? Should the United States fill the gap left by the decimated great powers? Should the United States intervene in anticolonial struggles worldwide?

Reconversion: The Home Front

The question of how to wind down World War II was equally pressing on the home front. No one knew exactly what the postwar social order would look like. Pessimists feared that, without the stimulant of wartime spending, the United States would plunge back into a depression. No one was certain how the 16.4 million World War II veterans, many of them traumatized by their experiences overseas, would integrate back into American society.

The 1946 film *The Best Years of Our Lives*, which won eight Oscars, captured the pensive mood. Three GIs return home to fictional Boone City, where they find their lives spinning out of control. Homer, who had been a high school football hero, struggles to come to terms with the amputation of both of his hands. Al, a banker, struggles to readjust and turns to drink. Fred, who has won the Distinguished Flying Cross for service as a bomber captain, is emasculated by his job as a drugstore soda jerk (the only work he can get) and divorces his dissatisfied wife when she has an affair with a better-off man. In the film's bleakest scene, Fred, having fled his unfaithful wife and troubled life, finds himself in a sprawling lot of decommissioned military planes, a flyer and his aircraft now without purpose.

ECONOMIC ANXIETIES *The Best Years of Our Lives* was the highest-grossing film of its time—and a close second in viewership to *Gone with the Wind*—in large part because it captured popular angst. Divorce was endemic in the United States, reaching a peak of 31 per 100 marriages in 1945.[17] Joblessness spiked. Many veterans, hoping to return to their prewar jobs, instead took unemployment pay. Former soldiers without work were eligible for twenty dollars a week in benefits for up to one year. Civilian workers—including millions of African Americans and women who had worked for defense contractors during the war—feared, with good reason, that they would lose their jobs during the postwar "reconversion."

Black defense workers faced a particularly insecure future. Many lost their jobs because of veterans' preferences in postwar hiring, which counted military service toward seniority. Black workers complained that because they had been the last hired during the war, they were the first to be fired afterward. Many women also found themselves unemployed, their jobs reassigned to returning veterans, many of whom had little experience in the civilian workforce.

Corporate profits had skyrocketed during the war and afterward, but after V-J Day (the day marking Japan's surrender and the war's end), when production slowed, wages stagnated. Workers, who had benefited from overtime pay during the war, found themselves with lighter paychecks as employers reinstated the forty-hour week. President Truman contended that profitable firms could afford to pay workers more. "Wage increases are . . . imperative," he argued in October 1945, "to cushion the shock to our workers, to sustain adequate purchasing power and to increase national income."[18] Business leaders reacted bitterly, arguing that Truman had capitulated to organized labor and that industry could not afford pay hikes. The National Association of

Manufacturers warned of "a wage-price spiral" and blamed the "labor monopoly" for "rais[ing] the prices of the things you need."[19]

Even more troubling was the prospect of mass unemployment. Would the United States tumble back into another depression? Union leaders, like Walter Reuther, head of the powerful United Automobile Workers (UAW), demanded that the federal government enact a full employment policy, including public works programs to build housing and provide work for the jobless. "We have but to mobilize for peace the resourcefulness and technical know-how which put the B-29 into the skies over Tokyo and sent the atomic bomb crashing into Hiroshima," stated Reuther optimistically, "and we can wipe out the slums and sub-standard housing, both rural and urban."[20] At war's end, nearly four in five Americans surveyed believed that "it should be up to the government" to ensure employment "for everyone who wants to work." Congressional Democrats, with Truman's support, began drafting "full employment" legislation, taking up the motto "sixty million jobs."[21]

THE GREAT STRIKE WAVE The postwar tension over wages and security sparked the most intensive wave of labor unrest in American history. As soon as the ticker tape parades ended, unionists took to the picket lines. In the year following the end of the war, 4,630 work stoppages involving over five million workers affected nearly every sector of the U.S. economy. In late 1945, 200,000 General Motors workers walked out and would not return to work for 113 days.[22] In early 1946, some 93,000 meatpackers and 750,000 steelworkers went on strike; 180,000 electrical workers shut down every Westinghouse and General Electric plant in the United States and Canada. "The picketing in the larger plants," lamented Charles E. Wilson, GE's chief executive, "was literally hundreds of people, actually joining hands and going around in an ellipse in front of the plant so that nobody could get through."[23] GE executives were particularly flummoxed by the fact that the public seemed to be on the workers' side. Veterans, still in uniform, joined picket lines. Police officers often showed more sympathy to the strikers than to their bosses. Ministers and priests blessed the protesting workers. Management seemed, at least for the moment, to be on the wrong side of history.

The strike wave continued through the spring, leaving few sectors of the economy untouched. In April, 400,000 coal miners in Pennsylvania, West Virginia, Kentucky, Alabama, Illinois, and Iowa stopped work for forty days. And in May, 300,000 railway workers struck, paralyzing the nation's vast transportation system.[24] Tens of thousands of other workers—among them truckers, printers, lumberjacks, and clerical workers, even professional baseball players—also walked out of their jobs, demanding better pay, benefits, and more security.

Few of the strikes were violent: federal labor laws prevented employers from brutally attacking striking workers as they had in the labor upheavals of the 1890s or the 1930s. Moreover, employers seldom had recourse to "scabs," the slang for replacement workers. During demobilization, despite fears of joblessness, no huge reserve army of the unemployed stood ready to replace striking workers. In addition, the 1935 National Labor Relations Act had enshrined the principle of collective bargaining in the law, and the Truman administration used its clout to bring employers and union leaders to the negotiating table.

Resolving labor unrest proved challenging. In November 1945, President Truman assembled a national labor-management conference to lay "a broad and permanent foundation for industrial peace and progress," but despite his best efforts, the negotiations failed.[25] In early 1946 he created a federal fact-finding board to gather statistics on company profits and wages, hoping that hard data would serve as the basis for compromise. But he also wielded the power of government to shut down the railway workers strike, blaming it on "men within our own country who place their private interests above the welfare of the nation." Truman temporarily nationalized the railroads.[26]

Even if unionists regretted Truman's response to the railroad strike, they had little reason to be unhappy with the overall results of the strike wave. In late March 1946 an agreement between the UAW and General Motors raised wages by 18.5 cents per hour, a substantial gain. The United Steelworkers and the United Electrical, Radio and Machine Workers (UE) quickly accepted the same wage hike. The following year General Motors and the UAW would agree to cost-of-living allowances (COLA) that pegged wages to inflation, ensuring stability. This set a pattern that would play out in many other industries over the next few years, culminating in the "Treaty of Detroit," a five-year contract that Reuther negotiated with General Motors and Ford in 1950. The treaty gave workers high wages, ongoing COLA increases, excellent health benefits, and a generous pension plan, in exchange for a promise of peace on the shop floor.

THE FAILURE OF FAIR EMPLOYMENT PRACTICES Not all workers benefited equally from the rise in wages and benefits after the great strike wave. African American workers, though they had made inroads in defense industries during World War II, were concentrated in the most menial jobs. They faced widespread discrimination at work. Whole sectors of the economy—particularly skilled, clerical, retail, and professional employment—remained nearly completely closed to them. Even industries that accepted black workers, like automobile manufacturing, steelmaking, and meatpacking, stuck them in the most unpleasant or dangerous jobs, lifting engines and spraying paint in car plants, stoking red-hot furnaces in steel mills, or cutting open cow carcasses in meat processing factories.

Ever since A. Philip Randolph's threatened March on Washington in 1941, civil rights activists had put jobs and freedom at the center of their agenda. In 1944 a coalition of nearly one hundred unions, civil rights organizations, and religious groups created an umbrella organization to lobby for a permanent Fair Employment Practices Committee. Leading the group was Anna Arnold Hedgeman, a formidable intellectual and astute organizer who had begun her career in the early 1920s with hopes of becoming a schoolteacher in her hometown, St. Paul, Minnesota. Since the school

Anna Arnold Hedgeman A longtime civil rights activist, Hedgeman led the effort to create a permanent Fair Employment Practices Committee to prevent racial discrimination in the workplace.

district was overwhelmingly white with only a few thousand black residents, St. Paul's school board simply wouldn't allow an African American to teach white students.

Instead, she made a career in the segregated world of social services. She got a job working at the "Negro" YWCA in Springfield, Ohio, and quickly moved up the ranks, taking executive positions at YWCAs in Jersey City, Harlem, and Brooklyn. Living in Harlem and Brooklyn during the Depression, she moved leftward politically, investigating the poor working conditions of black laundresses and domestic servants, joining "Do not buy where you cannot work" boycotts of white-owned stores, supporting the March on Washington movement, and spearheading a campaign against segregated blood banks during the war.

Hedgeman and her group lobbied Congress, wrote op-eds, and sponsored mass rallies around the country, focusing on early 1946, when Franklin Delano Roosevelt's Fair Employment Practices Committee (FEPC), a temporary agency, would dissolve. They won the support of President Truman and former first lady Eleanor Roosevelt, but their battle was uphill nonetheless. Congress refused to create a permanent FEPC in February 1946. Facing a filibuster by southern Democratic senators, FEPC supporters mustered only forty-eight votes, well short of the two-thirds needed to bring the bill to the floor. In the House, a bill to make the FEPC permanent languished in committee. Senator Theodore Bilbo (D-MS), in one of his politer moments, lashed out at the FEPC as a "damnable" law, one that "forced" black and white "affiliation and association" based on "the craziest, wildest, most unreasonable illogical theory."[27]

Bilbo found allies who didn't share his fiery rhetoric but nonetheless ferociously opposed civil rights in the workplace. Pro-business Republicans saw the FEPC as unjust interference with employers' decisions to hire, promote, and fire at will. The Dixie-GOP coalition prevailed—and it would win a steady streak of victories for the next two decades. Between 1944 and 1963, FEPC proponents introduced 114 fair employment bills in the House and Senate. All of them were buried in committee hearings or filibustered to death.

Frustrated by the stalemate in Congress, civil rights activists pushed for state and local antidiscrimination laws. Between 1944—when New York State passed a law forbidding discrimination by race, ethnicity, and religion—and 1963, two dozen states, all of them in the North and West, passed their own Fair Employment Practices laws. Sometimes those laws were weak, the result of business opposition to regulation. But particularly in states with growing black populations, like New York and New Jersey,

civil rights laws gained broad Democratic support and the votes of pluralities or majorities of Republicans.

THE 1946 MIDTERM ELECTIONS The global uncertainty, labor unrest, civil
rights struggles, and economic instability of 1946 galvanized Truman's opponents on
both left and right. The president's position on the railway strikes alienated many in his
party's sizable labor wing. Several union leaders, among them the UAW's Reuther and
the Steelworkers' head Philip Murray, considered organizing a separate labor party, like
those in Western Europe. Drained after months of strikes, exhausted unionists had little inclination to spend their energy getting out the vote in the 1946 midterms. Civil
rights groups complained that Truman was too weak to challenge the Dixie-GOP coalition. To the right, hawks argued that Truman was wobbly in the face of Stalin's aggression and all too willing to sacrifice business interests to a grasping labor movement.

The Republican Party, sensing opportunity, ran a strong slate of congressional candidates. Voters of all persuasions chortled at the pun, "to err is Truman." In the weeks
leading up to the midterm elections, the Frost advertising company, a firm working
for the Republicans, came up with a simple slogan that captured the anti-Truman
mood: "Had enough?"[28] In a November landslide, Republicans gained control of both
the Senate and the House for the first time since 1930. Of the seventy-seven most liberal members of the House up for reelection, only thirty-six won.

Congress and Truman faced off again and again over the next two years, threatening many of the New Deal's achievements. Liberals like T.R.B., the pseudonymous
columnist for *The New Republic*, bemoaned the harsh political climate. "This Congress brought back an atmosphere you had forgotten or never thought possible," he
wrote. "Victories fought and won years ago were suddenly in doubt."[29] In 1947 and
1948, Truman wielded the veto sixty-two times. But Congress, truculent, especially on
domestic labor and economic policy, overrode him fifteen times, more than any president to date other than the woefully inept Andrew Johnson, who succeeded Abraham
Lincoln in 1865.

**TAFT-HARTLEY, OPERATION DIXIE, AND THE "RIGHT TO
WORK"** Truman's congressional opponents pushed an aggressive agenda to unravel
the New Deal, beginning with legislation to weaken the 1935 National Labor Relations Act. The leader of the antiunion effort, Ohio senator Robert Taft, nicknamed
"Mr. Republican," had been elected to the Senate in the anti-Roosevelt midterm election of 1938. Over his three terms in office, he accepted some New Deal programs,
including Social Security and public housing, but he was a fierce critic of any legislation
that might strengthen labor.

The Taft-Hartley Act, passed in June 1947, gave the president the authority to intervene in strikes to protect national security. It empowered states to pass "right to
work" laws that allowed workers in unionized companies to opt out of membership. It
required all union leaders to sign affidavits stating that they were not members of the

Communist Party. It forbade "secondary strikes," walkouts by workers in one firm in support of striking workers in another. And most significantly, it limited unions' use of the "closed shop," a practice that required that all workers in a firm that had elected union representation be members of that union and pay dues. President Truman denounced the legislation as "vindictive," argued that it would "restrict the proper rights of the rank and file of labor," and vetoed it.[30] But the Dixie-GOP alliance stood united and overrode Truman's veto, 68–25 in the Senate and 331–83 in the House.

Antilabor campaigns played out with special intensity at the state and local levels, particularly in the South and Mountain West, where over the next two decades, nineteen states would pass right-to-work laws that thwarted unionization. In the 1940s in Phoenix, Arizona, Chamber of Commerce leaders successfully led campaigns to lower business taxes, fought to limit the bargaining power of the city's once-powerful trade unions, and used the promise of a "favorable business climate" to attract companies fleeing the old industrial cities of the Northeast and Midwest.[31] The result was an extraordinary economic boom in sparsely populated Arizona, as companies seeking low-wage workers began relocating factories there in the 1950s.

Labor's biggest defeats came in the states of the Old Confederacy. Operation Dixie, a CIO organizing effort that began in 1946, brought more than two hundred organizers to textile, furniture, steel, and cotton-processing plants in Virginia, the Carolinas, Georgia, and Alabama. Many were committed to both racial equality and unionism—a double threat to Jim Crow. Operation Dixie organizers reached out to black and white workers alike, arguing that union efforts would bolster everyone's wages and benefits.

Southern business elites used Taft-Hartley as a powerful weapon to fight the CIO campaign: right-to-work laws, enacted in Alabama, Arkansas, Florida, Georgia, Mississippi, North Carolina, South Carolina, Tennessee, Texas, and Virginia by the early 1950s, weakened organizing drives. Accusations of Communism, sometimes true, discredited union organizers. Southern antiunionists also resorted to time-tested appeals to white supremacy. David Clark, who edited the *Textile Bulletin*, an industry publication, compared Operation Dixie's organizers to the "carpetbaggers" of Reconstruction and argued that the CIO "seeks to place Negroes upon the basis of social equality with whites."[32] Evangelical pastors circulated leaflets at factory gates accusing unionists of being godless Communists. In many towns, vigilantes attacked organizers. Local police departments, often in the pocket of industrialists, arrested and jailed unionists, and local magistrates sentenced many to hard labor on chain gangs. Operation Dixie collapsed in the late 1940s. Union membership in most of the South remained low for decades afterward.

Cold War, First Moves

Truman faced big hurdles in Congress when it came to labor, but on foreign policy he was able to build a bipartisan coalition of support. In 1946 and 1947 the United States and the Soviet Union jostled for power, first in the eastern Mediterranean and the Middle East. Greece, devastated by German occupation, exploded into full civil war, its robust Communist party battling traditional monarchists and fascist sympathizers for control. The United States and its allies worried about Soviet pressure on Turkey to control the Dardanelles, a strategic maritime link between the Black Sea and the Mediterranean, a nexus between Russia, Europe, and the Middle East. Tensions spread eastward to Iran, where United States, British, and Soviet troops tensely occupied a country that was supposed to be moving toward independence. The Soviet Union supported a rebellion led by ethnic Azeris in northern Iran, an area bordering the USSR, and refused to withdraw its troops from the contested region, despite a 1943 agreement to do so. The fate of Iran mattered perhaps even more than Turkey and Greece because of its vast oil deposits.

THE TRUMAN DOCTRINE AND THE ORIGINS OF CONTAINMENT

In early 1947 the Truman administration stepped in, with Dean Acheson, now undersecretary of state, playing a key role. Acheson made a forceful case for aggressive engagement in Greece and Turkey. The bishop's son framed his foreign policy analysis in moral terms. "We are met at Armageddon," he argued. "Like apples in a barrel infected by one rotten one, the corruption of Greece would infect Iran and all to the East. It would also carry infection to spread through Asia Minor and Egypt, and to Europe through Italy and France."[33] It was neither the first nor the last time that Communism would be compared to a contagion that needed to be quarantined or contained. Both abroad and at home, policy makers justified anti-Communism as a necessary cure for a disease that could destroy the United States and the world.

Acheson provided the president with the blueprint for what would be called the Truman Doctrine. On March 12, 1947, in his first major foreign policy address since the disastrous midterm elections, Truman stood before Congress, requesting $400 million to shore up Greece and Turkey, on the grounds that "it must be the policy of the United States to support free peoples who are resisting attempted subjugation by armed minorities or by outside pressures."[34] Acheson wrote much of the speech because Truman was dissatisfied with early drafts. "I want no hedging in this speech," stated Truman. "This was America's answer to the surge of expansion of Communist tyranny. It had to be clear and free of hesitation or double talk."[35] Simple and strong, the address depicted the fate of two small countries as a matter of slavery and freedom, vital to the future of democracy. On May 15 the aid bill passed by overwhelming majorities in the House and Senate, Truman's first big bipartisan victory in the "do nothing Congress."

The principle behind the Truman Doctrine—that Communism was a contagion that needed to be quarantined wherever it sprang up—would guide American foreign policy for the next two decades. In the summer of 1947, George Kennan, writing anonymously as "Mr. X" in the pages of the journal *Foreign Affairs*, fleshed out what came to be called the strategy of "containment." A rising star in the State Department after his "long telegram," Kennan offered a simple, compelling rationale for the escalating

Cold War Europe

Cold War, asserting that "the innate antagonism between capitalism and socialism" motivated the Soviet Union. The USSR, believed Kennan, would be relentless and creative. Soviet "political action is a fluid stream which moves constantly, wherever it is permitted to move, toward a given goal. Its main concern is to make sure that it has filled every nook and cranny available to it in the basin of world power." If Moscow was patient, opportunistic, and aggressive, argued Mr. X, the key to defeating the Soviets would be the "adroit and vigilant application of counterforce at a series of constantly shifting geographical and political points, corresponding to the shifts and maneuvers of Soviet policy."[36] Kennan thus defined containment.

THE NATIONAL SECURITY ACT In July 1947, Congress enacted the National Security Act, a sweeping reorganization of American military and intelligence services. The law established a new cabinet position, the secretary of defense, who directed a new agency, the National Military Establishment (renamed the Department of Defense in 1949). It created a new military branch—the U.S. Air Force—and empowered the Joint Chiefs of Staff (the top officers of the army, navy, and air force) to coordinate military operations. The law also established the National Security Council (NSC), to advise the president on foreign policy, and the Central Intelligence Agency (CIA), to direct espionage overseas. In 1948 the NSC gave the CIA the power to engage in clandestine operations abroad, targeting governments and organizations that threatened American political or economic interests. Truman and Congress had created a vast, centralized American security state unprecedented in American history.

THE MARSHALL PLAN In 1947 the Truman administration—under a new secretary of state, General George C. Marshall—elaborated on the Truman Doctrine, with an eye toward strengthening Western Europe. Marshall was Truman's first strong secretary of state, a man of supreme self-confidence. He had first seen military action in the Philippines in 1902, served again in France during World War I, and rose quickly up the ranks. In 1939, Roosevelt named him army chief of staff. A master of both logistics and strategy, Marshall rose in prestige because of his leadership during World War II.

Marshall worked closely with Acheson and Kennan, whom he named to direct the Department of State's new Policy Planning Staff. Together they laid the groundwork for the next phase of the Cold War: an unprecedented infusion of economic aid to Western Europe. The European Recovery Program, quickly dubbed the Marshall Plan at President Truman's insistence, promised $13 billion in aid to the war-torn Western European countries. When Marshall announced the plan in June 1947, at Harvard's commencement, he described it as necessary to prevent "economic, social, and political deterioration of a very grave character." He emphasized the plan's humanitarian side. "Our policy is not directed against any country or doctrine but against hunger, poverty, desperation, and chaos." Still it built firmly on the Truman Doctrine. The president called the aid to Greece and Turkey and the Marshall Plan "two halves of the same walnut," which linked capitalism and democracy. The purpose of aid to Europe, Marshall went on, "should be the revival of a working economy in the world so as to permit the emergence of political and social conditions in which free institutions can exist."[37] He did not have to mention the Soviet Union, and he did not.

The Marshall Plan, however, faced an uphill battle in Congress. Senator Robert Taft led the opposition. Over his three terms in office, he had controversially opposed American intervention in World War II, denounced Japanese internment, and argued that fears of Soviet domination were overblown. Reaching beyond his shrinking iso-lationist circle, Taft led a chorus of Republicans who denounced the Marshall Plan as "a bold socialist blueprint" and a costly boondoggle.[38] Why should Americans channel billions into what Taft denounced as a European T.V.A.?

Despite the opposition, Marshall, a celebrated military man, retained public good-will. He rallied pro-business Republicans, internationalists, anti-Communists, and liberals, all of whom found something to like in the plan. For corporations, it could expand the market for American exports. So long as the funds were not used for state-run enterprises, Europe could become fertile ground for American investment. For internationalists, the plan would reinforce the historic ties between the United States and Europe. For anti-Communists, it would stabilize European economies, weakening the influence of Communist parties and thwarting Soviet plans to extend their reach westward. For liberals, the plan was a humanitarian effort of the highest order, build-ing infrastructure, creating jobs, and spurring consumerism throughout Europe.

By early 1948 the Marshall Plan had stalled in Congress, a victim of bitter parti-san division. The Republican majority in the House and Senate did not want to hand the unpopular president a victory in an election year. But events in Central Europe in February shifted the debate. In early 1946, Czechoslovakia, free from German con-trol, had created a multiparty government after a closely contested election—the prime minister was a Communist since his party had won a plurality of votes, but the pres-ident and foreign minister were not. In February 1948 the fragile government split. Within days the Soviets stepped in, toppled the president, and installed a pro-Moscow regime. Two weeks later the foreign minister was murdered. General Lucius Clay, who oversaw the occupation of Germany, warned that the events in Prague signaled "a sub-tle change in the Soviet attitude," at once "faintly contemptuous, slightly arrogant, and certainly assured."[39] Secretary of State Marshall warned of the gravity of the situation in Central Europe. In that context, advocates of the Marshall Plan pushed successfully for its enactment.

A blend of humanitarian and social democratic rhetoric, fear-mongering, and stra-tegic anti-Communism shaped Truman's Cold War foreign policy. He and his advisers were New Dealers enough to describe American foreign policy in the soaring rhetoric of Roosevelt's Four Freedoms. They were Cold Warriors enough to shift their aims to one version of freedom—free enterprise—at the expense of a more inclusive social democratic politics. And they were astute enough politically to capitalize on a sense of anxiety to build political will. For a few critical years in the second half of the 1940s, the ideal of expanding the New Deal worldwide collided with the imperatives of making a world safe for capitalism, in a climate of escalating fear. Ultimately security and enterprise would trump social democracy.

The Election of 1948

The struggles over labor, civil rights, and Communism shaped the election of 1948, a four-way race against incumbent Harry Truman. It was the first presidential election since 1932 without Franklin Roosevelt on the ticket. Two of Truman's opponents had defected from the ranks of the Democratic Party, a reminder of the instability of Roosevelt's governing coalition.

HENRY WALLACE AND THE PROGRESSIVE INSURGENCY On the left stood former vice president Henry Wallace. A quixotic figure, he had gained the support of the New Deal's left flank during his time as vice president. "Some have spoken of the 'American Century,'" Wallace proclaimed in 1942. "I say that the century on which we are entering—the century which will come out of the war—can be and must be the century of the common man."[40] He was arguing with Henry Luce, the influential publisher of *Time* and *Life* magazines, who had envisioned an "American Century," when the United States would "exert upon the world the full impact of our influence, for such purposes as we see fit and by such means as we see fit."[41]

Wallace was the administration's strongest advocate of full employment, federal health insurance, and guaranteed annual wages, all programs that conservative Democrats and the GOP saw as dangerously socialistic. In 1944 FDR, facing pressure from party insiders who feared that Wallace could assume the presidency in the likely event that the ailing FDR died in office, named Truman his vice-presidential nominee, demoting Wallace, as the embittered vice president saw it, to secretary of commerce.

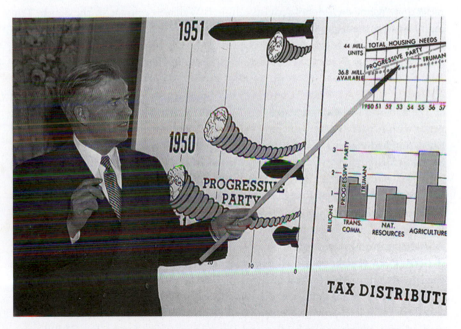

Henry Wallace A staunch New Dealer and former vice president, Wallace challenged President Truman from the left in the 1948 presidential election. Here, he presents the Progressive Party budget, pledging to cut military spending and expand social services.

Wallace, a restless seeker (he had flirted with various religions, from Catholicism to Theosophy), wandered further leftward, never veering from his agenda as an internationalist, advocate of human rights, and friend of labor. Rather naïvely, he found much to commend in the Soviet Union, even if his critics unfairly charged that he was a Communist or a Communist dupe. Wallace used his position at Commerce to challenge Truman's foreign policy, denouncing the new president as a militarist. Finally, in September 1946, he publicly criticized British prime minister Winston Churchill for his belligerent stance toward the Soviet Union. Truman, furious, insisted on Wallace's resignation.

Unchained from the administration and using his new position as editor of *The New Republic* as a bully pulpit, Wallace railed against Truman, accusing him of capitulating to business interests, of unnecessary belligerence toward the Soviets, and of failure on civil rights and labor. After traveling the country in 1946 and 1947, giving speeches to rapturous audiences, he decided to mount a third-party effort for the presidency. As the Progressive Party candidate, he surrounded himself with left-liberal New Dealers and, to his later chagrin, with members of the Communist Party, who saw in his foreign policy and staunch New Dealism an opportunity to revive the Popular Front. Wallace fearlessly defended civil rights on a tour through the South. He was frequently pelted with tomatoes and eggs but refused to relent on his position that "the poll tax must go."

Wallace ran an uphill battle. Most CIO unions had made their peace with Truman after he vetoed the Taft-Hartley Act. They put their formidable resources behind his reelection. While civil rights activists admired Wallace's courage in the South, Truman had won the fealty of black voters; hardly any black newspapers endorsed Wallace. But Truman's civil rights position spurred another revolt, this one from the right. Southern Democrats found little to like in the president's pro–civil rights program.

THE DIXIECRAT REBELLION White Southerners found themselves dismayed at Truman and increasingly uneasy with the Democratic Party itself. FDR had kept peace within party ranks by deferring to powerful southern Democrats. New Deal legislation had mostly frozen out African Americans, in exchange for southern votes. Social Security had excluded farm laborers and domestics, the two occupations that employed most African Americans. The administration of welfare, unemployment insurance, and old age assistance was left in the hands of state and local officials who blatantly discriminated against blacks. The Federal Housing Administration refused to underwrite home mortgages in racially mixed neighborhoods. The Agricultural Adjustment Administration's farm subsidies went to property owners, not to renters, sharecroppers, or debt peons, all disproportionally black. FDR even refused to back antilynching legislation for fear of alienating southern Democrats.

One of the bitterest pills was the 1944 Servicemen's Readjustment Act, popularly called the GI Bill. It provided returning veterans with unemployment compensation, medical care, educational subsidies, and access to mortgage funds. The GI Bill sent a generation of men and some women back to school, made home ownership a possi-

Dixiecrats Members of the Alabama delegation to the 1948 Democratic National Convention howled in protest when the party adopted a pro–civil rights platform. They would walk out of the convention and shift their support from President Harry Truman to South Carolina governor Strom Thurmond, who ran on the States' Rights Democratic ticket.

bility for the masses, and built a suburban middle class. It helped prevent a postwar depression. But most of its benefits did not reach black veterans. Many colleges and universities refused to admit blacks, or they let in a token number. And few blacks could use GI Bill housing benefits, because banks, real estate brokers, and housing developers openly discriminated against them.

Some northern Democrats pushed their party to support civil rights for African Americans. At the 1948 convention, Minneapolis mayor Hubert H. Humphrey roused liberals with his argument that "the time has arrived in America for the Democratic Party to get out of the shadow of states' rights and walk forthrightly into the bright sunshine of human rights."[42] Southern delegations were outraged. When the convention supported Humphrey's position, many walked out, while others led an unsuccessful effort to replace Truman with Georgia senator Richard Russell, a congressional powerhouse and staunch segregationist. After the convention, many southern Democrats rallied behind South Carolina's governor, Strom Thurmond, the insurgent candidate of the new States' Rights Democratic Party, nicknamed the Dixiecrats.

Thurmond had begun his career as a staunch New Dealer, supporting Social Security, jobs programs, and a federal minimum wage but never wavering from his commitment to white supremacy. At twenty-two, Thurmond had fathered a daughter, Essie Mae, with Carrie Butler, a sixteen-year-old black girl who worked for his family, though it would be decades, after Thurmond's death in 2003, before the story became public. Running against Truman, he declared that not even the U.S. Army "could admit the nigger race into our theaters, into our swimming pools, into our homes, and into our churches."[43] But increasingly Thurmond cast his lot with pro-business opponents of civil rights, adopting their argument that antidiscrimination laws threatened economic liberty. It was a position that would lead Thurmond, over his later career, to seal the Dixie-GOP marriage and eventually to defect to the Republican Party himself in 1964.

TRUMAN'S ELECTORAL COALITION The odds seemed long against Truman's reelection. Not only did he face mutiny in his own party; his Republican opponent was the well-regarded governor of New York, Thomas Dewey, who had run against Roosevelt in 1944 and won 46 percent of the vote nationwide. Dewey represented the moderate wing of his party. A strong supporter of civil rights, he had signed a strong state antidiscrimination law in 1944. An internationalist, he strongly supported the United Nations and opposed Robert Taft and the Republican isolationists. Dewey also supported liberal programs such as public housing, generous unemployment insurance, government-funded highways, and Social Security. As he argued, "anybody who thinks that an attack on the fundamental idea of security and welfare is appealing to people generally is living in the Middle Ages."[44]

How could Truman beat Dewey if the Democratic electorate split? Truman's advisers boldly gambled that enough southern Democrats would remain loyal to the party to neutralize Thurmond's challenge. They poached key constituents from Wallace's shaky coalition, including organized labor. Some left-led unions supported Wallace, but radical unionists were weak in 1948, hobbled by factionalism and anti-Communism. Mainstream union leaders, who had been lukewarm to Truman in 1946, now backed him loyally because he took their side in the debate over Taft-Hartley. Many unions used their money and troops to get out the vote for Truman.

The president needed more votes, both among progressive whites who might lean toward Wallace and especially among black voters who, because of their mass migration northward, were increasingly powerful, particularly in closely contested northern states. In 1948 journalist Henry Lee Moon published an influential book called *Balance of Power: The Negro Vote*. Moon, a brilliant young writer, one of the first black graduates of Ohio State's prestigious journalism program, was just the man for the job. He had covered racial politics for various papers, including *The New York Times*, since the mid-1930s. During World War II he had worked as a writer for the CIO, traveling to the South to publicize its union-organizing campaigns. In 1947 he became the NAACP's chief publicist. Moon's argument was simple: black voters, who had long supported the party of Lincoln but had recently defected to the Democrats, might switch back. Their votes could decide the fate of mayoral, congressional, and statewide elections, even the presidency.

Truman used his executive power to move forward on civil rights. He cared about winning black votes but also worried about America's international reputation. In October 1947 the President's Committee on Civil Rights, which Truman had created a year earlier, issued a report, *To Secure These Rights*. The committee argued that "domestic civil rights shortcomings are a serious obstacle" to America's influence in the postwar world.[45]

In July 1948, Truman boldly circumvented Congress and issued Executive Orders 9980, which banned discrimination in the federal workforce (in effect creating a permanent FEPC), and 9981, which desegregated the U.S. military. Echoing the language of the Double Victory campaign, Truman insisted that the armed forces maintain "the highest standards of democracy, with equality of treatment and opportunity."[46] Behind the scenes, many top military leaders quietly supported the move: it was costly to maintain separate barracks, separate dining halls, and even separate blood banks for black and white soldiers. In the fall—mostly off the radar of the white-owned news media but covered at length by the black press, Truman became the first major Democratic candidate to campaign in black neighborhoods, in both Harlem and North Philadelphia, hoping to appeal to black voters in closely contested states.

Neither Wallace nor Thurmond did particularly well. Both won about 2.5 percent of the vote. Wallace did badly even among the groups he saw as his base—organized labor and blacks. Thurmond won a majority of voters in Alabama, Louisiana, Mississippi, and South Carolina, but Truman swept the rest of the South. Republican Thomas Dewey scarcely benefited from the split ticket. He had run a lackluster campaign. In a low-turnout election, Truman lost some closely contested states, including Dewey's New York, Michigan, and Pennsylvania, but he eked out a victory in others, among them Ohio, Illinois, and California. Whether black votes put him over the top is uncertain, but it is clear that Truman moved fast on civil rights because he believed they mattered.

Few pundits believed that the Dixiecrat defection would be lasting. For the moment, the South remained solidly Democratic. The Dixie-GOP alliance would continue to weaken labor and thwart civil rights legislation, leaving the president little room to maneuver on domestic issues. For the next four years, international conflicts would take priority in Washington. Truman and Congress would find common cause in the aggressive pursuit of the Cold War at home and abroad.

Anti-Communism at Home

For President Truman, the crusades against Communism abroad and at home were inseparable. Well before his 1948 campaign, he had laid the groundwork for an aggressive campaign against the "red menace." In March 1947, just after he announced the Truman Doctrine, the president signed Executive Order 9835, creating loyalty review boards to ferret out federal employees who were "disloyal to the Government of the United States." This category included the vanishingly small number who called for violent revolution or engaged in espionage against the United States. But the order also covered many more—those affiliated with any group "designated by the Attorney General as totalitarian, fascistic, communistic, or subversive."[47] Over the next several years, such investigations would extend to government contractors and, at the state and local levels, to public employees of all stripes, from teachers to traffic engineers. About twelve hundred federal government workers lost their jobs during the Truman administration because of suspected disloyalty and, though precise figures are hard to assemble, thousands more at the state and local levels.

ROOTS OF ANTI-COMMUNISM The anti-Communist crusade had deep roots, extending back to the battles in the 1880s and 1890s against anarchists and radicals who organized among immigrants in big cities like New York and Chicago. It was fueled by the systematic crackdown on dissent and the imposition of strict censorship laws during World War I. It intensified in fears of Bolshevism after the 1917 Russian Revolution and in crackdowns on suspected Bolshevik sympathizers in the immediate postwar years. During the 1920s, the Red Scare targeted labor activists, suspected anarchists, and socialists. It took new form during the New Deal. By the 1936 election, right-wing critics of Roosevelt regularly denounced the recognition of labor's bargaining rights, government job-creation and housing programs, Social Security, unemployment insurance, and aid to dependent children as Communist-inspired, ignoring their roots in homegrown, American reform politics dating back to the Progressives.

As the world hurtled toward World War II, the U.S. government had hunted suspected radicals. In 1938, Representative Martin Dies (D-TX) drafted legislation creating a special House Committee on Un-American Activities to investigate radical insurgencies. Dies and his committee targeted pro-Nazi groups but singled out the larger network of Socialist and Communist activists, during a period when the left had unprecedented influence on mainstream politics, intellectual life, and labor unionism. The 1940 Smith Act criminalized any activities or publications "advocating, advising, or teaching the duty, necessity, desirability, or propriety of overthrowing or destroying any government in the United States by force or violence," a law that brought members of pro-Nazi organizations as well as leftists to federal courts for trial.[48] After the war, as the American alliance with the Soviet Union quickly frayed, Smith Act prosecutions almost exclusively targeted members of Socialist and Communist organizations.

The key player in investigating suspected subversives was the Federal Bureau of Investigation. Founded in 1908, the FBI expanded substantially under J. Edgar Hoover, the secretive director who took over the agency in 1924 and would go on to lead it for forty-eight years. Beginning in 1939, Hoover ordered the agency to compile a secret "Security Index" of individuals perceived to be dangerous to the United States. That list grew to 26,000 names by 1954. By 1960 the FBI had compiled a total of 430,000 dossiers on organizations and individuals suspected of subversion. Using new technologies of surveillance, the FBI cultivated informants—more than 109,000 in 1953 alone—who monitored radical organizations and dissidents and watched over defense plants and other sites deemed to be vital to national security. The FBI sometimes eavesdropped on meetings and sent undercover agents to infiltrate left-leaning groups.

THE COMMUNIST PARTY AND ITS CRITICS The FBI paid special attention to members of the Communist Party (CP) and a number of affiliated organizations. Small in number and shrinking, CP membership had peaked at around 100,000 during the Depression. The party had enjoyed a revival during World War II, when the United States and the Soviet Union were allies. But it shrank after the war, in part because of the party's strict rules, its expectation that members would devote their lives to the movement ("every evening to Party work"), and the rigid partisan discipline imposed by Moscow as the Cold War intensified.

About 40 percent of the party's membership lived in New York. Some were "fellow travelers," who were sympathetic to Communist goals, like Congressman Vito Marcantonio, a fiery Italian American who represented mostly Italian and Puerto Rican East Harlem and won voters with his energetic commitment to civil rights, his support for organized labor, and in the late 1940s, his critique of the Cold War. Ben Davis, Jr., a lawyer and one of the few blacks to hold elective office in the country—he was elected to New York's city council in 1943—was also a Communist. But in most places outside New York, Communists had little success at the ballot box. Unlike in Europe, where Communist parties became major political players in the postwar years, America's CP remained on the electoral fringe.

Mostly frozen out of office, Communists embedded themselves in labor unions or volunteered for groups seeking social change, particularly in the struggle for civil rights. Many black activists and intellectuals, even those with little sympathy for Communists, could not help but admire their commitment to racial equality. Dorothy Height, a devout black churchwoman who would have a distinguished career in the YWCA and in black women's groups, rejected Communists' atheism but was attracted by their energetic efforts on behalf of racial equality. "I went to all kinds of Young Communists groups' meetings, I was in everything," she recalled, "but I knew I was not and never would be a Communist."[49]

THE VARIETIES OF ANTI-COMMUNISM Even though some liberals and leftists admired the CP, many could not stomach party members' secrecy and their uncritical support for Moscow's shifting party line. The CP lost many followers for good when, in 1939, it endorsed the Hitler-Stalin pact, opposing intervention against Nazism, then changed positions again a little more than a year later when Germany invaded the Soviet Union. The harsh realities of life under Stalin's rule alienated many on the left. Some of the most pronounced critics of Communism in the United States came from the small but vocal Socialist Party and various socialist sects that denounced the Soviet Union's lack of democracy, its bureaucracy, and its industrial policies.

An even larger contingent of anti-Communists was liberal. Americans for Democratic Action, founded in 1947 by longtime New Dealers on the Democratic Party's left, railed against Communism. Mainstream Democrats saw the New Deal as a compelling alternative to both laissez-faire economics and Communism, providing for social welfare and a well-regulated economy while upholding the primacy of individual rights and the sanctity of private property. "What we saw in the Russia of the thirties," wrote historian Arthur Schlesinger, Jr., in his spirited defense of liberalism, *The Vital Center*, a 1949 best seller, "was a land where industrialization was underwritten

by mass starvation, where delusions of political infallibility led to the brutal extermi-
nation of dissent, and where the execution of heroes of the revolution testified to some
deep inner contradiction in the system."[50]

Religious beliefs also fueled anti-Communism. The most vocal critics of the Soviets
were Roman Catholics, who denounced Russia as a haven of atheism and who singled
out the persecution of religious minorities and the state control of religious expression.
In 1930 Fulton J. Sheen, America's most influential priest, a brilliant philosopher and
theologian, launched a popular radio program, realizing that he could reach a bigger
flock with new media than with arcane theological treatises. Over the air in 1948, he
offered an eleven-part denunciation of Communism, which he turned into a popular four-book series. In 1951, the year he was named a bishop, he launched his most
successful venture, a television show, *Life Is Worth Living*, eventually reaching about
thirty million viewers a week. He warned his viewers of the evils of the Soviet Union
but also of their own moral laxity. Communism, he argued, "is not to be feared just because it is anti-God, but because we are Godless; not because it is strong but because
we are weak, for if we are under God, then who can conquer us?"[51] It was commonplace
on Sundays for Catholics to pray for their coreligionists behind the iron curtain. In
1952, Pope Pius XII issued a proclamation consecrating Russia to the Virgin Mary,
leading Catholics worldwide to pray for the "conversion of Russia."

HUAC AND THE ANTI-COMMUNIST CRUSADE Red-baiting worked well
at the ballot box. In 1946, for example, an ambitious California politician, Richard
Nixon, won election to the House by denouncing his Democratic opponent, Jerry
Voorhis, as a Communist. When he ran for the U.S. Senate four years later, he trounced
his opponent, Helen Gahagan Douglas, by labeling her the "pink lady," compiling a
"pink sheet" that compared her votes with those of Vito Marcantonio. According to
Nixon, she had voted with Marcantonio 353 times, in his view evidence of her Communist sympathies. He called her "pink right down to her underwear."[52] For Nixon,
conflating liberals and leftists was political gold.

Not surprisingly, Congressman Nixon found his way to the House Un-American
Activities Committee (HUAC). In the spring of 1947, he joined HUAC's high-profile investigation of the United Electrical Workers, a left-dominated union. HUAC
provided a forum for conservative southern Democrats and pro-business Republicans
to lambaste unions and civil rights activists as pawns of Moscow, and to undermine
left-leaning critics of the American economy.

HUAC also extended its hearings to Communism in Hollywood. In October
1947 the committee investigated forty-one prominent actors, actresses, screenwriters,
and directors. The hearings began with friendly testimony from Walt Disney and from
Screen Actors Guild head Ronald Reagan, a B-movie actor who had put more energy
into union politics than into his onscreen career. Ten witnesses refused to testify and
were cited for contempt. Over the next several years, HUAC investigated the directors
of films such as *The Best Years of Our Lives*, *Gentleman's Agreement*, which criticized
anti-Semitism and racism in housing, and *Salt of the Earth*, which chronicled the strug-

gles of Mexican-born mine workers. HUAC targeted nearly every type of cultural producer—poets, artists, novelists, even comic book writers—based on the assumption that they used their art to indoctrinate the masses.

HUAC traveled around the country, holding hearings in major cities, with special interest in teachers and professors, government workers, and labor organizers. Sometimes those hearings backfired. In Detroit, for example, HUAC chair John Wood (D-GA) targeted left-leaning auto unionists and civil rights activists. But during HUAC's visit to Detroit in October 1953, four of the first six witnesses he subpoenaed were African American, infuriating black Detroiters and leading to a dramatic confrontation. Coleman Young, a black labor leader (and two decades later Detroit's first black mayor), took the stand and faced down Wood. Young had imbibed radical politics at a local barbershop in his childhood neighborhood on the city's west side, and in the 1940s he had lost jobs at Ford and the post office for his outspoken efforts in support of unionization. A talented organizer and speaker, Young moved into CIO leadership, supported Henry Wallace, and in 1951 was a founder of the leftist National Negro Labor Council, which pushed for workplace civil rights and challenged the expansion of the auto industry into the Jim Crow South. Young chided Wood for using the term "nigra." When Congressman Donald Jackson (D-CA) suggested that Young was downplaying the progress of blacks, Young snapped back: "You can't tell me that Jim Crow doesn't exist in California."[53] He became a folk hero.

An Escalating Cold War

Many were the crimes and many the victims of America's domestic crusade against Communism, but the Cold War abroad took a greater toll. While the United States continued to send economic aid and military support to Europe, the struggle against Communism intensified elsewhere in the world, particularly East Asia. The collapse of Japanese imperial rule in Manchuria spurred a civil war in China between the Nationalists, led by the unpopular and corrupt Chiang Kai-shek, and insurgents led by Communist Mao Zedong. The Soviets, who shared a long border with China, had a complex and troubled relationship with the country, supporting both Mao and Chiang in their struggle against Japan during World War II. Stalin also kept a distance from Mao, uncertain that China was ready for Communism. Truman and his advisers saw China as a sidelight in the Cold War and calculated that the cost of intervention in the bitter civil war far outweighed any possible geopolitical gains.

That decision backfired. In 1949, Mao and the Communists won control of the mainland, leaving Chiang and his supporters to retreat to the island of Taiwan (also known as Formosa), where they would establish a government-in-exile. The Truman administration then faced the searing accusation that it had "lost" China. Dean Acheson, now serving as secretary of state, took the brunt of the criticism, with Republicans calling for his resignation. The charge would haunt the Democrats for decades to follow and would indelibly shape the next phase of the Cold War in Asia.

Making a Nation

The Cold War at Home

From

Red Channels

The Report of Communist Influence in Radio and Television (1950)

The right-wing magazine *Counterattack* published the pamphlet *Red Channels* to spread fear that Communists had infiltrated America's broadcast networks and were using programming to indoctrinate unsuspecting viewers. It listed 151 journalists, executives, actors, and producers as "Red fascists and their sympathizers." Many studios and broadcasters blacklisted these suspected Communists, causing them to lose their jobs.

In indoctrinating the masses of the people with Communist ideology and the pro-Soviet interpretation of current events, the Communist Party, with set purpose, uses not only Party members, but also fellow-travelers and members of Communist adjuncts and periphery organizations. It is the Party's boast that for every Party member there are at least 10 "reliables," dupes or innocents who, for one reason or another will support its fronts. Our so-called "intellectual" classes—members of the arts, the sciences and the professions—have furnished the Communist Party USA with the greatest number in these classifications. . . .

Dramatic programs are occasionally used for Communist propaganda purposes. A few documentary programs produced by one network in particular have faithfully followed the Party line. Several commercially sponsored dramatic series are used as sounding boards, particularly with reference to current issues in which the Party is critically interested: "academic freedom," "civil rights," "peace," the H-Bomb, etc. . . .

With radios in most American homes and with approximately 5 million TV sets in use, the Cominform and the Communist Party USA now rely more on radio and TV than on the press and motion pictures as "belts" to transmit pro-Sovietism to the American public. . . .

The Communist party has made intensive efforts to infiltrate every phase of our life, and because of its great propaganda value has concentrated on radio and television. Networks, individual stations, advertising agencies, "package producers," radio-TV unions and even the trade press have been more and more "colonized" by the Party. The "colonists" need not be party members or even deliberate cooperators. It is sufficient if they advance Communist objectives with complete unconsciousness.

Coleman A. Young

Testimony before the Committee on Un-American Activities, U.S. House of Representatives, Hearings in Detroit, Michigan (1952)

Young, an African American activist in Detroit, drew HUAC's suspicion because of his affiliation with left-leaning civil rights and labor organizations. Young's combative answers attracted media attention and helped him launch a successful political career. In 1973 he won election as Detroit's first black mayor.

Mr. TAVENNER. . . . I desire to ask you the question which I have asked other witnesses: Are you now a member of the Communist Party?

Mr. YOUNG. I refuse to answer that question, relying upon my rights under the fifth amendment, and, in light of the fact that an answer to such a question, before such a committee, would be, in my opinion, a violation of my rights under the first amendment, which provides for freedom of speech, sanctity and privacy of political beliefs and associates, and, further, since I have no purpose of being here as a stool pigeon. . . .

Mr. TAVENNER. You told us you were the executive secretary of the National Negro Congress——

Mr. YOUNG. That word is "Negro," not "Niggra."

Mr. TAVENNER. I said, "Negro." I think you are mistaken.

Mr. YOUNG. I hope I am. Speak more clearly.

Mr. WOOD. I will appreciate it if you will not argue with counsel.

Mr. YOUNG. It isn't my purpose to argue. As a Negro, I resent the slurring of the name of my race.

Mr. WOOD. You are here for the purpose of answering questions. . . .

Mr. POTTER. . . . We are here to find out the extent of the Communist activities in this area. You are in a position to help and aid, if you will, but the attitude you are taking is uncooperative to such an investigation.

Mr. YOUNG. I am not here to fight in any un-American activities, because I consider the denial of the right to vote to large numbers of people all over the South un-American, and I consider—— . . .

Mr. TAVENNER. Do you consider the activities of the Communist Party un-American?

Mr. YOUNG. I consider the activities of this committee, as it cites people for allegedly being a Communist, as un-American activities. . . .

Questions for Analysis

1. According to *Red Channels*, how do Communists manipulate public opinion?

2. What are Young's objections to the HUAC investigation?

3. Consider the different assessments of Communism and civil liberties in these two documents.

Cold Warriors President Harry S. Truman (*center*) transformed America's role in the postwar world, with the assistance of Secretary of State Dean Acheson (*left*) and Secretary of Defense George Marshall (*right*), depicted here in 1950.

By 1950, hoping to deflect criticism, Acheson adopted a hard line on China. Although Mao had signaled that he would welcome a rapprochement with the United States to serve as a counterweight with the Soviets, even a hint of diplomacy with the new regime was impossible. Supporters of Chiang Kai-shek—the "China lobby"—pressured the United States to recognize the Nationalists in Formosa as the sole legitimate Chinese government. Rather than viewing Mao's People's Republic of China as a potential rival with the Soviet Union and pitting the two regimes against each other, Acheson and the Truman administration treated the new regime as a Soviet ally.

In the wake of the Chinese revolution, Truman and Acheson made two momentous decisions that would embroil the United States in two devastating wars. In May 1950, during a visit to Paris, Acheson pledged that the United States would support the French in their struggle to preserve their colony, Indochina, against Vietnamese revolutionaries led by Ho Chi Minh. Thus began a quarter century of American engagement in Vietnam. And in June, the United States, with the backing of the UN, launched a massive military operation in Korea that led to a devastating three-year war that would worsen U.S. relations with both the Soviet Union and China, ravage large parts of the Korean peninsula, and leave nearly two million combatants and civilians dead.

THE KOREAN WAR Few places seemed more remote and less central to the Cold War than the former Japanese colony of Korea. In 1945, after the Japanese defeat, the Americans and the Soviets divided the country in half, as Soviet troops occupied the area north of the thirty-eighth parallel and the United States controlled the region to the south. Like many postcolonial regimes, Koreans were bitterly divided over their political future: authoritarian but generally incompetent nationalists under Syngman Rhee gained power in the south and the brutal, pro-Soviet regime of Kim Il Sung controlled the north, both hoping to govern a unified Korea after the occupations ended.

On June 25, 1950, Kim Il Sung launched a surprise attack on the South. The North Koreans were well armed, disciplined, and ruthless. Kim had Stalin's backing and a formidable arsenal from his Soviet benefactors. Kim also believed, without warrant, that his invasion of the South would spur an anti-Rhee insurgency, bringing the civil war to a decisive close. Rhee's regime was indeed fragile. His party had been defeated in April elections, and the United States was, for a time, unwilling to do much to prop up his rule. Both Stalin and Kim had good reason to believe that the United States, which had been bolstering its military presence elsewhere in Asia, would not bother to interfere. In January, responding to criticism about the loss of China, Acheson delivered a major speech in which he announced the creation of a "defense perimeter" in East Asia, pledging that the United States would respond to any aggressive military action within its boundaries. Notably, he did not include Korea.

Within days after crossing the thirty-eighth parallel, North Korean troops rolled through Seoul, the capital and largest city in the south, and advanced toward Pusan, on the southeastern tip of the peninsula. The Truman administration responded readily. Truman got the UN Security Council to issue a resolution denouncing North Korean aggression. It passed because the Soviets were, at the time, boycotting the UN for its refusal to seat the People's Republic of China on the Security Council. Truman then proceeded with military engagement that he called a "police action" in Korea without going to Congress for a declaration of war. The decision set a precedent of ignoring Article I, Section 8 of the Constitution, which gave Congress the authority to declare war. Thereafter most of America's wars, including Vietnam, would be the result of presidential action, without prior congressional declaration.

Truman argued that the "police action" was necessary given the possibility of Communist expansion in Asia. It was also expedient, defusing the political charge that he had "lost" China. "If this was allowed to go unchallenged," recalled the president of the North Korean invasion, "it would mean a third world war, just as similar incidents had brought on the second world war."[54]

Truman's decision proved, at first, tremendously popular. His approval rating, which had plummeted in the aftermath of the Chinese revolution, skyrocketed. The president's critics on both left and right joined the cause. For liberals—including Henry Wallace, who opposed the Truman Doctrine—the war was necessary to uphold the UN resolution and bring democracy to the Korean peninsula. For others across the political spectrum, war was necessary to prevent future Communist aggression. Even Taft and the embattled isolationists supported intervention in Korea.

Truman dispatched Pacific commander General Douglas MacArthur to devise a plan to push back the North Koreans and within days ordered the deployment of troops in South Korea. MacArthur was anything but cautious, and the administration gave him great license to conduct the war according to his own instincts. In the short run, that decision to give MacArthur a free hand seemed a brilliant move. But in the long term, it proved disastrous both militarily and diplomatically.

On September 15, 1950, MacArthur directed one of the riskiest invasions in modern military history, a landing at Inchon Bay. The sea at Inchon saw huge tidal fluctuations; at low tide much of the bay was a mudflat. Ships could carry troops close to shore only a few times a month without the risk of being stranded. The troops needed to make landfall by scaling a huge seawall. The gamble, however, paid off. Inchon was poorly defended, and the landing allowed American troops to flank the North Korean troops. The American public hailed MacArthur for turning the fortunes of the war around.

From then on, the situation on the ground worsened rapidly. MacArthur decided to launch air and ground attacks north of the thirty-eighth parallel and threatened to bring troops up to the Korean-Chinese border. In response, the new People's Republic of China began massing troops on the border and joined in aid of the North Koreans in early November. Although MacArthur boasted that the war would be over by Christmas, the next few months were devastating. The North Koreans and their Chinese allies drove the UN troops back south of the thirty-eighth parallel in some of the bloodiest battles in any modern war; nearly ten thousand American soldiers were injured or killed. In late November, in one of the biggest slip-ups in his presidency, President Truman offhandedly suggested that the United States was considering the use of nuclear weapons in Korea. This drew howls of protest from America's allies.

In January and February 1951, MacArthur and the American troops succeeded in pushing the Chinese and North Koreans back to the thirty-eighth parallel, opening up the possibility for a cease-fire, which Truman and Acheson were considering as a prelude to negotiations. But MacArthur wanted much more—nothing short of a complete victory in North Korea and the unconditional surrender of China. To make his case, MacArthur held unauthorized interviews with the news media, criticizing his own commander-in-chief. Hinting that he did not trust Truman, the vain MacArthur suggested that he himself negotiate directly with the Chinese. At home, hawks on the president's right hailed MacArthur's aggressive stance and lambasted Truman for not heeding his advice. Truman and Acheson were furious at what they saw as the general's reckless posturing and insubordination and decided to relieve MacArthur of his command. On April 11, 1951, that decision went public. The general returned home a hero, while Truman's critics shredded the decision as capitulation to Communism.

Over the next two years, the war in Korea bogged down: it was not a limited engagement as Truman had promised; nor was it punctuated by many decisive victories for either side. The United States stepped up air attacks on North Korean troops and targets, eventually dropping some 635,000 tons of bombs on the peninsula, more than it had used in the whole Pacific theater during World War II. Nearly every urban

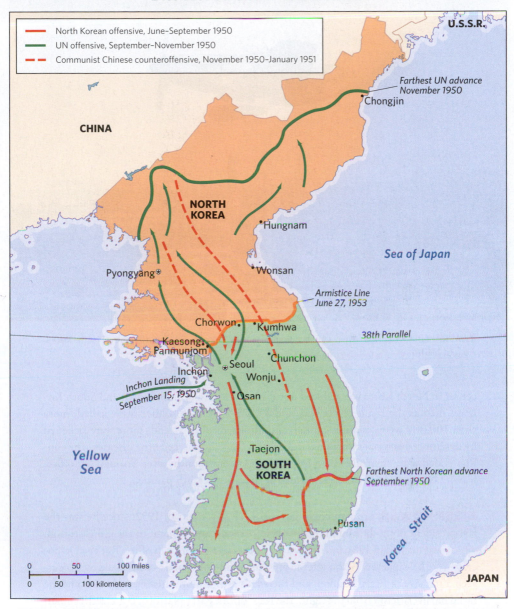

The Korean War 1950–1953

Legend:
- North Korean offensive, June–September 1950
- UN offensive, September–November 1950
- Communist Chinese counteroffensive, November 1950–January 1951

U.S.S.R.

CHINA

Farthest UN advance
November 1950

Chongjin

NORTH
KOREA

Hungnam

Sea of Japan

Pyongyang

Wonsan

Armistice Line
June 27, 1953

Chorwon • Kumhwa

38th Parallel

Kaesong
Panmunjom

Chunchon

Inchon • Seoul
Wonju

Inchon Landing
September 15, 1950

Osan

Yellow
Sea

Taejon

SOUTH
KOREA

Farthest North Korean advance
September 1950

Pusan

Korea Strait

JAPAN

0   50   100 miles
0 50 100 kilometers

The Korean War An American bomber releases napalm fire bombs over North Korea, August 1951.

center in North Korea was reduced to rubble. At least a million North and South Koreans died as the result of the war, and 33,629 American soldiers were killed; more than 100,000 were seriously injured; and hundreds of thousands more were sickened by dysentery, bacterial infections, and other water- and insect-borne diseases. The conflict ended with an armistice on July 27, 1953, a few months after Truman left office, leaving North and South Korea divided at the thirty-eighth parallel.

EISENHOWER Truman could have run for reelection in 1952, since he was the last president not to be bound by the twenty-second amendment to the Constitution, which was ratified in 1951 and limited presidents to two terms in office. But the Democrats were beleaguered. Although the president had unleashed a costly Cold War, overseen a massive military buildup, and fueled an anti-Communist crusade at home, he faced harsh criticism from the right. The Republican Party platform criticized Truman and Acheson's containment policy for leaving "countless human beings to a despotism and Godless terrorism." It predictably denounced the Truman administration for having lost China and fumbled the Korean War. It also sanctimoniously announced that "there are no Communists in the Republican Party," suggesting that Truman's party, for all of its zealous anti-Communism, was somehow teeming with leftists.

The Republicans chose a candidate who seemed highly qualified to carry forth America's Cold War aggressively: retired general Dwight David Eisenhower. A career military man who had become the mostly ceremonial president of Columbia University in 1948, he neither had political experience nor obvious partisan inclinations. Both parties had courted him.

On the campaign trail, Ike took a bellicose position, pledging to fight for the "liberation" of those who lived under Communist tyranny. In practice, Eisenhower's foreign policy differed little from his predecessor's. Both Truman and Eisenhower were committed to the policy of containment and maintained a large standing military. Both supported the National Security Act, and both supported the expansion of the CIA and its power to operate in secrecy.

McCARTHYISM Tensions with the Soviets, the Chinese revolution, and the Korean War all intensified the domestic crusade against the red menace. The anti-Communist movement got a new face and a new name with the activities of a formerly obscure first-term senator. After three undistinguished years in office, Joseph McCarthy (R-WI) discovered the political value of red-baiting. First elected to the Senate in the anti-Democratic wave of 1946, McCarthy was a devout Roman Catholic, a short-tempered alcoholic and gambler, and like many in the GOP, a strong pro-business voice. He supported Taft-Hartley, allied himself closely with the home building industry, and used his position to denounce public housing as a threat to free enterprise.

Not until 1950 did McCarthy blast himself onto the national stage, at an unlikely venue: a Lincoln Day address to a group of Republican women in Wheeling, West Virginia. "The State Department is infested with communists," he charged. "I have here in my hand a list of 205—a list of names that were made known to the Secretary of State as being members of the Communist Party and who nevertheless are still working and shaping policy in the State Department."[55] The charges stung because, at that moment, McCarthy's fellow Republicans were accusing Dean Acheson and the State Department's China hands—its experts on the region—of treason for aiding and abetting the Chinese revolution. Although McCarthy's numbers were slippery, his charges prompted the Senate to launch its own investigations of subversion in the federal government and even in the U.S. military.

McCarthy initially riveted the nation with his investigations of reds, but eventually he lost the support of the news media, a growing segment of the public, and president Dwight Eisenhower. Eisenhower had remained silent as McCarthy ascended to the national stage. But the president grew embarrassed by McCarthy's bombast. In March 1953, CBS news reporter Edward R. Murrow, a pioneering investigative journalist and hardly a Communist sympathizer, dispassionately unraveled McCarthy's techniques, demonstrating that many of the charges that he had hurled were based on unreliable testimony, secondhand evidence or rumor, and outdated information. But McCarthy, unstoppable, turned his attention to the military, accusing the army, navy, and air force of harboring Communists and other subversives.

McCarthy's inflammatory charges prompted the media to dig into the story for themselves. By the fall, Murrow was on the trail of Milo Radulovich, an air force lieutenant who fell afoul of a military regulation that found an individual a "security risk if he has close and continuing associations with communists or people believed to have communist sympathies."[56] Radulovich, who had no leftist affiliations, faced dismissal because he refused to cut ties with his father, who had once belonged to a Communist front organization, and his sister, who was thought to be subversive because of her support for liberal causes. Under pressure after Murrow's exposé, the air force reinstated Radulovich.

By early 1954, McCarthy was under siege both from the new Democratic majority in Congress and from fellow Republicans whose backing he had lost. Millions of Americans tuned into the thirty-six-day-long Army-McCarthy hearings, broadcast by the three major television networks between April and June 1954. Shabby, often unshaven, and embittered, McCarthy was a made-for-TV villain, harshly interrupting the proceedings with his shrill demand, repeated again and again, for "point of order."

Behind the scenes, Eisenhower unraveled McCarthy's plans by squashing his efforts to subpoena key military officials and withholding key information from the investigation. Finally, on June 9, McCarthy lashed out against the army's attorney, the whip-smart and poised Joseph Welch, accusing his law firm of employing a Communist. In words that would forever scar McCarthy, Welch snapped back, "I think I never really gauged your cruelty or your recklessness." When McCarthy continued his aggressive line of questioning, the exasperated Welch finally asked, "Have you no sense of decency, sir, at long last? Have you left no sense of decency?" McCarthy fought back, but Welch interrupted again, stating that he was finished. The audience burst into applause, leaving McCarthy stunned.[57]

Even with McCarthy discredited, the anti-Communist battle was far from over. HUAC continued to hold hearings, and suspected Communists faced ongoing interrogations. Investigators at the state and local level continued to ferret out suspected Communists. The Philadelphia board of education, for example, fired several teachers who pleaded their Fifth Amendment rights when HUAC held hearings on Communism in the public schools.

All together, about ten to twelve thousand suspected Communists lost their jobs, usually because they refused to cooperate with investigations or renounce the Communist Party. Those without U.S. citizenship were often deported. Two suspected Communists, Ethel and Julius Rosenberg, were executed after being convicted of conspiracy to commit espionage on behalf of the Soviet Union. The Rosenberg trial generated an intense controversy over whether two innocent Americans had been convicted. Later evidence suggested that Julius had indeed passed secrets to the Soviets, though it is less certain that the information jeopardized American security and warranted the death penalty.

More commonly, uncooperative witnesses or those convicted of membership in subversive organizations faced jail time. Folk singer Pete Seeger, who helped popularize the civil rights anthem "We Shall Overcome" and had been a Communist through 1950, paid the price for defying his interrogators. Called before HUAC in 1955,

Seeger offered to talk about his music and even to sing, but he refused to answer questions about his political affiliations: "I think these are very improper questions for any American to be asked, especially under such compulsion as this."[58] Convicted of contempt of Congress, Seeger was sentenced to a year in prison, and though he only served a day, his successful career was derailed. For seventeen years, he was barred from appearing on television and was turned away from major concert venues. Many of his recordings disappeared from stores.

Although the anti-Communist crusade barely slowed, Eisenhower's presidency seemed tranquil. The United States had risen to economic prominence. Observers celebrated American prosperity and consumerism. But the Cold War did not abate. Beneath a thin veneer of consensus and self-congratulation, the unresolved tensions of the Truman years persisted, particularly the poisonous divisions of race and the realities of an economy and consumer society that had brought unprecedented wealth to the United States but relied on workers and citizens, at home and abroad, who seldom saw the direct benefits of their hard work.

Suggested Reading

Anderson, Carol. *Eyes off the Prize: The United Nations and the African American Struggle for Human Rights, 1944–1955* (2003). Shows how civil rights activists linked their domestic struggles with global humanitarian efforts.

Borgwardt, Elizabeth. *A New Deal for the World: America's Vision for Human Rights* (2005). Explores how politicians, lawyers, and activists attempted to export Roosevelt's Four Freedoms.

Boyle, Kevin. *The UAW and the Heyday of American Liberalism, 1945–1968* (1995). A history of one of America's most influential unions and its efforts to shape national politics.

Craig, Campbell, and Fredrik Logevall. *America's Cold War: The Politics of Insecurity* (2009). A sweeping narrative of anti-Communist foreign policy, with attention both to global strategy and to domestic interests, from 1945 to 1989.

Crespino, Joseph. *Strom Thurmond's America* (2012). A vivid biography of the Dixiecrat who fused segregationism, antilabor politics, and staunch support for the growing military-industrial complex—and in the process created the Sunbelt.

Cumings, Bruce. *The Korean War: A History* (2010). An indispensable overview of Korean civil conflict, the country's entanglements with China and the United States, and the brutal war that ensued.

Leffler, Melvyn P. *A Preponderance of Power: National Security, the Truman Administration, and the Cold War* (1992). A foundational analysis of the origins of the Cold War.

McCullough, David. *Truman* (1993). This definitive biography moved Truman out of FDR's shadow.

Schrecker, Ellen. *Many Are the Crimes: McCarthyism in America* (1998). The politicians and intelligence officials who led a decades-long crusade against the American left, at a high cost to civil liberties.

Westad, Odd Arne. *The Global Cold War: Third World Interventions and the Making of Our Times* (2005). How the United States and the Soviet Union struggled for supremacy by intervening in independence movements and civil wars in Asia, Africa, and Latin America.

Chapter Review

Review Questions

1. How did the United Nations envision the postwar world order?

2. What were the strengths and weaknesses of the American occupation of Germany and Japan?

3. Why did the United States and Soviet Union end their wartime alliance?

4. What explains the strike wave in late 1945 and 1946?

5. What was the impact of the Taft-Hartley Act?

6. What was the Truman Doctrine?

7. Why did President Truman face such stiff opposition in the election of 1948?

8. Outline the views of anti-Communists in the late 1940s.

9. Why did the United States decide to intervene in the Korean War?

10. How did Senator Joseph McCarthy lose his credibility?

Key Terms

Postwar Prosperity and Its Discontents

✳

1946–1960

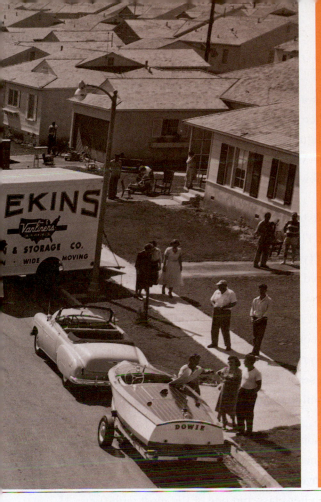

Fifth Avenue between 42nd Street and Central Park South bustled with commerce in the fall of 1946, the sidewalks packed with fashionable shoppers like Betty Goldstein, a stylish journalist who often spent part of her lunch hour checking out the latest ready-to-wear fashions. Business had picked up fast when the war ended, in part because of pent-up demand and unprecedented savings rates during the war. Without many opportunities to spend their wages wartime workers had squirreled away their paychecks in savings bonds and bank accounts, totaling some $150 billion. Even though she was just a few years out of college, Betty had money to spend. One of her favorite places was the luxurious Bergdorf Goodman store just a few blocks from her office. She was not prone to extravagance, but she adored black cashmere sweaters and occasionally splurged on high-end items, like her favorite accessory, a pair of Gucci gloves.[1]

Betty's office, at 11 East 51st Street, occupied a once-grand townhouse. As she climbed the building's imposing granite steps, a Bergdorf bag in hand, it was possible, if you did not know her Jewish name, to imagine her as the great-granddaughter of John Pierce, the Granite King, the nineteenth-century magnate who had built the magnificent stone edifice as a monument to his wealth. Or perhaps she was an Astor, the old-money mercantile family who had lived at 11 East 51st just a few decades earlier, before the rich moved farther uptown.

The Granite King or the Astors would have cringed if they had ever returned to their ancestral home. The obsequious servants were long gone, their hush supplanted by the click of typewriters and frequent outbursts of heated debate. Their house had suffered, at least from the viewpoint of Gilded Age America, a grim fate: it was now the headquarters of the United Electrical, Radio, and Machine Workers of America, known as the UE. Between 1946 and 1952, Betty worked as a reporter for the *UE News*, the union's muckraking newspaper. "She bubbled over with energy," one of her friends recalled of those days. Despite her fashion sense, she was no Astor. She "talked in spurts, rarely finishing a sentence, her mind racing so fast the words couldn't keep up with it."

Born in 1921 in Peoria, Illinois, Betty had grown up in comfort. Her father owned a successful jewelry business. Her mother, who had written for the local daily before having children, stayed at home to raise her and her two siblings. One of the smartest students in her class and one of the most ambitious—"I want success and fame," she told a classmate—she left Peoria behind for elite, all-female Smith College. Smith's atmosphere mixed New England propriety, intellectual rigor, and at the time, a zeal for social justice. Her professors, many of them liberal internationalists, some even Socialists and Communists, did not protect their students from the world. By her junior year, Betty was taking courses on social policy, learning about psychology, and studying economics. On the recommendation of one of her professors, she spent most of the summer of 1941 at the Highlander Folk School in rural East Tennessee, a sort of summer camp for radicals that trained generations of civil rights and labor activists, where students read the poetry of the Harlem Renaissance, learned about Indian nationalist Mohandas K. Gandhi, and debated the tactics of sit-down strikes and draft resistance.

< Families moving into newly built houses in Lakewood, California, a suburb of Los Angeles, in 1953 (*previous page*).

By the mid-1940s, Betty had discovered her lifelong passions—labor, politics, and feminism. Her prose was sharp and invariably radical. She lauded the CIO for giving workers "a power of their own to match that of their bosses." She believed that union wages and job security would give women financial independence and access to the booming postwar consumer culture. But she also worried about the rightward turn in American politics. She watched with anger as the UE saw its membership plummet under the Taft-Hartley Act. She lambasted HUAC, which hounded suspected Communists in the labor movement, many of them her colleagues. Nearly everything that she did the next fifty years would touch

Betty Goldstein (Friedan) In 1942 Betty Goldstein graduated from Smith College, where she honed her writing skills and gained a passion for social justice, laying the groundwork for her career as a labor journalist and feminist advocate.

on these issues, beginning with her work as a labor journalist in the 1940s, as a political organizer in Queens in the 1950s, and—under her married name, Betty Friedan—as the best-selling author of *The Feminine Mystique* and founder of the National Organization for Women in the 1960s. In the aftermath of the postwar anti-Communist crusade, she downplayed her radical past, but it indelibly shaped her career.

Postwar Prosperity

Betty worked for the UE during one of the longest economic booms in American history. The gross domestic product had increased by 4.8 percent in Truman's last four years. The national unemployment rate fell before reaching an all-time low of 2.9 percent in January 1953. Globally, the United States enjoyed unchallenged industrial power. By the late 1940s, more than half of the world's manufactured goods were American-made, including four-fifths of all cars. Almost two-thirds of the world's oil bubbled up from American soil, and more than half of the world's steel was forged in American foundries.

Postwar prosperity lifted the wages of tens of millions of American workers, in large part because big companies and powerful unions had successfully bargained for generous employment contracts. At the peak, in 1953, over a third of all American workers belonged to unions, including most of those in defense production, auto assembly, electrical manufacturing, steelmaking, and meatpacking. In the industrial belt that extended from New England down the Eastern Seaboard, across the Appalachians through the coal mining towns of Pennsylvania and West Virginia, and along the southern Great Lakes, unionization rates topped 50 percent. Even nonunion workers benefited. To compete with unionized firms and attract the best workers, many nonunion employers raised pay and offered good benefits.

LEFT BEHIND: AFRICAN AMERICANS AND FARMWORKERS Not everyone benefited from the postwar boom equally. African Americans had made big advances in wartime defense industries but saw only incremental gains in the two decades afterward. In the South—which recruited northern manufacturers looking for low-wage workers—blacks were usually frozen out of industry altogether. Regardless of their skill and experience, blacks were stuck on the bottom rung of the corporate ladder, in dangerous, unpleasant jobs, hauling heavy equipment, doing janitorial work, and stoking furnaces. Beginning in the late 1940s, many of those entry-level jobs disappeared, as companies like General Motors replaced unskilled workers with new "automated" labor-saving technology. Unlike whites, blacks had few chances to move up the ladder. Only 67 out of 11,125 skilled workers at GM were black in 1960. Without discrimination, many would have qualified for those jobs.

As Americans grew wealthier during the postwar boom, they bought more food. Food producers scrambled to meet a nearly insatiable demand for flash-frozen, canned, and ready-to-eat processed foods. Meat consumption skyrocketed, leading to the consolidation of small farms into enormous enterprises that factory-farmed chickens and pigs and mass-produced beef and dairy products. Growing demand for fruit and vegetables also transformed farming. In places like California's Central Valley, with rich soil but an arid climate, irrigation transformed farms into places where lettuce, tomatoes, grapes, and a huge variety of fruits and vegetables could be grown most of the year. In the 1930s, writer Carey McWilliams described the region's farms as "factories in the fields." By 1945, California had 5,939 farms of more than one thousand acres each, covering nearly twenty-five million acres.[2] American growers also expanded their investments overseas. United Fruit and Dole purchased produce from a network of vast plantations in Latin America, the Caribbean, and the Pacific islands, eager to capitalize on Americans' growing demand for tropical fruits like bananas, grapefruits, and pineapples, formerly luxury items.

Agribusinesses at home and abroad depended on a ready supply of cheap labor. Southern farms still relied on methods of labor dating back to emancipation, trapping blacks as debt peons and sharecroppers in conditions of near bondage. California re-

Chronology

1947	Congress of Racial Equality launches Journey of Reconciliation
1948	*Sipuel v. Regents of the University of Oklahoma*
	Shelley v. Kraemer
1950	*McLaurin v. Oklahoma State Regents*
	Sweatt v. Painter
	Age of marriage reaches historic low
1951	Window air conditioners introduced
	Mattachine Society founded
1952	Restriction of homosexuals from entering the United States
	Dwight D. Eisenhower (Republican) elected president
	United States tests first hydrogen bomb
1953	CIA-backed coup in Iran
	Senate hearings on juvenile delinquency begin
1954	*Brown v. Board of Education of Topeka, Kansas*
	CIA-backed coup in Guatemala
1955	*Rebel Without a Cause* and *Blackboard Jungle* open
	Daughters of Bilitis founded
	Montgomery Bus Boycott
1956	Interstate Highway Act
	Southern Manifesto
	Allen Ginsberg's poem *Howl* released
	Dwight D. Eisenhower (Republican) reelected president
1957	*Roth v. United States*
	Levittown housing protest
	Little Rock Central High School protest
1959	Fidel Castro takes power in Cuba

lied on migrant farm laborers, many Mexican, who lived in converted chicken coops, cabins, trailers, or poorly ventilated huts. In fields and orchards, they were exposed to harmful pesticides and chemical fertilizers. The bracero program peaked in the mid-1950s, with some 450,000 Mexican guest workers crossing the border per year to work on American farms. American agribusinesses also relied on an army of landless peasants who picked coffee beans and fruit in Guatemala, cut sugarcane in Cuba and Jamaica, toiled on pineapple plantations in Hawaii, and harvested cocoa and coffee beans in Colombia.

Unlike industrial workers, whose wages, hours, and working conditions were regulated under New Deal legislation and often protected by vigilant unions, American farmworkers were on their own. They did not have the right to collective bargaining. Growers punished those who complained about their working and living conditions, sent injured or ill workers back to their homelands rather than treating them, and turned over labor union organizers to the authorities for deportation. Farmworkers also did not have a minimum wage. They were not eligible for Social Security. Growers profited from large government agricultural subsidies but did not pass the benefits down to their workers.

THE "FAMILY WAGE" AND WOMEN WORKERS For all the travails of agricultural workers, most commentators could not help but notice that a large share of white, blue-collar workers—especially those in unionized industries—were better off than ever. By 1960, about 60 percent of American households, including most of those headed by unionized workers, belonged to the middle class, earning between $5,000 and $10,000 per year, depending on family size. Colonies of cottages and hunting cabins, owned by auto- and steelworkers, sprang up in the northern Great Lakes, in the Alleghenies and Poconos, and along the Jersey shore. Sociologists talked of the "embourgeoisement" of American workers, arguing that as they grew wealthier, America would become a classless society. They believed conflict between workers and bosses would soon become a thing of the past.

For the most part, blue-collar workers expected a "family wage," namely that a male breadwinner's single paycheck should be large enough to support his wife and family. During the immediate postwar years, many unions supported a suspension of seniority rules so that men who had fought in the war could move back into their former jobs, even if that meant laying off women workers. For their part, many women welcomed the opportunity to leave behind assembly lines, to return home and have children.

Over her long career, Betty Friedan wrote about a lot of topics, but she took special interest in women's issues, especially the situation of women workers. After a brief period of resettlement in 1946 and 1947, when factories laid off women and hired returning servicemen in their places, women's employment began to rise again. By 1953, 48 percent of single women worked, as did 26 percent of married women, comprising a larger part of the workforce than they had during World War II. Single women needed paychecks; if their husbands had died in the war or returned disabled, their families depended on women's work. The family wage was insufficient for a growing number of households, which could not subsist on one check alone.

Betty Friedan had a special vantage point on these changes. Her employer, the United Electrical Workers, represented more women than any other union in the country. No industry had been more feminized than electrical manufacturing. Sophisticated aircraft required elaborate electronics; so too did tanks and jeeps and cars. The military and the general public had an insatiable demand for radios. While manufacturers sometimes resisted hiring women workers until circumstances forced them to do so, electrical manufacturers valued female laborers.

Electrical workers were also among the best organized and best paid in the country. When Betty started working for the UE, it was the third-largest industrial union in the country and one of the twelve out of thirty-five CIO unions led by Communists. The UE represented more than 600,000 workers, including those employed by the industry's giants, General Electric, Westinghouse, and RCA. Few unions put more energy into helping advance women workers. UE organizers pushed for equal pay for equal work, demanded the protection of seniority for women workers, and negotiated for still-unheard-of maternity leave policies, so that women could resume working after they had children. For Betty, the UE was part of a "revolution" in women's work, one that could be a model for improving the lives of all Americans.

The generational legacy of women's workforce participation in World War II set the stage for the women's movement of the 1960s and 1970s. Older married women who had gone to work for the first time during the war saw their young daughters join them. Those daughters might have taken time out of the workforce in the late 1940s and early 1950s to marry and have their own daughters and sons, but after childbearing, their wartime skills and a booming economy brought them back to paid employment. In 1956 the average age of women workers was forty; it had been thirty-two in 1940. By the 1960s, the granddaughters of women who had gone to work in World War II could point to two generations of working women as role models. Betty Friedan celebrated those changes. "Men," she wrote in one of her first articles, published in 1943, "there's a revolution cooking in your own kitchens—revolutions of the forgotten female who is finally waking up to the fact that she can produce things besides babies."

The Baby Boom

The expansion of women's paid work came into collision with postwar norms about gender roles and the family. The period from the mid-1940s to the early 1960s saw a celebration of the male-headed nuclear family, one that belied the gradual change in the relationship of women and the workplace. At its core was a profound and still unresolved conflict: how should women negotiate paid labor outside the home with the demands of childrearing? For all the shifts in labor, domestic life remained women's domain. The normative mother would watch over her children in new informal "family rooms" that replaced the formal parlors of houses built between the 1840s and the 1920s.

Magazines geared to housewives, such as *Family Circle*, *Good Housekeeping*, and *Better Homes and Gardens*, saw their circulation skyrocket. *Good Housekeeping*'s subscription base doubled between 1943 and 1962, reaching over five million. In those pages, women could discover new recipes, read helpful hints for cleaning and household organization, and peruse advertisements for detergents, appliances, and child care products. And if they fretted about relationships, whether with their boyfriends, husbands, or kids, they could turn to advice columns, most notably those by the pseudonymous Ann Landers (launched in 1942) and Abigail Van Buren (launched in 1956), which were syndicated in papers nationwide and, from the mid-1950s to the end of the century, written separately by Esther Lederer and Pauline Phillips, twin sisters, originally from Iowa.

YOUNG NEWLYWEDS The family-centered culture of the postwar years resulted from a profound demographic shift that remade American households and the nation's very landscape. In 1950 the age of marriage fell to a historic low: the average woman married at 20.3 years, and the average man at 22.8. Along with marriage came children: families grew larger between the mid-1940s and the early 1960s, reaching an average of four children per woman of childbearing age. Even with more women in the paid labor market, heterosexual marriage and stay-at-home motherhood remained the norm and the ideal.

For most of American history, marriage had often been primarily a legal matter, bringing two families and their property together. But in the twentieth century—especially after World War II—many Americans came to see marriage as a vehicle for emotional fulfillment. The days of arranged marriages or loveless partnerships for the sake of children and inheritance faded as the marital bond was affective and emotional. In the 1940s and 1950s, clergymen, psychologists, and journalists used a new term, *companionate marriage*, to describe the new normal. Men and women were bonded by love, even if marriage was still legally a contractual relationship. A happy marriage should produce children—that went without saying—but it should also be personally fulfilling for both husband and wife.

Betty joined that trend. At age twenty-six, rather late for a woman of her generation, she married Carl, a theatrical producer. For Betty, the reasons for marriage were simple. She described herself as having "a pathological fear of being alone," but even more than that, she saw marriage as a vehicle for emotional fulfillment. In a paper she had written at Smith, she made what was a bold statement for the time: "marriage means togetherness." Like many marriages, however, Betty's was not a model of togetherness. She and her husband frequently argued. Having a family also came at a cost to her professional career. When she lost her job at the UE in 1952, she attributed it to the fact that she was pregnant with her second child. She resented that, despite her commitment to feminism, she remained the primary caregiver. Still, as a young mother, she remained politically engaged in the semisuburban housing development in Queens where she lived between 1950 and 1956. There, while her children frolicked in the garden, she organized mothers to protest rent hikes, push for civil rights, and improve the local school's curriculum.

SPOCK Many of the young parents who were Betty's neighbors had come of age during the austerity of the Depression and the shared sacrifice of war. During the ordeal, they had made do with hand-me-down clothes. During the war, they had often been left to fend for themselves with Daddy off to war and Mommy working in factories, growing the Victory Garden, or mobilizing civilian defense. After nearly two decades of scarcity, emotional and economic, postwar parents put more energy than ever into raising happy, comfortable children.

Millions looked for advice on how to bring up baby, and they turned to experts other than their parents or grandparents. The most influential was Dr. Benjamin Spock. The son of an elite Connecticut family, Spock had attended Yale, graduated at the top of his class at Columbia Medical School, and spent six years studying and undergoing psychoanalysis in the 1930s, while beginning his career as a pediatrician. In 1946, Spock exploded the conventional wisdom—the emphasis on discipline, structure, and denial in childrearing—in *The Common Sense Book of Baby and Child Care*. He assumed a gentle, reassuring tone: "Bringing up your child won't be a complicated job if you take it easy, trust your own instincts, and follow the directions that the doctor gives you."[3] Spock also reinforced the notion that young mothers should stay at home with their children, one that even Betty Friedan took to heart. No book, other than the Bible, sold more copies. By the best estimate, about one-fifth of all American households in the postwar years had Spock on their bookshelves. One journalist described the book as one that "many mothers clutch like a pacifier" because it so relieved their anxieties.[4]

A Nation of Homeowners

Americans had long valued domesticity and home ownership, but for most Americans through World War II, owning a home had been an unattainable dream. From 1929 to 1945, private housing development in the United States had nearly halted. The banking collapse during the Depression—not to mention the decline in most Americans' wages and savings—crippled the housing industry. During World War II, the federal government had diverted construction materials to the defense industry. Skilled workers found jobs building aircraft or contributing to the military's rapid construction of barracks, airstrips, and temporary encampments on the ground in Europe and the Pacific.

THE FEDERAL GOVERNMENT, HOME OWNERSHIP, AND RACE

Still, the federal government had laid the groundwork for the postwar housing boom in the depths of the Great Depression. In 1933 the Home Owners Loan Corporation made low-interest financing available to those who wanted to buy or repair their homes. In 1934, Roosevelt signed a law creating the Federal Housing Administration (FHA), which brought the government into the mortgage market. The FHA guaranteed mortgages, allowing lenders to offer long-term (usually thirty-year) loans with low down payments (usually 10 percent of the asking price). As late as the 1920s, home buyers had had to put as much as 50 percent down on a home and pay off the remaining amount in a period of about five years. Finally, the 1944 GI Bill extended low-interest home loans to returning veterans. The impact of these programs was nothing short of spectacular. Home ownership rates skyrocketed, from about 40 percent of all Americans in 1930 to over 60 percent in 1960. Builders scrambled to meet Americans' almost insatiable demand for new homes.

The housing boom came with one big restriction: keep "undesirables" out. During the 1920s, as African Americans began to migrate into American cities, housing developers devised strategies to keep new developments all white. Racially restrictive covenants, part of the language in deeds to most houses built between the 1920s and the late 1940s, used blunt language: "This property cannot be occupied by Negroes" or "colored" or "Ethiopians" (all terms referring to people of African descent) or "Orientals" or "Malays" or "Hindus" (people of Asian descent). Many covenants specified that properties could be sold or rented to "Caucasians only" (a term that referred to the alleged origins of Europeans in the Caucasus Mountains of Russia). "Semites," people of Jewish descent, usually appeared on the list of undesirables as well.

Racial categories also shaped federal housing policy. Beginning in the mid-1930s, the Home Owners Loan Corporation prepared "security maps" that determined what neighborhoods were eligible for government-backed home loans. The maps used a four-color scheme, designating areas as green (A), blue (B), yellow (C), and red (D). Neighborhoods colored green were the "best," blue were "still desirable," yellow were "definitely declining," and red were "hazardous." The presence of even a handful of blacks ensured a D rating. Only whites could get loans in top-ranked neighborhoods, including almost all the new suburbs that sprang up after World War II. Blacks, on the other hand, found themselves frozen out.

With these guidelines in place, real estate brokers considered it unethical to support racial integration. From the 1930s through the 1960s, the National Association of Real Estate Boards stated that realtors "should never be instrumental in introducing to a neighborhood a character of property or occupancy, members of any race or nationality, or any individual whose presence will be clearly detrimental to property values in a neighborhood."[5] Lest there be any confusion, an industry brochure offered guidance:

> *The prospective buyer might be a bootlegger who would cause considerable annoyance to his neighbors, a madam who had a number of call girls on her string, a gangster who wants a screen for his activities by living in a better neighborhood, a colored man of means who was giving his children a college education and thought they were entitled to live among whites. . . . No matter what the motive or character of the would-be purchaser, if the deal would institute a form of blight, then certainly the well-meaning broker must work against its consummation.*[6]

The result was the vast new suburbs that appeared almost overnight in places like Park Forest, Illinois, and Lakewood, California. The famous Levittowns, the first on former farmland on New York's Long Island, the second just outside Philadelphia, were all white. Their developer, William Levitt, used the newest mass-production technology, with standardized components, to build new houses quickly and inexpensively. Levittowns attracted GIs and other first-time home buyers eligible for FHA and VA

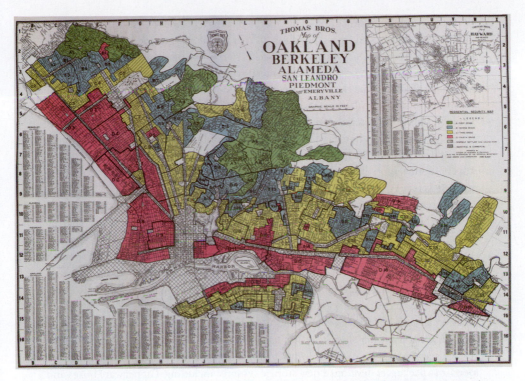

HOLC Redlining Map In the mid-1930s the Home Owners Loan Corporation prepared "residential security maps" of major cities around the country, like this one for Oakland and Berkeley, California, in 1937. These maps rated neighborhoods by color (blue, green, yellow, and red) to provide guidance for mortgage lenders. Lenders were eager to offer mortgages in blue and green neighborhoods but were reluctant to make loans in "risky" red neighborhoods. Areas with even a small number of racial minorities were marked red, thus making it difficult or impossible for African Americans, Hispanics, and Asians to get mortgages.

loans. Levitt's brokers refused to show homes to prospective black homeowners, even though blacks were eager to move to new houses in the job-rich suburbs. In Pennsylvania, Levittown even turned away a group of black World War II veterans who showed up in uniform.

Life in the Consumers' Republic

One value that suburbanites held as dearly as segregation was privacy. Urban apartments were cramped, especially during the housing shortages of the Depression and World War II. People jostled together on sidewalks, subways, and buses. Because green space was at a premium, urbanites crowded together, sometimes tens of thousands at a time, on beaches, in parks, and at amusement parks.

By contrast, huge swaths of lawn separated suburban houses. Children played in backyard sandboxes and on swing sets instead of public playgrounds. Over the course of the 1950s and into the 1960s, private backyard swimming pools and neighborhood swim clubs (which, of course, reflected racial segregation) replaced public pools. The only major public events that brought suburbanites together out of doors on a regular basis were youth sports leagues and high school sporting events, both of which proliferated in the child-centered culture after World War II.

Postwar suburban homes were small universes of children, appliances, toys, food, and fulfillment. Manufacturers scrambled to cater to the needs of suburban families. Advertisers attempted to create new desires. Stores offered a cornucopia of exciting new goods for every member of the family.

The center of activity was the eat-in kitchen, which often had large windows overlooking the backyard, where Mom could watch the children play while preparing meals. The kitchen showcased the latest consumer technologies, from electric toasters to power blenders, both introduced after World War II. Homeowners with enough money could install one of the newly invented electric dishwashers. New electric garbage disposal systems allowed Mom to scrape off the dishes and wash the waste down the drain. The most useful kitchen appliance of all was General Electric's 1947 combination refrigerator-freezer, substantially larger than earlier stand-alone refrigerators or older iceboxes, where blocks of ice, used for cooling, took up much of the space. As refrigerator-freezers dropped in price, innovative manufacturers produced frozen foods and packagers developed new storage systems, including Tupperware boxes and cellophane sandwich bags.

TUNING IN: TV AND MASS CULTURE Usually adjoining the kitchen was the family room, an informal gathering place, new to postwar houses, where the family could relax. There children's board games filled the shelves and toys littered the carpet. Carefully arranged furniture gave everyone a view of the newest and most popular household appliance, the television.

For decades, inventors had experimented with the tubes and circuitry and broadcast technologies for what would become television, but as late as the 1930s, TVs were still a bizarre, futuristic novelty. In 1946, after more than four years of making radios and radar and other electronic equipment for the military, RCA, a leading electronics manufacturer, expanded its production of TVs, encouraged that year by the licensing of twenty-six new television stations by the Federal Communications Commission.

At first, TV was a luxury item, even as broadcasters began to build a communications infrastructure and manufacturers put vast resources into improving the technology. In 1948 the Democrats and Republicans welcomed the televised coverage of their conventions, but only about 3 percent of Americans, most of them wealthy, had televisions. Still, the innovations paid off: by 1960, about 44 million American households—nine in every ten—had a television.[7] TVs were affordable and ubiquitous.

Television had all sorts of unexpected impacts on American society. As TV watching took off, movie theaters began to close, although for a time, "drive-in" theaters, where viewers could watch movies in the privacy of their cars, flourished. Live theaters, music venues, and even sports arenas saw attendance drop. Radio listenership began to decline, although fears of radio's death were greatly exaggerated. Because more and more Americans spent more and more time in their cars, radio had a captive and growing audience. Listening to the radio and watching TV, with the family and maybe some close friends, changed how Americans interacted in public.

With only three networks broadcasting, there was a limited repertoire of shows for people to watch. Television created a sense of commonality among Americans. Whether you lived in Dubuque, Iowa, or Los Angeles, California, or Florence, Alabama, whether you were a stranger, a family member, or a co-worker, you could talk about what you watched last night. Americans led more private lives, but at coffee klatches and cocktail parties, at barbecues and in bars, at the grocery store and at the desk, everyone could talk about TV.

On January 19, 1953, the day before President Eisenhower's inauguration, more than two-thirds of America's television-watching households turned to NBC's slapstick comedy *I Love Lucy*, to watch a hapless husband pace around a hospital waiting room as he waited for his goofy wife to give birth. The show coincided, happily on the same night, with news announcements about the birth of the first son of costars Lucille Ball and Desi Arnaz.[8]

TV also gave a boost to consumer culture, especially for children. Mass TV was only a few years old when companies realized that children spent hours a day in front of the small screen. In 1951 toymaker Hasbro broke new ground with commercials for Mr. Potato Head, the first toy to be advertised on TV. Over the next few years, toy companies introduced new products during children's shows and began spinning off kids' clothing, memorabilia, and toys from popular movies and programs. The sales of coonskin caps skyrocketed after Disney's successful 1955 film *Davy Crockett*. And Disney launched a full line of Mickey Mouse hats, musical instruments, records, and posters from its popular variety show, *The Mickey Mouse Club*.

TV watching was the most visible manifestation of what many prominent social critics called "mass culture," one that crushed individualism and group identities. Elites fretted that American culture would become "lowbrow," a term popularized in the 1950s. (It had originated in the science of craniology, to describe the wide brows and low foreheads that nineteenth-century scientists believed characterized intellectually inferior people.) Norman Cousins, the editor of the *Saturday Review of Literature*, argued that TV was "such an assault against the human mind, such a mobilized attack on the imagination, such an invasion against good taste as no other communication medium has known."[9] Even riskier, worried other mass culture critics, if every American watched the same three commercial networks, listened to near-identical newscasts, and watched the same advertisements, they would be subject to manipulation and propaganda.

For all the fears of mass culture, television, especially in its early days, played a critical role in shaping Americans' understanding of their own society, politics, and the world. Early television programs offered lengthy news stories and detailed coverage of political events. In 1950, Senator Estes Kefauver (D-TN) invited cameras into Senate hearings that he led on crime, moving the issue to center stage in policy debates. Kefauver became a national figure and, in 1956, was the Democratic Party's vice-presidential candidate. TV also brought issues that were remote to many Americans right into their living rooms, from haunting film footage of nuclear explosions to images of civil rights protesters facing off against club-wielding police. TV did provide mindless entertainment. It made the fortunes of advertisers. But for better or worse, it also became a political force. Politicians rose and fell on camera. Social movements could vault from obscurity to global prominence if the news cameras turned in their direction.

AIR-CONDITIONED AMERICA TV was but one technology that kept people indoors. The window electric air conditioner, first sold in 1951, transformed everyday life, particularly in the South and Southwest. Tens of millions of Americans thereafter drew their windows shut on muggy evenings, relaxing in the artificially cool air. As one observer put it in 1959, "people have just decided that it's part of the American standard of living, something we're all entitled to, just as we're entitled to heat in the winter and food on the table."[10] By 1970 more than half of all houses in the South had air conditioners, as did nearly every store, movie theater, restaurant, hospital, and hotel. In new housing developments, front porches became shrunken appendages or disappeared altogether. Who needed to sit outside when relief came at the turn of a switch?

Climate control had its biggest effect on industry and commerce, where it had been in use, on a very limited scale, since the turn of the century. Firms could now safely locate factories in places where the heat would otherwise wilt workers, damage fragile equipment, or overheat motors. Phoenix, Arizona, where temperatures regularly rose to 110 degrees in the summer, had just 65,000 people in 1940. It grew sevenfold in the next two decades, the desert blooming with defense manufacturers lured by cool indoor air and, just as important, a "favorable business climate," made possible by loose regulation, low taxes, and, under Taft-Hartley, open shop laws.[11]

AUTOMOBILITY Suburbanites depended on automobiles to navigate the sprawling, decentralized landscape. It was difficult to walk to shops, sports, and schools. Many new suburbs did not have sidewalks. Few had traditional pedestrian-oriented downtowns; even fewer had good public transit systems. Instead, stores clustered in privately owned shopping malls, surrounded by vast parking lots.

No industry prospered more in the postwar years than auto manufacturing, and no company more than General Motors, then the largest corporation in the United States. During the war, GM had become a massive defense contractor, turning its factories, almost overnight, over to the production of aircraft engines, tanks, armored vehicles, the amphibious "duck" transport vehicle, and ammunition and torpedoes. When the war ended, GM made the transition back to civilian production with extraordinary success. Within a few years, the company's five passenger car divisions, each marketed toward buyers of a different socioeconomic status—Chevrolet, Pontiac, Oldsmobile, Buick, and Cadillac—captured more than 40 percent of the domestic car market. The

1949 models, the first to be totally reengineered inside and out to reflect a new post-war aesthetic, were GM's proudest. Thousands gathered at New York's Waldorf Astoria hotel to view the "sleek and sybaritic specimens of automotive splendor," among them a $30,000 Cadillac, the most expensive car ever built. GM also introduced its newest innovation, the Dyna-Flow automatic transmission.

In the fifteen years following World War II, car ownership more than doubled, from 28.2 million in 1945 to 61.7 million in 1960. That year 77 percent of American households owned a car.[12] The rise of the car had enormous economic implications, particularly for the consumption of oil and gas. Between 1948 and 1972, American petroleum consumption tripled. And although the United States had produced most of its own oil in the first half of the twentieth century, it depended more and more on foreign oil beginning in the 1950s, when about 10 percent of American oil came from overseas. By the 1970s, 36 percent of American oil was imported.[13]

Eisenhower's Middle Ground

Who was responsible for postwar American prosperity? What policies would strengthen the national economy? Business and politics had coexisted in tension for most of the first half of the twentieth century. Progressives had railed against monopolies and the corruption of government by big business. New Dealers argued for a mixed economy, using the power of government to create jobs, construct infrastructure, and provide a favorable climate for organized labor. But since the great strike wave of 1946, the Dixie-GOP coalition had advocated trimming the sails of organized labor. Eisenhower took their side.

Eisenhower's cabinet, gibed *The New Republic*, the nation's most influential liberal periodical, consisted of "eight millionaires and a plumber."[14] Treasury Secretary George Humphrey was a corporate lawyer. Secretary of Commerce Sinclair Weeks, a wealthy manufacturer, pledged "to create a 'business climate' in the nation's economy."[15] Secretary of Agriculture Ezra Taft Benson, the first Mormon cabinet member, was closely allied to agribusiness, worked to roll back New Deal farm aid, and sought to expand America's export markets to benefit large-scale corporate farms with the capacity to transport produce overseas. The plumber, Martin Durkin, Eisenhower's only Democratic appointee, lasted less than eight months as secretary of labor, his sympathy for organized labor out of sync with the new administration's politics.

The most controversial of Eisenhower's nominees was Charles E. Wilson, also known as "Engine Charlie," the chief executive of General Motors. Wilson's experience overseeing a vast, multinational corporation struck Eisenhower as ideal for the job of secretary of defense. Despite Eisenhower's blessing, many senators doubted that Wilson could separate his financial interests from the demands of government service. He held some $2.5 million in GM stock, and after he was nominated, he made headlines when he stated that he would not divest himself from his company's holdings, despite the fact that GM was a major manufacturer of military vehicles.

Wilson was blunt and, for a CEO, not particularly well versed in public relations. When asked if he would be willing to make a decision with "extremely adverse" effects on his company, he replied brusquely, "Yes sir, I could. I cannot conceive of one." He elaborated on the point, stating that "for years I thought what was good for our country was good for General Motors and vice versa. The difference did not exist. Our company is too big. It goes with the welfare of the country."[16]

The Senate conducted Wilson's nomination hearings in secret, as was commonplace with sensitive military and foreign policy appointments. But word of his testimony leaked out. An unnamed senator attributed these words to Wilson: "Certainly. What's good for General Motors is good for the country," leading to a firestorm of controversy.[17] To many commentators, Engine Charlie gave voice to the untamed power of corporate America. Wilson and Eisenhower spent days attempting to correct the record, and under pressure, Wilson reluctantly agreed to sell his GM stock. After he was confirmed, the Senate released the transcript of his hearings, which included the correct quotation.

Over his two terms in office, Eisenhower attempted a high-wire political act: straddling the New Deal and business interests. Eisenhower believed in "limited government," balancing the federal budget and opposing federal aid to public education, which he saw as best left to the localities and states. Still, with the exception of two years, 1953 and 1954, he had to collaborate with a Democratic majority in both the House and the Senate.

The majority of both parties—Democratic and Republican—supported massive government expenditures to expand the national infrastructure and bolster the military. Large majorities of Americans also supported programs to provide a safety net for the elderly, workers, and poor. "Should any political party attempt to abolish Social Security, unemployment insurance, and eliminate labor laws and farm programs," Eisenhower pointedly argued, "you would not hear of that party again in our political history."[18] Eisenhower presided over Social Security's expansion in the mid-1950s and supported efforts to broaden a signature New Deal program, the minimum wage, to include more workers. He also signed legislation in 1954 to fund "urban renewal" programs, including new civic centers, hospitals, universities, and middle-income housing in cities.

THE MILITARY-INDUSTRIAL COMPLEX From the beginning of his term in office, Eisenhower was ambivalent about America's enormous defense budget. His secretary of state, John Foster Dulles, directed his international strategy. A lawyer, the scion of an establishment family, and a fierce anti-Communist, Dulles shared Eisenhower's interest in cutting expenditures while maintaining American superiority over the Soviet Union. In an influential 1954 memo, he called for a reduction in costly American ground forces and instead preparation for "massive retaliation" against the Soviets. That would entail substantial funding for research and development and lucrative government contracts to electronics and aircraft firms to develop new missiles.

On November 1, 1952, the United States tested its first thermonuclear, or hydrogen, bomb, a weapon that was exponentially more powerful than the bombs dropped on Hiroshima and Nagasaki, creating a three-mile wide fire cloud. In 1953 the Soviets responded with their own H-bomb test, leading to a further acceleration of the arms race. When Eisenhower entered office, the United States had about fifteen hundred nuclear warheads; by the end of the 1950s, it had nearly six thousand nuclear weapons. To demonstrate American nuclear superiority, the United States detonated close to three hundred nuclear weapons in the 1950s in weapons tests. At the same time, Eisenhower reduced the number of standing troops by nearly 700,000, a considerable cost savings.

Defense spending during the Eisenhower years spurred development, mostly in suburban and rural areas. Grumman, a major aircraft manufacturer, located a huge plant on Long Island, the cutting edge of massive industrial and residential sprawl. A flood of federal military contracts enriched aircraft, electronics, and related firms that turned Orange County, California, into a magnet for engineers, electrical workers, and assemblers from all over the United States. Southern senators and congressmen, using their seniority, were particularly adept at securing federal contracts for firms in their districts.

THE INTERSTATE HIGHWAY SYSTEM In the name of national defense, Eisenhower also launched the largest public works program in American history, the

The Interstate Highway System

construction of the interstate highway system, which Congress authorized in 1956 by passing the Interstate Highway Act. The idea of interconnecting the United States with a vast web of superhighways dated back to the 1920s, when the federal government began providing states with funds to construct better roads. During the Cold War, planners called for the expansion of highways to encourage the decentralization of vital industries to prevent a single nuclear attack from crippling American defense capabilities. Everyone liked the idea. Members of Congress could channel the money to their districts. Real estate developers would profit immensely from developing land near interstates for shopping, fast food, and industry. Manufacturers—still reliant on the costly and aging railway system (even most automobiles were shipped by train)—could now use the more flexible and less expensive trucking industry to bring goods to market. The interstate highway system would eventually span nearly 48,000 miles and open vast areas to metropolitan sprawl.

ANTI–NEW DEALERS ON THE RISE   Opponents of the New Deal were encouraged by Eisenhower's pro-business rhetoric but demoralized by his support for liberal social programs and substantial federal spending. Cultivating members of the Dixie-GOP coalition, they continued their crusade against organized labor, fighting unionization efforts in the South and Southwest. They fashioned a double-edged campaign to elevate the reputation of big business while fomenting antigovernment sentiment, all in the name of an abstract principle, "free enterprise."

The pioneer in selling free enterprise, scarcely known to the American public, was a GE executive named Lemuel Ricketts Boulware. Born at the turn of the century in a small Kentucky town, Boulware graduated from the University of Wisconsin, where he was a baseball star, before seeing battle as an infantry captain in World War I. He was ideally suited for the corporate world of the 1920s: a team player who took the jobs he was assigned and excelled in them—accountant, purchasing agent, comptroller, factory and marketing manager, and corporate vice-president. During World War II, he served as vice-chairman of the War Production Board. It was the perfect résumé for his high-level position at General Electric, one of America's largest and most prestigious corporations, overseeing labor relations in the wake of the 1946 strike wave.

Boulware's real strength was marketing. *Fortune* magazine described him as "a jovial, fast-talking man, [who] combines the folksiness of a Kentucky farm background with the fervor of a washing machine salesman."[19] At GE, Boulware sold a good that he truly believed in. "Management is in a *sales* campaign to determine *who* will run business and the country, and to determine if business and the country will be run *right*," he wrote in 1946.[20] The stakes were high. If management didn't win, he argued, the country would slouch into socialism.

Boulware learned valuable lessons in marketing from business organizations' efforts to thwart Franklin Delano Roosevelt's pro-labor and regulatory policies. Depression-era groups like the Liberty League had foundered because they were too insular, too defensive, and too naïve politically to have much influence. Boulware came up with new tactics and a new script. At GE, he directed a campaign to win the hearts and minds of both the general public and the GE workforce.

GE popularized the concepts of then-radical right-wing economists through catchy brochures and articles. Boulware personally funded early conservative think tanks, including the Mont Pelerin Society, a group of business leaders and economists, well outside the mainstream, who promoted an ideology of free markets. Boulware supported libertarian economists and theorists, among them Friedrich von Hayek and Milton Friedman, who argued against economic regulation and federal spending. But those ideas would matter only if they made their way from the elite down to the masses. To get the job done, Boulware's team prepared pro–free enterprise pamphlets that they distributed to workers. Other business groups, most prominently the National Association of Manufacturers, launched their own campaigns, with PR men drafting magazine articles, films, sermon guides, and even school curriculums.

Lemuel Ricketts Boulware A brilliant marketer, Boulware helped shape General Electric's antilabor strategy in the postwar years. Under Boulware's direction, GE prepared pro-free enterprise advertisements and hired Hollywood actor Ronald Reagan as the firm's spokesman.

Ever innovative, Boulware adapted quickly to the new medium of television and in 1954 hired Ronald Reagan, a minor but charming Hollywood celebrity, who found his calling as the smiling face of GE. Reagan genially hosted *The General Electric Theater*, a popular evening television program. He used his role to hawk GE products but also to promote Boulware's ideology of free enterprise. Reagan traveled to GE plants and addressed business groups around the country as an inspirational speaker, challenging Communism, criticizing unions, and celebrating capitalism.

God's Country

Boulware, Reagan, and other defenders of free enterprise had prominent foes, particularly among religious leaders. Advocates of the Social Gospel, a prominent movement within mainstream Protestant denominations, supported workplace safety regulations, minimum hours and wage laws, and unionization. They worried about greed, materialism, and exploitation in industrial America. Likewise Roman Catholic leaders had, since the late nineteenth century, criticized big business for mistreating workers, paying them poorly, and threatening family security. Catholics were among the staunchest supporters of organized labor. Priests and bishops alike regularly attended labor rallies and blessed striking workers. But by the 1950s, a growing segment of religious Americans, many Protestants and a small but vocal minority of Catholics, began to cast their lot with free enterprise, largely because they saw it as a bulwark against Communism.

The postwar years marked a resurgence of godliness in the United States, which by midcentury had a greater percentage of religious believers and regular churchgoers than any other country in the industrialized West. Social scientists might have believed that the West marched inevitably toward rationality and secularism, but church membership figures did not bear that out. In 1940, 64 million Americans belonged to religious congregations; by 1960, 114 million, or about four in five Americans, did.

A growing number of Americans—many of them self-proclaimed fundamentalists (who believed in the literal interpretation of the Bible) or evangelicals (who attempted to bring new souls into a personal relationship with Jesus)—set out to remake American society. Although they were often depicted as old-fashioned or backward-looking, they were anything but traditional, especially in their use of technology. New organizations like Billy James Hargis's Christian Crusade and Carl McIntire's American Council of Christian Churches used radio and television to call on Americans to repudiate immorality and reject any compromise with "the Devil" of Communism.

Many evangelicals joined forces with those who defended the principle of free enterprise. McIntire, who had split from the mainstream Presbyterian Church in the 1930s, railed against debauched film and music and Communism at home and abroad. He elevated free enterprise to a biblical principle, and he was not alone. "The blessings of capitalism come from God," wrote Reverend James Fifield, one of the most influential theological defenders of the free market. "A system that provides so much for the common good and happiness must flourish under the favor of the Almighty."[21] For Fifield and McIntire, government programs that restrained economic liberty violated God's law. By the early 1960s, McIntire broadcast his message over more than five hundred radio stations nationwide, and the words of ministers like Fifield filled the pages of church bulletins and sermon guides. They provided seemingly godly reinforcement to Boulware and Reagan.

In combination, the corporate and religious advocates of free enterprise were remarkably successful. The stock figure representing big business, with his top hat and monocle, gave way to benign corporate figures like the zippy, futuristic Reddy Kilowatt, a figure representing progress. The grouchy Scrooge had been supplanted by the cheerful Reagan, while the Jesus who proclaimed that "it is easier for a camel to go through the eye of a needle, than for a rich man to enter the kingdom of God" lost out to a gospel of prosperity that preached wealth as a sign of divine favor.

Teens, Sex, Anxiety

But for all the sunny optimism personified by Ronald Reagan, the Eisenhower years were riddled with anxiety, particularly concerning children and especially teens. Over the 1950s, journalists stoked fears of an epidemic of "juvenile delinquency." Newspapers ran lurid headlines about teen gangs, even though crime rates remained level between the early 1930s and the early 1960s, and murder rates had plummeted from their peak in the first years of the Great Depression. Still, reports of teen antics, whether schoolyard brawls or minor acts of vandalism, took on outsize importance as evidence of a generation run amok. By the mid-1950s, parents fretted that their children had disappeared into a youth subculture of comic books, tawdry movies, sexualized music, and raunchy dress. Those fears of teenage rebellion dovetailed with a deep-rooted panic about sexuality and morality.[22]

TEENAGE REBELS Most unsettling to parents was that their children seemed to be rejecting traditional notions of propriety. Middle-class boys began wearing tight T-shirts and blue jeans, clothes that had been long associated with the working class. Girls' skirts hiked upward, and their bathing suits showed more skin. And

Teenagers During the post–World War II years, popular culture centered on young people, like these teenagers at a high school "sock hop" in 1953. Parents worried about juvenile delinquency and adolescent sexuality and tried to supervise their high school-aged children closely.

increasingly, boys and girls danced together, rather too closely for their parents' liking, to new rock 'n' roll music, which seemed to overturn longtime racial norms, drawing from black rhythm and blues music and expressing sexual urges with a degree of candor that shocked an older generation.

Many parents had believed that the suburbs would protect their children from the temptations of the city, but the private, car-centered world of postwar suburbia and more disposable income than ever gave teens new freedoms. In particular the car allowed adolescents to escape parental supervision, listen to rock 'n' roll music, and engage in sexual experimentation without the risk that Mom or Dad would find out. To assuage parental fears, suburban police departments patrolled "lovers' lanes" where teenagers parked and kissed and wooded parks where kids gathered to smoke.

Teenage rebellion, however worrisome to parents, was good for Hollywood. Two 1955 films, *Rebel Without a Cause* and *Blackboard Jungle*, attracted teens and outraged their parents. The protagonist of *Rebel*, the jean-clad, rakish James Dean, became a teenage heartthrob, even if the film's message reinforced the familiar refrain of adolescents driven to ruin by overbearing moms and emasculated dads. *Blackboard Jungle* featured Hollywood's first rock 'n' roll soundtrack, headlined by Bill Haley and His Comets' hit "Rock around the Clock." Fifties youth saw themselves in a new way: as a generation defined in opposition to the stodgy culture of their parents. For the next few decades, the script of youth rebelling against authority, of fighting for freedom against conformity, would shape nearly every aspect of American politics, consumer culture, and family life. It was the precondition for the youth rebellions that would explode in American cities and on American campuses throughout the 1960s.

COMIC BOOKS AND THE "SEDUCTION OF THE INNOCENT" The panic over rebellious youth played out in advice columns, in films, and especially in the corridors of the national capitol. In 1953, Senator Estes Kefauver (D-TN), who had become famous with his televised hearings on crime, launched a full-scale investigation of juvenile delinquency, joining forces with Senator Robert Hendrickson (R-NJ). In April 1954 the major networks halted regular programming to broadcast Hendrickson and Kefauver's lurid hearings on comic books and their impact on children.

The star witness at the comic book hearings, psychiatrist Fredric Wertham, took the stand to summarize his best-selling book, *Seduction of the Innocent*. Wertham warned that comic books lured children to commit violent acts and engage in deviant sexual practices. "It is my opinion," he testified, "without any reasonable doubt and without any reservation, that comic books are an important contributing factor in many cases of juvenile delinquency."[23] He even argued that Batman and Robin, the crime-fighting superhero and his boy sidekick, promoted homosexuality. Within a few years, more than a dozen states passed laws regulating comic books, religious groups led comic book burnings, and the hundred-million-dollar-a-year comic book industry imposed strict self-censorship. It seemed a victory for Hendrickson, Kefauver, and Wertham that comic book circulation steadily dropped thereafter. But the menaces facing America's youth abounded.

THE LAVENDER SCARE Wertham's fears about Batman and Robin reflected a deeper concern over what seemed to be, at midcentury, rampant homosexuality. At the time, most gays and lesbians kept their sexual identities hidden. The risk of disclosure was too great: they would lose their jobs, be ostracized by family and neighbors, and sometimes be sent to mental hospitals. Mainstream medical doctors and psychiatrists classified same-sex attraction as a serious mental illness. Against the odds, gays and lesbians found companionship and community in gay-oriented taverns, coffeehouses, dance halls, and theaters in nearly every major city. For a time, peaking in the 1920s, authorities tolerated gay urban life, even if they seldom approved of it, so long as it remained confined to theater districts, working-class neighborhoods, and racially mixed areas.

But the growing public presence of gays in cities led to calls for the regulation of sexual "immorality." By the 1930s, many municipalities began to crack down on patrons of gay establishments for "disorderly conduct." In some cities, authorities shut down restaurants and bars that served patrons who appeared to be homosexual. Hollywood also censored homosexuality. Under the 1934 Hays Code, an agreement among major movie studios, films could not depict gay or lesbian characters or even discuss the topic.

Still, gay subcultures thrived, especially in single-sex environments, including the military. During World War II, the U.S. armed forces forbade same-sex relations but did not single out gay men or lesbians on the basis of their identities. Around military bases, gay soldiers could usually find bars or clubs where they could meet discreetly. Many, especially from rural areas and small towns, were thrilled to discover that they were not alone in their desires.

The growing visibility of homosexuals provoked a crackdown after the war, fueled by fears of subversion more generally. What came to be called the "lavender scare" (referring to a color that was popularly associated with gays and lesbians) played out side by side with the anti-Communist crusade. In 1950, prompted by Senator Joseph McCarthy, the U.S. Senate launched an investigation into homosexuality in the federal government. Gays and lesbians, his Senate committee contended, were susceptible to blackmail. They might give up military secrets to protect their secret sexual identities. The committee went further: "the presence of a sex pervert in a Government agency tends to have a corrosive influence on his fellow employees. These perverts will frequently attempt to entice normal individuals to engage in perverted practices."[24] In 1952, Congress passed a law that forbade homosexuals (classified as "psychopaths" in the legislation) from entering the United States. Even applicants for tourist visas had to attest that they were not homosexual.

In 1953, President Eisenhower issued an executive order requiring government agencies, the military, and private companies with government contracts to purge all suspected homosexuals. The FBI worked closely with local police forces to gather information about homosexuals and the businesses that catered to them. Military investigators often confiscated mail, followed soldiers home, or simply acted on rumors, using the information they gathered to justify discharging thousands of gays and lesbians.

Homosexuals expelled from the armed forces paid a high price. They were usually ineligible for GI Bill benefits, and without honorable discharge papers, they often had trouble finding work.

Many thousands more suspected gays came under the supervision of state and law enforcement officials and prosecutors. Around the country, police raided gay bars and coffee shops, arresting thousands of people, mostly gay men, on vague charges of disorderly conduct. Undercover police officers also engaged in entrapment schemes, propositioning gay men and then charging them with public lewdness. In Washington, about a thousand suspected gays and lesbians were arrested each year on various charges. In Philadelphia, over the 1950s, police arrested nearly a hundred gays each month, most of them in bar raids. Antigay witch-hunts touched nearly every state in the country. In 1955 and 1956, for example, the police in Boise, Idaho, interviewed more than fourteen hundred people in efforts to hound out suspected homosexuals.[25]

The stigma of homosexuality, the risk of prosecution, and the danger of losing a job did not destroy gay culture, particularly in big cities. Lesbians could go to bookstores and magazine stands to find sensationalistic novels—called pulp fiction because they were printed on cheap paper—with titles like *Women's Barracks*, *Odd Girl*, and *The Third Sex*. The most popular books sold millions of copies. Gays and lesbians alike scouted out friendly bars and restaurants, whose proprietors often paid off the police to remain open. Certain remote parks and beaches that were hard for police to patrol also became informal gathering places, particularly for gay men.

The frustrations, indignities, and dangers of gay life led a small but growing number of activists to form what they called "homophile" organizations to change the negative perceptions of gays in medical textbooks and the media, and to reform antihomosexual laws. The two most prominent were the Mattachine Society, founded in 1951 (named after a masked figure in medieval theater), and the Daughters of Bilitis founded in 1955 (named after one of the companions of Greek poet Sappho). These groups mostly worked behind the scenes, providing gays and lesbians safe places to meet, engaging in educational efforts, and quietly laying the groundwork for what would become a mass movement a few decades later.

Even amid the repression of the postwar years, some noteworthy legal changes undermined censorship laws and created openings for gay and lesbian activists and writers. In 1953 postal officials in Los Angeles confiscated copies of the first issue of *ONE: The Homosexual Magazine*, a homophile publication. The headline that prompted the censorship was the cover story headline, a two-word question: "Homosexual Marriage?" A year later postal authorities impounded the magazine once again on grounds that its content was obscene. *ONE*'s publisher filed suit, challenging the federal government. In the meantime, in its landmark *Roth v. United States* decision (1957), the Supreme Court issued a broad ruling defining obscenity as material that violated "contemporary community standards," leaving the exact definition vague. The court applied that reasoning to *ONE* in a 1958 ruling, allowing the magazine, and by implication other gay periodicals, to circulate freely.

The most prominent obscenity case involved Allen Ginsberg's book-length poem, *Howl*, published in 1956. Ginsberg, a disillusioned Columbia University dropout and poet, joined New York's gay scene in Greenwich Village, a neighborhood where men could find companionship in unmarked speakeasies and immigrant bathhouses. Like many budding poets, he found his way to San Francisco, where the North Beach neighborhood, with its tawdry burlesque bars and its mix of sailors on furlough and young men on the make, provided a bit of a refuge for gays. The center of gravity in North Beach was City Lights, a bookstore and publisher, run by the poet Lawrence Ferlinghetti.

In 1956, City Lights released *Howl*, to some notoriety. In the poem, Ginsberg evoked the gritty city, with its casual mixing of the races, free sex (including an explicit line about homosexuality), and plentiful drugs. San Francisco's district attorney ordered copies of *Howl* confiscated, on the grounds that it was obscene, and arrested Ferlinghetti and the City Lights bookstore manager, leading to a lengthy criminal trial. In 1957 a California judge ruled that however offensive the poem was, it was of "redeeming social importance" and could not be censored.

When it came to policing juvenile delinquents or gays, or censoring lascivious comic books or homophile magazines, it was hard to enforce conformity. By the late 1950s, encouraged by the shift in obscenity laws, mainstream publishers began to capitalize on gay-and-lesbian–themed books. The demand was too big for them to ignore. Filmmakers began to push at the boundaries of sexuality, and musicians even more so. The market for rebellious books, music, and movies was vast, ever changing, and extraordinarily lucrative, one part of a seemingly insatiable consumer culture in the postwar years.

The Black Freedom Struggle

Of all of the rebellions that remade post–World War II America, none was more unsettling to the status quo than the African American insurgency against segregation and inequality. The civil rights movement, which peaked in the postwar years, touched on nearly every facet of American life. Investigative journalists, lawyers, and academics published books and articles chronicling America's past and present of racial injustice and discrimination. Activists demanded that black Americans have full access to postwar prosperity, well-paying jobs, high wages, and the consumer marketplace. They challenged one of the taken-for-granted aspects of modern American life: the nearly complete racial segregation of America's housing. They resisted racially separate and unequal education. They demanded the right to vote and the right to political representation. And they began, slowly, to win major victories.

JIM CROW PUBLIC ACCOMMODATIONS From the late nineteenth through the mid-twentieth centuries, from coast to coast, north and south, restaurants and bars that served whites usually refused service to any dark-skinned customer. In the South, blacks were subjected to Jim Crow laws that forbade them from sitting at the same lunch counters or using the same bathrooms and drinking fountains. Blacks and whites could not ride in the same train cars. Blacks had to give up their seats to

white passengers on trolleys and buses. Movie theaters throughout the country excluded blacks altogether or confined them to seats in the "crow's nest," the balcony,
most distant from the big screen. Public swimming pools everywhere were closed to
blacks or open to them only on special "colored" days, after which the pools would be
drained and refilled. Along the Rio Grande River and in parts of southern California,
Mexican Americans complained of "Juan Crow," local discriminatory practices that
still kept them out of white establishments.

Even wealthy travelers of the wrong complexion could not buy their way out of
Jim Crow. Robert Joseph Pershing Foster, a black doctor from Louisiana, had to carry
his surgical tools and a portable operating table to his patients' houses because white-
run hospitals would not admit him. Frustrated, on April 1, 1953, he headed west to
Los Angeles in search of better work. But even with a full wallet, Foster drove the
few-thousand-mile-long trip between Monroe, Louisiana, and Los Angeles nonstop
because he couldn't find motels that would put him up. Sometimes the rejections were
polite. "Oh my goodness," proclaimed a motel clerk. "We forgot to turn on the no-
vacancy sign." Sometimes he was greeted with a scowl. And once in L.A., though he
was an experienced surgeon, he could only find a job working for an insurance company, going door to door to perform health exams on policyholders. It would take Foster years to find a job that matched his skills. [26]

SEGREGATION UNDER SIEGE   Foster's struggles represented the everyday
indignities that blacks faced. Those indignities—getting kicked out of a restaurant,
having to ride at the back of the bus, not being able to swim in a public pool—seemed
especially egregious when the United States presented itself as the world's arsenal of
democracy. At the same time, assumptions about racial difference and inferiority came
under siege. During the 1930s, leading scientists began challenging the very notion of
race as unscientific. Anthropologist Franz Boas argued that race was a cultural construct rather than a biological reality. Sociologists, like St. Clair Drake and Horace
Cayton, published highly regarded books and popular articles that chronicled the effects of segregation and discrimination. Nearly everyone was familiar with Gunnar
Myrdal's best-selling *An American Dilemma* (1944), which argued that racial discrimination violated the "American creed," a tradition of egalitarianism that ran throughout American history from the founders to the present day.

Those books and articles helped shift elite opinion about race, but it would take a
lot more to undermine centuries of racial segregation. It would take what the leader of
the March on Washington, A. Philip Randolph, called "pressure, more pressure, and
still more pressure."[27] Much of that pressure, when it came to public accommodations,
was at first informal. Authorities in Birmingham, Alabama, for example, reported
eighty-eight cases of blacks occupying "white" places on city buses during the year
following September 1941. White transit riders in Baltimore, Detroit, and Atlanta,
among other cities, complained about black passengers deliberately jostling whites.
Uniformed soldiers returning from service in the Pacific or Europe often responded
angrily when confronted with Jim Crow on buses and at lunch counters.

ORGANIZING AGAINST JIM CROW The struggle against segregation did not remain unorganized for long. In 1946 the National Association for the Advancement of Colored People (NAACP), the nation's leading civil rights group with nearly a half million members, published a "how to" list for those who wanted to challenge segregated restaurants in northern cities: "If refused service, ask to see the manager. . . . If you have no witnesses, call the police." And finally: "Be polite at all times. Avoid creating a disturbance either in the establishment refusing service or the police station."[28]

Beginning in the 1940s, small bands of activists launched organized challenges to segregation. Leading the way was the Congress of Racial Equality (CORE). Founded in Chicago in 1942 by a group of black and white theology students, CORE directed its first protests against restaurants in the Windy City that turned away blacks. Creative and fearless, CORE members staged sit-ins, occupying restaurants and, when they were denied service, refusing to leave. CORE was especially influenced by what was happening a world away in India, where the nationalist leader Mohandas K. Gandhi faced off against British colonizers by marching and engaging in nonviolent civil disobedience—that is, refusing to obey laws they considered unjust, and refusing to use violence against the police and military who tried to stop them.

CORE had a string of victories throughout the North in the mid-1940s, sitting-in at restaurants and roller-skating rinks in Cleveland, wading-in at segregated pools in Philadelphia and Fort Lee, New Jersey, and joining protests against jobs and housing discrimination. One of CORE's key organizers in the postwar years, Bayard Rustin, graduated from traditionally black Lincoln University, worked as a labor organizer, and spent part of World War II in jail for refusing to serve in the military. After the war, he was a tireless organizer in the South. "I traveled all over the country creating all kinds of demonstrations, sit-ins in restaurants, theaters, hotels, barbershops, and the like," he recalled.[29] Rustin, who was gay, also knew another form of discrimination—in 1953, he was arrested and convicted for having sex with a man—though he would not join the struggle for gay rights until late in his life.

In 1947 sixteen CORE members, eight black and eight white men, including Rustin, embarked on what they called the Journey of Reconciliation, the most daring act of civil disobedience of the time. The sixteen riders boarded southbound buses from Washington, D.C., into Virginia and North Carolina, refusing to obey Jim Crow rules. Several, including Rustin, were arrested in North Carolina and sentenced to work on a chain gang for their blatant violation of the law. The Journey of Reconciliation did not attract a lot of media attention, but Rustin and several other riders would shape the ongoing civil rights struggle.

THE MONTGOMERY BUS BOYCOTT The movement to challenge segregated transportation took a dramatic turn in 1955. Rosa Parks, a seamstress in Montgomery, Alabama, refused to give up her bus seat to a white passenger. Parks was not simply tired after a long day of work. She was a longtime civil rights activist, committed to undermining Jim Crow. Born in 1913 in Tuskegee, Alabama, her family was part of the Marcus Garvey movement. Most black women of her generation were destined to do manual labor, but Parks graduated from high school (rare for black women in her state), married, and moved to Montgomery. From young adulthood, she was involved in civil rights. In the early 1930s, she and her husband had supported the Scottsboro Boys, a group of young men falsely accused of raping a white woman. At age thirty, she joined the local branch of the NAACP, serving as its secretary. Within a year, she took leadership of what became a nationwide campaign to bring justice to six white Alabama men who admitted kidnapping and gang-raping Recy Taylor, a black Alabama woman, but who faced no charges for their crime.

Working for the NAACP brought Parks into contact with a nationwide movement. She learned of civil rights protests in the pages of the NAACP's magazine, *The Crisis*. And she made connections with local and national activists. In the summer of 1955, just a few months before she was arrested for refusing to give up her seat, Parks had attended the Highlander Folk School in rural Tennessee where Betty Friedan had spent part of the summer of 1941. Scores of black passengers had refused in the past to give up their seats, but Parks's case sparked a mass movement.

In the aftermath of Parks's arrest, Montgomery activists planned a boycott of the city's bus system. A young minister, only twenty-five years old, Martin Luther King, Jr., rose as spokesman for the boycotters. Montgomery's leaders gathered in his living room and used his church for meetings. King, the son of one of Atlanta's most prominent ministers and already a brilliant preacher, was the ideal public face for the boycott. E. D. Nixon, the head of Montgomery's NAACP and Parks's close colleague, used his organization's national network to publicize the case.

Parks, King, and Nixon did not act alone. Local women provided the backbone of the boycott. Seasoned northern activists, including Bayard Rustin, headed south to provide their own lessons from more than a decade of organizing. And perhaps even more important, the Montgomery struggle attracted the national news media. In the age of television in particular, it was difficult for Americans to ignore Jim Crow and the struggle against it. But even with the pressure of unfavorable media coverage, and with some of the most talented organizers in the country, Montgomery's bus company and its white elites did not capitulate easily. The boycott would last nearly a year before Rosa Parks could sit wherever she wanted on the bus without fear of arrest.

SEPARATE AND UNEQUAL EDUCATION The events in Montgomery occurred amid an even higher-stakes battle in the civil rights struggle: the struggle for racial equality in public education. Just a little over a year before Rosa Parks refused to give up her seat, the U.S. Supreme Court ruled, in *Brown v. Board of Education*, that racially segregated public schools were unconstitutional. The battle over separate, unequal schools was harder fought than the battle to desegregate lunch counters and buses, and the victory was far from complete.

Educational credentials mattered more than ever in postwar America. For most of the early twentieth century, overall school attendance and graduation rates had been low: only about 25 percent of Americans born in 1900 graduated from high school. But as the economy grew more complex, fewer Americans worked with their hands. More worked in jobs that required at least basic reading, mathematical, and writing skills. The high school diploma became an essential credential for many jobs. As a result, between 70 and 80 percent of baby-boom generation children born between 1945 and 1965 graduated from high school.[30] College attendance and graduation rates also rose steadily after World War II, largely because white, male veterans used GI Bill funds to pay for college.

But the benefits of education were unevenly distributed. Black and Hispanic children were far more likely to attend underfunded, segregated schools, and in rural areas where nonwhite students worked the fields, school districts did not even open high schools for them. And even though racial minorities were technically eligible for the GI Bill, the program was administered in a discriminatory fashion. Most institutions of higher education, particularly in the South, refused to admit African Americans. Instead, most blacks who made it to college attended historically black institutions, long the training ground for the small black elite of doctors, engineers, ministers, and professionals. The most elite white institutions admitted few if any blacks. Princeton's class of 1961, for example, had one black student.

Despite all the obstacles they faced, African Americans put a high value on education. Black educational attainment had risen steadily since the early twentieth century, in part driven by the vast migration of African Americans to cities. There black children could attend high school, even if most of them were stuck in vocational or industrial courses. For all these problems, they came, like most Americans in the mid-twentieth century, to demand more than a rudimentary education, fully aware that employers put a greater premium on well-educated workers.

But for minorities nearly everywhere in the United States, the reality of separate, unequal education dashed their expectations. Black and Hispanic schools were usually shabby and overcrowded, often lacking basic facilities like libraries, gymnasiums, and sometimes even indoor plumbing. This pattern had been ratified in the 1896 Supreme Court decision *Plessy v. Ferguson*, which permitted racial separation so long as the facilities serving blacks and whites were nominally equal, which was almost never the case.

Teachers in segregated schools worked hard managing overcrowded classrooms. In rural areas, it was not uncommon for classrooms to mix older and younger students together. The situation in big cities was grim in another way. In 1950s-era Chicago, for example, black students regularly attended schools with fifty to sixty students per class, and many schools held two-part or double-shift school days. African American teachers mentored the brightest students, often visited families at home, and sometimes used their meager paychecks to buy supplies. Other than ministers, they were often the most revered members of their communities. But white-led school boards almost always paid nonwhite teachers less than their white counterparts and until the 1950s, even in the most open parts of the country, refused to let them teach white students.

THE NAACP'S MARCH ON THE COURTS Civil rights activists had challenged segregated schools in a piecemeal way beginning in the 1890s, but the protests escalated in the North during World War II and afterward. During the 1940s, black parents agitated against racially separate schools in Hillburn, Hempstead, and New Rochelle, New York; Trenton, Montclair, and Princeton, New Jersey; and Dayton and Hillsborough, Ohio. Taking the lead in most of these cases were black mothers who coordinated school boycotts. The NAACP, which had begun a legal attack on segregated schools in the 1930s, provided the parents with legal assistance and used its newspaper, *The Crisis*, to spread word of the protests.

Some of the riskiest cases—given the intransigent white opposition to integration—played out in the Old Confederacy. In Clarendon County, South Carolina, for example, local activists stepped up their protest against separate schools between 1947 and 1949, first demanding access to bus transportation, then filing petitions challenging separate schools. The protesting parents faced reprisals, in some cases losing their jobs. The Reverend Joseph DeLaine, who coordinated the campaign, lost his job, lost his house to arsonists, and fled the state.

Thurgood Marshall led the NAACP's march through the courts. A native of Baltimore and the grandson of slaves, Marshall had attended Howard University Law School before setting up a private practice in his hometown. In 1940, Marshall, only thirty-two, began a distinguished career as a civil rights attorney with the NAACP. Immensely talented, he immediately took on some of the organization's most prominent cases. Also on the team was the talented Robert L. Carter, a graduate of two historically black universities, Lincoln in Pennsylvania and Howard Law School in Washington. Carter traveled to out-of-the-way places like Cairo, Illinois, to challenge school segregation. He also worked closely with expert witnesses, including the black psychologist Kenneth Clark, who testified in the Clarendon County case about the damaging psychological impact of segregation on black students.

The NAACP fought segregated education on many fronts in the late 1940s and won early victories in three cases involving universities. In *Sipuel v. Regents of the University of Oklahoma* (1948), Marshall and the NAACP persuaded the U.S. Supreme Court to overturn a state law that made it a misdemeanor to educate black and white students together. The NAACP brought another case, on behalf of George McLaurin, a black student who had been admitted to Oklahoma's graduate school of education. The school's administrators cordoned off a special section of the library and cafeteria for McLaurin, where he would not come into contact with white students. They assigned him to desks placed just outside the doors to his classrooms, where he could listen to lectures without mingling with his classmates. In *McLaurin v. Oklahoma State Regents* (1950), the Supreme Court found that McLaurin could not get an equal education if he remained physically separated from his fellow students. The same day, in *Sweatt v. Painter*, the court ordered the University of Texas to admit Heman Sweatt, a black applicant, to the flagship University of Texas law school.

THE *BROWN* DECISION These victories whittled away at the "separate but equal" principle that had been in place since the *Plessy* decision. The NAACP now had some good precedents for taking on the biggest challenge of all, the widespread practice of officially segregating primary and secondary schools south of the Mason-Dixon

Line. Working closely with local parents in Clarendon, South Carolina; Wilmington, Delaware; Prince Edward County, Virginia; Washington, D.C.; and Topeka, Kansas; the NAACP began to file suit in federal courts, laying siege to the entire system of separate education.

In 1953 the Supreme Court heard arguments in these five cases, bundled together, with Oliver Brown of Topeka as the first-named plaintiff. Brown's daughter, Linda, had been denied admission to the all-white school just a few blocks from her home. Kansas was one of five states outside the South with laws on the books that permitted racially separate schools.

Taking on the entire system of segregated education was risky, even if the courts were more open to civil rights than they had ever been. Civil rights advocates worried that the high court would be reluctant to overturn *Plessy*, on the grounds of judicial restraint, and would instead issue a compromise decision. They also lacked confidence that Chief Justice Fred Vinson would be able to bridge the court's divisions. But in September 1953, while the court deliberated, Vinson died.

The fate of *Brown* fell into the hands of the man whom President Eisenhower nominated to fill Vinson's spot: California governor Earl Warren. A moderate Republican, Warren had been an effective governor. Despite his party affiliation, he supported many New Deal programs, including welfare, economic regulation, and federal infrastructure spending, which greatly benefited his rapidly growing home state. Warren's red flag, for those who knew his past, was his support for the internment of Japanese Americans during the Second World War, a decision that he later came to regret.

Warren came to the bench with no judicial experience. His political background, however, proved to be his greatest asset. A skilled politician, he had an instinct for building coalitions and a willingness to forge compromises. Unlike many of his fellow justices past and present, he was not steeped in any legal theory. A pragmatist, he believed in deciding what was right and developing his legal rationale from there. On May 17, 1954, he announced a unanimous ruling that "in the field of public education, the doctrine of 'separate but equal' has no place. Separate educational facilities are inherently unequal."[31] Warren acknowledged Kenneth Clark's argument that segregation created "a feeling of inferiority" among black students, an argument important for bringing social science to bear on what, in the hands of another chief justice, could have been a narrower, strictly legal ruling.

Warren's politics, however, led him to proceed cautiously when it came time for the court to rule on how *Brown* would be implemented. Fearful of backlash, the court ruled in 1955 that segregated school districts had to comply with the *Brown* decision "with all deliberate speed." Those four vague words became a license for southern school districts to move forward at their own pace. In the border states, many districts acted quickly to abolish segregated schools. In northern districts, beginning in New York City in 1957, activists began to challenge the existence of segregated "neighborhood schools," where black students were segregated because of where they lived, not because of laws that required segregation. By the early 1960s, protesters and litigators in more than two hundred northern districts were using *Brown*'s language to demand rapid desegregation.

In the South, change happened slowly if at all. Some districts, like Greensboro, North Carolina, implemented token desegregation programs, admitting a handful of black students to formerly all-white schools but leaving racial patterns otherwise unchanged. Many more Southerners openly resisted *Brown*. In 1956, 101 members of Congress issued the "Southern Manifesto," declaring the *Brown* decision "a clear abuse of judicial power."[32] Southern state legislatures passed laws intended to thwart integration. Several allowed for the closing of integrated schools; others refused to commit state education funds for desegregation efforts. A common subterfuge was the introduction of "freedom of choice" laws that formally ended segregation, but made it difficult for African Americans to attend white schools. Many conservative activists outside the South endorsed such plans. In 1959, Prince Edward County, Virginia, simply disbanded its public schools, turning white schools into private academies and leaving black children locked out.

President Eisenhower expressed his misgivings about civil rights. Earl Warren later recounted a strange after-dinner conversation he had had with the president during the *Brown* deliberations. "These are not bad people," Eisenhower told Warren, commenting on southern whites. "All they are concerned about is to see that their sweet little girls are not required to sit alongside some big overgrown Negroes."[33] Privately, Ike called his nomination of Warren "the biggest damn fool mistake I have ever made."[34] For Ike, civil rights would only come gradually, through change of hearts and minds. The very idea of imposing civil rights orders rubbed against his belief in limited government.

LITTLE ROCK But events at the beginning of the 1957 school year forced Eisenhower to act. The school district in Little Rock, Arkansas, admitted nine black students to the city's Central High School, a token effort to demonstrate compliance with the *Brown* ruling. But for many Arkansas residents and their grandstanding governor, Orval Faubus, nine students was nine too many. Faubus ordered the Arkansas National Guard to cordon off the high school. When the students attempted to enter the school building, guardsmen turned them away. Crowds of angry whites taunted the students. And the television cameras caught it all, projecting the images of angry whites screaming at well-dressed black schoolchildren to a worldwide audience.

Eisenhower summoned Faubus to a personal meeting and insisted that the governor relent and open Central High School. Under court order, Faubus withdrew the National Guard troops. But the situation worsened. Three weeks later, when the black students entered the school through a service entrance, an angry mob surrounded the school. In response to the chaos, Eisenhower federalized the Arkansas National Guard, taking it out of Faubus's control, and dispatched one thousand members of the elite 101st Airborne unit to Little Rock to restore order.[35] The president was furious at Faubus's insubordination but even more worried about the impact of Little Rock on America's image abroad. Secretary of State John Foster Dulles warned Eisenhower that the events at Central High were "ruining our foreign policy."[36] In his memoirs, Eisenhower wrote that the disorder in Little Rock "could continue to feed the mill of Soviet propagandists who by word and picture were telling the world of the 'racial terror' in the United States."[37]

Under federal supervision, the nine students enrolled and Little Rock quieted, but resistance to *Brown* did not slow down. Whether by tokenism or by violent resistance, by closing down schools and opening private, whites-only academies, or simply by ignoring the Supreme Court's orders, southern public officials flouted the law. By 1964 only 2 percent of black children in the South attended racially integrated schools.[38] It would take more than a decade of protest and violence to lay the groundwork for the sweeping federal civil rights and education reforms enacted in 1964 and 1965, which pried open the doors of Jim Crow schools.

OPEN HOUSING Breaking open America's housing market represented an even bigger challenge than desegregating its schools. Defenders of the "American way of life" celebrated consumer choice and America's high rates of home ownership, but for African Americans, the housing market remained largely closed. Beginning in the early 1940s, civil rights activists in Chicago, Detroit, St. Louis, Los Angeles, and elsewhere launched a battle in the courts against racially restrictive covenants. Finally, in 1948, a unanimous U.S. Supreme Court ruled in *Shelley v. Kraemer* that the clauses that forbade the use or occupancy of a property by race, religion, or ethnicity were unenforceable in court.

Fair housing activists did not rest content after *Shelley*. Armed with optimism, they tried to break down segregated suburbia. No target was more inviting than the famous Levittowns. African Americans had tried to buy and rent houses from developer William Levitt since the late 1940s, but his company turned them away, even evicting whites who had invited black friends to their homes in Long Island's Levittown. The NAACP unsuccessfully pushed the Eisenhower administration to back integration in Levitt's developments. Eisenhower and his aides believed that government should not interfere with business decisions. A renter or seller should have the freedom to choose renters or buyers.

Once again, "freedom of association" provided whites with a powerful rationale for their opposition to civil rights. Beginning in the 1950s, realtors around the country led the charge against efforts to desegregate housing. Their argument tapped the pro-business rhetoric of the era. The government was attempting to "force" private individuals and real estate companies to sell to minorities, violating "homeowner's rights" and businesses' "freedom of contract." Advocates of fair housing, in their view, were Communists, attempting to undermine free enterprise. Cold War concerns prompted Eisenhower to act on Little Rock, but Cold War rhetoric also became a powerful tool to discredit the civil rights struggle.

In the late summer and early fall of 1957, just as Little Rock exploded, racial violence shattered the quiet of Levittown, Pennsylvania. On August 13, 1957, William and Daisy Myers and their three children settled into a little house at the corner of Daffodil and Deepgreen Lanes. Within hours, hundreds of angry whites gathered outside their home, breaking its windows and clashing with the police. The skirmishes continued for several weeks, but the Myerses did not budge. Bill Myers, a World War II veteran, took to weeding his lawn with the bayonet on his military-issued rifle, asserting his dignity in the face of violence. Finally the protests abated. But white

From

Harry Henderson
The Mass-Produced Suburbs (1953)

Writing in *Harper's,* a popular magazine, journalist Henderson described the social and cultural life of postwar suburbs, drawing from interviews with new suburbanites and scholars who studied them. He emphasized the distinctive nature of postwar suburbia. Its residents, he argued, were well educated, well off, and friendly.

Since World War II, whole new towns and small cities, consisting of acres of near-identical Cape Cod and ranch-type houses, have been bulldozed into existence on the outskirts of America's major cities. Everybody lives in a "good neighborhood"; there is, to use that classic American euphemism, no "wrong side of the tracks." At first glance, regardless of variations in trim, color, and position of the houses, they seem monotonous; nothing rises above two stories, there are no full-grown trees, and the horizon is an endless picket fence of telephone poles and television aerials. (The mass builder seeks flat land because it cuts his construction costs.)

However one may feel about it aesthetically, this puts the emphasis on people and their activities. One rarely hears complaints about the identical character of the houses. "You don't feel it when you live here," most people say. One mother, a Midwestern college graduate with two children, told me: "We're not peas in a pod. I thought it would be like that, especially because incomes are nearly the same. But it's amazing how different and varied people are, likes and dislikes, attitudes and wants. I never really knew what people were like until I came here."

The populations differ strikingly from those of the older towns. The men's ages average 31 years; the women's about 26. Roughly 90 per cent of the men are veterans. Their major occupational classifications are managers, professionals, salesmen, skilled workers, and small business men. . . .

Buying or renting a home in one of these communities is, of course, a form of economic and personal screening. As a result, there are no poor, no Negroes; and, as communities, these contain the best educated people in America.

Socially, the outstanding characteristic of these people is their friendliness, warmth, and lack of pretentious snobbery. Outgoing and buoyant, they are quick to recognize common problems and the need for co-operation; one does not find the indifference, coldness, and "closed doors" of a long-established community. Nothing in these communities, to me, is more impressive than this uniform pattern of casual but warm friendliness and co-operation.

New York Times
Levittown Incident (1957)

In August 1957, *The New York Times* covered the protest and violence that greeted William and Daisy Myers, the first black family to move into Levittown, Pennsylvania, one of the country's most famous planned suburbs. Most news coverage of civil rights focused on the South, but the article's coverage of white-led protests showed that discrimination and racial violence were national problems.

The construction firm of Levitt & Sons mass-produced 17,500 homes in Levittown. L.I., and 15,500 in Levittown, Pa. It did not sell any of them to Negroes. Said President William J. Levitt: "As a Jew, I have no room in my mind or heart for racial prejudice. But . . . I have come to know that if we sell one house to a Negro family, then 90 to 95 per cent of our white customers will not buy into the community. That is their attitude, not ours."

Thus the Levittowns began as all-white communities. But the builders had no say over the resale of houses. Over the years a few in the older Long Island development have gone to Negroes without open protest by white Levittowners.

Recently, William Myers Jr., a 34-year-old Negro employed in near-by Trenton, N.J., paid $12,150 for a ranch-type house in the Dogwood Hollow section of Levittown, Pa. On the night of Aug. 13, two days after he started moving in, a crowd of 200 persons, mostly teen-agers, gathered outside the house. Some stones were thrown, breaking two windows. Police broke up the demonstration, but next night there was another. Gov. George M. Leader sent state troopers to guard the house. Anti-Negro elements formed a "Levittown Betterment Committee" to buy Mr. Myers out. Other elements called for tolerance. Demonstrations continued almost nightly.

Last Monday, Mr. Myers moved his wife and one of their three children into the house and said he was "here to stay." That night there was a demonstration so disorderly that police had to use force to break it up. Tuesday night another crowd gathered. Someone threw a rock and hit a policeman on the head; he suffered a concussion and a torn ear. The state police cracked down, forbidding gatherings of more than three persons in the area.

An uneasy peace descended on the neighborhood. It held during the week, with police guarding the Myers house. Whether it will last after the police leave remains to be seen. Said Mr. Myers: "We are churchgoing, respectable people. We just want a nice neighborhood in which to raise our family and enjoy life."

Questions for Analysis

1. How did Henderson see postwar suburbia as a new and different way of life?

2. What was William Myers's suburban dream?

3. How different were Levittown's first black residents from Henderson's white suburbanites?

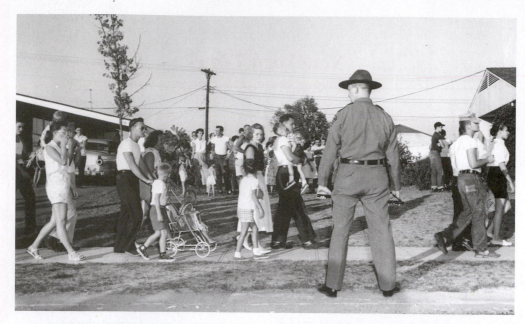

Levittown Protests In August 1957, William and Daisy Myers and their three children moved into a house in Levittown, Pennsylvania. They were the first African American family in the sprawling new suburb. For several weeks, white neighbors picketed, vandalized the property, and clashed with the police.

Levittowners had sent a chilling message: moving to their neighborhood would come at a high price. In most of suburban America, African Americans were unwilling to subject themselves to harassment, and whites were unwilling to sell.

The Covert Cold War

For Eisenhower, foreign policy took priority over domestic concerns like civil rights. Elected as a Cold Warrior, he surrounded himself with hawks. For his part, Engine Charlie proved a disappointing choice for secretary of defense. He was so gaffe-prone that his critics joked that he had introduced automatic transmissions at General Motors so he could drive with his foot in his mouth. While the president increased military spending, particularly to enhance America's nuclear capacity, his administration also entangled the United States in a series of proxy conflicts with the Soviets, mostly on the small stages of developing countries and former European colonies throughout the world.

IRAN Just as Eisenhower wound down the Korean War, he increased the power of the CIA. With thousands of operatives worldwide, the agency infiltrated foreign governments, spying on the nation's enemies. But the CIA became much more than a well-funded intelligence operation. Its operatives infiltrated revolutionary organizations and took sides in civil wars and domestic power struggles, particularly in former European colonies. It collaborated with authoritarian regimes, provided training and financial assistance to the police in pro-American countries, and engaged in covert operations against America's enemies.

In the summer of 1953, the CIA staged one of its most audacious covert operations, leading a coup in Iran, a major oil producer, vital to American economic interests. Iran's prime minister, Mohammad Mosaddeq, nationalized foreign-controlled petroleum operations in 1951 and collaborated closely with Iran's near neighbor, the Soviet Union. The CIA coup replaced Mosaddeq with Mohammad Reza Shah Pahlavi, who was both pro-American and ruthlessly authoritarian. The unpopular shah gave the Americans and the British a cut of oil revenues, accepted hundreds of millions in American aid for development, and made Iran, for the time, an anti-Soviet bulwark. The Iran coup became a blueprint for similar CIA-supported insurgencies elsewhere in the world, most prominently Indonesia in the late 1950s and the Congo in the early 1960s.

GUATEMALA The Cold War had made its way to the western hemisphere in the postwar years, but fighting leftism in Latin America was not at the top of the Truman administration's priorities. Indeed, those on the left side of the New Deal coalition found the new direction of Latin American politics was appealing. A burst of political reform between 1944 and 1946 brought the region from autocracy to democracy with real speed. Insurgent political movements, led by democratic leftists, inspired by the New Deal, Popular Front politics, and worldwide antifascism, toppled dictators, expanded voting rights, pushed for labor reforms, and demanded the redistribution of lands long held by wealthy planters. Reformers took power throughout Central and South America. By 1946, all but five countries in the region had democratically elected governments, mostly on the left.

Guatemala, a country of only about three million people, embodied both the promise of democracy in Latin America and, for the United States, the threat of leftism in the western hemisphere. In mostly rural Guatemala, a small, corrupt, wealthy planter elite, enriched by global demand for coffee and bananas, controlled the government in the early twentieth century. The majority of Guatemalans, many of Indian descent, lived in near-feudal conditions, dispossessed of their lands and forced into labor.

In 1944, Guatemalans toppled the autocratic regime of Jorge Ubico and a military successor. In the country's first-ever democratic election, they elected Juan José Arévalo, who promoted a version of social democracy, building a base in the countryside among landless and brutally exploited rural workers. Arévalo's successor Jacobo Arbenz, elected in 1951, instituted a sweeping land reform program, redistributing land long held by the planters and international investors. Arbenz authorized the appropriation of some 225,000 acres of land belonging to United Fruit, an American-based firm.[39]

In 1954, a CIA-backed coup toppled Arbenz, denounced as a Communist and loathed by the planter elite and the U.S.-based companies in Guatemala. Post–

Arbenz Guatemala became a case study in American Cold War policy in the developing world. Despite its rhetoric of democracy, the United States propped up authoritarian, anti-Communist regimes in the name of stability and security. To Eisenhower and his successors a dictatorial, pro–United States regime was more useful than a democratically elected government that threatened American economic or geopolitical interests.

On the ground in Guatemala oppression and instability flourished. The brutal regimes that succeeded Arbenz used the power of state to silence dissent, crush labor and land reform movements, and bolster the small elite that benefited from international investment. The United States did not merely tolerate such excesses under Eisenhower and his successors: it encouraged them in the name of freedom. In 1966, again with CIA support, Guatemala used advanced technology to gather information about dissenters. The regime created death squads and systematically began to "disappear" its opponents, using the tactics of kidnapping, torture, and assassination to silence dissent. This brutality provided a blueprint for the "dirty wars" conducted by American-backed dictatorships in Chile and Argentina in the 1970s and 1980s.

The Guatemalan coup and repression—like so many American Cold War ventures—had unintended consequences. While the United States hoped that Guatemala would modernize, serving as a model for other countries, many Latin American leftists took home a different lesson. If the results of democratic elections could be overturned by American intervention, then it would take other means to accomplish social and economic changes. For many on the left, that meant leaving New Deal–type programs to the side, rejecting elections, and instead seizing power outside the electoral process. Che Guevara, who led a Communist insurgency in Cuba, for example, promised that "Cuba will not be Guatemala."[40] On that island, revolutionaries overthrew the corrupt Batista dictatorship in 1959 and instituted reforms much like those in postwar Guatemala but without democratic institutions.

CUBA Cuba, the former Spanish colony, just ninety miles off the U.S. coast, had long been, in most respects, a dependency of the United States. In the mid-twentieth century, American investors dominated its economy and controlled its utilities, its extractive industries, and a sizable segment of its lucrative sugar production. American dollars flew thick in the sultry bars and luxury hotels along Havana's beaches. Three times since Cuba achieved its independence from Spain in 1898, the United States had sent troops to the island to protect American interests. In 1950, Cuba was in the hands of Fulgencio Batista, a former insurgent turned dictator. Batista had made his peace (and considerable profit) with outside economic interests, called off Guatemalan-style land reforms, and enjoyed little support outside the island's elite and the military.

In January 1959, less than two years from the end of Eisenhower's term in office, revolutionary insurgents led by Fidel Castro toppled Batista. At first, many Americans looked hopefully to Castro. He visited the United States in April 1959, met for three hours with Vice President Nixon, and stayed in a hotel in Harlem. But by the fall, relations with Castro began to sour when his regime embarked on an aggressive land reform policy. In the following months, Cuba confiscated nearly $1 billion in American holdings, signed a trade agreement with the Soviet Union, and recognized the People's Republic of China.

Eisenhower did not see anything to be gained by restoring Batista's unpopular regime to power, but he retaliated against Castro by imposing a trade embargo (including restricting the importation of Cuba's only lucrative cash crop, sugar) and freezing American aid. In the spring of 1960, he authorized the CIA to provide support and training for anti-Castro insurgents who hoped to assassinate Castro and stage a coup. By allying with the Soviets and Chinese and standing up aggressively to the United States, Castro made clear that he had learned from Guatemala: his regime would use military force, coercion at home, and aid from the Soviet bloc to ensure that he would not go the way of Arbenz. For the next several decades, Cuba would be the flashpoint of Cold War tensions in the western hemisphere.

Security and Insecurity

Eisenhower's America was a paradoxical place, prosperous yet insecure. America at midcentury underwent transformations that few fully understood but whose ramifications many felt. A new, youth-oriented culture threatened an older generation. Women working and gays gathering surreptitiously threatened the normative family, just as it seemed more invincible than ever. Business leaders and conservative elites promoted a doctrine of free enterprise out of fear that, even under a Republican president, big government was unstoppable. A mass insurgency, led by the country's long-oppressed African Americans, threatened to undermine one of the deepest American traditions, that of racial inequality. American global might was unsurpassed, yet the threat of nuclear war loomed over the world, and insurgencies in faraway places like Guatemala and Iran seemed to pose an existential threat to the United States. The postwar years marked the beginning of a struggle that shaped the politics of the next few decades, between dissent and conformity, between social welfare and free enterprise, between racial and sexual equality and tradition.

Suggested Reading

Cohen, Lizabeth. *A Consumers' Republic: The Politics of Mass Consumption in Postwar America* (2003). How Americans came to define themselves as "consumer citizens," and how policy makers encouraged suburbanization, shopping, and prosperity.

Coontz, Stephanie. *The Way We Never Were: American Families and the Nostalgia Trap* (1993). A readable account that debunks conventional wisdom about the mid-twentieth-century American family and gender roles.

Dudziak, Mary L. *Cold War Civil Rights: Race and the Image of American Democracy* (2000). Connects the civil rights struggle in the United States to international relations by showing how federal officials responded to civil rights protests to enhance America's reputation abroad.

Grandin, Greg. *The Last Colonial Massacre: Latin America in the Cold War* (2004). Shows how American anti-Communist foreign policy fostered authoritarian politics in a region on the brink of democratization.

Horowitz, Daniel. *Betty Friedan and the Making of "The Feminine Mystique": The American Left, the Cold War, and Modern Feminism* (2000). A biography of the feminist writer that documents links among labor, radical activism, anti-Communism, and feminism.

Igo, Sarah E. *The Averaged American: Surveys, Citizens, and the Making of a Mass Public* (2007). An innovative account of how ordinary Americans responded to opinion polls, surveys, and community studies that attempted to define what was normal in mid-twentieth-century America.

Johnson, David K. *The Lavender Scare: The Cold War Persecution of Gays and Lesbians in the Federal Government* (2004). Uses declassified government documents to uncover the history of federal investigations of suspected homosexuals.

Newton, Jim. *Eisenhower: The White House Years* (2011). The best biography of the general turned politician.

Phillips-Fein, Kim. *Invisible Hands: The Businessmen's Crusade Against the New Deal* (2010). Traces the history of the business leaders who campaigned against liberalism between the New Deal and the 1960s and fueled the rise of the New Right.

Shermer, Elizabeth Tandy. *Sunbelt Capitalism: Phoenix and the Transformation of American Politics* (2013). Explores the paradoxical history of a Sunbelt metropolis that depended on federal spending but whose leaders rebelled against regulation, welfare, labor rights, and taxation.

Chapter Review

Review Questions

1. Who did and did not benefit from the postwar economic boom?

2. How did American family structure change in the post–World War II years?

3. How did the federal government promote home ownership?

4. Describe the typical postwar suburban house.

5. Were President Eisenhower's domestic politics liberal or conservative?

6. What were business elites' major arguments against the New Deal?

7. What explains the rise in fears of juvenile delinquency in the 1950s?

8. Explain the Lavender Scare and its repercussions.

9. Discuss the major arguments that civil rights activists made against "separate but equal" education.

10. How did American involvement in the developing world reshape Cold War foreign policy?

Key Terms

The Feminine Mystique p. 45

family wage p. 48

United Electrical Workers (UE) p. 48

The Common Sense Book of Baby and Child Care p. 51

Home Owners Loan Corporation p. 51

Federal Housing Administration (FHA) p. 51

Levittowns p. 52

military-industrial complex p. 58

Interstate Highway Act p. 59

juvenile delinquency p. 62

"homophile" organizations p. 66

National Association for the Advancement of Colored People (NAACP) p. 69

Congress of Racial Equality (CORE) p. 69

Journey of Reconciliation p. 69

Montgomery Bus Boycott p. 69

Brown v. Board of Education of Topeka p. 70

Sipuel v. Regents of the University of Oklahoma p. 72

Shelley v. Kraemer p. 75

Guatemalan coup p. 79

A Season
of Change

✳

Liberals and the Limits of Reform, 1960–1966

John Lewis spent his twenty-first birthday, Sunday, February 21, 1961, in a Nashville jail. He didn't exactly plan it that way. That day Lewis, a student at American Baptist Theological Seminary in Nashville, was scheduled to give his senior sermon, a meditation on the tenth chapter of the Gospel of Matthew, in which Jesus proclaims, "Think not that I come to send peace on earth. I came to send not peace but a sword."[1] It was an apt passage for an earnest young man who pledged nonviolence but whose actions as a protester provoked violence.

The previous evening Lewis and twenty-five other civil rights activists, most of them students, had been arrested for blockading the entrance to Nashville's glittering Loew's Theater, where hundreds lined up to watch Cecil B. DeMille's epic film *The Ten Commandments*. It did not take years of theological education to see the hypocrisy of white theatergoers cheering at the liberation of Pharaoh's slaves and admiring Moses as he led his people to the Promised Land. Nashville's theaters—if they let in black patrons at all—forced them to sit in the "crow's nest," high in the balcony, far from the screen. Loews made black patrons enter via the outdoor fire stairs, "out in the cold and rain, past garbage cans and up rickety metal steps."[2]

The son of sharecroppers who worked the rich soil of Alabama's Black Belt but barely earned enough to survive, John Lewis was a precocious student on the path to one of black America's most prestigious occupations: the ministry. There weren't many black lawyers or doctors, engineers or accountants. Even bright young men like Lewis—if they were lucky enough to go to college—often found themselves working as shop clerks or railroad porters, jobs that were beneath their education. The pulpit, by contrast, offered prestige and, for those as talented as Lewis, the promise of a life of more than modest comfort.

The budding minister, however, did not follow a straight path through his studies. On February 27, 1960, just a year before he was arrested for blockading the Loew's ticket booth, he had spent his first night in jail, hauled away from a Woolworth's lunch counter and charged with disorderly conduct simply for asking to be served a meal. Lewis helped convene the fledgling Nashville Student Movement, inspired by the lunch counter sit-ins in Greensboro, North Carolina, earlier that month. After weeks of careful planning and training in nonviolent tactics by seasoned movement strategists, they launched a nearly month-long peaceful assault on Nashville's dime-store lunch counters. The 1960s sit-ins reprised tactics that civil rights activists had been deploying since CORE's protests at segregated Chicago diners during World War II.

In the years following the Montgomery Bus Boycott, Lewis and his fellow students had watched the battles against Jim Crow in the South wax and wane. They chafed at many of their elders' calls for patience. Many of Nashville's leading black ministers counseled the students against direct action. Lewis's own parents, still hopeful that their son would rise to respectability and leadership, were "shocked and ashamed" when they learned that he had broken the law and been hauled off to jail. "You went to school to get an education," wrote Amie Lewis to her son. "You should get out of this movement, just get out of that mess."[3]

< Civil rights and religious activists join Martin Luther King, Jr. (*third from left*) in the March on Washington for Jobs and Freedom, August 28, 1963 (*previous page*).

The real mess in Nashville resulted from white retaliation against Lewis and his fellow activists. Angry whites dumped food and put their cigarettes out on the backs of the nonviolent students as they patiently waited to be served. During one sit-in, they beat some of Lewis's friends as the police watched. But the violence in Nashville did not discourage the sit-in movement. Northern activists targeted chain stores, including Woolworth, Kress, and Kresge, with operations in Nashville and other southern cities. By March, Nashville's business leaders had reached a compromise with the movement: halt the protests and the lunch counters would be open to anyone who could pay. By the end of 1960, thousands of activists had joined sit-ins throughout the South. In October, Martin Luther King, Jr., was arrested after refusing to give up his seat at an Atlanta lunch counter.

Kennedy and the Liberal Revival

Many observers sensed change everywhere in 1960, not just at lunch counters. News reporters noted an awakening among both black and white youth, often expressed as a search for "authenticity" in a culture of conformity. In his best-selling 1956 book, sociologist C. Wright Mills criticized the "power elite," an interlocking system of military, business, and political leaders who shaped America's economy and politics. Mills believed that the challenge to established authority would come from a "new class" of well-educated youth in a prosperous America. "The Age of Complacency is ending," wrote Mills in 1960. "We are beginning to move again."[4]

The fundamental question was in what direction the United States would move. The answer remained far from clear. The protesters and counterprotesters in Nashville clashed over competing visions of what America should be. The struggle for civil rights was already reconfiguring party politics and raising fundamental questions about economics and political power. Should the New Deal, more than a quarter century old, be revivified or expanded? Was Eisenhower's pro-business vision right for the United States? For all their differences, members of both parties believed in aggressive engagement with Communism internationally. They fought mainly over who would wage the Cold War more effectively.

DEMOCRATS AND REPUBLICANS ADRIFT At the beginning of the 1960 campaign season, liberals were despondent, having lost the last two presidential elections. The New Deal had been tempered by more than a decade of stasis. Organized labor—still the Democrats' most powerful constituency—had seen its membership decline beginning in 1954. The party's southern wing had found common cause with the GOP over laws restricting labor, and the most rapid economic growth happened in the Sunbelt, especially in states with major defense contractors and attractive "right to work" laws that inhibited union organizing. Key Democratic constituencies also began to drift rightward. A majority of Catholics, who had reliably voted Democratic for decades, found Eisenhower attractive and rallied around conservative anti-Communists. White urbanites worried about growing black political and economic power, white suburbanites feared integration, and white southerners opposed the civil rights insurgency.

The GOP, despite eight years in the White House, faced its own troubles. The Eisenhower administration presided over a deep recession that began in 1959. It seemed paralyzed by the Communist takeover of Cuba. The outgoing president fretted about a bloated "military-industrial complex" that jeopardized the federal budget. Vice President Richard Nixon, the Republican frontrunner to succeed Ike, had spent eight years overshadowed by Eisenhower, who did not particularly like him. Rather than giving him much responsibility to shape policy, Ike sent Nixon around the country to events he couldn't be bothered to attend.

The Democrats cast about for a new presidential candidate, someone who could bridge the party's growing north-south divide and credibly challenge Nixon. That would not be Senate majority leader Lyndon Johnson, a Texan whom the party's reform wing reviled, even as it grudgingly admired him for his legislative prowess. It would not be two-time loser Adlai Stevenson. Southerners would not rally for Minnesota senator Hubert Humphrey because of his early and outspoken support for civil rights in 1948.

THE RISE OF JOHN F. KENNEDY Finally, Democrats rallied behind Massachusetts senator John F. Kennedy. At forty-three, he was one of the youngest contenders for the White House ever. His youthful good looks, and his comfort with the new medium of television, seemed to his admirers to embody change, even if liberals grumbled when he picked LBJ as his running mate. Still, Kennedy was a blank slate as the race for the presidency began. The scion of a wealthy Massachusetts family (his father had been FDR's ambassador to Britain), he had served with valor during World War II. With his family's financial backing, he had successfully run for Congress, winning the support of Boston's Irish Catholic–dominated political machine. In 1952 he won the first of two terms in the U.S. Senate, though he did not establish much of a record as a legislator. But influence in Washington came not just through writing laws or cutting deals. As a senator, Kennedy cultivated the Washington elite, published a Pulitzer Prize–winning series of vignettes of courageous political leaders, which had been ghostwritten by a family adviser, and appeared regularly on television news programs to opine on the political issues of the day.

Perhaps the most novel aspect of Kennedy's candidacy was that for all his Washington connections, he was a religious outsider, at least when it came to presidential politics. As one of the nation's most prominent Roman Catholics, Kennedy came to be revered among his coreligionists as he moved onto the national stage. Though Catholics

Chronology

1952	Immigration and Nationality Act
1957	Civil Rights Act
1960	Sit-in movement begins
	Student Non-Violent Coordinating Committee founded
	Barry Goldwater's *Conscience of a Conservative* published
	John F. Kennedy (Democrat) elected president
1961	Bay of Pigs invasion
	Freedom Rides
	Berlin Wall completed
1962	*Engel v. Vitale*
	National Farmworkers Association (later United Farm Workers) founded
	James Meredith enrolls at University of Mississippi
	Cuban Missile Crisis
1963	Birmingham, Alabama, civil rights protests
	Gideon v. Wainwright
	The March on Washington for Jobs and Freedom
	Malcolm X "Message to the Grassroots"
	John F. Kennedy assassinated
	Lyndon B. Johnson (Democrat) becomes president
1964	President Johnson declares "War on Poverty"
	Escobedo v. Illinois
	Civil Rights Act
	Freedom Summer
	Lyndon B. Johnson (Democrat) elected president
1965	Great Society
	Selma, Alabama, protests
	Voting Rights Act
	Elementary and Secondary Education Act
	Medicare and Medicaid enacted
	National Welfare Rights Organization founded
	Watts, Los Angeles, riot
	Hart-Cellar (Immigration) Act
1966	*Miranda v. Arizona*
	Black Panther Party founded
	Ronald Reagan elected California governor

made up more than one-fifth of America's population—and formed a powerful voting bloc in key, closely divided states like Illinois, Pennsylvania, and New York—they were underrepresented in higher office.[5] Like the last Catholic contender for the presidency, Al Smith in 1928, Kennedy faced deep-rooted suspicion, especially among conservative Protestants, that he would be a tool of the papacy. But much had changed in the intervening three decades: prominent Catholic clerics like Fulton Sheen appeared on national television, Catholic immigrants and their children had served valiantly in World War II and Korea, and the American Catholic bishops zealously fought Communism.

Still, Kennedy had to reassure voters who had qualms about his religion. During the campaign, he used a speech to the Greater Houston Ministerial Association to pledge his commitment to an America "where no religious body seeks to impose its will directly or indirectly upon the general populace or the public acts of its officials."[6] He and most religious leaders, for the moment, agreed that religious belief belonged in the private sphere, not in the public square.

Kennedy campaigned on the vague promise to "get America moving again." Though Eisenhower, Nixon, and Kennedy differed little on foreign policy, Kennedy chastised his Republican opponent for standing still while the United States "lost" Cuba. He accused Ike and Nixon of allowing a "missile gap" with the Soviets to widen, and promised to pursue the Cold War more aggressively.

On the campaign trail, Kennedy called for a renewal of public service. He was cautious. He called for a reduction in taxes, gradualism on civil rights, and business-friendly, pro-growth policies to pull the country out of the economic slump. Telegenic and composed, he swept the 1960 presidential debates, the first time candidates in a presidential election had sparred face-to-face. His message about the power of government as a force for positive change captured the imagination of many Americans. In one of the closest presidential races in American history, Kennedy beat Nixon by just a little more than 100,000 votes out of more than 68 million cast nationwide. Some scholars suggest that Kennedy's close victory in both Texas and Illinois was the result of ballot-box-stuffing by Lyndon Johnson's well-oiled political operation in Texas and Chicago's infamous Democratic machine.

THE KENNEDY TECHNOCRACY "The torch has been passed to a new generation of Americans," proclaimed Kennedy in his inaugural address. In soaring prose, he pledged that "we shall pay any price, bear any burden, meet any hardship, support any friend, oppose any foe to assure the survival and the success of liberty." Winning the Cold War would not simply be a matter of might. It would require uplifting the oppressed both at home and abroad. Kennedy called for sacrifice in a "struggle against the common enemies of man: tyranny, poverty, disease and war itself."[7]

Once in office, Kennedy established himself as the heir to Progressive reformers and New Dealers for his belief that the most effective government grew from a marriage of detached experts and government officials. In one of his most important addresses, in 1962, he summed up his philosophy of governance: "The fact of the matter is that most of the problems, or at least many of them that we now face, are technical problems, are administrative problems. They are very sophisticated judgments which do not lend themselves to the great sort of 'passionate movements,' which have stirred this country so often in the past."[8] He distanced his administration not only from the most passionate of movements, the struggle for civil rights, but also from the messiness of the legislative process. Instead, he sought the advice of the nation's most prominent economists, social scientists, and executives, particularly graduates and faculty of the most elite universities, including his alma mater, Harvard, his own version of Franklin Roosevelt's "brains trust."

When Kennedy asked James Tobin, a Nobel Prize–winning economist at Yale, to join his economic team, Tobin modestly demurred: "Mr. President, I am what you might call an *ivory tower economist*." Kennedy rejoined, "That's the best kind! Professor, I am what you might call an *ivory tower* President."[9] Kennedy believed that experts like Tobin, detached from the messy process of campaigning and lawmaking, would act in the national interest, not in their own self-interest.

Mostly uninterested in the details of domestic policy, Kennedy relied on his staff to set his agenda. His economic advisers persuaded him to adopt economic policies based on John Maynard Keynes's argument that government spending would stimulate economic growth. Like many political centrists, Kennedy at first prioritized government solvency through a balanced budget. But Tobin and Minnesota economist Walter Heller persuaded him that deficit spending would stimulate demand. Following their advice, he supported increased federal spending on the construction of schools, highways, and military bases. He also singled out "distressed areas" for federal aid, although critics complained that the administration just sent federal "pork" into districts to reward Democratic loyalists or to buy off critics.

Kennedy's tax policy was also Keynesian. His aides overhauled the federal tax code, creating a standard deduction, reducing tax-withholding rates, eliminating loopholes, and lowering the rate for the top tax bracket from 91 to 70 percent of individual income. Kennedy's economic team argued that lower taxes and a streamlined tax-collection system would stimulate consumer demand and spur growth. Getting tax reform through Congress was challenging. Many Republicans worried that tax cuts would unbalance the federal budget. Congress would not pass the new tax code until 1964.

Civil Rights

For all Kennedy's faith in the judgment of cool, detached experts, he could not ignore the intensifying African American struggle for civil rights. He himself had been lukewarm toward the civil rights insurgents of the 1950s. He only tepidly supported the Civil Rights Act of 1957. The first such law enacted in more than eight decades, it was mostly a symbolic gesture. The act called for voting rights for African Americans but contained no enforcement mechanisms. It also created a federal Civil Rights Commission to investigate discrimination and recommend reforms. Kennedy refused to join liberals who wanted the law to be stronger. During his 1960 campaign, to attract black voters, he gestured toward civil rights. He pledged to end discrimination in housing with "the stroke of a pen" and prepared campaign materials to be distributed to black churches that touted his successful effort to persuade Atlanta officials to release Martin Luther King, Jr., from jail after his sit-in arrest.

Civil rights was not, however, a priority for the new president. That was largely a matter of political calculation. Kennedy had long been mindful of the restive southern wing of his party. In 1948, as a first-term member of Congress, Kennedy had witnessed Dixiecrat Strom Thurmond's rebellion. As Kennedy set his sights on higher office, he distanced himself from civil rights legislation and assiduously cultivated southern Democrats, just as FDR had during the New Deal. His choice of Lyndon Johnson, a prominent southerner, as his vice-presidential nominee discomfited northern liberals.

"A GREAT SENSE OF HOPE" Even though civil rights advocates had good reason to worry about Kennedy and more so about Johnson, they still hoped that the Democrats would be more responsive than Eisenhower and Nixon to their demands. Kennedy had given the Democrats' liberal wing nearly full control over the 1960 party platform, which they used to push for aggressive civil rights enforcement. But behind the scenes, Kennedy reassured his party's southern lions that he did not consider the platform to be binding.

John Lewis was one of the many young people who believed that, despite his record, Kennedy would be an agent of change. "I watched Kennedy's inaugural address that January with a great sense of hope," recalled Lewis. "Here was this young, vibrant man who seemed to represent the future just by his energy and age. He didn't mention race or civil rights in his speech, but I assumed that was simply a matter of political expediency. I believed that *he* believed in what we all believed in—The Beloved Community."[10]

Kennedy could not have cared less about Lewis's vision of an interracial society. For him, civil rights was a political obstacle that bitterly divided the Democratic Party. Rather than taking a principled position in favor of racial equality, he awkwardly tried to appease southern segregationists, especially when it came to nominations to the federal bench. About a third of Kennedy's appointees to the Fifth Circuit—which included Alabama, Florida, Georgia, Louisiana, Mississippi, and Texas—had records upholding Jim Crow laws. But nodding to his party's liberal wing, Kennedy also nominated prominent blacks to district and appellate court posts in the North, including longtime NAACP attorney Thurgood Marshall, Philadelphia civil rights lawyer A. Leon Higginbotham, and Wade H. McCree, a reform Democrat from Detroit. Kennedy hoped, at least, that he could paste together a coalition big enough to stave off a Republican challenge in 1964 by giving a little bit to everyone.

In trying to lower the temperature of the civil rights debate, Kennedy devised and implemented many of his most significant initiatives outside the public eye. In April 1961, for example, he created the President's Committee on Equal Employment Opportunity, which worked mostly behind the scenes to draft federal regulations to address the problem of discrimination by federal contractors. In 1962, Kennedy signed a little-noticed executive order calling for vaguely defined "affirmative action" in hiring by government contractors. Kennedy hoped that given small victories, labor and civil rights groups would cool their demands for a full-blown antidiscrimination law and that perhaps the party's southern constituents would pay little heed to bureaucratic directives.

THE FREEDOM RIDES John Lewis was not satisfied with Kennedy's baby steps forward. Within months of the inauguration, it became clear to him that the White House would not take the lead on civil rights. Pressure had to come from below. Lewis and other activists made sure that it did. During Kennedy's first year in office, members of CORE, including several veterans of the 1947 Journey of Reconciliation, planned an assault on segregated interstate transportation. Beginning in April 1961, carefully trained interracial teams launched the Freedom Rides, traveling by bus across Virginia and the Carolinas, down to Georgia, Alabama, and Mississippi, refusing to give up their seats to whites and disregarding the ubiquitous "whites only" signs in bus terminals. The Freedom Rides attracted many youthful activists, including Lewis.

One of the key training exercises for the Freedom Riders was "role playing," in which potential riders tried out nonviolent responses to mock attacks. For Lewis—who had already been arrested five times—these were nothing new. But on May 4, in Rock Hill, South Carolina, Lewis and his fellow Freedom Riders found their skills tested when white thugs beat them in the bus terminal before the police dispersed the crowd. Lewis stumbled back onto the bus, his chest badly bruised and his head bloody.

The Freedom Riders (minus Lewis, who left for a few days for a fellowship interview) made headlines worldwide on May 14, when, just outside Anniston, Alabama, a group of white supremacists drove the bus off the road, lit it afire, and brutally beat the black and white passengers as they escaped. The photograph of the burning bus—on the front pages of newspapers worldwide—became an icon of southern intransigence. It accomplished the Freedom Riders' goal of putting the spotlight on white supremacy.

Battered and stunned, the Freedom Riders proceeded from Anniston to Alabama's largest city, Birmingham, in another bus, this time under police escort. But as the bus arrived at the city's main terminal, the police disappeared. Hundreds of whites converged on the Freedom Riders as they disembarked, beating them with bats, chains, and bricks. Some of Alabama's leading public officials had encouraged the mob violence, including the Birmingham police commissioner, Eugene "Bull" Connor, who had given the police orders to withdraw from the station just minutes before the Freedom Riders arrived.

Lewis and another group of Freedom Riders arrived in Birmingham on May 17, where they were arrested, imprisoned, and eventually shuttled to the Tennessee border in two unmarked cars. Lewis sat in the lead car, driven by none other than Bull Connor himself. Not intimidated, Lewis and his comrades sneaked back to Birmingham, intending to continue on their Freedom Ride. They didn't know that, embarrassed by the news coverage of the Rides, the Kennedy administration had quietly reached an agreement with Alabama governor John Patterson that the riders would be protected from further violence.

Freedom Riders White supremacists brutally beat Freedom Riders John Lewis (*left*) and James Zwerg when their bus arrived at the terminal in Montgomery, Alabama, on May 20, 1961.

But the Alabama state police did not cooperate. On May 20, in a grim reprise of the Birmingham bloodbath, the police once again left the Riders unguarded. As the bus arrived in Montgomery, they once again faced mob violence. White vigilantes pummeled Lewis and his fellow Riders, beat several reporters, and left John Seigenthaler, a high-ranking Kennedy administration official sent to monitor the protests, bloody and unconscious. Stationed just blocks from the bus terminal, the police deliberately ignored the rampage.

Kennedy was furious at Patterson but just as angry at the Freedom Riders. "Can't you get your god-damned friends off those buses?" Kennedy asked domestic policy aide Harris Wofford, a supporter of the civil rights movement.[11] Many commentators, north and south, accused the Freedom Riders of stirring up violence. But the Freedom Rides continued unabated through the fall, as hundreds of nonviolent protesters went to jail, especially in Mississippi.

COLD WAR CIVIL RIGHTS The president worried that, in the midst of the Cold War, the grisly images of beaten protesters and reports of Freedom Riders sentenced to hard labor in southern prisons would damage America's carefully manufactured international image. In the struggle to win the hearts and minds of the third world, the Soviets used images of beaten protesters and burning buses as proof that America was a sham democracy. The Freedom Rides threatened to unravel more than a decade's worth of American cultural diplomacy, which included black diplomats appointed to American embassies in Scandinavia, government-sponsored tours by black celebrities like jazz trumpeter Louis Armstrong, and black-themed programming on the Voice of America.

Another well-publicized racial incident in the fall of 1961 embarrassed Kennedy. Chad's ambassador to the United States, Malik Sow, was driving from New York to Washington, D.C., along Maryland's Route 40, when a roadside restaurant refused to serve him. "He looked just like an ordinary run of the mill nigger to me," stated the waitress who rebuffed him. "I couldn't tell he was an ambassador."[12] Mainstream publications, including *Life* magazine, made it "story of the week" in early December—another blow to America's reputation. The State Department intervened, reaching an agreement with dozens of Maryland restaurants that they would not discriminate.

Cold War Crises

The Route 40 incident starkly reminded Kennedy that Jim Crow and civil rights protests had international implications: they threatened the new administration's foreign policy. The Cold War intensified during Kennedy's first months in office. Despite Kennedy's rhetoric of change, he inherited a well-developed anti-Communist policy from his predecessors. He built on Truman's policy of containment, increased military spending, and continued Eisenhower's policy of fighting the Cold War in the developing world. However, Kennedy faced a series of escalating international crises on every front of the Cold War: Latin America, Europe, and Asia.

THE BAY OF PIGS Less than three months after inauguration day, Kennedy authorized an attempted coup in Cuba. The plan was not his—Eisenhower's CIA had hatched it. On April 17, 1961, fourteen hundred anti-Castro insurgents, trained and armed by the United States, made landfall at the Bay of Pigs. The CIA had mistakenly assumed that tens of thousands of Cubans would hail the liberators and join them in overthrowing the Castro regime. Establishing a beachhead in the marshy bay proved to be a strategic error. A popular uprising did not ensue, and Castro, fully aware of the plot, deployed the Cuban military and put down the insurrection within hours. The debacle deeply embarrassed Kennedy.

GERMANY, THE SOVIETS, AND EAST-WEST HOSTILITY In the meantime, the Soviets and the East Germans, emboldened by their perception of Kennedy's weakness, challenged the United States in Berlin. By the fall of 1961, they completed construction of the Berlin Wall, which separated Communist East Berlin from the American-controlled West. The wall became a symbol of East-West hostility. A humanitarian disaster, it prevented the movement of political refugees into West Berlin.

In the meantime, the Soviet Union stepped up support for insurgencies in Southeast Asia, Latin America, and central Africa.

Kennedy, who did not share Eisenhower's end-of-term misgivings about the military-industrial complex, greatly accelerated the production and deployment of nuclear weapons. In the summer of 1961 he expanded the military draft, stationed additional troops in Europe and Asia, pressed Congress to increase defense spending, and even urged ordinary Americans to build fallout shelters in case of an all-out war.

Despite his public warnings about the "missile gap," Kennedy was in an advantageous position vis-à-vis the Soviet Union. American airpower and weaponry were unsurpassed. The United States still had a substantially larger nuclear arsenal than the Soviets. Most Soviet nuclear weapons could not reach the United States. But the threat of nuclear war never seemed closer than during the weeks following October 14, 1962, when an American U2 spy plane discovered that the Soviet Union was installing intermediate-range ballistic missiles in Cuba, just ninety miles off the U.S. coast.

THE CUBAN MISSILE CRISIS The Cuban Missile Crisis had its origins earlier in the Kennedy administration. In early 1961, JFK had authorized the military to place nuclear missiles in Turkey and Italy, within range of Moscow and St. Petersburg. Khrushchev considered U.S. missiles near its border an "intolerable provocation." Kennedy also provoked the Soviets by stepping up the Cold War in Latin America, supporting efforts to assassinate Castro, and channeling aid to Castro's enemies elsewhere in Latin America. Finally, he authorized military exercises over the Caribbean to unsettle the Cubans and demonstrate American strength.

On October 16, Kennedy responded to the discovery of Soviet missiles in Cuba by pulling together ExComm, a group of key military and foreign policy advisers, and close aides, who held intensive secret meetings to plan a response to the crisis. Some Pentagon officials promoted the invasion of Cuba, arguing that the missile crisis offered the perfect opportunity to topple Castro, a position that Attorney General Robert F. Kennedy, the president's brother, also urged. Others made the case for a targeted strike against the missile sites. A third group called for negotiations.

ExComm members debated the strategic significance of the deployment of the missiles. In a memo to the president, aide Ted Sorensen wrote that the Cuban missiles, "even when fully operational, do not significantly alter the balance of power—i.e., they do not significantly increase the potential megatonnage capable of being unleashed on American soil, even after a surprise American nuclear strike."[13] But other advisers feared the deployment was the first step in expanding Soviet capacity for a retaliatory strike in the event of war.

On October 22, in a televised speech, Kennedy made the startling public announcement about the missiles. He issued an ultimatum, finding a middle ground in ExComm's deliberations. If Khrushchev didn't withdraw the missiles, the United States would enforce a blockade of Soviet shipments to the island. Nodding to the hawks, Kennedy also promised that the use of any Cuban missiles against any target in the Americas would be regarded "as an attack by the Soviet Union on the United States, requiring a full retaliatory response upon the Soviet Union."[14] Two days later, with the blockade in place, Soviet ships turned back.

Khrushchev reacted with fury, denouncing Kennedy. Privately, however, both sides were open to negotiation. In a letter to Kennedy on October 26, Khrushchev proposed to withdraw the Soviet missiles if the United States pledged not to invade Cuba. On the twenty-seventh he publicly demanded that the United States withdraw its own missile installations in Turkey. The administration accepted Khrushchev's terms to dismantle the Cuban installation under UN inspection and agreed not to take military action against Cuba. Neither Khrushchev nor Kennedy mentioned the secret agreement at the heart of the deal: the United States promised to later remove its missiles from Turkey. On October 28 the Soviet government announced that it would disassemble and remove the Cuban missiles.

Cuban Missile Crisis President John F. Kennedy (*left*) confers with Secretary of Defense Robert S. McNamara outside the White House during the Cuban Missile Crisis in October 1962.

The truce with Khrushchev was at best uneasy. The successful negotiations had prevented war and begun the process of gradually slowing the arms race. Over the next year, Kennedy and Khrushchev agreed to a partial test ban treaty, entered into negotiations over an arms reduction treaty, and set up the White House–Kremlin hotline, so the two leaders could talk directly in case of another crisis.

But the Kennedy administration continued to fight the Cold War on many fronts. Using "soft diplomacy," the United States funded large-scale economic development projects in South America and Southeast Asia. In 1961, just weeks after the inauguration, Kennedy announced the creation of the Peace Corps, a popular program that would send idealistic young Americans to work on education, disease eradication, and agricultural and engineering projects throughout the world.

But the Cold War intensified. The United States and the Soviet Union continued their proxy battles through direct military support and clandestine activities in places as diverse as Vietnam, the Dominican Republic, and the Congo. Most consequential was Vietnam, where the Kennedy administration simultaneously channeled substantial economic aid, provided military support to anti-Communist forces, and supported CIA covert action. Kennedy increased the number of American military advisers there from about 900 in 1961 to 16,000 in late 1963, but did not commit the United States to an all-out war. At the same time, the propaganda war between the United States and the USSR intensified and, increasingly, affected the struggle for civil rights on the home front.

"Where's the PEN, Mr. President?"

As the president directed his energies abroad, and moved slowly on civil rights, John Lewis expressed his growing frustration: "Where's the PEN, Mr. President?"[15] Throughout Kennedy's first and much of his second year in office, activists mailed thousands of pens to the White House to urge him to ban housing discrimination. Kennedy's staff warehoused the pens, and Kennedy did nothing, fearing the wrath of white voters who associated integrated housing with intermarriage and crime. But the pressure kept mounting. Kennedy could not dismiss hundreds of petitions from churches and celebrity endorsements of open housing. Members of CORE picketed new housing developments in Cleveland, New York, and Los Angeles. On the weekend before Thanksgiving, just after the 1962 midterm elections, timed to minimize controversy, Kennedy issued an executive order banning discrimination in all new housing constructed with federal funds. As Kennedy hoped, the order attracted little media attention.

Housing was one battleground in the multifront struggle for civil rights; public education was another. *Brown* continued to be a dead letter in the South, where public officials mostly ignored the ruling. In the North and West, however, civil rights activists used *Brown* to challenge segregated schools. In 1961 local officials in New Rochelle, New York—dubbed the "Little Rock of the North"—lost a court battle to maintain the town's segregated Lincoln primary school. Fired up by the victory in New Rochelle, activists took on segregated schools throughout the region. In 1962 the Englewood Movement, a diverse coalition of former Freedom Riders, activist lawyers, and black radicals, challenged segregated schools in a New Jersey suburb. By year's end, the NAACP was battling segregation in sixty-nine northern and western school districts. Over the next two years, hundreds of thousands of students in Chicago, Boston, Cleveland, and New York boycotted classes in segregated schools.

The Kennedy administration kept its distance from the northern school protests. But it could not ignore the media coverage of the University of Mississippi in September 1962, when James Meredith attempted to enroll. With legal support from the NAACP, Meredith won a Supreme Court ruling that struck down the university's discriminatory admissions policy. When he attempted to register for classes, however, Mississippi governor Ross Barnett encouraged defiance and, when violence erupted on the campus, refused to intervene. Angry mobs of white students, alumni, and area residents went on a rampage, injuring dozens of armed officials and killing two bystanders. The Kennedy administration deployed five hundred U.S. marshals, nationalized the Mississippi National Guard, and sent troops to quell the riot, before Meredith, under armed guard, enrolled.

BIRMINGHAM AND THE "NEGRO REVOLT" OF 1963 January 1, 1963, marked the centennial of the Emancipation Proclamation. Rather than celebrating, black America seemed to be in open rebellion. That spring Martin Luther King, Jr., and the Southern Christian Leadership Conference (SCLC) chose Birmingham, Alabama, as a target of protest. On May 3 thousands of black protesters, many of them schoolchildren, took to Birmingham's streets. King and his co-organizers anticipated that local law enforcement officials, led by Bull Connor, would react with violence, a prophecy that turned out to be grimly true. Connor ordered policemen to sic their dogs and firefighters to blast their hoses on protesters. The photos of the violence appeared on the front pages of newspapers worldwide.

From his Birmingham jail cell, where he languished after being arrested for demonstrating without a permit, King defended his strategy: "We know through painful experience that freedom is never voluntarily given by the oppressor; it must be demanded by the oppressed." In especially pointed words, he lambasted moderates, perhaps even the president himself. "I have almost reached the regrettable conclusion," wrote King, "that the Negro's great stumbling block in his stride toward freedom is not the White Citizens Councilor or the Ku Klux Klanner, but the white moderate, who is more devoted to 'order' than to justice."[16]

The demands of the oppressed intensified in the following months. In late spring and early summer, 758 demonstrations broke out throughout the country. In seventy-five southern cities, 13,786 protesters were arrested.[17] Not all the demonstrations followed the nonviolent course that King advocated. In Birmingham, shortly after the police attacks, angry blacks took to the streets, breaking windows and looting stores. Mass protests, many of them violent, broke out in northern cities beginning in May and continued through the summer. In Philadelphia, dozens of activists were arrested for occupying city hall and blockading construction sites that had no black workers. Militants, including members of a fledgling black power organization called the Revolutionary Action Movement, joined the demonstrations. Many young protesters could barely contain their anger. Mocking the misuse of police dogs, young men in Philadelphia marched with mastiffs and turned a famous civil rights anthem into a military style chant: "We . . . Shall . . . Over . . . Come."[18]

White supremacists reacted aggressively. In June 1963, Alabama governor George Wallace, who earlier that year used his inauguration address to call for "segregation today, segregation tomorrow, segregation forever," defiantly stood at the entrance of the University of Alabama's main building to oppose the enrollment of two black students. After high-level negotiations with the Kennedy administration, which wanted to avoid a Mississippi-style bloodbath, Wallace let them in.[19] In Mississippi, on June 12, 1963, white supremacists assassinated NAACP leader Medgar Evers in his driveway.

The Kennedy administration entered a state of crisis. The passionate movements that the president had neglected seemed unstoppable. When Kennedy dispatched staffers to visit northern cities that had erupted in protest, they returned with a warning. The situation there was explosive. The administration had come to realize that the domestic crisis was every bit as grave as its troubles abroad. In a nationally televised address on June 22, 1963, Kennedy announced that his administration would draft civil rights legislation, though he was light on the specifics.

If Kennedy expected that his announcement would put a lid on protests, he was wrong. The next day Martin Luther King, Jr., headlined the hundred-thousand-person Walk for Freedom in Detroit. Rather than celebrating Kennedy's shift on civil rights, King encouraged protesters to push harder, saving especially harsh words for those who demanded blacks to be patient. "Gradualism," King argued, "is little more than escapism and do-nothingism, which ends up in stand-stillism."[20]

THE MARCH ON WASHINGTON Few took the argument against gradualism more seriously than John Lewis. While King was marching in Detroit, Lewis worked with a coalition of longtime labor and civil rights activists, convened by A. Philip Randolph, to plan a massive civil rights demonstration in the nation's capital. The March on Washington for Jobs and Freedom, held on August 28, 1963, packed the Mall with 250,000 people. In a rousing speech, King delivered his famous line, "I have a dream," using soaring language to unify America in pursuit of a common goal, a society where everyone would be "judged by the content of their character, not the color of their skin."[21]

March on Washington for Jobs and Freedom About a quarter-million Americans, black and white, gathered in Washington, D.C., on August 28, 1963, to demand federal civil rights legislation. They called for antidiscrimination laws and the expansion of economic opportunities for African Americans.

The message of the March on Washington could not be boiled down to King's dream. The participants demanded well-paying, secure jobs and an end to workplace discrimination. A few weeks before the march, Randolph pulled together more than eight hundred union and civil rights leaders and gained the support of dozens of interracial unions. Tens of thousands of blue-collar workers—including meatpackers, department store stock handlers, auto assemblers, and steelworkers—packed buses rented by their unions. Thousands of unemployed men and women, their trips to Washington subsidized by unions and churches, joined them.

SNCC John Lewis prepared one of the march's most radical speeches. Only twenty-three, he was one of the founding members of the Student Non-Violent Coordinating Committee. SNCC members were impatient with the carefully choreographed, media-oriented events staged by King and the Southern Christian Leadership Conference. They were skeptical of the SCLC's top-down organizing style and its ministerial leadership. Ella Baker, who had begun her career organizing among domestic servants in Harlem during the Depression, counseled SNCC activists and reminded them that leadership was not solely a male prerogative. At their most acerbic, SNCC members derided King as "de Lawd" and called for a more democratic movement.

SNCC members settled in the most troubled parts of the Mississippi Delta and the Alabama Black Belt. They mostly worked off-camera, uninterested in staging media events. Instead, they went door to door, winning the trust of sharecroppers and domestics, establishing "freedom schools" to bring them literacy and local history and civics education, and encouraging them to vote. SNCC organizers faced everyday violence. Local authorities cracked down on them with impunity, forcing many to go underground. The Kennedy administration, though it supported voting rights in principle, turned a blind eye toward the everyday harassment of black would-be voters.

By 1963, Lewis and fellow SNCC members harbored no illusions about the president. In the speech he prepared for the March on Washington, Lewis minced no words: "American politics is dominated by politicians who build their career on immoral compromising." In his view, Kennedy's proposed civil rights legislation was too little and too late, a weak attempt to mollify protesters while thwarting more systemic change. He concluded with even stronger language, comparing the civil rights movement to General Sherman's march through Georgia during the Civil War.[22] At the last minute, Randolph and other march organizers persuaded Lewis to tone down his speech, for fear of alienating the president. "I've waited my entire life for this opportunity," Randolph told Lewis. "Please don't ruin it."[23]

Quivering with anger, Lewis delivered a somewhat tempered version of his speech, cutting a key sentence: "We will not wait for the President, the Justice Department, nor the Congress, but will take matters into our own hands and create a source of power, outside of any national structure, that could and would assure us of victory." After the march Randolph and King went to a White House meeting and gained the president's assurance that he would push hard for civil rights legislation.

Making a Nation

Passion and Politics

From

President John F. Kennedy

Commencement Address at Yale University (1962)

Kennedy used this graduation speech at Yale, one of America's most elite universities, to argue that America's economic and social problems were best solved not by passionate debate, partisanship, or public protest but by experts. He suggested that America should adopt practical, technical policies rather than being guided by partisan divisions. He expressed optimism about the positive role of government in bettering Americans' lives.

Calhoun and Taft . . . and their contemporaries spent entire careers stretching over 40 years in grappling with a few dramatic issues on which the Nation was sharply and emotionally divided, issues that occupied the attention of a generation at a time: the national bank, the disposal of the public lands, nullification or union, freedom or slavery, gold or silver. Today these old sweeping issues very largely have disappeared. The central domestic issues of our time are more subtle and less simple. They relate not to basic clashes of philosophy or ideology but to ways and means of reaching common goals—to research for sophisticated solutions to complex and obstinate issues. The world of Calhoun, the world of Taft had its own hard problems and notable challenges. But its problems are not our problems. . . .

What is at stake in our economic decisions today is not some grand warfare of rival ideologies which will sweep the country with passion but the practical management of a modern economy. What we need is not labels and clichés but more basic discussion of the sophisticated and technical questions involved in keeping a great economic machinery moving ahead. . . .

How do we eradicate the barriers which separate substantial minorities of our citizens from access to education and employment on equal terms with the rest?

How, in sum, can we make our free economy work at full capacity—that is, provide adequate profits for enterprise, adequate wages for labor, adequate utilization of plant, and opportunity for all?

These are the problems that we should be talking about—that the political parties and the various groups in our country should be discussing. They cannot be solved by incantations from the forgotten past. But the example of Western Europe shows that they are capable of solution—that governments, and many of them are conservative governments, prepared to face technical problems without ideological preconceptions, can coordinate the elements of a national economy and bring about growth and prosperity—a decade of it.

From

John Lewis
Wake Up America! (1963)

At twenty-three, John Lewis of the Student Non-Violent Coordinating Committee was the youngest speaker at the 1963 March on Washington. In this draft of his speech, he criticized the Kennedy administration and argued that African Americans had lost patience with the slow pace of change. The leaders of the march insisted that Lewis cut some of his most confrontational passages, because they feared alienating the president.

The revolution is at hand, and we must free ourselves of the chains of political and economic slavery. The nonviolent revolution is saying, "We will not wait for the courts to act, for we have been waiting hundred of years. We will not wait for the President, nor the Justice Department, nor Congress, but we will take matters into our own hands, and create a great source of power, outside of any national structure that could and would assure us victory." For those who have said, "Be patient and wait!' we must say, "Patience is a dirty and nasty word." We cannot be patient, we do not want to be free gradually, we want our freedom, and we want it now. We cannot depend on any political party, for both the Democrats and the Republicans have betrayed the basic principles of the Declaration of Independence.

We all recognize the fact that if any radical social, political and economic changes are to take place in our society, the people, the masses must bring them about. In the struggle we must seek more than mere civil rights; we must work for the community of love, peace and true brotherhood. Our minds, souls and hearts cannot rest until freedom and justice exist for *all the people*. . . .

Listen, Mr. Kennedy, listen, Mr. Congressman, listen, fellow citizens—the black masses are on the march for jobs and freedom, and we must say to the politicians that there won't be a "cooling-off period."

We won't stop now. . . . The next time we march, we won't march on Washington, but we will march through the South, through the Heart of Dixie, the way Sherman did. We will make the action of the past few months look petty. And I say to you, *Wake up America!!* . . . The black masses in the Delta of Mississippi, in Southwest Georgia, Alabama, Harlem, Chicago, Philadelphia and all over this nation are on the march.

Questions for Analysis

1. What did President Kennedy think about the relationship of history to the present?

2. Why did John Lewis state, "We cannot be patient"?

3. Compare Kennedy's and Lewis's views of how political change happens.

UNREST IN THE STREETS Over the fall of 1963, the movement followed the course that Lewis outlined, while the administration's efforts to push civil rights legislation moved forward haltingly. In Harlem the situation was so tense that a number of "near riots" broke out, usually sparked by arrests. Many northern police departments invested in military gear, preparing for what they believed was an inevitable race war. Blacks also reacted angrily in September, when four black schoolgirls died in a church bombing in Birmingham. Journalists called 1963 the year of the "Negro Revolt."

In October, John Lewis joined a protest at Rochdale Gardens, a massive apartment complex under construction in Queens, New York, where protesters formed blockades and chained themselves to cranes to protest the lack of black workers on the site. Lewis took the occasion to argue that "the Negro must revolt against not only the white power structure but also against the Negro leadership that would slow the Negro march to a slow shuffle."[24] Although Lewis remained committed to nonviolence and to integration, his words echoed those of Nation of Islam leader Malcolm X, who also joined the picket line at Rochdale Gardens that fall.

The Nation of Islam, a small African American religious sect founded in the early 1930s, had about 100,000 members at its peak. But its influence was greater than its size would seem to indicate because of Malcolm X's charisma and his unsettling and newsworthy message. Malcolm Little, raised in Detroit, had converted to the Nation while in jail for petty theft. He took the surname X, the single letter replacing the name of the family of slaveholders who had held his ancestors as chattel. Striking for his crisp dress and formidable oratorical skills, Malcolm argued that the white man was the devil, that blacks needed to take power into their own hands, and that integration was an impossible dream.

By late 1963, Malcolm X had more invitations to speak at public events than he could accept. He also wrote regularly for the black press and aired his views on national news programs; he disseminated one of his most important speeches, his November 1963 "Message to the Grassroots," through the new record label, Motown, produced by Detroit impresario Berry Gordy. The recording popularized Malcolm X's celebration of African and Asian revolutionaries. He lambasted the members of the civil rights establishment as "House Negroes" and "Uncle Toms" who "keep us passive and peaceful and non-violent."[25] He was particularly skeptical of King's version of civil rights. "There's no such thing as a nonviolent revolution. The only kind of revolution that is nonviolent is the Negro revolution. The only revolution in which the goal is loving your enemy is the Negro revolution. It's the only revolution in which the goal is a desegregated lunch counter, a desegregated theater, a desegregated park, and a desegregated public toilet; you can sit down next to white folks—on the toilet. That's no revolution."[26] Malcolm X did not reflect the majority opinion among African Americans, but he gave voice to the passion, anger, militancy, and race pride that many civil rights activists, even advocates of nonviolence like John Lewis, felt from Nashville to Birmingham to Queens.

President Johnson

Whether President Kennedy would have succeeded in calming the growing racial unrest and passing civil rights legislation are open questions, but there weren't many good reasons to be optimistic in late 1963. Kennedy was heading into what many expected would be a bruising reelection campaign, and he needed the support of southern Democrats. Many party leaders, including Lyndon Johnson, doubted that Kennedy had the skill to push any antidiscrimination law through Congress. Civil rights leaders feared that yet another empty, symbolic gesture would be coming from the White House.

KENNEDY'S ASSASSINATION Those questions would remain forever unanswered. On November 22, 1963, the president who had hoped that technocracy would trump passion was undone in one of the darkest moments of passion in American history when he was felled by an assassin's bullet. Riding in an open-top convertible through the streets of Dallas, Texas, Kennedy was targeted by a mentally ill drifter, twenty-four-year-old Lee Harvey Oswald.

The assassin's troubled past, including stints in the Soviet Union and Cuba, fueled all sorts of conspiracy theories, as did the fact that Oswald was shot dead on November 24, before he could be interrogated. While there is no evidence that anyone other than Oswald was involved in the assassination, some pointed their fingers at the Cubans, others at the Soviets, and still others at a shadowy criminal underworld of Mafia bosses angry because the president's brother, Robert, the attorney general, was investigating them. Some harbored the far-fetched belief that a cabal of Texans who wanted to plant Lyndon Johnson in the White House was responsible.

However plausible or ridiculous the assassination theories were, none would ever be proven or disproven. Each was a symptom of the trauma surrounding the death of a young, telegenic leader, in office less than three years. Kennedy's death took on near-mythic status in post-1963 America, in part because Americans projected their hopes and fears for the country onto the body of the slain president. What if? What if Kennedy had not died that November day?

JOHNSON'S RISE Lyndon Baines Johnson took the oath of office aboard *Air Force One* with Kennedy's widow, still wearing her bloodstained dress, at his side. He immediately promised to use his legislative skills to push through Kennedy's tax-reduction bill and free the civil rights bill from the quicksand of southern-dominated congressional committees and the steel trap of the filibuster. He also pledged much more: to expand voting rights to disenfranchised African Americans, to provide affordable higher education for "every boy and girl in this country, no matter how poor, or the color of their skin, or the region they come from," and to pass a national health insurance bill that Democrats since Roosevelt had advocated.[27]

Few liberals expected that President Johnson would be such a forceful advocate for the poor and disenfranchised. He had grown up in the Texas Hill Country, a poor area, home to mostly white hardscrabble farmers. For most of his childhood, rural Texas—like large parts of the South and Southwest—had been an economic backwater. The state's cotton production was declining. Most homes lacked electricity. Public schools, including the one near the border where Johnson had started his career as a teacher of mostly Mexican American students, were run-down and barely provided an education, particularly during planting and harvest season, when classrooms emptied.

The fortunes of Texas took a turn for the better during the New Deal, as powerful Democrats, including Johnson, channeled federal dollars to the Hill Country. When Johnson entered Congress in 1937, he badgered New Deal officials to extend power lines into the area. Rural electrification, along with federal funds for roads, hospitals, post offices, and schools, taught Johnson a lesson that he carried with him for the rest of his career: government could transform the lives of "forgotten" Americans, like his constituents and neighbors.

Johnson won election to the U.S. Senate in 1948, after a bruising and corrupt primary. A ruthless campaigner, he portrayed his opponent as soft on Communism and civil rights. In San Antonio and along the Rio Grande, Johnson's supporters stuffed the ballot box to give him an edge—only eighty-seven votes statewide.[28] But once he was in office, Johnson's popularity soared as he masterfully channeled federal aid to his home state. Joining his fellow senators Strom Thurmond of South Carolina, William Fulbright of Arkansas, and Richard Russell of Georgia, he ensured that the Sunbelt became a major recipient of defense spending, highway construction funds, and tax breaks to buttress its growing oil industry. Without massive public works, Texas and most of the South would have remained underdeveloped economically.

Early in his career, Johnson also positioned himself against even modest civil rights reforms. He voted against antilynching legislation and denounced legislation to create a permanent federal Fair Employment Practices Committee as the first step toward the creation of a "police state." But as he moved into the Senate leadership and set his sights on higher office, he began to shift his position on racial issues. If he wanted a chance at the White House, he needed to put some distance between himself and white supremacy. Unlike many southerners, Johnson supported the 1957 Civil Rights Act, even if he had made sure that the final law was weak.

THE CIVIL RIGHTS ACT OF 1964 Under Kennedy, LBJ had strengthened his civil rights portfolio, but most liberals did not expect much from him. They were proven wrong. Johnson's crowning achievement was the enactment of sweeping civil rights reforms. During his first six months in office, he forged a bipartisan coalition of northern and western Democrats and key Republicans to bypass his own party's southern wing. He used the blunt tools of deal making that he had learned in his time as the Senate majority leader. He threatened those who were lukewarm on the bill and cut deals with powerful Republicans, including Minority Leader Everett Dirksen, who brought along enough GOP votes to break the Democratic filibuster. The Civil Rights Act of 1964, enacted on July 2, forbade discrimination in commercial establishments and in both public and private schools. The act's lengthiest and most controversial section was Title VII, which forbade employers from hiring, promoting, and firing workers on the basis of "race, color, religion, sex, or national origin." It also created the Equal Employment Opportunity Commission (EEOC) to investigate claims of workplace discrimination.[29]

The Civil Rights Act was full of qualifications and hedges, the result of compromises to win the support of enough pro-business Republicans to overcome a filibuster, which under Senate rules at the time required sixty-seven votes. As a result, it left housing segregation untouched. The EEOC had the power to engage in "conciliation" with employers but could not bring lawsuits or file criminal charges against those who discriminated. If it detected a "pattern and practice" of workplace discrimination, it could refer cases to the Department of Justice for litigation.

Civil rights groups pushed aggressively for the act's enforcement. The NAACP and local attorneys began taking employers to court to force them to open jobs to black workers. Grassroots activists around the country used it to challenge trade unions that excluded blacks. Although the drafters of the Civil Rights Act had not spent much time discussing the prohibition against sex discrimination, women's groups began pushing for its enforcement. In 1966 the new National Organization for Women (NOW), whose founders included Betty Friedan, argued against the notion that a man should "carry the sole burden of supporting himself, his wife and family." It demanded "equal pay for equal work" and the rigorous enforcement of Title VII.[30]

Over the next few years, the Johnson administration expanded the reach of Title VII. In 1965, Johnson issued Executive Order 11246, which gave the newly created Office of Contract Compliance the power to terminate government contracts to firms that did not practice "affirmative action" in employment. What "affirmative action" meant would be defined in 1966 and 1967 in a series of policy experiments in four metropolitan areas that had been rocked by protests over workplace discrimination. In St. Louis, where civil rights protesters chained themselves to the Gateway Arch, then under construction, federal officials fashioned a "St. Louis Plan" that demanded that contractors provide evidence of their efforts to hire minorities. Similar plans were put in place in San Francisco, Cleveland, and Philadelphia after massive protests at construction sites there.

NORTHERN WHITE RESISTANCE Johnson had signed the Civil Rights Act just four months before that year's presidential election. He worried mightily about his prospects, with good reason. "We have lost the South for a generation," he told his aide Bill Moyers.[31] White voters in his home region called him a turncoat. There were also ominous signs for Johnson outside the states of the Old Confederacy. During the 1964 Democratic primaries, Alabama governor George Wallace, making his first run for the Democratic presidential nomination, swept predominantly white, blue-collar precincts in Gary, Milwaukee, and Baltimore, surprising many observers. He picked up 30 percent of the Democratic vote in Indiana, 34 percent in Wisconsin, and 45 percent in Maryland.

Whites all over the country were uneasy about civil rights. The crowd at Boston's 1964 St. Patrick's Day parade pelted NAACP officials with stones. Later that year, in a statewide referendum, California voters rolled back a civil rights law that forbade discrimination in the sale of housing by a two-to-one ratio. White parents in Brooklyn and Queens boycotted schools targeted for integration.

The negative reaction to civil rights built on a long history. Since the 1920s the movement of even a single black family into a white neighborhood in most northern cities had generated mob violence. In the twenty years following World War II, whites in Detroit had attacked hundreds of black homeowners. Hundreds of thousands of whites fled to the segregated suburbs rather than accept black neighbors. In Chicago in the 1940s and 1950s, huge white mobs protested integrated housing and regularly attacked black youths using city parks, beaches, and pools.

Northern politicians had long catered to the racial fears of their white constituents. Throughout the 1950s and early 1960s, elected officials in Illinois, Michigan, California, Connecticut, and New York had led a campaign against "welfare chiselers," just as the ranks of blacks receiving public assistance was rising. Big-city mayors like Chicago's Martin Kennelly and Richard J. Daley and Detroit's Albert Cobo defended segregation in public housing projects. And even the mildest efforts to desegregate public education met with fierce resistance by politicians and parents who supported "neighborhood schools," even though in the sprawling postwar metropolis, fewer and fewer white students lived within walking distance of schools, and by 1960 a majority already rode buses each day.

Opposition to civil rights ran deeper than local battles over turf and schools. Right-wing activists criticized civil rights and racial integration, arguing that antidiscrimination laws interfered with management's right to hire and fire at will. They denounced laws forbidding discrimination in housing as "socialistic" or "communistic" incursions on individual freedoms to sell or rent to anyone they pleased. In 1962 the National Association of Realtors released the "Home Owners' Bill of Rights," proclaiming that "the individual property owner, regardless of race, color, or creed, must be allowed under law to retain the right to determine acceptability of any prospective buyer or tenant of his property."[32] Civil rights legislation, they believed, interfered with the free market and violated the constitutional right to freedom of association.

The New Right

The reaction to civil rights was the most prominent part of a right-wing insurgency against liberalism that had been gaining strength since the 1950s. On a beautiful fall weekend in September 1960, a group of well-dressed young white people, mostly men, gathered for a photograph on the manicured lawn of Great Elm, the Sharon, Connecticut, family estate of William F. Buckley, Jr., the editor of a New Right periodical, the *National Review*. Although they had come of age when America was at its peak of global economic and political power, they were anything but self-congratulatory. For them, postwar America was facing grave "moral and political crises." Both Democrats and Republicans, they argued, were complacent about the international Communist threat. The United States was afflicted by spiritual decadence, aided and abetted by leaders of both parties who expanded the power of government and thus restricted individual freedom.

To address that crisis—and to harness the energy of their generation—the Sharon conferees issued a brief manifesto. "The Sharon Statement" listed a series of "eternal truths," with "the individual's use of his God-given free will" the foremost. Freedom depended above all on a market untrammeled by regulations. The statement warned that "when government interferes with the work of the market economy, it tends to reduce the moral and physical strength of the nation; that when it takes from one man to bestow on another, it diminishes the incentive of the first, the integrity of the second, and the moral autonomy of both."[33] The statement fused religious individualism and economic libertarianism, echoing Lemuel Boulware and Reverend James Fifield, the postwar popularizers of the gospel of free enterprise.

The activists whom Buckley gathered at Sharon formed an organization called Young Americans for Freedom (YAF), which grew steadily in the early 1960s, establishing beachheads on campuses from Notre Dame to Arizona State, from Yale to UCLA. YAF's members mobilized against Kennedy and, even more so, against Johnson's expansive domestic agenda. By the end of Johnson's presidency, YAF had at least seventy thousand members nationwide.

BARRY GOLDWATER The New Right insurgency found an intellectual and political leader in Barry Goldwater, an Arizona businessman turned Republican U.S. senator. A self-proclaimed frontiersman, he flew his own plane and belonged to an elite men's club whose members sometimes dressed in Native American garb. Goldwater romanticized frontier individualism, even though the development of the Sunbelt had been made possible by massive federal expenditures, especially for dams, electrification, airports, and highways. Most important, powerful Arizonans worked to attract several major military bases and dozens of defense contractors. In 1950, as federal dollars began to flow in, Phoenix was a dusty town of only fifty thousand on the edge of a vast, mostly empty desert; by the end of the century, it would be one of the nation's ten largest cities. Goldwater envisioned remaking America in the image of Phoenix, a place that put up few obstacles to business and protected a free market with a powerful military.

Goldwater's profile rose in the 1950s, as he traveled nationwide to address business groups about free enterprise and small government. In 1960, just months before the Sharon gathering, he turned a set of his speeches into what would become one of the most widely read political tracts of the twentieth century, *The Conscience of a Conservative*. Published by a right-wing vanity press, the book became a surprise best seller. By 1964, it had sold more than three million copies.

Goldwater offered a bracing view of post–World War II America. "Conservatives," he wrote, "are deeply persuaded that our society is ailing."[34] To him and his followers the United States was morally and spiritually bankrupt, its citizens seduced by the welfare state. Communism prevailed abroad because of America's effeminacy. Americans had lost the self-sufficiency and entrepreneurial energy that had made their country great. Politics and society needed wholesale renovation.

Goldwater was a radical individualist: "Every man for his individual good and for the good of his society is responsible for his *own* development."[35] He railed against the signature welfare programs of the New Deal, including Social Security, which he saw as soul-destroying. Welfare, he argued, "transforms the individual from a dignified, industrious, self-reliant spiritual being into a dependent animal creature without his knowing it."[36] The greatest hindrance to the fulfillment of human potential was nothing other than government itself: "Throughout history, government has proved to be the chief instrument for thwarting man's liberty."[37] Goldwater's moral critique of America and his staunch defense of free enterprise found him readers among evangelicals and Catholics, *National Review* subscribers, and members of the YAF and the Chamber of Commerce.

Goldwater and his supporters on the New Right were particularly upset by civil rights laws. The federal government, they argued, had unconstitutionally usurped the power of the states in service of experiments in "social engineering." Since the Supreme Court had decided *Brown v. Board of Education* in 1954, southern elected officials had couched their opposition to integration in terms of states' rights, a position that Buckley and the *National Review* endorsed. In 1958, Buckley's journal solicited subscriptions from the 68,000 members of the segregationist White Citizens' Councils—founded to resist the Montgomery Bus Boycott—on the grounds that "our position on states' rights is the same as your own."[38]

Goldwater himself professed support for the goal of racial integration: he claimed to believe in a color-blind America. But he vehemently opposed the *Brown* decision. Falling back on a narrow reading of the Constitution, he argued that education was a state and local prerogative and that any federal mandate that schools be desegregated was unconstitutional. As for the Civil Rights Act, he charged that it would hasten "the loss of our God-given liberties" and constituted "a special appeal for a special welfare."[39]

As civil rights leaders stepped up their demands, conservative writers reacted angrily. In 1963, the *National Review*'s Frank Meyer argued that the movement against segregation "was destroying the foundations of a free, Constitutional society."[40] Buckley called for the use of police repression to put down what he considered the lawless protests being led by Martin Luther King, Jr. The riots during the summer of 1964 only confirmed conservatives' belief that the civil rights movement had fostered a culture of lawlessness.

THE WARREN COURT AND ITS CRITICS Compounding the conservatives' sense of crisis was a string of Warren Court decisions on criminal rights. In *Gideon v. Wainwright* (1963), the court ruled that those charged with a crime had the right to legal counsel. Clarence Gideon, a Florida prisoner jailed for theft, had sent a handwritten petition to the court, arguing that he had been unfairly convicted because he could not afford a lawyer. After the ruling, the state retried Gideon and he won acquittal. Florida and many states instituted public defender programs to provide legal representation for the poor. In a follow-up case, *Escobedo v. Illinois* (1964), the court ruled that those charged with a crime had the right to counsel during police interrogations. The case foreshadowed the more famous 1966 *Miranda v. Arizona* decision, that those charged of a crime had to be read their rights, including the right to remain silent.

Critics of the court found more grist for their discontent in two cases involving prayer in schools. In *Engel v. Vitale* (1962) the court ruled that mandatory school prayer—still commonplace around the country—was unconstitutional. The case involved a complaint against the New Hyde Park, New York, public schools, where officials had replaced an explicitly Christian prayer with one that read simply "Almighty God, we acknowledge our dependence upon Thee, and we beg Thy blessings upon us, our parents, our teachers and our country. Amen."[41] A group of Jewish students objected to the words "Almighty God" and won their case on the grounds that such prayers violated the constitutional ban on the establishment of religion. A year later, in another controversial ruling, *Abington School District v. Schempp*, the court ruled on behalf of a group of Pennsylvania school students who challenged required Bible classes.

Conservatives denounced the court's civil rights, criminal justice, and religious freedom rulings. "They have put the Negroes in the schools," charged Alabama representative George W. Andrews. "And now they have taken God out."[42] Religious activists demanded a constitutional amendment to allow school prayer, which public opinion surveys showed that 77 percent of the American population supported. Barry Goldwater lamented that "our law enforcement officers have been demoralized and rendered ineffective in their jobs."[43] The John Birch Society, an organization that believed that the federal government and the courts were agents of Communist subversion and immorality, placed "Impeach Earl Warren" billboards on roadsides throughout the country.

FROM THE FRINGE TO THE MAINSTREAM The GOP, nominally the party of Lincoln, of Emancipation and Reconstruction, was long reviled in the South. But in 1964, Goldwater discovered the GOP's Promised Land: the Old Confederacy. Since 1960 the Republican National Committee had sent organizers to the South in what it called "Operation Dixie" (an ironic appropriation of the name of labor's postwar efforts to build unions in the South) appealing to southern whites disaffected by the civil rights movement. The defection of prominent Democrats, like South Carolina senator Strom Thurmond in 1964, only strengthened their position. Goldwater's support for states' rights and the freedom of association echoed southern white racists' growing use of color-blind rhetoric to prop up racial segregation and racial privilege.

Goldwater and his supporters also sharply criticized Cold War foreign policy. Containment, they insisted, was capitulation to Communism. The Soviet Union and its allies must be defeated, not simply cordoned off. Kennedy's policy toward Cuba and Germany evidenced America's weakness. Brent Bozell, editor of the *National Review*,

Barry Goldwater The insurgent Republican candidate for the presidency in 1964, Goldwater proudly highlighted his right-wing credentials, proclaiming that "extremism in defense of liberty is no vice."

argued that Kennedy should have torn down the Berlin Wall and invaded Cuba. Overseas economic development programs were both ineffective and unconstitutional. The founders, argued Goldwater, had not envisioned providing economic aid to other countries. The United States was exporting New Deal "socialism" rather than fighting for an all-out victory against the red menace. "American strategy must be primarily offensive," asserted Goldwater. "If we are to achieve victory," he continued, "we must achieve superiority in all of the weapons, military as well as political and economic."[44]

Goldwater summed up his arguments in his remarkable speech accepting the Republican nomination for the presidency at San Francisco in July 1964: "Extremism in the defense of liberty is no vice, moderation is no virtue."[45] The ideological purity of Goldwater's address fired up his supporters, but it left much of the GOP establishment cold. Henry Cabot Lodge, who had been Nixon's vice-presidential nominee in 1960, felt wholly out of place among Goldwater's supporters. "What in God's name has happened to the Republican Party!" he fumed while looking through a roster of delegates. "I hardly know any of these people!"[46] When Goldwater delegates pushed through a resolution denouncing the Civil Rights Act of 1964, it proved too much for moderate Republicans. Many walked out of the convention in protest.

The Republican Party's implosion boosted Johnson's campaign. Republican voters in northeastern and midwestern swing states—those attracted to Eisenhower's temperate Republicanism—were likely to stay home or even to vote for Johnson. Goldwater's denunciation of Social Security to an audience of Florida retirees gave Johnson another line of attack. Johnson also warned that the self-proclaimed extremist would likely plunge the country into nuclear war, a theme that animated his speeches and made its way into ads, including the justifiably famous "Daisy" commercial (aired only once) that showed a little girl pulling petals from a flower before a nuclear bomb exploded overhead. Even Goldwater's campaign slogan became the butt of jokes. "In your heart you know he's right" became "in your guts you know he's nuts."[47]

Johnson won the 1964 election in one of the greatest landslides in American history, with 61 percent of the vote. Goldwater won his home state and broke the Democratic Party's stronghold in the South, picking up majorities in Alabama, Georgia, Louisiana, Mississippi, and South Carolina. But the Democrats picked up their largest majorities in the House and Senate since 1936. Johnson would have a 155-seat margin in the House and 35 seats in the Senate.

The election results confirmed the views of those mainstream pundits who had denounced Goldwater and his supporters as far-right zealots. Social scientists, among them the influential Daniel Bell and Seymour Martin Lipset, saw Goldwaterites as the embodiment of a pathological "authoritarian personality," wholly out of touch with the liberalism that they believed defined the American political tradition. "When in our history has anyone with ideas so bizarre, so archaic, so self-confounding, so remote from the basic American consensus ever gotten so far?" asked eminent historian Richard Hofstadter after the election.[48]

But the political troops that Goldwater had mobilized, north, south, and west, remained optimistic after their crushing defeat. In the South, the Goldwater campaign had mobilized many whites to vote Republican for the first time ever. Goldwater volunteers, many of them women, held coffee klatches, fought to control school boards, and campaigned against rock 'n' roll music. Methodically, they built a conservative movement at the grassroots. On campuses, the YAF recruited ambitious conservative student leaders, many of whom would move into Republican leadership in the 1970s and 1980s, among them future vice president Dan Quayle. In the decades that followed, what seemed to most Republicans and Democrats to be the crackpot ideas of a few zealots would move into the mainstream.

The Great Society

Johnson had every reason to celebrate his overwhelming victory. Just after the election, while lighting the White House Christmas tree, he crowed that "these are the most hopeful times since Christ was born in Bethlehem."[49] The election returns gave him a mandate for the ambitious legislative agenda he had been preparing since his first State of the Union address, in January 1964, when he announced: "The administration today, here and now, declares unconditional war on poverty in America."[50] Johnson's Great Society initiative was far-reaching. The president assembled outside experts and administration insiders to draft civil rights legislation, provide unprecedented federal support for public education, reform immigration law, and protect the environment.

THE "DISCOVERY" OF POVERTY Even amid the postwar prosperity, tens of millions of Americans found themselves left behind. In the early 1960s, journalists, intellectuals, and academics had "discovered" poverty in America. In 1962, Michael Harrington, a young socialist intellectual who had begun his career in the Catholic Worker movement helping the homeless on New York's Lower East Side, published a best-selling account, *The Other America*, that documented poverty and called for action.

Poverty affected every section of America: in 1960 nearly a quarter of the nation's population was poor. By the middle of the twentieth century, small farmers, once perceived as the backbone of the country, were an endangered species. The rise of government-subsidized agribusiness displaced independent farmers in the nation's most fertile regions. Many small towns in the Plains hollowed out, as farmers migrated to cities. Poverty was commonplace in rural America, particularly in the southern Black Belt, in Johnson's rural Texas, on the Great Plains, and in the rich farmlands of California, where migrant farmworkers struggled to get by. Just as hard hit were the nation's old mining towns. The anthracite coal region, extending from Pennsylvania south through the Virginias and west through Kentucky and Illinois, was ravaged by job losses as the mines closed. The spotlight of John F. Kennedy's fall 1960 campaign through West Virginia had made Appalachia's tumbledown shacks and shoeless residents the icons of poverty.

Between 1947 and 1963, Detroit—the epitome of American industrial power—lost almost 140,000 manufacturing jobs, as companies moved plants south and west to lower costs and replaced workers with labor-saving machinery.[51] The once-bustling ports of Brooklyn and Oakland grew quieter, as stevedores lost out to container shipping and cross-country trucking. The aging northeastern rail lines—owned by century-old companies like the Pennsylvania Railroad, which teetered on the brink of insolvency—passed the crumbling ruins of textile mills in Philadelphia, Baltimore, and Trenton. The patterns of poverty also reflected the enduring color line: in 1960 close to half of all African Americans were poor.

POVERTY WARRIORS In the early 1960s, major philanthropies, led by the Ford Foundation, began to channel funds to community programs that targeted the poor. Both Kennedy and Johnson recruited sociologists and economists who studied poverty and used their ideas to develop a major federal antipoverty initiative. In 1964, Johnson appointed Sargent Shriver, President Kennedy's brother-in-law, to direct his War on Poverty. "The sky's the limit," Johnson told Shriver. "You just make the thing work period. I don't give a damn about the details."[52]

But a full-fledged war would require massive expenditures, and Johnson was unwilling to provide the funds. In 1964 he had successfully shepherded Kennedy's tax reform legislation through Congress, but it came at the price of trimming costs elsewhere in his budget. So Shriver gravitated toward relatively inexpensive programs. One was the Job Corps, modeled after the New Deal's Works Progress Administration and Civilian Conservation Corps, but with only a fraction of the funding. Job Corps programs attracted only a small percentage of the unemployed and underemployed and plopped them down into isolated camps with poorly trained supervisors and inadequate facilities.

The most controversial of the War on Poverty programs, Community Action, targeted impoverished urban neighborhoods, rural counties, and Indian reservations. Community Action Agencies (CAAs) were intended to give poor people a stake in the system by allowing them to oversee neighborhood organizations, preschools, health centers, and welfare offices. CAAs rested on the assumption that the "maximum feasible participation" of the poor would ultimately reduce poverty. Many CAAs, which operated with little government oversight, implemented controversial arts and theater programs; some engaged in political protests; and others created social service jobs for poor people. But CAAs did not receive enough funds or create enough jobs to make a

War on Poverty President Lyndon Johnson visits impoverished families in Appalachia to promote his proposed anti-poverty agenda, May 7, 1964.

dent in local poverty rates. And some of the programs, like Newark, New Jersey's, run by black power advocate and poet Amiri Baraka, became flashpoints of controversy.

The War on Poverty unleashed a political movement among the poor of a scale unseen since the Great Depression. In 1965 an interracial coalition of poor women challenged state laws that cut off families from receiving welfare. They worked with the support of attorneys who were funded under another Great Society program, Legal Aid, that provided legal assistance to the poor. In the South, local welfare administrators, eager to maintain the supply of inexpensive domestic workers, often denied black women benefits, even as they continued to support poor white women. Around the country, the National Welfare Rights Organization (NWRO), formed in 1965 and staffed predominantly by women, challenged intrusive home inspections to determine welfare eligibility. NWRO members demanded an increase in monthly payments so that they could afford better housing. Those efforts paid off. The Johnson administration streamlined welfare rules and increased stipends. The rolls of welfare recipients rose significantly in the mid- and late 1960s.

PUBLIC EDUCATION As a former teacher, Johnson put a special priority on public education to pull people from poverty. The newly created Office of Economic Opportunity (OEO) channeled hundreds of millions of dollars to community organizations to implement the Head Start program, to provide preschool education to disadvantaged children. Johnson also dramatically expanded federal funding for public education, which had long been left to the states and localities. The 1965 Elementary and Secondary Education Act (ESEA)—which Johnson signed "in the one room school house near Stonewall, Texas," with his first teacher, "Miss Kate," sitting at his side—provided a billion dollars to fund schools that served poor children. [53] By 1968, 94 percent of American school districts had received ESEA funds to build new schools, improve curricula, and hire teachers.

In addition, Johnson signed into law programs that offered federally guaranteed student loans and direct grants to needy students, making college affordable to many for the first time. Great Society programs funded university libraries, created national arts and humanities programs, trained nurses, and supported research in mental health, heart disease, stroke, and disease prevention. College campuses, flush with federal support, expanded rapidly in the late 1960s.

HEALTH CARE Also in 1965, Johnson succeeded where his predecessors had failed by creating federally subsidized health insurance programs for the elderly (Medicare) and the impoverished (Medicaid). President Franklin Roosevelt had used federal funds to build hospitals but had met with obstacles to providing universal government-funded health care. Harry S. Truman's efforts to create a national health insurance program had fallen to cries of socialism. Still, as a senator, Johnson worked mostly behind the scenes to increase federal spending on hospitals and medical research. But many liberals never gave up the hope of creating a broad national health system, and they pushed hard during the Kennedy and Johnson years.

Johnson was enough of a realist to make a case for something narrower than a national health plan. In 1964 he argued, "Every American will benefit by the extension of Social Security to cover the hospital costs of their aged parents."[54] Hospitalization costs had tripled since Johnson's first term in the Senate—from an average of $15 per day in 1950 to $45 a day in 1965. And as the United States grew wealthier, life expectancy had grown, leaving retirees to rely on a rickety system of charity or public hospitals or to raid their savings. Over half of elderly Americans had no health insurance at all in 1965. "We've just got to say that by God you can't treat grandma this way," Johnson put it in his inimitably folksy way.[55]

Johnson had higher ambitions than helping Grandma. He viewed federal health insurance as one of the greatest unfulfilled promises of the New Deal. If he passed it, he could outshine his Democratic predecessors. Drafted with Senator Wilbur Mills (D-OH), a master of taxation and budgeting, the final health care bill exceeded Johnson's expectations. In a "three layer cake," the program provided the elderly with hospital coverage, voluntary doctors' visits (which required an additional premium, with government subsidies if necessary), and insurance for the poor. Johnson signed the bill in Harry S. Truman's hometown, Independence, Missouri, on July 30, 1965.

Implementing Medicare and Medicaid proved to be a challenge. Many medical professionals, still concerned about "socialized medicine," threatened to boycott the program. Costs rose rapidly, outpacing inflation. But at least in terms of access, the programs met with immediate success. In 1965 one in five poor Americans had never been to the doctor; five years later, that figure had fallen to under 10 percent. Medicare proved especially popular among the elderly: all were covered by hospital insurance, and 93 percent chose the voluntary insurance for regular doctors' visits.[56] Within a few years of its enactment, Medicare became politically untouchable.

Expanding the Boundaries of Citizenship: Voting Rights and Immigration

Johnson's vision of a "great society" included more than alleviating poverty and providing economic opportunity. Since the end of Reconstruction, African Americans had lacked one of the fundamental rights of citizenship: the right to participate in the electoral process. And over the course of the late nineteenth and twentieth centuries, the United States had shut the nation's borders to people who were presumed to be inferior because of where they were born. One step to creating a more equal America was creating a more inclusive society.

"MASSIVE CONFRONTATION" IN MISSISSIPPI One of Johnson's most important tasks was to take care of some of the unfinished business of civil rights. During his first year in office, SNCC members stepped up their efforts for voting rights, recruiting hundreds of college students to run citizenship training programs, alternative "Freedom Schools," and voter registration campaigns in the South. In the Freedom Summer of 1964, thousands of black and white activists targeted the Mississippi Delta, one of the country's most isolated and impoverished regions. There Jim Crow took its most brutal form. A majority of Delta residents were black, but hardly any could exercise their basic citizenship rights: voting and serving on juries. Local landowners and public officials relied on violence to keep the population passive.

John Lewis, who had been elected SNCC chair, saw Mississippi as the last stand for voting rights. "Before the Negro people get the right to vote, there will have to be a massive confrontation," proclaimed Lewis, "and it will probably come this summer."[57] SNCC rejected the carefully staged, made-for-TV demonstrations that Martin Luther King and the SCLC had used to define the civil rights movement in the South. Their door-to-door, face-to-face efforts to build support for voting rights in the Delta lacked the drama that brought television cameras to places like Montgomery and Birmingham.

Key to SNCC's Mississippi campaign were activists like Robert Parris Moses, who adopted a self-effacing style, preferring to sit at the kitchen table in a shotgun shack instead of in a network news studio. Moses, educated at elite Hamilton College and Harvard, taught math and was one of the first black faculty members at the prestigious Horace Mann School in New York. In 1959, Moses had joined with Bayard Rustin in a demonstration for school integration, and in 1960, he headed to Atlanta to meet with Martin Luther King, Jr. There he found his calling: as a SNCC organizer in the Deep

South. By 1961, he had planted himself in the Delta, where he coordinated SNCC's efforts and worked to build a statewide network of civil rights groups.

Working for years behind the scenes, SNCC members were well known and despised by whites in the Delta, especially when they began to bring would-be voters to local courthouses to register. Just as unsettling was the flood of northern-born student activists, many of them white, who arrived during the summer of 1964 to staff Freedom Schools and voting campaigns. These Freedom Summer volunteers—living with black activists, socializing with them in the open, and sometimes breaking the taboo of interracial dating—outraged white locals. Increasingly, SNCC activists and Mississippi voters faced violent reprisals. On June 21, 1964, three Freedom Summer participants—James Chaney, Andrew Goodman, and Michael Schwerner—were kidnapped and murdered by white supremacists just outside Philadelphia, Mississippi.

SNCC activists grew increasingly restive in the face of brutal reprisals and glacial change. Many resented Washington liberals for supporting the goal of voting rights in principle but not providing material support for those on the ground. Although President Johnson had signed the Civil Rights Act, they still distrusted him profoundly. That distrust solidified during the 1964 Democratic National Convention, where the party refused to seat the Mississippi Freedom Democratic Party, an interracial delegation led by Fannie Lou Hamer. A sharecropper who stood up to the president and vice president, both of whom did not want to alienate Mississippi's all-white official delegation, Hamer made the evening news with her proclamation that "if the Freedom Democratic Party is not seated now, I question America."[58] For John Lewis, the convention debacle proved Johnson's treachery, "politics at its worst." Even as Johnson swept to office in November, Lewis viewed the convention as a "turning point," the beginning of a "loss of faith" in Johnson and in government.[59]

SELMA AND THE VOTING RIGHTS ACT Voting rights activists stepped up the pressure. In March 1965 dozens of prominent civil rights, religious, and labor leaders joined members of SNCC in a well-publicized voting rights march from Montgomery to Selma, Alabama. One activist, Detroit-born Viola Liuzzo, who came south to support the enfranchisement campaign, was shot and killed by Klansmen. On March 7, John Lewis, who organized the march, took his most brutal beating, as protesters attempted to cross the Edmund Pettus Bridge into Selma. The police attacked several hundred marchers, injuring nearly seventy, many severely. Lewis suffered a fractured skull. Two days later the marchers again confronted the police, before turning back from the Pettus Bridge.

On March 15, Lyndon Johnson addressed the nation, calling on Congress to pass comprehensive voting rights legislation. As he had with the previous year's Civil Rights Act, he worked to forge a bipartisan coalition to thwart a southern filibuster. The day after Johnson's speech, under federal military protection, the marchers headed on to Montgomery. The tide had turned in favor of voting rights, though it took Johnson's legislative skill to bring it to a vote. The act, which Johnson signed on August 6, 1965, prohibited the use of such devices as literacy tests and poll taxes to disenfranchise voters. Under Section 5 of the act, the federal government had to approve "any voting qualification or prerequisite to voting, or standard, practice, or procedure with respect to voting" in districts with a history of past discrimination.[60]

Civil rights activists began to push for the implementation of the new law and to gain political office themselves in the South. Fannie Lou Hamer ran an unsuccessful campaign for Congress but finally won a seat at the Democratic National Convention in 1968. The year after the Voting Rights Act passed, John Lewis left SNCC to coordinate a large-scale voter registration campaign in the South. With the federal government forcing southern districts to enfranchise blacks, with the Department of Justice challenging illegal electoral practices, and with thousands of volunteers assisting new voters, the Voting Rights Act transformed the color of American politics in a very short period of time. In 1965 fewer than 200 blacks held elective office; by 1970 the figure had more than tripled to 764. By 1980 almost two thousand African Americans held elective office nationwide. One of the beneficiaries of the act was John Lewis himself, who won election to Atlanta's city council in 1981 and to Congress in 1986, as the U.S. representative from Georgia's fifth district.

IMMIGRATION REFORM Johnson and his congressional allies were also committed to another major shift from exclusion to inclusion. In October 1965, Congress passed the Hart-Cellar Act, the most sweeping immigration reform in decades. Since 1924, America had had a restrictive quota system in place that favored immigrants from northern and western Europe. In the intervening years, the nation modified its immigration laws somewhat. During World War II, the United States lifted the ban on Asian immigration but admitted only a token 100 immigrants per country each year. The 1952 Immigration and Nationalities Act lifted racial restrictions dating back to the nineteenth century but kept discriminatory national quotas in place, and it restricted suspected "subversives" and the "immoral," including homosexuals, from entering the United States. In 1964, Congress eliminated the bracero program, largely responding to critics of the harsh treatment of migrant farmworkers.

The Hart-Cellar Act lifted nation-specific quotas on immigration, made provisions for family reunification, set aside places for skilled workers, and gave special status to refugees fleeing Communist rule. The law changed the complexion of immigration to the United States. By the 1990s, 29 percent of immigrants would be Asian, a striking turnaround from the days of Chinese and Japanese exclusion. About 6 percent of immigrants came from Africa, the first significant influx from that continent since slavery. Only 14 percent of immigrants originated in Europe.

Hart-Cellar, however, had unintended consequences for immigration from Latin America. It instituted the first numerical restriction on immigrants from the western hemisphere: a cap of 120,000 per year, not including spouses, parents, and children of U.S. citizens. Because that cap coincided with the end of the bracero program, it significantly reduced the ability of Mexicans legally to migrate to the United States. After 1965 the demand for Mexican labor in the United States did not abate, nor did

Mexican workers' interest in crossing the border to work. But under the new caps, many Mexican workers would have to cross the border without documentation.

Jobs and Freedom

For all the ambitions of Johnson's Great Society programs, they did not adequately address one of the root causes of inequality and poverty: the unequal economy. Despite an economic boom (unemployment fell below 4 percent between 1966 and 1969), millions of Americans remained trapped in poor-paying, insecure jobs. Labor and civil rights groups had long argued that remunerative work was a precondition for freedom. A just society required decent pay and humane working conditions.

HARVEST OF SHAME Farmworkers were near the bottom economically, trapped in insecure, dangerous jobs. The day after Thanksgiving in 1960, CBS had aired the documentary, *Harvest of Shame*, interviewing migrant workers and showing graphic images of their miserable housing, backbreaking labor, and bare cupboards. The film galvanized public support for efforts to improve conditions in the fields. In 1962, Cesar Chavez and Dolores Huerta founded the National Farmworkers Association (later the United Farm Workers, or UFW) to advocate for better wages and working conditions in California's Central Valley. Both had worked for the Community Service Organization, a grassroots group in California that challenged discrimination against Hispanics. Chavez had been a farmworker himself.

The UFW was not the first farmworkers' union, but it was the most visible and successful. UFW activists went from settlement to settlement, pressuring growers to provide decent housing to workers who often slept in converted chicken coops or in the open air. They demanded better wages. They improved conditions in many farm communities and, more than that, rallied thousands of farmworkers to demand even more systemic changes. In 1965, Chavez and Huerta led California grape pickers in a strike that would last nearly five years. They also built a broad base of support in college towns, churches, and big cities when they launched a well-publicized call to boycott grapes to put pressure on agribusinesses.

THE FREEDOM BUDGET Many labor and civil rights activists criticized what Bayard Rustin called Johnson's "skirmish on poverty." In late 1965, Rustin and A. Philip Randolph convened a group of prominent economists, labor unionists, and civil rights leaders who drafted the Freedom Budget, released in October 1966. The budget called for job creation programs to eliminate unemployment, a guaranteed annual income for poor families, and increased federal spending to eradicate slums, improve schools, and build public works.

Martin Luther King, Jr., sympathized with the Freedom Budget: he had called for a "bill of rights for the disadvantaged" that would expand opportunities for workers of all races. For King, the next stage in the movement was forging an interracial coalition committed to economic justice. He argued that "while Negroes form the vast majority of America's disadvantaged, there are millions of white poor who would also benefit from such a bill."[61] King also reached out—tentatively—to Chavez and the Farmworkers.

There was little political support for the Freedom Budget, but many activists, including King, turned their attention to improving pay and working conditions in the two sectors of the urban economy that grew in the 1960s: health care and public sector employment. In the manufacturing cities hemorrhaging industrial jobs and losing retail employment to the suburbs, hospitals and the government provided many of the new jobs. Orderlies, social workers, nurses, teachers, and sanitation workers—a growing number of them black and Puerto Rican—fought for better pay and benefits. King supported hospital workers' unions, including New York's 1199, which had helped bankroll the March on Washington. And he joined public employees, like Memphis's sanitation workers, in their fight for workplace dignity and better pay.

Black Power, White Backlash

Johnson had hoped that civil rights and antipoverty legislation would put a lid on protests in the streets. But in the mid-1960s, racial tensions escalated. Just weeks after Johnson signed the Civil Rights Act, riots broke out in three northern cities—Philadelphia, New York, and Rochester—sparked by clashes between blacks and the police. In August 1965 the mostly black Watts neighborhood of Los Angeles exploded after another police incident, just days after Johnson signed the Voting Rights Act. Thirty-four people died, most of them shot by law enforcement officials. Thousands of stores were looted and burned. When survey researchers interviewed Watts rioters, they discovered a deep well of frustration. Despite more than a decade of civil rights activism, they believed their situation to be worse than ever. Johnson was unsympathetic. He directed the FBI to investigate the possibility that Communists were behind the riots. (They were not.) And he fumed that blacks were ungrateful for his legislative victories.

BLACK NATIONALISM If Johnson had expected the black freedom struggle to wane after the passage of the Civil Rights and Voting Rights Acts, he was mistaken. By the mid-1960s, a growing cadre of black activists rejected civil rights laws as too little too late. White resistance had scarcely abated, blacks remained economically insecure, and schools and neighborhoods remained separate and unequal. SNCC, which had spent 1964 and 1965 agitating for voting rights and calling for inclusion in the political system, began to argue instead for black separation and self-determination.

Leading SNCC in its turn toward militancy and black nationalism was John Lewis's successor as SNCC's chair, Stokely Carmichael. A Trinidadian immigrant raised in New York, Carmichael had joined the Freedom Rides, attended the March on Washington, led voting rights efforts in Lowndes County, Alabama, and suffered beatings and jail several times. By 1965, Carmichael, like many members of SNCC, had given up hope that the Democratic Party would effectively represent black interests in the South or indeed nationwide.

In 1966, Carmichael helped found the Lowndes County Freedom Organization, with a crouching black panther as its symbol. A powerful orator who had learned the art at Harlem's speaker's corner and Howard University, Carmichael roused a crowd at a June rally in Greenwood, Mississippi: "The only way we gonna stop them white men from whuppin' us is to take over. We been saying freedom for six years and we ain't got nothin'. What do you want?" The crowd chanted, "Black Power! Black Power! Black Power!"[62]

Carmichael popularized a concept with deep roots in black politics, north and south. His call for self-determination echoed the Garvey movement in the 1920s and also built on the rhetoric of anticolonial movements in Africa and Asia. His demand for a black-run movement echoed A. Philip Randolph's call for an all-black March on Washington in 1941. But the two words *black power* were electric in 1966. They gave voice to growing dissatisfaction with liberalism, pessimism about the seeming permanence of white racism, and a sense that armed self-defense was necessary for black advancement.

The same year that Carmichael spoke of black power, CORE adopted a platform calling for black separatism. SNCC repudiated its signature strategy and called for the violent overthrow of white supremacy. That cry for self-determination echoed in the streets of many big cities in the summer of 1966, among them Chicago and Cleveland, which exploded in days-long uprisings, marked by clashes between young black men and mostly white police forces. In the next two years, inspired by the Lowndes County symbol of black political power, activists in Oakland, Harlem, Philadelphia, Des Moines, and many other cities created their own Black Panther Parties.

THE RESONANCE OF THE RIGHT By early 1966, political strategists began warning Johnson that a growing "white backlash" against civil rights threatened to reduce his congressional majority. In the midterm elections, Republicans made gains in both the House and the Senate, picking up seats in Georgia, Tennessee, and Texas. Many northern and western Democrats, sensitive to their constituents' fears of racial integration, riots, and crime (which they often conflated), rallied around candidates who opposed school integration and called for stiffer antiriot measures.

In the West, Californians elected Goldwater supporter and conservative business spokesman Ronald Reagan as governor in 1966 on a ticket that emphasized law and order, small government, and school prayer. Civil rights legislation, black power, and rioting had confirmed the Right's fears of a breakdown in civility. Johnson's expansion of educational spending affirmed their view that the federal government unconstitutionally trammeled local rights. And the Great Society's health and antipoverty programs added another layer of soul-destroying, initiative-sapping programs to those launched during the New Deal, or so they thought. Still, through the mid-1960s, it appeared that groups like the Young Americans for Freedom and the Goldwater wing of the Republican Party would remain gadflies, not become major political actors.

But even if a majority of Americans remained skeptical of the New Right's demands for individual freedom, states' rights, and small government, its message began to resonate more widely. Over the next ten years, the angry Republican delegates who supported Barry Goldwater's quixotic bid for the White House would find a more receptive climate for their political vision, as discontent on America's streets intensified and, especially, as the United States waded into the deep turmoil of Vietnam. An increasingly vocal minority of blacks found a receptive message for their calls for group power. Within a few years of Lyndon Johnson's triumphs, one of the most common questions in the United States was "Which side are you on?" That question would take on yet another dimension as Johnson fought a war abroad, one that came to be every bit as divisive as the wars that he fought on the home front.

✳

Suggested Reading

Dallek, Robert. *An Unfinished Life: John F. Kennedy, 1917–1963* (2001). A balanced account of the charismatic president and the personal and political obstacles that he faced.

Dobbs, Michael. *One Minute to Midnight: Kennedy, Khrushchev, and Castro on the Brink of Nuclear War* (2008). A gripping, minute-by-minute narrative of the Cuban Missile Crisis and its resolution.

Garcia, Matthew. *From the Jaws of Victory: The Triumph and Tragedy of Cesar Chavez and the Farm Worker Movement* (2012). A thorough and unsentimental account of the movement to improve conditions for Latino agricultural workers.

Jackson, Thomas F. *From Civil Rights to Human Rights: Martin Luther King, Jr., and the Struggle for Economic Justice* (2007). A close reading of the Reverend King's sermons, speeches, letters, and books that reveals the centrality of economics, labor, and poverty to his activism.

Joseph, Peniel. *Waiting 'Til the Midnight Hour: A Narrative History of Black Power in America* (2006). The most comprehensive history of the black power movement.

MacLean, Nancy. *Freedom Is Not Enough: The Opening of the American Workplace* (2006). How African Americans, Latinos, and women led the fight for jobs and freedom, and why business leaders and segregationists fought back.

McGirr, Lisa. *Suburban Warriors: The Origins of the New American Right* (2001). The rise of grassroots conservatism in Orange County, California, where middle-class white voters supported Barry Goldwater and Ronald Reagan.

Naftali, Timothy, Ernest May, and Philip Zelikow. *The Presidential Recordings: John F. Kennedy,* vols. 1–3, *The Great Crises* (2001). Fascinating insight into presidential politics from secret White House tape recordings.

Payne, Charles M. *I've Got the Light of Freedom: The Organizing Tradition and the Mississippi Freedom Struggle* (1995). A dramatic account of the civil rights movement in the Mississippi Delta, with attention to the churchwomen and youthful organizers who fought Jim Crow in one of its strongholds.

Sugrue, Thomas J. *Sweet Land of Liberty: The Forgotten Struggle for Civil Rights in the North* (2008). A detailed overview of the battle for racial equality outside the South from the 1920s through the 1990s.

Zelizer, Julian. *The Fierce Urgency of Now: Lyndon Johnson, Congress, and the Battle for the Great Society* (2015). How Congress overcame fierce resistance to enact Johnson's sweeping domestic agenda, including civil rights, voting rights, and Medicare.

Chapter Review

Review Questions

1. How did President Kennedy view the relationship between the federal government and expertise?

2. Why did the Kennedy administration move slowly on civil rights before 1963?

3. How did the White House resolve the Cuban Missile Crisis?

4. Why did journalists call 1963 the year of the "Negro revolt"?

5. How did Lyndon Johnson's views on civil rights evolve?

6. Explain northern white resistance to the black freedom struggle.

7. Discuss Barry Goldwater's arguments about the role of the federal government.

8. What were the key elements of the Great Society?

9. Explain the origins of the Voting Rights Act.

10. What were the links between jobs and freedom?

Key Terms

Civil Rights Act of 1957 *p. 91*

Freedom Rides *p. 93*

Bay of Pigs invasion *p. 95*

Cuban Missile Crisis *p. 96*

Peace Corps *p. 97*

Southern Christian Leadership Conference (SCLC) *p. 99*

March on Washington for Jobs and Freedom *p. 100*

Student Non-Violent Coordinating Committee (SNCC) *p. 101*

Nation of Islam *p. 104*

Civil Rights Act of 1964 *p. 106*

Young Americans for Freedom (YAF) *p. 109*

The Conscience of a Conservative p. 109

Miranda v. Arizona p. 111

Engel v. Vitale p. 111

Great Society *p. 113*

War on Poverty *p. 113*

Voting Rights Act *p. 119*

Hart-Cellar Act *p. 119*

United Farm Workers (UFW) *p. 120*

Black Panthers *p. 122*

May Day

✳

Vietnam and the Crisis of the 1960s

On May 1, 1968, Private First Class Lawrence James Merschel joined a "rat patrol" just outside Hue, the largest city in the narrow sliver of South Vietnam where the coastal lowlands meet the mountainous jungle that extends for hundreds of miles westward into Laos. Hue was a major center of Buddhist religious practice and an old imperial city with grand palaces and pagodas. Its imposing stone citadel stood watch over the city and offered vistas over the Perfumed River to the mountains in the west and the hazy lowlands along the China Sea to the east. By the spring of 1968, two-thirds of Hue lay in rubble, the smoke of burning jungles polluting its air. The din of helicopters and explosions of mortar fire penetrated the once-peaceful Buddhist temples. Hue and surrounding Thua Thien province became one of the bloodiest battlegrounds in the war for the future of Vietnam.[1]

The third of eight children, Larry Merschel grew up in the shadow of war. His parents, Peggy and Jack, met during World War II and married just before Jack shipped off to France. By the time Larry was born in 1948, the United States was engaged in a multifront battle against Communism. For young Larry, the Cold War was no abstraction. Throughout elementary and high school in Wayne, Pennsylvania, a comfortable Philadelphia suburb, he and his classmates learned—through slide shows and drills—how to protect themselves if the Russians launched an airstrike on their hometown. They formed single-file lines and marched into the school's basement fallout shelter, marked by distinctive yellow and black signs. There they practiced taking cover among the barrels of crackers and water, intended to nourish them as they waited out a storm of radioactive cinders.

In Larry's world, the Cold War was a matter not just of physical survival but of morality. At his home parish, St. Catherine of Siena, parishioners prayed for the "conversion of Russia." Young Catholics learned about the persecution of clerics like Joseph Cardinal Mindszenty in Communist-controlled Hungary. They celebrated the heroism of Tom Dooley, a Catholic medic who worked with refugees in Indochina, led the construction of hospitals in Vietnam, and worked with orphans in Laos, fighting what he considered to be the twin evils of disease and Communism. To Catholics, the Cold War pitted atheism and materialism against democracy and spirituality. It also mattered to Catholics that Vietnam's longtime postindependence leader, Ngo Dinh Diem, who had ruled from 1954 to 1963, was himself Catholic.

Larry was exactly the sort of young man whom the military hoped would enlist—morally serious and disciplined, with a strong sense of duty to his country. As a high school student, he was, as his sister Lisa described him, a "quiet, introspective young man." Like his father, a Sun Oil executive, Larry was tall, good-looking, and athletic, and although a bit taciturn, he exuded leadership. During his senior year at Radnor High School, he became cocaptain of the varsity basketball team and won his school's prize for "outstanding spirit and sportsmanship, ability and teamwork." In the fall of 1966, Larry started his freshman year at Villanova University, on a Navy ROTC scholarship. But the prospect of joining another team, for a cause far greater than that of glory on the basketball court, led Larry to enlist in the military. In April 1967, just before the end of his freshman year, he dropped his classes and headed off to basic training. "He felt that he was doing what had to be done," recalled his father, "and he felt he had to do this instead of attending college."

< Marines carrying their wounded comrades during a battle in South Vietnam, 1966 (*previous page*).

After basic training, Larry headed to Fort Campbell, Kentucky, to join one of the army's most celebrated units, the 101st Airborne. Renowned for their valor in World War II, deployed to put down unrest in the streets of Little Rock in 1957 and in Detroit ten years later, the men of the Screaming Eagles underwent especially rigorous training, including in the unit's signature skill, paratrooping. By the time of the Vietnam War, however, hardly any Airborne members actually dropped to battlefields by parachute. Most were deployed in infantry and cavalry units that fought side by side with regular troops on the ground or, by 1968, in airmobile units, delivering troops to battlefields by helicopter and leading search and destroy missions that targeted suspected havens of insurgents on the ground in South Vietnam. Larry trained as an infantryman, part of the 101st Airborne's Second Squadron, 17th Calvary. On February 20, 1968, he deployed in the Thua Thien province about one hundred miles south of the demilitarized zone that separated North and South Vietnam.

The Origins of the Vietnam War

The events that led to PFC Merschel's service in Vietnam had played out for more than a quarter of a century in the rice paddies and mountain jungles of Southeast Asia. During the 1940s, Ho Chi Minh, a charismatic Vietnamese revolutionary with close ties to the French Communist Party, launched an independence movement, challenged the Japanese occupation during World War II, and fought the restoration of French colonial rule afterward. Ho gained strong support in rural Vietnam, especially among peasants who resisted the huge landowners who had expropriated their land and forced them into conditions of near-servitude as tenant farmers and sharecroppers.

Ho appealed to President Truman for American support, but the president ignored his pleas. The United States resolutely supported its French ally's efforts to hang on to its Southeast Asian colony. As Ho's insurgency led to a widespread rebellion, the United States stepped up its involvement. Beginning in 1950, the Truman administration provided substantial economic and military support for the French. Depleted by two world wars, France simply could not mount a counterrevolution in Southeast Asia without aid. By 1954, U.S. funds covered about 80 percent of the French military efforts in Indochina.

DIEN BIEN PHU AND THE GENEVA ACCORDS Millions of dollars in foreign aid and hundreds of thousands of French troops proved no match for Ho's disciplined forces. The French military was unprepared for the guerrilla-style tactics of the Vietnamese revolutionaries. The war brought terrible casualties to both sides. Between 1946 and 1954, about 200,000 Vietminh and 70,000 French troops died. As casualties mounted, popular support in France for the counterrevolutionary struggle waned. The French nicknamed it "the dirty war." Finally, in April 1954, the French garrison at Dien Bien Phu fell to the rebels.

After months of negotiations in Geneva, an agreement temporarily partitioned Vietnam into the north, controlled by Ho Chi Minh and the Communist Party, and the south, led by Ngo Dinh Diem, a staunch anti-Communist and American puppet. The Geneva Accords called for a nationwide election in 1956 to create a unified government. Most of the major powers, including Britain, the Soviet Union, and China, signed the treaty, but the United States did not, for fear that, if the Vietnamese held elections, Ho Chi Minh would win.

NGO DINH DIEM AND CIVIL WAR IN VIETNAM   The Diem regime was corrupt and unstable. Vietnam was the second-largest recipient of American international aid for most of the 1950s. Diem and his supporters enriched themselves with American largesse. To shore up his legitimacy, Diem jailed his political opponents and staged a sham 1955 referendum in which he supposedly won the support of 96 percent of the South Vietnamese electorate. In 1956, he refused to hold the Vietnam-wide reunification election that had been required under the Geneva Accords. North and South Vietnam remained separate, with Ho establishing a capital in Hanoi, and Diem one in Saigon.

Perpetually insecure in his rule, Diem suppressed dissent and grew increasingly brutal. Still, the Eisenhower administration continued to support him. The United States provided training to the South Vietnamese police and military and dispatched a small force of military advisers to the country. Diem channeled U.S. economic development aid to cities, favoring his regime's cronies. He also empowered large landowners to consolidate their holdings and thus further impoverish the peasantry. Unpopular and autocratic, Diem's regime jailed, tortured, and murdered dissenters and censored opposition newspapers.

Diem's brutality drove growing numbers of Vietnamese, especially in rural areas, into the opposition. The Catholic Diem angered Buddhists—the majority religion—by marginalizing them in his regime. And even more consequentially, the Vietcong—a coalition of revolutionaries, nationalists, and opponents of Diem—gained control of villages throughout the countryside, winning over the peasantry by advocating land reform and opposing corruption. They used their growing strength to mount an insurgency against Diem's regime. In 1958 and 1959, rebels assassinated hundreds of Diem supporters, especially local government officials. The Diem regime stepped up its attacks on the opposition, and by 1960 a full-blown civil war had erupted in South Vietnam. The Vietcong and Buddhist dissenters, gathering under the banner of the National Liberation Front (NLF), deposed local officials who supported Diem, attacked rural landlords, appropriated land for the peasantry, and established bases throughout the countryside.

Chronology

1954	Vietnamese defeat French at Dien Bien Phu
	Geneva Accords
1960	Young Americans for Freedom founded
1962	Students for a Democratic Society founded
1963	U.S.-backed coup against Ngo Dinh Diem
1964	Gulf of Tonkin resolution
1965	Operation Rolling Thunder begins
	Watts, Los Angeles, riot
	Law Enforcement Assistance Act
1966	Fulbright hearings
1967	163 urban riots, including Newark and Detroit
	March on Pentagon
	Berrigan brothers begin breaking into Selective Service centers
1968	Tet Offensive
	Majority of Americans oppose the Vietnam War
	"Yip-In" at Grand Central Station
	President Johnson announces he will not seek reelection
	My Lai Massacre
	Martin Luther King, Jr., assassinated
	American troop deployment in Vietnam peaks at 535,000
	Columbia University protests

KENNEDY AND VIETNAM By early 1961, when John F. Kennedy took office, there were about nine hundred U.S. military advisers on the ground in Vietnam, providing tactical support to the South Vietnamese military and police. The Kennedy administration continued its predecessors' strategy of supporting the Diem regime but also began to lay the groundwork for greater American involvement in Vietnam. In the fall of 1961 the administration dispatched one of its most respected advisers, Walt Whitman Rostow, along with a key military adviser, General Maxwell Taylor, to assess the situation in South Vietnam.

Rostow, a Rhodes scholar and MIT economist, had a knack for distilling ideas down to simple formulations. He was said to have coined the phrase "New Frontier" to describe Kennedy's domestic agenda. Rostow had made his reputation as the most prominent advocate of "modernization theory," through his studies of comparative industrialization and the stages of economic growth. One of the key lessons he drew from economic history was that underdeveloped countries like Vietnam needed "benevolent authoritarianism"—dictatorships propped up by the United States—to build the institutions necessary for political stability and economic growth.[2]

What Rostow and Taylor found on their fact-finding trip was unsettling: they noted a "deep and pervasive crisis of confidence and a serious loss of national morale" in South Vietnam.[3] They argued for stepping up the deployment of American engineers, medics, and infantry to provide additional support for Diem's regime. Secretary of Defense Robert McNamara—who would serve both Kennedy and Johnson—concurred, arguing that "the United States should commit itself to the clear objective of preventing the fall of South Vietnam to Communism."[4]

McNamara, who joined the Kennedy administration after serving as Ford Motor Company's chief executive, encouraged the application of the latest thinking in planning, finance, and statistics to military strategy. He did not have much specific knowledge about Vietnam, but the numbers convinced him that the United States could easily handle the situation there. "It seems on the face of it," McNamara told Kennedy in November 1961, "absurd to think that a nation of 20 million people can be subverted by 15-20 thousand active guerrillas if the government and people of the country do not wish to be subverted."[5] McNamara believed that continued American economic aid would win the hearts and minds of the Vietnamese people, and that American military support would help Diem thwart the insurgents. In 1962 he returned optimistic from his first visit to Saigon, stating that "every quantitative measure we have shows that we are winning the war."[6]

Vietnam was not as central to Kennedy's Cold War aims as Cuba, Germany, and the Soviet Union, but the administration escalated spending and sent a growing number of military advisers to assist Saigon. The number of American troops in Vietnam rose to more than sixteen thousand at the end of 1963. In November 1963 the CIA cooperated with a military-backed coup against Diem. After the assassination of Diem and his brother Nhu, a dozen governments rose and fell in South Vietnam through 1965, all of them unpopular. The civil war intensified.

COVERT OPERATIONS AND THE GULF OF TONKIN When Lyndon Johnson assumed the presidency in late 1963, he inherited the mess in Southeast Asia. He kept Kennedy's foreign policy team mostly intact, and he agreed with those who argued that a victory in Vietnam was essential to American foreign policy goals. After two months in office, he authorized the military to engage in covert operations against the North Vietnamese. Over the summer of 1964, the White House began secret preparations to escalate the war in Vietnam, including planning for massive airstrikes on North Vietnamese supply lines.

The opportunity for that escalation came on August 2, after North Vietnamese patrol boats fired on two American destroyers in the Gulf of Tonkin. The ships were clandestinely supporting South Vietnamese operations along the coast. Johnson pledged harsh retaliation in the event of another attack. On August 4, after navy radar operators erroneously detected what they thought were torpedoes aimed at the American ships, the navy bombed North Vietnamese military targets. Johnson and his advisers hid their skepticism about the August 4 events—the president confidentially told aides that "those stupid, dumb sailors were just shooting at flying fish." But he used the event to get congressional authorization for "all necessary measures" to protect U.S. interests in Vietnam.[7]

Congress barely debated the Gulf of Tonkin resolution, which gave Johnson the authority to use military force in Vietnam. The resolution passed on August 7, unanimously in the House and with only two no votes in the Senate, from Alaska Republican Ernest Gruening and Oregon Democrat Wayne Morse. Gruening was the earliest national critic of the war, on the grounds that given the corruption of the South Vietnamese government, "the allegation that we are supporting freedom in South Vietnam has a hollow sound," and that "all Vietnam is not worth the life of a single American boy."[8] Morse believed that Congress was abrogating its responsibility, under Article I of the Constitution, to declare war. As he feared, the Gulf of Tonkin resolution became a blank check to the president to escalate an undeclared war. Johnson colorfully concurred that "it was like grandma's nightshirt, it covered everything."[9]

Lyndon Johnson's War

Johnson had a number of reasons for dramatically escalating the war. He cringed as Republicans excoriated the Democratic Party for being soft on Communism, and he desperately hoped to avoid a reprise of the GOP's damning critique of President Truman for "losing China" during the 1949 Communist-led revolution. Vietnam was, in the conventional Cold War view, an essential bulwark against the spread of Communism throughout Southeast Asia.

But Johnson's Vietnam strategy also grew from other, deeper motives that dated back to early-twentieth-century liberal internationalism, when leaders like Woodrow Wilson had justified foreign military engagements as necessary to bring civilization or democracy to the world. By the end of World War II, advocates of international economic development believed that bringing investment to the "backward" countries of Africa, Asia, and Latin America would simultaneously thwart Communism, expand the global market for American goods, and serve the humanitarian goal of eradicating global poverty.

In Johnson's most effusive moments, he described Vietnam as one front in the global war on poverty. He envisioned a Great Society in Vietnam. Building on one of the New Deal's signature accomplishments, he proposed a Tennessee Valley Authority to control flooding and generate electricity in the Mekong Delta. Rostow's vision of modernization spoke to Johnson's aspirations. Indeed, Johnson called Rostow "my intellectual" and promoted him to head the National Security Council in 1966. Like Rostow, Johnson believed that victory against the Vietcong was necessary to the larger strategy of containing Communism in Southeast Asia. And he saw it as an essential precondition for Vietnam's entry into the ranks of the developed world.

PUBLIC SUPPORT FOR THE WAR The first months of the war witnessed an outpouring of goodwill toward Johnson. The president's approval rating soared in the aftermath of the Gulf of Tonkin incident, and a sizable majority of Americans strongly supported the undeclared Vietnam War. How could the American public not support a war clearly rooted in Cold War imperatives, prompted by an apparently unjustified act of aggression against American troops, and defined as part of a plan to bring the benefits of economic development to an impoverished population?

Initially, support for the war was high across all demographic groups, particularly among younger Americans like Larry Merschel, who had reached adulthood during the 1950s and 1960s. In August 1965, a year after the Gulf of Tonkin resolution, Gallup found that 76 percent of Americans under 30 supported the war, compared to 64 percent of those 30 to 49, and only 51 percent of those over 49.[10] The oldest had lived through the horrors of both world wars; they acutely remembered World War II's more than 400,000 American casualties and 700,000 war-related injuries, and they recognized, in its aftermath, the long-term effects of postwar traumatic stress.

Contrary to clichés about youthful opposition to the war, the age gap in public opinion would hold fast for the remainder of the war, as support for the war declined among every demographic group. The number-one song on the pop charts in 1966, Barry Sadler's patriotic "Ballad of the Green Berets," celebrated one of the military's most famous units, those "fearless men who jump and die" in service of their nation.

THE AMERICANIZATION OF THE WAR Johnson and his key military advisers initially gained public support because they promised that the war would be quick and decisive. No one was more optimistic than General William C. Westmoreland, who commanded U.S. troops in Vietnam between 1964 and 1968. Westy, as he was nicknamed, oversaw military operations with brusque efficiency. A top graduate of West Point and a World War II veteran, he had also studied at Harvard Business School. "Westy was a corporation executive in uniform," argued historian Stanley Karnow. He evaluated military performance in quantitative terms, relying on detailed data to assess the threat of the North Vietnamese and Vietcong, and he used a grim metric of military success, the "favorable kill ratio."[11]

At the outset, Westmoreland believed that the United States could crush the Vietnamese rebellion through airpower and use "advanced technology to spare the troops an onerous offensive task."[12] Since World War II, American military planners had shared a nearly utopian faith in airpower as the key to American military might. The systematic application of American technology to war would reduce the number of American casualties while swiftly paralyzing North Vietnamese military production and halting enemy troop movements. American airpower had been crucial to victory in World War II against the technologically advanced Germans and Japanese, so it surely would allow the United States to prevail in a place that Johnson, off the cuff, called a "raggedy-ass, fourth rate nation."[13]

In February 1965 the North Vietnamese attacked the American air base at Pleiku, a city in the central highlands. The assault killed nine U.S. soldiers, injured many more, and destroyed a few dozen U.S. aircraft. The president responded angrily. "We have kept our gun over the mantel and our shells in the cupboard for a long time now," he stated. "And what was the result? They are killing our men while they sleep at night."[14] He pulled more than a gun from the mantel and authorized Operation Rolling Thunder, a massive airstrike on North Vietnamese military installations and industrial sites that also resulted in hundreds of thousands of civilian deaths. Rolling Thunder began the longest and most devastating aerial campaign in American military history. By 1968, the United States had dropped more than 3.2 million tons of explosives on Vietnam, more than the entirety of American bombing in both the Second World War and the Korean War.

But it soon became clear to Westmoreland that airpower would not be sufficient, especially in the large parts of rural South Vietnam that were under the control of the Vietcong, which embedded its troops in villages and hamlets. Just a few months after the United States launched Operation Rolling Thunder, Westmoreland requested a significant increase in ground troops. By late 1965 there were 185,000 American troops stationed in Vietnam, more than ten times the number in the last days of the Kennedy presidency. The Johnson administration also broadened the military draft, conscripting about 300,000 men per year from 1966 through 1968. All men between eighteen and twenty-five were eligible for the draft, but under a policy put in place after the Korean

Pro–Vietnam War Demonstration Members of the conservative Young Americans for Freedom demonstrate in support of the Vietnam War in Philadelphia, October 1965. That year a sizable majority of Americans, including young people, backed the war.

War called "manpower channeling," college and graduate students could get deferments while studying in a field considered to be vital to the national interest, such as physics. Those deferments extended to include the vast majority of college and graduate students. By January 1966, more than two million college students were able to defer military service.[15]

PACIFICATION In past colonial wars, including in the Philippines, the United States sought to pacify the civilian population, thereby weakening popular support for insurgent troops. In Vietnam, pacification took different forms at different points during the war. It consisted of American efforts to flush out the enemy combatants from Vietnamese settlements, displace rural populations to reduce the influence of the National Liberation Front, and restructure Vietnamese society through programs of economic development. The first phase of pacification began in the Diem years, with the advice of the Kennedy administration. South Vietnamese government officials created "strategic hamlets," forcibly relocating Vietnamese peasants there and fortifying them to keep out NLF forces. The program was costly and ineffective. Many peasants, who wanted nothing to do with the war, became active enemies of the Diem regime. They allowed the Vietcong to move surreptitiously in and out of villages. Even those unsympathetic with the rebels often refused to support the South Vietnamese regime because of their anger at the process of being uprooted, often more than once.

By 1966, the United States, now directly involved in Vietnam, launched its own version of pacification. Building on Johnson's lofty Great Society rhetoric about "civic action," American aid officials worked with the South Vietnamese government to launch a program of democratization and economic development in villages that had been ostensibly purged of the Vietcong. Americans encouraged local elections and pledged to win over local populations by sponsoring agriculture, rural electrification, and public health initiatives.

But the instability of the population—particularly the high mobility of refugees and villagers' continued suspicion of the Saigon government and its American backers—greatly hampered rural development efforts. The massive depopulation of rural provinces and the environmental devastation wrought by massive airstrikes and the use of toxic herbicides to clear forests hampered agricultural reform. Corrupt local officials pocketed American dollars, and the military had little interest in supporting development efforts. By 1968, the rural pacification program was a shambles.

The lion's share of the remaining development funds went to managing the rapidly growing refugee population. All together, about 3.5 million Vietnamese people were displaced during the war. Some had moved voluntarily to the periphery of American military bases, where black market economies boomed. Residents there provided cheap labor and goods and services, from foodstuffs to prostitution, to the soldiers on American bases. One Vietnamese woman recalled the "gold rush" mentality that drew many rural residents to military encampments. But far more Vietnamese were forced out of their villages. In NLF-controlled areas, residents who supported Diem fled persecution and assassination.

Many more fled the destruction wrought by ground war and especially by massive airstrikes and flamethrower attacks, using napalm, a gelatinous form of gasoline. Chemical defoliants, including Agent Orange, devastated some 20 percent of the land in South Vietnam—about the size of the state of Massachusetts—between 1965 and 1971. The roads of rural Vietnam teemed with haggard, hungry refugees, overwhelmingly women and children, often carrying little more than their clothes. With the agricultural economy destroyed, the dense, overcrowded refugee camps that housed many of the displaced could barely meet their needs. One study estimated that over half of all working-age refugees were unemployed.

ATTRITION Despite Johnson and Rostow's dream of a modernized Vietnam, economic development became a sidebar to the most important objective: eliminating the Vietcong and destroying North Vietnam's military and industrial capacity. The key to victory was attrition by weakening the enemy through sustained air attacks and relentless ground operations. At every step of the way, Johnson acceded to Westmoreland's requests to expand American ground forces in Vietnam and steadily escalate the bombing raids.

Together, the U.S. and South Vietnamese troops greatly outnumbered the North Vietnamese and Vietcong. Coupled with their technological capabilities, the superiority of the American forces was clear in the casualty rates. Westmoreland, for whom demography was destiny, offered a grim statistical tally of the number of dead and captured. Ten to twenty Vietcong and North Vietnamese soldiers died for every American. After comparing notes on six of Westmoreland's press briefings that he attended, war correspondent Ward Just found that the "sessions had a striking similarity. The recurring message—'The Americans were on the offensive, the North Vietnamese and the Vietcong were on the defensive. But there was no sign of a break. Any questions?'"[16]

SKEPTICS FROM WITHIN President Lyndon Johnson trusted Westmoreland's data, even as the war dragged on. For Johnson and his most steadfast advisers, statistics and faith in technology overrode more impressionistic assessments of what was happening on the ground in Southeast Asia. The skeptics were few and isolated at first. George W. Ball, an experienced foreign policy hand, played devil's advocate in Johnson's inner circle. An attorney who shared his colleagues' faith in expertise, Ball had worked for the federal government on and off since the New Deal. He joined the Kennedy administration in 1961 and a year later was promoted to undersecretary of state. During the Kennedy years, Ball had warned Taylor and Rostow that "the Vietcong were mean and tough, as the French learned to their sorrow."[17] But few were interested in Ball's analogy with France's anticolonial debacle. Surely the U.S. military could do better.

Ball posed hard questions about Johnson's decision to Americanize the war in 1964 and early 1965. At each moment when Johnson planned to escalate American engagement, Ball wrote a memorandum taking the contrary position. He proved to be remarkably prescient. The affairs of Vietnam, he argued, were not central to America's Cold War goals. Ball explicitly rejected the "domino" theory of Communism, namely that Communism spread by toppling regimes one by one. "The great captains of history," he wrote, "drew their lessons from complex chess, not simple dominoes."[18] He echoed arguments that were gaining currency among other foreign policy experts in the mid-1960s. Growing tension between the two dominant Communist powers—the Soviet Union and China—led to a reappraisal of some of the fundamental tenets of the Cold War. There was no single monolithic Communist threat but rather multiple centers of Communist power that could be played off against one another. Vietnam was a minor stage in a large geopolitical struggle.

Ball also argued that the costs of military engagement in Vietnam greatly outweighed any possible benefits. Ultimately, he believed, the Vietcong would prevail against the South Vietnamese and their American allies, even if conventional measures currently suggested that the revolutionaries were losing. The South Vietnamese, he argued, lacked the solidarity necessary to establish an enduring, stable government and prevail against a well-organized revolutionary insurgency.

In a crucial memo to President Johnson on July 1, 1965, just as the administration dramatically escalated the ground war, Ball put his position most bluntly: "The decision you face now, therefore, is crucial. Once large numbers of U.S. troops are committed to direct combat, they will begin to take heavy casualties in a war that they are ill-equipped to fight in a non-cooperative if not downright hostile countryside." He continued: "Once we suffer large casualties, we will have started a well-nigh irreversible process. Our involvement will be so great that we cannot—without national humiliation—stop short of achieving our complete objectives." Clinching his point in italics, Ball warned: *"Of the two possibilities, I think humiliation would be more likely than the achievement of our objectives—even after we have paid terrible costs."*[19]

President Johnson shared some of these concerns. Behind the scenes, in private conversations with Defense Secretary McNamara, he worried "that it is going to be difficult for us to very long prosecute effectively a war that far away from home."[20] But he ultimately rejected Ball's arguments. McNamara, Rostow, and most of Johnson's inner circle clung to a simpler Cold War orthodoxy. They took as a matter of faith that the South Vietnamese regime was legitimate and, if restructured slightly, could be popular. And they believed that American firepower and know-how made victory inevitable.

In October 1966, Ball finally resigned from the Johnson administration, the most prominent official to leave to date because of disagreements about the conduct of the war. James Thomson and Bill Moyers, both Johnson loyalists who broke with the president on Vietnam, had preceded him. The departure of dissenting voices left Johnson increasingly isolated, surrounded by a group, among them Rostow, that political scientist Larry Berman called a "closed circle of decision making." But even that circle shrank, as other high-level officials resigned, including McNamara in 1967 and UN ambassador Arthur Goldberg in 1968.

Johnson's stubborn insistence that the Vietnam War was justified, necessary, and winnable generated greater skepticism outside the executive branch, even among some of his erstwhile political allies. As early as the summer of 1965, some key Democratic members of Congress began expressing concern about the escalation of American troop commitments, among them Senators Mike Mansfield (D-MT) and Richard

Johnson and Fulbright On July 28, 1965, the day he announced the deployment of 125,000 troops to Vietnam, President Lyndon Johnson (*right*) confers with Senator J. William Fulbright, chair of the Senate Foreign Relations Committee and one of the staunchest critics of his foreign policy.

Russell (D-GA). Those divisions came to light in January 1966, when Senator William Fulbright (D-AR) opened up hearings on the Vietnam War, giving a prominent pulpit to the war's critics.

Fulbright had been one of Johnson's closest allies and, at the president's bidding, had whisked the Gulf of Tonkin resolution through the Senate. But over the course of 1965, he had grown increasingly critical of the value of American intervention in regional wars overseas, including in the Dominican Republic, where Johnson had sent 23,000 American troops to put down a leftist insurgency in 1965, and Vietnam. Fulbright's Foreign Relations Committee hearings, which were covered extensively on national television, gave credence to the growing chorus of voices critical of the war. In 1966 and 1967 more members of Congress, many with impeccable anti-Communist credentials, argued against Johnson's war. In early 1967, Senator Robert F. Kennedy (D-NY) called for negotiations to end the war, earning the moniker "Ho Chi Kennedy" from the hawkish *Chicago Tribune*, whose editors, like many on the right, would settle for nothing less than total victory.[21]

The Antiwar Movement

Fulbright, Kennedy, and Ball—despite their disagreements with the president—did not reject the larger aims of the war. They believed that the United States needed to prevail against Communism, and they argued that the war in Vietnam could, unintentionally, impede America's larger foreign policy aims. But growing numbers of Americans rejected both the war and, in the process, America's Cold War foreign policy.

In March 1965, several months before Democratic congressmen raised concerns about the war, University of Michigan faculty and students held a teach-in on the Vietnam War, the first of thousands of such events held nationwide over the next several years. In April a broad coalition of religious and secular activists led a 25,000-strong march in Washington to oppose the war. One of the largest antiwar demonstrations to that date, it was a polite affair that attracted "more babies than beatniks," according to *The New York Times*.[22]

Opponents of the war represented different generations, acted on divergent motives, and disagreed on goals and tactics. Almost all the war's early critics came from the religious and political lefts. Since World War II, a dedicated band of activists, working through pacifist groups like the Fellowship of Reconciliation (FOR) and the War Resisters League, had argued for a militant, nonviolent resistance to war. They had mobilized quickly after Johnson announced Operation Rolling Thunder. "In the name of God, STOP IT!" pleaded FOR members to the president in April 1965.[23] Some were socialists who saw American military power as a tool of oppression. Others believed in the fundamental immorality of state-sanctioned violence. Still others, like Women Strike for Peace, offered a maternalist critique of the war, arguing that as mothers, they had their sons' and the nation's best interests at heart. But whatever their ideological differences, these groups collaborated in the struggle against the war, signing petitions and staging local and national protests.

RELIGION AGAINST THE WAR Essential to the antiwar effort were members of traditional peace churches, especially the Quakers, the Mennonites, and the Brethren. Their more radical members joined protests, but most of them worked quietly behind the scenes, gathering medical supplies to assist Vietnamese refugees, printing antiwar pamphlets, and setting up centers to counsel young men on conscientious objection to the draft. Mainstream Protestants, Reform Jews, and a growing number of Catholics added their voices to the chorus of opposition. As early as November 1965, the Union of American Hebrew Congregations, speaking for Reform Jews, called for a cease-fire and a negotiated settlement. In 1966 an ecumenical group of leading clerics, including Reinhold Niebuhr, Martin Luther King, Jr., Rabbi Abraham Heschel, Yale chaplain William Sloane Coffin, Jr., and Catholic priests Philip and Daniel Berrigan, joined forces to create Clergy and Laity Concerned About Vietnam, a group that would broaden the antiwar mobilization even further.

Especially prominent in the movement were Catholic antiwar activists, many of them priests and nuns who had been radicalized in the postwar years by the Catholic Worker movement, which embraced both pacifism and a commitment to help the poor. Part of a left-wing theological insurgency in the church, they challenged Catholics' reflexive anti-Communism. Priests like the Berrigans envisioned themselves as prophets against war and organized some of the most dramatic protests of the period.

In October 1967, Philip Berrigan led the first of what would be at least one hundred protests at Selective Service centers in the next several years, pouring blood on draft cards in "a sacrificial and constructive act" to protest "the pitiful waste of American and Vietnamese blood, 10,000 miles away."[24]

THE RISE OF THE STUDENT MOVEMENT The most visible opposition to the war arose on American college campuses. In the mid-twentieth century, war had remade American higher education. After World War II, military veterans, who had benefited from the GI Bill, flooded American universities. Most were older than the average college student, had families, and finished their coursework quickly. The Reserve Officer Training Corps (ROTC), a program to prepare college men for military leadership that had been created in 1916, expanded rapidly during the early years of the Cold War. By 1955, it had chapters on 313 American campuses.[25]

Many university faculties had grown somewhat more conservative after the war. McCarthyism had suppressed campus radicals. Scholars in the new field of American civilization emphasized the consensual nature of American politics and society; political scientists resuscitated the theory of American exceptionalism; business schools expanded rapidly; and physicists and chemists conducted secret research for the military and for firms that were contracted to improve weapons, radar, and other military technologies. By the time that the Vietnam War escalated, professors at Columbia, Penn, Michigan, Wisconsin, Chicago, and Berkeley engaged in high-level, classified research on chemical and atomic weaponry or military electronics systems. American universities proved central to the Cold War.

But it would be on campus that the Cold War consensus began to crack. Colleges were havens for political dissenters, reformers, the offbeat, and the eccentric. In the 1940s and 1950s, socialist students held earnest discussion groups at the City College of New York. Social Gospel Christians ran many campus ministries and sponsored

March on the Pentagon On October 21, 1967, a diverse crowd of about 100,000 converged on the Department of Defense headquarters to protest the Vietnam War.

events at the campus YMCA and YWCA at the University of Texas. Students frequented bars featuring folk music and coffee houses where they earnestly discussed existential philosophy and beat poetry.

THE NEW LEFT For the battered American left, campuses held potential, particularly in the early 1960s, when students began to organize around issues such as civil rights and the nuclear arms race. Students at Michigan, CUNY, Madison, and Berkeley had joined CORE's protests against segregated restaurants and lunch counters; and campus chapters of the National Committee for a Sane Nuclear Policy (SANE) proliferated. In 1962 a small band of socialists, closely allied with the labor movement, held a retreat in Port Huron, Michigan, and formed Students for a Democratic Society (SDS), with hopes of expanding their ranks by recruiting a younger generation of activists, especially those who had come of age in the postwar years.

It seemed an uphill battle. Since the 1930s, various socialist groups had aligned against the Communist Party over its allegiance to Moscow. But other than their disdain for Stalin and the Soviet Union, postwar socialists were a fractious lot, quibbling over minute differences in their interpretations of Marx, Lenin, Trotsky, and their latter-day heirs. A culture of disputation, however, created a vital intellectual infrastructure that nurtured leftist writers, even as their ranks dwindled. Radical theorists appeared in lively little journals like *Partisan Review* (founded in 1934), *Dissent* (1954), and *New America* (1960). Even if the American left was minuscule, its influence could be felt on campuses, in union halls (Oakland, Chicago, and Detroit had very active socialist groups), and in countercultural neighborhoods in big cities and college towns, including Greenwich Village, Austin, Ann Arbor, and San Francisco. The mainstream media took leftist intellectuals seriously. Many left-leaning writers, including Irving Howe, Dwight Macdonald, Michael Harrington, Betty Friedan, and Langston Hughes, their skills honed in the leftist press, penned articles for periodicals as diverse as *The New Republic*, *The New Yorker*, *Christian Century*, and even *Fortune*.

The Port Huron Statement, SDS's founding manifesto, articulated a broad set of principles in sweeping moral language that fused together elements of socialism, liberalism, and religious perfectionism, while eschewing the old partisan rhetoric of the left. Rather than advocating class struggle or denouncing state socialism, it called for "a democracy of individual participation" that would undermine the "depersonalization" of a modern bureaucratic society: "We would replace power rooted in possession, privilege, or circumstance by power and uniqueness rooted in love, reflectiveness, reason, and creativity." The statement's authors railed against what they considered the "crust of apathy" and the "inner alienation that remain the defining characteristics of American college life"; they blamed the "cumbersome academic bureaucracy" and those scholars whose work directly benefited corporations and the military.[26]

Some SDS activists formed the Economic Research and Action Project (ERAP), which sent students to work with white Appalachian migrants in Chicago and poor blacks in Newark. Organizing among the poor was difficult and frustrating and attracted only a small cadre of organizers. Most stayed on campus, hopeful that students would become the vanguard of revolutionary change.

Nothing fueled the rise of SDS more than the Vietnam War. In 1965 SDS chapters began to proliferate on campuses. At Swarthmore College, for example, SDS mobilized a third of the student body in February to protest Operation Rolling Thunder. In April, about 15,000 SDS members marched on Washington, demanding a cessation of the war. By 1966 and 1967, student radicals led campus protests against defense industries that recruited on campus, professors who conducted secret military research in their campus labs, and ROTC programs. At SUNY Buffalo and Wisconsin, protesters targeted Dow Chemical, which manufactured Agent Orange, a chemical defoliant used in Vietnam. Nearly everywhere that SDS had more than a handful of members, it coordinated teach-ins and protests against the war. The group's membership reached a peak of about 100,000 nationwide by early 1968, with more than three hundred chapters and perhaps another million or so loosely affiliated followers.

SDS was a decentralized organization that put as much value on process as outcomes. An anonymous SDS member quipped, "Freedom is an endless meeting," leading another to offer the hopeful embellishment that "talk helps people consider the possibilities open for social change."[27] SDS members did a lot of talking, but spoke without a single voice. On some campuses doctrinaire Maoists were able to commandeer chapters. And many anti-Communist "old leftists" fretted that student radicals were naïve in their support of revolutionaries like Che Guevara and Ho Chi Minh, whose portraits graced the walls of many dorm rooms and communal houses. But most SDS members were motivated less by revolutionary romance than by a sense that the "establishment" or "the system" needed to be challenged, be it in the form of university regulations of student behavior like parietals (rules that forbade members of the same sex from staying in each other's rooms overnight and that set curfews for female students) or the ability of the military to recruit on campus.

HIPPIES AND YIPPIES "Make love, not war." The popular slogan denoted the blurry boundaries between the antiwar movement and a loosely organized counterculture, one that celebrated personal liberation and fulfillment through sex or psychedelic drugs or music. Todd Gitlin, an early SDS leader and later a prominent sociologist, viewed the counterculture as a "less risky, more pleasurable" diversion from politics, "the Sixties' version of the fraternity-sorority culture of the Fifties."[28] For many young people, politics became a fashion statement: wearing long hair, loose clothes or none at all, beads, and sandals seemed a rebuke to businessmen in their wool suits and housewives in their A-line dresses.

There was a frivolity to the "hippie" culture that emerged in big cities in the mid-1960s, but to worried parents, it made the "juvenile delinquents" of the 1950s seem tame. Hippies took over San Francisco's Golden Gate Park for a "love-in" during the summer of 1967, stripping off their clothes, dancing, and shocking observers by doing what was usually done behind closed doors. In March 1968 thousands of young people, many of them disinhibited by smoking marijuana or dropping acid (the nickname for the hallucinogenic lysergic acid diethylamide), gathered for a "Yip-In" at New York's Grand Central Station, coordinated by members of the Youth International Party. Known as the Yippies, the colorful group, more theater troupe than political party, was

Making a Nation

The Morality of War

From

Lyndon Johnson

Peace Without Conquest (1965)

In early 1965, President Johnson dramatically increased the number of American troops in Vietnam. In this April 7 speech at Johns Hopkins University, he explained his rationale for the war in Vietnam. He asserted that victory in Vietnam would prevent the spread of Communism and lift the Vietnamese people from poverty through economic modernization.

Viet-Nam is far away from this quiet campus. We have no territory there, nor do we seek any. The war is dirty and brutal and difficult. And some 400 young men, born into an America that is bursting with opportunity and promise, have ended their lives on Viet-Nam's steaming soil.

Why must we take this painful road?

We are there because we have a promise to keep. Since 1954 every American President has offered support to the people of South Viet-Nam. We have helped to build, and we have helped to defend. Thus, over many years, we have made a national pledge to help South Viet-Nam defend its independence.

And I intend to keep that promise. . . .

We are also there to strengthen world order. Around the globe, from Berlin to Thailand, are people whose well-being rests, in part, on the belief that they can count on us if they are attacked. To leave Viet-Nam to its fate would shake the confidence of all these people in the value of an American commitment. . . . The result would be increased unrest and instability, and even wider war.

We are also there because there are great stakes in the balance. Let no one think for a moment that retreat from Viet-Nam would bring an end to conflict. The battle would be renewed in one country and then another. The central lesson of our time is that the appetite of aggression is never satisfied. To withdraw from one battlefield means only to prepare for the next.

These countries of southeast Asia are homes for millions of impoverished people. . . . They are often wracked by disease, plagued by hunger, and death comes at the early age of 40.

Stability and peace do not come easily in such a land. Neither independence nor human dignity will ever be won, though, by arms alone. It also requires the work of peace. . . . Now there must be a much more massive effort to improve the life of man in that conflict-torn corner of our world.

The vast Mekong River can provide food and water and power on a scale to dwarf even our own TVA.

The wonders of modern medicine can be spread through villages where thousands die every year from lack of care. . . .

And these objectives, and more, are within the reach of a cooperative and determined effort.

Paul Potter

Naming the System (1965)

Ten days after Johnson's "Peace Without Conquest" speech, Potter, president of Students for a Democratic Society, addressed 25,000 people at an antiwar rally in Washington. He rebutted Johnson, arguing that the Vietnam War was destructive and immoral.

Most of us grew up thinking that the United States was a strong but humble nation, that involved itself in world affairs only reluctantly, that respected the integrity of other nations and other systems, and that engaged in wars only as a last resort.

The incredible war in Vietnam has provided the razor, the terrifying sharp cutting edge that has finally severed the last vestige of illusion that morality and democracy are the guiding principles of American foreign policy. . . . The further we explore the reality of what this country is doing and planning in Vietnam the more we are driven toward the conclusion that the United States may well be the greatest threat to peace in the world today.

The pattern of repression and destruction that we have developed and justified in the war is so thorough that it can only be called cultural genocide. I am not simply talking about napalm or gas or crop destruction or torture, hurled indiscriminately on women and children . . . upon the first suspicion of rebel activity. That in itself is horrendous and incredible beyond belief. But it is only part of a larger pattern of destruction to the very fabric of the country. We have uprooted the people from the land and imprisoned them in concentration camps called "sunrise villages." Through conscription and direct political intervention and control, we have destroyed local customs and traditions, trampled upon those things of value which give dignity and purpose to life.

Vietnam, we may say, is a laboratory ran by a new breed of gamesmen who approach war as a kind of rational exercise in international power politics. It is the testing ground and staging area for a new American response to the social revolution that is sweeping through the impoverished downtrodden areas of the world.

For in a strange way the people of Vietnam and the people on this demonstration are united in much more than a common concern that the war be ended. In both countries there are people struggling to build a movement that has the power to change their condition. The system that frustrates these movements is the same. All our lives, our destinies, our very hopes to live, depend on our ability to overcome that system.

Questions for Analysis

1. Why did President Johnson believe that the United States had no choice but to defend South Vietnam?

2. Why did Potter see America as a threat to peace?

3. Compare Johnson's and Potter's understanding of America's role in the world.

led by Abbie Hoffman. The Yip-In, which the Yippies described as "a spring mating service celebrating the equinox," ended badly when some rowdy members of a collective called Up Against the Wall Motherfuckers climbed up to the station's trademark wall clock and pulled off its hands, announcing that they wanted to "fuck time"—the perfect excuse for hundreds of New York police to surge through the station in a bloody rampage that left hundreds injured and dozens arrested.[29]

The Yippies' founder, Abbot Howard (Abbie) Hoffman, famous for his bushy hair and flamboyant hats, was a jester with a serious mission: to mock the venality of power and celebrate its Dionysian alternative. A bit older than most of his followers, he had imbibed the "hep" culture of the beats as a college student in the late 1950s and, by the mid-1960s, proffered a gleefully subversive variant of youthful protest. "The goal now," he wrote in *The Realist*, one of hundreds of underground radical and countercultural newspapers that circulated in the late 1960s, "is to disrupt an insane society." He and his comrades practiced that disruption again and again. In one of the Yippies' most celebrated "happenings," Hoffman and his comrades tossed dollar bills from a balcony onto the floor of the New York Stock Exchange, bringing the whole operation to a halt as stock traders scrambled to scoop up the money.

The streets became stages in a theater of protest. Hoffman's comrade Paul Krassner described one antiwar demonstration with glee: "Throwing cow's blood. A costumed mock wedding of Military and Big Business. Overturning garbage cans. Painting a Rolls Royce in Day-Glo while the chauffeur cowers at the wheel in disbelief. Blocking traffic. Turning in false fire alarms. This was the Vietnam equivalent of Watts."[30]

For student radicals and hippies alike, the Vietnam War represented the ultimate perversion of the system. Out-of-touch, power-hungry liberals like Lyndon Johnson and the foreign policy establishment misled the public. War enriched major military contractors who funded defense research at leading universities, with the collusion of corrupt professors, deans, provosts, and presidents. Vietnam was a racist war, fought against people of color who were struggling for their own self-determination. And the war machine fed on the bodies of young men—American and Vietnamese—who sacrificed their lives for the establishment.

DRAFT RESISTANCE By 1967, many young men, some persuaded by the arguments of antiwar politicians and activists, others simply self-interested, found ways to keep from being drafted. Most of those who avoided service were well-to-do, well educated, or well connected. Young men from privileged families found all sorts of ways to avoid being shipped to Southeast Asia, from using their families' political clout to join the National Guard (whose units were seldom deployed abroad) to finding sympathetic doctors to document health problems that would render a draftee unfit for service. In 1968, when the Selective Service narrowed the criteria for graduate school deferment to men in training in medicine, dentistry, or divinity, applications to medical schools and seminaries skyrocketed.

Some half-million draftees petitioned to be recognized as conscientious objectors, claiming that they had moral reasons for opposing military service. In past wars, most COs had been members of traditional peace churches such as the Quakers. But by the mid-1960s, Reform Jews, Roman Catholics, and even agnostics claimed that they had moral reasons for opposing the war, if only they could convince a Selective Service board, an easier task in many cosmopolitan cities and college towns than in much of middle America. All together, 170,000 draftees, more than 100,000 more than in World War II, won conscientious objector status. Between 30,000 and 50,000 young men resisted the draft by leaving the country, most taking refuge in Canada and Scandinavia.

A Working-Class War

As a result of widespread draft avoidance, those at the bottom of the socioeconomic ladder fought the war: the sons of America's fading industrial cities, its marginal farms, and its impoverished backcountry. About 80 percent of the 2.5 million who served in the military during the war came from working-class and poor families.[31] Many volunteers, especially those from places that had been left behind in the changing economy, saw service as a steady paycheck and an alternative to underemployment. This was a sharp contrast with World War I, when many college students joined the "preparedness" movement and zealously signed up to join the military. At that time many working-class men were deemed too unhealthy or too unintelligent to serve in the military. It contrasted sharply with World War II, in which widespread mobilization included the wealthy, the middle class, and the working class. Vietnam was a young man's war, fought disproportionately by high school dropouts and young men with diplomas but with few hopes of attending college. The average age of an infantryman in Vietnam was only nineteen, compared to twenty-six during World War II. Young men could be drafted at age eighteen but—until the Constitution was amended in 1971—only those twenty-one or older could vote.

The disproportionate number of soldiers and war dead who came from working-class families gave resentment a class tinge. "I'm bitter," recalled a firefighter who lost his son in Vietnam. "You bet your goddamn dollar I'm bitter. It's people like us who gave up our sons for the country."[32] Not surprisingly, support for the war strongly correlated with education: despite the prominent antiwar movement on campuses, those who had attended college were consistently more likely to support the war than their counterparts with a high school degree or less.

AFRICAN AMERICANS AND THE WAR If students became the most visible opponents of the war, African Americans, whether on campus or off, were the war's earliest and most steadfast critics. In the 1960s, many blacks had looked hopefully to the military, the only substantially integrated institution in the United States. For black men in particular, enlisting offered an escape hatch from the grim urban economy or from the dying world of southern farm labor. Military service promised training, long-term health and pension benefits, and respect. In 1966 the Johnson administration launched Project 100,000, an antipoverty program that lowered military entrance requirements to provide opportunities to underemployed men. Of the 350,000 men who entered the program (it exceeded its numerical target), 41 percent were black, and about 40 percent of them were deployed to combat. Many black commentators viewed Project 100,000 in conspiratorial terms, and statistics from the first two years of the war did nothing to alleviate their concerns. Between 1964 and early 1967, African Americans suffered over 20 percent of U.S. casualties in Vietnam, although they made up only about 11 percent of the population. That imbalance was only temporary. Over the course of the entire war, blacks were not grossly overrepresented among the troops or the war dead. All together, blacks made up 12.5 percent of American casualties in Vietnam.

Racial tensions among the troops ran high, even though the military had been officially integrated since 1948. Black soldiers found it hard to advance through the ranks. They regularly complained of harassment by drill sergeants and officers. Petty arguments between black and white soldiers often exploded into brawls. Black soldiers were more likely to face courts-martial and were overrepresented in the ranks of those with less-than-honorable discharges. In the military's top ranks, African Americans made up only 2 percent of officers. Many career white officers had come of age while the military was officially segregated and now adjusted only slowly to the change. Not surprisingly, blacks on the front lines in Vietnam began to embrace the rhetoric of the black power movement. Some painted black panthers and clenched fists on their helmets. Others joined Black Brothers United, one of many underground groups that gave soldiers a vehicle for dissenting from the war.

CIVIL RIGHTS AND THE WAR For their part, civil rights activists were, initially, badly split over the war, but for tactical more than ideological reasons. Many leaders of the SCLC, including Martin Luther King, Jr., shared misgivings about the war but feared that if they publicly opposed President Johnson, they would jeopardize civil rights legislation. One of the movement's key strategists, Bayard Rustin, who had been jailed for resisting the draft during World War II, took an equivocal stance on Vietnam. He criticized the war but counseled King and other civil rights activists to keep their antiwar sentiments quiet, for fear of alienating Johnson and other Democrats. CORE took a similar stance. By a narrow margin at its 1965 annual meeting, it passed a resolution denouncing the war, but at the urging of its leader, James Farmer (who like Rustin had been a war resister during World War II), tabled it for fear of alienating the civil rights movement's liberal allies.

Rustin and Farmer were increasingly out of touch with the rank and file in their organizations, who saw Vietnam as the latest example of a people's struggle for self-determination. As early as 1954, the singer and prominent leftist Paul Robeson had compared Ho Chi Minh's rebellion to slave uprisings, calling him the "Toussaint L'Ouverture of Indochina." Robeson worried that "Negro sharecroppers from Mississippi" would be dispatched "to shoot down brown-skinned peasants in Vietnam—to serve the interests of those who oppose Negro liberation at home and colonial freedom abroad."[33] If Robeson was a lonely voice in the 1950s, by the following decade black activists commonly made similar arguments. They depicted the war as one that served the interests of whites, threatened people of color, and relied on black Americans to do the dirty work.

As the war ground on, some prominent black public figures took a stand against Johnson's war. Among them was the heavyweight boxing champion Muhammad Ali, who declared himself a conscientious objector in early 1966, memorably stating that "I ain't got no quarrel with them Viet Cong." Antiwar activists embellished the quote, adding the phrase, "No Viet Cong ever called me nigger."[34] Ali was convicted of draft evasion in 1967, stripped of his heavyweight title, and banned from professional boxing, though he appealed the charges successfully and, in 1970, returned to the ring.

In a highly publicized April 4, 1967, sermon at New York's venerable Riverside Church, the Reverend Martin Luther King, Jr., urged an end to hostilities in Vietnam. "Surely this madness must cease. We must stop now. I speak as a child of God and brother to the suffering poor of Vietnam. I speak for those whose land is being laid waste, whose homes are being destroyed, whose culture is being subverted. I speak for the poor of America who are paying the double price of smashed hopes at home, and dealt death and corruption in Vietnam."[35]

Critics denounced Ali as un-American and railed against King for confusing his message. *The Washington Post* editorialized that King "has diminished his usefulness to his cause, his country, and his people."[36] But black celebrities like comedian Dick Gregory, singer Eartha Kitt, and actor Harry Belafonte, as well as black power activists including Stokely Carmichael and Angela Davis, joined King and Ali in their outspoken opposition to the war.

War at Home: The Urban Rebellions

The pronouncements of popular figures like Ali and King no doubt shaped black public opinion, but so too did events on the home front. The Americanization of the Vietnam War coincided with one of the most sustained periods of violence in American domestic history, what many called the "war at home." Between 1964 and 1967, hundreds of American cities exploded in riots. In the worst of the "long hot summers"—1967—uprisings occurred in 163 American cities and towns, ranging from Detroit in July, where 43 people were killed, 17,000 arrested, and tens of thousands of buildings destroyed, to small towns like Plainfield, New Jersey, Nyack, New York, and Wadesboro, North Carolina.

"OCCUPYING FORCES" For those participating in the riots, Vietnam represented a touchstone. The Detroit riots broke out when police raided an illegal after-hours bar that was hosting a party for two black servicemen returning from the war. In Plainfield, undercover investigators reported that rioters praised Muhammad Ali and talked of self-determination against "occupying forces." National Guard units put down disturbances in Cincinnati and Tampa. Troops from the 101st Airborne, Larry Merschel's unit, joined the Michigan National Guard and the local and state police to put down the rebellion on Detroit's streets. Altogether 17,000 armed officials deployed in the Motor City. It was impossible not to compare the sight of jeeps and tanks in the streets and choppers hovering over America's burning cities to images from the war in Vietnam.

Many black critics of the war made explicit comparisons between Vietnam and American inner cities. Echoing decades-old critiques of American foreign policy by Marcus Garvey and W. E. B. Du Bois, Stokely Carmichael, the leading voice of the black power movement, argued that "we must recognize that Detroit and New York are also Vietnam."[37] One of the most outspoken critics of the war, Carmichael called the president a "buffoon" and Defense Secretary McNamara "a racist."[38]

By 1967 Carmichael and many black radicals viewed Vietnam as a potential ally in a global war of liberation. Blacks must "align ourselves with people of color around the world who are also oppressed," he argued. "The enemy around the world is the same." Carmichael saw both American inner cities and Vietnam as "occupied territories" whose residents mobilized for self-determination.[39] In Vietnam, peasants struggled against western colonialism, and in the United States, blacks struggled against "internal colonialism." Overseas possessions and inner cities alike were, in this view, places where whites enriched themselves by extracting resources and exploiting labor. For black radicals, the urban riots were nothing less than rebellions against white America's occupying forces: shopkeepers who got rich by charging high prices for inferior products and the police who brutalized blacks and suppressed dissent.

LAW AND ORDER POLITICS The confluence of campus unrest and urban rioting fueled the alarm that the United States was out of control, plagued by disorder, and in need of policies to reinstate law and order. In 1964, Republican presidential candidate Barry Goldwater had argued that liberals aided and abetted disorder in the streets, and he called for a stronger police presence to restore safety and security, especially in America's cities. By 1966, the upsurge of campus protests and urban riots fueled calls for crackdowns on public dissent. That year California voters overwhelmingly elected to the governorship Ronald Reagan, who had run a campaign criticizing the ongoing campus rebellion at the University of California, Berkeley, the insurgency on the streets of Watts, and the growing black power movement. "Will we allow a great university to be brought to its knees by a noisy, dissident minority?" asked Reagan as he announced his campaign in January. "Will we meet their neurotic vulgarities with vacillation and weakness?"[40] His own answer was a clear no.

Johnson did not take the criticism lightly. In 1965, a month after Watts burned, he signed the Law Enforcement Assistance Act (LEAA), which provided unprecedented grants to local police forces. In its first two years, most of LEAA's $300 million went to riot preparation. With federal funds, local police departments purchased armored vehicles, tear gas, and high-powered rifles, preparing themselves to put down possible rebellions. The administration also provided training in antiriot techniques modeled after military counterinsurgency campaigns in Korea, Guatemala, and Vietnam. Around the country, police departments created paramilitary special weapons and tactics (SWAT) teams to control city streets. LEAA funding expanded exponentially in the next decade and a half. By 1981, the federal government had channeled more than $8 billion into a growing, federally-backed law enforcement system.

Behind the scenes, the Johnson administration also authorized the enhanced surveillance of antiwar and black radical organizations. J. Edgar Hoover, the FBI director, had spent decades investigating suspected Communists and gays; it was a small step from the Kennedy administration's approval of Hoover's wiretap of Martin Luther King, Jr. Cooperating with local police forces, FBI informants infiltrated student, antiwar, and black power organizations.

Many infiltrators were agents provocateurs, who goaded radicals into plotting acts of violence. One black power group, the Revolutionary Action Movement, was brought down in the summer of 1967 after revelations that its members plotted the assassination of black moderate leaders—a harebrained scheme devised by an infiltrator. And in 1968 a group of Philadelphia SDS members were arrested in a plot to blow up the Liberty Bell after the police "discovered" incriminating evidence that they themselves had planted. Johnson authorized the CIA to launch Operation Chaos, an extensive program of spying against domestic opponents of the war, surreptitiously gathering information on hundreds of thousands of American citizens.

The Collapse in Public Support for the War

Efforts to curb dissent did little to change public opinion on the Vietnam War. Between 1965 and 1968, public approval fell sharply. Nothing played a greater role in fueling skepticism than the powerful, uncensored images of bloodshed that appeared in newspapers and, especially, on the televised evening news. One journalist called Vietnam "the living room war," for the ubiquity of images of dead and maimed bodies that shaped the public consciousness of the war. Every week beginning in 1967, *Life* magazine published the high school yearbook pictures of young American men killed in Vietnam. Gruesome photographs from the legion of photojournalists who accompanied the troops in Vietnam appeared in daily newspapers and on the evening news—soldiers burning thatched cottages with Zippo lighters; a young, naked girl screaming after being hit with napalm; a Vietcong rebel being executed at point-blank range on the streets of Saigon; a bloodied American soldier carrying a critically injured comrade over his shoulders. Previous wars had been equally horrible, but the tragedies of Vietnam were unfiltered, and to audiences accustomed to World War II–era newsreels or to the sanitized heroism of popular war films, they were shocking.

THE RISE OF THE ANTIWAR MAJORITY Opinions about the Vietnam War varied by sex, race, class, and region. Men were more likely to be hawks; women, doves. Residents of the Southwest—the part of the country that had been remade by the postwar military-industrial complex—supported the war more strongly than their counterparts elsewhere. Southerners, who sent disproportionately more young men to war than the rest of the country, were more likely to support de-escalation.

But by early 1968, a majority of Americans—men and women, from all regions—opposed the Vietnam War, and most wanted it to end quickly, though they had different explanations as to why. Some had come to believe that it was unwinnable; others that it was morally wrong. Some opposed the war because they thought it was being fought with inadequate resources; in their view, the United States was too soft. Those who opposed the war also diverged greatly on the means to ending it. A minority called for an immediate withdrawal from Vietnam, but just as many believed that the United States should dramatically escalate its airstrikes to accomplish a swift and decisive victory. On the extreme, some, including General Curtis Le May, who would be tapped by the independent George Wallace as his vice-presidential candidate in 1968, called for the use of nuclear weapons.

Opposition to the war did not, however, entail sympathy with the antiwar movement. Antiwar protesters proved even less popular than Johnson and the war. One of the most popular bumper stickers in 1968 was "America love it or leave it." Those who chanted "Ho, Ho, Ho Chi Minh, the Viet Cong are gonna win," or who defaced the American flag with peace signs, were considered a threat to society. The "do-goodniks" and "longhairs" who led antiwar demonstrations seemed "un-American." Many who opposed the war also opposed what they saw as the erosion of respect for authority.

DUMP LYNDON   The combination of urban unrest, escalating campus protest, and a seemingly unwinnable war all hurt the presidency of Lyndon Johnson. But the most consequential opposition came from within the ranks of his own party. Though he had been elected in 1964 by one of the most substantial margins in American history, his prospects had greatly dimmed a few years later. By 1967, Democratic opposition to Vietnam had coalesced into a "Dump Lyndon" insurgency on the party's left, though it seemed unlikely that any major Democrat would jeopardize his career by challenging the incumbent.

That changed on November 30, when Senator Eugene McCarthy (D-MN) announced that he would be the anti-Johnson standard-bearer: "I am concerned that the Administration seems to have set no limit to the price it is willing to pay for a military victory."[41] McCarthy was an unlikely candidate. An unusually cerebral politician, he read Latin, wrote poetry, and steeped himself in Roman Catholic social teaching. Virtually unknown outside his home state of Minnesota, he had not been a major player in the Senate; nor had he been prominent among the president's critics. McCarthy's campaign slogan, "He stands alone," suggested a man of conscience, which he was, but also a politician without the ability to make the alliances necessary for success on the partisan battlefield.

McCarthy's campaign to unseat Johnson, as improbable as it was, galvanized liberal opponents of the war. Thousands of students went "clean for Gene," shaving their beards, cutting their hair, and replacing their countercultural garb with starched shirts, ties, or dresses, as they joined his New Hampshire primary campaign. On March 12, 1968, when McCarthy picked up 42 percent of the Granite State's Democratic primary vote and won a majority of the state's delegates, the Johnson campaign reeled.

Tet and Bloody 1968

As Johnson weighed his political future, PFC Larry Merschel prepared for his deployment to Vietnam. Merschel supported the war and volunteered for the army out of a sense of duty. But he had the misfortune of being deployed to Vietnam in early 1968, during the worst few months of the war's worst year. American troop deployment reached its peak that May, at 535,000. That year 16,543 Americans died in action, making up more than a quarter of all American casualties in the entire war. More than 27,000 South Vietnamese troops died in battle in 1968, as did an estimated 200,000 North Vietnamese and Vietcong fighters. It was also the costliest year of the war, with U.S. military expenditures in Vietnam topping $77 billion.

On January 1, 1968, as Merschel and his fellow troops at Fort Campbell, Kentucky, celebrated the New Year, the president offered a cautiously optimistic prognostication from his ranch in Johnson City, Texas. "We are very hopeful that we can make advances toward peace. We are pursuing every possible objective. We feel that the enemy knows that he can no longer win a military victory in South Vietnam. But when he will reach the point where he is willing to give us evidence that would justify my predicting peace this year—I am unable to do so—that is largely up to him."[42] The very same day Ho Chi Minh rallied his own people, offering his own resolution. Hanoi Radio broadcast his poem:

> This Springtime certainly will be more joyous than all such previous seasons,
> For news of victories will come from all parts of the country.
> North and South (our people and our soldiers) will compete
> in the anti-American struggle.
> Forward we go,
> And total victory will be ours.[43]

Both Johnson and Ho were wrong. The New Year would bring only the most tenuous advances toward peace, and total victory for no one.

THE TET OFFENSIVE   The Vietnam War took an abrupt turn in early 1968. The National Liberation Front had been planning a massive surge for months. At three in the morning on January 31, the first day of Tet, the Vietnamese holiday that marked the lunar New Year, a commando squad of nineteen National Liberation Front insurgents attacked the American embassy in Saigon, killing two military police officers, blasting the embassy door with antitank shells, and battling American soldiers and a helicopter force. Saigon was the most prominent of more than a hundred cities and towns that the North Vietnamese Army and the Vietcong targeted, among them five of the six largest cities in the South and 36 out of 44 provincial capitals. They caught American military leaders off guard.

The goal of the Vietnamese revolutionaries at Saigon and elsewhere in the Tet Offensive was not to achieve total victory, despite Ho Chi Minh's rhetoric. The insurgents were vastly outnumbered and weakened by years of heavy losses. Instead they hoped to humiliate and demoralize the South Vietnamese government and its American allies, and force a de-escalation of the war by bringing the United States back to the negotiating table.

The Tet Offensive was audacious but short-lived. At the U.S. Embassy, American troops killed all the attackers and secured the facility within hours of the raid, though not without drama. The military police protecting the grounds were unprepared, and two died. The fighting was chaotic. An American soldier threw a pistol up to an unarmed embassy official through a second-floor window, who used it to repel one of the attackers as he ran up the stairs. By midday, rubble and corpses littered the embassy gardens. In a stiff public statement after the embassy siege had ended, General Westmoreland declared victory, claiming that the Communists' "well laid plans went afoul." But the televised coverage of the attack and its aftermath undermined Westmoreland's credibility.

The Tet Offensive lasted for only a morning in Saigon, and in many cities and towns, the rebels lost within hours or days. But in some parts of the country, fighting extended for weeks. Among the most bitterly contested places was Hue, a city of 140,000. Despite its strategic location, Hue fell astonishingly quickly to the rebels on January 31. More than three weeks of horror followed. After hoisting the yellow and red Vietcong flag aloft at the citadel in the heart of the city, the occupying forces engaged in a bloodbath, eventually shooting, clubbing to death, or burying alive supporters of the South Vietnamese regime. The death toll from the massacre was, from the outset, contested. Those sympathetic to the Vietcong claimed that 300 or 400 traitors died; the U.S. military estimated that rebels slaughtered somewhere between 2,800 and 5,700 public officials, military leaders, clergy members, merchants, and intellectuals.

Retaking Hue proved to be more difficult than repelling the attack on the American embassy in Saigon. For most of February, the United States bombed Hue and strafed it with gunfire. U.S. and South Vietnamese troops fought insurgent forces block by block. More than 13,000 of the city's 17,000 dwellings were destroyed or seriously damaged, and thousands of civilians died, maimed by shrapnel, crushed by rubble, or felled by gunfire. About 116,000 Hue residents fled to makeshift refugee camps in the nearby countryside. The South Vietnamese and U.S. troops would not recapture the city until February 25.

By Westmoreland's grim metric, the Americans and the South Vietnamese won a clear victory at Hue. Several thousand enemy troops died, and only a few hundred Americans. But images of the battle for the citadel in Hue—broadcast on the evening news for weeks in the United States—told a different story. The reports of television journalists accompanying U.S. troops in the streets of Hue added to the sense of a brutal and unwinnable war. From February 1968 onward, a dwindling minority of Americans supported it.

On February 27 the respected CBS news anchor Walter Cronkite, who had just returned from Saigon and Hue, declared that "the bloody experience of Vietnam is to end in a stalemate."[44] The same day General Earle Wheeler, chairman of the Joint Chiefs of Staff, requested the deployment of as many as 206,000 more American

The Vietnam War, 1964–1975

CHINA

NORTH VIETNAM

U.S. air raids 1966–1968, 1972

•Dien Bien Phu

Hanoi• ⊗ •Haiphong

BURMA (MYANMAR)

Gulf of Tonkin

Gulf of Tonkin incident August 1964

Thanh Hoa•

LAOS

Hainan

•Vinh

Vientiane•

Mekong R.

•Dong Hoi — **Demilitarized zone**

17th Parallel demarcation line Geneva Accords, July 1954

Invasion of Laos February–March 1971

Hue ⊗ *Tet Offensive January–February 1968*

THAILAND

•Da Nang

Thua Thiem

⊗ *My Lai massacre March 1968*

BATTLE OF HUE, JANUARY 30–MARCH 3, 1968

South China Sea

0 2 4 miles
0 2 4 kilometers

HUE

Perfume R.

Camp Eagle•

CAMBODIA

•Pleiku
Qui Nhon•

Ho Chi Minh Trail

Invasion of Cambodia April–June 1970

SOUTH VIETNAM

South China Sea

Na Trang•

Phnom Penh•

Gulf of Thailand

Saigon• ⊗ *Tet Offensive January–February 1968 Surrender of South Vietnam April 30, 1975*

Mekong Delta

⊗ Major battles or actions
— U.S. and South Vietnamese offensives
— North Vietnamese offensives
--- North Vietnamese supply routes

0 100 200 miles
0 100 200 kilometers

troops to Vietnam. Behind the scenes, top foreign policy advisers and military leaders—and even Westmoreland himself—began to question their assessment of the war's progress. Almost since the start of Tet, they had privately acknowledged that the offensive had weakened the South Vietnamese and served as a political and psychological boon for the Vietcong. Wheeler's request for a massive surge of troops generated an intense debate at the highest levels of government and in foreign policy circles. The call

The Battle of Hue American troops, including an injured soldier, take cover in Hue on February 6, 1968, during the first week of a nearly month-long struggle for control over the ancient South Vietnamese city.

for negotiation and cease-fire, only a year ago a position held by a minority of liberals, gained traction.

On March 26, 1968, Johnson convened a private White House meeting with the "Wise Men," a blue-chip group of foreign policy advisers who had served various presidents since Franklin Roosevelt. Among them were former secretary of state Dean Acheson; former ambassador both to the UN and to South Vietnam, Henry Cabot Lodge; and former undersecretary of state George Ball. Acheson argued that the United States needed to disengage from Vietnam, and those assembled concurred. Almost a year and a half after he had resigned, Ball felt vindicated. "I share Acheson's view. I have felt that way since 1961—that our objectives are not attainable. In the U.S., there is a sharp division of opinion. In the world, we look very badly because of the bombing. That is the central defect in our position."[45]

On March 31, two months after the Tet Offensive began, Johnson gave a nationally televised speech that shocked the nation. "We are prepared to move immediately toward peace through negotiation. So tonight, in the hopes that this action will lead to early talks, I am taking the first step to de-escalate the conflict. We are reducing—substantially reducing—the present level of hostilities. And we are doing so unilaterally, and at once." As the speech wound to a close, Johnson announced, "I shall not seek, and will not accept, the nomination of my party for another term as President."[46]

GROUND WAR IN THUA THIEN Larry Merschel deployed to Vietnam on February 20, 1968, a little over a month before Johnson's stunning announcement. He joined his 101st Airborne comrades near Hue in Thua Thien province. Hue's hinterlands remained among the bloodiest battlegrounds of the war. During the early 1950s, Thua Thien had been a base of resistance to French colonialism, and in the late 1950s and early 1960s a center of Buddhist-led dissent against the corrupt and brutal South Vietnamese governments. As the civil war in Vietnam escalated, Thua Thien had provided some of the strongest support for the National Liberation Front. Even the village of My Thuy Phuong, where the 101st Airborne established Camp Eagle, its major base of operations in the region, was a hotbed of Vietcong support during the Tet Offensive.

General Westmoreland identified the region from Thua Thien northward to the Demilitarized Zone as key to post-Tet American strategy. Nearly half of all American troops deployed in Vietnam in 1968 were stationed there. After Tet, North Vietnamese and Vietcong troops took refuge in the jungles and hamlets outside Hue. American military planners, fearful of another attack on the city, worked to flush out the rebels. A month after Larry Merschel arrived, the 101st Airborne engaged in efforts to cordon off Vietcong troops, digging trenches around suspected havens, using flares to light up suspected enemy "nests," and attacking those who attempted to sneak through the lines.

Merschel's unit, the Second Division, 17th Calvary, went on "rat patrols" in the lowlands between Hue and the coast, seeking out insurgents by jeep and by foot in the marshes and jungles along the "Street Without Joy," the bleak, refugee-laden Highway 1 that connected Hue with points northward. Along with these search-and-destroy missions to capture or kill suspected insurgents, American and South Vietnamese officials recruited locals to create pro-Saigon local governments, police the communities, and lay the groundwork for economic redevelopment. The battle for Thua Thien became one of the longest ground operations of the war.

DISILLUSIONMENT AMONG THE TROOPS Nearly every soldier had his horror stories from the forests and hamlets of South Vietnam, and most of them did not make the news. Instead, soldiers recounted their experiences in letters home and, using their own cameras and tape recorders, documented the war themselves. What they experienced and reported gave the lie to optimistic prognostications about favorable kill ratios and American invincibility. If many Americans on the home front felt a "credibility gap" between Johnson's statements and news coverage of the war, soldiers in the Indochinese jungles and swamps experienced it directly.

The troops on the ground in Vietnam also voraciously consumed the American print media. Although the military's own publications echoed official pronouncements on the war, most soldiers had access to American periodicals and, through them, learned of the raging home front protests and debates. In the spring of 1968, they knew that most Americans opposed the war, that antiwar protests proliferated, and that even mainstream politicians questioned the war. With Johnson and his close advisers shifting the administration's own position, confusion and tensions on the battlefields grew. What did Johnson's March 31 speech mean? Would the war end? What would the next president do?

Johnson's March 31 speech reverberated in Thua Thien. In letters home, twenty-year-old Larry, too young to vote, conveyed some of his own discomfort, though he did so in a light tone. "I can't have any say in who runs our government. I can't vote. I'd get arrested and heavily fined if I was caught drinking beer," he wrote. "But here I am—somebody is always getting unfairly treated, so I'll bear the burden with a smile."

The Spirit of Rebellion

In April 1968, as Larry and the 101st Airborne dodged bullets and shells in Thua Thien, disturbing news came from home. On April 4, in Memphis, Tennessee, Martin Luther King, Jr., was assassinated. More than one hundred American cities exploded in the most intense days of rioting in American history. The most extensive looting and burning happened in Washington, D.C., only a mile from the White House. A pall of smoke from burning buildings darkened the skies over the nation's capital. In Baltimore, riots lasted for four nights, and six people died. And in Chicago, which had already been ravaged by an uprising in 1966, eleven died in several days of discontent.

Campus protests exploded. In the semester that began the month of the Tet Offensive, major protests (involving at least a thousand people) erupted on more than two hundred campuses throughout the United States. On fifty-nine of those, students took over campus buildings. Students on at least another thousand campuses held smaller demonstrations or teach-ins, most directed toward the Vietnam War.

The antiwar movement also intensified on campuses with large populations of first-generation college students. They were the working- and lower-middle-class cousins, the brothers and sisters and classmates of the men fighting in Vietnam. Students marched at Wayne State University in Detroit and at Temple in Philadelphia, at historically black Jackson State University in Mississippi, and at Catholic Fordham and St. Louis Universities. Even at conservative Villanova, where Larry Merschel had matriculated, students began to raise their voices in opposition to the war and invited antiwar priest Daniel Berrigan to campus.

REVOLT AT COLUMBIA   No campus got more press in the spring of 1968 than Columbia University, where students shut down the campus for eight days beginning on April 23. Since late March, members of Columbia's SDS had staged confrontational protests there, led by a charismatic junior, Mark Rudd. Born to a middle-class Jewish family in suburban New Jersey, Rudd had been a hardworking, disciplined high school student with a proclivity for math. But as an undergraduate, the confluence of the civil rights struggle and the anti-Vietnam insurgency radicalized him. In the winter of 1968, he visited Cuba and returned further resolved to be an agent of revolutionary change.

Over the spring semester, Rudd and his comrades in SDS, named the "Action Faction," stepped up protests. Rudd sent a letter to Columbia president Grayson Kirk, listing student demands, including the cessation of defense research on campus. Rudd memorably signed off, "Up Against the Wall Motherfucker," a salutation that outraged the staid President Kirk.[47]

On April 23, SDS members took a further step toward revolution. They marched against what they saw as faculty complicity with the war (a defense research center on campus) and racism (a gymnasium under construction in Morningside Park, bordering Harlem, that would be closed to community members). Over the next eight days, students occupied several campus buildings, briefly held the dean of the college hostage, and raided and pilfered the president's office. On April 24 a faction of black students ousted white protesters from the main classroom building and renamed it Malcolm X Hall. University officials, fearful that Harlem residents would riot, closed off the campus to outsiders.

On campus, the occupation generated an intense debate and counterprotests. Nearly two thousand students signed a petition denouncing the occupation, calling themselves the Majority Coalition; antiprotest students blockaded the main administration building, with hopes of starving out the student protesters. Sympathizers delivered takeout food—Mark Rudd's mother even dropped off a freshly cooked dinner for her son. Faculty members, some sympathetic with SDS, others fearful of violence, unsuccessfully attempted to broker a compromise between the protesters and the administration.

At two a.m. on April 30, more than eighteen hundred police officers raided the Columbia campus under the cover of darkness and arrested hundreds of students. They were particularly sensitive to the black students: an all-black unit of the police force peacefully led protesters out of Malcolm X Hall. But the late-night raids quickly turned bloody. Many police officers, resentful of what they saw as privileged students who lacked respect for authority, put black tape over their badges and took the license of anonymity to beat the protesters indiscriminately, even as they lay limp on the ground. About 150 students were injured. Dozens of faculty attempted to serve as peacekeepers; some of them were beaten and arrested too. That day Columbia SDS called for a general strike, and on May 1 the university suspended classes. For most of May and early June, at the paralyzed campus students skipped classes and many boycotted graduation ceremonies.

"MANY VIETNAMS" Latin American revolutionary Che Guevara was a hero to Rudd and to student protesters worldwide. His familiar face graced countless pamphlets and posters. But nothing solidified Che's reputation more than his 1967 critique of the Vietnam War. "How close and bright would the future appear if two, three, many Vietnams flowered on the face of the globe," argued Che, "with their quota of death and their immense tragedies, with their daily heroism, with their repeated blows against imperialism, forcing it to disperse its forces under the lash of the growing hatred of the peoples of the world!"[48]

Students worldwide saw their universities and cities as some of Che's "many Vietnams." At the beginning of the 1967–68 academic year, British students had engaged in a general strike at many major universities; and in the spring of 1968, demonstrations rocked campuses from Tokyo to Mexico City, from Berlin to Bombay. Youthful protesters in Prague challenged the Soviet occupation of Czechoslovakia. Media coverage of the protests worldwide brought the student protesters together virtually, as they challenged governments, denounced the war in Vietnam, and for a time felt a part of something that transcended their local concerns.

The biggest day for worldwide protests was May Day, the traditional occasion for leftist and pro-labor parades. That day students in Paris barricaded the streets of the Left Bank and began a monthlong battle with the police. Unlike students at Columbia, Jackson State, or Swarthmore, French students had a broad base of support, as hundreds of thousands of workers joined in solidarity, holding a nationwide general strike.

REBELLION IN THE RANKS   The spirit of rebellion made its way into the ranks of soldiers in Vietnam in countless ways, even among those who had little in common with protesters at Columbia or in Paris. Soldiers founded underground newspapers and magazines that viciously criticized officers and the war itself. Black power pamphlets circulated widely. Closeted gay soldiers circulated their own newsletter. Many soldiers adorned their helmets with peace signs or black panthers, signaling their sympathy for dissenters at home. And still others held late-night rap sessions on the morality of war. The letters column of *Playboy* became a public forum for anonymous GIs to report on their experiences, denounce their officers, and argue about military strategy.

For its part, the military did everything in its power to keep up the morale of GIs. The United States bankrolled dozens of large clubs on or near South Vietnamese bases, with booze, beer, and slot machines. (Gambling generated an estimated $23 million in revenue per year.) American and Filipino rock bands, well-known American actors, actresses, and comedians, and dancers and strippers entertained soldiers on bases and at off-base clubs. The army slapped together gymnasiums and movie theaters, installed pizza ovens and soda and popcorn machines, and even subsidized ice cream factories. Soldiers received their pay in "military payment certificates," a form of scrip that quickly became currency in Vietnam's rapidly expanding black market, to which military officials mostly turned a blind eye. Prostitution proliferated—in plain sight—in the settlements surrounding military bases.

But the military's efforts to boost morale fell short. The grim conditions in South Vietnam greatly demoralized troops, and many turned inward to express their frustration. Many soldiers began to escape by using marijuana, which was cheap and readily available in Saigon and in the hastily built trading centers that sprang up around American bases. Although there are no good estimates, internal military studies suggest that by the end of 1968, probably between a third and half of soldiers frequently smoked pot. About 1.5 million soldiers went AWOL (absent without leave) during the war, and some 450,000 left the military with a less-than-honorable discharge, many for insubordination, drug use, and petty crimes.

Tensions flared between the frontline troops and the GIs "in the rear," in support units on bases that seldom saw direct combat. Racially charged brawls erupted in mess halls and bars, echoing the struggles in the streets on the home front. At the extreme, the post-1968 years witnessed a significant increase in "fragging," anonymous attempts to injure or kill officers, often through the use of fragmentation grenades. By the military's conservative estimate, at least a few hundred fraggings occurred during the war.

THE MY LAI MASSACRE Other soldiers turned their wrath on the South Vietnamese. Brutal attacks on civilians and rapes became alarmingly commonplace. Officers regularly covered up wartime atrocities, even if they were often common knowledge among the troops. One happened shortly after the end of the Tet Offensive, in a small hamlet called My Lai, in the Quang Ngai province, about 150 miles southeast of Hue, where the Vietcong had a strong base of indigenous support. The countryside was especially dangerous, and dozens of U.S. soldiers had been killed or maimed by landmines surrounding rebel bases. On March 16, 1968, an army unit, led by Lieutenant William Calley, raided My Lai, a suspected Vietcong haven. The military's intelligence was wrong: there were no rebel troops or caches of weapons to be found, just hundreds of terrified civilians.

Ordered to cordon off My Lai and capture combatants, Calley and his troops went on a rampage, killing somewhere between 347 and 504 villagers, most of them women and children. Calley himself herded about fifty villagers into a trench and killed them with automatic rifle fire at close range. Several elderly men died by bayonet, and troops shot women praying for their lives in the back. U.S. soldiers mutilated bodies, and raped some of the women and a child. The event would not be reported until 1969. After a lengthy investigation and court-martial, Calley was convicted of murder, though he only served a short sentence and went free on appeal.

The blood and gore, the terror of stumbling upon a landmine or walking into a snipers' nest, the horror of killing and watching civilians and comrades die, the anxiety and distrust among the troops themselves, the dehumanization of Vietnamese civilians as "gooks"—strained even the most disciplined soldiers. And for what? Putting one's body on the line for a war that fewer and fewer Americans on the home front supported seemed senseless.

At the end of 1968, someone prominently posted an antiwar petition that read simply, "Fuck War" at the 101st Airborne's Camp Eagle. Among others, Steve Sherlock, a Screaming Eagles officer who had enlisted as a "super war supporter," signed it.[49] Maybe, after months of slogging through the "Big Muddy," Larry Merschel would have agreed with the petition's sentiment too, though he probably would not have cared much for its language.

But he would not have the chance to sign. On May 1, 1968, while part of a search-and-destroy mission four kilometers northwest of Hue, Larry died when fragments from an exploding antitank mortar mutilated his body. He was buried in a closed casket. His parents begged to see their son one last time. The army would not let them.

✳

Suggested Reading

Appy, Christian G. *Patriots: The Vietnam War Remembered from All Sides* (2003). Gripping oral histories of 135 people whose lives were transformed by the Vietnam War, including American and Vietnamese soldiers, military leaders, journalists, antiwar protesters, and civilians.

———. *Working-Class War: American Combat Soldiers and Vietnam* (1993). Shows that in Vietnam, unlike past wars, soldiers from the lowest rungs of the economic ladder bore the burden of military service.

Bradley, Mark Philip, and Marilyn B. Young, eds. *Making Sense of the Vietnam Wars: Local, National, and Transnational Perspectives* (2008). A collection of essays by leading historians who write about the war using archives in the United States, Vietnam, China, and the Soviet Union.

Cullather, Nick. *The Hungry World: America's Cold War Battle Against Poverty in Asia* (2010). How America used economic development policy from India to Vietnam's Mekong Delta as a tool of counterinsurgency.

Foley, Michael S. *Confronting the War Machine: Draft Resistance During the Vietnam War* (2003). Explores the ideology and strategy of the antiwar movement.

Isserman, Maurice, and Michael Kazin. *America Divided: The Civil War of the 1960s* (2011). The best single-volume overview of social movements and their impact on national politics in a tumultuous decade.

Logevall, Fredrik. *Embers of War: The Fall of an Empire and the Making of America's Vietnam* (2012). A distinguished diplomatic historian traces the consequences of America's fateful decision to support the French in its battle against Vietnamese independence.

Young, Marilyn. *The Vietnam Wars, 1945–1990* (1991). A classic, deeply researched, and impassioned account of America's long and troubled engagement with Southeast Asia.

Chapter Review

Review Questions

1. Explain the impact of Ngo Ninh Diem's regime on the coming of the Vietnam War.

2. Why did President Johnson decide to Americanize the Vietnam War?

3. Evaluate George Ball's position on American military policy in Southeast Asia.

4. What was the appeal of left-wing politics on American campuses in the mid-1960s?

5. What were the differences and similarities between the counterculture and the New Left?

6. Who served in the military during the Vietnam War?

7. Explain the ways black radicals compared the urban uprisings and Vietnam.

8. Why did public support for the war in Vietnam decline so sharply in 1968?

9. What explains the difficulties that the U.S. military faced in Thua Thien province?

10. Why did students at Columbia and other universities revolt in the spring of 1968?

Key Terms

Geneva Accords *p. 130*

Vietcong *p. 130*

National Liberation Front (NLF) *p. 130*

Gulf of Tonkin incident *p. 132*

Americanization *p. 134*

Operation Rolling Thunder *p. 135*

pacification *p. 136*

domino theory *p. 137*

Fulbright hearings *p. 139*

conscientious objection *p. 140*

Students for a Democratic Society (SDS) *p. 142*

Port Huron Statement *p. 142*

Economic Research and Action Project (ERAP) *p. 142*

Yippies *p. 143*

Law Enforcement Assistance Act (LEAA) *p. 150*

Operation Chaos *p. 151*

Tet Offensive *p. 153*

Hue, Battle of *p. 154*

My Lai Massacre *p. 161*

Which Side Are You On?

The Battle for Middle America, 1968–1974

C armen Roberts, a thirty-one-year-old mother of two, became a political activist for the first time in the spring of 1970. She lived in a quiet lower-middle-class neighborhood in northeastern Detroit, about as close to the suburbs as you could get without crossing the city line. Married young to a truck driver, she was a stay-at-home mom who took pride in her impeccably neat living room and her lush front lawn. Stylish in a late-1950s sort of way, and though some of her friends wore miniskirts and bell-bottoms, the latest fashions did not tempt her. She liked her world just so.[1]

As hard as she tried, Roberts couldn't cocoon her family from social and political change. The neighbors' older children grew their hair long. She found their insouciant style and loud music upsetting. Even more ominous was the racial unrest that seemed to move closer and closer every year. Detroit had been a racial battleground for decades. Whites resisted integration by attacking black newcomers to their neighborhoods more than two hundred times in the period since World War II. Many more fled the "Negro invasion" and headed to the suburbs. By 1970, Detroit was on the brink of becoming a majority black city. Roberts and her neighbors hunkered down on their patch of segregated turf.

Whites had long dominated Detroit politics, but African Americans fought to be heard. In the late 1950s, blacks began to win elections to the city council and school board and used their positions to fight for civil rights. Other insurgents worked outside the system. Young black activists had taken over the campus newspaper at Wayne State, the city's major public institution, and turned it into a voice of black militancy. During Detroit's 1967 riot, someone had sprayed the words *Black Power* on a street, catching the attention of news helicopters. Someone else painted black a statue of Jesus at the local Catholic seminary. Tellingly, the local archbishop decided to leave the altered statue intact.

The black insurgency intensified after the riot. Local activists Milton and Richard Henry took African names, Gaidi and Imari Obadele, and formed the Republic of New Afrika, demanding that the U.S. government turn over land for the new country. In 1968 and 1969 a group called the League of Revolutionary Black Workers staged wildcat strikes at the city's Dodge and Chrysler plants, protesting systematic racial exploitation in the workplace.

Black and white students fought for power in Detroit's schools. At Mackenzie High School, black students walked out in October 1968, demanding an Afrocentric curriculum. At Cooley High School, which had been nearly all white through the mid-1960s, white students fought integration. At the beginning of the 1969–70 school year, they hurled bricks, beer cans, and bottles at their black classmates, shouting "get out of our school, Nigger!"[2]

Detroit's school board scrambled to deal with the unrest. On April 7, 1970, it announced a modest plan to integrate the city's schools. Carmen Roberts was furious that her son, who had just started at Denby High School, and her daughter, who walked to nearby Columbus Elementary, might have to transfer, all for the sake of what she believed was a dangerous effort in social engineering. Roberts and about 750 other white parents gathered to protest at the public school headquarters when the plan was announced. She called it "the day my life was to be altered from that of a complacent housewife to an active alert housewife."[3]

< Richard Nixon leaving the White House by helicopter on August 9, 1974, just after he resigned the presidency (*previous page*).

The Election of 1968: Democratic Fracture

Carmen Roberts represented the sort of voter whom the various candidates for the White House fought to win beginning in 1968—and even more so in the midterm elections of 1970 and the presidential election of 1972. White, working class, and urban, they had been the bedrock of the Democratic Party, but they had grown increasingly disaffected with civil rights, urban unrest, student rebellion, and the Vietnam War. Although working-class voters remained in the Democratic Party camp in 1968, they began shifting rightward with momentous consequences for national politics.

For over three decades, the Democratic Party had held together a fractious coalition across region and race. Blue-collar whites and African Americans in the North supported the party of the New Deal and turned out in large numbers for Kennedy and Johnson. Roman Catholics mostly remained on the Democratic side, attracted by the party's pro-labor policies and its support for the family wage. Republicans enjoyed their deepest support among suburban and rural Protestants in the Northeast, the Great Plains, and the West. The GOP's pro-business politics ensured a loyal following among small business owners and corporate executives alike.

Domestic strife, and the unpopular war, threatened to upend the political order. Southern whites, still overwhelmingly Democratic, rebelled against Johnson and their party's northern wing. Union members in the North, among the most reliable Democrats, grew uneasy with student rebellion and black unrest. The Democrats could count only on African American voters to turn out huge majorities for their candidates. On the right side of the aisle, Republicans sensed a real opportunity to break up the Democratic coalition for good.

THE DEMOCRATIC CHALLENGERS Lyndon Johnson's announcement in March 1968 that he would not run for reelection left his fellow Democrats scrambling. Their first challenge, an impossibly difficult one, was to manage the party's deep divisions over Vietnam. Eugene McCarthy had captured the antiwar vote in the early primaries, but his constituency of young, well-educated voters was small, and he did not have the political skill to expand it. The Minnesota senator appeared elitist to many blue-collar voters, and he would not gain the support of many unions, especially those whose members continued to support the war. Southern whites saw him as just another meddling northern liberal. McCarthy did support civil rights legislation, but it was never his priority, and as a result, he did not have much appeal for black voters. He had succeeded in persuading Johnson of the political costs of the Vietnam War, but that single issue would not be enough to sustain a winning candidacy.

McCarthy paved the way for Robert F. Kennedy, a candidate with an impressive résumé and a compelling story of personal transformation. In the 1950s, Kennedy had established his "law and order" credentials as a Democratic staff attorney working with anti-Communist Wisconsin senator Joseph McCarthy, then as chief counsel to the

Senate's investigation of the corrupt Teamsters Union leader, Jimmy Hoffa. Serving as attorney general in his brother's administration, RFK played a part in nearly every major presidential decision, including the Cuban Missile Crisis, the drafting of civil rights legislation, and the wiretapping of Martin Luther King, Jr. After his brother's death, RFK moved leftward, first as a critic of the Vietnam War, then as a passionate defender of the downtrodden, whether Hispanic farm workers or American Indians, whose reservations he insisted on visiting during the 1968 primaries despite the advice of his staff who saw nothing to be gained by targeting their votes.

Beginning in late 1967, Democratic activists led a "Draft Kennedy" movement, but RFK was reluctant to stand against the incumbent in what would probably have been a losing effort. But after McCarthy's impressive showing in the New Hampshire primary, Kennedy stepped in. McCarthy's supporters were outraged at what they saw as Kennedy's opportunism. Kennedy proved to be a formidable campaigner. He attracted enormous crowds at his rallies, sometimes emerging from the fray with his shirt ripped and hands bloodied by enthusiastic supporters.

Kennedy tried to hold together the fraying Democratic coalition of working-class whites and African Americans. To whites, he promised to crack down on urban crime; to blacks, he pledged his unwavering commitment to civil rights and federal job creation programs. He also pledged to use federal funds to rebuild decaying neighborhoods, like New York's Bedford-Stuyvesant, where he had spearheaded a community redevelopment effort with substantial foundation funds. And over time, by campaigning against the war, he won the trust of many left-liberal Democrats who agreed with McCarthy but saw him as unelectable.

On April 4, 1968, Kennedy's most impressive campaign moment came in downtown Indianapolis, where just before a rally, he got news of Martin Luther King, Jr.'s, assassination. He climbed to the roof of a car and, speaking without notes, offered a poignant, personal reflection on King's death. "We can do well in this country. We will have difficult times; we've had difficult times in the past; we will have difficult times in the future. It is not the end of violence; it is not the end of lawlessness; it is not the end of disorder. But the vast majority of white people and the vast majority of black people in this country want to live together, want to improve the quality of our life, and want justice for all human beings who abide in our land." He continued, "Let us dedicate ourselves to what the Greeks wrote so many years ago: to tame the savageness of man and make gentle the life of this world."[4] When Indianapolis proved to be one of the biggest major cities that did not riot that week, many credited Kennedy.

Few party insiders believed that Kennedy could carry the convention despite his name and charisma. Only fourteen states held Democratic primaries in 1968. The majority of delegate slots went to party regulars. Still Kennedy campaigned with intensity, hoping that if he won some of the biggest primaries, he might sway a closely contested convention. In May he headed to California, a must-win state. There he met with striking farmworkers, greeted voters in riot-torn Watts, and campaigned among working-class whites. At the Ambassador Hotel in Los Angeles on June 4, he celebrated his

Chronology

1966	National Organization for Women (NOW) founded
1968	Robert F. Kennedy assassinated
	Miss America protest in Atlantic City
	Chicago Democratic National Convention protests
	George C. Wallace runs most successful third-party campaign since 1912
	Richard M. Nixon (Republican) elected president
1969	Stonewall protests
1970	*Time* magazine names middle Americans "Men and Women of the Year"
	Happiness of Womanhood (HOW) founded
	Hardhat protests
	Goldberg v. Kelly
1971	*Swann v. Charlotte-Mecklenburg Board of Education*
1972	Equal Rights Amendment passes Congress
	STOP ERA campaign launched
	The Watergate break-in
	Richard M. Nixon (Republican) reelected
1973	*Our Bodies, Ourselves* published
	Roe v. Wade
	Keyes v. School District no.1, Denver, Colorado
1974	*Milliken v. Bradley*
	President Nixon resigns

victory with a call for an end to "the divisions, the violence, the disenchantment" that plagued the United States during the election year.[5]

Early on the morning after victory, as Kennedy greeted workers in the hotel kitchen, a mentally ill man, Sirhan Sirhan, who had been stalking him for weeks, shot and killed him. Sirhan, a Palestinian, was bitter about Kennedy's support for the State of Israel. The assassination of a second Kennedy, coming less than two months after Martin Luther King's death, seemed to many an apocalyptic portent, a sign of a country gone mad.

HUBERT HUMPHREY The frontrunner all along was Vice President Hubert Humphrey. Revered by members of the Democratic Party's liberal wing during the 1940s and 1950s, Humphrey had begun his career in Minneapolis. Elected mayor in

1945, he drafted the city's antidiscrimination ordinance, one of the nation's first. At the 1948 Democratic National Convention, he electrified liberals and outraged the Dixiecrats with his bold criticism of states' rights. Humphrey pushed for full employment policies, which would use government funds to create jobs for the unemployed. He built especially close ties with industrial unions.

By 1968, however, Humphrey had lost his luster. Despite his own misgivings about the Vietnam War, which he kept private, he loyally stood by Lyndon Johnson, alienating antiwar Democrats. As the stand-in for the incumbent, he won support from the party establishment, including big-city mayors like Richard Daley in Chicago, the heads of major unions, and southern power brokers, who could not bear the thought of Kennedy or McCarthy in the White House. Humphrey had not bothered to run in the Democratic primaries, instead gaining support through surrogate "favorite son" candidates like Florida senator George Smathers and Indiana governor Roger Branigin. After RFK's death, it was a foregone conclusion that he would be the Democratic standard-bearer in the fall.

THE SIEGE OF CHICAGO   For all of his confidence that he would be the party's nominee, Humphrey faced insurgencies from both left and right. On the left, tens of thousands of protesters—Yippies, Black Panthers, and antiwar activists—descended on the Democratic National Convention in Chicago. Spearheading the protests was Tom Hayden, a restless young activist who had grown up in Royal Oak, Michigan, a conservative middle-class suburb of Detroit, where the most prominent landmark was the Shrine of the Little Flower, anti–New Dealer Father Charles Coughlin's home parish.

As a student at the University of Michigan, Hayden had embarked on a search for authenticity. In June 1960 he decided to hitchhike across the country, "trying to mimic the life of James Dean."[6] He recalled that he was "interested in the bohemians, the beatniks, the coffeehouse set, the interracial crowd but I wasn't really part of them." He found himself and his political calling in Berkeley, where he fell in with a group of radical students and joined Martin Luther King, Jr., in a protest at the 1960 Democratic convention in Los Angeles. That fall he returned to Michigan, committed to building a student movement for social change.

Like so many white students on the left, Hayden gravitated toward the civil rights struggle. In 1961 he joined SNCC, and later that year he was arrested with seven other Freedom Riders in Albany, Georgia. Fired up by his experience, he helped found Students for a Democratic Society and drafted large parts of the Port Huron Statement in the spring of 1962. Two years later he led the group of SDS members who launched the Economic Research and Action Project, its antipoverty campaign, in Newark, New Jersey.

By 1965, Hayden turned away from antipoverty to antiwar organizing and visited Hanoi to express his support for negotiations to end the war. He helped the National Mobilization Committee to End the Vietnam War (known as "the Mobe," a coalition of about one hundred antiwar groups) to plan its October 1967 March on the Pentagon.

In the months following the Pentagon protest, the Mobe began planning for a massive demonstration at the Democratic convention in Chicago, intended once and for all to discredit the party of Lyndon Johnson. Hayden and Rennie Davis, another SDS veteran, led the organizing effort.

The other dramatis persona in the events unfolding in Chicago was Mayor Richard J. Daley, a formidable politician who controlled the city's Democratic machine. The product of Chicago's rough, Irish Catholic Bridgeport neighborhood, he had spent his childhood with street toughs who fiercely protected their turf, particularly from blacks who lived in nearby neighborhoods. Daley represented a brand of Democratic urban politics that had mostly disappeared: he used his office to reward his followers with patronage jobs and city contracts, while punishing his opponents by depriving their neighborhoods of prompt trash pickup and snowplowing.

For all his rough edges, Daley was an astute businessman who channeled federal urban renewal funds to massive, modern downtown and lakefront developments, pleasing the city's corporate leaders while creating more blue-collar jobs for his supporters. To showcase Chicago, he ordered the construction of huge redwood fences to shield journalists and delegates from the sight of the blighted neighborhoods that they would pass on their way to the convention.

For Daley, the convention protests affronted his street-brawling side and threatened his plans to market Chicago. For months before the convention, the Chicago Police Department's Red Squad infiltrated antiwar groups as far away as New York. The Yippies facetiously threatened to dump LSD into the city's water supply (public works officials estimated that it would take five tons to have any effect); Daley stationed police officers at the city's water treatment plants. The week before the convention federal judge William J. Lynch, Daley's former law partner, denied protesters permits to march in the streets or sleep over in the city parks. To control media coverage of demonstrations, Daley refused to provide electrical service to power cameras outside the convention hall.

On August 28, anticipating an all-out clash with the ten thousand protesters who had gathered in Grant Park, along Chicago's lakefront, Daley dispatched about eleven thousand police officers to the streets around the convention hotel, with thousands of National Guardsmen on standby. Under the glare of television cameras, over the hum of power generators, Hayden and his fellow protesters chanted, "The whole world is watching, the whole world is watching." A phalanx of police officers in full riot gear, most of whom had removed their badges so they couldn't be identified, charged into the crowd, shouting, "Kill! Kill! Kill!" They tear-gassed, beat, and arrested hundreds. Hayden and six fellow organizers (nicknamed the "Chicago Seven") were charged with conspiracy in a case that would wend its way through the courts for five years, before they won acquittal.[7]

Coming after summers of rioting, months of campus sit-ins and protests, and the chaos after King's assassination, the events in Chicago seemed irrefutable proof that the country was at the brink of collapse. If the Democrats could not maintain order at their own convention, how could they be trusted to govern the country? The protests inadvertently spurred demands for law and order. A majority of Americans—and huge majorities of whites—believed that the Chicago police had responded appropriately to the provocations of Hayden, the Mobe, and the Yippies.

INSURGENCY ON THE RIGHT: GEORGE WALLACE   The cry for law and order galvanized Humphrey's opposition on the right. In February, Alabama governor George C. Wallace announced that he would run for the presidency as an independent, denouncing government violations of "states' rights," railing against campus protests, and calling for a more aggressive use of American airpower in Vietnam. "We're gonna have a police state for folks who burn the cities down," pledged Wallace.[8] After the debacle in Chicago, Wallace polled favorably with more than 20 percent of voters. By late September, he polled so well among northern, urban, working-class whites—the sorts of folks who cheered on Daley—that major unions, led by the United Automobile Workers, ran advertisements reminding voters that Wallace had a long antiunion record. Wallace's ratings fell in October, in part because his vice-presidential nominee, General Curtis LeMay—nicknamed "Bombs Away LeMay" by his detractors—had called for the use of nuclear weapons in North Vietnam. Still, in the November election Wallace picked up six southern states, including the four that Goldwater had won in 1964, the best showing for an independent presidential candidate since Theodore Roosevelt's Bull Moose candidacy in 1912.

Nixon and the "Silent Majority"

The beneficiary of the tumult in 1968 turned out to be the eventual Republican nominee, Richard Nixon, who accepted his nomination at the Republican convention in Miami, held just a week after the clashes in Chicago but almost eerily peaceful by contrast. There, to the roar of delegates, Nixon pledged to speak for "the great majority of Americans, the forgotten Americans, the non-shouters, the non-demonstrators. They are not racists or sick; they are not guilty of the crime that plagues the land. They are black and they are white—they're native born and foreign born—they're young and they're old. They work in America's factories. They run America's businesses. They serve in government. They provide most of the soldiers who die to keep us free. They give drive to the spirit of America. They give lift to the American Dream. They give steel to the backbone of America."[9] This sort of populist language offered a respectable gloss on Wallace's vitriolic denunciations of crime, riots, and student protest.

Nixon's nomination marked a remarkable turn in his political fortunes. Just four years earlier he had decided not to seek the presidency, but during the 1964 election, he had begun resuscitating his career. He refused to take sides in the bitter feud between the party's moderate establishment and its Goldwater-led insurgents. Although he was associated with the party's Eisenhower wing, he had a track record as a vehement anti-Communist, going back to his days in HUAC. The Goldwaterites admired his

Nixon on the Campaign Trail, 1968 Eager to reach white voters who were alienated from cities, civil rights, and black power, Richard Nixon aggressively campaigned in suburban areas during the 1968 presidential campaign.

staunch anti-Communism. They especially appreciated that he stumped for Goldwater, rather than remaining on the sidelines, as did many moderate Republicans. Still, in 1968, Nixon was not the top choice of either the GOP's moderates or its right wing.

ROMNEY, ROCKEFELLER, AND REAGAN In 1968, Nixon survived a bruising Republican primary season that was a battle for the future of the Republican Party. He had staked out the middle ground between the favored moderates, Michigan governor George Romney and New York governor Nelson Rockefeller, and the heartthrob of the right, California governor Ronald Reagan. Romney had made his name as an auto executive. He cared about balanced budgets most of all, but he also took positions that put him toward his party's left. He had no love for organized labor, but supported collective bargaining rights and, as governor, signed a law that recognized Michigan's public employee unions. Although he was a member of the Mormon Church, which relegated black congregants to second-class status (until 1977, blacks could not serve as bishops, one of the most important church offices), Romney strongly supported civil rights. But he proved to be an inept candidate, doomed by his shifting position on the Vietnam War. First he supported it; then he questioned it; then he told reporters that on a visit to Southeast Asia, he had been "brainwashed" by military officials. In late February, he dropped out, leaving Rockefeller to make a half-hearted run for the White House as the moderate standard-bearer.

Reagan, two years into his first term as California's governor, emerged as Nixon's most serious challenger. In 1964 he had enthusiastically campaigned for Goldwater, denouncing "the schemes of the do-gooders" and "those who would trade our freedom for the soup kitchen of the welfare state."[10] In 1966, riding a national antiliberal wave, he had handily defeated incumbent governor Edmund "Pat" Brown, a close ally of Presidents Kennedy and Johnson. Reagan blamed Brown for the uprisings in Watts and on the campus of the University of California, Berkeley, where "the ringleaders should have been taken by the scruff of the neck and thrown off campus permanently."[11]

Reagan railed against student radicals, visibly cringing as he described the lurid scene at a Berkeley dance: "The hall was entirely dark except for the light from two movie screens. On these screens the nude torsos of men and women were portrayed from time to time in suggestive positions and movements. Three rock and roll bands played simultaneously. The smell of marijuana was thick throughout the hall. There were signs that some of those present had taken dope. There were indications of other happenings that cannot be mentioned here." And he offered a damning critique of the collapse of moral authority. "How could this happen on the campus of a great university? It happened because those responsible abdicated their responsibilities."[12]

Reagan captured the imagination of the right, but even those uneasy with uppity students and gyrating torsos feared that he did not stand a chance of election. He was inexperienced and too closely associated with Goldwater's disastrous campaign. Reagan entered the convention with only a small percentage of votes. Party regulars—including Goldwater—lined up behind Nixon, who won the nomination on the first ballot.

NIXON'S VICTORY   In Nixon, Humphrey faced a shrewd opponent. Determined to avoid the mistakes of his losing presidential bid in 1960, Nixon hired a team of brilliant ad men and strategists. The most talented among them was Roger Ailes. Only twenty-six, Ailes had made his name by transforming the image of Mike Douglas, a square Philadelphia television host, into a national celebrity. Nixon—edgy, sweaty, seldom photogenic—was an even more challenging client. To burnish Nixon's image as a man of the people, Ailes carefully staged "town meetings." The local media seldom learned that the events were packed with rank-and-file Republicans whose questions were screened in advance to put Nixon in the best light.

Nixon's team produced brilliant campaign spots, with ominous music and shots of angry protesters and rubble-strewn streets that captured Americans' anxieties about civil disorder. One ad, alluding to fears of sexual predation, showed the nude torso of a mannequin. Another showed a Vietnam battlefield strewn with dead bodies. The GOP spent almost twice as much as the Democrats on commercials.

Humphrey had one major advantage. In 1968, buoyed by government spending on the war and social programs, the economy was booming. Unemployment stood at only 3.6 percent, the lowest since 1953. Humphrey and his campaign team played on themes familiar to Democratic voters since the New Deal, depicting the Republicans as out-of-touch elitists. The vice president highlighted his party's long support for So-

The Election of 1968

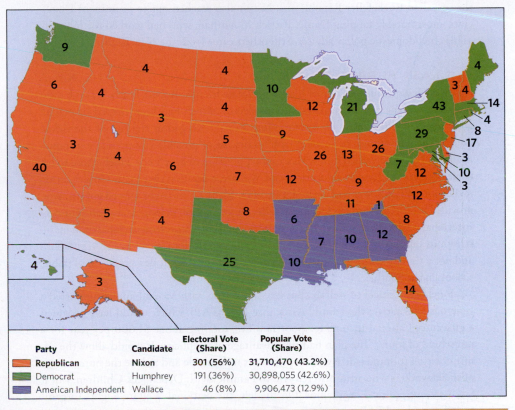

Party	Candidate	Electoral Vote (Share)	Popular Vote (Share)
Republican	Nixon	301 (56%)	31,710,470 (43.2%)
Democrat	Humphrey	191 (36%)	30,898,055 (42.6%)
American Independent	Wallace	46 (8%)	9,906,473 (12.9%)

cial Security, the minimum wage, and pro-labor policies. He promised that he would keep America prosperous.

The election would not be decided on bread-and-butter issues, however. Humphrey got only 41.7 percent of the popular vote. Nixon eked out a victory with 42.3 percent. Wallace picked up most of those remaining. Nixon did not win a mandate, although more than 58 percent of the voters had repudiated Humphrey. Still, the Democrats held on to solid majorities in both the House and Senate. Liberalism was far from dead. Despite the strong economy, voters rejected the status quo.

Nixon in Power

Nixon's election did not immediately signal a rightward lurch. The new president had to work with a solidly Democratic House and Senate. He also had to balance his own party's competing interests carefully. To do that, he put together a political team that defied easy political characterization. Some of his most trusted advisers and high-profile appointments came from the GOP's moderate Rockefeller/Eisenhower wing, the so-called Rockefeller Republicans. Nixon also reached out to prominent Democrats, most notably tapping Daniel Patrick Moynihan, who had worked for Johnson, as his chief domestic policy adviser. Still others came from the New Right.

THE LAST HURRAH OF THE MODERATE REPUBLICANS

Nixon's closest campaign aide and one of his few intimate friends, Robert Finch, was the most prominent of the new administration's moderates. Finch had been elected lieutenant governor of California in 1966, outpolling Ronald Reagan at the top of the ticket. During the convention, he made Nixon's short list of possible vice-presidential nominees, and Nixon rewarded him with a cabinet position of his choice. Finch chose to become Secretary of Health, Education, and Welfare, a position that many Goldwaterites reviled after Eisenhower had created it in 1953. Many on the right viewed government-provided health insurance as socialistic, federal intervention in local education as unconstitutional, and welfare a reward for indolence, but Finch represented a bipartisan mainstream in support of each. He used his position to push for stricter health regulations and, for a time, was the administration's advocate for the swift desegregation of public schools in the South.

Finch was critical of welfare, but in conjunction with Moynihan, he supported a generous alternative, the Family Assistance Plan (FAP), which would have provided a guaranteed annual income for poor families, totaling about $1,600 per year for a household of four.[13] The plan had the advantage of simplicity. It would allow the administration to standardize welfare payments nationwide and reduce the bureaucracy of social workers who administered Aid to Families with Dependent Children. But it faced serious political headwinds. On the left, the National Welfare Rights Organization considered FAP payments insufficient and denounced its requirement that aid recipients find work. Critics on the right argued that it was a handout to the undeserving. Congress failed to pass FAP.

Other moderates joined Finch in the administration. For secretary of transportation, Nixon named liberal Massachusetts Republican John Volpe, who would go on to oversee significant increases in federal spending on public transit and the creation of the federal rail system, Amtrak. Nixon even appointed his former rival, Michigan governor George Romney, as Secretary of Housing and Urban Development, a cabinet post that Johnson had created as part of his Great Society reforms. Nixon, in the words of *The New York Times*, had appointed "a team of moderates."[14]

NIXON'S RIGHT FLANK

Nixon also rewarded his party's right-wing insurgents. Their biggest prize was Vice President Spiro T. Agnew, who had begun his career as a moderate but then shifted sharply to the right while serving as Maryland governor. By the time Baltimore exploded in a riot after Martin Luther King, Jr.'s, assassination, Agnew had become a staunch advocate of law and order politics and a bitter critic of the student left, civil rights, and black power. Speaking just after the riot, Agnew lambasted the "circuit-riding, Hanoi-visiting . . . caterwauling, riot-inciting, burn-America-down type of leader," claiming that "some hard things needed to be said."[15] As vice president, he fired up the right wing with florid speeches denouncing the "thieves and traitors" who led campus uprisings and the "nattering nabobs of negativism" who denounced American foreign policy.[16]

Nixon also reserved places for right-wing activists in his speechwriting and policy staffs. The most notable was Patrick Buchanan, the scion of a Catholic, New Deal family, who vehemently repudiated liberalism and became one of the administration's loudest voices on the right. Nixon's special counsel was Harry Dent, a steely South Carolinian and former aide to Senator Strom Thurmond, the erstwhile Dixiecrat. Dent would be a key figure in helping the administration orchestrate its "southern strategy" to win over whites who were angry about civil rights.

Rebellion and Repression

Nixon had promised to restore order, but America during his first term was far from peaceful. Cadres of activists—many convinced that the United States was on the brink of revolution—turned their energies toward mobilizing the people. Some put their hopes in the Black Panthers, who called for a global struggle against capitalism and imperialism. Still others celebrated the Weather Underground, a minuscule but tightly disciplined band of revolutionaries who plotted spectacular acts of violence to destabilize the United States, in hopes of spurring a mass uprising. In March 1970 the Weather Underground accidentally blew up a Greenwich Village townhouse where they were constructing a bomb. Later that spring Weathermen took credit for bombing the New York City police headquarters. In July, as Weather activists dispersed and went into hiding, spokesperson Bernardine Dohrn issued a "Declaration of War," arguing that "revolutionary violence is the only way" to overcome "the frustration and impotence that comes from trying to reform this system."[17]

The escalating revolutionary rhetoric fueled growing repression against dissenting groups of all varieties at all levels of government. Nixon authorized the secret infiltration of antiwar, black power, and student organizations, expanding the Counter Intelligence Program (COINTELPRO) that dated to the Eisenhower presidency. Local police forces created their own special squads to spy on activists and wreak havoc. Undercover law enforcement infiltrators, posing as militants, hatched violent schemes to frame dissidents, including assassination plots—fueling the revolutionary fervor of activists while providing evidence of their danger to society. Police exploited intergroup rivalries, often goading militants to attack members of competing organizations for their ideological deviations. The presence of informants tore apart radical organizations. Paranoid for good reason, some radical groups brutally interrogated and occasionally murdered suspected "snitches."

Law enforcement officials made extra efforts to pursue black radicals, with bloody results. In 1969 alone, 27 Black Panthers were murdered and 749 arrested. In an incident that generated international outrage, Chicago police, working with an FBI informant, targeted Black Panther leader Fred Hampton. In a police raid early in the morning of December 4, 1969, police shot Hampton, asleep and possibly drugged to keep him from waking, three times, twice in the head at point-blank range.

The year 1970 brought little peace, as activists again stepped up protests around the country, and law enforcement officials responded with violence. The two most brutal incidents happened at the end of the spring semester, during a wave of campus protests against the war in Southeast Asia. On May 4, Ohio National Guardsmen, patrolling the Kent State campus, shot four unarmed students and injured nine others during a campus protest. Eleven days later, just after midnight on May 15, local and state police swept through Mississippi's Jackson State University campus, attempting to disperse an angry crowd of students, shooting into a crowd and shattering all the windows in a woman's dormitory. Two died, one shot by the police, the other trampled in the chaos that ensued. Twelve others were injured.

CONSTRUCTION PROTESTS AND THE RISE OF AFFIRMATIVE ACTION

If Nixon hoped to silence the most radical dissenters, he also looked to calm less disruptive forms of dissent. In May 1969, in response to nonviolent civil rights protests at construction sites in Pittsburgh, Philadelphia, and Oakland, Nixon administration officials issued orders calling for "affirmative action" in government contracting that mandated "goals and timetables" for the hiring of minority workers as a condition of winning federal contracts.[18] Overnight, federal officials monitored hiring at construction sites and soon would do so in defense plants and in thousands of firms that produced everything from paper to cars to missile components.

Behind the affirmative action plan were two of Nixon's moderate appointees, Arthur Fletcher, one of the administration's several high profile black officials, and Labor Secretary George Shultz, a well-respected University of Chicago economist. For his part, Shultz was concerned that skilled workers kept wages high by excluding black workers. He hoped that affirmative action would ultimately drive down wages, especially on costly government construction projects. Nixon saw affirmative action as a cost-free form of "crisis management," hoping it would prevent urban unrest. Some of Nixon's political advisers believed inaccurately that they could win black votes. Nixon oversaw the expansion of the Office of Minority Business Enterprise and appointed several former civil rights activists, including CORE's James Farmer, to administration positions. He also reached out to black celebrities like Jackie Robinson in an unsuccessful effort to create a "black silent majority."[19] Nixon's seasoned campaign operatives had less principled motives, arguing that affirmative action could be a wedge to divide two key Democratic Party constituencies, white unionists and African Americans.

WHITE VOTERS

The partisan allegiance of white voters, already up for grabs in 1968, became an obsessive concern with Nixon's aides. How could they win over people like Carmen Roberts? Pundits and pollsters provided contradictory advice, sometimes shoring up the moderates, sometimes the New Right. On one side were the respected analysts Richard Scammon and Ben Wattenberg, who argued in their influential 1970 book, *The Real Majority*, that American politics "shows signs of splitting into two battlefields: the old economic one and the new social one that deals with crime, drugs, racial pressure, and disruption." They argued that political success for the Republicans depended on winning the "unyoung, unpoor and unblack." Candidates needed to "listen to the center" and be *responsive* to the real majority of voters— without being repressive to minorities."[20]

On the other side was Kevin Phillips, an impatient young campaign strategist who had worked for Nixon in 1968. In an influential *Washington Post* article and subsequent book, Philips identified a "New Republican majority," comprising whites in the South, in the West, and in suburbs everywhere. That majority was increasingly conservative on welfare, crime, and civil rights. Phillips's advice was to veer rightward, capturing the anger represented by George Wallace, and to look southward to capture disaffected white Democrats.

In the White House, Nixon aides diverged considerably on what strategy to pursue. Moderates like William Safire, Nixon's lead speechwriter, argued against the Phillips strategy, making a case that the Republicans needed a national rather than a sectional strategy. But many of Nixon's other political operatives, among them Harry Dent and political whiz kid John Ehrlichman, made a forceful case to the contrary: Nixon would seal a victory in 1972 if he repudiated school desegregation, open housing, and affirmative action. Dent pushed Nixon to win the support of the right by appointing "strict constructionist" judges. Nixon ultimately sided with the latter, bolstered by journalists' discovery of "white backlash."

THE REVOLT OF THE MIDDLE AMERICANS In January 1970, *Time* magazine named white "middle Americans" its "Men and Women of the Year," hailing their "silent but newly felt presence" and their battle for "a system of values that they see assaulted and mocked everywhere."[21] In New York, journalist Pete Hamill, hanging out in bars, had documented the "revolt" of the white lower middle class in an article that circulated widely among Nixon's advisers. And a slew of reporters inspired by Hamill documented "middle-class rage" and "backlash" among angry "white ethnics," a new umbrella category to describe Catholic, working-class residents in hard-luck neighborhoods in Boston, Brooklyn, Philadelphia, Chicago, and Detroit.[22]

In each of these places, the story seemed to be racial resentment pure and simple. Residents pointed their fingers toward African Americans who were moving into their neighborhoods and, as a result of the newly instituted affirmative action programs, competing for their jobs. For them, civil rights laws were special favors to help blacks at their expense. "If I hear the four hundred years of slavery bit one more time," one of Hamill's informants griped, "I'll go outta my mind."[23] Just as ethnics had established themselves in American society as a result of perseverance, hard work, and discipline, so too should blacks lift themselves up, without the aid of special pleading or special preferences, they thought.

THE HARDHAT PROTESTS In the late 1960s and early 1970s, America seemed to be a nation of binaries: white or black, right or left, patriot or protester, housewife or hippie. These combustible resentments exploded dramatically on May 8, 1970, on Wall Street. There a group of youthful protesters gathered to mourn the recent Kent State shootings. During their lunch break, a few hundred "hardhats"—construction workers—charged toward the protesters, shouting "All the way, USA" and "Love it or leave it." Wall Street office workers cheered from the sidelines as the construction workers singled out "longhairs"—those who, more than their comrades, bent gender categories—beating and kicking them, while police officers stood aside. Only six construction workers were arrested after the melee that they had started. "These hippies are getting what they deserve," said hardhat John Halloran in the midst of the fracas.[24]

For the next few weeks, hardhats took to the streets in Pittsburgh, Buffalo, and San Diego, culminating in a massive protest on May 20, coordinated by Peter Brennan, the head of the Building Trades Council of Greater New York, whom Nixon would later appoint as secretary of labor. One hundred thousand white workers took to the streets, waving banners that read "God bless the Establishment" and "We support Nixon and Agnew." The president crowed, "Thank God for the hard hats."[25] He made political hay out of the protests, presenting construction workers as true conservatives, even if most trade unionists opposed Nixon's economic programs and many hated the war.

Hardhat Protests On May 20, 1970, construction workers building the World Trade Center in lower Manhattan demonstrated in support of President Nixon. It was the last of a series of protests that had begun twelve days earlier.

Undermining Integration

How could Nixon's efforts to reach disaffected whites succeed with the administration's moderates pushing for programs like affirmative action for racial minorities, school integration, and open housing? The first test came in the spring and summer of 1970, when residents of Warren, Michigan, a blue-collar suburb of Detroit where only 28 residents out of 180,000 were minorities, rebelled against George Romney and the Department of Housing and Urban Development (HUD). The face-off began with HUD's decision to withhold a housing grant of almost $3 million until Warren implemented a plan to fight housing discrimination. Warren, the mayor pledged, would not be "a guinea pig for integration experiments."[26] When Romney visited Warren to explain the policy in July, a jeering crowd greeted him and he left under police escort. That fall Warren residents voted to refuse to accept any federal housing funds that required integration.

Nixon was furious at Romney, but throughout the fall and winter the housing secretary continued to promote residential integration. Romney, warned presidential aide John Ehrlichman, "keeps loudly talking about it in spite of our efforts to shut him up." Nixon replied tersely, "Stop this one."[27] But Romney did not shut up and would not resign, even when Nixon offered him the ambassadorship to Mexico. By 1971, Nixon's conservative aides fumed about HUD. Pat Buchanan recommended that the administration "tie the hands of HUD," lest Nixon become "the last worshipper in the Church of Integration before it closes down for good."[28] Nixon refused to fire Romney but instead weakened HUD's suburban housing programs and pledged that his administration opposed "forced integration."

SCHOOL INTEGRATION Even more vexing to the administration was the problem of racially segregated education. Under the 1964 Civil Rights Act and the 1965 Elementary and Secondary Education Act, the federal government required school districts, mostly in the South, to dismantle racially separate schools. In January 1969, Robert Finch pledged that there would be "no erosion of the guidelines."[29] The Department of Health, Education, and Welfare would withhold funds from school districts that practiced segregation. Using more than a billion dollars in federal funds, Finch created local desegregation councils, bringing together prominent white politicians, black ministers, and other civic leaders to make plans to dismantle Jim Crow schools.

Many southern school districts complied quickly—forced to do so by the threat of losing federal aid. At the same time, many whites opted out by withdrawing their children from newly integrated schools. In Mississippi, private school enrollments tripled between 1968 and 1970, especially in small towns in the Delta with large black populations. In Indianola, for example, nine hundred students applied for admission to the "seg academy" in 1969, to avoid desegregation.[30] To make the school affordable, local elites raised money for scholarships to help needy white students attend. Ten years later only 10 percent of Indianola's public high school students were white.

For opponents of integration, however, private education was no panacea. Only about 15 percent of white students across the South attended private academies. Most couldn't afford to do so. As districts came under orders to shut their all-black schools—and shuttle black students to formerly all-white buildings—southern opposition to desegregation began to take new forms. Even as they told survey researchers that they were "colorblind" and did not mind sending their children to racially mixed schools, many southerners simply picked up and moved across city lines when court-ordered desegregation plans were implemented, a tried-and-true tactic borrowed from the North.

But in some of the region's largest school districts, whites could not flee. In Nashville, Tennessee; Jacksonville, Florida; and Charlotte, North Carolina, to name three, school districts extended across entire metropolitan areas. In the 1971 *Swann v. Charlotte-Mecklenburg Board of Education* decision, the Supreme Court upheld a school desegregation plan in Charlotte—a school district that included the central city, the suburbs, and outlying rural areas. Finding a school that was not under the court order essentially meant leaving the county altogether. So Charlotte residents put forth another argument: they advocated sending children to their "neighborhood schools" rather than busing them to other sections of town to accomplish integration. Because neighborhoods were deeply segregated by race, a neighborhood school was usually a single-race school. Charlotte adopted a plan that minimized travel but maximized integration, and the resistance died down quickly. By the mid-1970s, Charlotte became one of the few racially diverse large school districts.

BUSING Quickly and fairly peacefully integrated, Charlotte proved exceptional. In 1971 a Gallup poll found that 76 percent of respondents nationwide opposed the "busing of Negro and white school children from one school district to another."[31] It did not matter that by 1970, nearly half of all American public school students rode buses to school (only about 2 to 4 percent as part of desegregation plans). Antibusers defended the invented "tradition" of children walking or riding their bicycles to school, avoiding the charge that they were motivated by race. Black activist Julian Bond acerbically rebutted, "It's not the bus, it's us."[32]

The staunchest opposition to busing was north of the Mason-Dixon line, where women like Carmen Roberts rallied to protect their own segregated schools. In most northern metropolitan areas, black students were clustered in a handful of school districts. Since the early 1960s, the NAACP had significantly stepped up its legal challenge to northern school desegregation, although the law remained unsettled. Robert Carter, a longtime attorney for the NAACP, pushed the courts to move past *Brown* and its emphasis on "intentional" segregation. After *Brown*, federal judges had regularly ordered desegregation when it could be proved that districts had intentionally fostered racial segregation. But if there was no smoking gun that a district had deliberately excluded blacks—even if it was all white—the courts were reluctant to intervene. The existence of racially segregated schools, under Carter's theory, justified state action, regardless of whether school district boundaries had been drawn with discriminatory intent.

Finally, in the late 1960s and early 1970s, several court cases gained national attention. The two most important involved public schools in Denver and Detroit; both would make their way to the Supreme Court. In their argument on behalf of desegregation in the Denver public schools (*Keyes v. School District no. 1, Denver, Colorado*, 1973), NAACP attorneys succeeded in getting the Supreme Court to accept the "Keyes presumption," that if a district had engaged in segregation in one part of town, it would be presumed to have engaged in systematic racial discrimination, unless it could prove otherwise. Denver consequently had to institute a district-wide integration plan.

In Detroit, the NAACP decided to address the issue of metropolitan school segregation head-on. In an important 1971 federal district court case, *Milliken v. Bradley*, NAACP attorneys challenged racial segregation in Detroit and fifty-three surrounding school districts. They argued that federal and state policies were responsible for the "containment" of black students in urban schools and, at the same time, for maintaining a ring of all-white districts around the city. Federal district judge Stephen Roth agreed with the plaintiffs, concluding that state action was responsible for ending educational segregation, and that only a metropolitan-wide school desegregation plan could remedy the persistence of separate and unequal education for black and white students. Roth's decision would be appealed all the way up to the Supreme Court, which would hear arguments on the case in 1974.

THE ANTIBUSING MOVEMENT Roth's decision unleashed a firestorm of protest. Now, it seemed, entire metropolitan areas would be subjected to court-ordered busing. Prominent elected officials denounced the ruling. Senator Robert Griffin (R-MI) proposed an antibusing amendment to the U.S. Constitution, drawing support from both Democrats and Republicans. Nixon, sensitive to the issue, denounced "forced busing" and told Finch's successor, Elliot Richardson, "to do what the law requires and not one bit more."[33] In March 1972, Nixon supported a national moratorium on school busing. Not to be outdone, Alabama governor George Wallace, mounting a campaign for the Democratic presidential nomination, railed against busing as the "most asinine and cruel thing I've ever heard of."[34] Amid the busing dispute, Wallace won the Michigan Democratic primary, sweeping all the majority-white precincts in Detroit, including Carmen Roberts's neighborhood.

On the ground, Roberts and her comrades around the country organized a grassroots antibusing campaign. The very acronyms that the antibusers chose for their organizations—Mothers Action Detroit (MAD), the National Action Group (NAG), and the National Association for Neighborhood Schools (NANS)—symbolized righteous, angry motherhood. Antibusing activists spoke not just as voters or taxpayers or citizens or homeowners but as moms. Who could be opposed to women who were, in the words of one of Roberts's comrades-in-arms, "just looking out for the good of their children"? One popular bumper sticker, targeting the judge who decided the *Milliken* case, read, "Roth is a Child Molester."[35]

NIXON AND THE COURTS Roberts and her colleagues were guardedly optimistic as *Milliken* made its way to the U.S. Supreme Court. The Nixon administration

Carmen Roberts　An opponent of school integration and an antifeminist organizer, Carmen Roberts, center wearing sunglasses, leads an antibusing protest in Detroit in the early 1970s.

slowly shifted the balance of power on the court rightward, especially on civil rights. In June 1969, Nixon nominated Warren Burger, a well-known conservative and a strict constructionist, to succeed the retiring Earl Warren as chief justice. Nixon made special efforts to win the loyalty of southerners. When another Supreme Court seat opened in the fall of 1969, Nixon nominated Clement Haynsworth, a South Carolina judge whose segregationist record was so egregious that seventeen Republicans and the majority of Democrats voted him down. Nixon rejoined by putting up G. Harrold Carswell, who had a long history supporting racial segregation, including turning a public golf course in Florida private so that blacks could not tee up alongside whites. When Carswell's nomination failed as well, Nixon thundered that both judges had been "falsely charged with being racists" and rejected because of "the accident of their birth, the fact that they were born in the South."[36] Seeking to avoid controversy, Nixon nominated Harry Blackmun, a well-respected lawyer and close friend of Warren Burger, to the court. His confirmation generated little debate.

In 1971, Nixon nominated two more conservatives to the bench. The first, Virginia lawyer Lewis Powell, had a strong case. He had headed both the Chamber of Commerce and the American Bar Association. His impeccable conservative credentials as a defender of "free enterprise" earned him the suspicion of labor groups but scarcely enough to derail his nomination. Powell's civil rights record was also troubling. From 1953 to 1961, he had chaired the Richmond, Virginia, board of education. He had distanced himself from those who called for "massive resistance" to *Brown* but did nothing to comply with the Supreme Court decision. When he left office, only two of about 23,000 black children in Richmond attended school with whites. But unlike Carswell and Haynsworth, Powell had not spoken out in defense of segregation. He had criticized Martin Luther King, Jr., not over his goals but rather because he disagreed with the tactic of civil disobedience, which he linked to "organized lawlessness and even rebellion."[37] Powell did not have much respect for the black freedom struggle, but his defense of law and order provided no smoking gun. He won the Senate's approval with only one dissenting vote.

William Rehnquist, an Arizonan with close ties to Barry Goldwater, was far more controversial. His nomination hearing focused on a memo that he had written as a clerk for Justice Robert Jackson during the deliberations over *Brown v. Board*. "I realize that it is an unpopular and unhumanitarian position, for which I have been excoriated by 'liberal' colleagues," wrote Rehnquist, "but I think *Plessy v. Ferguson* was right and should be re-affirmed."[38] Rehnquist claimed that he was speaking for Jackson, but the justice was long dead. Rehnquist's critics pointed to his later, public criticism of the Warren Court for disregarding precedent. Some witnesses also testified that during the late 1950s and early 1960s, Rehnquist had harassed black and Hispanic voters at polling places. He successfully dodged the criticisms and won nomination, though with twenty-six no votes, including those of three moderate Republicans.

The shifting composition of the court bolstered Roberts and the antibusing movement. In its 5–4 1974 *Milliken v. Bradley* decision, the Supreme Court struck down Roth's plan for cross-district busing, leaving local school district boundaries and administrative fragmentation wholly unchallenged. Four of the five in the majority were Nixon appointees: Chief Justice Burger and Associate Justices Blackmun, Rehnquist, and Powell. Associate Justice Thurgood Marshall issued a blistering dissent: "It may seem the easier course to allow our great metropolitan areas to be divided up into two cities—one white, the other black—but it is a course, I predict, our people will ultimately regret."[39]

The Personal Is Political

The mothers' crusade against busing touched on deep, primal fears of a society transformed not just by race but by new gender roles. For the conservative and the conventional, busing represented just one threat to parental control and the traditional family. It was bad enough, as Ronald Reagan had memorably put it, that hippies "dress like Tarzan, have hair like Jane, and smell like Cheetah."[40] But it was not just hippies who were subverting traditional notions of masculinity and femininity. In the second half of the 1960s, many high school students began to challenge school dress codes. In Oak Lawn, a Chicago suburb, girls walked out of class in early 1967 to demand the right to wear miniskirts. Boys began to grow their hair long, in a style that had been viewed as feminine since the mid-nineteenth century. In small towns and conservative suburbs, schools expelled young women for wearing blue jeans instead of demure dresses. Wearing pants was inherently mannish, wearing revealing clothing was too sexual, and both were in their own ways subversive. Civil liberties groups took up the cause of these students, and by 1970, in the face of lawsuits and bad publicity, school districts began grudgingly to accept a range of dress styles in the classroom.

RADICAL FEMINISM Radical feminism offered an even more subversive challenge to gender norms. In September 1968 a group of self-described radical feminists burst onto the scene in a theatrical protest during the Miss America pageant in Atlantic City. There protesters tossed the symbols of female oppression, including girdles, false eyelashes, and high-heeled shoes, into a "Freedom Trash Can" as news cameras recorded the scene. Contrary to subsequent myth, the protesters did not burn any brassieres. The event culminated in the coronation of a sheep as Miss America.

Robin Morgan, a young activist, had pulled together the Atlantic City event, along with members of her new protest group, the Women's International Terrorist Conspiracy from Hell, or WITCH. The group—like the Yippies, which Morgan had briefly joined—was deliberately, humorously subversive. Morgan, who had begun her career as a popular child actress (she appeared in a 1950s-era family show, *I Remember Mama*), was the perfect spark for the Atlantic City protest. She was an experienced—if jaded—new left activist, who had protested the Vietnam War, written for underground newspapers, and embraced the counterculture.

Morgan came to reject what she called the "counterfeit male-dominated left."[41] She had good reason. The left-wing social movements of the 1960s were riddled with sexism. In 1965, when Mary King and Casey Hayden drafted a manifesto calling for the equal participation of women in SDS activities, men at the meeting laughed and shouted them down: "She just needs a good screw."[42] In 1966 women in Students for a Democratic Society rebelled when they were left to cook and clean at the annual meeting, while men drafted resolutions and prepared speeches. The popular antiwar slogan "Girls say yes to boys who say no" offered a one-sided view of sexual freedom: women could either reward the rebellious with sexual favors or be denounced as "bourgeois" or "uptight."[43] Stokely Carmichael's infamous edict that the "only position for women in SNCC is prone," and Eldridge Cleaver's celebration of "pussy power" in the Black Panthers, seemed to condone a culture of sexual predation.[44]

In 1970, Morgan edited a best-selling collection of essays by leading feminists, *Sisterhood Is Powerful*, and with a group of feminists took over an underground magazine called *Rat*, where she issued an angry manifesto, "Goodbye to All That." Morgan lambasted those men who "degrade and destroy women by almost everything they say and do." For her, men on the left were just as culpable as those in power. "White males are most responsible for the destruction of human life and environment on the planet today. Yet who is controlling the supposed revolution to change all that? White males." Change would come only through a revolution "led by, *made* by those who have been most oppressed: black, brown, yellow, red, and white *women*—with men relating to that the best they can."[45]

The phrase that seemed to best encapsulate radical feminism's distinctive ideology was "the personal is political." It had been popularized by Carol Hanisch, another Atlantic City protester, who grew disaffected with flamboyant, media-focused protests. In a 1970 article, Hanisch captured one of radical feminism's key messages: what happened in the kitchen, in the bedroom, and in personal relationships reflected larger power dynamics in society. "One of the first things we discover," wrote Hanisch, "is that personal problems are political problems. There are no personal solutions at this time. There is only collective action for a collective solution."[46]

Off camera, that collective action took concrete form, in hundreds of women's medical clinics and bookstores, mostly in big cities and college towns. Feminists did their real work circulating mimeographed pamphlets and articles

Feminists March for Equality On August 26, 1970, thousands of feminists marched down New York's Fifth Avenue, the largest women's rights demonstration since the early-twentieth-century suffrage protests.

like "The Myth of the Vaginal Orgasm" or leading "consciousness raising groups," where women could meet and share their stories of oppression, sexual violence, and repressed longing. "Herstory" groups began rewriting the past with women at the center, recounting the histories of abolitionists like the Grimké sisters, the workers killed in the Triangle Shirtwaist Fire, and suffragists like Alice Paul.

Nothing was more personal and more political than the body. Radical feminists, for all their differences over strategy, found common ground by focusing on women's sexuality, reproduction, and health. In 1970 twelve feminists, calling themselves the Boston Women's Health Book Collective, compiled a short book, *Women and Their Bodies*. Nancy Miriam Hawley, one of the original authors, had organized a women's health class in Boston, taught by women for women. Traditional male doctors did not listen; women had no voice in managing their own health. "We weren't encouraged to ask questions, but to depend on the so-called experts. Not having a say in our own health care frustrated and angered us. We didn't have the information we needed, so we decided to find it on our own."[47] There was such a hunger for woman-centered health advice, on topics like pregnancy, menstruation, and abortion, that the book, despite its bland title, sold 250,000 copies. It was repackaged in 1973 as *Our Bodies, Ourselves*, eventually going through nine editions and reaching tens of millions of readers.

GAY LIBERATION   One of the controversial topics covered by the Boston Women's Health Book Collective was lesbianism. Same-sex attraction, with all the taboos surrounding it, had been an undercurrent in American popular culture and national politics throughout the postwar years. Gay and lesbian protesters, like those who regularly gathered at Independence Hall in Philadelphia in the mid-sixties, dressed conservatively, seldom talked in public about their sexual desires, and made their demands politely.

Homophile activists, like their counterparts in the black freedom struggle, also looked to the courts for recognition of their rights. Franklin Kameny, a leader in the Mattachine Society, recommended that "discriminatory laws and regulations be tested in the courts" and noted that "the Negro went to the courts and Southerners still don't like him. He nevertheless now has his basic rights."[48] Over the 1960s, encouraged by the expansion of minority rights in federal courts, homophile groups joined in suits defending gay publications from obscenity prosecutions.

One of the key attorneys who developed the strategy was David Carliner, a civil libertarian who had been expelled from the University of Virginia law school in the 1940s after he was arrested for distributing Communist literature. In the 1960s, Carliner challenged "moral turpitude" arrests, fought in the courts for gays who were fired because of "immoral conduct" off the job, and took on the important case—eventually decided by the Supreme Court—of a gay man, Clive Boutilier, who had been deported from the United States because of his sexuality. Carliner, hardened by years of fighting uphill battles, argued that change would come slowly: "Brick by brick, and stone by stone, the law is built. The homosexual is consigned to slow and piecemeal progress."[49]

By the late 1960s, however, many gays and lesbians were less patient than Carliner. Gay districts in big cities expanded over the decade, and although homosexuality was still frowned upon by many activists on the left, gays took inspiration from the tactics of the new left and began to protest. On June 27, 1969, several days of unrest broke out in Greenwich Village, after New York police raided the Stonewall, a gay speakeasy. The raid took a dark turn when one patron, fearful of being arrested and exposed, leaped from a window and impaled himself on a fence below. In the aftermath of the raid, thousands gathered on the street in front of the bar. *The Village Voice* wrote, "The gay brigade emerged from the bars, back rooms, and bedrooms of the Village." The protests lasted for three nights, as angry gays hurled bricks and bottles at the police, chanting "I'm a faggot and I'm proud of it!" and "Gay Power!"[50]

Gay power—like radical feminism and black power—was decentralized and local. In 1973 there were about eight hundred gay and lesbian organizations around the country, most in big cities and college towns. Gay enclaves, like Greenwich Village or the Castro in San Francisco, Boystown in Chicago, and Washington Square West in Philadelphia, quickly became oases of gay life. Their bookstores, dance clubs, bars, movie theaters, and bathhouses catered to gay newcomers and many out-of-towners who fled the still-closeted suburbs and small towns, even if just for a night or weekend.

With homophobia still rife in their ranks, civil rights and black power groups gave a mixed reaction to gay liberation. Many traditional feminists like Betty Friedan warned that lesbianism would erode popular support for feminism. But some prominent figures shifted their positions. In jail in 1970, Huey Newton of the Black Panthers listened to an audiotape in which French writer Jean Genet—who was sympathetic to black power—lamented the homophobic slurs that Newton's comrades regularly hurled. "How would you feel being called a 'nigger'?" Genet asked. "How do you think I feel hearing these words?"[51] Newton, shaken by Genet's heartfelt criticism, reappraised his stance and called for an alliance with the Gay Liberation Movement. "The terms 'faggot' and 'punk' should be deleted from our vocabulary," he instructed.[52]

LIBERAL FEMINISM AND THE ERA Radical feminists and gays were the most visible faces of sexual liberation, and because of that they were a lightning rod for criticism. Newscasts took a mocking tone when it came to women's liberation activists. Eric Sevareid of CBS called feminism a "disease." One of the most influential news anchors, Howard K. Smith of ABC, began a story on feminism with a quote from Spiro Agnew: "Three things have been difficult to tame: the oceans, fools, and women."[53] Feminism was a complicated movement, but in the eyes of the news media and many gullible viewers, it boiled down to "bra burning," man hating, and lesbianism. But radicals, however newsworthy, were always a small minority of feminists.

Many feminists rejected the tactics and ideology of the women's liberation movement and kept their distance from sexual liberation of any variety. Betty Friedan, for one, viewed radical feminism and lesbianism as a distraction from NOW's agenda of formal equality, preferring the tactics of litigation and lobbying to theatrical protests. Mostly behind the scenes, on presidential commissions, and in reform organizations, liberal feminists fought for the full participation of women as equals to men in American politics and the economy. And by the late 1960s, they put their energy into fighting for the Equal Rights Amendment to the Constitution, a demand of feminists since the 1920s, when suffragist Alice Paul had launched the ERA movement.

Advocates of parity between the sexes had long found their staunchest allies in the Republican Party. From 1940 through 1972, the GOP platform endorsed the ERA. The amendment's staunchest opponents at that time came not from the political right but from trade unionists who feared that it would undermine special laws that protected women workers from long hours and dangerous labor. Indifference and outright opposition had kept the ERA trapped in congressional committees for almost a half century after Paul drafted it: only twice between the 1920s and 1960s did the bill make it to a full vote of the House or Senate, only to be quickly torpedoed. Still, there had been some bright moments for ERA advocates, including President Eisenhower's public endorsement in 1958.

For working-class women, equality in the workplace was especially remote. Women trade union activists strenuously fought for civil rights and, just as important, for dignity on the job. Myra Wolfgang, who had organized women workers in the auto industry, was one of the more creative tacticians. She fought to open all-male jobs in the Big Three car companies to women. She engaged in a sit-down at Michigan's state capitol to demand an increase in the minimum wage. In 1967 she decided to go after one of the most visible targets of all—Hugh Hefner's Playboy Clubs—as her seventeen-year-old daughter Martha went undercover as a "Bunny" to investigate working conditions. Feminists like Wolfgang found the very premise of Hefner's operations humiliating (Hefner, she argued, wanted women to be "obscene but not heard"), but she was especially outraged that Playboy's "bunnies," all "bare but not hare," worked long hours and had to subsist on their tips alone.[54] In 1969 she succeeded in winning union representation for Playboy Club workers in Detroit.

But Wolfgang, like many labor feminists, remained skeptical of the ERA until its passage in 1972, not because she believed in the inferiority of women but because she feared that employers would use equal rights as a pretext to speed up women's work and assign them to dangerous jobs. Women, she argued, were protected by special woman-only laws that limited overtime and put restrictions on physically demanding work. "It would be desirable for some of these laws to be extended to men," she testified, "but the practical fact is that an Equal Rights Amendment is likely to destroy the laws altogether rather than bring about coverage for both sexes."[55]

Still, by the early 1970s, the ERA had overwhelming bipartisan support. The language of the amendment, scarcely changed since Alice Paul had drafted it, seemed uncontroversial: "Equality of rights under the law shall not be denied or abridged by the United States or by any State on account of sex." President Nixon and most Republicans backed it. Labor groups hoped it would improve working conditions and wages, and Democrats, some stalwarts like Wolfgang excepted, unified around it. On March 22, 1972, eighty-four senators voted for the ERA.[56]

ANTIFEMINISM   Whether radical or liberal, feminism came under fire in the early 1970s. Antifeminist activists organized against the ERA, rallied against sexual liberation, fought the legalization of abortion, and denounced feminists and their supporters as out-of-touch radicals who hated men and subverted womanhood. They tied all these threads together with a call for traditional femininity and a celebration of motherhood.

The most visible antifeminist, Phyllis Schlafly, had been raised in a large, wealthy, and devout Roman Catholic family in St. Louis. She was a bright student, earning her bachelor's degree at Washington University and her master's at Harvard. Armed with a sharp pen, she became a leading right-wing activist. During the 1960 election, she denounced Nixon for his liberal position on civil rights. She made her name with her 1964 pro-Goldwater best seller, *A Choice Not an Echo*, a conspiratorial book that targeted the Eisenhower/Rockefeller wing of the Republican Party. Written with real flair, it argued that "secret kingmakers" had taken over the GOP nominating process, favoring candidates who capitulated to liberals. Her own party had become a shadow of the New Deal, accepting massive government expenditures, profiting from the welfare state, and pursuing an "America Last foreign policy" that let Communists seize power and rule unchecked.[57] Heavy on paranoia and short on evidence, the book excited right-wing insurgents. More than nine in ten delegates at the 1964 Republican convention claimed to have read the book, which sold more than three million copies.

Schlafly had little patience for the Nixon administration and even less for the bipartisan coalition in the Senate that had overwhelmingly voted to support the Equal

Antifeminists Phyllis Schlafly (*center*), founder of STOP ERA, leads a protest against the Equal Rights Amendment outside the White House, February 4, 1977.

Rights Amendment. She had already expressed her skepticism on the latter in a February 1972 essay, "What's Wrong with 'Equal Rights' for Women." She described equal rights as antithetical to the family, "the basic unit of society, which is ingrained in the laws and customs of our Judeo-Christian civilization." The family "assures a woman the most precious and important right of all—the right to keep her own baby and to be supported and protected in the enjoyment of watching her baby grow and develop."[58] The ERA, she argued, would destroy the two-parent family by undermining traditional gender roles, and most of all, it would deprive women of the favored position that they deserved. Women would lose the protection of men and would be forced to use disgusting men's bathrooms and to put their lives on the line in American wars. It was an argument that bore some resemblance to Wolfgang's insistence on protective legislation, except that it valorized motherhood and housework over paid labor, and traditional masculinity over equality of pay.

In September 1972, Schlafly launched the STOP (Stop Taking Our Privileges) ERA campaign, taking the battle against feminism to the states. It seemed at first, like most of Schlafly's efforts, more than a little quixotic. The ERA seemed unstoppable. By mid-1973, twenty-eight states had already ratified the amendment. But behind the scenes, Schlafly inspired grassroots organizers. Her group trained activists to testify before state legislators and provided them with compelling talking points. She argued that advocates of the ERA were elitists, out of touch with everyday women, with those who worked hard, struggled to survive, and needed all the protection they could get. To religious women—an increasingly key constituency—Schlafly and her allies warned that the ERA spearheaded a radical agenda to withhold protection from the innocent, especially the unborn, and to promote homosexuality. That many ERA supporters had also advocated reproductive rights and sexual freedom only confirmed the link that Schlafly made.

The STOP ERA movement found support among Catholics, evangelicals, and small women's organizations that emerged to challenge feminism and the sexual revolution. One such group was Happiness of Womanhood (HOW), founded in Kingman, Arizona, in 1970 as a counterpart to NOW. HOW founder Jacquie Davison, a mother of six, argued that "housewives have been called leeches, parasites and even legal prostitutes by some in the liberation movement. It's time for housewives who object to such insults to pull on the combat boots and battle those dragging the word 'housewife' through the mud."[59] In 1972, HOW members led the charge against the ERA, testifying before Congress and sometimes engaging in less polite forms of protest. During California's contentious debate over the ERA, HOW sent boxes of live mice to legislators who supported the amendment, with a simple cover letter: "Do you want to be a man or a mouse?"[60]

Carmen Roberts was a fan of Schlafly and a member of HOW. In a 1974 interview, using language that echoed Schlafly's, she criticized "libbers" for being disconnected from "the majority of women in the United States." Photographed in her impeccable living room, standing behind a vacuum cleaner, Roberts celebrated the joys of childrearing and housekeeping. She warned of the dangers of women's liberation. "What happens to a man and his masculinity when you are now his equal?" she asked. Women were already powerful, she believed, precisely because they were superior to men. "Women have always been placed on a pedestal in this country," she argued. "To make her equal is to make her stoop to equality as far as I am concerned."[61]

Roberts saw "forced busing" as one in a series of interrelated issues that threatened "family unity and togetherness," including the ERA, taxation, and crime. In 1973, Northeast Mothers Alert (NEMA), Roberts's antibusing group, joined a legal challenge to a Michigan law that mandated sex education in the public schools. Providing support to NEMA was the Center for the Public Interest, a conservative legal advocacy organization. It had been created, along with the right-wing think tank the Heritage Foundation, in 1973, with funds from a group of Goldwater supporters, among them Joseph Coors, a Colorado brewer, and Richard Mellon Scaife, a wealthy Pittsburgh businessman.

Roberts feared that a conspiracy of government officials, educators, and feminists sought to undermine parental control of their children. "Parents must and do have a right to guide the moral development of their children without interference from the state, from the schools, or from militant women's liberationists," she argued.[62] The battle against sex education and reproductive rights, like that against busing, was an attempt to protect the family from a multifront attack.

However forceful her arguments on behalf of the "traditional family," Roberts pursued a political career that belied her stay-at-home rhetoric. She traveled nationwide giving speeches, leaving her children in the care of her husband. After she was elected to the city school board, she earned her high school degree and went on to nursing school, all while her daughter was still at home. Like so many conservative women who made a career denouncing feminism, she was an unacknowledged beneficiary of a movement that had made it acceptable for mothers to pursue an independent career outside the home.

NIXON'S RESPONSE President Nixon found the shifts in gender and sexuality bewildering. Although he seldom raised the issues publicly, he felt freer behind the scenes to express his opinion that "homosexuality, dope, immorality are the enemies of strong societies." In his view, "homosexuality destroyed" the Greeks and contributed to the fall of Rome, because "the last six Roman emperors were fags."[63] But even if Nixon's views were intemperate, there was little support for gays in the political mainstream. In the 1970s only a few politicians—mostly from big cities, many of them minorities, like New York's Bella Abzug, Shirley Chisholm, and Ed Koch; Philadelphia's Robert Nix; and Oakland's Ronald Dellums—supported legislation that forbade discrimination against gays. Their legislative efforts went nowhere.

If Nixon mostly ignored the sexual revolution, he could not so easily pass over calls for the ERA, which enjoyed deep support in his own party. Even First Lady Pat Nixon endorsed it. But Nixon found himself buffeted by competing advice on the amendment—just as he had been on civil rights. Ever since his first run for office, he had been on the record as a supporter of the ERA, but a lukewarm one at best. As the proposed ERA wended its way through Congress, he sidestepped the issue, neither endorsing the amendment again nor repudiating his past position. The executive branch was split. Some political advisers saw support for the ERA as a way to win wavering women voters; the most moderate welcomed it as the culmination of decades of Republican efforts; and still others were skeptical or outright critical. Nixon's congressional liaison viewed the ERA as "insane," and conservative speechwriter Pat Buchanan wrote, "One prays the silly amendment would perish."[64] For the moment, Buchanan did not speak for his party's majority, but women like Carmen Roberts and Phyllis Schlafly, organizing at the grassroots, would fight the ERA for a decade—and in the process remake the Republican Party.

ROE V. WADE For activists on Nixon's right, the Supreme Court remained a fickle ally. In 1970, in *Goldberg v. Kelly*, the Burger Court held that states could not cut individuals' welfare and disability payments without a hearing, and in a close decision in 1971, it liberalized capital punishment laws. For many, the Burger Court's defining case was *Roe v. Wade*. Roe was the pseudonym of plaintiff Norma McCorvey, a thirty-five-year-old Dallas woman who challenged the Texas state law that forbade abortions. She had lived a hard life. Married at sixteen to an older man, McCorvey ran away from her abusive marriage, lost custody of her first child to her mother, and gave up her second to adoption. In 1969 she found herself pregnant again, and without much support other than a string of lousy jobs, she decided to procure an abortion. She was

Making a Nation

Equal Rights for Women?

From

League of Women Voters of California
Yes ERA! (1974)

In a photocopied pamphlet for widespread distribution, the women's political organization made the case for the ratification of the Equal Rights Amendment. The league highlighted persistent discrimination against women and contended that the ERA would end second-class status for women in the United States.

Feminists contend that woman's anatomy is only part of her destiny and the image of women as submissive and dependent beings doesn't accurately describe their diverse personalities and capabilities. To continue to categorize and limit one-half of the Americans in this country is to deny our society talents which it desperately needs.

When women look for employment, they find that a woman is paid less than a man for the same job; they find themselves in dead-end jobs with no room for advancement. The average woman worker in 1970 earned only 60% of what a man does (a smaller percentage than in 1950), yet nearly 70% of all American women who work do so because of economic necessity.

Implicit in our legal system is an attitude that women are incapable of caring for themselves.

In a nation where women are in the majority and are able to articulate their ideas, it was inevitable that an Equal Rights Amendment would emerge as an idea whose time had come. Overwhelming evidence shows that sex discrimination under the law exists in America, particularly in areas of legal rights, education and employment.

What the ERA will do:

The ERA will create a greater range of opportunities for both men and women. It will stop federal and state sanction of discrimination against men and women on the basis of sex.

Specifically, it will;

—create equal educational opportunities in publicly supported schools for both men and women students and strengthen laws against sex discrimination in education

—strengthen laws against sex discrimination in employment so that workers will be hired and judged on the basis of individual merit

—make all credit backed by federal funds or insurance available on the basis of ability to pay, not on the basis of sex

—provide equal access to military service for men and women and guarantee equal eligibility for benefits

—insure that men and women get the same social security benefits

—erase laws that prohibit women from controlling property, mortgages, or insurance.

Phyllis Schlafly

What's Wrong with "Equal Rights" for Women? (1972)

A longtime supporter of Barry Goldwater, a conservative Roman Catholic, and founder of the STOP ERA movement, Schlafly argued that "women's libbers" were out-of-touch elitists who wanted to undermine traditional motherhood and marriage. In her view, the ERA would harm women.

The "women's lib" movement is *not* an honest effort to secure better jobs for women who want or need to work outside the home. This is just the superficial sweet-talk to win broad support for a radical "movement." Women's lib is a total assault on the role of the American woman as wife and mother, and on the family as the basic unit of society.

Women's libbers are trying to make wives and mothers unhappy with their career, make them feel that they are "second-class citizens" and "abject slaves." Women's libbers are promoting free sex instead of the "slavery" of marriage. They are promoting Federal "day-care centers" for babies instead of homes. They are promoting abortions instead of families.

Why should we trade in our special privileges and honored status for the alleged advantage of working in an office or assembly line? Most women would rather cuddle a baby than a typewriter or factory machine. Most women find that it is easier to get along with a husband than a foreman or office manager. Offices and factories require many more menial and repetitious chores than washing dishes and ironing shirts.

Women's libbers do *not* speak for the majority of American women. American women do *not* want to be liberated from husbands and children. We do *not* want to trade our birthright of the special privileges of American women—for the mess of pottage called the Equal Rights Amendment.

Modern technology and opportunity have not discovered any nobler or more satisfying or more creative career for a woman than marriage and motherhood. The wonderful advantage that American women have is that we can have all the rewards of that number-one career, and still moonlight with a second one to suit our intellectual, cultural or financial tastes or needs. . . .

If the women's libbers want to reject marriage and motherhood, it's a free country and that is their choice. But let's not permit these women's libbers to get away with pretending to speak for the rest of us. Let's not permit this tiny minority to degrade the role that most women prefer. Let's not let these women's libbers deprive wives and mothers of the rights we now possess.

Questions for Analysis

1. What did members of the League of Women Voters see as the biggest problems confronting American women?

2. Why did Phyllis Schlafly think women deserve special protections?

3. Contrast the two positions on the value of the Equal Rights Amendment.

unable to make a claim of rape (one of the few grounds for legally ending a pregnancy in Texas) and found no clinics to provide the service. A young, inexperienced, but ambitious lawyer, Sarah Weddington, took on McCorvey's case, which wended its way, over a three-year period, to the U.S. Supreme Court.

In the years leading up to *Roe*, feminists had moved the issue of reproductive rights to the center of their agenda. In the early 1960s, after a spate of gruesome birth defects caused by thalidomide, an antinausea drug that many women took during pregnancy, a group of doctors and medical reformers pushed for less restrictive abortion laws. They found sympathetic legislatures in fourteen states that passed laws between 1967 and 1972 permitting therapeutic abortions in the case of fetal deformities or risks to the mother's health. Radical feminists—building on their demand for women's bodily autonomy—pushed further.

In 1969 members of the New York chapter of the moderate National Organization for Women and the radical collective Redstockings demanded the legalization of abortion on feminist grounds, arguing that, as in the case of sexual relations, women should be able to control their own bodies. Making the personal political, they led demonstrations and held public events in which women spoke out about their experiences with coerced sex and unwanted pregnancies. Others, like the National Association for the Repeal of Abortion Laws (later the National Abortion Rights Action League, or NARAL), founded in 1969, appealed to deep American traditions of individual liberty, defining abortion as a right. But its legislative efforts were halting. Only New York, Hawaii, Alaska, and the District of Columbia loosened abortion laws. So NARAL and affiliated groups took to the courts. By 1971 about seventy abortion cases were at some stage of litigation in state and federal courts.

In 1972 the Supreme Court heard two sets of oral arguments on *Roe*, and in 1973 it upheld the right to abortion during the first twelve weeks of pregnancy by a 7–2 vote. The court found that while the Constitution "does not explicitly mention any right to privacy," the court had recognized "a right of personal privacy" in previous cases, including *Griswold v. Connecticut*. In his concurring opinion, Justice Potter Stewart stated even more forcefully that "we recognize the right of the individual, married or single, to be free from unwanted governmental intrusion into matters so fundamentally affecting a person as the right of a woman to decide whether or not to terminate her pregnancy." Among Nixon's appointees, only Rehnquist voted no, a harsh blow to the GOP's right wing.[65]

After the *Roe* decision, the abortion rate rose steadily, reaching an all-time peak in 1980 of 359 abortions for every thousand live births. The debate over abortion also intensified, swirling around two competing sets of rights: the "right to choose" and the "right to life." This dichotomy continued to define the debate, even if the majority of Americans in the aftermath of *Roe* saw abortion in far more complicated terms: as a tragedy that was sometimes necessary, as something to be avoided but not banned outright. Both sides in the abortion debate borrowed language and strategies from the civil rights movement. They demanded that the government protect the rights of an oppressed group (women) or a voiceless minority (fetuses), engaged in lobbying and legislative efforts to transform state law, used religious rhetoric to win supporters,

and especially in the case of antiabortion activists, deployed the tactics of civil disobedience and, sometimes, disruption and violence. Nixon sided with advocates of
the "right to life," arguing for "the sanctity of human life, including the life of the yet
unborn."[66]

The Election of 1972 and Watergate

Abortion was but one of a series of contentious issues that swirled around the election of 1972, along with feminism, school desegregation, and backlash politics. Vying
to obstruct Nixon's path to reelection was a Democratic Party in flux. The party's left
pushed for a rewriting of party rules to prevent debacles like the failure to seat the
Mississippi Freedom Democratic Party in 1964 and the triumph of pro-Humphrey
party bosses in 1968. The reformers made the nominating process more democratic
than ever before. They required the party to expand the representation of blacks,
women, and youth and to choose convention delegates from the grassroots rather
than at the statewide level. This time around the party's primaries and caucuses would
have real significance: party regulars would have control of nothing close to a majority of the delegates. The results were stunning: the diverse Illinois delegation to
the 1972 convention included civil rights firebrand Jesse Jackson but not dealmaker
Mayor Richard Daley. One stalwart Democrat complained, "There is too much hair
and not enough cigars at this convention."[67]

The primary season was raucous for the Democrats. Hubert Humphrey, still
tainted from his 1968 loss, ran a lackluster campaign as the establishment candidate,
garnering the support of organized labor but little enthusiasm otherwise. Two senators faced off: Edmund Muskie from Maine, a well-respected moderate who was initially viewed as the frontrunner, and George McGovern from South Dakota, a former
history professor and longtime critic of the Vietnam War. Alabama governor George
Wallace made his most credible run for office yet, winning Democratic primaries in
Florida, Tennessee, and North Carolina, and finishing second in Indiana, Wisconsin,
and Pennsylvania, before he was shot in Laurel, Maryland on May 15. Paralyzed from
the waist down, Wallace dropped out of the race but not before achieving sweeping victories in Maryland and Michigan, where he won every predominantly white precinct
in Detroit, including Carmen Roberts's.

Nixon's advisers were not, however, satisfied to watch the Democrats bloody themselves politically or to benefit from the fissures between the party's youthful reformers
and its old guard. Rather, they did their best to rig the outcome, building on a set of
strategies they had developed during Nixon's first months in office.

DIRTY TRICKS The linchpin of Nixon's efforts to undermine his political foes
was the wonderfully named Committee to Re-elect the President, or CREEP, which
included key White House aides and party operatives. CREEP was ruthless. In
July 1969, Massachusetts senator Edward M. Kennedy drove his car off a bridge in
Chappaquiddick on Martha's Vineyard, resulting in the death of the young woman

in the car with him; thereafter CREEP began its own investigation, hoping to doom Kennedy's chances of ever running for the presidency. Beginning in 1970, it launched surreptitious efforts to raise funds from major corporations in $100,000 increments, raking in about $20 million. It put pressure on donors to pay up before April 7, 1972, when a law requiring the disclosure of campaign contributors would come into effect. A Wall Street broker, under indictment, delivered his contribution, $200,000, wholly in cash, in a briefcase to CREEP's treasurer. Much of CREEP's money ended up in a Mexican bank account where it could not easily be traced.

CREEP also set up a "dirty tricks" operation, using funds to support elaborate espionage efforts against major Democratic Party figures. Its operatives went undercover into Democratic campaigns, stealing campaign documents and planting false rumors about candidates. A CREEP operative obtained press credentials so that he could fly in Democratic candidate George McGovern's plane and eavesdrop. CREEP held fake rallies for Nixon's opponents, letting the real campaigns pay the bills, and distributed incendiary, false campaign literature. To discredit Muskie, whom Nixon's advisers saw as the most serious threat, CREEP operatives fabricated a letter attributed to Muskie that used the ethnic slur "Canucks" to refer to French Canadians, and CREEP spread rumors that Muskie's wife was a loose-tongued alcoholic. Muskie shed tears at a press conference responding to the accusations, making him appear weak and "unpresidential." After that his candidacy struggled. During the Florida primary, where Muskie faced George Wallace, CREEP circulated a flyer asking voters to "Help Muskie in Busing More Children Now."[68]

One of CREEP's dirtiest tricks occurred in May, just after George Wallace was shot. Nixon hatched a scheme involving his aides H. R. Haldeman and John Ehrlichman to plant a story "that a McGovern/Kennedy person did this. Know what I mean? Rumors are going to flow all over the place. Put it on the left right away."[69] Nixon's henchmen broke into the apartment of Arthur Bremer, Wallace's would-be assassin, planting McGovern brochures and, in the process, disrupting a criminal investigation.

The secret White House Special Investigations Unit, created in the summer of 1971, worked hand in glove with CREEP. The unit ran under the supervision of Nixon policy advisers John Ehrlichman, Charles Colson, and E. Howard Hunt, all of whom had been architects of Nixon's strategy to capitalize on white backlash. Nixon ordered his aides to compile an "Opponents List" of people never to be invited to the White House and, more ominously, an "Enemies List" of prominent celebrities, journalists, political analysts, and politicians to be thwarted by any means necessary.

G. Gordon Liddy, a shadowy espionage expert, led many of the unit's efforts to discredit Nixon's enemies. Dressed as workmen (their nickname was "the plumbers"), they broke into the office of the psychiatrist of Daniel Ellsberg, a defense analyst who had released classified documents about the Vietnam War, and attempted to break in to the Brookings Institution, a liberal think tank. Nixon's critics were also subjected to one of the stealthiest and most troubling dirty tricks: the White House ordered the IRS to investigate the tax returns of think tanks, including Brookings, as well as liberal lobbyists, journalists, professors, and other political foes.

THE DOWNFALL OF A PRESIDENT Those crimes might never have come to light had it not been for a bungled break-in on the evening of June 17, 1972, at Democratic National Committee (DNC) headquarters in Washington's posh Watergate Hotel. Five well-dressed men, carrying surveillance equipment, were caught just outside the office of DNC chairman Lawrence O'Brien. Two of them had address books with E. Howard Hunt's name in them. The following day a pair of young, ambitious journalists at *The Washington Post*, Bob Woodward and Carl Bernstein, got wind of the arrests and began their own investigation. But in the meantime, Nixon denied any knowledge of the break-in, fired his aides associated with the event, and behind the scenes—and also illegally—ordered the CIA to pressure the FBI to stop investigating the break-in. It seemed, for the moment, that the botched burglary would be soon forgotten.

Nixon's opponent in 1972 was widely perceived as the most left leaning of the Democratic candidates, South Dakota senator George McGovern. A decorated World War II veteran, former history professor, and longtime critic of the Vietnam War, McGovern had the support of the Democratic Party's reformers and also benefited from Edmund Muskie's tumbling campaign. McGovern was, however, no radical. "I can present liberal values in a conservative, restrained way," he asserted. "I see myself as a politician of reconciliation."[70] He pledged to govern from the middle.

Many pundits and politicians worried that McGovern would not appeal to the Democratic Party's blue-collar base. "The people don't know McGovern is for amnesty, abortion, and legalization of pot," stated Missouri senator Thomas Eagleton, in a widely quoted statement that was unattributed to him, just after McGovern won the Massachusetts primary. Once "middle America—Catholic middle America, in particular," learned of it, "he's dead."[71] Middle America proved not to be very tolerant of McGovern or of Eagleton, who would later be McGovern's vice-presidential nominee, until he withdrew after press reports that he had undergone shock therapy for depression.

Eagleton's quip took on a life of its own, turned alliterative by Nixon's surrogates, who accused McGovern of being in favor of "acid, amnesty, and abortion." McGovern did support amnesty for those who fled overseas to avoid the draft, but he never endorsed LSD or even the legalization of marijuana, and he was opposed to the Supreme Court decision on abortion, which he thought was a matter best left to the states. But McGovern's actual positions did not matter once Nixon ran him through the thresher. The Yippies' endorsement of McGovern and the demand by Democratic delegates, despite McGovern's pleading for "moderation," for floor votes on then-controversial issues like gay liberation, allowed Nixon's campaign to brand McGovern as hopelessly out of touch with the American mainstream.

Nixon won the 1972 election in one of the greatest landslides in American political history, taking all but Massachusetts and the District of Columbia. But the Watergate break-in, mostly ignored during the election, moved back to the front pages afterward. Woodward and Bernstein, the *Washington Post* reporters, had been following CREEP's paper trail, filing reports about its shadowy bank accounts, and getting inside information from an informant nicknamed "Deep Throat," whose identity—

Mark Felt, the associate director of the FBI—would not be revealed until 2005. Felt, whom Woodward and Bernstein had first met after the attempted assassination of Wallace, proved an invaluable source, confirming many of their stories and pointing them to the very heart of the Nixon administration. Woodward and Felt's meetings were right out of the pages of a thriller. When Woodward wanted to meet his informant, he placed a flowerpot on his balcony. To avoid surveillance, the journalist walked, took taxis, and traced circuitous routes through the city. Felt, fearful of wiretaps, met with him late at night in Washington parking garages. "They are underhanded and unknowable," Felt described Nixon and his team.[72]

In early 1973, the Watergate cover-up began to unravel. In January the Watergate burglars were tried before federal judge John J. Sirica, a Republican, a Nixon supporter, and a tough jurist nicknamed "Maximum John" for his willingness to dole out long sentences. During the Watergate trials, he asked pointed questions, sometimes maddening the defendants' attorneys. "I had no intention of sitting on the bench like a nincompoop and watching the parade go by," he later recalled.[73] The jury found the five burglars guilty.

At the same time, Senator Mike Mansfield, the Senate majority leader, launched a bipartisan investigation of the Watergate affair, with a respected southern conservative, North Carolina senator Sam Ervin, as the chair of the hearings. Behind the scenes, Solicitor General John Dean and CREEP member Jeb Magruder testified before a grand jury, pulling investigators closer to the Oval Office. In March a fearful Nixon invoked executive privilege, stating that no one in his administration would testify before the hearings, but he was on dubious legal grounds. In April, just after forcing his aides Haldeman and Ehrlichman to resign, and firing his counsel, John Dean, Nixon urged Colson to refuse to answer questions about the burglaries: "You say we were protecting the security of this country."[74]

In the summer of 1973, testimony before Ervin's committee—especially by Dean— was damning to Nixon, revealing CREEP's nefarious activities, including the plumbers' break-ins and wiretapping. The other startling revelation was that since 1970, President Nixon had recorded some 3,700 hours of conversations in the White House. In October, under pressure, Nixon turned over some of the tapes to Judge Sirica, including one that had been recorded just three days after the Watergate break-in; it included an eighteen-and-a-half-minute deletion. In October Nixon agreed to the appointment of a special prosecutor, Harvard law professor Archibald Cox; but on October 20, 1973, in what came to be called the Saturday Night Massacre, he fired Cox from the position. Further undermining the administration's credibility, Vice President Spiro Agnew had resigned just ten days earlier, on non-Watergate-related charges: he had accepted bribes while governor of Maryland and evaded taxes.

Watergate dominated the news nearly every day, weakening Nixon and, more important, further undermining public trust in government. Little else that occurred in late 1973 and the first half of 1974 restored any of it. On April 30, Nixon released redacted transcripts of the tapes but still held back from a full release, continuing to invoke executive privilege. That claim went before the U.S. Supreme Court, which unanimously ruled on July 24, 1974, that the president's assertion of "privilege depends solely on the broad, undifferentiated claim of public interest in the confidentiality of such conversations." A narrow assertion of privilege, based on the "need to protect military, diplomatic, or sensitive national security secrets," would have been acceptable as well, but in this case, the administration made no such claim.[75] The court ordered the tapes released, and Nixon complied. Facing charges of impeachment from the House of Representatives, he resigned the presidency on August 8, 1974.

Watergate proved a landmark in domestic politics. Public faith in government at all levels had been plummeting ever since Lyndon Johnson's "credibility gap" on the Vietnam War. Nixon's malfeasance solidified public sentiment that politicians were inherently corrupt and that government could not be trusted. Nixon also unwittingly reinforced a broader sensibility—forged in the polarized domestic politics of the late 1960s and early 1970s—that whatever side you were on, government was on the other. For the right, government had sided with the hippies and pornographers, the busers, rioters, and abortionists. For the left, it had abused police power in order to silence dissent, whether by the Panthers or by the Yippies.

That corrosion of the public trust made it more difficult for government, under Nixon and beyond, to respond to the most sweeping and consequential changes of the 1970s: the collapse of postwar economic growth, the restructuring of the American economy, the rise of increasingly autonomous global corporations, the steady rise in economic inequality, and the erosion of American power in the world.

Suggested Reading

Cobble, Dorothy Sue. *The Other Women's Movement: Workplace Justice and Social Rights in Modern America* (2004). How working-class women shaped feminist demands for pay equity, child care, and work-family balance.

Critchlow, Donald. *Phyllis Schlafly and Grassroots Conservatism: A Woman's Crusade* (2005). A political biography of the founder of STOP ERA and one of the most influential conservatives in the last third of the twentieth century.

Kabaservice, Geoffrey. *Rule and Ruin: The Downfall of Moderation and the Destruction of the Republican Party from Eisenhower to the Tea Party* (2012). An account of the fall of the moderate Rockefeller wing of the GOP.

Kornbluh, Felicia. *The Battle for Welfare Rights: Politics and Poverty in Modern America* (2007). How women welfare recipients shaped both a social movement and the Nixon administration's welfare reform efforts.

Lassiter, Matthew. *The Silent Majority: Suburban Politics in the Sunbelt South* (2006). Shows how the suburban residents of Charlotte and Atlanta reshaped American politics in the 1960s and 1970s by emphasizing color blindness, merit, and the market.

Perlstein, Rick. *Nixonland: The Rise of a President and the Fracturing of America* (2008). A sweeping account of the political conflict in America between 1964 and 1974 and the president who made his career by appealing to embittered white, middle-class Americans.

Rosen, Ruth. *The World Split Open: How the Modern Women's Movement Changed America* (2000). An overview of liberal and radical feminists and their impact on American life in the 1960s and 1970s.

Self, Robert O. *All in the Family: The Realignment of American Democracy Since the 1960s* (2012). An account of how debates about family, gender, and sexuality moved to the center of American political debate and fueled the rise of a new, assertive conservative movement.

Skrentny, John David. *The Minority Rights Revolution* (2002). A comprehensive account of how policy makers responded to the demands of African Americans, women, gays and lesbians, the disabled, Hispanics, Asians, and white ethnics for civil rights.

Stein, Marc. *Sexual Injustice: Supreme Court Decisions from Griswold to Roe* (2010). How the nation's highest court ruled on privacy, obscenity, birth control, homosexuality, interracial marriage, and abortion.

Chapter Review

Review Questions

1. How did the Democratic candidates for the presidency in 1968 differ?

2. Describe the events on the streets outside the Democratic National Convention in Chicago.

3. How did Richard Nixon manage the divisions between the Republican Party's moderate and right wings?

4. Why were white "middle Americans" so angry?

5. Explain the shifting position of the federal government on housing and school integration in the early 1970s.

6. What did feminists mean when they said "the personal is political"?

7. What explains the rise of the gay liberation movement?

8. In what ways did the STOP ERA movement succeed?

9. How did the Supreme Court explain its decision in *Roe v. Wade*?

10. What led Richard Nixon to resign from the presidency?

Key Terms

National Mobilization Committee to End the Vietnam War (Mobe) *p. 170*

Silent Majority *p. 172*

Rockefeller Republicans *p. 176*

Family Assistance Plan (FAP) *p. 176*

Weather Underground *p. 177*

COINTELPRO *p. 177*

affirmative action *p. 178*

hardhat protests *p. 180*

Swann v. Charlotte-Mecklenburg Board of Education *p. 182*

Milliken v. Bradley *p. 183*

radical feminism *p. 186*

Stonewall riots *p. 188*

liberal feminism *p. 189*

Equal Rights Amendment *p. 189*

STOP ERA *p. 191*

Goldberg v. Kelly *p. 193*

Roe v. Wade *p. 193*

National Organization for Women (NOW) *p. 189*

Committee to Re-elect the President (CREEP) *p. 197*

Watergate *p. 199*

A Season of Darkness

✳

The Troubled 1970s

John "Book" Ksionska left the bleak anthracite-coal-mining town of Shenandoah, Pennsylvania, in the early 1950s. The old mines, mostly tapped out, were closing, and many of the people who stayed behind were too elderly or sick to work, stooped from crawling through the mine shafts or ravaged by black lung disease. Book didn't have to travel far to find a new opportunity. At twenty-nine, he was one of the first workers in the new U.S. Steel Fairless Works plant, a massive complex that sprawled over 3,900 acres along the Delaware River in the rapidly growing suburbs between Philadelphia and Trenton, New Jersey. Book started in the furnace, a young man's job, hot and grueling, but still a step up from the mining job he had held for a few years after serving in World War II. Book was a proud union man who moved up the ranks to become an officer in the United Steel Workers of America (USWA) Local 4889, and he benefited from the good wages, seniority, health insurance, and a generous pension plan that the USWA had negotiated. Eventually he advanced to running a crane at the plant's dock.[1]

With his paycheck, he could easily afford one of the new houses that had appeared virtually overnight in the suburbs surrounding the plant. U.S. Steel built some of its own workers' housing, modest single-family detached homes just beyond the factory gates. And William Levitt had just planted one of his massive Levittowns nearby, with a wide variety of houses priced for the broad middle class: steelworkers and schoolteachers, accountants and engineers. "It was like a future city being born," Book recalled. "There were no layoffs, just new plants and businesses opening up." Book bought a brand-new house in 1952 for about $12,000. After paying it off for thirty years at just $69 per month, he owned it outright.

"I came along at a time when you could still buy something for a dollar," Ksionska, in his late fifties, told a reporter for *The Philadelphia Inquirer* in 1983. He lived comfortably, taking up golf and spending his time off fishing and hunting. With thirty years seniority by then, his job was safe, and his pension was guaranteed. Still, he couldn't hold back his gloom: despite his hard work, his children lived in a world that was a lot less secure than his. Fairless Works shed workers by the thousands, one of whom was his son Jim. "But someone like my son, where can he go? The times have turned around. It reminds me of the days before I came here, when I was a miner."

Jim Ksionska followed in his father's footsteps. A blue-collar child of suburbia, he took his first full-time job at the Fairless Works in 1974, right after graduating from high school. The pay and benefits were too good to resist—and with a recommendation from Book, the job was his for the asking. Still, the next nine years were rough, as the steel industry faltered and the economy fluctuated wildly. In 1975, U.S. Steel laid off 2,300 workers at the plant; in 1982, it laid off another 3,500. "I've been in and out of there so often, I feel like a yo-yo," Jim lamented. During one layoff, he found temporary work in the kitchen at a local country club, learning to cook. The holidays in 1982 were grim: a local charity gave away about five hundred turkeys to laid-off steelworkers, and as the economic slump dragged on, many relied on a local food bank to provide for their families. It was especially tough for Jim, who had a toddler at home and a monthly mortgage payment ten times his father's. Many of his neighbors had a hard time keeping up payments on their homes.

< By the late 1970s, New York's rundown South Bronx had become a national symbol of urban disinvestment and crisis (*previous page*).

Between 1974 and 1982, interest rates for thirty-year mortgages had steadily risen from about 9 percent to nearly 15 percent. Desperate for a paycheck, some of his friends drove to Atlantic City to work in the casinos; others left their families and headed to the Sunbelt in search of work. But they were often disappointed. The economy was in a deep recession, and if they were lucky enough to find work, their paychecks were usually slimmer than those they had brought home from U.S. Steel.

The War's End

The one thing that Jim Ksionska did not have to worry about was being sent overseas. His father had served in the navy in World War II, and many of his older friends had done their time in the Big Muddy. But by the time he graduated from high school, in 1974, the war in Vietnam was winding down, and the draft was over. The war's long end had begun in 1968, with the collapse of public support for military intervention in Southeast Asia. During the presidential election that year, the question was not whether the war would end, but which candidate would end it sooner. During his first campaign for the White House, Richard Nixon had suggested that he might take a different course of action than Hubert Humphrey and Lyndon Johnson, hinting at a "secret plan" to end the Vietnam War and, much to the surprise of many observers, calling for the abolition of the draft and the creation of an all-volunteer military. "A system of compulsory service that arbitrarily selects some but not others," he argued in October 1968, "simply cannot be squared with our whole concept of liberty, justice, and equality under the law."[2]

Nixon did not, however, have a secret plan, and the war would grind on for nearly seven more years. He and his advisers did not share Johnson's fatal optimism that the war was winnable, but they were in a bind, caught between a skeptical public, a demoralized military, and a vocal contingent of hawks, many in the GOP, who could not tolerate a unilateral American withdrawal. How could the United States emerge from the debacle without appearing to capitulate to the North Vietnamese? In Nixon's first year of office, ten thousand American troops died, more casualties than in any year but 1968. As the war intensified, opposition mounted. October and November 1969 witnessed the largest antiwar protests to date. Nearly a million people took to the streets in major cities calling for a moratorium on bombing and an end to the war.

VIETNAMIZATION The Nixon administration viewed the protesters as a nuisance. But whatever Nixon thought of the antiwar movement, he was sensitive to public opinion. In November 1969 he announced plans to "Vietnamize" the war, which would entail a steady reduction of American ground troops while channeling even more military aid to the South Vietnamese army. "The defense of freedom," stated

Nixon, "... is particularly the responsibility of the people whose freedom is threatened. In the previous administration, we Americanized the war in Vietnam. In this administration, we are Vietnamizing the search for peace."[3] In late 1971, as the United States continued to draw down troops, Nixon suspended the draft, defusing one of the major sources of domestic discontent. By the spring of 1972, about 74,000 American troops remained in Vietnam—about an eighth of the number stationed there in 1968.

Vietnamization did not, however, bring an end to hostilities. As ground troops headed home, Nixon ordered the escalation of air raids on suspected Vietcong supply lines, including the secret bombing of targets in neighboring Laos and Cambodia. These military operations were unauthorized by Congress and hidden from the public and even from many of the president's close aides for four years. In early 1970 the United States launched a massive airstrike on northern Laos, bordering Vietnam. Although Cambodia was neutral, the United States began bombing there in March 1969 and over the first year dropped 110,000 tons of bombs on the country.

While the bombing continued, the North Vietnamese and United States engaged in secret negotiations to end the war that met with frustration again and again, for more than three years. Nixon and his advisers believed that the stepped-up air attacks would weaken North Vietnamese resolve and allow the United States to negotiate from strength. That proved to be a serious miscalculation. "The [North] Vietnamese were very tough—true believers in Communism," recalled General Vernon Walters, a state department adviser involved in the negotiations.[4]

"PEACE WITH HONOR"   Guiding Nixon's foreign policy was the former Harvard professor Henry Kissinger, a German Jew who fled Nazi persecution in 1938, served with U.S. forces in World War II, and earned three degrees at Harvard, including a Ph.D. in government. Charming and, by the accounts of most of his admirers and critics, opportunistic, Kissinger had a steel-trap memory, an unsurpassed mastery of diplomatic history (he knew what Metternich whispered to Castlereagh), and a wealth of connections in both political parties. He had advised the Kennedy and Johnson administrations, even though he was known as a conservative. In the mid-1960s he gravitated to the power center of the GOP, allying first with presidential aspirant Nelson Rockefeller, then shifting his allegiance to Nixon. In 1969, Nixon named him his national security adviser, and four years later, promoted him to secretary of state.

Kissinger's Vietnamese counterpart was the Communist Party official Le Duc Tho. A steely negotiator, he won Kissinger's grudging admiration for his "subtlety, his acumen, his iron self-discipline."[5] In late 1969, Kissinger proposed an armistice in exchange for the release of American prisoners of war, and a concession that allowed Hanoi to retain control over large parts of rural South Vietnam. But South Vietnamese leader Nguyen Van Thieu refused to allow Communists to control parts of his countryside. Le Duc Tho had little incentive to cede ground to the weak and unpopular South Vietnamese government.

In 1972, after Hanoi launched a ferocious attack just across the demilitarized zone separating North and South Vietnam, the Nixon administration again stepped up its air war, hopeful that the United States would finally demoralize the North Viet-

Chronology

1967	Six Day War
1969	Vietnamization
1970	Postal, auto, and mine workers' strikes
	Earth Day
	Environmental Protection Agency created
	Clean Air Act
	United States bombs Cambodia and Laos
1971	United States goes off gold standard
	Nixon issues wage and price controls
	Attica, New York, prison uprising
1972	Nixon visits China
	Lordstown, Ohio, General Motors strike
	Strategic Arms Limitation Treaty (SALT)
	Clean Water Act
1973	Endangered Species Act
	United States backs coup against Allende in Chile
	Yom Kippur War
	Organization of the Petroleum Exporting Countries (OPEC) oil embargo begins
1974	Truckers' strike
	Gerald R. Ford (Republican) becomes president
	President Ford pardons Nixon
	Whip Inflation Now
1975	United States withdraws troops from Vietnam
1976	Jimmy Carter (Democrat) elected president
1977	New York blackout and riots
1978	International Banking Act
	National Energy Plan
1979	Levittown, Pennsylvania, gas riot
	Iranian hostage crisis begins
1980	Depository Institutions Deregulation and Monetary Control Act

namese and bring them back to the table. Over the summer, Le Duc Tho and Henry Kissinger resumed negotiations, and in October, just weeks before the U.S. presidential election, they reached a tentative agreement: the North would cease fire in South Vietnam, while the United States would halt the bombings and promptly withdraw its remaining troops. North and South would be reunified, and elections would be held.

Kissinger even held out the promise of American funding for the reconstruction of Hanoi. At an October 26 news conference, Kissinger crowed, "Peace is at hand."[6]

But weeks later the agreement dissolved. The South Vietnamese government balked, in part because Thieu feared that the Communists would prevail in post-reunification elections. To satisfy him, Nixon and Kissinger offered new terms: as a condition for the U.S. withdrawal, Thieu would remain in power. Le Duc Tho refused, and negotiations halted. In December the air force launched a Christmas campaign against Hanoi, dropping 36,000 tons of bombs on the North Vietnamese capital over a twelve-day period, the most intense air attack of the entire war. Once again Kissinger and Tho negotiated and finally, on January 23, 1973, reached an agreement that differed little from what had been on the table in the summer and early fall.

On January 27, the parties announced a cease-fire, but the war did not end. The United States continued bombing Cambodia. Thieu and the South Vietnamese army, still propped up by American military aid, resisted North Vietnamese control in rural areas, and skirmishes continued to break out. Nixon had promised "peace with honor," but the situation for the next twenty-seven months was bloody, and the resolution disastrous. In April 1975 the Khmer Rouge, led by the genocidal dictator Pol Pot, took control of bomb-ravaged Cambodia; later that month Thieu fled Saigon after a North Vietnamese offensive. On May Day, more than a decade after Lyndon Johnson had Americanized the war, seven years to the day after Larry Merschel's death, and five years after Nixon had begun Vietnamization, the United States evacuated the American embassy by helicopter, and Saigon became Ho Chi Minh City.

New Directions in the Cold War

While the war in Southeast Asia dragged on, Nixon and Kissinger turned their attention to Moscow and Beijing. Nixon was a Cold Warrior but in many respects an unorthodox one. Since the 1960s, foreign policy experts had challenged the conventional view of the Cold War as a bipolar struggle, pointing to deep tensions within the ostensibly monolithic Communist bloc, particularly the Sino-Soviet conflict. This more nuanced view of Communism came from the think tanks, leading international relations scholars, and even a growing cadre of Republicans who had long accused the Democrats of losing China and being soft on Communism. In 1966 the Ripon Society, an influential group of GOP moderates, released a report calling for a "searching re-examination" of policy toward Beijing, including reconsidering the position that Taiwan was "the only 'legitimate' government of all China."[7] It was a message that neither mainstream Republicans nor President Johnson heeded for the moment, but it reflected new thinking among analysts in both parties who had begun to see Communism as polycentric, and who began to argue that the United States should jettison the simplistic Cold War binaries of the previous quarter century.

The evidence of a fractured Communist world was abundant. The Russians and Chinese coexisted uneasily. In 1962, Sino-Soviet relations had worsened when the

USSR sided with India in a border dispute with the Chinese. Most ominously, China and the USSR periodically struggled over questions of territory and sovereignty, particularly along the jagged border that separated northwestern China from the Soviet territories along the Ussuri River. In March 1969 the Red Army and the Chinese People's Liberation Army skirmished along the Ussuri, with hundreds of casualties. The Soviets threatened to attack Chinese nuclear facilities in the region. As fears of a Sino-Soviet war spread, the Chinese and Soviets managed to resolve the conflict, but mutual mistrust and hostility remained deep.

THE OPENING TO CHINA The Nixon administration decided to exploit the situation. In July 1971, Kissinger made a bold gambit. While on a diplomatic visit to Pakistan, he secretly flew to Beijing to meet with Chinese premier Zhou Enlai. The outreach to China was risky because the United States still recognized Taiwan as the sole legitimate Chinese government, and at the very time of Kissinger's trip, it had taken a vocal position against the admission of the People's Republic of China to the UN Security Council.

Mao and Nixon In a celebrated gesture of reconciliation, President Nixon traveled to China in late February 1972 and met with Communist Party chairman Mao Zedong.

Kissinger found Zhou to be "one of the two or three most impressive men I have ever met," and the two talked for almost twenty hours.[8] The wide-ranging conversation was remarkable for its candor: Zhou demanded that the United States grant self-determination to Asian countries and leave the fate of Taiwan to the People's Republic of China. He bluntly told Kissinger that "American friends always like to stress the dignity, the honor, and the face of the U.S. . . . the best thing for you would be to withdraw all your armed forces lock, stock, and barrel and withdraw all other foreign forces and do so on your own initiative. That would be the greatest honor." Kissinger listened but argued for a go-slow approach to U.S.-Chinese relations: "We should not destroy what is possible by forcing events beyond what the circumstances will allow."[9] But the two leaders found common ground in Zhou's description of the Soviets as "greedy and menacing to the world."[10] They agreed on an extraordinary next step: President Nixon would visit China, meet with Mao Zedong and Zhou, and begin redefining U.S.-Chinese relations.

Nixon's visit to China in February 1972 was a made-for-television event, complete with carefully staged footage of the president shaking hands with Mao Zedong and walking along the Great Wall. All three major networks spent four hours covering the historic banquet that brought together the leaders of both countries. Nixon toasted Zhou and Mao: "This is the day, this is the hour for our two peoples to rise to the heights of greatness which can build a new and better world."[11] Zhou offered a more poetic description, praising the two powers for bridging "the vastest ocean in the world, 25 years of no communication" between the United States and China.[12] Later China donated two rare giant pandas to the National Zoo in Washington. Two quite different critics, however, found nothing great about the opening to China. The right-wing commentator Clarence Manion called Nixon's China policy "madness" and called the president "an anti-communist 'also ran.'"[13] And the Soviets considered Nixon's "shock" nothing short of "collusion" with the Chinese, with "grave consequence for the Soviet people."[14]

In May, with the triumphant tour to Beijing just behind him, Nixon traveled to Moscow for a summit with the Soviet leader Leonid Brezhnev, the culmination of nearly three years of behind-the-scenes negotiations. From 1969 to 1972, the two superpowers had engaged in Strategic Arms Limitation Talks (SALT). In 1970 the rivals settled a dispute over a Soviet naval base in Cuba. And in 1971 they reached an accord over the governance of Berlin, lowering some barriers to travel between East and West. The China trip had given Kissinger and Nixon more clout with the Soviets. A deal with the United States would be a counterweight to the Washington-Beijing thaw. Nixon's summit with Brezhnev resulted in the first Anti-Ballistic Missile (ABM) Treaty. Optimistic observers hailed the summit as the beginning of "détente," a warming of relations between the two rivals.

THE COLD WAR IN LATIN AMERICA: CHILE Détente did not, however, bring a halt to the brushfire wars against Communism, particularly in the developing world. There the Cold War had devastating consequences. Nixon stepped up his predecessors' policy of providing military aid and support to anti-Communist regimes, often through covert operations directed by the CIA. Latin America was of particular concern. In 1970 the Chilean people elected Salvador Allende, a leftist and staunch critic of the United States. That year the CIA backed a failed coup, providing money, weapons, and other support to rightist military leaders. Kissinger was particularly worried about what would happen if Allende remained in power. Chile "could end up being the worst failure of the administration—'our Cuba'—by 1972," he warned, suggesting that he would be blamed for losing another American ally to the Communists.[15]

Once in office, Allende nationalized about five hundred firms, some of the largest owned by the United States, expanded the Chilean welfare state, and allied with Cuba. Nixon responded by imposing economic sanctions on Chile in 1971. Behind the scenes, the United States worked to destabilize Allende's regime, providing support to authoritarian forces and encouraging a military coup on September 11, 1973, in which Allende was killed and replaced by the dictator Augusto Pinochet. Pinochet's regime was brutal: the army assassinated a few thousand Allende supporters, arrested and tortured an estimated thirty thousand more, harassed antigovernment journalists (killing one American reporter), and silenced many labor and community organizations critical of the regime.

Pinochet turned the country into a petri dish for a new, harsh economic experiment promoted by the "Chicago boys," a group of neoliberal economists, most of them trained at the University of Chicago. The Chicago boys called for strict austerity measures, the privatization of welfare programs, the lifting of tariffs, and efforts to curb the influence of trade unions. Chile's economy expanded significantly in the second half of the 1970s and early 1980s, but so did poverty and inequality, particularly in the sprawling, squalid slums outside Santiago. In ways that no one, except perhaps the Chicago boys themselves, anticipated, the Chilean economic experiment would shape economic policies in the United States just a few years later.

Economic Shifts

America's rise to global power in the twentieth century was military but even more so economic. Since World War II, the United States had dominated the production of cars, steel, electronics, and oil, exported its consumer goods worldwide, and attempted to impose American-style development in Latin America, Asia, and Africa. But by the 1970s, American economic power was fading. Unemployment rose steadily, as did inflation. American investments flowed overseas, and consumers depended more than ever on imports. Few understood the scope of the momentous economic shifts that were remaking the domestic economy and reshaping America's place in the world. Even fewer understood their causes.

For the most part, Nixon and his administration accepted the pro-growth economic consensus that had prevailed since the 1940s. They began as Keynesians, in practice, if not in name. Government spending and tax policy together, they believed, were tools that, if used carefully, would perpetuate steady economic growth. "Let's build some dams," stated Nixon in 1969, to stimulate the economy.[16] After some deliberation, and facing congressional pressure, Nixon ended his first year by reducing taxes, mostly by increasing the personal exemption and cutting rates for the poorest Americans. At the same time, the administration bolstered spending. Fiscal conservatives, those who called for reducing taxes and government spending at the same time, were for the moment on the sidelines.

STAGFLATION A shaky and unpredictable economy began to erode the foundations of growth economics. Unemployment rose steadily from 3.4 percent during Johnson's last full year in office to 6.1 percent in December 1970.[17] The composition of the labor force also changed. The number of working-age Americans skyrocketed as the baby boomers graduated from high school and college. Women entered the workforce in rising numbers. And by the early 1970s, new immigrants, particularly from Latin America, entered the labor force in growing numbers, an unexpected consequence of the 1965 Hart-Celler Act. Between 1964 and 1970 alone, 10.1 million new workers entered the U.S. labor force, and they were younger, more racially and ethnically diverse, and more female than ever before. Those workers were, however, poorly paid. In 1970, Hispanic workers earned only 55 cents for every dollar earned by whites. The same year women workers earned only 59.4 cents for every dollar earned by men.

Inflation rates, which had held between 1 and 1.6 percent annually between 1959 and 1965, began to creep upward in the late 1960s, in part because of the expense of the Vietnam War. In 1970 annual inflation was close to 6 percent; the increase in consumer prices was even greater. It was not supposed to be this way: mainstream economists held that unemployment and inflation were inversely correlated—inflation up, unemployment down, and vice versa. Pundits deployed a new word in the early 1970s, "stagflation," to describe the stagnant economy, with rising inflation and falling employment.

THE UNITED STATES AND THE GLOBAL ECONOMY The position of the United States in the global economy eroded. After World War II, it had taken the Western European nations and Japan two decades to recover from the demographic and economic devastation of war, even with massive financial aid, including funds from the Marshall Plan. The United States and its allies channeled money to the "developing world," in hopes of bolstering economies and creating markets for American-made goods, but those efforts were halting. And the Soviet bloc regimes had anemic industrial economies, held back by creaking industrial technologies. Russia's factories were mostly state-of-the-art for the 1920s and 1930s, when the country had undergone massive industrialization; Poland, East Germany, and Yugoslavia had rebuilt after World War II, but largely on the Soviet model rather than adopting the new, automated technologies that revolutionized Western manufacturing. And China was still overwhelmingly agricultural.

By the late 1960s, the economic balance of power had begun to shift. Germany and Japan saw huge growth in steel, auto, and home appliance manufacturing. Taiwan, the bulwark of Chinese resistance to Mao, benefited from a massive infusion of U.S. aid. Soon its electronics industry made inroads into Western markets. South Korea, a significant recipient of American economic support after the Korean War, invested in massive new steel mills and also began to compete with the United States.

American trade policy also spurred economic development overseas. In the early 1960s, President Kennedy signed legislation that rewarded American firms for opening new plants in Europe and eliminated import tariffs. American companies got tax breaks for importing parts produced abroad for domestic production. European and Asian manufacturers produced goods more cheaply; their industries were heavily subsidized by the state, and American firms ramped up their foreign investments, with long-term consequences for the domestic economy.

Gradually, the balance of trade—the difference between the value of the goods and services that the United States sold abroad versus what it imported—shifted. The U.S. trade surplus began to dwindle in the late 1950s, the result of economic recoveries abroad and currency policy. The 1944 Bretton Woods agreements had made the American dollar, pegged to gold, the bedrock of the global economy. In the world economy of the late 1950s and 1960s, the strong dollar, which made American exports more expensive, began to bite into the ability of American manufacturers to sell overseas. Conversely, U.S.-based firms and consumers took advantage of the strong dollar to import Asian- or European-made goods cheaply. American dollars flooded into Western Europe and East Asia, where industrial development, spurred by the rapid expansion of import markets in the United States, accelerated. The United States began to pay more for goods and services from overseas than it took in, and gradually America's global industrial dominance began to wane. In 1971 the United States had a negative balance of trade for the first time since 1893.[18]

WAGE AND PRICE CONTROLS Washington's economic, monetary, and trade policies had set the stage for the economic crisis of the 1970s, but Congress and the White House struggled to come to grips with these changes. Nixon knew that his political fate turned on the domestic economy, even if he preferred to put his energies into diplomacy. In his January 1971 State of the Union address, he promised "a new prosperity: more jobs, more income, more profits, without inflation and without war."[19] That year the administration made curbing inflation its top priority. When steel prices rose by 12 percent in January, Nixon threatened Bethlehem Steel, the industry's leader, by calling off talks to limit steel imports from Europe. Bethlehem cut its price increase by half. And to curb high construction costs in the unionized building trades where average wages and benefits had risen 18 percent over the previous year, Nixon suspended the 1931 Davis-Bacon Act, a law requiring that workers on government contracts be paid the "prevailing wage," usually the union-negotiated wage.

The secretary of labor crowed that the suspension of Davis-Bacon hit unions "the way a two-by-four gets the attention of a mule."[20] With his big stick, Nixon created a Construction Industry Stabilization Committee and restored Davis-Bacon on the condition that union carpenters, electricians, plumbers, and others working on government projects accept lower wages and benefits. In August 1971, Nixon froze wages and prices for ninety days, a move that angered the unions but was immensely popular with the public because inflation slowed considerably.

The Nixon administration also faced a currency crisis that threatened the economy. With inflation rising quickly, foreign investors dumped dollars for gold, destabilizing money markets. So in August 1971 the administration undid the Bretton Woods agreement, unhitching the U.S. dollar from gold and allowing the dollar to float on world currency markets. Bankers at the IMF circulated a mock obituary: "R.I.P. We regretfully announce the not unexpected passing away after a long illness of Bretton Woods, at 9 P.M. last Sunday. Bretton was born in New Hampshire in 1944, and died a few days after his 27th birthday. . . . The fatal stroke occurred this month when parasites called speculators inflated his most important member, and caused a rupture of his vital element, dollar-gold convertibility."[21] The death of Bretton Woods dramatically reshaped international money markets. Within months, the value of the dollar fell on world markets by 13.5 percent against the West German mark and 16.9 percent against the Japanese yen. To strengthen America's balance of trade, the administration put a 10 percent surcharge on all imports.

The Oil Shock

Nixon's greatest economic challenge involved the oil market. For the entire postwar period, the United States had been both the world's leading producer and consumer of petroleum. The American economy depended on cheap oil. The rise of suburban America was based on the family house and car. In 1970 more than four in five Americans owned at least one car. Most of them were gas-guzzlers. The average passenger car traveled only 13.6 miles per gallon. The expansion of industry to rural areas, especially the Sunbelt, was made possible by the rapid growth of the interstate highway system, unleashing a massive cross-country trucking industry that also depended on inexpensive fuel. Even the asphalt used as a cheap paving material was petroleum-based. Oil heated houses, powered factories, and generated electricity to keep American home appliances and lights glowing. Agribusiness depended on gasoline to fuel massive industrial tractors. Rural communities sprayed oil on unpaved roads to control the dust. Plastic toys, appliances, and bottles, made from petroleum derivatives, were ubiquitous.

OPEC AND ISRAEL Gas hungry, the United States came to rely more and more on overseas oil sources. Domestic oil production peaked in 1970 at nine million barrels a day. With domestic production slowing, demand continued to rise. American oil imports doubled over the next three years alone. A growing share of that oil came from the vast deposits controlled by the member nations of the Organization of the

Petroleum Exporting Countries (OPEC). Founded in 1959, OPEC brought together Kuwait, Iran, Iraq, Saudi Arabia, and Venezuela to control oil prices and regulate production. As a result, the fate of motorists in Levittown, aircraft manufacturers in Los Angeles, and air-conditioning users in Arizona increasingly depended on events half a world away. By 1973, 42 percent of American oil imports came from the Middle East.[22]

Oil politics increasingly revolved around one tiny country, a nation without any petroleum fields of its own but one of America's most important allies: Israel. Ever since President Harry S. Truman recognized the new state of Israel in 1949, the country had taken on outsize significance in American foreign policy. Many liberals saw the new Jewish state as a humanitarian project, a necessary refuge for the millions of European Jews who had survived the Holocaust and then huddled in displaced persons camps for years after the war. Cold Warriors across the political spectrum saw Israel as a strategic ally, a pro-U.S. bastion in a region where the Soviets were making significant inroads. American Jews, about 2 percent of the population, were initially divided over the merits of Zionism, a movement for Jewish nationalism that dated to the nineteenth century. By the 1970s the prominent Jewish intellectual Norman Podhoretz, on an odyssey from leftist to neoconservative, noted an "extraordinary development—the complete Zionization, as it might be called, of the American Jewish community."[23] His measure of this was the overwhelming support of American Jews for the Israeli state. Some Christians, especially fundamentalists, also zealously promoted the state of Israel. They saw the Jews as the legitimate heirs to the biblical Promised Land, and their resettlement and the ensuing regional conflict as the unfolding of God's plan. This unlikely coalition propelled bipartisan support for Israel. By 1974, Israel was the largest recipient of American foreign aid.

Israel's Arab neighbors fiercely contested its boundaries and viewed the new state as illegitimate. The 1947–49 war for Israeli independence had led to the dispossession of millions of Palestinians, whose land and homes Israel appropriated for new settlements. Palestinians called the period *al-Naqba* or the Catastrophe. Border skirmishes, especially with Syria, were frequent in the 1950s and 1960s. Egypt and Israel disputed control over the Sinai Peninsula. Displaced Palestinians based in the West Bank (an area to the west of the Jordan River, controlled by the Kingdom of Jordan) challenged Israeli authority and demanded the right to return to their lands.

The struggles culminated in Israel's Six Day War with Egypt, Jordan, and Syria, in June 1967. Israel took control over most of the Sinai, East Jerusalem, including Jerusalem's Old City, the West Bank, and the Golan Heights. In the aftermath of the war, hundreds of thousands of Palestinian refugees fled to Jordan. The Israeli occupation of the Sinai, which had been in Egyptian hands for millennia, fueled already-intense anti-Israeli sentiment throughout the region. Israel drew new boundaries, and the tensions in the region continued.

A little more than six years later, on October 6, 1973, on the Jewish holy day of Yom Kippur, Egyptian forces advanced across the Suez Canal into the Israeli-controlled Sinai Peninsula, and the Syrians raided the contested Golan Heights, catching the Israelis off guard. Nearly three weeks of fighting ensued; Israel pushed back the Syrians in just a few days, then advanced north into Syria and bombed Damascus. The struggle with Egypt was longer and bloodier: it took a few weeks and substantial American military support to push Egyptian troops back to the Suez. Many surrounding Arab countries sent troops to support the Egyptians and Syrians, and both the United States and the Soviet Union provided substantial military aid to their respective allies. Tensions between the Americans and the Soviets were greater than they had been since the Cuban Missile Crisis, threatening to unravel détente. The Pentagon put American troops on a worldwide alert. Over the next several years, the United States would substantially increase its military support of Israel.

THE OIL CRISIS Although the war ended with a tenuous cease-fire in late October, Saudi Arabia used its power over oil production to punish the United States for its support for Israel. On October 16 the Arab oil states raised oil prices dramatically and the next day announced that they would curtail oil production by 5 percent per month, escalating future oil prices. On October 20, as the United States stepped up military support for Israel, OPEC announced an oil embargo, banning oil shipments to the United States and several of its allies. The embargo, which would last until March 1974, brought disastrous results.

In early November 1973, as the embargo began to take effect, President Richard Nixon addressed the nation in prime time, presenting "a very stark fact: We are heading toward the most acute shortages of energy since World War II."[24] He encouraged Americans to turn down their thermostats by six degrees to conserve energy. He asked airlines to reduce flights by 10 percent. Announcing "Project Independence," to free America from its reliance on foreign oil, Nixon called for reducing the speed limit on interstate highways to 55 miles per hour, and he halted a federal program to convert coal-fueled electrical generation plants to oil. The Senate nearly passed legislation calling for the coupon rationing of gasoline, just as the country had rationed consumer goods during World War II. To prepare, the White House ordered the Bureau of Printing and Engraving to print between ten and fifteen billion coupons.

The oil embargo hit home for Book and Jim Ksionska and their neighbors. Between Thanksgiving and the New Year, the subdivisions around Fairless Hills usually glowed with Christmas lights. Residents festooned their rooflines with brightly colored bulbs and their shrubbery with blinking white lights that looked like snowflakes. But "Christmas 1973," reported a local newspaper, "was a season of darkness."[25] Everyone switched off the lights to save energy.

December was a dark month in other respects as well. Every business that depended on oil—and that was nearly all of them—suffered. Crude oil prices had risen a stunning 470 percent since January 1973. The Big Three auto companies and major airlines announced layoffs just before the holidays; trucking companies reduced shipments during the peak holiday season; farmers halted plowing. School districts closed for winter break early, to save on fuel costs. And as gas prices rose, the cost of just about everything else did too.

The Oil Crisis Service stations around the country, like this one in Portland, Oregon, ran out of gas during the OPEC oil embargo that began in October 1973.

Christmas 1973 was just the beginning of a bleak winter. The supply of gas dropped and prices skyrocketed. Customers, hundreds deep, waited for hours in line to fill up their cars. Gas station attendants came to work with pistols to protect themselves during the brawls that regularly broke out among impatient commuters cutting the lines. "These people are like animals foraging for food," stated a gas station attendant. "If you can't sell them gas, they'll threaten to beat you up, wreck your station, run you over with a car."[26] Gas siphons became popular items, the fuel tanks of cars parked overnight on city streets the targets. In one prominent heist, bandits "gasjacked" an ARCO tanker at gunpoint, stealing all 8,500 gallons of fuel and abandoning the truck.[27]

The situation grew worse in the New Year. In February 1974 about 100,000 independent truckers, demanding a reduction in gas prices, went on strike, blockading the nation's highways for eleven days. Using their citizens' band (CB) radios to coordinate protest convoys—and to dodge law enforcement officials—the truckers were the most visible face of rebellion against the oil shock. With food deliveries cut off, grocery store shelves quickly emptied. Eventually several state governors deployed National Guard units to keep the roads open, prevent violence at roadside rest areas, and restore shipping.[28]

In the meantime, gas grew even scarcer: about one-fifth of all American service stations in February had none at all. To control the lines, the nation implemented a gas rationing system: gas stations would be open on alternate days to cars with license plates ending in even and odd numbers. The long lines were one symbol of changing times, but for many Americans the independent truckers became heroes of resistance. Over the next few years, CB radios exploded in popularity and songs like C. W. Mc-Call's 1975 hit "Convoy" celebrated "a thousand screamin' trucks" who broke the speed limit and faced off "smokies" (police officers) "as thick as bugs on a bumper" as they barreled across the country.[29]

Recession and Disillusionment

The oil shock plunged the domestic economy—already shaky—into what observers called the "great recession." Unemployment rose to 5.4 percent in January 1974, and even more unsettling, inflation skyrocketed, reaching 12 percent. The unprecedented combination weakened consumer confidence and led to sharp rises in joblessness. The stock market collapsed, losing 37 percent of its value between March and December 1974.

The instability of the markets coincided with instability in the U.S. government. When President Gerald Ford assumed office after Nixon's resignation on August 9, 1974, he sought, in vain, to restore confidence in both government and the economy. On September 8, Ford attempted to put the crimes of his predecessor behind him when he pardoned Richard Nixon, shielding the former president from any Watergate-related criminal charges. In awkward prose, Ford told Americans that "my conscience tells me clearly and certainly that I cannot prolong the bad dreams that continue to reopen a chapter that is closed."[30] The controversial decision doomed his long-term political prospects but allowed him to turn his attention to the other unfinished business that Nixon had left him: the cratering economy.

WHIP INFLATION NOW A little more than a month after he pardoned Nixon, Ford took the occasion of one of his first major policy speeches to rally the country around a campaign to "Whip Inflation Now," calling for a nationwide voluntary effort to conserve energy, eliminate waste, and support the administration's efforts to stimulate investment. "Through the courtesy of such volunteers from the communication and media fields," stated Ford, "a very simple enlistment form will appear in many of tomorrow's newspapers along with the symbol of this new mobilization, which I am wearing on my lapel. It bears the single word WIN. I think that tells it all. I will call upon every American to join in this massive mobilization and stick with it until we do win as a nation and as a people."[31] The branding effort was a success—but in ways that Ford had not intended. Hard-nosed critics, like Federal Reserve head Alan Greenspan, denounced WIN as a publicity stunt that "didn't reflect any practical, conceivable policy that could be implemented." He doubted that any voluntary efforts would curb inflation.[32] But still, the White House issued hundreds of thousands of red and white lapel buttons that read WIN. Chain stores promoted WIN in their ads. Inflation rates continued to rise.

"A PROFOUND SENSE OF DIS-ILLUSIONMENT" To pessimists, and there were many, the oil shock, raging inflation, and high unemployment symbolized a larger problem facing the country: the American century, a long period of unsurpassed economic and diplomatic power, seemed to be over. In June 1974 a Gallup poll had found a "profound sense of disillusionment, even despondency," among Americans. For the first time, survey researchers reported that a majority of Americans "considered their future bleaker than their past."[33] Americans were turning inward, expressing less concern about America's engagement in the world and more about domestic problems. That inward turn came at a moment when America's place in the world was in profound flux. The economy was shaped, more than it had been in decades, by shifts in the global economy. Kokomo was affected by Kuwait; Toledo by Toyota City; Levittown by London.

Whip Inflation Now President Gerald R. Ford announces his anti-inflation campaign on October 8, 1974, holding up the prototype for the Whip Inflation Now lapel pins that the government circulated by the millions to publicize the effort.

Jim Ksionska might not have taken the job at Fairless Works if he had known the troubles that were undermining the American steel industry. Given the state of the economy in 1974, when he graduated from high school, he considered himself lucky to get a union job, close to home. But steelmaking, one of America's most formidable industries since the nineteenth century, was a bellwether of the sweeping changes in the global economy. Steel, used in skyscrapers and bridges, car chassis and engines, forklifts and forks, toasters and turntables, had made the fortunes of some of America's wealthiest dynasties, including the Mellons, Carnegies, and Fricks. Steel manufacturing had also indelibly shaped America's landscape, from the iron mines in northern Minnesota and Montana to the coal seams in Pennsylvania, West Virginia, and Kentucky. Its impact could be seen in the vast shroud of soot that turned Pittsburgh's day into night. Steel's power showed in the vast mills, like Book and Jim Ksionska's Fairless Works, that extended in an industrial belt from Baltimore to Bethlehem to Pittsburgh to Youngstown, Cleveland, Detroit, Gary, and Chicago.

The rise of global competition—aided and abetted by American trade and currency policy—pushed domestic steel into crisis. European steel firms sometimes sold their product (already relatively cheap because of the strong dollar) at a loss in the United

States to undercut their domestic competitors. American-based steel manufacturers lobbied unsuccessfully for trade protections and, in the meantime, introduced new labor-saving technologies and cut their workforces to remain profitable. Still, the market share of steel produced abroad rose steadily. By 1977 about one-fifth of American steel was imported, and many of the old cities with steel mills began to lose population and rot away.

One of the casualties—it died a slow death—was the Fairless Works plant. Built in 1951, it employed between 7,000 and 10,000 workers during its first two decades. But between 1975 and 1982, its managers fired a total of 5,800 of those workers; the remaining few thousand, including Book Ksionska, took wage cuts. In 1985, Fairless Works employees walked out, subsisting on the union strike fund at $60 per week and winning only token concessions. Book, protected by seniority, hung on to his job until retiring in 1988. Within a few years, the plant had almost completely shut down.

The Fairless Works story played out with grim regularity throughout industrial America. Shipbuilding moved overseas to the Baltic. Auto parts suppliers jumped to Canada, taking advantage of the weak Canadian dollar. The auto industry, trapped in its big car/big oil paradigm, began to lose market share to Japanese and European competitors who built small, fuel-efficient cars. "The man with a wife and four kids and a shaggy dog can't get into a Vega," remarked Mack Worden, GM's vice-president of marketing in 1974, explaining his company's reluctance to expand its line of compact cars.[34] He misunderstood both family structure (families were shrinking) and the demand for fuel efficiency in an era of economic trouble.

By the mid-1970s, as the auto industry continued to reel from competition, American Motors, the weakest of the industry's firms, put out the Gremlin and the Hornet, two small cars—one with special denim interiors—that failed miserably. In 1972, Ford pioneered its compact Pinto, which had a defect that sometimes caused the car to explode when hit from behind. General Motors began working on a successor to the Vega, the tinier and tinnier Chevette, introduced in 1979. But the interventions proved too timid. American Motors struggled for survival and eventually went defunct in 1987. Chrysler declared bankruptcy in 1979 and had to be bailed out by the federal government. General Motors and Ford steadily lost market share to Toyota, Datsun, and Volkswagen and in the process shed tens of thousands of jobs and closed dozens of plants to remain viable.

ECONOMIC RESTRUCTURING AND LABOR UNREST American industries struggled mightily in the new global economy of the 1970s, haltingly adapting to price controls, new currency rules, and intensifying international competition. As profit margins diminished, companies began to speed up production and cut labor expenses. The goal was straightforward: to produce more goods at less expense. For decades, companies had been experimenting with new technologies to replace workers with machines. The advent of new computer technologies spurred the process. Assembly lines, once bustling with life, grew increasingly mechanized. And low-skill, entry-level jobs began to disappear. At the same time, managers worked the remaining workers harder. In many industries, companies pitted two plants against each other, a process called parallel production. The plant that achieved a higher output would get additional resources; the loser would face cutbacks and sometimes be closed.

Workers responded angrily. Between 1970 and 1974, America saw more labor strife than in any period since the Great Depression. Nearly nine million workers, including Book Ksionska, walked off their jobs in 1,670 separate strikes. In March 1970 about 180,000 postal workers nationwide struck for two weeks, leading to the deployment of National Guard units to deliver mail. The following month 40,000 coal miners stopped working, demanding better conditions and health care coverage. Many of them suffered work-related injuries and debilitating chronic diseases, like black lung, which came from breathing coal dust. That fall the United Automobile Workers led a massive, two-month-long strike against General Motors. The auto manufacturer lost $1 billion in profits, and the UAW nearly went bankrupt. But in the end, the union achieved many of its goals, including higher wages and a "thirty years and out" deal that allowed workers who had been with the company three decades or more to retire with full pensions.

The wave of labor unrest was not simply confined to heavy manufacturing. The United Farm Workers, which had spent years organizing the mostly Mexican field hands working the orchards and vineyards of California's Central Valley, stepped up its call for an international grape boycott, collaborating with churches and student groups and unions. In 1970 they succeeded in forcing California grape growers to offer better wages and working conditions.

None of those strikes seemed as much a sign of the times, however, as the March 1972 shutdown of the Chevrolet Vega plant in Lordstown, Ohio. Lordstown's workers were young—their average age was only twenty-four—and they lived in a culture infused with youthful rebellion. To a local journalist, they looked just like hippies: "Many wear their hair shoulder length, have grown mustaches or beards and come to work in hip-hugging, bell-bottomed trousers. They are probably better educated than any generation of workers in the history of American industry. They were taught to question traditional values and encouraged to stand up and be counted." Whereas many of the old auto plants were segregated by race, black and white workers mingled on the shop floor at Lordstown, and many would drink and smoke together after work.[35]

Journalists called Lordstown the "workers' Woodstock," but there was not a lot of love on the assembly line. The General Motors Assembly Division (GMAD), nicknamed "Get Mean and Destroy" by assembly workers, set production quotas at 100 Vegas an hour, compared to 55 cars an hour at most auto plants. With a partially assembled car passing by workers every thirty-five seconds, there was no time to pause. Facing pressure to move at almost superhuman speed for eight hours (or more with overtime), workers resisted, deliberately slowing down the assembly line, challenging the authority of supervisors, and sometimes sabotaging cars. Speedup was a failure: many Vegas came off the assembly line shoddily assembled or with missing parts. Workers "just want to be treated with dignity," stated Gary Bryner, the twenty-nine-year-old

"Dangerous Curve" A cartoon protesting the speedup of assembly lines at the Chevrolet Vega plant in Lordstown, Ohio. In March 1972, angry Lordstown workers walked out in a three-week strike to demand better working conditions.

president of the Lordstown UAW local. "That's not asking a hell of a lot."[36]

Finally, in March 1972, after months of unrest, Lordstown workers walked out for three weeks in one of the most acrimonious strikes of the era. In the end, GMAD increased the size of the workforce and reinstated workers who had been fired for disciplinary reasons. Vega production, a little slower, went on. The work stoppage cost General Motors nearly $150 million and was, for most commentators, a sign of "blue-collar blues," the nagging insecurity and discontent of speedup in an age of growing international competition.[37]

Speedup was only one tool to reduce labor costs. Another tried and true method was to relocate factories to low-wage regions, places where workers were not unionized, taxes were low, and local governments were lax in their enforcement of workplace safety laws. Since 1950 capital had been fleeing the heartland of American industrialism, the old cities of the Northeast and the Midwest, for the low-tax, antiunion South, aided by a massive reorientation of federal defense and infrastructure spending toward the Sunbelt. Powerful southern Democrats had long used the power of their seniority in Congress to steer appropriations toward their districts. Places like Phoenix, Arizona, and Orange County, California, once economic backwaters, became major centers of defense production. Old defense centers like Detroit and Chicago were hobbled. Massive federal subsidies to the oil industry, which grew under Eisenhower, Kennedy, and Johnson, fueled economic growth in Texas and Louisiana, turning sleepy Houston into a boomtown. And new shipping technologies—particularly container shipping by truck, which required access to superhighways—led to the decline of the dense, crowded ports of Brooklyn, Philadelphia, Baltimore, New Orleans, and Oakland. A shipping boom remade the part of the swampy Meadowlands of northern New Jersey into the Port of Newark. Likewise, Newport News, Virginia, and the port of Los Angeles took advantage of abundant land, rail lines, and access to interstate highways to expand. But these new megaports, heavily mechanized, did not create enough jobs to replace those that disappeared from the rotting old wharves.

By the early 1970s, many firms were looking even further afield to cut costs. Major textile firms set up new production facilities in the Dominican Republic and Hong Kong. Electronics manufacturers, in search of cheap female labor and loose regulations, began to expand plants abroad. RCA, the major television, radio, and phonograph producer in the United States, had shifted production several times. During World War II, it had cut employment in its flagship Camden, New Jersey, plant and moved jobs to Bloomington, Indiana, lured by low taxes and a ready supply of women workers from the region's declining farm economy. In the mid-1960s, RCA opened a plant in Memphis, Tennessee, a state with few union workers and low wages. And in 1968 it opened a massive facility in Ciudad Juárez, Mexico, part of Mexico's free trade region, just across the Rio Grande from El Paso, Texas. Donald Baerresen, an economist who promoted the Mexican border to American firms, highlighted the "large supplies of relatively inexpensive, unskilled labor located close to the United States."[38] By 1973, 168 other American electronics firms had located just south of the border. Left behind were tens of thousands of American workers living in places with the shells of old, redbrick factory buildings where light bulbs, radios, and televisions had once been made.

The Environmental Crisis

For a century and a half, the rise of cities and factories, industry and suburbs, railroads and personal cars had altered the American landscape. Each of these economic and population shifts had dramatic environmental consequences. Book Ksionska had left behind the declining anthracite region of Pennsylvania, with its huge slag heaps, for the brand-new Fairless Works, which had replaced thousands of acres of farms and wetlands with parking lots, furnaces, and warehouses. He traded up one environmental disaster for another. Lifeless ponds that held the steaming water discharges from the plant's cooling system now surrounded the site of the steel mill.

The nearby Fairless Hills and Levittown neighborhoods, like most American suburbs, were an environmental mess. Developers bulldozed forests and meadows to build new housing. Residents poured tons of fertilizer on their lawns, which ran into local streams, leading to massive algae blooms that sucked oxygen out of the water. They sprayed insecticides to kill off lawn-eating bugs and used DDT to exterminate the mosquitoes that made summers miserable. In a 1962 best seller, *Silent Spring*, Rachel Carson described an environmental disaster that was painfully close to home: right in the backyard. DDT was decimating suburban bird populations. And what about people? Carson issued a stark warning. "If we are going to live so intimately with these chemicals—eating and drinking them, taking them into the very marrow of our bones—we had better know something about their nature and their power."[39]

Over the postwar years, more and more Americans came into contact with wilderness, industrial, and postindustrial landscapes, usually through their car windows. What they saw ranged from the sublime to the degraded. The advent of the interstate

Pollution In the early 1970s, Congress enacted strict environmental regulations intended to curb air and water pollution at industrial sites like the Jones and Laughlin steel plant in Aliquippa, Pennsylvania, on the Ohio River, pictured here in September 1973.

highway brought more Americans than ever into remote forests, seashores, and mountains. Road trips also took them through some of the grim manufacturing zones in places like Cleveland, so polluted that the Cuyahoga River, filled with flammable chemicals, caught on fire in 1948, in 1952, and again in 1969. In Los Angeles, "acrid blue-gray air" would descend over the metropolitan area for weeks at a time, obscuring the beautiful mountain views and causing what doctors called "smog disease," with symptoms including burning throats and a shortness of breath.[40] In the suburbs, it was possible to see firsthand the transformations wrought by the bulldozer in the countryside. "They paved paradise to put up a parking lot," sang Joni Mitchell, in a popular hit.[41] Over the course of the 1960s and 1970s, the suburbs became the hotbed of "quality of life" politics, which included demands that open land be protected from sprawl.

From steel mills to fast-food restaurants, from burning rivers to mountains enshrouded in smog, it was impossible to ignore the human impact on the environment. By the 1960s, Americans began to pressure politicians to protect fragile landscapes from development and open them to tourism. President John F. Kennedy created the

National Lakeshore and National Seashore system to protect coastlines and open them to recreational use. Johnson's Great Society expanded these commitments. In 1964, Johnson signed the Wilderness Act, protecting nine million acres, most of it already owned by the federal government. This was followed in 1965 by the Water Quality Act, which curbed industrial and agricultural discharge into lakes and rivers, and in 1968 by the Wild and Scenic Rivers Act, to protect pristine waterways. None of these laws was particularly effective, but they signaled a new federal commitment to environmentalism and led activists to push for more.

THE ENVIRONMENTAL MOVEMENT By the late 1960s, longtime preservation and conservation groups like the Sierra Club, founded in California in 1892, competed for influence with more militant organizations, influenced by the tactics of other activist groups. The Environmental Defense Fund (founded in 1967), for example, used the courts—imitating the strategies of civil rights litigations—to challenge polluters, mounting lawsuits against DDT manufacturers and other industrial polluters. Friends of the Earth (founded in 1969) took its cue from the counterculture and antiwar movements, mobilizing supporters with back-to-the-earth rhetoric and engaging in disruptive protest. The Natural Resources Defense Council (founded in 1970) lobbied for environmental regulations and deployed scientists to produce expert reports critical of pollution, overpopulation, wildlife loss, and nuclear power.

What was most striking about environmentalism was its broad appeal. At a moment when the nation seemed irreconcilably divided over war and peace, civil rights, and feminism, it gave bipartisan support to protecting the land, water, and air. Nothing made that clearer than Earth Day, April 22, 1970, when over 20 million Americans in places as diverse as Green Bay, Wisconsin, and Birmingham, Alabama, gathered to demand action on the environment. No single day of protest in American history brought together so many people: Earth Day dwarfed the March on Washington in 1963 and the massive march against the Vietnam War in October 1969.

Although counterculturists and student leftists dominated some Earth Day events and captured the headlines for their dramatic protests—for example, dumping gallons of oil into the fountain at Standard Oil's San Francisco headquarters—most Earth Day events were ecumenical affairs. Philadelphia's Earth Day, one of the country's largest, with thirty thousand participants, included suburban parents and schoolchildren, hippies, church leaders, college students, and members of the Chamber of Commerce, which underwrote the event. Politicians of both parties jostled for prominence, including Democratic presidential hopeful Edmund Muskie and Senate minority leader Hugh Scott. Nearly two-thirds of members of Congress gave speeches at Earth Day events around the country. Beat poet Allen Ginsberg led Philly's crowd with chants, environmental crusader Ralph Nader denounced corporations for polluting rivers, and Pete Seeger, Judy Collins, and the cast of *Hair* performed.

The major news media covered Earth Day more extensively than any event other than the moon landing and presidential funerals. The popular morning television program *Today* dedicated four shows to the environment, leading off with host Hugh

Downs declaring, "Our Mother Earth is rotting with the residue of our good life. Our oceans are dying, our air is poisoned. This is not science fiction. And it is not the future; it is happening now and we have to make a decision now."[42]

ENVIRONMENTAL REGULATION Behind the scenes, businesses complained to Nixon, who was an ambivalent environmentalist at best. "In a flat choice between jobs and smoke," he reassured corporate leaders who worried about the cost of implementing clean air measures, jobs would win. To auto executives Lee Iacocca and Henry Ford II, Nixon denounced environmentalists as not "really one damn bit interested in safety or clean air. What they're interested in is destroying the system."[43]

But business lobbyists could not stop the bipartisan well of support for environmental legislation. In the fall of 1969, Congress passed the National Environmental Policy Act, and in the summer of 1970, Nixon used an executive order to create the cabinet-level Environmental Protection Agency. That year, Nixon signed the Clean Air Act, restricting both industrial and automobile emissions. In 1972 the EPA banned DDT, and it would use its powers to enforce a panoply of new environmental regulations. That year Congress also passed several key laws, including the Clean Water Act and the Marine Protection, Research, and Sanctuaries Act, which brought places like the Santa Barbara Channel, San Francisco Bay, and Boston Harbor under federal jurisdiction. Capping the wave of legislation, in 1973 Congress passed the Endangered Species Act, bringing federal protection to hundreds of creatures, from tiny snail darter fish to giant elk. Many states—including Republican-controlled Massachusetts, New Jersey, California, and New York—passed their own environmental regulations, putting strict controls on land use, setting aside funds for the creation of state parks and wilderness areas, and in the case of California, capping auto and industrial emissions.

The Urban Crisis

The shift in policy gave rise to a guarded optimism about the environment, but on the other "crisis" of the 1970s—the travails of American cities—the pessimism was crushing. The old Rust Belt cities hemorrhaged jobs and population and struggled to provide city services. On the West Coast, Oakland struggled to remain solvent, as companies decamped to "greenfields"—undeveloped sites—in the East Bay. Back east, Philadelphia raised local income taxes to deal with a growing budget deficit. In Detroit, the city's first black mayor, Coleman Young, elected in 1973, cut city employment and closed dozens of parks and recreation centers. In Baltimore, city efforts staved off a budget crisis by cutting funding to the police, leading to an outbreak of the "blue flu" in 1974. With most police calling in sick, looters took to the city's streets, cleaning out stores and vandalizing properties.

NEW YORK IS BURNING Worst hit of all was New York. The city lost 600,000 jobs between the mid-1960s and mid-1970s. The housing market collapsed as landlords in decrepit neighborhoods like Manhattan Valley, the Lower East Side,

Urban Crisis In the 1970s, New York and other major cities faced intense racial conflict and rising crime rates. In response to calls for law and order, in 1979 New York increased the police presence on its subways.

and Harlem simply walked away from their buildings, unable to pay for costly repairs. About ten thousand apartments per year in the early 1970s were left empty. Many property owners decided it was more lucrative to collect insurance than to rent at a loss, leading to an epidemic of arson. Large parts of the South Bronx burned to the ground.

Population loss and disinvestment gutted New York's tax base. The city had long provided excellent social services to its residents, including a network of city-run hospitals, a well-managed public housing authority, and one of the world's only twenty-four-hour public transit systems. But the infrastructure groaned with age, and the city teetered on the brink of insolvency.

The streets of big cities like New York, Philadelphia, and Los Angeles also filled with the mentally ill and homeless, many of whom had been released from psychiatric hospitals. Advocates of deinstitutionalization hoped that community-based health centers would deliver services more humanely, but budget cuts made that impossible. The bleak setting of abandoned apartment buildings, trash-strewn streets, and graffiti-covered trains served as the grim backdrop for Martin Scorsese's apocalyptic 1976 film, *Taxi Driver*, whose protagonist, Travis Bickle, passes through seamy Times Square bitterly describing the scene: "All the animals come out at night—whores, skunk pussies, buggers, queens, fairies, dopers, junkies, sick, venal. Someday a real rain

Making a Nation
Working-Class Rebels

From

Pete Hamill
The Revolt of the White Lower Middle Class (1969)

Just after President Nixon was inaugurated, Hamill, a New York–based journalist and the son of working-class Irish immigrants, set out to Brooklyn and Queens to document white backlash politics. He sat at bars and interviewed white ironworkers and carpenters and bartenders, who talked about their economic insecurity, expressed their resentment against taxes and welfare, and often blamed African Americans for their troubles.

They call my people the White Lower Middle Class these days. It is an ugly, ice-cold phrase, the result, I suppose, of the missionary zeal of those sociologists who still think you can place human beings on charts. It most certainly does not sound like a description of people on the edge of open, sustained and possibly violent revolt. And yet, that is the case. All over New York City tonight . . . men are standing around saloons talking darkly about their grievances, and even more darkly about possible remedies. Their grievances are real and deep; their remedies could blow this city apart. . . .

But basically, the people I'm speaking about *are* the working class. That is, they stand somewhere in the economy between the poor—most of whom are the aged, the sick and those unemployable women and children who live on welfare—and the semi-professionals and professionals who earn their way with talents or skills acquired through education. The working class earns its living with its hands or its backs; its members do not exist on welfare payments; they do not live in abject, swinish poverty, nor in safe, remote suburban comfort. They earn between $5,000 and $10,000 a year. And they can no longer make it in New York. . . .

The working-class white man feels trapped and, even worse, in a society that purports to be democratic, ignored. The tax burden is crushing him, and the quality of his life does not seem to justify his exertions. He cannot leave New York City because he can't afford it, and he is beginning to look for someone to blame. That someone is almost certainly going to be the black man. This does not have to be the situation, of course. If the government were more responsive to the working-class white man . . . there would be a chance to turn this situation around. The working-class white man does not care if a black man gets a job in his union, as long as it does not mean the loss of his own job, or the small privileges and sense of self-respect that go with it. . . .

It is a tragic situation, because the poor blacks and the working-class whites should be natural allies. Instead, the black man has become the symbol of all the working-class white man's resentments.

Studs Terkel

Interview with Gary Bryner (1975)

The journalist Studs Terkel traveled around the United States conducting oral histories with American workers. One of them, Gary Bryner, was the twenty-nine-year-old president of United Automobile Workers Local 1114, which represented workers at the General Motors plant in Lordstown, Ohio, during a period of intense labor unrest. Bryner described his youthful co-workers and their discontent with their working conditions.

Someone said Lordstown is the Woodstock of the workingman. There are young people who have the mod look, long hair, big Afros, beads, young gals. The average age is around twenty-five—which makes a guy thirty over the hill. I'm a young union president but I'm an old man in my plant.

The almighty dollar is not the only thing in my estimation. There's more to it—how I'm treated. What I have to say about what I do, how I do it. It's more important than the almighty dollar. The reason might be that the dollar's here now. It wasn't in my father's young days. I can concentrate on the social aspects, my rights. And I feel good all around when I'm able to stand up and speak up for another guy's rights. That's how I got involved in the whole stinkin' mess. Fighting every day of my life. And I enjoy it.

Guys in plants nowadays, their incentive is not to work harder. It's to stop the job to the point where they can have lax time. Maybe to think. We got guys now that open a paper, maybe read a paragraph, do his job, come back, and do something else. Keeping himself occupied other than being just that robot that they've scheduled him to be.

If the guys didn't stand up and fight, they'd become robots too. They're interested in being able to smoke a cigarette, bullshit a little bit with the guy next to 'em, open a book, look at something, just daydream if nothing else. You can't do that if you become a machine.

Thirty-five, thirty-six seconds to do your job—that includes the walking, the picking up of the parts, the assembly. Go to the next job, with never a letup, never a second to stand and think. The guys at our plant fought like hell to keep that right.

There was a strike.

The strike issue? We demanded the reinstitution of our work pace as it was prior to the onslaught by General Motors Assembly Division. The only way they could do it was to replace the people laid off.

Questions for Analysis

1. What were the major grievances of the white men whom Hamill interviewed?

2. Why were Bryner's coworkers at the Lordstown plant dissatisfied with their jobs?

3. How did these "middle Americans" respond differently to the cultural and economic changes of the 1960s and 1970s?

will come and wash all this scum off the streets."[44] Bickle's New York captured what many believed was the apocalyptic end of urban America.

One apocalypse was barely averted during the grim winter of 1974–75, as New York City's bond market collapsed. Crushed by debt, the city teetered on the brink of bankruptcy before state and federal officials offered billions in loans to pay the city's bills. The bailout, however, exacted a high price. The city drastically cut public services, deferred maintenance on the run-down subway system, let parkland revert to nature, cut welfare expenditures, laid off police officers, firefighters, and teachers, and trimmed municipal workers' wages. Life in New York got harder.

The city's underfunded and demoralized police could not respond to rising crime, the city's hospital system struggled to serve hundreds of thousands of uninsured patients, and population and job flight continued unabated. New York hit bottom in August 1977 when, after a massive power outage, tens of thousands of city residents took to the streets, looting stores and setting more than a thousand fires. City officials estimated that $1 billion in property was destroyed.

THE "WAR ON CRIME"   In 1975, *Time* magazine lamented that cities had become "canyons of fear."[45] Between 1965 and 1975, rates of violent crime soared. Scholars debated the extent and magnitude of lawlessness in the United States: Was the sharp increase in burglary or assault an artifact of better reporting or an actual measure of growing violence? Was the pervasive fear of crime the result of lurid news coverage by local television news programs competing for viewers with a strategy of "if it bleeds, it leads"?

One crime statistic could not be ignored. The number of murders in the United States doubled in just fifteen years, from 10,000 in 1965 to over 20,000 in 1980.[46] Horrible stories of grisly serial murders grabbed the headlines and became the subject of a burgeoning genre of "true crime" best sellers, fueled by the voyeuristic coverage of the California cultist Charles Manson, who ordered his followers to commit seven murders in 1969. The sadistic Houston killer Dean Corll kidnapped, tortured, and killed at least twenty-eight adolescent boys between 1970 and 1973. Ted Bundy went on a murderous spree in Washington State and Utah in 1974. Mass murders were far from normal, but they occupied an outsize place in the American imagination of the 1970s. America seemed to be in the grip of remorseless killers.

Calls for law and order had been on the rise since the mid-1950s, even before any measurable increase in crime rates occurred, stoked by fears of an epidemic of comic-book- and Hollywood-fueled juvenile delinquency. When the Warren Court expanded the rights of the accused in *Miranda* and other criminal procedure cases, conservatives argued that the courts coddled criminals rather than punishing them. The fear of lawlessness intensified with urban unrest and campus disorder, leading politicians across the political spectrum to capitalize on fears of crime. But how to respond to growing crime was a matter of debate. Liberals called for economic assistance to the poor, arguing that poverty caused crime. In 1968, Congress passed gun control legislation with a large bipartisan majority, hoping to curb the increase in firearm-related deaths. The 1968 Omnibus Crime Control and Safe Streets Act committed billions to the fight against crime, most of it to fund local police departments.

Still, crime, especially violent crime, rose. By the early 1970s, fear of criminality had turned into a full-fledged panic, with conservatives and liberals alike calling for "law and order" measures, including stricter law enforcement and stiffer sentences for convicted criminals. New York led the way. New York governor Nelson Rockefeller, who had long emphasized rehabilitation and antipoverty efforts to curb crime, changed his position: "Once the orderly structure of society is breached, where does it end?"[47] Politicians and police departments turned their attention to illicit drugs, especially marijuana, heroin, and cocaine. In 1973, Rockefeller supported the nation's strictest antidrug laws.

Also in the 1970s, Congress and the states began introducing mandatory minimum sentencing laws, particularly for drug offenses. By 1980 seventeen states had introduced laws limiting parole, resulting in longer jail stays. The result was a staggering increase in the number of prison inmates, many serving longer sentences than ever. In 1970 about 322,300 Americans were arrested on drug-related charges, compared to more than 1,375,600 in 2000. Young black men were disproportionately represented among those arrested and incarcerated.

Calls for law and order also resuscitated demands for the death penalty. During the postwar period, public support for capital punishment had fallen in the United States, as it did in most Western countries. No American was executed between 1966 and 1976. In 1972 the Supreme Court narrowed the legal basis for capital punishment, ruling that in practice, the death penalty was arbitrary and that methods of execution violated the constitutional ban on cruel and unusual punishment. But in 1976 the Supreme Court, with several conservative members appointed by President Nixon, opened a window for the reinstitution of the death penalty. Utah put the murderer Gary Gilmore to death by firing squad in 1977, and within a few years, thirty-seven states had modified their laws and resumed capital punishment.

One of the few growth industries during the 1970s and early 1980s was incarceration. In most respects, the prison system in the United States was a mess. Jails were old and run-down and, by the early 1970s, hotbeds of rebellion. In 1967 there were five prison riots in the United States, a figure that rose each year, peaking at forty-eight in 1972. The biggest was the uprising at upstate New York's Attica Prison in 1971, which left thirty-nine dead. Attica and the prisoners' movement put a harsh spotlight on the conditions in America's jails, leading to growing litigation to improve prison conditions. This, combined with court-ordered caps on the number of prisoners per facility, the dramatic increase in arrests and convictions, and the panic over crime, fueled a steady increase in prison construction over the next thirty years. While the federal government dealt with stagflation, and while cities and states imposed austerity budgets, spending on prisons grew exponentially.

Support for tough crime measures was truly bipartisan. Massachusetts senator Edward M. Kennedy, who was on the Democratic Party's left, was an early and staunch supporter of mandatory sentencing laws. Governor Jerry Brown in California, a well-known liberal, joined conservatives in the state legislature in instituting tough sentencing requirements and supporting the construction of dozens of new jails. California's debt for prison construction rose from $763 million to $4.9 billion between the mid-1970s and the late 1980s.[48] Massive barbed-wire-enclosed prison complexes sprang up all over the country, mostly outside big cities, often built at the behest of legislators from dying small towns and agricultural communities who were eager to create jobs in their districts.

Political Reform

The fear of decline loomed over the United States by the mid-1970s, even if it remained one of the wealthiest countries in the world. The signs of collapse were everywhere: a president had resigned in disgrace, and the country had lost the war in Vietnam, run out of gas because of OPEC, and lost market share to Toyota. Inflation and unemployment hit record highs. The environment was poisoned, the cities were dying, and predators lurked everywhere. And government—from corrupt Nixon to bankrupt New York—seemed to be failing.

For some politicians, the crisis presented opportunity. In the wake of the Watergate scandals—and general disaffection with the presidency—Congress passed a series of reforms intended to curb presidential power. The War Powers Resolution (1973) reinforced Congress's power to authorize military intervention; the Budget Impoundment and Control Act (1974) created the Congressional Budget Office and limited the president's power to overrun congressionally approved budgets; and the Privacy Act (1974) restricted the government's ability to collect and disseminate personal information. In the months after Nixon's resignation, in an attempt to curb political corruption, Congress instituted strict campaign finance reforms, put limits on individual spending on elections, established a system of public funding for presidential campaigns that would remain in place for the next thirty-four years, and created the Federal Election Commission to monitor campaign spending.

THE WATERGATE BABIES The so-called Watergate babies, most of them moderate Democrats, swept into office in the midterm elections of 1974. In the House and Senate they promised to sweep the halls clean with the brooms of reform. One of the major reforms they enacted was limiting the filibuster, reducing the number of votes required to bring a debate to cloture in the Senate from 67 to 60; another was the abolition of the House Un-American Activities Committee. They also reorganized the seniority rules in the House and Senate that had allowed long-serving members, mostly from the South, to dominate congressional committee chairmanships.

The Watergate babies did more than restructure Congress; they also worked to create a third way between New Deal and Great Society liberalism, of which they were skeptical, and pro-business Republicanism, which they embraced. In Colorado, Gary Hart (who had been a key campaign operative for George McGovern) made a successful run for the U.S. Senate in 1974, appealing to voters as a moderate who would work on "quality of life" issues, most notably environmental protection. Hart, like many of these "new Democrats," as they came to be called, argued for shrinking government, stepping back from controversial and expensive social programs, and unleashing an entrepreneurial spirit. "We're locked into these '60s definitions of liberal-conservative which don't work anymore," he argued. "The issues of the '70s are not liberal or conservative, they are not left-right issues . . . and they will not yield to 'New Deal thinking.'"[49] Hart decisively beat the incumbent Republican, picking up a wide swath of self-proclaimed moderates from both parties.

The "new Democrats" (who would sometimes be called "Atari Democrats" in the 1980s, named after a popular first-generation video game manufacturer) argued that their party's future lay in empowering a high-tech economy rather than in continuing to shore up a decaying manufacturing sector. They saw trade unions—still one of the Democratic Party's most powerful groups—as an obstacle to pro-business policies. And they believed that Democrats needed to distance themselves from "special interest" groups, including labor but also racial minorities, if they wanted to succeed nationally. Many older northeastern and midwestern Democrats remained skeptical, but around the country, "new Democrats" began winning office at the state and local levels.

THE RISE OF JIMMY CARTER The post-Watergate reform impulse—and the widespread sense of political, economic, and international crisis—opened the way to a most unlikely president: Jimmy Carter, an engineer, peanut farmer, and Southern Baptist lay preacher. He often returned to his hometown, Plains, Georgia, to lead Sunday school classes while he was both Georgia's governor and the U.S. president. Carter emerged from a crowded pack of candidates in 1976 to win his party's nomination and victory against the unpopular incumbent, Gerald Ford. Carter was the first president to declare that he was "born again," reaffirming his Baptist faith as an adult. He represented a growing segment of Americans, many in the Sunbelt, who practiced evangelical Christianity and proudly proclaimed their faith publicly.

Carter's overt religiosity stood in sharp contrast with nearly every president of the twentieth century, all of whom practiced their Christianity quietly, occasionally appearing at Sunday services, but seldom arguing that their faith informed their politics. John F. Kennedy had to pledge that he would not be a tool of the Catholic Church; Carter, by contrast, reminded voters that his politics were guided by his religion. Carter's morality came to the limelight in, of all places, the pages of *Playboy*, where he told readers that he was a sinner who had committed "adultery in my heart" by looking lustfully at women other than his wife. In the White House, Carter called for family values, arguing that "we need a stable family life to make us better servants of the people" and even suggesting that Department of Housing and Urban Development staffers who "are living in sin" get married.[50] Carter's cultural conservatism allowed him to pick up southern voters and religious whites who had begun to defect to the GOP in the late 1960s.

The Carter Presidency

For all the novelty of being a born-again Christian in the White House, Carter faced economic and global crises for which his religion did not offer many answers. The problem of stagflation persisted throughout the late 1970s, and increasingly, Carter adopted a politics of austerity: reduce government expenditures to curb inflationary impulses. In his inaugural address, he set a somber tone. "We have learned that 'more' is not necessarily better," he stated, "that even our great Nation has its recognized limits."[51] His presidency unfolded in the shadow of Vietnam and the disillusionment of Watergate. Carter was no wheeling-and-dealing, grandiose politician like Lyndon Johnson. As he taught Bible lessons, he seemed to inhabit a moral world far, far away from Nixon's. With his background as a farmer and a nuclear engineer, he exuded a technical competency that the bumbling Gerald Ford had lacked.

A TECHNOCRAT IN THE WHITE HOUSE It was that last quality, his penchant for technocracy, that seemed to distinguish Carter the most. Kennedy had admired scientists and economists and delegated policy making to them. Johnson had disdained "the Harvards" who dominated Kennedy's administration, preferring the arm-twisting and cajoling of congressional deal making. Nixon was a mix of the two. He had professors like Kissinger and Shultz in his cabinet and took a strong hand in foreign policy, but he was happy to leave most of the details of domestic policy to his staff, checking in only when it affected his political prospects. Carter, by contrast, was obsessively concerned with detail. He micromanaged every aspect of his administration's social, economic, and foreign policy. That proclivity showed up in the pages of the 178-page report of Carter's Urban Policy Research Group, a turgid document that focused on an issue that was not very high on the president's list of priorities. The president read every page, underscoring key passages with a ruler and jotting down comments in his neat handwriting in the margins.

Carter also employed a rhetoric of postpartisanship. During his campaign, he had distanced himself from the "Washington mess," emphasizing the need for "limits" to government reach, echoing Republican criticism of the Great Society. Likewise, Carter rejected "selfish special interests" that were a "menace to our system of government," echoing Republican criticism of civil rights activists, labor unions, and liberal reform groups that had supposedly captured policy making. He and his advisers also echoed the GOP's silent majority strategy, appealing directly to disaffected white middle-class voters, the "average, hard-working American" who struggled to make ends meet by working hard in "homes, factory shift lines, beauty parlors, barber shops, livestock sales barns, and shopping centers."[52]

At first, it seemed that Carter would focus on unemployment, which remained doggedly high—over 7 percent—when he entered office.[53] Early in his term, Carter called for stimulus spending, most notably through a modest tax rebate (it would average about fifty dollars per household) and federal efforts to curb unemployment, including full employment legislation that labor and liberals had been demanding since World War II. Carter also supported government-funded job training to bolster the fortunes of those displaced by collapsing industry. Under pressure from big-city mayors and civil rights leaders to do something about the urban crisis, he pledged support for comprehensive urban reform.

Carter's job-creation record was mixed at best. He expanded the 1973 Comprehensive Employment and Training Act, which created about 725,000 federal jobs at its peak in 1978. But he dropped the tax rebate within months of introducing it, on the grounds that it was expensive and unnecessary as unemployment rates temporarily fell. He found political support for the full-employment law (sponsored by two liberal lions, former vice president Hubert Humphrey and Congressman Augustus Hawkins [D-CA], one of the few African Americans in the House and a staunch ally of organized labor) but at the cost of compromise on its provisions. By the time it made its way through the House and Senate, it was little more than symbolic. Carter's comprehensive but underfunded urban reform provided only about $600 million of new urban spending. His urban policy was a warmed-over version of Nixon's: fund small-scale community development organizations that had the will but not the capacity to address the mass of urban problems that they faced.

INFLATION AND AUSTERITY All these programs ultimately fell to Carter's budgetary ax. A little more than a year into office, the administration turned its attention from the unemployment side of stagflation to the inflation side. The annual inflation rate skyrocketed, rising from 6.5 percent in 1977 to 11.3 percent in 1979. Carter's political response to inflation was confused. He attempted to curb wage and price increases, calling for controls on both, a failed reprise of Nixon's policy. By 1978 he called for austerity measures. He embraced arguments from the political right that blamed government deficits for the economy's troubles.

Leading the charge toward austerity was Carter's chief inflation adviser, the Cornell University economist Alfred Kahn, who advocated dramatic reduction in government spending. Carter proposed cuts to social programs, a reduction in the federal workforce (he promised to hire one government worker to replace two who quit or retired), and cost controls on government contracts. Kahn advocated free market reforms. Greater competition, he argued, would weaken trade unions, lower wages, and curb inflation. "I'd love the Teamsters to be worse off," he argued. "I'd love the automobile workers to be worse off."[54]

The economy worsened. When Carter took office, unemployment had been at 7.1 percent. It fell to 5.8 percent—still high—in 1979, before returning to 7.1 percent again in 1980.[55] The value of the dollar plummeted, increasing the cost of American imports, most notably oil, thus driving up the prices of many commodities. Inflation also skyrocketed, rising 14.8 percent between March 1979 and March 1980, the largest increase since the lifting of price controls after World War II.[56]

DEREGULATION Like the Watergate babies, Carter offered a critique of bureaucracy that was a softer version of conservative critiques of the New Deal and Great Society. He pledged to institute "comprehensive" government reform, including the streamlining of bureaucracy, the reduction of paperwork, and most consequentially, the rollback of government regulation. "One of my Administration's major goals," Carter stated, "is to free the American people from the burden of over-regulation."[57] To that end, he directed Kahn to oversee his deregulation efforts. "I have more faith in greed than in regulation," Kahn argued.[58] When it came to regulation, he believed that the costs often outweighed the benefits. Of environmental regulations, Kahn contended, "the cost per life—say per year of additional life expectancy—is just astronomical."[59]

With Kahn's guidance, the Carter administration put up hurdles to new regulations, including a regulatory review council that would conduct cost-benefit analyses of any proposed regulations and give businesses a strong voice in future regulations. Carter also pushed for legislation to lift controls on airlines, deregulate the trucking industry, and weaken communications regulations, allowing for the proliferation of competing telephone companies rather than large regional monopolies. Most significant, he called for a rollback of Depression-era banking regulations. Without exaggeration, he called deregulation "the greatest change in the relationship between Government and business since the New Deal."[60]

Many would later associate deregulation with a right-wing political agenda. Carter's call for free markets and Kahn's paeans to greed warmed the hearts of conservatives like Barry Goldwater, who enthusiastically supported deregulation as a necessary first step to dismantling big government. The National Association of Manufacturers, which had fought New Deal labor laws and Nixon-era environmental laws alike, lined up behind Carter's plans. But deregulation also had staunch supporters on the left. Consumer advocate Ralph Nader, who had crusaded for environmental regulations, joined Carter on the grounds that competition would lower prices and give consumers more choice in the marketplace. Senator Edward Kennedy (D-MA), to the left of Carter on most issues, led the Senate in pushing for deregulation in trucking to cut overhead and reduce prices. Even though many on the left would later regret deregulation, consumer advocates and key liberals were decisive players in the process.

Perhaps the most consequential shift was in banking. In 1978, Carter signed the International Banking Act, which allowed foreign-held banks to acquire American banks and compete for business in the United States. Even more important was the Depository Institutions Deregulation and Monetary Control Act, signed by Carter in 1980, which ushered in a new era of financialization by loosening credit, lifting interest-rate ceilings on bank deposits, and allowing financial institutions to create interest-bearing checking accounts and offer adjustable-rate mortgages. The act also allowed savings and loans to issue credit cards. With the lifting of interest-rate ceilings, lending institutions could expand the availability of credit to borrowers who had once been considered too risky.

Credit cards, once symbols of wealth because banks limited them to customers able to make their payments, proliferated in the 1980s and 1990s. By 1984 more than half of all American households had credit cards. Savings and loan institutions and consumer banks dramatically expanded lending to higher-risk customers, increasing their profits but also creating a spiral of indebtedness and a decline in individual and household savings. The decline in financial sector regulations played out with grim consequences in many households that got bogged down in debt. And it laid the groundwork for two future financial crises, the savings and loan crisis in 1987 and the collapse of major investment banks because of predatory mortgage lending in 2008.

THE ENERGY CRISIS Of all of the economic problems that Carter inherited from his predecessors, the most difficult involved energy. He was inaugurated during one of the coldest winters in modern American history, a chill that coincided with a severe natural gas shortage. America grew increasingly dependent on foreign oil in the 1970s: by the time Carter entered office, more than half of American petroleum came from foreign sources. At first, Carter echoed Nixon's earlier calls for conservation. In his first televised address, in April 1977, he appeared in the White House library, seated casually, wearing a cardigan sweater. He called for a "comprehensive energy policy," arguing that solving America's energy problems was the "moral equivalent of war."[61]

A few months later Carter announced the National Energy Plan (NEP), which called for conservation, energy efficiency standards for appliances and cars, the development of alternatives to fossil fuels, taxes on firms that continued to use petroleum and natural gas, and the lifting of price ceilings on oil and gas. The NEP generated intense controversy. Republicans saw it as big government interference in a market best left to its own devices. They resisted any efforts to use the tax system to encourage conservation. Still, with bipartisan support, a weakened NEP passed in November 1978, with Carter's energy efficiency measures in place, and a plan gradually to lift the price ceiling on oil and gas, but without a tax to discourage consumption. But the NEP would face troubles from the get-go, mainly because its emphasis on conservation through the uncapping of gas prices collided directly with the administration's war on inflation.

THE IRANIAN REVOLUTION Within weeks of Carter's signing of the NEP, the United States faced even bigger problems. In late 1978 oil production in Iran came to a virtual halt when Islamic fundamentalists challenged the regime of the shah, Mohammad Reza Pahlavi. The United States had propped up the shah since 1953. An autocrat, Pahlavi and his supporters had grown rich on petrodollars. He attempted to Westernize Iran while using his secret police to brutalize and censor his political foes. His chief opponent, the fundamentalist Ayatollah Ruhollah Khomeini, led a resistance from exile in nearby Iraq. In the mid-1970s the popular resistance to the shah intensified, culminating in massive demonstrations in Tehran in 1978. Huge student-led strikes and violent street protests shut down the capital for weeks at a time. The crisis in Iran caught the Carter administration—and nearly every American foreign policy expert—off guard. They had all embraced the view of the shah's regime as secular and modernizing, as symbolized by the luxury resorts along the Persian Gulf and the glittering, high-end shops in downtown Tehran.

In early 1979 the shah fled Iran, leaving huge construction projects unfinished and the country unstable. The Ayatollah Khomeini returned from exile and took leadership, drafting an Islamic constitution. Like the shah, he cracked down brutally on dissent, but unlike the shah, he denounced the United States as the root cause of his country's problems.

The crisis in Iran—and an OPEC decision to increase oil prices—precipitated an energy crisis every bit as severe as the one in 1973–74. Carter was never one to sugarcoat a grim scenario. In April 1979 he announced that the "nation's energy problem is serious—and it's getting worse."[62] His proposed solution—the immediate decontrol of oil prices, along with a windfall tax on oil company profits—satisfied no one. Gas prices shot up by over 50 percent in the first half of 1979, and Carter's anti-inflation policy met its limits.[63]

"NO GAS, MY ASS" Six years after the first oil shock, history seemed to be repeating itself, but even more grimly: gas lines once again, angry drivers waiting for hours to pay $1.79 per gallon if there was any fuel left at the pumps. On June 23, 1979, a balmy Saturday afternoon, that anger flared up just a few miles from Book Ksionska's house. That afternoon Denny Riley, a twenty-one-year-old trucker, rounded up a group of his friends who pulled their rigs into the Levittown intersection known as Five Points, a major crossroads with four gas stations. Blaring their air horns and blasting music, they slowed to a halt. The disruption attracted a crowd. Within hours about five hundred people gathered, cheering and waving homemade banners. Bill Brown, a friend of Riley's, pulled up in his rig, and when the police asked him to move along, he defiantly leaped to the top of his cab and waved at the cheering crowd. By evening the crowd grew restive: the police arrested sixty-nine demonstrators.

On Sunday several trucks and a larger, angrier crowd, about two thousand strong, gathered again at Five Points, along with three hundred police officers. As the police attempted to disperse the crowd, hitting people and trucks with nightsticks and chasing protesters with police dogs, tempers flared. Protesters chanted "No gas, my ass!" and tossed firecrackers into the air, pelted the police with stones and bricks, broke service station windows, attacked gas pumps, and lit a car and van on fire.[64] One hundred seventy-nine people were arrested, including a trucker who was charged with running over a police officer's hand. "What happened to Levittown's tranquility?" worried *Newsweek*.[65]

MALAISE Just three weeks after the Levittown gas riot, President Carter gave his "malaise" speech, which would become a defining moment of his presidency. On the evening of July 15, he offered a somber portrayal of a national crisis that was, at core, existential rather than political or economic, though he never actually used the word *malaise*. "Why have we not been able to get together as a nation to resolve our serious energy problem?" he asked. To answer that question, he met with ordinary Americans, clerics, and community leaders, soliciting their advice. After weeks of listening, he concluded: "It is a crisis of confidence. It is a crisis that strikes at the very heart and soul and spirit of our national will. We can see this crisis in the growing doubt about the meaning of our own lives and in the loss of a unity of purpose for our Nation."[66] Though

Carter hoped the speech would spur a call for national renewal—and for a moment it did bolster his popularity—it became an epitaph for postwar America.

The events that played out in late 1979 and early 1980 constituted a depressing coda. In November 1979, when Carter permitted the exiled shah to come to the United States for cancer treatment, a group of radical Islamic activists stormed the American embassy in Tehran and took fifty-two Americans hostage. The hostage crisis would play out for 444 days, gripping the American public and fueling a sense that the United States was indeed powerless worldwide. On April 24, 1980, the president authorized a rescue mission that failed spectacularly, with eight U.S. soldiers dead and no hostages freed. For Carter, the crisis—replayed nightly on the evening news—was at least as devastating as the Tet Offensive had been for Lyndon Johnson, a sign of presidential and, by implication, national impotence.

The Turn to the Right

That year Carter would face a political opponent who promised an easy answer to America's crises. He was Ronald Reagan, the longtime right-leaning Republican candidate who promised a new, assertive style of leadership: "I will not stand by and watch this great country destroy itself under mediocre leadership that drifts from one crisis to the next, eroding our national will and purpose."[67] Counter to Carter's ruminations about America's malaise, Reagan exuded confidence. Facing the crisis in Iran, he promised swift military action. Reagan swept the election, winning 50.8 percent of the popular vote to Carter's 41 percent. Independent, former moderate Republican John Anderson picked up 6.6 percent. But the 1980 election was less a moment of resolution than the opening of a new period of political turmoil.

The United States had lurched rightward in the sixteen years since Barry Goldwater challenged Lyndon Johnson. That rightward turn resulted in part from grassroots organizing by Republican insurgents, but it was also the consequence of long-brewing suspicions of government rooted in the debacles of Vietnam and Watergate. For all their differences, Carter and Reagan shared a bipartisan consensus that government was too big and regulation too burdensome. They shared a belief that austerity measures could restore the nation's economy. And they both advocated market-friendly policies that would encourage competition. That bipartisan consensus—as much as the unresolved struggles over family, race, and culture—would reshape American politics for the next three decades.

Just a few years before Reagan won election, the writer Michael Harrington argued that "America is moving vigorously left, right, and center all at once."[68] Even if 1980 marked a rightward turn in national politics, the political climate was still muddled. In Book and Jim Ksionska's suburban Philadelphia district, voters had backed Carter by a narrow margin in 1976 and joined the Reagan sweep in 1980 and again in 1984. But presidential politics offered only one glimpse into the fluid political world of the time. In 1978 voters in the Ksionskas' district elected a moderate Democratic Watergate baby and staunch environmentalist. In 1980 they voted him out of office. But two years later, amid the troubles at Fairless Works and a deep recession, they reelected the Democrat, who ran ads featuring closed factories.

For the next several years, Harrington's dictum held true: Congress switched control from Democratic to Republican and back again. The new Republican president pushed domestic and foreign policy rightward but faced more limits than his fervent supporters had expected. Centrist Democrats gained influence and refashioned their party, rejecting Carter's gloomy rhetoric but embracing many of his administration's ideas about austerity, bureaucracy, and regulation. And in the meantime, more and more Americans lived like the Ksionskas, stuck in the political middle, uncertain of their economic futures or their political identities. In its 1985 hit, the band Camper van Beethoven captured the ambiguity of the age: "Everything seems to be up in the air at this time."[69]

Suggested Reading

Cowie, Jefferson. *Stayin' Alive: The 1970s and the Last Days of the Working Class* (2010). How presidential politics, economic policies, and popular culture fragmented social democracy and led to a new politics of inequality.

Gottschalk, Marie. *The Prison and the Gallows: The Politics of Mass Incarceration in America* (2006). Examines the public policies that led the United States to build a massive prison system and incarcerate a greater proportion of its citizens than nearly any other country in the world.

Kalman, Laura. *Right Star Rising: A New Politics, 1974–1980* (2010). A sweeping account of a critical period of political, legal, and economic transition.

Kruse, Kevin. *One Nation Under God: How Corporate America Invented Christian America* (2015). The backstory to the rise of right-wing Christianity and its critique of the federal government.

Matusow, Allen. *Nixon's Economy: Booms, Busts, Dollars, and Votes* (1998). How the president and policy makers struggled with stagflation, trade deficits, and rising unemployment.

Rome, Adam. *The Genius of Earth Day* (2013). How a diverse coalition of Democrats and Republicans, student leftists and suburbanites, religious leaders and counterculturalists created a mass environmentalist movement.

Sargent, Daniel J. *A Superpower Transformed: The Remaking of American Foreign Relations in the 1970s* (2015). Explains how the Nixon, Ford, and Carter administrations struggled to reorient the Cold War, manage globalization, and push for human rights.

Schulman, Bruce J., and Julian E. Zelizer, eds. *Rightward Bound: Making America Conservative in the 1970s* (2008). Explorations of how ethnicity, religion, and grassroots activism challenged liberalism and redefined the role of the government.

Chapter Review

Review Questions

1. How did the United States end the Vietnam War?

2. Why did Henry Kissinger and Richard Nixon decide to open relations with the People's Republic of China?

3. What was stagflation, and how did it transform the economy?

4. Explain the origins of the oil crisis of 1973–74.

5. Why were Americans so pessimistic about the state of the country in the mid-1970s?

6. Why did so many workers go on strike in the period from 1970 to 1974?

7. How did policy makers respond to growing concerns about the environment?

8. Explain the dramatic increase in incarceration in the United States beginning in the 1970s.

9. How did President Carter differ from his Democratic predecessors?

10. What was deregulation, and why did members of both political parties support it?

Key Terms

Vietnamization *p. 207*

Anti-Ballistic Missile (ABM) Treaty *p. 212*

détente *p. 212*

stagflation *p. 214*

Organization of the Petroleum Exporting Countries (OPEC) *p. 216*

Six Day War *p. 217*

Yom Kippur War *p. 217*

oil embargo *p. 218*

Project Independence *p. 218*

"great recession" *p. 220*

Whip Inflation Now (WIN) *p. 220*

Earth Day *p. 227*

Environmental Protection Agency (EPA) *p. 228*

Watergate babies *p. 234*

"New Democrats" *p. 235*

International Banking Act *p. 238*

Depository Institutions Deregulation and Monetary Control Act *p. 238*

National Energy Plan (NEP) *p. 239*

"malaise" speech *p. 240*

Iranian hostage crisis *p. 241*

The New Gilded Age

*

1980–2000

In 1994 Betty Dukes took a five-dollar-per-hour part-time job as a cashier at Wal-Mart. The national chain targeted places like her hometown, Pittsburg, California, an industrial city on the Sacramento River Delta that had reached its economic peak in the mid-twentieth century. The town's racially diverse, mostly blue-collar residents liked Wal-Mart for its friendly employees, its long opening hours, and most of all, its rock-bottom prices. It was expensive living in northern California, even in a gritty working-class town. Buying their food, clothing, electronics, and household supplies at Wal-Mart helped many families, barely getting by after they paid their rent or mortgage, make ends meet at the end of the month.[1]

Betty's job didn't pay much, but the retail sector was one of the few options open to women like her, without a lot of skills and education. And for a devoutly Christian woman, Wal-Mart seemed like an ideal employer. She admired what she called the "visionary spirit" of the company's founder, Sam

Walton. Wal-Mart promoted an ideology of family and faith and prided itself on being a big company with the heart of small-town America.

Betty worked hard at Wal-Mart, and after her first year, she earned a promotion to a full-time position and a modest raise. In 1997, having compiled a sterling record, she became a customer service manager. Still she grew frustrated with her position in the company. She was a manager in name only. She still got paid by the hour, just a little above minimum wage, despite her experience. She was particularly upset to watch as the company provided special training for male employees and promoted them to salaried positions. She wanted to move up to a better job, but her boss refused. Adding to her growing bitterness, she discovered that she earned fifty cents an hour less than another customer service manager, a man, who had less experience than she did.

Betty complained, first to the store manager and then, when he brushed her off, to Wal-Mart's regional office. Things took a turn for the worse. Her supervisor started keeping close track of her comings and goings. The scrutiny was unusual. If she returned a minute or two late from a break, it went down on her record. One day when she called in sick (using one of the sick days allowed under company policy), she got an earful. Citing a detailed list of minor infractions, the company demoted her in 1999, putting her back to work at the cash register and cutting her hours. She took a pay cut too. In 2000 she filed a lawsuit against Wal-Mart, accusing the chain of discrimination. Her lawyers found other women workers with similar stories at Wal-Mart stores throughout the country. The suit was a class action, filed in federal court in California. Betty and the other plaintiffs eventually lost their suit in the U.S. Supreme Court in 2011 on technical grounds. But the story revealed much about the transformation of American politics and economics in the late twentieth century.

Pittsburg's Wal-Mart was store number 1615 of more than three thousand Wal-Marts worldwide. In 1962 an enterprising businessman, Sam Walton, had launched the first, Wal-Mart Discount City, in tiny Rogers, Arkansas. Walton, the son of a land appraiser, had grown up comfortably in Missouri. After college and military service, he started his career in retail, purchasing and running small variety stores in Arkansas, Kansas, and Missouri. By

< President Ronald Reagan addresses the 1984 Republican National Convention (*previous page*).

Betty Dukes Wal-Mart emerged as the largest private employer in the United States in the late twentieth century, paying low wages to its heavily female workforce. Betty Dukes, pictured here outside its Pittsburg, California, store, launched a class-action lawsuit contesting Wal-Mart's discriminatory practices.

the early 1960s, he was ready to start his own chain. The timing was right. In 1962, when Walton opened his first Wal-Mart, three other discounters—Kmart, Target, and Woolco—opened their first stores as well. The last third of the twentieth century saw a proliferation of discount stores. Discounters like Wal-Mart made their money by keeping prices low but selling a high volume of goods.

Wal-Mart took advantage of shifts in the national economy. Walton could not have created his nationwide retail empire without the benefit of decades of federal programs. Rural electrification during the New Deal had opened the way for the expansion of business and manufacturing in places like Arkansas. Federally funded highways facilitated the quick and inexpensive shipping of clothes, food, and household items by truck from warehouses to stores. Federal labor laws, dating back to the 1947 Taft-Hartley Act, made it hard for retail workers to form unions, particularly in states like Arkansas.

Sam Walton opened his first stores in rural areas, where he found a ready source of low-wage workers, most of them women, victims of the collapsing agricultural economy. Having a low-wage workforce was key to his strategy to shave every penny he could from his company's overhead. His first stores— and the factories and warehouses that supplied them—were nearly all in areas with weak unions. His home base, Arkansas, was a deeply antiunion state. It had added a right-to-work amendment to its constitution in 1944, and immediately after the passage of Taft-Hartley in 1947, it had rushed through a right-to-work law. Throughout his career, Walton fiercely fought organized labor.

At the center of Wal-Mart's marketing was an idealized image of its small-town roots. Wal-Mart described its workers as "family," and in its early years, it often hired multiple generations of workers, from grandparents to grandchildren. Walton also promoted Christian values among the workforce. Beginning in the 1970s, he funded college courses in free enterprise, eventually at more than seven hundred state universities and Christian colleges, mostly in the South and lower Midwest. Walton also promoted an ethic of "service" among his company's mostly female workforce. "Mr. Sam calls this 'Servant Leadership,'" declared Sam's *Associate Handbook* in 1990, the manual distributed to all the firm's employees.

But for all his support for family values, Walton was no fan of the family wage. Over his career, he fought to keep the minimum wage low, and he cut costs by purchasing goods from suppliers that relied on poorly paid workers, increasingly overseas. He also fought to reduce corporate and individual taxes and to loosen international trade barriers. By the time he died in 1992, he had turned his firm into America's largest employer, with 371,000 employees at 1,928 stores. And the policies that he promoted enjoyed bipartisan support. The rise of Wal-Mart's America was the consequence of dramatic political shifts that had roots in the postwar years, but that accelerated beginning in the 1980s.

The Reagan Revolution?

The economy was on everyone's mind in the early 1980s. With unemployment over 7 percent, interest rates pushing 20 percent, and inflation sky high, the prognosis was grim. In his final debate with President Jimmy Carter in late October, Ronald Reagan asked, "Are you better off than you were four years ago? Is it easier for you to go and buy things in the stores than it was four years ago? Is there more or less unemployment

Chronology

1978	California's Proposition 13 and tax revolt
1979	Soviet-Afghan war begins Nicaraguan revolution
1980	Iran-Iraq war begins Ronald Reagan (Republican) elected president
1981	President Reagan shot Professional Air Traffic Controllers Organization (PATCO) strike AIDS epidemic begins
1982	Nuclear freeze movement
1983	Strategic Defense Initiative announced Operation Urgent Fury
1984	Ronald Reagan (Republican) reelected
1986	*Bowers v. Hardwick* Immigration Reform and Control Act Iran-Contra affair
1987	AIDS Coalition to Unleash Power (ACT UP) founded Reagan and Gorbachev agree to arms reductions
1988	George H. W. Bush (Republican) elected president
1989	Tiananmen Square protests in Beijing Fall of the Berlin Wall Operation Just Cause
1991	Operation Desert Storm
1992	William J. Clinton (Democrat) elected president
1993	North American Free Trade Agreement (NAFTA) signed into law
1994	Contract with America Rwandan genocide
1996	Personal Responsibility and Work Opportunity Reconciliation Act William J. Clinton (Democrat) reelected president
1998	Google.com founded House of Representatives votes to impeach President Clinton
1999	Gramm-Leach-Bliley Act

in the country than there was four years ago? Is America as respected throughout the world as it was?"[2] It was a simple and powerful rebuke to Carter's presidency.

Sixteen years after Barry Goldwater had gone down to defeat and pundits had declared the New Right dead, the United States elected one of its most conservative presidents ever. Carter picked up 41 percent of the vote, winning only six states and Washington, D.C. Reagan took the returns as a mandate for sweeping change. Reprising arguments that he had made since he was a spokesman for General Electric in the 1950s, he stated in his inaugural, "In the present crisis, government is not the solution to our problem; government is the problem."[3]

Though Reagan had decisively defeated Carter, polls suggested that a sizable majority of Americans did not share his philosophy of government. He came to office with a Republican majority in the Senate, the first in nearly twenty-five years, but the House was still solidly Democratic. Despite talk of a "Reagan Revolution," the American electorate supported programs that Reagan had long denounced, including Social Security, assistance to the poor, federal funding for public schools, and Medicare and Medicaid.

Still Reagan moved forward aggressively on his agenda. Less than a month after he took office, he pledged "to put the nation on a fundamentally different course, a course leading to less inflation, more growth, and a brighter future for all of our citizens."[4] That course included a 30 percent cut in income and corporate taxes, significant cuts in federal social programs, and a tight monetary policy to reduce inflation.[5]

THE TAX REVOLT Reagan subscribed to the theory that tax cuts would unleash corporate investment, which would then "trickle down" to ordinary citizens in the form of more jobs and higher wages. Taxpayers, he believed, would work harder if they could keep more of their paychecks, and as a result, the economy would grow. By this reasoning, it followed that even if tax rates were lower, more revenue would flow into federal coffers. In other words, tax cuts would pay for themselves.

Reagan was inspired by Representative Jack Kemp (R-NY) and Senator William Roth (R-DE), who had introduced legislation in 1977 to cut federal income tax rates by 30 percent. The tax-cutting agenda got a boost from Arthur Laffer, a young conservative economist at the University of Southern California who had worked in the Nixon and Ford administrations. In 1974, Laffer became famous on the right for the "Laffer curve," a graph that he drew on a napkin to illustrate his hypothesis that high taxes discouraged work. Tax cuts, he argued, would encourage productive activity and, in time, increase tax revenue. Few economists took the Laffer curve seriously, but rightwing politicians did. Jude Wanniski, a conservative editorialist at *The Wall Street Journal*, wrote that the Laffer curve "set off a symphony" in Reagan's mind; he believed "instantly that it was true and would never have a doubt thereafter."[6]

The first battleground of the tax revolt was Reagan's home state of California. There in 1978 voters overwhelmingly approved Proposition 13, a statewide referendum that cut state property taxes by 57 percent and required all municipalities to put property tax increases up for a vote. Prop 13 was the brainchild of wealthy businessman Howard Jarvis, a longtime anti–New Dealer and Goldwater supporter who had spent most of the 1960s and 1970s organizing against taxes. The Constitution, he argued, did not call for the protection of "life, liberty, and welfare or life, liberty, and food stamps."[7] Jarvis inspired tax rebels in solidly Democratic Massachusetts, where in 1980 a majority voted for Proposition 2½, a ballot initiative that capped local property tax increases.

Whether the tax revolt would go viral remained an open question well into the 1980s. Many moderates and liberals worried that tax cuts would have unintended negative consequences. They could point to California's public schools, which received most of their funding from property taxes. In many communities, voters without school-aged children were often reluctant to support property tax increases, and school funding dropped. The pinch was especially sharp in those older industrial cities and suburbs, like Betty Dukes's Pittsburg, whose public schools struggled with budget cuts because of the steady decline of the town's fishing, canning, and steel industries. Over the 1980s and 1990s, California's public schools suffered—districts put off maintenance, cut teacher pay, and tolerated crowded classrooms to make ends meet. Around the country, many voters were not yet ready to join Jarvis's rebellion.

REAGANOMICS On February 18, 1981, President Reagan announced a comprehensive economic plan, with four prongs: a cut in federal spending, a reduction in income taxes, economic deregulation—accelerating and expanding programs begun under Carter—and a tightening of the money supply. Cutting domestic programs would wean Americans from their "dependency" on government. Fiscal tightening would reduce inflation. Reagan promised that if his program was enacted, the federal budget would be balanced by 1984. Lifting "haphazard and inefficient regulation" would, in his view, spur corporate investment and job creation. He also called for creating a program of "tax incentives for investment," allowing investors larger and faster tax write-offs, on the untested assumption that companies would use tax savings to expand production and hire new workers. At the same time, however, he pledged to strengthen the national defense, a particularly costly priority.[8] "The whole thing is premised on faith," explained David Stockman, a former congressman from Michigan who directed Reagan's Office of Management and Budget. "On a belief about how the world works."[9]

Many did not share Reagan's faith. Fiscally conservative Republicans were skeptical of arguments for deep tax cuts. For decades, the GOP had staunchly supported balanced budgets, which meant increasing taxes if spending rose. Many worried that if tax revenue fell, Reagan would not be able to sustain his promise to bolster the nation's defense. During the Republican primaries, his leading opponent, George H. W. Bush, had denounced Reagan's ideas as "voodoo economics." Some economists warned that tax cuts would fuel inflation. Reagan faced an uphill battle in Congress.

On March 30, 1981, John Hinckley, a mentally ill twenty-five-year-old from a wealthy Texan family, attempted to assassinate the president. Reagan, gravely injured but conscious, survived the assault, and did so with characteristic humor and grace. He bantered with doctors and told his wife, Nancy, "Honey, I forgot to duck." After an outpouring of public sympathy, Reagan's approval ratings skyrocketed. He and his advisers used the goodwill to build momentum for his economic plan.

Reagan's tax and budget passed in August 1981, with the support of most Republicans and a small number of Democrats, nearly all of them from the South. Even if most Americans did not share Reagan's optimism that tax cuts would pay for themselves, most liked the idea of paying a little less every April 15. Many middle-class American taxpayers had seen their tax rates rise during the 1970s, not because they were wealthier but because inflation had bumped them into higher tax brackets. Reagan's reform would, for a time, reduce the effect of "bracket creep."

Reagan's tax cuts, however, benefited the wealthy far more than the middle class. The top tax rate, for the top earners, fell from 71 percent of income to just 28 percent. The tax rate on capital gains fell from 28 to 20 percent, and corporate tax rates fell from 46 to 35 percent. The result was a staggering increase in the annual income of the wealthiest Americans. The top 1 percent of income earners saw their annual after-tax income rise 256 percent in real dollars between 1976 and 2006.[10] By contrast, over that same period, the poorest fifth of the population saw an income increase of only 11 percent. Over the long run, the benefits of tax cuts did not "trickle down" from the rich to middle- and working-class Americans.

Reagan's tax cuts did not pay for themselves. The president's faith in the Laffer curve proved misguided. Over the 1980s, federal deficits skyrocketed, exacerbated by dramatic increases in defense spending, which constituted nearly a quarter of the 1982 budget. Domestic spending also proved difficult to trim. A tenth of federal spending went to servicing the federal debt, and the government could not fail to meet its fiscal obligations without triggering an economic crisis. Forty-eight percent of the federal budget went to Social Security and Medicare, programs that enjoyed broad bipartisan support. Only about one-fifth of the federal budget consisted of discretionary programs, ranging from infrastructure projects like the expensive interstate highway system to education spending, and a panoply of mostly small antipoverty programs. Even drastic cuts to those programs would not substantially reduce the deficit. Between 1981 and 1989, federal debt tripled, reaching $2.8 trillion.

Deregulation also had unintended consequences. Reagan used the power of the presidency to weaken the enforcement of environmental regulations (many passed less than a decade before he entered office). Secretary of the Interior James Watt loosened regulations that limited commercial mining, cattle grazing, and oil and gas extraction on federal lands. Several regulatory agencies, including OSHA, the EPA, and the FDA, cut the number of inspectors to enforce regulations protecting worker safety, water supplies, and food. The loosening of SEC regulatory oversight of Wall Street encouraged insider trading scandals in the mid-1980s. Executives like Michael Milken and Ivan Boesky made fortunes by getting advance word of pending mergers and acquisitions and using that information to buy stocks before their prices shot upward.

Congress and the administration also rewrote regulations governing savings and loan (S&L) associations, allowing them to expand their pool of investments to include risky mortgages and loans, most notably lifting the cap on mortgage interest rates. For most of their history, S&Ls had been conservative with their investments and local in their orientation. In the new loosely regulated financial regime, S&Ls grew exponentially and gambled on tempting but often unwise investments, from remote vacation housing developments to hastily constructed strip malls. When many of those investments failed, S&Ls collapsed. Nearly sixteen hundred S&Ls failed between 1980 and 1994, most of them in 1987 and 1988. Eventually the costs of bailing out those institutions exceeded $150 billion.

The Social Safety Net

Reagan's wing of the Republican Party had been fighting the New Deal for decades and mostly losing. But now that they were in power, they trained their sights on social welfare spending, beginning with Social Security. Since 1935, Social Security had become the costliest domestic program. Many Americans viewed its central provisions—old age and disability insurance—as inalienable rights. Social Security had support in both parties. President Eisenhower had enacted reforms that dramatically expanded its rolls. In 1972, President Nixon authorized the adjustment of Social Security payments to the cost-of-living index. As a result, during the inflationary 1970s, Social Security spending skyrocketed.

SOCIAL SECURITY REFORM The Republican right had long despised Social Security as an expensive welfare program that bolstered big government and stifled the free market. In the 1950s and 1960s, Reagan denounced the Social Security payroll tax as coercive and instead backed a voluntary system of savings for retirement. It was a principled position but deeply unpopular. In 1976, Reagan had suffered a stinging defeat in the Florida Republican primary because of his support for privatizing Social Security. Politically astute, he began shifting his position in the late 1970s, publicly stating his support for Social Security but calling for a radical overhaul of the program.

In May 1981, Reagan proposed raising the eligibility age for Social Security to 67. (Seniors at that time were eligible for partial payments at 62½ and full payments at 65.) He also argued for reducing Social Security checks by 25 percent for those who took early retirement. It was one of the biggest miscalculations of his presidency. Democrats howled in opposition. "It is a rotten thing to do, a despicable thing," stated Speaker of the House Thomas P. O'Neill, a Boston liberal whose mostly blue-collar constituents revered the New Deal.[11] By the 1980s, the elderly were living longer, voted at higher rates than younger people, and had an effective voice through Washington lobbyists, particularly the American Association of Retired People, which had millions of members and the resources to fight. In a crushing 96–0 vote on May 20, the Senate rejected Reagan's plan. It was an early reminder of the limits of the "Reagan Revolution."

Embarrassed by his defeat, Reagan appointed a commission to reform Social Security. In 1983 the president and Congress agreed to a payroll tax hike to bolster the funds available to pay beneficiaries. For the moment, the Social Security system was solvent (though rising life expectancies and the graying of the baby boom generation would put pressure on the system a few decades in the future). It would not be until the 2000s that the Republicans, this time with control over both the White House and Congress, would revive the idea of privatizing Social Security, and again they would fail decisively.

AID TO FAMILIES WITH DEPENDENT CHILDREN Reagan, however, had some success in chopping less popular social welfare programs. Since the 1950s, conservatives had criticized Aid to Families with Dependent Children (AFDC), the program commonly known as welfare, which mostly supported impoverished single mothers and their children. They argued that AFDC created a culture of "dependency," discouraging poor people from engaging in paid labor outside the home. Many blamed welfare for unleashing a culture of immorality that broke down families and destroyed the work ethic. The program's supporters countered that it had played a role in reducing overall poverty rates, which had fallen by half between 1959 and 1979. In fact, poverty rates remained below 10 percent through the economically troubled 1970s.[12]

There was no evidence of a causal relationship between welfare, joblessness, and family structure. Beginning in the early 1970s, AFDC payments steadily declined, and they would continue to fall in value for twenty-five years. Unlike Social Security, AFDC was not indexed to inflation. As a result, between 1973 and 1989, the value of an average monthly welfare check fell by 40 percent. Welfare payments seldom proved sufficient to support a family. By the 1980s, the vast majority of welfare recipients engaged in paid labor, often off the books, to make ends meet. Welfare also had little impact on family structure. It was true that fewer and fewer Americans married; those who did saw marriages dissolve into divorce more frequently; and a steadily growing percentage of children were born to single women. But these patterns held across all socioeconomic groups, whether or not they received welfare checks.

Many Americans saw welfare in racial terms. Though the majority of AFDC recipients throughout the period were white, media accounts of poverty focused on African Americans, in part because they were concentrated in cities, as were most news outlets. Surveys showed that many whites believed that blacks were ungrateful, happier to take "handouts" than to work hard, and inherently lazy. Black welfare mothers, the argument went, lived extravagant lives on the proceeds of their AFDC checks, while hardworking white Americans barely made ends meet.

Reagan offered his own version of the story, featuring a fictitious "welfare queen." "There is a woman in Chicago," he proclaimed during his 1976 campaign. "She has 80 names, 30 addresses, 12 Social Security cards, and is collecting veterans' benefits on four non-existing deceased husbands." Reagan's story brought audiences to their feet, but it was a fabrication, woven together from a country music song and news reports about a Chicago woman in the early 1970s who had used four aliases and earned about $8,000 fraudulently.[13]

THE LIMITS OF WELFARE REFORM For all his antiwelfare rhetoric, Reagan found it difficult to cut many of the programs on his list. Medicare and Medicaid were popular among hospital administrators and doctors because they enabled poor and elderly patients to pay their bills. Food stamps, another War on Poverty initiative, had wide bipartisan support. Big-city Democrats knew that many of their working-class and poor constituents benefited from the program. Senators from agricultural states, many of whom were Republicans, supported food stamps because their use expanded the market for produce and meat.

To many Reagan critics, cutting support to the poor was heartless. When the Department of Agriculture issued a directive in the fall of 1981 that ketchup could be considered a vegetable—a response to Carter and Reagan administration cuts to the National School Lunch Act, a popular but costly Truman-era program that provided subsidies to schools to feed needy students—critics mocked the president. Welfare activists, many of them veterans of the civil rights and feminist movements of the 1960s, staged hunger strikes and marched on welfare offices, fighting against what they called Reagan's "war on the poor." For the moment, they had enough congressional allies to hold back Reagan's proposed cuts. Reagan did not eviscerate aid to the poor, but his antiwelfare rhetoric played a key role in further delegitimizing already unpopular welfare programs.

By the mid-1980s, conservative think tanks, encouraged by Reagan's policies, began to draft welfare reform programs that called for mandatory work requirements for AFDC recipients, time limits on welfare payments, and further funding cuts. In one of the most important—but largely unnoticed—social policy experiments of the 1980s, the Reagan administration issued waivers that allowed states to modify welfare laws and institute work requirements. Several states with Republican governors, most notably Pennsylvania, instituted punitive new welfare laws. Those experiments would lay the groundwork for nationwide welfare reform efforts in the 1990s.

JOBS AND URBAN POLICY The administration had only limited success in cutting welfare, but Reagan's budgetary ax fell on programs that helped poor people find work. The Comprehensive Employment and Training Act (CETA), signed by Nixon in 1973 and expanded by Carter, had provided job training for the unemployed, ex-convicts, and impoverished youth. The Reagan administration replaced CETA in 1982 with the underfunded Job Training Partnership Act, which provided incentives to private employers to train workers. All together, the administration cut federal labor market programs drastically, from $15.6 billion in 1980 to only $5 billion in 1985. If poor people were to escape welfare, they would have to fend for themselves.

But the administration did not do much to improve the fortunes of low-wage workers. In June 1981, Reagan and Congress set the minimum wage at $3.35 per hour. It would not increase again until April 1990. During that period, the value of the minimum wage fell by 44 percent. Workers in the economy's most rapidly growing sectors, including unskilled service work and retail employment, often had to take more than one job to make ends meet. Working-class families were particularly hard hit. By the end of the 1980s, a full-time minimum wage job was insufficient to lift a family of four out of poverty. For employers like Wal-Mart, the minimum wage was a boon. It allowed them to keep prices low and profits high.

URBAN SPENDING The conservative administration also cut urban spending. Many big cities were losing population, and with it congressional seats and clout in Washington. By 1980 a plurality of Americans lived in suburbs. And it was there that Reagan and the Republicans had made some of their biggest electoral gains. Urban spending, in their view, was a zero-sum game: unworthy urban residents benefited while hardworking suburbanites paid the bill. Federal urban spending fell from 12 percent of the budget in 1980 to only 3 percent in 1990. But those spending cuts came at a time when many urban problems were worsening. Urban infrastructure was crumbling. One of the most unsettling problems was the sharp increase in homelessness, the result of inadequate housing, the unstable economy, cuts in welfare spending (especially for single people), and the deinstitutionalization of the mentally ill. By best estimates, 500,000 to 600,000 people were without homes in 1987. Many blamed Reagan administration policies, but the president deflected criticism by arguing that "people who are sleeping on the grates . . . the homeless . . . are homeless, you might say, by choice."[14]

REAGAN AND LABOR One of the biggest economic shifts in the last quarter of the twentieth century was the disappearance of well-paying jobs—particularly union jobs with relatively good wages and benefits. Nearly as many union members had voted for Reagan as for Carter in 1980. Reagan was also the only president who had been a union member. From 1947 to 1952, and again in 1959–60, he had been president of the Screen Actors Guild, which negotiated wages, a generous pension plan, and health care benefits for its members.

But Reagan forever altered the trade union movement during his first year in office. In August 1981 the Professional Air Traffic Controllers Organization (PATCO), a union that had endorsed Reagan, voted to strike. Reagan threatened to fire PATCO members who did not return to their jobs within forty-eight hours. The strike was illegal, and Reagan used law and order rhetoric to call them back. "What lesser action can there be?" he responded when a journalist asked why he had taken such a strong position. "The law is very explicit. They are violating the law."[15] Nearly eleven thousand remained off the job and, much to their surprise, Reagan followed through. He fired them and called in military personnel to oversee the air traffic system. Conservatives hailed Reagan for showing his mettle and for striking a blow against organized labor.

Organized labor had been gradually declining since the 1950s, but Reagan's response to PATCO emboldened employers to stand up to striking workers. Between the end of World War II and 1980, there had been only three years with fewer than two hundred major strikes. Between 1981 and 2014, only two years (1981 and 1982) had more than one hundred strikes. In Reagan's last year in office, there were only forty.[16] Union membership declined steeply, from about a quarter to a sixth of the workforce. The private sector was hardest hit: in 1990 only about 8 percent of its workers were unionized.

One of the beneficiaries of the PATCO strike was Wal-Mart. Sam Walton's first wave of expansion had largely been in nonunion states in the South and lower Midwest. When workers organized to demand better pay, the firm fiercely resisted. In early 1982, when warehouse workers at the company's Searcy, Arkansas, facility petitioned for a union election, Sam Walton made a personal visit. One warehouse worker pointed out that the firm paid $1.50 an hour more in a Texas facility. Walton bluntly replied, "I can hire you for less in Arkansas." One worker recalled that Walton intimidated them. "He told us that if the union got in, the warehouse would be closed." The Searcy workers decided to keep their jobs and voted down the union. PATCO had taught them a harsh lesson: if they as much as supported a union, their livelihoods were in jeopardy.[17]

Sam Walton began to expand his retail empire well outside its base in the South and in the border states. Between 1980 and 1992, the chain added more than sixteen hundred stores, many in places like Pittsburg, California, that had once been hotbeds of union organizing. During the Truman and Eisenhower years, Pittsburg's steelworkers, chemical industry workers, and dockworkers, most of them men, had been among the best paid in the country. In 1991, when Wal-Mart opened there, workers like Betty Dukes, mostly women, had no one to bargain for better wages or to protect them from discriminatory employers. They were left to their own devices. They started at the minimum wage—only $4.25 per hour that year. They worked irregular hours, did not get overtime pay, had little vacation time, and received no health benefits. Many Wal-Mart workers were so poor that they qualified for food stamps.

Religious Revivals

Ronald Reagan always put economic issues first. But over the course of his administration, he gave voice to the concerns of some of his staunchest supporters, members of the burgeoning religious right. Reagan was not particularly devout. He had come of age in Hollywood, a place that many conservative Christians saw as the fount of immorality. He had divorced and remarried and was never an attentive father. As governor of California, he had signed into law one of the most liberal abortion laws in the country.

But Reagan and his advisers were attuned to major changes in American religious practices and affiliations during the 1960s and 1970s. Mainstream Protestant denominations saw their membership drop, while evangelical churches exploded. Between 1970 and 1985, the Southern Baptists saw a membership increase of 23 percent. The Assemblies of God, a Pentecostal denomination whose members spoke in tongues, grew by 300 percent in the same period. By 1980 about 20 million viewers regularly tuned in to programs such as Jim and Tammy Faye Bakker's *PTL Club*, Pat Robertson's *700 Club*, and Jerry Falwell's *Old Time Gospel Hour*. In the 1980s more than

110,000 of America's estimated 400,000 churches were evangelical or fundamentalist.[18] "It was a wonderful time for Christianity," remembered Jan Lindsey, who evangelized on college campuses.[19]

Evangelical religion thrived in part because it responded to frustrations and uncertainties in the United States and the world. Jan Lindsey and her husband Hal discovered that their audiences responded with enthusiasm to the prophetic message that the world was entering its final days. Drawing parallels between apocalyptic biblical prophecies and current events, Hal Lindsey's 1970 book, *The Late Great Planet Earth*, sold 28 million copies within two decades. The calamities of global wars, the clash between the United States and the Soviets, and especially conflicts in the Middle East were all portents of the End Times, the moment when earth would be ruled by the Antichrist, Jesus would return, and the true believers would be raptured, leaving the troubled earth and joining the Lord. Lindsay's books were popular because they gave meaning to the incomprehensible.

THE RELIGIOUS RIGHT Those who opted to "choose Jesus Christ as their personal Lord and Savior" also began to make the personal political, denouncing liberalism, homosexuality, abortion, crime, and pornography, and blaming liberal politicians for enabling a culture of permissiveness. Many ministers wove political messages into their sermons: those who were saved by Jesus had a responsibility to save society from the temptations of sexual liberation and the collapse of the family.

It was but a small step from calls of personal responsibility and respect for authority to denunciations of "secular humanism," a term popularized by another best-selling evangelical author, Francis Schaeffer. Over the course of the 1970s and 1980s, many on the religious right began to step up their political involvement. Their rhetoric reprised themes from the postwar years—the dangers of godless Communism, juvenile delinquency, and homosexuality. But these themes took on a new urgency in the shadow of the struggle for civil rights, the rise of the counterculture, the feminist insurgency, and sexual liberation movements.

The new phase in the politicization of conservative churchgoers dated to court challenges to religiously affiliated segregated academies in the 1970s. In *Green v. Connally* (1971), the Supreme Court ruled that religious institutions that discriminated on racial grounds could not claim tax-exempt status under the Internal Revenue Code. For much of the 1970s, the ruling was only loosely enforced, leading to a proliferation of all-white Christian schools in the South. By the mid-1970s, however, civil rights groups demanded that the IRS enforce *Green*. When the IRS revoked the tax-exempt status of Bob Jones University, a fundamentalist institution in South Carolina that forbade racial mixing, conservative critics howled that the government was infringing on religious freedom. In 1978 the IRS tightened its rules and began to hold hearings to determine whether segregated Christian academies should be eligible for tax exemption.

Paul Weyrich, a conservative political activist, had been trying to mobilize evangelicals since 1964 with limited success. Weyrich, a Catholic, began his career as a congressional staffer, supported Goldwater, and worked closely with anti–New Deal business groups. In 1974, joining with Colorado brewing magnate Joseph Coors, Weyrich founded the Heritage Foundation, a conservative think tank. Heritage promoted free enterprise and rallied against the minimum wage, welfare programs, and labor unions. Still, it was difficult to rouse working- and middle-class Americans around a pro-business agenda. Weyrich had a hunch that he could do better by stirring up popular discontent around religious and cultural concerns.

At first, mobilizing evangelical Christians was an uphill battle. "I utterly failed," he recalled of his early efforts to create a conservative Christian political movement. But much to his surprise, the new IRS rules sparked a mass mobilization. "What changed their mind," recalled Weyrich, was "Jimmy Carter's intervention against the Christian schools, trying to deny them tax exemption on the basis of so-called de facto segregation."[20]

Religious and racial resentment proved a potent combination. Ministers denounced the IRS for enforcing "racial quotas." They argued that the IRS directive was proof that secularists were using government power to silence religious expression. In 1979, Weyrich met with the televangelist Jerry Falwell and launched the Moral Majority, which raised nearly $100 million in its first two years and claimed to have registered nearly ten million conservative voters. "If you would like to know where I am politically," stated Falwell, "I am to the right of wherever you are. I thought Goldwater was too liberal."[21]

The Reagan administration rewarded the Moral Majority. In 1982 it intervened in the Bob Jones University controversy, reversing the IRS decision to deny the school tax-exempt status. The Bob Jones battle ended up in the Supreme Court, which issued an 8–1 decision upholding the IRS. Bob Jones would not get a tax exemption. The ruling was a blow to Reagan, who faced charges that his administration endorsed racism.

Reagan also appointed prominent religious conservatives to his administration. James Watt, the secretary of the interior, used his bully pulpit to promote Christian ideas. In an address to Falwell's Liberty University, Watt called for a "Christian revolution."[22] But he was more concerned with curbing environmental regulations than with spreading the Gospel. Surgeon General C. Everett Koop, appointed in 1982, had joined the crusade against "secular humanism" and was a staunch opponent of abortion. In 1984 the conservative preacher James Robison opened the Republican convention, and Falwell called Reagan and his administration "God's instruments in rebuilding America."[23] But in practice, Reagan often disappointed the religious right.

ABORTION POLITICS Evangelicals stepped up their mobilization against abortion in the late 1970s and 1980s, moving it to the center of the conservative agenda. The antiabortion movement demanded the recognition of the personhood of the fetus. It denounced feminists and their emphasis on women's reproductive freedom. It depicted abortion as a selfish choice. And it called for a reassertion of traditional male authority.

Neither side in the debate captured the complicated attitudes of most Americans toward reproduction and abortion. Most Americans, including religious believers, were ambivalent about abortion, particularly late in pregnancy. They viewed it as a tragedy, best avoided but sometimes unavoidable. Public opinion surveys consistently showed that a majority of Americans believed that the decision to terminate a pregnancy should be a private choice, decided by a woman in consultation with a counselor, minister, or family member. In 1981 and 1982, polls showed that only about one-third of Americans wanted to ban abortion.[24] But abortion politics was intensely polarized. Both sides could point to one striking pattern: the rate of abortions in the United States had increased steadily—rising from about 20 per 1,000 in 1973 to a peak of 29 per 1,000 in 1980.[25] For religious opponents of abortion, this was incontrovertible evidence of moral decay. For supporters, it was a proof that legalized abortion met a demand. To turn back abortion, the pro-life movement would turn to the courts.

AIDS Religious politics also shaped the Reagan administration's response to one of the gravest health crises of the twentieth century. In 1981 doctors began noticing that young men, many of them gay, appeared with unexplained symptoms, among them virulent pneumonia and a rare cancer called Kaposi's sarcoma. Within a few years, the disease, named acquired immunodeficiency syndrome (AIDS), would go from a medical oddity to an epidemic. One of its early victims was Stuart Garcia, a brilliant, charismatic Texan who entered Columbia University the fall that Reagan was elected. President of Columbia's student government, Stuart was, in the words of a classmate, "one of those people who seemed destined to do something important."[26] He also had a lively life off campus, joining gay dance parties at downtown nightclubs. But his health took a turn for the worse the year after he graduated. In 1985 he began coughing violently and was hospitalized, the first of many times. Less than a year later, after struggling with 106-degree fevers and excruciating pain, he died. He was twenty-three.[27]

Stuart was one of 11,932 Americans to die of AIDS in 1986. But federal support for AIDS research remained a low priority. In 1983 the administration rebuffed health officials from eleven cities who asked for support to manage the epidemic. The federal Public Health Service, whose director pledged that year to make AIDS a priority, suffered budget cuts for the next few years. In September 1985 the president mentioned AIDS publicly for the first time but again trimmed funds for AIDS research. In the spring of 1986, a few months before Stuart's death, Reagan asked Surgeon General Koop to issue a report on the disease. Koop's report called for abstinence, monogamy, and condom use. The last angered some religious conservatives. Secretary of Education William Bennett denounced "condom-mania" as "a species of self-delusion."[28]

AIDS remained near the bottom of the list of presidential priorities. Under pressure, the president created a committee to investigate AIDS in 1987, including several prominent conservative religious leaders. But his decision to name one gay doctor to the panel angered many of his conservative allies. The administration, argued Senator Gordon Humphrey (R-NH), "should strive at all costs to avoid sending the message to society—especially to impressionable youth—that homosexuality is simply an alternative lifestyle."[29]

In the meantime AIDS activists stepped up pressure on the president. In October 1987 a half million protesters marched in New York, convened by a new organization, the AIDS Coalition to Unleash Power (ACT UP). Over the next several years, AIDS

The AIDS Crisis Protesters in Washington, D.C., on June 1, 1987, challenge the Reagan administration's inaction on the AIDS epidemic.

activists would pressure Congress to substantially increase AIDS funding. In the next decade, they would embark on a massive AIDS education effort and would successfully advocate the loosening of pharmaceutical regulations to allow for early testing of promising medications on AIDS patients.

TURNING THE COURTS RIGHTWARD Reagan gave only symbolic support to religious conservatives' drive for a constitutional amendment to outlaw abortion. But the administration worked through the courts to push a conservative agenda that encompassed abortion and much more. That began with his court appointments. In 1981 he nominated the first woman justice to the Supreme Court, Sandra Day O'Connor. Many conservative advocates worried: although she was a favorite of Barry Goldwater, her positions on abortion and women's rights were suspect. Still, she won Senate approval with overwhelming bipartisan support. She would be one of Reagan's few moderate appointees. In the next few years, the Department of Justice implemented an unprecedented process to screen potential judges for their views on regulation, abortion, affirmative action, and criminal procedure. By 1989, Reagan had named 344 of

714 federal district and appeals court judges. His appointees were the youngest of any twentieth-century president, the average just under fifty years old. They were almost uniformly to the right of federal judges named by Reagan's predecessors.[30]

In the late 1970s and 1980s, many states and localities, under pressure from religious groups, passed laws to discourage abortions. Reagan directed the Department of Justice to support these laws. But the administration's intervention did not tip the scales. In *Akron v. Akron Center for Reproductive Health* (1983), the Supreme Court struck down a city ordinance that had required doctors to inform women that the fetus "is a human life from the moment of conception" and set a twenty-four-hour waiting period for women who planned to have an abortion.

The administration continued to challenge *Roe v. Wade*. In 1986, Solicitor General Kenneth Starr argued *Thornburgh v. American College of Obstetricians and Gynecologists* (1986), defending a Pennsylvania law that required doctors to inform women that abortion was risky, to file detailed reports, and to favor live births over abortion if the fetus was at a late stage of development. The court was bitterly divided. In a 5–4 decision, it struck down the restrictions. "The states are not free, under the guise of protecting maternal health or potential life, to intimidate women into continuing pregnancies," wrote Justice Harry Blackmun for the majority. In their dissent, Justices William Rehnquist and Byron White denounced *Roe v. Wade* as "fundamentally misguided." Advocates of reproductive freedom celebrated the narrow victory but worried that if the Court shifted rightward, *Roe* might be overturned.

Another 1986 decision, *Bowers v. Hardwick*, this one involving gay sex, cheered conservatives. The case involved two Georgia men who were arrested for engaging in consensual oral sex. The case gave the court another opportunity to consider the "right to privacy," which the court had found and protected in its contraception and abortion cases. Did that right extend to homosexuality? In a strongly worded majority opinion, the court ruled no. Justice Byron White, writing for the majority, argued that the Constitution did not protect "a fundamental right to engage in homosexual sodomy." Giving legal recognition to gay sex, concurred Chief Justice Warren Burger, would "cast aside millennia of moral teaching."[31]

SUPREME COURT POLITICS   In the wake of these contentious cases, Reagan got the opportunity to reshape the Supreme Court. Each nomination was more contested than the one before. In 1986 he elevated William Rehnquist, the court's most conservative member, to the position of chief justice. To fill Rehnquist's seat, Reagan nominated a crusading right-wing jurist, Antonin Scalia, who had made his name as a proponent of "textualism"—the notion that judicial interpretations should rely on a narrow reading of original legislative texts. Both won Senate approval but with significant Democratic defections.

A year after Scalia joined the high court, Reagan nominated Robert Bork to fill another vacancy. Bork, a controversial law professor and former solicitor general in the Nixon administration, argued that the Supreme Court had wrongly decided the landmark *Brown v. Board of Education* case because it relied on social science. He had opposed the Civil Rights Act of 1964. And he criticized *Roe v. Wade* for relying on a "right to privacy" that was not enumerated in the Constitution.

In the past, most Supreme Court nomination hearings had been brief and uncontroversial. Bork's was not. Feminists, civil rights leaders, and liberal law professors lined up to testify against him. Senator Edward Kennedy, brother of the slain president, offered one of the harshest critiques. "Robert Bork's America is a land in which women would be forced into back-alley abortions, blacks would sit at segregated lunch counters, rogue police could break down citizens' doors in midnight raids, children could not be taught about evolution."[32] Bork was feisty and often arrogant during his confirmation hearings. That hurt him. After weeks of bitter public debate, the Senate rejected his nomination, 58–42. Reagan then successfully nominated a soft-spoken conservative, Anthony Kennedy, to fill the seat, and since he lacked Bork's baggage, the Senate quickly confirmed him. Later federal judicial nominees learned from Bork's experience. Fearful that they would be "Borked," they dodged controversy, refusing to disclose their positions on hot-button issues like abortion and affirmative action.

"Peace Through Strength"

For Reagan, no issue was as pressing as the battle against Communism. He had long argued that the United States would prevail in the Cold War only by flexing its military might. In the 1950s he had criticized the policy of containment. In the 1960s he supported Barry Goldwater's position that the United States should consider using nuclear weapons in Vietnam. In the 1970s he denounced Nixon's opening to China and détente with the Soviet Union. Arms reduction treaties, he contended, appeased the Soviets and jeopardized American security. During his first term, he drew his core foreign policy advisers from the most prominent critics of détente. Many—like Alexander Haig, the secretary of state, William Casey, the CIA director, and Caspar Weinberger, the secretary of defense—were proponents of "peace through strength," advocating militarization rather than negotiation with the Soviets.

Reagan had blamed his predecessors for a lack of resolve in confronting America's enemies abroad. A case in point was the Iranian hostage crisis, which entered its 444th day when Reagan was inaugurated on January 20, 1981. Just after he was sworn in, he learned that the Iranian government had released the American hostages. The resolution to the crisis was the result of Carter's behind-the-scenes diplomacy, but the timing benefited Reagan. It gave him a clean slate on his first day in office.

THE DEFENSE BUILDUP Reagan began by significantly increasing defense spending, one of the priorities in his first budget. It rose from 5.3 to 6.4 percent of the gross domestic product between 1981 and 1989. The administration channeled funds into constructing expensive new bombers, including research for a high-tech "stealth" bomber that would evade conventional radar. Reagan also authorized the deployment of 572 new intermediate-range nuclear missiles in Western Europe, within easy striking distance of the Soviet Union.

Reagan's nuclear policy was particularly unpopular in Europe, where mass protests against Euromissiles erupted in 1982. On the home front, Americans were also concerned about the arms race. By the summer of 1982, nearly two-thirds of Americans supported a "nuclear freeze," calling for both superpowers to halt the construction and deployment of new weapons. In July one million Americans, many members of liberal religious organizations, marched in New York City in support of a freeze, the largest demonstration in American history.

In early 1983 the Reagan administration's relations with the Soviets were icier than ever, and the president escalated the war of words. He continued to assert that the USSR was on the brink of military supremacy, despite mounting evidence that the Soviet regime was weak and unpopular, its military technologies inferior, and its economy in crisis. In a speech before the National Association of Evangelicals in March, Reagan spoke of "sin and evil in the world" and pointed to the Soviet Union as an "evil empire." He denounced the nuclear freeze as "a very dangerous fraud."[33]

That same month, Reagan announced the Strategic Defense Initiative (SDI), calling for the creation of a space "shield" of X-rays and lasers to protect the United States from incoming nuclear missiles. He rejected the long-standing American doctrine of "deterrence of aggression through the prospect of retaliation." In the context of the "evil empire" speech, some commentators feared that SDI would be cover for the United States to build a first-strike capability against the Soviet Union. Few scientists believed that Reagan's program was feasible. Critics nicknamed SDI "Star Wars," suggesting that it was no more real than science fiction. Budget hawks argued that SDI would be an expensive boondoggle, costing as much as a trillion dollars. But Reagan did not let it go. The program would survive until the early 1990s, when the Bush administration and Congress dramatically cut funding for the program to balance the federal budget. The Clinton administration would dismantle it in 1993.

One of the unintended consequences of the arms buildup was that it stimulated a boom in research and development and military technology. Suburban Boston, Silicon Valley, and Los Angeles were flush with federal dollars, pulling them out of the economic slump sooner than most of the rest of the country. Federal spending also launched a high-tech economy. Universities introduced student-accessible computer centers in the early 1980s, the personal computer went from a novelty item to a mass-produced necessity in less than ten years, and microchips transformed everyday electronics. The number of jobs for electrical engineers and computer scientists skyrocketed. By the early 1990s, local area networks and the Internet began connecting computers into what would be later named the World Wide Web.

The rise and success of American high-tech industries did not result from tax cuts and deregulation. In fact, no American industries relied more on government spending than did computing, electrical engineering, and communications equipment. All had emerged as the result of Cold War–era federal spending on science and research, much of it defense-related. Federal research funding for Cold War–related research and development programs took off in the 1980s, after stagnating during the fiscally troubled Nixon and Carter years. Between 1982 and 1988, federal research and development spending nearly doubled. By the decade's end, 40 percent of all research and development in the computing industry was federally funded; nearly half of communications technology research—including the systems that were the basis of the Internet—came from the federal government. Government programs also bankrolled university laboratories, computer science, and electrical engineering. In 1985 alone, computer science programs received 83 percent of their funds from the federal government.[34] Members of Congress jostled for federal appropriations to their districts, hoping to become the "next Silicon Valley," the computing industry's hub outside San Francisco.[35] Those efforts paid off in the 1980s, when the influx of government spending to contractors and universities fueled the rise of the Route 128 corridor outside Boston, the Research Triangle in North Carolina, and the semiconductor center of Austin, Texas.

America in the World

While the administration pushed to win the arms race, it put more resources into winning the Cold War around the world. The United States aggressively intervened in civil wars in the Middle East and Latin America. The administration hoped to overcome the "Vietnam syndrome" but faced widespread public and congressional skepticism about its counterinsurgency operations. To end-run around public opinion, the administration stepped up covert operations, with disastrous consequences.

THE VOLATILE MIDDLE EAST Politics in the Middle East were especially volatile in the 1980s. The Reagan administration's foreign policy there did not help. In Afghanistan, Shi'ite Muslims, inspired by the Iranian revolution, rose against the Soviet-backed Communist regime in 1979, resisting efforts to secularize the country. The USSR responded by sending troops, embarking on what would be a ten-year war. About 25,000 Soviet troops died, most in brutal ground combat. Four hundred thousand Afghans died in Soviet airstrikes. Many considered the Afghan war to be the Soviet equivalent of Vietnam—costly, bloody, and unwinnable.

When the war broke out, the Carter administration had authorized modest CIA support for the anti-Soviet uprising, but the Reagan administration stepped up the effort. CIA operatives secretly provided weaponry to the mujahideen, a force controlled by Afghan warlords. The CIA also collaborated closely with Islamic groups in neighboring Pakistan, where the rebels established bases. While Reagan viewed the mujahideen as "freedom fighters," his administration ended up empowering Islamic radicals in both Pakistan and Afghanistan who would later turn against the United States, embroiling the country in its own long, inconclusive war in Afghanistan a little more than two decades after the Soviets launched theirs.

Nearby, the United States found itself entangled in the Iran-Iraq war, a brutal eight-year conflict that began in 1980 and ended in a stalemate, with over 400,000 dead. The Reagan administration allied itself with Iraq and its autocratic leader,

Saddam Hussein. In 1982 the State Department removed Iraq from its list of terrorist nations and encouraged a robust market exchanging American arms for Iraqi oil. Reagan administration officials, concerned that the Iranian theocracy would get access to Iraq's vast oilfields, overlooked Hussein's use of illegal chemical weapons and his brutal repression of dissent. A 1983 memo captured America's view that "any major reversal of Iraq's fortunes" would be "a strategic loss for the West."[36] Reagan administration officials hoped, in vain, that with American aid, the Hussein regime would become less repressive.

Reagan faced equally daunting challenges in Lebanon. Since gaining its independence from France in 1943, the country had struggled to hold together a government that included its rivalrous Muslim minority, divided between Sunnis and Shi'ites, its substantial Christian population, and its minority Druze. In the 1970s and early 1980s, it was torn by civil war. Skirmishes between bordering Israel and Syria added to the tension, as did the presence of Palestinian Liberation Organization (PLO) forces near the Lebanese-Israeli border and in Beirut. In June 1982 the United States supported Israeli attacks on the PLO in Lebanon. In August, Reagan made the momentous decision to send U.S. Marines there as part of a peacekeeping force: "In no case will our troops stay longer than 30 days."[37] But they stayed longer, and the situation worsened. In October 1983 a suicide bomber attacked a U.S. barracks at the Beirut airport, killing 241 Americans. The United States did not retaliate. For three and a half months afterward, Reagan pledged to keep marines in Lebanon as long as they were needed. If American troops withdrew, he argued in early February, "we'll be sending one signal to terrorists everywhere: They can gain by waging war against innocent people."[38] But faced with congressional opposition and public skepticism, Reagan backtracked, and on February 7, 1984, the United States pulled out of Lebanon.

"ROLLBACK" IN LATIN AMERICA AND THE CARIBBEAN   The Reagan administration was particularly concerned with what it considered to be Soviet "expansionism" in Latin America and the Caribbean. Its primary targets were leftists in El Salvador and Nicaragua. El Salvador was embroiled in a bloody civil war, led by revolutionaries who challenged its corrupt military leadership and demanded reforms to redistribute agricultural land to the impoverished peasantry. El Salvador's authoritarian government, which Reagan supported, brutally silenced dissent. In 1980, El Salvadoran death squads had murdered the popular Roman Catholic archbishop Oscar Romero, a critic of the regime, and had raped and murdered four American-born nuns who worked with the country's impoverished peasants.

Throughout the 1980s, the United States provided funding and training for El Salvadoran counterinsurgency forces, often with bloody results. In December 1981, El Salvadoran troops massacred more than eight hundred people in El Mozote, executing men and boys and gang-raping women and girls before killing them and burning the village. The El Salvadoran government denied its involvement, and the Reagan administration maintained, despite abundant evidence to the contrary, that reports of the massacre were "not credible." Reagan administration officials saw El Salvador as

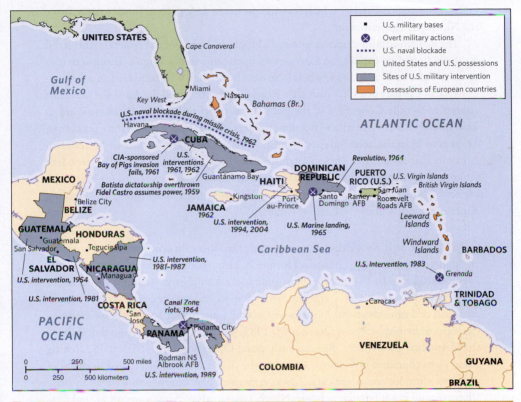

The United States in the Caribbean and Central America, 1954–2004

- ■ U.S. military bases
- ⊗ Overt military actions
- ••••• U.S. naval blockade
- United States and U.S. possessions
- Sites of U.S. military intervention
- Possessions of European countries

UNITED STATES

Cape Canaveral

Gulf of Mexico

Miami

Key West   Nassau

Bahamas (Br.)

U.S. naval blockade during missile crisis 1962

Havana

ATLANTIC OCEAN

CUBA

CIA-sponsored Bay of Pigs invasion fails, 1961

U.S. interventions 1961, 1962

Guantánamo Bay

Revolution, 1964

DOMINICAN REPUBLIC

PUERTO RICO (U.S.)

U.S. Virgin Islands

British Virgin Islands

MEXICO

Batista dictatorship overthrown Fidel Castro assumes power, 1959

HAITI

San Juan   Roosevelt Roads AFB

Belize City

Kingston

Port au-Prince

Santo Domingo

Ramey AFB

BELIZE

JAMAICA 1962

Leeward Islands

GUATEMALA

HONDURAS

U.S. intervention, 1994, 2004

U.S. Marine landing, 1965

Windward Islands

BARBADOS

Guatemala

San Salvador

Tegucigalpa

Caribbean Sea

EL SALVADOR

NICARAGUA

U.S. intervention, 1981–1987

U.S. intervention, 1954

Managua

U.S. intervention, 1983

Grenada

U.S. intervention, 1981

COSTA RICA

Canal Zone riots, 1964

TRINIDAD & TOBAGO

PACIFIC OCEAN

San José

Caracas

PANAMA

Panama City

VENEZUELA

GUYANA

0   250   500 miles
0   250   500 kilometers

Rodman NS Albrook AFB

U.S. intervention, 1989

COLOMBIA

BRAZIL

an opportunity to avoid the "mistakes" made in Vietnam. "El Salvador represents an experiment," a military report stated, "an attempt to reverse the record of American failure in waging small wars, an effort to defeat an insurgency by providing training and material support without committing American troops to combat."[39]

NICARAGUA The administration was most concerned with Nicaragua where, in 1979, a left-wing insurgency, the Sandinistas (named for the early twentieth-century Nicaraguan revolutionary Augusto Sandino) had overthrown dictator Anastasio Somoza, whose family had ruled the country for over six decades. The Sandinistas had military and economic ties with Cuba but also deep support in the Catholic Church, particularly among proponents of liberation theology, a movement led by priests and nuns who argued that the church needed to side with the poor against exploitative landowners and autocratic governments.

In November 1981, Reagan authorized $19 million to train and arm the Nicaraguan Contras, the counterrevolutionary opponents of the new Sandinista government.

Aid to the Contras, however, was unpopular, especially among Americans who feared that the small Latin American country might become another Vietnam. In December 1982, Congress approved the Boland Amendment (named for the Massachusetts congressman who sponsored it), which forbade the use of U.S. defense funds to overthrow the Nicaraguan government.

The Reagan administration exploited a loophole in the Boland Amendment: it did not forbid ongoing funding to CIA covert operations in Nicaragua. Those activities came to light in March 1983, when a Soviet ship struck a mine placed in a Nicaraguan harbor as part of a CIA plan that Reagan had authorized. In April the president attempted to rally Congress and the public to support military and economic aid to what he called Latin America's "freedom fighters." "El Salvador is nearer to Texas than Texas is to Massachusetts," argued Reagan. "Nicaragua is just as close to Miami, San Antonio, San Diego, and Tucson as those cities are to Washington."[40] The president attempted to calm fears that, as his critics put it, "El Salvador is Spanish for Vietnam." He told "those who invoke the memory of Vietnam, there is no thought of sending American combat troops to Central America."[41]

GRENADA Still, Reagan hoped to overcome the "Vietnam syndrome," and he found an opportunity to do so in Grenada, a former British colony of about 100,000 residents in the Caribbean. In 1979 a Marxist regime had taken charge. Reagan warned about ties between Grenada, Cuba, and the Soviet Union and asserted that Grenada's construction of a nine-thousand-foot runway would allow Soviet bombers easy access to the western hemisphere. On October 25, 1983, just after a military coup destabilized the Grenadine government, Reagan authorized Operation Urgent Fury, dispatching about eight thousand military personnel to the island. Several dozen died in the brief war, including sixteen Americans. It was America's first international invasion since Vietnam, and it was popular at home. Nearly two-thirds of Americans supported Reagan's decision.

THE IRAN-CONTRA CRISIS With the memory of Vietnam still vivid, Congress and the public remained unwilling to support Reagan's efforts to destabilize Nicaragua. In December 1984, Congress enacted a revised Boland Amendment, forbidding the United States to provide any aid to the Contras. In an end run around the Boland Amendment, the National Security Council (NSC) launched new schemes to support the Contras. NSC head Robert McFarlane negotiated a deal with Saudi Arabia to provide funds to the Contras, about $2 million per month in 1985.

Later that year McFarlane (who resigned from the NSC in December 1985), his successor, retired Admiral John Poindexter, and an NSC aide, Marine Lieutenant Colonel Oliver North, launched an even more elaborate and bizarre plan to fund the Contras. The United States sold arms secretly to Iran, quixotically hoping to empower pro-Western Iranians while prolonging the bloody Iran-Iraq war. As a quid pro quo, the United States asked the Iranian regime to pressure Lebanon to release seven Americans being held hostage by militants there. The plot grew more twisted. The proceeds from the arms-for-hostages deal would be channeled through intermediaries in Israel to cover up the American connection and sent to the Contras.

The scheme began to unravel in October 1986, when a plane delivering arms to the Contras crashed in Nicaragua. Over the next month and a half, investigative journalists began to piece together the story. In mid-November, the president denied that the United States had been behind the Iran-Contra affair, stating that his administration "did not—repeat—did not trade arms or anything else for hostages."[42] But evidence mounted to the contrary. On November 25 the president and his attorney general, Edwin Meese, stunned the nation by reporting that the essence of the story was true, that Poindexter was resigning, and that the White House was setting up a special committee to investigate. In December, Reagan named Lawrence Walsh, a well-respected attorney, as an independent counsel to investigate the case. The House and Senate launched their own investigations. The president's popularity plummeted, although no evidence emerged that he had been aware of the plan.

Between 1987 and 1990, investigations proceeded. Eleven Reagan administration officials were ultimately convicted, but most received light sentences. Poindexter and North had their convictions overturned on an appeal. And the remaining six defendants, including McFarlane and former defense secretary Caspar Weinberger, were pardoned by Reagan's successor, George H. W. Bush, in late December 1992, shortly before his term ended.

GORBACHEV AND REAGAN Between 1985 and 1991, events in Moscow fundamentally altered the direction of the Cold War. The Soviet regime had been dysfunctional for years. Its situation worsened in the early 1980s when the elderly and ill premier, Leonid Brezhnev, died. His successors, part of the Communist Party's entrenched, aging leadership, Yuri Andropov and Konstantin Chernenko, both died in office. Their passing marked a generational shift. In March 1985, Mikhail Gorbachev, only fifty-four, rose to power as secretary general. He vowed to institute reforms to deal with the sclerotic Soviet economy and the inept and unpopular bureaucracy that oversaw it.

Gorbachev inherited the costly Afghan war. He also faced growing insurgencies in Eastern Europe, most notably in Poland, where Solidarity, led by labor leader Lech Walesa, had been challenging the Communist regime since the late 1970s. Solidarity drew strong support from the Catholic Church, including Cardinal Karol Wojtyla, who would be named Pope John Paul II in 1978. The Soviet economy could not meet the needs of the nation's population. Its farms were vast but so unproductive that the nation needed to import much of its grain. Its antiquated factories lumbered along with unmotivated workers manning aging machinery. The populace, especially in big cities, suffered crippling shortages of everything from green vegetables to shoes.

Gorbachev instituted a series of long-overdue reforms, intended to shore up the crumbling Soviet regime. He began by announcing a policy of *glasnost* or openness. His regime lifted strict censorship rules, allowing newspapers to report on Russia's dire social and economic problems. Soviet dissidents, who had long faced persecution, exile, or harsh sentences in work camps, suddenly found public outlets for their essays. At the same time, Gorbachev took modest steps toward democratization, allowing for contested elections in the Soviet Union's far-flung ethnic republics, unwittingly unleashing currents of nationalism.

For all Reagan's skepticism about the Soviet Union, he was more hopeful than many of his advisers about Gorbachev. In November 1985 the two leaders met in Geneva. The discussion was inconclusive, but both leaders came away from the meeting impressed with each other. They scheduled a second summit, to take place in Reykjavik, Iceland, the following October.

At that meeting, both sides discussed arms reduction proposals. Reagan started from a position of strength. He put on the table a several-year-old proposal known as the "zero option," which previous Soviet leaders had rejected. Under the zero option, the United States would not station intermediate-range nuclear missiles in Western Europe if the Soviets withdrew theirs from Eastern Europe. To Reagan's surprise, Gorbachev accepted the offer and pushed even further. The Soviet premier proposed that both countries reduce their stronghold of nuclear weapons by 50 percent. Reagan rejoined by proposing that both countries eliminate their strategic nuclear weapons, but only if the United States could maintain an arsenal for self-defense. Gorbachev countered by calling for an elimination of all nuclear weapons by 1996. The two leaders met privately—without their aides—to discuss the plan further, but they hit a wall. Gorbachev demanded that the United States give up its SDI system. Reagan refused. The talks ended in an impasse.

In the meantime, Gorbachev intensified his reforms. He pushed for *perestroika*, a program of economic restructuring that loosened central control over the economy. Gorbachev also allowed for the formation of privately run businesses. And in a reform unimaginable just a few years earlier, Gorbachev allowed foreign investors to form partnerships with state-controlled firms.

Reagan's position on the Soviet Union was quickly shifting, in part because by 1987 he had replaced most of his hardline advisers (several of whom had resigned during the Iran-Contra scandal) with Nixon- and Ford-era supporters of détente. He remained open to further negotiations with Gorbachev, but he continued to criticize the Soviet Union publicly and offered support to Eastern European dissidents. In June 1987 he stood at the Brandenburg Gate separating East and West Berlin and issued one of his boldest challenges to date: "General Secretary Gorbachev, if you seek peace, if you seek prosperity for the Soviet Union and Eastern Europe, if you seek liberalization: Come here to this gate! Mr. Gorbachev open this gate! Mr. Gorbachev tear down this wall!"[43]

In December, Gorbachev and Reagan met again, this time in Washington. Gorbachev had begun winding down the costly Afghan war, was continuing to push for reforms, and hoped to reach an agreement with the United States, in part to reduce the heavy economic burden of militarization. He agreed to set aside, for the moment, his concerns about Star Wars, in part because the U.S. Congress, dominated by Democrats, had slashed SDI funding. Both sides agreed to substantial reductions of intermediate-range arms. Reagan's popularity soared, although not among right-

Reagan in Berlin At the Brandenburg Gate in West Berlin, on June 12, 1987, President Ronald Reagan calls on Soviet premier Mikhail Gorbachev to tear down the Berlin Wall.

wing Republicans who believed that he had betrayed his principles. Senator Jesse Helms (R-SC), a longtime Reagan supporter, told reporters, "The President doesn't need to discard the people who brought him to the dance." William F. Buckley, Jr., wrote that Reagan had "disappointed" him.[44]

G. H. W. Bush and the Currents of Republicanism

Nineteen eighty-eight seemed at first a hopeful year for the Democrats. Reagan Republicans had never warmed to Vice President George H. W. Bush. The son of a patrician Connecticut senator, Bush had a long résumé when he moved into the White House. His career reflected the shifting currents of Republicanism in the last third of the twentieth century. He had unsuccessfully run for office in 1964, opposing the Civil Rights Act. Two years later he reinvented himself as a moderate, winning election to Congress from suburban Houston.

For the next fourteen years, Bush aligned himself with the Rockefeller-Nixon wing of the GOP, taking moderate positions on civil rights, the legalization of abortion, and the Equal Rights Amendment. Nixon rewarded him for his loyalty by naming him ambassador to the United Nations in 1970. During the 1970s, Bush built a foreign policy portfolio, supporting Nixon's policy of détente, serving as U.S. envoy to China and CIA director under President Ford. In 1980, as the favored candidate of Republican moderates, he lost to Reagan but accepted the vice presidency and served loyally, though he was overshadowed by his boss and distrusted by his party's right wing.

The GOP's conservatives never warmed to Bush, although he tried hard to win their support. To prove his right-wing bona fides during the 1988 primaries, he pledged—much to his later regret—that he would never raise taxes, a position far stronger than Reagan's. He strongly opposed abortion and gun control, repudiating his once moderate views. And he pledged to appoint strict conservatives to the federal bench.

Bush's Democratic opponent, Massachusetts governor Michael Dukakis, was a centrist who ran on the slogan "competence, not ideology," but Republicans branded him as out of the mainstream. Bush portrayed Dukakis as the anti-Reagan, someone who would be weak on national defense and raise taxes. In a controversial ad, with strong racial overtones, the GOP depicted Dukakis as soft on crime, blaming him for furloughing a convicted murderer, Willie Horton, who raped a woman when he was out of jail. Bush crushed Dukakis, winning in forty states.

From Cold War to Gulf War

Given his résumé, George Bush made foreign policy his top priority. But no one could have predicted the extraordinary events that played out in his first year in office. In April and May 1989, thousands of Chinese students gathered in Beijing's immense Tiananmen Square to call for democracy in China. On June 3–4 the Chinese regime brutally put down the protest, killing some three thousand demonstrators, injuring thousands more, and jailing leading dissenters. Bush, familiar with China from his time there in the 1970s and committed to maintaining good relations with the emerging economic superpower, resisted efforts to punish China's leaders. In 1990 he supported and Congress authorized legislation that renewed China's "most favored nation" trading status, ensuring the continued flow of cheap Chinese goods to the United States. American economic interests in China trumped the anti-Communist agenda.

THE REVOLUTIONS OF 1989 Events in Eastern Europe over the next few months were even more surprising. In August 1989, Polish dissidents toppled the Communist regime in Warsaw. Solidarity's Lech Walesa formed the country's first non-Communist government since the end of World War II. Nationalists in the Soviet Baltic republics of Estonia, Latvia, and Lithuania all declared independence from the Soviet Union. On November 9, after days of protests in Berlin, East German students swarmed the Berlin Wall, tearing down the most prominent symbol of the Cold War. Later that month hundreds of thousands of pro-democracy demonstrators gathered in Prague, demanding free elections, which lifted the dissident poet Václav

Havel to the presidency. In December, Romanian rebels assassinated Communist leader Nicolae Ceaușescu and his wife. The following year, Communists lost control in Yugoslavia, in the process unleashing intense ethnoreligious conflicts that single-party rule had suppressed. In Moscow, Mikhail Gorbachev struggled against Communist Party regulars who hoped to restore order in the Soviet empire. In 1991 his government fell.

The abrupt end to the Cold War led congressional Democrats to demand a "peace dividend" in the form of dramatic defense budget cuts. But the Bush administration found itself in the position of dealing with the messes that the previous administration had left behind in Latin America and the Middle East. In Panama, General Manuel Noriega had been a useful conduit for aid to the Contras, but he ran a kleptocracy, enriching himself through arms and narcotics trafficking. In December 1989, Bush authorized Operation Just Cause, sending 28,000 American troops to depose Noriega. The invasion was quick: Noriega was captured and brought to the United States, where he was convicted on drug charges.

THE PERSIAN GULF WAR The Middle East was even messier. In the aftermath of the Iraq-Iran war, Saddam Hussein attempted to consolidate his power and fill his country's depleted coffers. Like Noriega, Hussein was no longer useful to the United States, but worse, he aggressively threatened American interests. He set his sights on neighboring Kuwait, a small, oil-rich nation on the Persian Gulf. In August 1990, Iraqi troops invaded and conquered the sheikhdom. The combined nations controlled one-fifth of the world's oil supplies.

The United Nations condemned the invasion of Kuwait. With hopes of forcing a nonmilitary solution, the UN also called for a global embargo on trade with Iraq. In August, Bush announced the deployment of 230,000 troops to the region and assembled a thirty-five-nation coalition to push back Iraq. The coalition included several Middle Eastern countries, among them Bahrain, Egypt, Saudi Arabia, Syria, and the United Arab Emirates. Eventually more than a half-million troops would serve in the Persian Gulf.

Iraq was isolated politically and crippled by the embargo, unable to sell its oil internationally. In November the UN pledged swift military action if Iraq did not vacate Kuwait by January 15. But Saddam Hussein was unrelenting. In Baghdad his military captured thousands of Western hostages, threatening to use them as "human shields" in the event of a war.

On the home front, Bush faced skepticism, especially among congressional Democrats. The memory of Vietnam still loomed over national politics. In December the House of Representatives passed a resolution that emphasized the need for the president to get congressional authorization before starting a war. In January 1991 the Bush administration—buoyed by polls showing growing public support for military action against Iraq—decided to go before Congress to ask for approval for "emergency powers." James Baker, the secretary of state, argued that the president would "be making

The United States in the Middle East, 1947–2012

a big mistake to undertake a war as big as this" without putting it to a vote. He also wanted to overcome the "debilitating post-Vietnam hangover."[45]

In early January the House and Senate held an intense two-day debate on a possible war. The House passed a resolution of support by a comfortable 250–183 margin, but the Senate vote was a razor-thin 52–47. Two Republicans opposed the intervention, but ten Democrats supported it. Nine of the ten Democrats were from the Sunbelt, and they included some of the party's moderate and conservative luminaries, among them future vice president Al Gore, future Senate majority leader Harry Reid, and future presidential candidate Joseph Lieberman.

On January 16, Bush authorized Operation Desert Storm, a massive airstrike on Iraq. The Bush administration carefully managed media coverage of the unfolding war. Echoing language from World War II, officials talked of the "liberation" of Kuwait. And remembering Vietnam, they put tight reins on journalists, requiring them to travel with military escorts and preventing them from photographing the wounded and dead. During the Vietnam War, television viewers had seen grisly photographs from the front lines, but during the Persian Gulf War, news broadcasts carried visuals of aerial bombing campaigns, showing the night sky of Baghdad flashing with explosions.

On February 24, American-led ground forces stormed Iraqi troops, who beat a hasty retreat. The ground war lasted a mere hundred hours. Only 148 Americans were killed in combat. By best estimates, about 25,000 Iraqi soldiers died. The swift, decisive victory against Iraq seemed to put the "Vietnam syndrome" finally to rest. Bush's popularity skyrocketed. American flag sales jumped, and Americans placed ribbons on their cars reading "I support our troops." But the administration withdrew troops

The Gulf War President George H. W. Bush welcomes troops returning home to South Carolina after service in the Persian Gulf, March 17, 1991.

from Iraq with Saddam Hussein's regime still in power. The Bush administration had decided against a prolonged military engagement in Iraq.

The Low-Wage Economy

The celebrations at the end of the Gulf War could not mask troubles in the domestic economy. Stagflation was a distant memory, but unemployment remained stubbornly high. It reached a postwar peak of 9.7 percent in 1982 and would not fall below 5 percent until the economic boom of 1997–2001. Even more troubling, most Americans suffered stagnating or falling incomes. Between 1979 and 2012, productivity (the amount of output per worker) increased by 74.5 percent in the United States, but the median worker saw only a 5 percent increase in wages. For the lowest fifth of workers, wages actually fell during the period. Gaps in household wealth widened significantly. Nearly all the gain in wealth went to the top 10 percent of the population, largely the consequence of Reagan's tax cuts. Much of that growth benefited the top 1 percent, largely because of the sharp drop in capital gains taxes. Throughout the 1980s, America grew poorer and less equal.

CUTTING COSTS   As Americans' incomes stagnated and fell, American businesses began to adapt to the needs of thrifty consumers. Discount retailers like Wal-Mart introduced innovative warehousing and marketing practices to cut costs. Wal-Mart pioneered barcode technology, which allowed the company to keep track of every transaction and to trim overhead. As it grew, Wal-Mart also benefited from its massive purchasing power. To keep prices low, it pitted manufacturers against one another, forcing them to cut production costs or lose its business. The company wrapped itself in the mantle of patriotism but pushed for the deregulation of international trade laws so that it could procure even less expensive goods from overseas manufacturers.

By 1990 more than half the clothes sold in the United States were manufactured abroad, mostly in Latin American and Asian sweatshops where poor pay, long hours, and lax environmental and safety regulations drove down costs. American consumers benefited from the flood of low-priced goods onto the market. After 1978 clothing prices rose more slowly than the consumer price index. Beginning in the early 1990s, the price of women's clothes, the largest segment of the market, dropped sharply.[46]

Those manufacturers that remained in the United States—particularly food producers that operated on a low profit margin—also began a quest for cheap labor and loose regulation. Tyson Foods, which started as a family business in Springdale, Arkansas, and did not go public until 1963, emerged as a giant in chicken processing. A supermarket executive hailed Tyson as "light-years ahead of the industry in taking chicken and giving you another product out of it."[47] In the 1980s, Tyson sold twenty-six varieties of chicken patties and even attempted (unsuccessfully) to market a "giblet burger." Over the next decade, it had bought out dozens of competitors, taking advantage of newly deregulated financial markets.

Expansion of Wal-Mart, 1967–2006

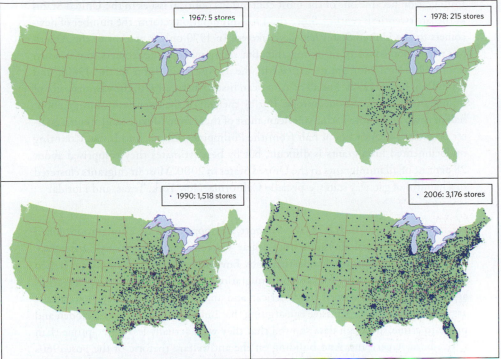

- 1967: 5 stores
- 1978: 215 stores
- 1990: 1,518 stores
- 2006: 3,176 stores

Like many fast-growing firms in the last two decades of the twentieth century, Tyson combined two strategies. It took advantage of government subsidies to expand, lobbying for tax breaks for its new facilities. In its home state, Arkansas, it found an ally in Governor William Jefferson Clinton. Like many governors competing to attract investment and jobs, Clinton offered Tyson substantial tax incentives to keep its factories in state. In exchange, Tyson executives generously contributed to his campaign coffers. Between 1988 and 1990 alone, the Clinton administration provided Tyson with $7.8 million in tax breaks.

The second strategy was to ruthlessly cut labor costs. Tyson, like Wal-Mart and other major firms, expanded in places with weak unions. It successfully resisted unionization among chicken processors, truckers, and warehouse workers. By the mid-1990s, Tyson and many other food-processing firms began recruiting Mexican and Guatemalan immigrants, most of them undocumented, to work in their factories. To keep wages low, they openly violated immigration and labor laws.

Immigration

Immigration became one of the most contentious political issues in the United States in the late twentieth century. Since the 1965 immigration reform, the number of new-comers to the United States had skyrocketed. In 1970 only 5 percent of the American population consisted of immigrants. But the numbers of newcomers rose steadily: 4.5 million legal immigrants arrived in the 1970s, 7.4 million in the 1980s, and 9.1 million in the 1990s. For all of American history before 1970, the vast majority of immigrants had come from Europe. But by the end of the twentieth century, about half of newcomers were Latin American, most of them from Mexico, and about a quarter originated in Asia, about half from the Philippines, China, and India. Counting undocumented immigrants is difficult, but by best estimates they comprised about 28 percent of all immigrants in the United States in 2000. Most immigrants clustered in a handful of gateway states, especially California, New York, Texas, and Florida.

DEBATING IMMIGRATION Support and opposition to immigration defied conventional political divisions. Blue-collar workers, including many Democrats, feared that immigrants would take their jobs. Environmental organizations, concerned with population growth, demanded immigration restriction. Cultural conservatives argued that new arrivals were un-American and unassimilable. Many reprised nativist arguments from the Progressive era, arguing that immigrants were disease-ridden and prone to crime, although data showed that they were actually less crime-prone than native-born Americans. And building on the antiwelfare rhetoric of the post-1960s years, anti-immigrant activists argued that newcomers cost taxpayers when they collected food stamps, disability benefits, and unemployment insurance. But economists showed that immigrants paid more in payroll taxes than they drew in public support.

Defenders of immigration celebrated America's growing diversity. Many churches—especially the Roman Catholic Church—took a strong pro-immigrant stand. Latin American immigrants were overwhelmingly Catholic, and they filled the pews when many native-born parishioners were leaving the church. By the end of the century, Hispanics comprised about one-third of all Catholics in the United States. Pentecostals and Mormons, both rapidly growing denominations, also proselytized in immigrant communities. Business leaders, many of them Republican, were among the most vocal advocates of immigration. Big firms like Tyson joined small businesses—builders, restaurateurs, nursing home owners, and landscapers—to oppose immigration restriction. They worried that native-born workers were unwilling to do menial jobs like skinning chickens, busing tables, washing dishes and floors, mowing lawns, and changing bedpans.

IMMIGRATION REFORM In 1986, Congress passed the Immigration Reform and Control Act (IRCA). IRCA contained a patchwork of provisions, giving a little to all sides in the immigration debate. It legalized about three million undocumented immigrants who had been in the United States since 1982, required employers to verify the immigration status of their employees, and tightened border controls, greatly expanding the U.S. border patrol. But Reagan and Bush administration officials only sporadically enforced verification laws. "We got here to get government off the backs of hard-working businessmen," noted one Reagan administration official, "not to add to their burdens."[48] Loose enforcement encouraged employers to seek out undocumented immigrants for low-wage labor. It also encouraged a black market in false identification papers. At one Tyson plant in Tennessee, ninety workers used the same California ID as proof of citizenship.[49]

IRCA's emphasis on tightening the border actually encouraged undocumented immigrants to stay in the United States. Most Latin American migration had been circular—many migrants were "birds of passage" who crossed the border when they needed work and returned home when they had earned enough. Tough border restrictions halted that circular migration, because migrants worried that if they returned home, they might not be able to reenter the United States.

The steady growth in undocumented workers, particularly in California, spurred an intense anti-immigrant backlash in the 1990s. In 1994, California voters approved

Border Security As immigration from Latin America increased, the U.S. military and border patrol stepped up patrols along the U.S.-Mexico border, searching vehicles and apprehending undocumented immigrants.

Proposition 187, a law that excluded undocumented immigrants from health care, welfare, and public education. Although a federal court ruled 187 unconstitutional, it inspired anti-immigrant legislation throughout the country. In 1996, Congress passed a law denying Social Security, disability, unemployment, Medicare, and welfare to immigrants during their first five years in the United States, regardless of their legal status. Many localities began enacting anti-immigrant ordinances, among them English-language-only laws. But the public remained deeply divided on immigration at the turn of the twenty-first century. The Democrats tended to be more open to immigrants, while the Republicans were split between pro-business advocates of immigration reform and cultural conservatives who feared that newcomers would dilute the American national character. The only policy that both parties supported was tightening border controls and reducing the number of undocumented immigrants. The number of immigrants removed from the United States rose sharply in the 1990s, reaching a peak of over 1.8 million people in 2000.

Politics and the Slumping Economy

The legacy of Reaganomics came to haunt Bush in the early 1990s. Having inherited massive deficits and $2.8 trillion in federal debt, Bush faced a choice between two Republican doctrines: to balance the budget or to keep taxes low. He was inclined toward the first but beholden to the second. On the campaign trail, hoping to win over skeptical conservatives, he had impetuously promised: "Read my lips. No new taxes." Bush, however, had to abide by the terms of a 1981 law that required the sequestration of federal funds and a government shutdown beginning in October 1990 if a balanced budget could not be achieved by 1993. Reagan had signed the law when he was infatuated by the Laffer curve. Bush was stuck having to comply. It was mathematically impossible to reduce the deficit without increasing revenues.

Bush's 1990 budget called for various "users' fees," a euphemism for taxes. Conservative critics, led by House minority whip Newt Gingrich, howled. Through the summer and fall of 1990, Bush and the Democratic leadership hammered out a compromise that included spending cuts and a gas tax increase, but Congress refused to enact it. Democrats were happy to weaken Bush in a midterm election year, and the Republicans would not accept the tax increase. In October, with no agreement in sight, the federal government shut down for three days. Finally, in late October, Bush and congressional leaders brokered a deal, modestly increasing taxes on upper-income earners. The budget passed, just a few weeks before the midterms, with a majority of Democrats supporting Bush. Bitter Republicans complained that Bush had sold out the principles of Reaganism and held it against him for years to come.

The deficit was only one of the economic woes facing Bush. Beginning in the fall of 1990, the economy fell into recession. The stock market was volatile, interest rates were creeping upward, and unemployment rose steadily, reaching a peak of 8.2 percent in February 1992. For many Americans, already financially insecure, the recession hit hard.

The economy—and Bush's turnaround on taxes—dominated the 1992 election. Bush fended off a primary challenge from angry right-wing commentator Pat Buchanan, but he faced another threat during the general election. Many Republican voters gravitated toward an independent candidate, the Texas billionaire Ross Perot. A conservative on social policy and an advocate of less regulation and low taxes, Perot hearkened back to the mid-twentieth-century Republicans like Robert Taft in his call for economic protectionism. Bush had just negotiated the North American Free Trade Agreement (NAFTA) with Mexico and Canada, which Perot contended would create a "giant sucking sound" of American jobs lost to Latin America.[50]

CLINTON AND THE DEMOCRATIC LEADERSHIP COUNCIL Bush also met a formidable opponent in the Democratic nominee, William Jefferson Clinton, the Arkansas governor. Clinton was the most prominent member of the Democratic Leadership Council (DLC), a group of insurgent Democrats founded in 1985 who argued that for the Democratic Party to survive, it needed to move rightward on civil rights, foreign policy, and especially economic policy. DLC members argued that liberals had lost touch with the majority of voters, particularly white working- and middle-class men. Their goal was to persuade centrists "to change the party rather than changing parties."[51]

In the late 1980s, the DLC fashioned a "third way" politics, embracing conservative arguments about the need for a robust anti-Communism. They supported aid to the Contras and bucked mainstream Democrats by backing Bush during the Gulf War. DLC members also echoed the Republican critique of welfare as corrosive of the work ethic. They distanced themselves from affirmative action and worried that white voters saw the party as captive to minority "special interest" groups.

The DLC was particularly attractive to younger Democrats from the Sunbelt. Its first six chairs were all from southern or border states, where Democrats felt particularly vulnerable to Republican challengers. Many other DLC members represented wealthy suburban districts, whose voters rejected Reagan's social conservatism while embracing his tax cuts and pro-business policies. The DLC's pro-business politics attracted substantial corporate support. By 1991–92, of its one hundred "sustaining members," fifty-seven were corporations and another twelve were professional and trade associations.[52]

In 1990, Clinton took the helm of the DLC, using it as a platform to launch his campaign for the presidency. He traveled the country, met with wealthy donors, and tapped the DLC's new think tank, the Progressive Policy Institute (PPI), to prepare position papers for his candidacy. The PPI's name was a nod to early twentieth-century reform politics, inspired by Theodore Roosevelt's Progressive Party, adapting "basic American political principles to changing circumstances."[53] The PPI and the DLC emphasized the need for "post-partisan" politics, calling for a third way between New Deal–Great Society liberalism and Reagan Republicanism.

At its 1990 conference, the DLC laid out its principles in the "New Orleans Declaration," a document that became a blueprint for Clinton's candidacy. The "Democratic

Party's fundamental mission," it stated, "is to expand opportunity, not government." This meant embracing pro-business policies, including free trade, a streamlined, business-friendly tax code, and government subsidies for high-tech research and development. It criticized welfare for maintaining the poor "in dependence." Finally, the DLC echoed Republican calls for "individual responsibility," arguing for "preventing crime and punishing criminals, not in explaining away their behavior."[54]

On the campaign trail, Clinton pitched himself as a bipartisan defender of "middle-class" values and interests. "The change I seek and the change we must all seek isn't liberal or conservative. It's different and it's both."[55] That meant repackaging many Republican ideas. Clinton defended government's role in society but criticized "tax and spend" politics. He argued that welfare should be "a second chance, not a way of life." Playing to culturally conservative white voters, he made headlines for criticizing Sister Souljah, a black rapper, for allegedly endorsing black-on-white violence. And in a particularly melodramatic moment, he left the campaign trail to preside over the execution of a mentally retarded black man, Ricky Ray Rector, who had been convicted of murdering an Arkansas police officer.

It was far from clear whether the electorate shared Clinton's centrist vision. Independent candidate Ross Perot ran a lackluster campaign but still managed to pick up 19 percent of the vote, much of it from conservative voters angry at Bush's decision to raise taxes. Clinton benefited from the split vote and picked up 43 percent of the vote, most of it from traditional Democratic voters, including African Americans, union members, and a plurality of women. Despite his efforts to win whites, he picked up only 39 percent of their votes, although he did win five southern states, the best Democratic showing there since 1976.

Clinton and Political Triangulation

In office, Clinton engaged in what commentators called the politics of "triangulation," appealing to cultural liberals, fiscal conservatives, and big business all at once. It proved to be a challenging task. Many on Clinton's left hoped he would deal with wage stagnation and joblessness. They looked to two appointees on Clinton's left, both professors: Harvard's Robert Reich (who had been a Rhodes scholar with Clinton) was secretary of labor; and the Berkeley economist Laura D'Andrea Tyson chaired the Council of Economic Advisers. Both highlighted growing inequality and called for federal funding for job training and stimulus spending to create public sector jobs.

"BUDGET HAWKS" Reich and Tyson were drowned out by Clinton's pro-business advisers, led by Robert Rubin, who left his job at investment bank Goldman Sachs to serve as head of Clinton's National Economic Council; Lloyd Bentsen, a DLC member and former Texas senator who was Clinton's secretary of the treasury; and budget director (and later chief of staff) Leon Panetta, a centrist who had begun his career as a Republican and Nixon staffer, then switched parties.

These "budget hawks" persuaded Clinton to prioritize deficit reduction. They argued that a balanced budget would bring confidence to bond markets and lower interest rates, thus loosening credit, allowing homeowners to refinance their homes, and jump-starting the economy. "We're all Eisenhower Republicans," Clinton told his advisers just three months after he was inaugurated. ". . . We stand for lower deficits and free trade and the bond market. Isn't that great?"[56]

Republicans had their own reasons for supporting deficit reduction. House Speaker Newt Gingrich, one of the most ambitious and conservative Republicans of his generation, represented a suburban district outside Atlanta. In 1983 he founded the Conservative Opportunity Society to promote free-market policies, pressuring Reagan from the right. In 1990 he was elected House minority leader. Gingrich believed that deficit reduction "changes the whole game . . . You cannot sustain the old welfare state inside a balanced budget."[57]

Clinton's first budget, in 1993, was a compromise between Democrats and Republicans, not unlike Bush's 1990 budget agreement. It called for modest tax increases, caps on discretionary spending, and a slowdown in the growth of Medicare, one of the costliest items in the budget. But the deficit hawks persuaded Clinton to jettison his middle-class tax cut and trim most of the stimulus spending that liberals had demanded. The bill squeaked through Congress.

NAFTA In late 1993, Clinton pushed through NAFTA, lending his support to the trade treaty that President Bush had negotiated with Mexico and Canada. Free trade had been a top priority of the DLC. Many major corporations, including Wal-Mart (whose board members included Clinton's wife Hillary until she resigned before the 1992 campaign) and Tyson Foods (which had funded both Clinton and the DLC), wanted to lower trade barriers so they could import cheaply produced goods and expand their markets abroad. The Business Roundtable, a major lobbying group, mobilized 2,400 member corporations to lobby for NAFTA. Major manufacturers and retailers also joined the effort.

Most Republicans supported NAFTA, but it faced stiff opposition among Democrats, who argued that it would accelerate "runaway jobs" to Mexico, where companies would have easy access to cheap labor without the burdens of environmental and safety regulations. Clinton countered that NAFTA would encourage American "competitiveness" and, over time, expand American firms' market share. NAFTA passed with only 27 Democratic votes in the Senate and 102 in the House. As NAFTA's critics had feared, the treaty fueled the dramatic expansion of American firms south of the border.

HEALTH CARE REFORM Clinton was confident that he would win bipartisan support for another key policy, health insurance reform. Health care costs had skyrocketed to 12 percent of the gross domestic product in 1992. In the 1970s and 1980s, employer spending on wages had increased by only 1 percent, controlling for inflation.

But employer health-benefit costs had risen by 163 percent. Almost 38 million Americans were uninsured, a stark contrast to every other Western democracy, all of which had enacted some form of national health insurance in the twentieth century.[58] Polls showed strong public support for systemic reform.

During his first week in office, Clinton put together a health reform team, led by his wife Hillary, a shrewd lawyer but an inexperienced politician. Over the next eight months, the group met secretly, arousing suspicion, and in September it issued a thirteen-hundred-page proposal. The plan reflected the market-oriented political shifts of the previous fifteen years. It left the responsibility for health insurance in the hands of private employers but called for a system of "managed competition" that would give government a role in negotiating lower premiums. Many big corporations supported the plan, especially one of its key features, an "employer mandate" that required all employers to provide insurance. They worried that, in the absence of a mandate, companies that opted out of providing health care would have an advantage over those that did provide it. Most small businesses, however, opposed Clinton's plan, because they kept costs low by not providing insurance to their employees.

Small business groups intensively lobbied Congress. So did the health insurance industry, fearful of cost controls. Republicans, hoping to deprive Clinton of a victory, put pressure on wavering members. They all capitalized on the health plan's complexity. As one health care reform supporter noted, "If you're explaining it, people's eyes glaze over. If you're attacking it, you only need that one rhetorical salvo." That one salvo was "government-run health care."[59] By early 1994 the tide had turned against Clinton's plan, which critics labeled as socialistic. Republicans painted a picture of a bloated government bureaucracy rationing health care and restricting access to doctors. The health care reform collapsed. Thereafter the number of uninsured Americans rose and medical costs continued to skyrocket. Most Americans remained unhappy with the health care system, but there was little incentive to reform it after Clinton's plan died.

The Contract with America and Welfare Reform

Six weeks before the 1994 midterm elections, Republicans issued the Contract with America. The high point of postwar conservatism, it called for a constitutional amendment that would require a balanced budget and limit taxation. It promised to promote businesses by trimming regulations and passing a 50 percent cut in capital gains taxes. It reiterated law and order themes dating back to the 1960s, including expanding the use of the death penalty and providing more funds for law enforcement and prison construction. It built on Reagan's war on welfare, calling for "a tough two-years-and-out" limit on benefits and "work requirements to promote individual responsibility." It promoted "family reinforcement" through tax credits for children, adoption, and elder care. And, as a first step toward fulfilling Barry Goldwater's decades-old dream of the privatization of Social Security, it advocated tax-sheltered retirement accounts.[60]

GINGRICH AND CLINTON The Republicans swept the 1994 midterm elections, winning 54 seats in the House and 9 in the Senate. For the first time since 1954, Republicans controlled the entire legislative branch. Under the leadership of new Speaker Newt Gingrich, the House aggressively pushed the Contract with America. The Republicans united around an austerity budget that included significant cuts to federal education funding and Medicare, combined with tax cuts for the highest-income earners. Clinton fought back, calling the GOP proposals "anti-family" and focusing on Medicare, which was very popular among the elderly.

Congress set a deadline of November 14, 1995, for a budget agreement. If a budget was not passed, government offices would be unfunded, and the federal government would shut down. On November 13 negotiations between Republican leaders and the president broke down. The government shut down for five days in November and for twenty-two days in December and January. Gingrich and the Republicans—who had been uncompromising throughout the process—took a political hit. By sizable margins, the public blamed Gingrich and the GOP for the gridlock. Finally, in early January, under pressure, Republicans agreed to a compromise, accepting modest cuts in social programs and leaving their proposed tax cuts on the table.

In his 1996 State of the Union address, President Clinton made the Reaganesque proclamation, "The era of big government is over." During that election year, Clinton moved rightward on social issues, hoping to outrun the Republicans. He announced his support for the Defense of Marriage Act, a law that defined marriage as a union between a man and a woman. He stepped up his calls for personal responsibility. And most consequentially, he found common ground with the Republicans over one of the core issues in the Contract with America: welfare reform.

ENDING WELFARE AS WE KNOW IT Since his days in the DLC, Clinton had argued for "personal responsibility." He and conservatives alike argued that poverty was the result of dysfunctional families, parents who lacked the motivation to work, and teens who engaged in crime and promiscuous sex. Behind all these changes was an overgenerous welfare system. Poor people needed a dose of "traditional values" like thrift, deferred gratification, and work discipline.

This criticism of welfare focused mostly on urban African Americans, who lived in communities that had been the hardest hit by disinvestment and depopulation. Since the 1950s old industrial cities had been ravaged by the flight of jobs. Residential segregation by race remained stubbornly high: between 1940 and 1990, it had hardly changed. The sociologist Douglas Massey wrote an influential book in 1993 describing the pattern as "American apartheid," noting that in most major cities, blacks and whites lived almost completely separate lives. Real estate brokers refused to show houses to minorities in suburban communities, often places where the best-paying jobs were concentrated. African American children were trapped in racially segregated, crowded, underfunded schools. Many inner-city communities were also ravaged by mass incarceration. In the 1990s about a third of black men in their twenties were in jail or on probation or parole. Employers seldom hired men with a criminal record.

The conservative critics of welfare focused on culture. The influential political scientist Lawrence Mead argued that blacks have a "deep conviction that they have to 'get things from white people' if they are to live a decent life." He also claimed that blacks had abandoned the work ethic of their grandparents' generation. "In that era, working hard and going to church were much of what black culture meant. Today, tragically, it is more likely to mean rock music or the rapping of drug dealers on ghetto street corners." Welfare reform, he argued, would change all that.[61]

In 1996, President Clinton and Speaker Gingrich negotiated the Personal Responsibility and Work Opportunity Reconciliation Act. A triumph of bipartisanship, it abolished AFDC, replacing it with a new program called Temporary Assistance for Needy Families (TANF). Nodding to Clinton's emphasis on work, the act provided states with funds for job training. Nodding to Gingrich, it also provided grants to pro-marriage programs, many run by churches. It was telling that ending poverty was not even listed as one of the law's primary goals. As Representative E. Clay Shaw (R-FL), one of the bill's sponsors, argued, TANF was about discipline. "You're going to have some who are just not going to be able to make it," he stated. Welfare reform "presented a certain amount of pain for not being able to take control of your life."[62] The reform forced individuals to fend for themselves, whatever the consequences might be.

Welfare reform grew out of the failure of policy makers to grapple with the wrenching structural changes that had created persistent, concentrated urban poverty. The new, daunting eligibility rules discouraged many needy parents from applying for TANF, even though they were eligible for support. In the decade following the enactment of TANF, welfare rolls nationwide dropped by nearly 60 percent. By contrast, poverty rates fell modestly in the late 1990s, mostly because of economic growth, not because of welfare reform. But those modest gains came at the price of growing insecurity. A 1999 study of poor families in thirteen states reported finding "evidence of lives made harder by the loss of cash assistance." To make ends meet, families often missed rent and utility payments.[63] Many resorted to unregulated day care programs or left their children with grandparents so they could find work. When poverty began rising again in 2001, their situation would get worse.

The Boom and Income Inequality

Even if the poor struggled during Clinton's second term, the American economy was stronger than it had been in more than two decades. In 1997 unemployment fell below 5 percent, the first time since 1973. It would eventually fall to 3.9 percent in 2001. The boom of the 1990s proved the old adage that rising tides lift all boats. In 1999 median household income in the United States reached an all-time high (in 2000 real dollars) of $42,418. Every racial and ethnic group saw increases: black household income reached a peak of $33,447, and Hispanics $30,439. The increase, however impressive, proved to be temporary. During the recession of the early 2000s, household incomes stagnated and, in real dollars, fell again.[64]

Distribution of Income Gains in the United States, 1979–2006

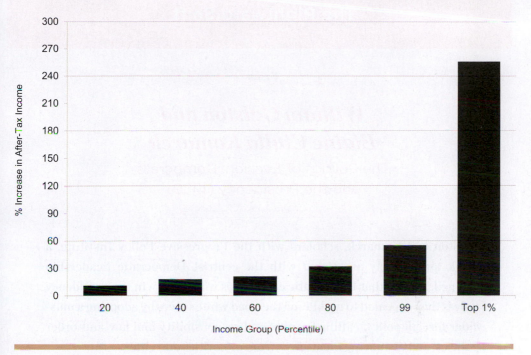

The increase in income in the late 1990s did not overcome the longer-term trend of dramatically worsening inequality in the United States. Between 1979 and 2006, the poorest fifth saw only an 11 percent after-tax income increase; the second and middle fifths saw an 18 percent increase and 21 percent increase respectively, and the fourth fifth saw a 32 percent rise. At the top, the gains were much greater. Those with income in the eightieth to ninety-ninth percentiles saw a 55 percent income increase; and the top 1 percent saw a 256 percent rise.[65]

TAX CUTS In the late 1990s, a bipartisan consensus emerged around policies that benefited the wealthiest Americans and particularly big businesses. Republicans targeted estate taxes, which Senator Trent Lott (R-MS) described as "a monster that must be exterminated."[66] Both Clinton and Republicans supported a reduction in capital gains taxes on stocks, home sales, and other investments. Clinton pushed for some modest benefits for middle-income taxpayers, including a tax credit for education expenses. In 1997 an overwhelming bipartisan majority passed the Taxpayer Relief Act, which cut taxes by about $400 billion. The law reduced capital gains taxes from 25 to 20 percent, a boon to wealthy Americans, for whom stocks, bonds, and real estate

Making a Nation

The Rightward Shift

From

William Galston and Elaine Ciulla Kamarck

The Politics of Evasion: Democrats and the Presidency (1989)

Galston and Kamarck, scholars with the Progressive Policy Institute, a think tank closely associated with the centrist Democratic Leadership Council, argued that Democratic candidates would not win the presidency unless they appealed to middle-of-the-road white voters by adopting a muscular foreign policy, calling for personal responsibility and law-and-order policies, and distancing themselves from minorities and elites.

The Democratic Party's 1988 presidential defeat demonstrated that the party's problems would not disappear, as many had hoped, once Ronald Reagan left the White House. . . . Democrats must now come face to face with reality: too many Americans have come to see the party as inattentive to their economic interests, indifferent if not hostile to their moral sentiments and ineffective in defense of their national security.

Since the late 1960s, the public has come to associate liberalism with tax and spending policies that contradict the interests of average families; with welfare policies that foster dependence rather than self-reliance; with softness toward the perpetrators of crime and indifference toward its victims; with ambivalence toward the assertion of American values and interests abroad; and with an adversarial stance toward mainstream moral and cultural values.

During its heyday, the liberal governing coalition brought together white working-class voters and minorities with a smattering of professionals and reformers. Over the past two decades, however, liberal fundamentalism has meant a coalition increasingly dominated by minority groups and white elites. . . .

What is to be done? . . .

Above all, the next Democratic nominee must convey a clear understanding of, and identification with, the social values and moral sentiments of average Americans. . . . The consistent use of middle-class values—individual responsibility, hard work, equal opportunity—rather than the language of compensation would also help. And finally, the American people overwhelmingly believe that the central purpose of criminal punishment is to punish—to express our moral outrage against acts that injure our community. The next Democratic nominee cannot appear indifferent to the victims of violent crime. . . .

Newt Gingrich, Dick Armey, and the House Republicans
Contract with America (1994)

In 1994, a group of leading congressional Republicans issued the Contract with America. A mix of economic libertarianism and moral conservatism, the document set the party's governing agenda for the next few decades.

Within the first hundred days of the 104th Congress, we shall bring to the House Floor the following bills: . . .

The Fiscal Responsibility Act. A balanced budget/tax limitation amendment and a legislative line-item veto to restore fiscal responsibility to an out-of-control Congress. . . .

The Taking Back Our Streets Act. An anti-crime package including stronger truth in sentencing, "good faith" exclusionary rule exemptions, effective death penalty provisions, and cuts in social spending . . . to fund prison construction and additional law enforcement. . . .

The Personal Responsibility Act. Discourage illegitimacy and teen pregnancy by prohibiting welfare to minor mothers and denying increased AFDC for additional children while on welfare, cut spending for welfare programs, and enact a tough two-years-and-out provision with work requirements. . . .

The National Security Restoration Act. No U.S. troops under UN command and restoration of the essential parts of our national security funding to strengthen our national defense. . . .

The Job Creation and Wage Enhancement Act. Small business incentives, capital gains cut and indexation, neutral cost recovery, risk assessment/cost-benefit analysis, strengthening of the Regulatory Flexibility Act and unfunded mandate reform. . . .

The Common Sense Legal Reforms Act. "Loser pays" laws, reasonable limits on punitive damages, and reform of product liability laws to stem the endless tide of litigation.

The Citizen Legislature Act. A first-ever vote on term limits to replace career politicians with citizen legislators.

Questions for Analysis

1. What did Galston and Kamarck see as the appropriate role for government?

2. How did Gingrich and Armey reconcile their calls for a smaller government and lower taxes and spending with their push for a stronger military and anticrime programs?

3. Both reform Democrats and Republicans fashioned their appeal to voters on "values." Consider the commonalities and differences between their recommendations.

holdings comprised a greater share of household earnings than the majority of Americans. It also sheltered estates worth $1 million or less from the taxation, benefiting about 1 percent of the population.

THE DOT-COM BOOM Stock prices skyrocketed in the 1990s, greatly surpassing corporate profit rates and increases in productivity. The end of the twentieth century witnessed a wave of lucrative mergers and acquisitions. Some of the biggest growth came in new high-tech industries, particularly firms based in Silicon Valley that had long been nurtured by Cold War spending but now developed civilian applications, including high-definition screens and microchips. The biggest advance was the creation of the World Wide Web, building on decades of advances in networking and telecommunications technologies for the military.

Investors were particularly attracted to new "dot-com" firms that proliferated on the Internet, spurring massive speculation. In 1995, Jeff Bezos founded Amazon.com, the first large-scale online bookstore; in 1998, Sergey Brin and another Ph.D. student at Stanford launched the search engine Google.com. Investors, hoping to strike it rich, flooded new startups with funds. The value of high-tech stocks increased fivefold between 1995 and 2000. Recent college graduates flocked to high-tech centers in Silicon Valley, Austin, and Seattle. But in 2000 the dot-com economy collapsed, triggered by a bubble of investment in unstable startup companies. Some firms, like Google, Yahoo, and Amazon, would survive, but many smaller enterprises collapsed, and the tech economy remained volatile for several years afterward.

FINANCIAL DEREGULATION The most sweeping transformations in the 1990s involved the deregulation of the financial sector. Here too Clinton found common cause with conservative Republicans. Beginning in 1995, the president's economic advisers pushed for a "financial services modernization," including repeal of one of the signature New Deal regulations, the Glass-Steagall Act, which forbade banks to speculate in stocks and real estate using individual depositors' money. Glass-Steagall also prohibited banks from owning firms that sold securities. Clinton's aides knew that "allowing banks to engage in riskier activities like securities or insurance could subject the deposit insurance fund to added risk."[67] It was a risk that they were willing to take.

In 1999, Clinton signed the Gramm-Leach-Bliley Act, which undid Glass-Steagall's regulations. The financial services industry immediately took advantage of the new circumstances. New "megabanks," often organized into nominally separate legal entities, engaged not only in traditional activities such as lending, but also in brokerage, investment banking, insurance, asset management, and the creation of securities and derivatives markets. Over the next eight years, banks created all sorts of new high-risk financial products, without close regulatory scrutiny.

The riskiest involved home mortgage lending, one of the Clinton administration's top priorities. In 1995 the president launched National Homeownership Day, offering a new rationale about personal responsibility. "You want to reinforce family values in America, encourage two-parent households, get people to stay home?" Clinton answered his own question: "Make it easy for people to own their own homes and enjoy the rewards of family life and see their work rewarded. This is a big deal."[68] By the late 1990s, lenders, including Washington Mutual, New Century, and Countrywide, began targeting working-class and minority communities with high-interest loans, often with substantial up-front closing costs and hidden fees. The loans were immensely profitable but also incredibly risky.

Predatory loans were especially appealing to those working Americans whose wages had stagnated or fallen. To cover rising costs—a child's college tuition, a major home repair, or medical bills—a growing number of homeowners took out home equity loans, borrowing against the value of their house. In the meantime, loosely regulated financial institutions bundled mortgages together as securities and sold them on the secondary market, at great profits. So long as housing prices continued to rise and the profits to be made from securitized mortgages went up, lenders grew more and more lax in their standards. The market would begin collapsing in 2007, with devastating consequences for home buyers who suffered foreclosures, and for investors who were left holding nearly worthless assets.

Impeachment

For most of Clinton's second term, however, few worried about the future. The economy seemed unstoppable. But the news media and public were distracted by lurid scandals that engulfed the president and dominated the headlines. Early in his term, Clinton's conservative opponents spun out a number of charges against him, the most serious involving allegations of corruption around Whitewater, a complex Arkansas real estate deal in which Clinton had invested. In 1994, Chief Justice William Rehnquist named Kenneth Starr, a lawyer in the Reagan and Bush administrations, to investigate the charges as an independent counsel. He would find no wrongdoing involving Whitewater.

Complicating the situation, in 1994 an Arkansas woman named Paula Jones filed a civil suit against the president, charging him with sexual harassment. To conservative critics, who saw Clinton as a libertine (Gingrich had once called him a "counterculture McGovernik"), the Jones suit was grist for the mill. The president, hoping to quash Jones's suit, claimed executive immunity. In 1997 a federal court ruled against him, allowing the suit to proceed.

In late 1997, Jones's attorneys got word of something they hoped would help their case. Clinton and Monica Lewinsky, a presidential intern in her early twenties, had had oral sex in the White House. Clinton's liaison with Lewinsky began during the government shutdown in November 1995. Over the two years, the two met occasionally, with Lewinsky performing oral sex on the president nine times. They sometimes engaged in phone sex. Their clandestine meetings might have remained secret, except that Lewinsky began confiding the affair to Linda Tripp, a disgruntled former White House secretary, who secretly recorded the conversations.

In November 1997, Jones's attorneys deposed Clinton in the ongoing suit. When asked if he had had sex with Lewinsky, Clinton stated, "I have not had sex with that woman." Starr, having failed to prove the Whitewater allegations but eager to prove that the president was unethical, shifted gears. He accused the president of perjury, for lying in his deposition. To make his case, Starr called Lewinsky before a grand jury, where she confirmed that she had performed oral sex on the president. Starr entered into evidence Lewinsky's semen-stained blue dress.

On September 11, 1998, Starr produced a 453-page-long report on every aspect of Clinton's relationship with Lewinsky, replete with sexually explicit details. In the next three months, the House of Representatives investigated the charges against Clinton and, on December 19, voted to impeach him on grounds of perjury and obstruction of justice. Clinton went on trial in the Senate, which needed a two-thirds majority to remove him from office. For thirty-seven days, the Senate debated the charges against him. On February 12, 1999, the impeachment failed. Only 45 senators, all Republicans, voted to convict him of perjury, and only 50 of obstruction of justice. Most Americans thought Starr had overreached his authority, and while many disapproved of Clinton's conduct, his approval ratings remained high.

Foreign Affairs

During the Clinton impeachment furor, few Americans paid much attention to international relations. A major survey conducted in late 1998 showed that only 2 to 3 percent of respondents ranked foreign policy as a primary concern. When asked to name the "two or three biggest foreign policy problems facing the United States today," the most popular response was "I don't know."[69] The lack of interest was in part the consequence of the end of the Cold War, in part a sharp decline in American media coverage of international relations in the 1990s. Many newspapers had closed or downsized their overseas bureaus.

Many of the foreign policy controversies of the Clinton years seemed distant to the American people. A civil war in Rwanda led to the genocidal killing of some 800,000 Tutsi by the Hutu majority in the spring and summer of 1994. The United States made no significant response. The administration also faced major humanitarian crises in the former Yugoslavia, which was torn apart by a brutal civil war. In 1994 and 1995, Serbian leader Slobodan Milošević ordered the massacre of thousands of Bosnian Muslims and displaced tens of thousands more. The United States supported the United Nations, which sent several thousand peacekeeping forces there. Some members of Congress called for more aggressive action, but there was little public support for a military engagement in the Balkans. In early September 1995, Clinton committed American troops to engage in airstrikes on targets around the Serbian capital, Sarajevo. In November the United States brokered the Dayton accords, imposing a cease-fire in the region.

In 1998 the United States faced a more ominous challenge from Al Qaeda, an extremist Muslim group led by Osama bin Laden, the wealthy son of a Saudi Arabian oil magnate. Bin Laden established a base of operations in Afghanistan and, from there, directed terrorist attacks on American targets. In August that year Al Qaeda took credit for the bombing of U.S. embassies in Kenya and Tanzania, which killed more than three hundred people. In retaliation, Clinton authorized airstrikes on an Al Qaeda base in Afghanistan and a factory in Sudan, suspected to be producing arms for Bin Laden's organization. Neither involved any major military engagement—Clinton was wary of committing troops to fight the terrorist organization. But in the late 1990s, CIA operatives, who closely monitored suspected terrorist groups throughout the Middle East, began to warn that Al Qaeda was planning an attack on targets in the United States. In October 2000, Al Qaeda operatives bombed the *USS Cole*, a destroyer stationed in the Persian Gulf, killing seventeen American marines.

At Century's End

American intelligence agencies were on high alert on December 31, 1999. Just two weeks earlier, border patrol agents at the Canadian border had stopped an Algerian national with a car full of explosives and timers. In Seattle, where protesters had taken to the streets to protest the World Trade Organization meeting in 1998, city officials were so fearful of violence that they canceled the city's New Year's fireworks display. Around the country, with the millennium looming, paranoid Americans girded themselves for the chaos that they expected would break out when the Y2K bug prevented computer systems from recognizing dates beginning with 20 rather than 19. Rumors had been spreading for months that a massive computer shutdown would freeze the nation's power grid, shut down banks and air traffic control centers, and crash the economy.[70] Those fears proved unfounded.

On New Year's Eve a quarter-million revelers crowded the Strip in Las Vegas, a place where gambling palaces had boomed during the economic upswing in the late 1990s. About a million gathered in New York's Times Square, despite a blizzard that struck the city the night before. The city, flush with money just a quarter century after it declared bankruptcy, dispatched thousands of workers on overtime to clear the sidewalks and streets. Limousines lined up at chic restaurants like Windows on the World, perched atop the World Trade Center, which had five thousand bottles of champagne—about two bottles per guest—ready for revelers.

On the New Year, which fell on a Saturday, many workers, hungover from the night before, stumbled to work. Many Wal-Mart associates did not get the day off. At the beginning of 2000, the world's single largest retailer now operated 1,821 discount stores, 650 SuperCenters, and 450 Sam's Clubs in the United States and 850 more overseas. Many of them were open twenty-four hours, 365 days a year. Wal-Mart also chose January 1, 2000, to launch a new online venture. Consumers could order more than 600,000 items online, a larger inventory than in most of its brick-and-mortar stores.

President Bill Clinton welcomed in the millennium: "Seldom in our history and never in my lifetime has our Nation enjoyed such a combination of widespread economic success, social solidarity, and national self-confidence, without an internal crisis or an overarching external threat."[71] The days of stagflation were remote. The Cold War was over. The United States was not at war, despite lingering fears of a terror attack. But the moment was fleeting. In the next several years, the country would be entangled in two wars. The contradictions of the 1990s boom—extraordinary wealth but deepening inequality—would become untenable. Intense partisan divisions would erode social solidarity. Deregulation and financial speculation would culminate in the greatest economic crisis since the Great Depression. America was still freighted by the burdens of the long twentieth century, unable to resolve the tensions between its promise of opportunity and its pervasive economic insecurity, its optimism and its deep-seated fears, its unsurpassed military power and its unease with the devastation of war, its persistent divisions of race and ethnicity. Americans at the new millennium hoped to overcome the past. But the past would indelibly shape their future.

Suggested Reading

Brands, H. W. *Reagan: The Life* (2015). A comprehensive biography of the most influential Republican of the second half of the twentieth century.

Frieden, Jeffry A. *Global Capitalism: Its Rise and Fall in the Twentieth Century* (2006). A readable overview of international capital flows, trade and currency policies, economic crises, and the rise of globalization.

Geismer, Lily. *Don't Blame Us: Suburban Liberals and the Transformation of the Democratic Party* (2014). Probes how the Democratic Party sought to counter the new right by appealing to white professionals living in high-tech suburbs.

Katz, Michael B. *The Price of Citizenship: Redefining the American Welfare State* (2001). Examines the political debates and policy experiments that resulted in "ending welfare as we know it."

Lichtenstein, Nelson. *The Retail Revolution: How Wal-Mart Created a Brave New World of Business* (2009). A labor and economic history of the world's largest retailer and its rise.

Patterson, James T. *Restless Giant: The United States from Watergate to Bush v. Gore* (2007). A sweeping, well-crafted political and social history of the last quarter of the twentieth century.

Rodgers, Daniel T. *Age of Fracture* (2011). A masterful intellectual history of how notions of consensus and the common good gave way to a celebration of choice, individual freedom, and cultural difference.

Tichenor, Daniel. *Dividing Lines: The Politics of Immigration Control in America* (2002). Places recent debates about immigration restriction in their long historical context.

Wilentz, Sean. *The Age of Reagan, 1974–2008* (2008). A fast-paced, sometimes polemical account of how conservatives remade American politics and how liberals responded.

Chapter Review

Review Questions

1. Explain Ronald Reagan's economic policy.

2. What social programs did the Reagan administration propose to cut and why?

3. How did the religious right become a powerful political force?

4. What satisfied and disappointed conservatives about Supreme Court decisions in the 1980s?

5. What were the causes and consequences of the Reagan administration's involvement in Nicaragua?

6. Explain the changing relationship between Ronald Reagan and Mikhail Gorbachev.

7. Why did the United States decide to intervene in Kuwait and Iraq in 1991?

8. What factors contributed to the expansion of low-wage jobs in the late twentieth century?

9. How did the Democratic Leadership Council help shape President Clinton's agenda?

10. Explain the creation of Temporary Assistance to Needy Families in 1996.

Key Terms

Laffer curve *p. 250*

Professional Air Traffic Controllers Organization (PATCO) strike *p. 256*

Green v. Connally p. 258

AIDS Coalition to Unleash Power (ACT UP) *p. 260*

Akron v. Akron Center for Reproductive Health p. 262

Bowers v. Hardwick p. 262

Strategic Defense Initiative (SDI) *p. 264*

Boland Amendment *p. 268*

Operation Urgent Fury *p. 268*

Iran-Contra affair *p. 269*

Operation Just Cause *p. 273*

Operation Desert Storm *p. 275*

Immigration Reform and Control Act (IRCA) *p. 278*

Proposition 187 *p. 280*

Reaganomics *p. 280*

North American Free Trade Agreement (NAFTA) *p. 281*

Democratic Leadership Council (DLC) *p. 281*

Contract with America *p. 284*

Personal Responsibility and Work Opportunity Reconciliation Act *p. 286*

Gramm-Leach-Bliley Act *p. 290*

United We Stand, Divided We Fall

❋

Since 2000

Chapter

8

atricia Thompson lived a hard life in one of the poorest cities in America, New Orleans. Born in 1956, she lost her mother when she was four and grew up with her struggling grandmother. "I've seen the hungry days," she recalled. "I've seen the days with no lights and water in the house.... I wouldn't wish my childhood on a dog." When she was seventeen, she left her grandmother and moved into the St. Thomas public housing project, a place that embodied all the contradictions of the New Deal. St. Thomas had been built to provide modern, affordable homes to working-class residents, but it was completely segregated by race, cut off from the surrounding city.[1]

Inspired by civil rights activists, Patricia Thompson worked to make St. Thomas a better place to live—an uphill task in the 1980s and 1990s, when federal housing support was collapsing, buildings were crumbling, and life for poor people like her got harder. In the mid-1980s, as crime was rising, it took police more than twenty-five minutes to respond to emergency calls in the project. But Thompson strove to make life better for herself, her six children, and her community. She helped start a health clinic and got a job working on a foundation-sponsored project to reduce teen pregnancy. Then in 1996 the New Orleans Housing Authority got funds from a Clinton administration program called Hope VI to demolish St. Thomas and replace it with mixed-income private housing. By 2001, most of the project had been bulldozed, and its more than three thousand residents scattered throughout the city. A new Wal-Mart would be built just a few blocks away. Thompson moved to another project. In the early 2000s she worked for a church doing social services. She earned about $200 a month.

On August 27, 2005, Thompson and her neighbors got word that a major hurricane was headed right toward New Orleans. About 80 percent of the city's residents evacuated, but many, like Thompson, could not. "I had one dollar in my pocket," she told an interviewer. "I did not have a vehicle, so there was no way for us to get out." That year more than a quarter of New Orleans residents, most of them black, did not own a car. The city's public transit system had struggled for decades with cuts in federal and state funding, and like many states, Louisiana did not have an extensive intercity bus or rail system. For those left behind as the storm approached, the scene was chaotic: "People are trying to get water, people are trying to get food. People are trying to steal cars, whatever they can do to help themselves and get out of that city." Without a car, and without money, Thompson was stuck.

In one respect she was lucky: she lived in a sturdy brick building, perhaps the only advantage of living in a housing project in a city of mostly wood-frame houses. She weathered the 140 mph winds that buffeted the city, staying on the second floor above the raging floodwaters that covered about 80 percent of the city when the levees broke. But when the electricity and power went out, she couldn't stay. Her daughters joined a crowd that went into a Wal-Mart to scavenge for food. "At this point, it's not stealing," she stated, "it's survival." Finally Thompson and her family headed to the Crescent City bridge, hoping to cross to Jefferson Parish, a community where she had relatives and that had not been flooded as badly by the hurricane. There she and hundreds of others were turned back by the police at gunpoint. She joined a huge crowd of people who gathered outside the city's convention center, where the Federal Emer-

< In the aftermath of the shooting of Michael Brown in Ferguson, Missouri, in 2014, protests against police shootings spread nationwide. In a photo from the *St. Louis Post-Dispatch's* Pulitzer Prize–winning coverage of the protests, demonstrator Cheyenne Green holds onto her flag as a man tries to grab it (*previous page*).

Patricia Thompson A public housing resident from New Orleans, Patricia Thompson (*center*) joins other Hurricane Katrina survivors testifying before Congress about their ordeal, December 6, 2005.

gency Management Agency (FEMA) provided meager rations. There was not enough to eat, so she and her daughters went back to abandoned stores to find food. She recalled the grim scenario of sleeping on the city's streets: "People were dying all around us. We were sleeping next to human feces and urine. All around you watching people die, watching them scream for help." More than eighteen hundred people died during the hurricane, most of them in New Orleans.

Patricia Thompson bore the heavy burdens of history. Her life had been shaped indelibly by the politics and policies that remade the United States in the hundred years leading up to the fateful day when the hurricane struck. She lived in a city whose social geography had been shaped by a long history of segregation, one that had been only partially undone by the civil rights legislation that passed when she was just a child. She lived in buildings that had been constructed as part of an experiment in providing "decent housing" for millions of Americans during the Great Depression, World War II, and the postwar years. But as these projects suffered decades of disinvestment, her quality of life deteriorated. And she had lived through a free-market revolution that put faith in the private sector to revitalize communities like St. Thomas. She had found work and support through foundations and churches, the nonprofit organizations that stepped in, with few resources but a lot of goodwill, to address the needs of the most disadvantaged Americans at the turn of the twenty-first century. Hurricane Katrina was not only a personal disaster for Patricia Thompson and many other residents of America's Gulf Coast; it was also one of the most important domestic political crises in a crisis-torn period in American history. It was a natural disaster whose worst effects were almost entirely man-made.

The Election of 2000

Katrina was a defining moment for the administration of President George W. Bush. Just five years earlier Bush had been the Republican nominee for the nation's highest office, but was by no means the frontrunner. Both he and the Democratic nominee, Albert Gore, Jr., hailed from states that bordered hurricane-ravaged Louisiana. Both candidates came from distinguished political families; both were sons of the 1960s, still shadowed by the Vietnam War; both had had elite educations; both were devout Christians; and both believed, to differing degrees, in reducing the size of government. One was the heir of Ronald Reagan and the son of a past president. The other was hoping to take over the reins of power from a popular incumbent.

Gore had graduated from Harvard in 1969 and volunteered to serve in the army, knowing he stood a strong chance of being dispatched to Vietnam. He worked as a military journalist but spent most of his enlistment stateside, eventually putting in just a few months in Southeast Asia. Five years later he won election to Congress from Tennessee, and in 1986, following in his father's footsteps, he won election to the U.S. Senate. Like many southern Democrats, Gore aligned himself with the Democratic Leadership Council, where he worked with Bill Clinton. In 1992, Clinton tapped him as his running mate. As vice president, Gore established a record on environmental issues and on science and technology. Well respected for his intelligence, he was a centrist and, like President Clinton, an advocate of streamlining government, cutting deficits, and using governmental power to help business.

Bush, the grandson of a Connecticut senator and son of President George H. W. Bush, had graduated from Yale in 1968. Eager to demonstrate his patriotism but reluctant to take the risk of being sent to Vietnam, he volunteered for the Air National Guard. At that time, few guard members were dispatched to the war. Bush remained a reservist for six years, earned an MBA at Harvard, and entered the oil business. In

Chronology

2000	*Bush v. Gore* George W. Bush (Republican) becomes president
2001	Economic Growth and Tax Relief Reconciliation Act 9/11 attacks USA PATRIOT Act War in Afghanistan begins No Child Left Behind Act
2003	Operation Iraqi Freedom
2004	Abu Ghraib torture reported George W. Bush (Republican) reelected president
2005	Social Security privatization fails Hurricane Katrina
2008	Great Recession Barack Obama (Democrat) elected president
2009	American Recovery and Reinvestment Act
2010	Affordable Care Act
2011	United States sends troops to Libya
2012	Barack Obama (Democrat) reelected president

1978 he tried—and failed—to follow his father's path by running for Congress. Unsuccessful as a politician, he was well connected among the Texas business elite and, by the early 1990s, quite wealthy. He invested in real estate and was part owner of the Texas Rangers baseball team. But his itch to follow his father's footsteps and win political office persisted. In 1994 he rode a well-funded campaign to win the governorship of Texas and, during the 1990s boom, laid the groundwork for his nomination as Republican candidate for the White House in 2000.

GORE AND THE DLC Most pundits thought that Gore had a clear shot at the Oval Office. His boss, President Clinton, had survived the impeachment proceedings and remained a popular figure. The economy was stronger than it had been in decades. Since 1964 every winning Democratic candidate had hailed from the South. Key Democratic operatives did not expect Gore to sweep the Old Confederacy, but they hoped that he would appeal to enough southern voters to win his home state, Tennessee, and perhaps Arkansas and a few others.

Gore, a longtime advocate of a smaller and "smarter" government, chose as his running mate a fellow member of the Democratic Leadership Council, Joseph Lieberman. The Connecticut senator was known for his hawkish foreign policy, his willingness to break ranks and vote with the Republicans, and his deep support on Wall Street. On the campaign trail, Gore offered his own version of what had become conventional wisdom among centrist Democrats, namely that running on competence would be more effective than appealing to Democratic "special interests" or reviving New Deal and Great Society politics. Gore distanced himself from President Clinton, preferring to run his campaign without the incumbent's assistance. Still he followed Clinton's script closely, pledging to fight for "middle class families and working men and women."[2]

It was a sign of how much the Democratic Party had changed that rather than pushing for higher wages or stronger unions as New Deal Democrats had done, Gore echoed a familiar Republican refrain: cut taxes for the middle class. On the campaign trail, he pledged to enact business-friendly policies, although his call for stricter environmental regulations worried business leaders, particularly in the heavy industries dependent on oil and coal. Gore was also candid about his religion, using stump speeches to call for more government support to faith-based organizations. As a campaigner, however, he was stiff and came across as arrogant, particularly during the presidential debates, when he implausibly claimed that he had invented the Internet.

BUSH'S CHRISTIAN CAMPAIGN

Bush—whose politics were considerably to the right of his father's—promised large tax cuts and pledged to reform Social Security. In this respect, he was Reaganesque. But unlike his father or Reagan, he foregrounded his evangelical Christianity on the campaign trail. "I feel like God wants me to run for president," he said to Reverend James Robison, a prominent televangelist.[3] When asked during a Republican primary debate who his favorite philosopher was, he immediately named Jesus Christ. Many on the religious right—who had felt marginalized since the Reagan years—rallied around Bush. He publicly stated his opposition to abortion, medical research on embryos, and gay marriage.

As he moved onto the national stage, Bush highlighted another side of his faith: "compassionate conservatism." Some critics, like Republican pundit David Frum, were skeptical of the concept, seeing it as a transparent effort to win over moderates. "Love conservatism but hate arguing about abortion? Try our new *compassionate conservatism*—great ideological taste now with less controversy." During his acceptance address to the Republican National Convention, Bush defined the term: "Government . . . can feed the body. But it cannot reach the soul." Rather than encouraging entitlement, government should empower the poor and the faith-based organizations that helped them: "My administration will give taxpayers new incentives to donate to charity, encourage after-school programs that build character, and support mentoring groups that shape and save young lives."[4]

BUSH V. GORE

The choice between Bush and Gore was unappealing to many voters. Some gravitated toward Green Party candidate Ralph Nader, who was running for president for the third time. A longtime environmental activist who had made his reputation challenging unsafe cars and environmental degradation, Nader argued that both parties were beholden to "oligarchs" who "subordinate democracy to plutocracy." The Gore camp worried that in a close race, "Nader's Raiders" would attract disaffected liberals. In the last few days of the race, Gore stepped up his own populist rhetoric, charging that a Bush victory would result in "a massive redistribution of wealth from the middle class to the wealthiest few." Bush responded by charging Gore with engaging in "class warfare."[5]

Only about half of eligible voters turned out on Election Day. The election revealed deep fissures in the electorate. Bush swept the South, including Gore's home state. He also picked up nearly every state in the Mountain West, where his small government rhetoric was popular. Gore, for his part, won throughout the Northeast, particularly in racially diverse metropolitan areas. The most notable gap separated men and women: Gore picked up about 11 percent more of the female vote than did Bush. Nader picked up only 2.7 percent of the vote, but just enough to tip the balance away from Gore in one key state: Florida.

On the evening of November 7, 2000, presidential candidates George W. Bush and Albert Gore, Jr., huddled with their families and close political advisers, anxiously watching the election returns. As evening turned to morning, the results remained inconclusive. More than 100 million Americans had voted, yet the outcome was too close to call. Gore had eked out a tiny margin nationwide—about 540,000 votes over Bush—and had won 266 of the 270 Electoral College votes needed for victory, compared to Bush's 246. The election eventually hinged on the returns in Florida, which initially showed Bush ahead by about 500 votes. Both campaigns sent teams to Florida to attempt a full recount. The balloting process had been full of problems. In one Florida county, several thousand votes had been accidentally cast for conservative independent candidate Pat Buchanan because of a flawed ballot. Both sides debated whether to count ballots with "hanging chads," the result of problems with outdated punch card technology.

The election ended abruptly on December 12 when the Supreme Court called for an end to the Florida recount, leaving Bush with several hundred votes more than Gore in that state. The *Bush v. Gore* decision was without precedent. Writing for the court's 5–4 majority (all five yes votes were cast by Nixon and Reagan appointees), associate justice Antonin Scalia stated: "The counting of votes of questionable legality does in my view threaten irreparable harm to petitioner [George W. Bush], and to the country, by casting a cloud on what he claims to be the legitimacy of his election." The decision shocked legal observers across the political spectrum, but it brought the contested election to a close. Without Florida, Gore lost the Electoral College 271–266, the closest margin ever. He conceded to Bush.

Bush in Office

During Bush's first few months in office, "compassionate conservatism" seemed to top his list of priorities. He devoted a lengthy section of his inaugural address to the theme. He pledged that his administration would reflect the diversity of America, and he appointed more women, Asian Americans, Hispanics, and African Americans to his cabinet than had any of his predecessors. But his cabinet choices reflected more than a symbolic commitment to diversity. His secretary of labor, Elaine Chao, was married to one of the most conservative senators, Mitch McConnell (R-KY). Unlike most past labor secretaries, she had no experience with organized labor, and her record was staunchly anti-union. Bush's secretary of the interior, Gale Norton, was a former mining industry lobbyist and a vehement critic of environmental regulation. Norton supported opening federal lands to oil extraction and mining. And Bush's foreign policy team, dominated by Vice President Richard Cheney and Secretary of Defense Donald Rumsfeld, called for rolling back the multilateral strategies of the first Bush and Clinton administrations. They argued that the United States should revive Reagan's Star Wars program and use American military force abroad to accomplish "regime change."

EDUCATION REFORM Bush prioritized domestic issues at first. Three days after his inauguration, he delivered a comprehensive education reform plan to Congress called No Child Left Behind (NCLB). For a conservative politician, it was a bold expansion of federal power over education, which had been almost completely the responsibility of states and localities until Lyndon Johnson's Great Society. NCLB required standardized testing to measure educational progress and imposed "accountability" on school districts for their students' academic achievement. The federal government would reward districts and states that saw an improvement in test scores with greater funding. If test scores failed to improve, the law allowed parents to send their children to better schools in their districts. And if test scores stagnated or declined, NCLB required school districts to reorganize or close "failing schools."

No Child Left Behind enjoyed broad bipartisan support. Republicans hailed it for making schools more competitive. Democrats supported it because it increased federal education spending, particularly in poor districts. But NCLB generated intense controversy in practice. Many teachers disliked having to "teach to the test." And many state and local education officials found it difficult to improve test scores. Cheating scandals—often instigated by principals fearful of losing funding—erupted in many districts, including Atlanta, where an investigation found that teachers had changed student answers to improve test scores. Over the next dozen years, Congress would amend but not end NCLB. Under pressure to show "metrics" of progress, school districts closed schools with low test scores. New education entrepreneurs—many with the backing of major investors and private foundations—developed special school curriculums to help students pass standardized tests. And advocates of the privatization of public education used NCLB's emphasis on test scores to argue (without much data to prove their point) that turning public schools over to the private sector would lead to better scores and greater student success.

FAITH-BASED INITIATIVES Bush also expanded federal grants to religious groups. His first executive order created the White House Office of Faith-Based and Community Initiatives. He pledged that "when we see social needs in America, my administration will look first to faith-based programs and community groups, which have proven their power to save and change lives."[6] In another executive order, Bush exempted religious organizations that received federal funds from regulations that forbade discrimination.

Bush named a conservative Democrat, John DiIulio, to direct the faith-based initiatives, but he resigned after eight months. DiIulio had had in mind a program that would fund churches like Patricia Thompson's in New Orleans to work with the truly disadvantaged. But instead, the program became intensely politicized. "There is no precedent in any modern White House for what is going on in this one: complete lack of a policy apparatus," complained DiIulio. The administration's political team "talked and acted as if the height of political sophistication consisted in reducing every issue to its simplest black and white terms for public consumption, then steering legislative initiatives or policy proposals as far right as possible."[7]

No presidency had been as explicitly religious as Bush's. He brought leading evangelicals into his inner circle, among them speechwriter Michael Gerson and attorney general John Ashcroft (who swiftly ordered that the classical statues in the Department of Justice be draped because of their nudity). Bush began his cabinet meetings with a prayer. Speechwriter David Frum—who was Jewish—was discomfited when he discovered that for White House staffers, "attendance at Bible study was, if not compulsory, not quite uncompulsory either."[8]

President Reagan and the first President Bush had greatly disappointed religious conservatives, but George W. Bush did not. On his second day in office (which coincided with the twenty-eighth anniversary of *Roe v. Wade*), he addressed a pro-life group and announced that he would institute a "gag rule" that forbade the use of government funds for any international organization that provided abortion services or lobbied on behalf of abortion rights. Later that year he issued an order banning federal funding for scientific research using embryonic stem cells derived from embryos that were left over from the process of in vitro fertilization. Scientists used these cells in their search for cures for Parkinson's disease and diabetes. "At its core," stated Bush, "this issue forces us to confront fundamental questions about the beginnings of life and the ends of science." For the president, the answer was clear: "human life is a sacred gift from our creator."[9] Bush also supported the teaching of "intelligent design" in classrooms, an alternative to evolution.

Bush's explicitly religious positions won the enthusiastic support of evangelical Christians. "This is the most receptive White House to our concerns and to our perspective of any White House that I've dealt with," stated Richard Land, the head of the Southern Baptist Convention. "In this administration, they call us, and they say, 'What is your take on this? How does your group feel about this?'"[10] Evangelicals, who had not turned out in high numbers during the 2000 election, would be Bush's most avid supporters for the next several years. Grateful that they had support at the highest levels of government, conservative Christians mobilized to reelect Bush in 2004 and to use that election to push statewide referenda on key conservative causes, most notably laws restricting same-sex marriage.

TAX POLICY Bush's most consequential domestic accomplishment was an overhaul of the tax system, one that was far more sweeping than Reagan's. After his father veered from his "no new taxes" pledge in 1990, it had become orthodoxy among Republicans that even a modest increase in taxes would be political suicide. Even though the Reagan tax cuts had had mixed results and the Clinton tax reforms preceded the most sustained economic boom since the 1960s, Republicans now argued that taxation was stalling economic growth. Bush promised "tax relief," reprising arguments from the 1970s and 1980s that cutting taxes would spur investment, create jobs, and improve the economy. The administration also echoed the supply-side economics that had been in vogue among Republicans since the 1980s: namely, that tax cuts would increase income and, as a result, boost government revenue over time.

In June 2001, the president signed the Economic Growth and Tax Relief Reconciliation Act. The law had sailed through the Republican-controlled House of Representatives and passed the closely divided Senate with the support of several Democrats, mostly conservatives from southern states. An immensely complicated law—the result of intense lobbying by business interests—it cut taxes by $1.35 trillion over a ten-year period. It reduced the top tax rate from 39.6 to 35 percent, expanded tax shelters for retirement plans, and gave a rebate of a few hundred dollars to everyone who had paid taxes in 2000. One of the law's most far-reaching measures was a planned reduction in the federal estate tax over a ten-year period, before its complete elimination in 2010. Bush's tax reforms would, however, expire in 2011, at which point the law would have to be reauthorized. Bush and the law's proponents hoped that, by then, the tax cuts would be politically impossible to repeal.

Bush's tax cuts had the same effects as Reagan's: they brought windfalls to the wealthiest taxpayers. About 45 percent of the total tax reductions went to the richest 1 percent of taxpayers; only 13 percent went to the bottom 60 percent. The result was that income inequality, which had been steadily growing since the 1970s, worsened. By 2005 one scholar found that "the richest three million people had as much income as the bottom 166,000,000."[11] The wealthy did very well, but incomes for most other Americans continued to stagnate or fall.

Bush's assumption that rich taxpayers would use their tax savings to create jobs and spur economic growth proved to be wrong. Instead, they fueled a speculative boom in real estate and in stocks and bonds. Many of the richest Americans invested in hedge funds and speculated on risky and exotic financial instruments like derivatives that only a handful of financial experts fully understood. Banks poured trillions into collateralized debt obligations, particularly home mortgages that had been bundled into securities and sold with the promise of high returns. Since 1999, investment banks and hedge funds had been poorly regulated. The Bush administration cut funds and weakened the enforcement power of the Securities and Exchange Commission and other regulatory agencies. The result was a wild west of speculation that made many wealthy investors phenomenally rich.

In a grim repetition of 1980s history, reality again disproved the Laffer curve hypothesis that tax cuts would pay for themselves by increasing income and federal revenue. Instead, federal revenue dropped. By 2002 the Clinton-era surplus had disappeared. In 2004 the federal deficit peaked at $375 billion, a record high. To his critics, Bush had become a "big government conservative," who cut taxes for the rich while escalating federal spending. Among his administration's biggest outlays would be military spending. During his first seven months in office Bush had focused on domestic concerns. No one expected that he would soon become a wartime president.

9/11

The skies along the eastern seaboard were crystal clear on Wednesday, September 11, 2001. Around eight a.m., nineteen hijackers took control of four passenger jets in a carefully calculated plan to terrorize the United States. They turned two aircraft, laden with jet fuel, into giant missiles, flying them into the upper stories of the twin towers of New York's World Trade Center. They flew a third into the Pentagon, the headquarters of the Department of Defense, just outside Washington. Passengers in the fourth plane got news of the previous attacks and struggled with its hijackers; the plane crashed in a field in rural western Pennsylvania. In New York, hundreds of firefighters and police officers rushed to the twin towers, tending to the injured and helping thousands of workers escape. Just before ten a.m., in a terrible roar, the first World Trade Center tower, weakened by fire, collapsed. The second fell about half an hour later. All together 2,977 people died on 9/11, most of them in New York.

AL QAEDA The terrorist organization responsible for the 9/11 bombings, Al Qaeda, was well known to American intelligence officials. Its leader, Osama bin Laden, had grown up in one of Saudi Arabia's wealthiest oil families and had been drawn to Afghanistan in the 1980s, during the bloody war against the Soviet occupation. Al Qaeda based its operations in the rugged mountainous region along the Afghan-Pakistani border.

Al Qaeda's rise was one of the many perverse results of the Cold War. During the 1980s, the Central Intelligence Agency had funded Bin Laden's fighters against the Soviets. But when the Cold War thawed, Bin Laden's funding dried up. In the early 1990s, enraged by the Persian Gulf War, by the American use of his native Saudi Arabia as a military base, and by ongoing American support for Israel, Bin Laden declared war against the United States. Al Qaeda also recruited throughout the Islamic world, attracting small but fiercely dedicated followers, mostly young men, committed to holy war.

The 9/11 assault was the most brutal in a string of Al Qaeda attacks on American targets. In 1993 Al Qaeda had detonated a truck bomb at the World Trade Center, killing six people. In 1998 it took responsibility for attacking the American embassies in Nairobi, Kenya, and Arusha, Tanzania, which killed several hundred more. And in 2000 Al Qaeda operatives suicide-bombed the *USS Cole*, a destroyer docked in Yemen, killing seventeen American sailors.

Fighting Al Qaeda had not been one of the Bush administration's top priorities. When Bush took office, intelligence officials were less concerned with the risks that Al Qaeda posed on the home front than with its potential to inflame tensions and religious conflict in the volatile Islamic countries of the Middle East, Africa, and Indonesia. During the spring and summer of 2001, Bush's foreign policy team began to discuss a long-term plan to neutralize Bin Laden's organization, but they did not anticipate that Al Qaeda was planning a massive attack on American soil. The bipartisan federal commission that later investigated 9/11 noted that during the summer of 2001, American intelligence officials received "a stream of warnings" of an impending attack, perhaps "something very, very, very big."[12] But the Bush administration ignored them.

HOMELAND SECURITY AND THE WAR ON TERROR Within days of the attack, President Bush announced an aggressive response. "Our war on terror," he told Congress on September 20, "begins with Al Qaeda but it does not end there. It does not end until every terrorist group of global reach has been found, stopped, and defeated." He pledged to use "every means of diplomacy, every tool of intelligence, every instrument of law enforcement, every financial influence, and every necessary weapon of war" to thwart the threat of terrorism.[13] This was the strongest language that any president had used since the Cold War. Bush warned that the struggle would not result in any quick victories, but by suggesting that the United States would target "every" terrorist group and use "every" means at its disposal to defeat them, he set impossibly high expectations for victory. Unlike national armies, terrorist organizations were decentralized and elusive. They used the Internet to recruit members worldwide. They communicated using encrypted messages, often through decoy websites that were difficult to track. They went underground and reorganized when they were threatened. New groups sprang up, particularly in fractious countries like Afghanistan, Pakistan, and Syria, often evading detection until they acted.

Would Americans commit to an all-out struggle against such a hard-to-define enemy? At first, the answer seemed to be yes. Bush's popularity skyrocketed after 9/11. Sales of American flags took off, and surveys showed the public to be more hawkish then it had been in decades. Commentators suggested that, for the first time since the 1960s, Americans seemed united around a common cause.

The Bush administration and Congress moved quickly to mobilize public opinion. In October, Congress hastily drafted and passed the USA PATRIOT Act (an acronym for Uniting and Strengthening America by Providing Appropriate Tools Required to Intercept and Obstruct Terrorism). The sweeping piece of legislation expanded the power of intelligence agencies to gather information about suspected terrorists. It allowed national security officials to intercept the electronic communications of American citizens suspected to be supporting terrorist activities. And it created a special Foreign Intelligence Surveillance Court that operated in secret to authorize federal investigations. The administration also created a secret domestic surveillance program—

one that would not be revealed to the public for four years. In the search for "sleeper cells" and potential terrorists, intelligence officials intercepted millions of telephone calls and Internet communications, installed spy software on computers and telecommunications devices, and demanded that Internet providers and telephone companies hand over records to the government.

More public security measures only added to the fear of imminent attack. The new Department of Homeland Security issued color-coded warnings of possible terrorist threats, signaling to the public that another 9/11 could happen at any moment. Airports instituted elaborate security screening procedures, under the supervision of the new federal Transportation Security Administration. The budget for homeland security skyrocketed, transforming local law enforcement. Flush with federal grants, police departments purchased expensive military equipment, including armored cars, tanks, and armor-piercing weapons.

In the name of fighting the war on terror, the Bush administration also empowered the CIA to detain suspected conspirators at secret centers. To give investigators as much leeway as possible, the Department of Justice issued a special memo in September 2002 that permitted the use of interrogation techniques that fell afoul of international treaties and domestic laws forbidding torture. John Yoo, a Harvard-educated attorney who worked at Justice, argued that suspected terrorists were not protected by due process provisions. Bush authorized the creation of "military tribunals"—outside the judicial system—to investigate terrorists. In early 2002 the government began constructing a secret prison, in Guantánamo Bay, Cuba, to hold suspected terrorists for indefinite periods. The U.S. held suspects at "black sites," unnamed prisons in Lithuania, Iraq, Thailand, Afghanistan, Poland, and Romania, where the CIA could interrogate and torture detainees without having to comply with American law.

TORTURE AND HUMAN RIGHTS The administration reinterpreted a federal law that banned torture by offering the narrowest possible definition: Torture consisted only of "the most extreme acts" that were "equivalent in intensity to the pain accompanying serious physical injury, such as organ failure, impairment of bodily function, or even death."[14] That loose definition put the United States at odds with international human rights laws that forbade the use of violence against prisoners. And it gave interrogators license to deploy new techniques such as waterboarding (simulating the act of drowning) to force prisoners to talk. CIA operatives waterboarded the key planner of the 9/11 attacks, Khalid Sheikh Muhammad, 183 times in a single month. In an effort to gain "total control" over detainees, they also used such tactics as sleep deprivation (forcing prisoners to stay awake for days at a time), mock executions, and forced rectal feeding. One prisoner was confined in a coffin-sized box for eleven days. Others were sodomized. In 2014, a congressional committee would issue a scathing report, presenting evidence that the "CIA's use of its 'enhanced interrogation techniques' was not an effective means of acquiring intelligence or gaining information from detainees."[15]

The Wars in Afghanistan and Iraq

Afghanistan became the first international battleground in Bush's war on terror. The country was under the control of the Taliban, Islamic fundamentalists who had also provided a haven for Bin Laden and his Al Qaeda operation. Brutal and repressive, the Taliban imposed strict religious rule on the war-torn country, destroying non-Muslim religious sites, forbidding the formal education of girls, and suppressing what they considered to be godless Western culture. Less than a month after 9/11, the Bush administration deployed American troops in Afghanistan, ordered air attacks on Taliban bases, and provided assistance to the Northern Alliance, a loose confederation of anti-Taliban forces. By the end of 2001, the Taliban had been routed. Hundreds of suspected terrorists were captured and shipped to America's military prison at Guantánamo Bay, where they would be held indefinitely, without access to lawyers or the right to communicate with the outside world, their lack of rights justified on grounds of a "national emergency." Bin Laden, however, remained at large, and the region remained unstable. During the 2002 fiscal year, the United States deployed 5,200 troops in Afghanistan. By 2008, nearly 31,000 troops were stationed there.

Regime change proved expensive. In early 2002 Bush announced a "Marshall Plan" for the reconstruction of Afghanistan that included funding for military training, public education, and public works. "We're working hard in Afghanistan," he declared. "We're clearing minefields. We're rebuilding roads. We're improving medical care." The rhetoric echoed a call by Lyndon Johnson for a TVA for Vietnam's Mekong Delta and met with a similar fate. The new Afghan regime, propped up by American aid, struggled with corruption and faced intense opposition in much of the country. Al Qaeda and other anti-American groups hid in the impenetrable mountains bordering Pakistan. The Taliban regrouped and skirmished with Afghan troops and their American allies, gradually regaining control in many regions. Just as the Russians found themselves bogged down in a costly effort to take control of Afghanistan in the 1980s, so did the United States see few positive long-term results from its costly engagement there.

IRAQ Behind the scenes, the Bush administration set its sights on another major target, Saddam Hussein's Iraq. His oil-rich dictatorship had not been involved in the 9/11 attacks and opposed fundamentalists like the Taliban and Al Qaeda. But from Bush's first days in office, his foreign policy advisers had warned, even if they lacked evidence, that Saddam Hussein was working to build weapons of mass destruction (WMD) in a bid to extend his power in the region.

Many Bush administration officials saw the resolution of the 1991 Persian Gulf War, which had left the dictator in power, as a failure. After the Gulf War, the United Nations had instituted an economic embargo on Iraq and forbidden arms trades with Saddam Hussein's regime. In the late 1990s, a group of conservative foreign policy experts—several of whom would later assume top positions in the Bush administration—began arguing that the United States should oust Saddam Hussein as a part of a larger post–Cold War project to depose anti-American regimes worldwide. Secretary of Defense Rumsfeld, his chief deputy, Paul Wolfowitz, and Vice President Dick

Cheney, the hawkish former senator from Wyoming and former Nixon and Ford aide, put Iraq at the top of the Bush administration's foreign policy agenda well before 9/11.

THE "AXIS OF EVIL" By late 2001, with the Taliban out of power in Afghanistan, Bush turned his attention toward "regime change" elsewhere in the world. In his 2002 State of the Union address, he singled out Iraq, Iran, and North Korea. "States like these and their terrorist allies," he argued, "constitute an axis of evil, arming to threaten the peace of the world. By seeking weapons of mass destruction, these regimes pose a grave and growing danger." His rhetoric echoed Ronald Reagan's "evil empire" statement by making a moral case for an aggressive foreign policy. In the wake of 9/11, Bush explicitly linked these regimes to the threat of violent attacks on the United States. "They could provide these arms to terrorists, giving them the means to match their hatred." Bush's strong language alarmed many of America's allies, who believed that it was a call for war.[16]

No place embodied the "axis of evil" for Bush more than Saddam Hussein's Iraq. That regime, argued Bush, "continues to flaunt its hostility toward America and to support terror."[17] The administration's hawks argued that Saddam Hussein destabilized the Middle East, continued to threaten American economic interests there, and jeopardized America's ally, Israel. They also believed that a post–Saddam Hussein Iraq would serve as a beacon for democracy throughout the Middle East. Bush also began to make a case for the necessity of preemptive warfare. "If we wait for threats to materialize, we will have waited too long," he told graduates of West Point in June 2002. "We must take the battle to the enemy, disrupt his plans, and confront the worst threats before they emerge. In the world we have entered, the only path to safety is the path of action, and this Nation will act."[18]

SELLING THE WAR Over the summer and fall of 2002, Bush and his advisers began making the case for military engagement, on the grounds that Saddam Hussein was building weapons of mass destruction and supporting terrorism. Independent observers were skeptical that Iraq had developed WMD, or even had the capacity to do so, in large part because the country's economy had been hobbled by UN sanctions. But the president insisted otherwise. In a September 2002 address, Bush forcefully argued: "The Iraqi regime possesses biological and chemical weapons, is rebuilding the facilities to build more . . . [and] is seeking a nuclear bomb and with fissile material could build one within a year."[19] Administration officials deflected arguments that there was no evidence for these claims. "We don't want the smoking gun to be a mushroom cloud," warned national security adviser Condoleezza Rice in a statement that the president and other administration officials would repeat.[20]

Behind the scenes, some Bush administration officials were skeptical of war with Iraq. Secretary of State Colin Powell worried that it would require a massive commitment of American ground troops and lead to a costly, long-term engagement. As Powell had memorably told the president, "You are going to be the proud owner of 25 million people. You will own all their hopes, aspirations and problems. You'll own it all."[21] The cost of reconstructing Iraq would be high, and Powell doubted that the

U.S. military had the capacity to oversee a transition to democracy in a regime that was bitterly divided by religious sectarianism and that lacked the institutions or history of democratic governance. Powell argued that continuing sanctions against Iraq would keep Saddam Hussein in check.

Some Republicans—including several veterans of the first Bush administration—made the case that going after Saddam Hussein would detract from efforts to target Al Qaeda. Liberal critics argued that a war in Iraq was a crude political ploy to mask the administration's failure to capture Bin Laden. Toppling the Iraqi dictator would provide more tangible evidence of victory against terror than the ongoing clandestine operations against Al Qaeda. Activists on the left resuscitated the Vietnam analogy and suggested that Bush, a former petroleum industry executive, was willing to spill "blood for oil" and that Vice President Cheney had financial interests in companies that would profit from the reconstruction of Iraq.

Throughout the second half of 2002 and early 2003, Bush and his foreign policy team took every occasion to reiterate their argument that Saddam Hussein possessed WMD. Most major newspapers and television news programs reported the administration's arguments uncritically, creating what diplomatic historian Fredrik Logevall called a "permissive context" for entering a war.[22] Both *The New York Times* and *The Washington Post* would later apologize for burying stories that presented evidence that contradicted the administration's position.

That permissive context set the tone for legislation authorizing the president to conduct military action against Iraq, which passed with large majorities in both the House and the Senate and was signed by President Bush on October 16, 2002. The public—still fearful of terrorism—rallied behind the call for war. Liberal internationalists, including many in the Democratic Party's mainstream like former president Clinton, echoed the Bush administration's position on Iraq. The "liberal hawks" used periodicals like *Slate*, *The New Republic*, and *The New York Times* to call for war.

Bush clinched his argument in his State of the Union address in January 2003. Although UN inspectors had found no evidence that Saddam Hussein's regime had WMD, Bush cited a British intelligence report that Iraq "had sought significant quantities of uranium from Africa" and had attempted to acquire aluminum tubes for the construction of nuclear weaponry. When Colin Powell addressed the United Nations in late January, he presented what he called incontrovertible evidence that Saddam Hussein had weapons facilities and was harboring key Al Qaeda leaders. Both claims proved false. A few years later Powell retracted his remarks, claiming that he had been fed misleading intelligence. But it was too late.

Powell, who was highly regarded, persuaded many Americans that the administration's case was valid. But most of America's allies remained skeptical of American claims about WMDs and concerned that a war in Iraq would destabilize the Middle East. Of the major powers, only Great Britain supported Bush. British prime minister Tony Blair shared Bush's moral argument in favor of toppling autocratic regimes and pledged to join the United States. The Americans and the British tried but failed to win United Nations support.

"Mission Accomplished" President George W. Bush, wearing a flight jacket, poses with sailors aboard the *USS Abraham Lincoln*, May 1, 2003, after his "Mission Accomplished" speech about the Iraq War.

OPERATION IRAQI FREEDOM With the backing of a hodge-podge "coalition of the willing" that included Britain, Australia, and about forty small countries that offered mostly symbolic support, Bush decided to buck the United Nations. On March 17, 2003, the president warned Saddam Hussein that if he did not step down, the United States would attack. Two days later the United States deployed about 140,000 troops in what the Pentagon called Operation Iraqi Freedom. The Iraqi army, badly trained, was caught by surprise by what Secretary Rumsfeld called a strategy of "shock and awe." Massive airstrikes broke Iraqi lines, and U.S. troops marched into the heart of the country. Within five weeks, Baghdad had fallen, and Saddam Hussein had gone into hiding.

His swift collapse seemed to vindicate the strategy of "regime change." On May 1, 2003, dressed in a flight suit, President Bush appeared on the *USS Abraham Lincoln*, an aircraft carrier stationed off the coast of San Diego. Under a banner that read "Mission Accomplished," he announced the end of major combat operations and hailed the "liberation of Iraq" as "a crucial advance in the campaign against terror." America and its allies were the agents of liberty. "In the images of celebrating Iraqis," he continued, "we have also seen the ageless appeal of human freedom."[23]

"MISSION ACCOMPLISHED" Bush's speech was ill timed. Within months it became clear that the war in Iraq was far from over. Saddam Hussein had brutally held together a country that was deeply divided by religion and ethnicity. The "liberation" of Baghdad was followed by intense sectarian violence. Sunni and Shi'ite Muslims struggled for power; rebels attacked both Iraqi government forces and American troops; and news of car bombings dominated the headlines. Bush and his aides, however, remained optimistic about the possibility of a democratic Iraq and increased the number of American troops in 2004 to maintain order until the country stabilized.

The rationale for the Iraq War quickly crumbled away. Investigators searched for evidence that Saddam Hussein had stockpiled WMD. Military and intelligence officials scoured factories, rifled through Iraqi government records, and interviewed former government officials, scientists, and military leaders, but they found no evidence of such weapons. They also looked long and hard for a smoking gun that Hussein had bankrolled Al Qaeda. They found nothing. In a particularly tasteless filmed skit at the 2004 White House Correspondents Association dinner, President Bush scuttled through the White House in a spoof search for WMD, even crawling under the Oval Office desk.

The situation in Iraq worsened over the next several years. The country plunged into civil war, and its weak American-supported government could not contain the disorder. In mid-2005 the Department of Defense reported about 500 "weekly security incidents" in Iraq, most of them bombings. The number increased to 1,000 in the summer of 2006 and peaked at 1,600 in June 2007. By 2008, after a "troop surge," about 250,000 American troops were committed to the Iraq War.[24] Because the military relied on reservists and volunteer forces (there was no draft during the Iraq War), many troops were ordered to extend their tours of duty, a move that was particularly unpopular among the ranks. The number of violent incidents declined for a time after the surge, but Iraqis lived in constant fear of car bombings, kidnappings, and shootings.

ABU GHRAIB In April 2004 grim photographs from Abu Ghraib, a notorious prison long operated by the Saddam Hussein regime, further discredited the American war effort. Nearly three-quarters of the prisoners held there by American forces had committed no crimes. For months reports had been filtering out through human rights organizations that the military and the CIA were systematically torturing Iraqi prisoners, administering brutal, sometimes fatal beatings, hanging them by their wrists and leaving them dangling, and raping them. The story exploded when *The New Yorker* magazine investigated the story and obtained photographs of soldiers, male and female, laughing as they abused inmates, sexually molested them, walked them naked on dog chains, and punched them. The most striking photograph showed a hooded Iraqi prisoner standing on a cardboard box, with wires attached to his fingers, toes, and penis. All together eleven U.S. soldiers were tried and convicted for their participation in the Abu Ghraib incident.

Some of those charged asserted they had acted with the approval of their superiors, and evidence mounted that higher military officials had condoned abuse and torture

Rumsfeld at Abu Ghraib Secretary of Defense Donald Rumsfeld meets with soldiers at the Abu Ghraib prison near Baghdad, May 13, 2004, shortly after revelations that U.S. soldiers had abused and tortured prisoners there.

in Abu Ghraib, Guantánamo, and other secret U.S. prisons. Bush and other administration officials denounced the abuses and attributed them to a few "bad apples." But the prison abuses occurred in a permissive atmosphere resulting from administrative decisions dating back to 2001 that justified torture and held that the United States was not bound by human rights accords or the laws of war when dealing with suspected terrorists.

The situation in Iraq scarcely fit the ideal of "liberty" that Bush and his advisers had imagined. The country's infrastructure had collapsed. Its economy was a shambles. And the war exacted a huge price in lives. Between 2003 and 2011, about 4,500 Americans and, by conservative estimates, between 100,000 and 200,000 Iraqis (some estimates reached over 600,000) died because of war-related injuries. Instability in Iraq fueled the growth of terrorist and radical Islamic organizations. About half of all terrorist incidents worldwide in the 2000s occurred in post-invasion Iraq. Saddam Hussein himself was tried, convicted, and executed by the Iraqi government in 2006, but no one saw the new regime as a beacon of liberty or the source of stability in the Middle East. The invasion and occupation of Iraq proved a costly foreign policy failure.

The Limits of Conservatism

The cost of pursuing the two wars was immense. Between 2001 and 2012, Congress appropriated $1.4 trillion for the wars in Afghanistan and Iraq, but as one analyst argued, "those figures vastly understate the total costs." By conservative estimates, the United States paid another $3.5 trillion for costs such as foreign aid to the war-torn countries, interest on money borrowed to pay for increased military expenses, and medical and disability expenses for veterans.[25]

During past wars, presidents had evoked the concept of shared sacrifice, rallying the population to buy war bonds, accept rationing, or pay for military expenditures through increased taxes. During the Iraq War as well, it became commonplace in political speeches, editorials, and in public discourse to call for supporting American troops. Uniformed armed service members got priority seating on airlines, cheers at sporting events, and countless rallies in high school gyms. But increasing taxes to pay for the massive military expenditures was out of the question in an era of "no new taxes." The federal budget deficit skyrocketed, and the Bush administration and Congress, already primed to cut domestic programs in the service of small government, axed spending in many areas, including scientific research, transportation infrastructure, and regulation.

"POLITICAL CAPITAL" AND SOCIAL SECURITY REFORM The 2004 election was closely fought, as Bush faced off against Senator John Kerry (D-MA). A decorated Vietnam veteran, Kerry had initially supported the Iraq War, but by 2004, as the war dragged on, he expressed skepticism about its goals. Kerry, a moderate, also criticized the Bush administration's positions on abortion, stem cell research, and homosexuality. The campaign was ugly. A group of Vietnam veterans, funded by right-wing donors, claimed, without basis, that Kerry had lied about his service in Vietnam. Evangelical Christians mobilized around gay marriage and abortion. And a conservative Catholic bishop denied Kerry—a practicing Catholic—communion because of his position on reproductive rights.

Bush pledged, if reelected, to stay the course. The election would occur less than two years after he launched the war in Iraq. Although the war's critics grew more vocal, Bush did not face the systematic opposition that had hampered Lyndon Johnson. American taxpayers did not feel the pinch of wartime spending or domestic sacrifice. Young men had no fear that they would be drafted. By the standards of World War II, Korea, and Vietnam, the American body count was small.

After a decisive election victory, Bush crowed, "I earned capital in this campaign, political capital, and now I intend to spend it."[26] At the top of his list was the privatization of Social Security. For decades, Republicans had targeted the program, one of the last survivors of Franklin Delano Roosevelt's New Deal. Goldwater had argued for its dismantling, and Reagan had attempted and failed a radical restructuring of the program. In the 1990s Bush had told members of the Cato Institute, a libertarian think tank, that privatizing Social Security was "the most important policy issue facing the United States today."[27]

He made the case that Social Security was irreparably broken and would collapse because of the rapidly aging population. He proposed to privatize the program, calling for the creation of "personal accounts" that would allow individuals to divert funds from payroll taxes to the stock market. Supporting Bush were a series of corporate and conservative think-tank-sponsored "AstroTurf" (as compared to grassroots) organizations like "For Our Grandchildren" and "Alliance for Worker Retirement Security." But those organizations were no match for the broad opposition that Bush faced from Democrats, from mass membership organizations like the American Association of Retired People, and from the public more widely. Social Security, as it had been under Reagan, was still a "third rail," politically untouchable. Bush's plan went nowhere.

KATRINA When Hurricane Katrina hit the Gulf Coast in August 2005, the Bush administration was caught off guard. The president was on vacation at his ranch in Crawford, Texas, and remained there two days after the hurricane struck. Even though the evening news showed horrific photographs of people trapped on their rooftops in Pascagoula, Mississippi, and New Orleans, bloated bodies floating through debris-strewn canals, and chaos outside the New Orleans Superdome, where more than twenty thousand people crowded in a makeshift refugee camp with few provisions, Bush said nothing until the fourth day after the storm hit.

Bush's silence was a sign less of personal insensitivity (which many felt at the time) than of bureaucratic failure, a consequence of the administration's shifting priorities. The Federal Emergency Management Agency (FEMA), which was responsible for disaster relief, was ill prepared to respond to Katrina. Created by President Carter in 1979, FEMA had been folded into the Department of Homeland Security after 9/11. The agency became a second-tier organization in a huge national security bureaucracy, ill managed and politically marginal. Disaster relief took second place to counterterrorism efforts. No one knew exactly what power FEMA had or how it should respond. Two days after the hurricane struck, Marty Bahamonde, the only FEMA official on the ground in New Orleans, sent an urgent message to Michael Brown, the head of FEMA, reporting that the situation was "past critical" and noted that people were running "out of food and out of water at the dome." Brown sent a terse reply four minutes later. "Thanks for the update. Anything I need to do or tweak?"[28]

On Wednesday, August 31, *Air Force One* flew over the Gulf Coast on its track from the president's Texas ranch back to Washington. On Friday, September 2, Bush toured the Mississippi coast, infamously praising Brown for doing "a heckuva job." Only then did the federal government begin to send relief dollars and federal assistance to the devastated region. After a harrowing week struggling to survive on the streets of New Orleans, Patricia Thompson was finally evacuated on Saturday, September 3. She resettled in College Station, Texas, where she found work at an elementary school and financial assistance and housing through a local evangelical church.

Rebuilding after Katrina would be a gargantuan task. The hurricane had wiped out several towns on the Gulf Coast, killed more than 1,800 people, destroyed 160,000 houses and apartments, and left $108 billion of damage in its wake. In its aftermath, the Bush administration decided to turn New Orleans into a model of privatization.

Hurricane Katrina Milvertha Hendricks, eighty-four, draped in the American flag, waits with other Hurricane Katrina victims outside the New Orleans convention center, September 1, 2005.

In September the president announced the creation of a "Gulf Coast Opportunity Zone" in which he waived federal air quality control and trucking safety regulations. He also waived a federal law that required contractors on government projects to be paid the local prevailing wage. Rather than putting federal money into the reconstruction of housing, the administration created Katrina trailer parks, leaving it to the private sector to provide, or not, affordable housing in the long term. Rebuilding New Orleans happened painfully slowly, especially in the neighborhoods that had been home to the city's poorest residents. The city grew wealthier and whiter after Katrina.

Post-Katrina relief efforts also relied heavily on faith-based community organizations. Hundreds of faith groups, with budgets ranging from a few hundred to a few million dollars, attempted to fill the gap left by the federal government. But Katrina tested their capacity. A detailed study of more than two hundred religious groups found that they "did not have sufficient trained staff, resources, or protocols to provide more than limited and short-term assistance."[29]

One of the most consequential post-Katrina experiments, which won the support of the Bush administration and both centrist Democrats and most Republicans, was a plan to privatize New Orleans's public schools. Scott Cowen, the president of Tulane University, argued that Katrina offered "a once in a lifetime opportunity" to transform public education.[30] Ten years after the hurricane, nine out of ten students in New Orleans attended charter schools, run by nonprofit organizations. Although educators intensely debated whether charter schools were more effective than public schools—the best evidence showed that there is little difference in educational outcomes—reformers saw the Crescent City as a laboratory for school reform that could be replicated nationwide.

DEREGULATION AND THE FINANCIAL CRISIS The economy of the early 2000s, more than in the past, rested on a volatile foundation: the housing market. Wages remained stagnant throughout the period, but housing prices skyrocketed, in large part because interest rates reached an all-time low. Federal Reserve chairman

Alan Greenspan, who had directed central monetary policy since the 1980s, used the tool of interest rate cuts to curb inflation and stimulate economic growth. But in the early 2000s, as the economy slowed, he took an even more drastic measure. The Federal Reserve steadily cut the prime rate, the interest that banks charged for interbank loans. It bottomed out at 1 percent between 2002 and 2004, the lowest since the early 1950s. Greenspan's rationale was that lower interest rates would fuel a housing boom. Ready credit would lead to a rise in home values. Homeowners would benefit from the growing equity in their properties and spend more, bolstering the economy.

Greenspan's actions set off a mad scramble in the housing market. Lower interest rates attracted first-time homebuyers. Those who already owned homes rushed to refinance their mortgages. Many gambled that their houses would continue to appreciate and took home equity loans, which they used to make home improvements, pay for skyrocketing college tuition expenses, or cover extraordinary health care expenses. The home became a sort of ATM, a source of easily available cash, so long as home values continued to rise.

Thousands of new mortgage origination firms sprung up virtually overnight, taking advantage of the seemingly boundless market. "Lending standards," wrote one analyst, "became almost comical. Buyers could get a mortgage with no income and no assets. Paperwork was scant."[31] Predatory lenders often overcharged customers, relied on fraudulent home appraisals, and hid exorbitant fees. They offered adjustable-rate mortgages that lured borrowers with low interest rates that quickly escalated to several points above the prime rate. Many of those lenders targeted minorities who had long suffered from discrimination in home lending. A group of housing economists found that in 2006 more than a quarter of all loans nationwide charged unusually high interest rates, "including 49 percent and 39 percent of loans made to African Americans and Hispanics, respectively."[32]

Wall Street investors fueled the madness. They took advantage of loose regulations, particularly the Clinton administration's repeal of the Glass-Steagall Act in 1999. They basked in the antiregulatory fervor of the Bush administration. The federal agencies that regulated banking and financial firms turned a blind eye toward risky lending practices. Sheila Bair, a moderate Republican who chaired the Federal Deposit Insurance Corporation (set up during the New Deal to protect depositors from bank failures), called for a tightening of mortgage lending rules but faced fierce opposition from Wall Street and from within the Bush administration itself. "I frequently found myself isolated in advocating for stronger regulatory standards," she recalled. From the Federal Reserve to the boardrooms of major banks, everyone believed that "market forces" would lead firms to "self-regulate."[33] Major financial firms, among them Countrywide Financial, Citigroup, Wells Fargo, JPMorgan Chase, and Lehman Brothers, bundled together risky loans and sold them as securities to eager investors. As long as real estate prices continued to rise, everyone seemed to be a winner. Consumers bought more; investors earned high returns; investment banks made massive profits.

The mortgage market began to collapse in 2006, when lenders ratcheted the interest on adjustable-rate mortgages upward. For the first time in years, housing values began to drop. Places like Euclid, Ohio, a working-class suburb just east of Cleveland, were the canaries in the coal mine. Euclid was exactly the sort of community that predatory lenders targeted: its residents, hurt by the collapse of the region's industrial economy and the rise of the low-wage service sector, earned moderate incomes. Nearly a third of Euclid's residents were African Americans who hoped to own their own homes in a suburb that had long excluded them. In 2006 and 2007 alone, lenders initiated foreclosures on more than six hundred houses in Euclid as homeowners saw the monthly payments on their adjustable-rate mortgages rise 50 percent or more. The city of Euclid installed alarm systems in some vacant houses to keep out scavengers and squatters. It spent more than a million dollars maintaining the foreclosed properties and mowing lawns.

By 2008, what happened in Euclid was happening everywhere in the United States. Housing values plummeted, and more than a million homes were lost to foreclosure nationwide that year, as homeowners struggled to meet payments. The collapse in confidence in securitized, high-risk mortgages devastated some of the nation's largest banks and lenders. The home financing giant Fannie Mae alone held an estimated $230 billion in toxic assets. In September 2008 the giant investment banking firm Lehman Brothers collapsed, sparking panic across the economy. The entire banking system teetered on the brink. Lending came to a virtual halt, and consumer spending plummeted. Wall Street firms panicked, and the stock market plummeted. In November the Federal Reserve used $800 billion to buy up mortgage debt, to save major banking institutions.

The Election of 2008

The economic crash and the disaster of Iraq weighed heavily on the presidential election in 2008. President Bush was deeply unpopular. Wall Street was reeling. Homeowners faced record foreclosure rates. Many commentators worried that Americans would make a run on banks in a grim repetition of the early years of the Great Depression. The political climate aided the Democratic Party. Two years earlier Democrats had swept the midterm elections, winning control of both the House and the Senate for the first time since 1994.

THE CANDIDATE OF "HOPE AND CHANGE" The Democratic nominee, Barack Obama, had risen from political obscurity, launching a presidential campaign just two years after he had been elected to the U.S. Senate from Illinois. His background was unusual: he was born in 1960, when interracial marriage was taboo in much of the United States and forbidden in most of the South, to a white mother and an African father. Obama had grown up in Hawaii and graduated from Columbia University before working for almost three years as a community organizer on Chicago's South Side. He achieved his only significant victory when he persuaded the Chicago Housing Authority to remove asbestos from the Altgeld Homes, a low-income housing project. Frustrated at the limitations of organizing, Obama attended Harvard Law School and became the first black editor of the *Harvard Law Review*. There

The 2008 Election Barack Obama often attracted large, racially diverse, and youthful crowds at his campaign rallies, like this one in Oakland, California, on March 17, 2007.

he succeeded in winning the support of liberal students who saw him as one of their own, black students who believed he would advance the goals of civil rights, and conservative students who trusted him because he took their ideas seriously and gave them voice on the law review's editorial board. It was a formula for bipartisanship—respect your opponents and use your skills of persuasion to win them over—that would be a model for his political career.

In 1991, with his law degree in hand, he moved back to Chicago, worked on a voting rights campaign, practiced law, and taught courses at the University of Chicago Law School. In 1996 he was elected to the Illinois State Senate, representing one of the most liberal districts in the country. In Springfield, Obama reached out and befriended some Republicans, even as he voted fairly consistently against them. By 2003, when he set his sights on the U.S. Senate, he had moved to the center of the Democratic Party. On most issues—welfare reform, regulation, and economic policy—his policy choices were fairly close to Bill Clinton's. Only on foreign policy issues did he veer toward his party's liberal wing, initially opposing the Iraq War and criticizing Bush's surveillance and detention policies.

In 2008 Obama ran for president as a fresh-faced alternative to the Washington status quo, pitching himself as a candidate who would bring the country together after a period of divisiveness. Since his national debut as a keynote speaker at the Democratic National Convention in 2004, he had pitched himself as a reconciler, drawing from his own interracial family history to make the point. The audience roared when he called out, "There's not a liberal America and a conservative America; there's the

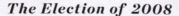

The Election of 2008

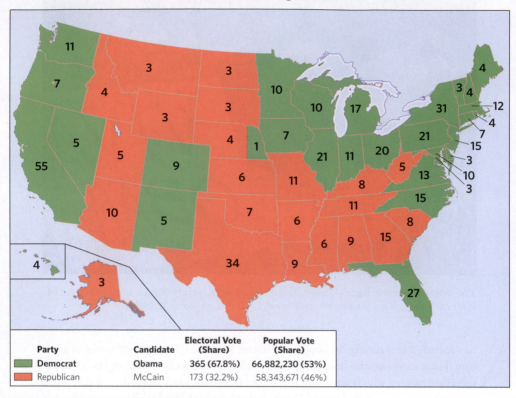

Party	Candidate	Electoral Vote (Share)	Popular Vote (Share)
Democrat	Obama	365 (67.8%)	66,882,230 (53%)
Republican	McCain	173 (32.2%)	58,343,671 (46%)

United States of America. There's not a black America and white America and Hispanic America and Asian America; there's the United States of America. The pundits, the pundits like to slice and dice our country into red states and blue states: red states for Republicans, blue states for Democrats. But I've got news for them, too. We worship an awesome God in the blue states, and we don't like federal agents poking around our libraries in the red states."[34]

Many Democrats in 2008 were skeptical that a majority white nation would elect a black president. During the primaries, Obama faced a formidable opponent, the New York senator and former first lady Hillary Rodham Clinton, who pledged to return the country to the economic prosperity and peace that it had enjoyed during her husband's presidency. But Obama electrified Democratic audiences with his call for "hope" and "change." Clinton denounced the concepts as gauzy, played on her experience as a policy maker and senator, and argued that she had the maturity and experience to win. In a closely fought season of primaries and caucuses, Obama edged out Clinton and won the nomination.

THE MAVERICK Obama faced a divided Republican Party and a weak Republican candidate. John McCain had occasionally bucked his party's right wing, and he had earned their skepticism as a result. He had been a prisoner of war in Vietnam, married into a wealthy Arizona family, and enjoyed a long career in the Senate. But he faced an uphill battle. He defined himself as a "maverick," attempting to create a little distance between himself and the Bush administration. McCain launched his campaign with an advertisement that evoked the 1960s, contrasting images of protest in the streets with his valiant service in the military. It was not a propitious beginning. In late August he made the electrifying announcement that he had chosen a virtually unknown Alaska politician, Sarah Palin, as his running mate. But he stumbled in the weeks that followed, as the economic crisis exploded. In September, when Lehman Brothers collapsed, he maintained that "the fundamentals of our economy are strong," before backtracking and making the ill-advised decision to suspend his campaign for a few days.[35]

Obama ran his campaign around the vague but appealing slogan, "Change We Can Believe In." Surrounding himself with talented advisers, he raised more money than any candidate to date and ran a sophisticated campaign, pioneering the use of new technologies to identify voters and bring them to the polls on election day. Obama's campaign events drew enormous crowds, and his supporters—younger and more racially diverse than the population as a whole—were highly motivated. He won the election with a clear majority of the electorate and a greater percentage of the vote than any Democratic presidential candidate since 1964.

Obama and the World

Obama's rise to the presidency seemed to herald the emergence of a new Democratic majority and a fundamental reorientation of U.S. domestic and international politics. He promised to reverse the previous administration's foreign policy, its penchant for secrecy, and its expansion of executive powers. In large part because of this promise, Obama won the 2009 Nobel Peace Prize, even though to that date, he had virtually no experience in international relations.

President Obama promised to withdraw American troops from Iraq. In December 2011, the last American troops would leave a country that was still ravaged by sectarian civil war, ruled by a corrupt, unstable regime, and crippled by a dysfunctional economy. The war, launched eight years earlier, had utterly failed in all its goals, other than toppling Saddam Hussein. Everyday life in Baghdad was still punctuated with car bombings. Iraq was a haven for terrorist organizations.

Obama attempted to tread a fine line between all-out war for regime change and limited interventions. He kept some key Bush administration programs in place. Breaking from a campaign pledge, he failed to close the American detention facility at Guantánamo Bay in Cuba. He continued the war on terror, authorizing the use of drones to assassinate "enemy combatants" in nonwar zones, even some who were American citizens. He continued the Bush administration's expansion of surveillance against dissenters and suspected terrorists at home and abroad. His administration fought efforts, pushed by civil liberties organizations, to restrict a National Security Agency program to mine data from cell phone companies and Internet providers. The president also dramatically escalated the war in Afghanistan, at the same time pledging to withdraw American forces by late 2014. He deployed American troops in Libya in 2011, assisting rebels during a bloody civil war to overthrow dictator Muammar Gaddafi. But after the "regime change" occurred, he pulled American troops out. Post-Gaddafi Libya remained unstable and terror-ridden.

Obama and the Limits of "Change"

Taking office in the midst of the Great Recession, Obama pledged to undo the Bush administration's tax and regulatory policies that favored big business and banking. Yet he appointed a team of economic advisers who were comfortable in the world of high finance. His treasury secretary, Timothy Geithner, had run the New York Federal Reserve during the lead-up to the 2008 crash, and had close relationships to major bankers, financiers, and hedge fund managers. The head of Obama's National Economic Council, the economist Larry Summers, had played a crucial role in deregulating the financial sector as secretary of the treasury during the Clinton administration, and had worked as a consultant for a major hedge fund. Obama created a Council on Jobs and Competitiveness, headed by former General Electric chief executive Jeffrey Immelt, who had overseen a downsizing of his company's employment in the United States and massive investment in China. Obama resisted calls for the prosecution of bankers and financiers whose investment strategies—and whose illegal manipulations of the mortgage market—had led to the financial collapse in 2008. To do so, he and his advisers argued, would be divisive.[36]

Faced with a strong Republican opposition and divisions within his own Democratic Party in Congress, Obama's policy options were limited. And he was also fundamentally cautious, unwilling to engage in the messy deal making and horse trading that had allowed past presidents like Lyndon Johnson to push controversial legislation through a reluctant Congress. In early 2009 he signed the American Recovery and Reinvestment Act (also known as the stimulus package), an $800 billion program to launch "shovel ready" infrastructure projects and provide additional funds to states for education, public works, and other job creation programs. The stimulus funds were well below what mainstream economists believed was necessary to spark growth in the stagnant economy, but Obama did not have the political clout to push through anything larger.

OBAMACARE Obama's signature program was health insurance reform, a longtime Democratic Party goal. About 15 percent of the population, many of them low-wage workers, had no health insurance. An injury or serious illness could be catastrophic. Many on the party's left hoped for a national health care system like those in

Britain or Canada, but Obama forged a program that incorporated Republican ideas. His policy team, learning lessons from Clinton's failed reform in the 1990s, reached out to potential opponents. Obama won the support of the insurance industry, big pharmaceutical companies, and major corporations. His plan was modeled heavily on one first devised by conservative policy analysts at the Heritage Foundation and implemented in Massachusetts under Republican governor Mitt Romney, Obama's future Republican challenger.

By 2010, when the administration drafted the legislation, it faced a disciplined and unwavering Republican Party. Pulling the GOP rightward was the Tea Party, a conservative insurgency that had challenged Obama's legitimacy almost from his first day in office. Tea Party activists tarred him as un-American, a crypto-Muslim, or a black power activist. Many believed that he was an illegitimate president on the false charge that he had been born outside the United States.

The Tea Party's biggest target was health care, which they branded as "Obamacare." They charged that the president's program would create "death panels" that would decide whether to provide health care to elderly patients or let them die. Reprising themes from the Cold War, they charged that Obama was a "socialist" or a "communist" who was using health care reform as the first step to creating a totalitarian government. The Tea Party also targeted Republican officials whom they saw as insufficiently conservative, labeling them as Republicans in Name Only (RINOs) and supporting insurgent candidates in congressional races.

Obama's health care program passed Congress with no Republican votes. Still, many Republicans who opposed "Obamacare" faced angry Tea Party opponents during the 2010 primaries. Establishment Republicans, including those who had long supported presidents Reagan and Bush, lost to primary challengers from the right. In Utah, Mike Lee, a Tea Party favorite, unseated the establishment Republican senator Robert Bennett. In Kentucky, Rand Paul, a longtime libertarian, defeated a once-popular Republican secretary of state and went on to win a Senate seat. In the House, far-right Republicans formed the Tea Party caucus, using their clout to pull their colleagues even further rightward. For the next several years, House and Senate Republicans would do everything in their power to torpedo health care reform, passing dozens of resolutions calling for its appeal and filing lawsuits challenging parts of the bill in federal courts. Still Obamacare survived the sustained challenges. In late 2013, despite serious problems in the online enrollment system, nearly 7.3 million Americans enrolled in the insurance program, more than the law's backers had predicted.

THE BUDGET No issue generated greater partisan struggle than the federal budget. Republicans fought the Obama administration on nearly every aspect of federal spending, reprising arguments dating back to the 1980s that Democrats were profligate spenders. In 2010, Republicans forced an economic crisis over raising the federal debt ceiling, something that had been raised routinely, with little political controversy, under past Republican and Democratic presidents. Obama reached out to congressional Republicans and accepted a compromise that incorporated almost all Republican demands for dramatic cuts in federal spending while not increasing taxes, even on the richest Americans.

By 2010, Obama had turned his attention away from programs to stimulate the economy to an emphasis on deficit reduction. Many economists, notably Nobel Prize winner and *New York Times* columnist Paul Krugman, argued that the country would recover from the recession more quickly if the federal government spent more on public works and job creation, as it had during the Great Depression and World War II. But after thirty years of austerity and deficit reduction policies—under Democrats and Republicans alike—building political will for Keynesian interventions was close to impossible.

THE LIMITS OF BIPARTISANSHIP Throughout his first term, Obama continued to hope that he could somehow bridge the deep partisan divide—just as he had back in his days as a law student at Harvard—by treating his political opponents with respect and conceding to at least some of their demands.[37] But his efforts yielded few victories. Despite an economic policy that continued to favor big business, his staunchest critics came from the right. His military policy, his commitment to "nation building" in Libya, his authorization of the assassination of Osama bin Laden, and his expansion of drone attacks were criticized by some left-leaning intellectuals, but not even the most bellicose foreign policy satisfied vast sections of the political right.

Although the recession officially ended in mid-2009, many Americans struggled to make ends meet. Obama had presided over a gradual improvement in the economy. Unemployment rates slowly fell beginning in 2009. The mortgage market remained tight, but housing prices leveled off, and in some parts of the country, they rose. Obama's policies, however, did little to address the pressing question of inequality. The economic recovery exacerbated the pattern of growing gaps between the rich, whose incomes steadily rose, in large part because of a booming stock market, and the middle and working classes, who faced a sluggish job market and falling wages. Between 2009 and 2012, incomes of the top 1 percent grew by 31.4 percent. But for the remaining 99 percent, incomes grew by only 0.4 percent.[38]

Persistent economic inequality sparked discontent on the political left. On September 17, 2011, a small group of protesters set up an encampment in Zuccotti Park, a small plaza in the heart of New York's financial district. They called themselves Occupy Wall Street (OWS) and vowed to hold major banks responsible for the ongoing economic crisis. Within weeks, a few hundred people had set up tents, and thousands more joined regular protests on the surrounding streets. In mid-November, the city of New York evicted the protesters, but Occupy movements took over public spaces in several other big cities and some college campuses throughout the fall and winter.

The Occupy movement took its inspiration from 1960s campus teach-ins and civil rights sit-ins, but also took advantage of new social media to spread its message worldwide. In Zuccotti Park, protestors set up a generator to power computers that they used to post photos, videos, and documents on Twitter, Tumblr, and Facebook. OWS activists did not, however, speak with a single voice—some wanted bank reform, others encouraged Americans to support small local businesses, some called for a repeal of austerity measures, and others demanded the overthrow of capitalism. For all of their differences—and their lack of a coherent program—OWS activists claimed to speak for the vast majority of people, versus the wealthiest 1 percent of the population. Their slogan, "We are the 99 percent," gave voice to those discontented at the persistence of inequality. By early 2012, the Occupy movement had dispersed, but it had succeeded in focusing attention on the widening wealth and income gaps in early twenty-first-century America.

In 2012, Obama handily won reelection against Republican Mitt Romney, who launched his political career after running Bain Capital, an investment firm that bought, restructured, and sold companies, a process that often left workers unemployed. Obama depicted Romney as an out-of-touch elitist. But even after Obama's decisive reelection, his second term would be full of unresolved challenges. Republicans continued to control the House of Representatives, using their position to block many of the president's key initiatives. After gaining control of the Senate in the 2014 midterm elections—benefiting from a low turnout among Democratic-leaning younger and minority voters—the Republicans vowed to continue to obstruct Obama's domestic initiatives. In the meantime, the administration struggled with ongoing instability in Egypt and Syria and worsening conditions in Iraq. Even with Bin Laden dead and Al Qaeda hobbled, new extremist organizations emerged in the Middle East, most prominently the Islamic State of Iraq and Syria (ISIS), which led brutal attacks on non-Muslim villages and towns in Kurdistan and western Iraq. In 2014, Obama announced that he would step up military assistance to Iraqi troops fighting ISIS. During each of these foreign policy crises, the president took a more cautious approach than Bush—unwilling to embroil the United States in another prolonged war but also unwilling to stand aside.

The Burden of History

Obama was not a transformational president, as his most fervent supporters hoped and as his staunch enemies feared he would be. He was ultimately constrained by a past that was not of his own making. The United States had been moving toward greater economic inequality since the 1970s. The grim plight of workers whose wages stagnated was the result of the collapse of organized labor, the rise of right-to-work policies, the massive flight of capital to low-wage regions around the world, and the emergence of a low-wage service sector economy at home. The Great Recession was the consequence of thirty years of financial deregulation under Democratic and Republican administrations alike.

In the Obama years, Americans intensely debated the nation's place in the world. At a moment of extreme partisanship, both parties showed signs of division over centuries-old questions about internationalism and isolation. Should the United States support regime change in places like Syria, torn by civil war? Or should it keep its distance, avoiding entanglement in another Iraq, another Vietnam? Should American foreign policy continue to be shaped by a moral vision of the United States as a global beacon of freedom? Or should the United States define its interests narrowly

Making a Nation

The 1 Percent

From

Joseph S. Kalinowski

The Truth about Income Inequality (2012)

Kalinowski wrote this essay for the *Tea Party Tribune*, a right-wing website. Echoing conservative arguments about "job creators" and "takers," he contends that the "1 percent" of wealthiest Americans create jobs and improve the quality of life of the vast majority of the population. Proposals to increase taxes on the rich, he argues, would unjustly redistribute wealth and, in the process, hinder the ability of the richest Americans to fuel economic growth.

There are two things we need to realize about this pie that makes up the 1% and 99%.

The pie is both fluid and dynamic.

Fluid in that the top 1% is consistently changing. Research shows the top 1% of the pie is ever changing. Turnover among the top 1% is estimated to be roughly 20% to 30% on an annual basis.

This is an important point because it captures the essence of the American dream. If one works hard, the benefits of that hard work will pay off and an individual will build wealth and security for themselves and their family.

Redistribution does not support this thesis. Attempting a forceful unification, taking from the 1% and distributing to the 99% will stymie those risk takers, entrepreneurs and future leaders. By eliminating the motivation to reach the status of the 1% in the name of helping the 99%, the outcome will ultimately harm those that redistribution is portraying to protect.

The pie is dynamic as well . . . In reality, the pie is ever growing, and while many individuals may never reach the 1%, there needs to be an understanding that the success of the 1% greatly influences the living standards of the 99%.

Many of our grandparents never entertained the thought of having a television or an automobile. Many of our parents never dreamed of personal computing and cell phones. Today I observe my four year old son using an iPad with great ease. One needs to consider those great achievements of the 1% er's that founded Apple, Microsoft, Ford Motor, Wal-Mart and the many other business people that have improved the quality of life for so many 99% er's. In fact, there has been work done showing an inverse relationship between income inequality and employment and poverty.

Chuck Collins

The 99 Percent Spring (2012)

Collins, a staff member at the Institute for Policy Studies, a left-leaning think tank, documents growing disparities in wealth. Here he argues that the political system benefits the top 1 percent at the expense of everyone else. He is critical of tax breaks for investors and trade policies that encourage overseas investment. He demands political reforms that help working Americans cut household debt and raise wages.

The richest 1 percent now owns over 36 percent of all the wealth in the United States. That's more than the net worth of the bottom 95 percent combined. This 1 percent has pocketed almost all of the wealth gains of the last decade.

In 2010, the 1 percent earned 21 percent of all income, up from only 8 percent in mid-1970s. The 400 wealthiest individuals on the Forbes 400 list have more wealth than the bottom 150 million Americans.

These trends among the 1 percent are bad for the rest of us. Concentrated wealth translates into political clout—the power to use campaign contributions to rent politicians and tilt the rules of the economy in their favor.

Web sites dramatizing the "We are the 99 percent" movement are full of personal stories of young people who are saddled with debt and no futures, and middle class families that have seen the American Dream collapse around them, losing jobs, homes, and hopes for the future.

"I used to dream about becoming the first woman president," one woman wrote. "Now I dream about getting a job with health insurance."

Reading these stories, I'm struck that the underlying conditions that have squeezed millions of Americans aren't going away. The current political system, captured by large corporations and the wealthy, is incapable of responding to their needs.

The "99 to 1" dichotomy may strike some folks as polarizing and inaccurate. Yet it's a powerful lens for understanding what's happened to our society and economy over the last several decades. The rules guiding our economy have been skewed to benefit the 1 percent at the expense of the 99 percent. These rules include tax policies, global trade agreements, and government actions that benefit asset owners at the expense of wage earners.

We must defend ourselves from the bad actors—the built-to-loot companies whose business model is focused on shifting costs onto society, shedding jobs, and extracting wealth from our communities and the healthy economy.

Questions for Analysis

1. Why does Kalinowski oppose increasing taxes on the "1 percent"?
2. What economic policies does Collins support?
3. What do Collins and Kalinowski view as a healthy economy?

These United States   On the fiftieth anniversary of the March 7, 1965, clash with state police on the Edmund Pettus Bridge in Selma, Alabama, President Obama stands with veterans of the Selma to Montgomery march for voting rights.

and act only when directly threatened? American foreign policy was still shaped, in fundamental ways, by the moral absolutism of the Cold War, an approach that was reinvigorated during the war on terror. But a countercurrent—not the majority—was chastened by the excesses of Abu Ghraib and Guantánamo and called for a reinvigoration of a lost American commitment to human rights.

Obama embodied one of the most enduring legacies of the long twentieth century, the growing recognition of African Americans in American politics. It is impossible to imagine the rise of a black president without considering the black freedom struggle of the post–World War II years. Obama looked up to civil rights leaders like U.S. representative John Lewis, who had begun his career sitting-in at movie theaters and lunch counters. Many commentators argued that Obama's election marked the rise of a "postracial" America, the dawn of a "post-civil-rights era."

But it was not so easy to overcome America's long history of racial injustice. By every measure, racial gaps remained vast, leaving people like Patricia Thompson with few opportunities for upward mobility. At the beginning of Obama's second term in office, 73 percent of whites but only 43 percent of blacks and 46 percent of Hispanics owned their own homes. The typical black household had only $5,677 in wealth (including savings accounts, real estate, and stock market investments); Hispanics had $6,325 in wealth. The comparable measure for white households was $113,149. The typical white household was twenty times wealthier than the typical black or Hispanic household.[39] Black unemployment rates have remained one and a half to two times that of whites since the 1950s—regardless of the state of the economy. And Hispanics, now 16 percent of the nation's population, comprise 28 percent of Americans living beneath the poverty line. One of the most pressing unresolved problems—the overrepresentation of blacks among those stopped by the police, arrested, and jailed—exploded in protests in 2014 after a police officer in Ferguson, Missouri, shot an unarmed black man, and when New York City police officers attempted to arrest a man for selling loose cigarettes and in the process choked him to death.

Well into the twenty-first century, the promises of the twentieth—equality, opportunity, and justice—remained only partially fulfilled. Martin Luther King, Jr., memorably stated that "the arc of the moral universe bends toward justice." But just as often, as modern American history shows, that arc veers off course. Modern America was shaped by the struggles of countless ordinary men and women, seeking to improve their communities, to achieve age-old ideals of equality and justice. But it was also shaped by a relentless drive toward self-interest. That struggle between individual interest and social responsibility remains the enduring contradiction of modern American history.

Suggested Reading

Frey, William. *Diversity Explosion: How New Racial Demographics Are Remaking America* (2014). How the new immigration of Latinos and Asians, along with changing ideas about race, are changing the color of America.

Hyman, Louis R. *Debtor Nation: The History of America in Red Ink* (2011). The rise of consumer credit and the deregulation of banking that led to the 2008 financial crisis.

Huret, Romain, and Randy J. Sparks, eds. *Hurricane Katrina in Transatlantic Perspective* (2014). Leading historians consider race, federal policy, urban redevelopment, and economics in New Orleans.

Mayer, Jane. *The Dark Side: The Inside Story of How the War on Terror Turned into a War on American Ideals* (2008). A prizewinning account of the Bush administration's decision to fight terrorism through secret detention centers, torture, and expanded surveillance.

Packer, George. *Assassins' Gate: America in Iraq* (2005). A narrative history of America's long engagement with the Saddam Hussein regime and the decision of the George W. Bush administration to launch the Iraq War.

Piketty, Thomas. *Capital in the Twenty-first Century* (2014). A rigorous economic analysis of the rise of inequality in the United States and the west.

Rajan, Raghuram G. *Fault Lines: How Hidden Fractures Still Threaten the World Economy* (2010). How the 2008 economic crisis arose from stagnant wages, educational inequality, and financial policies that encouraged risky investments.

Remnick, David. *The Bridge: The Life and Rise of Barack Obama* (2010). A detailed account of how a former community activist and Illinois state senator rose to be America's first African American president.

Skocpol, Theda, and Vanessa Williamson. *The Tea Party and the Remaking of Republican Conservatism* (2011). Drawn from interviews with Tea Party members, two political scientists chart the rise of the antigovernment insurgency.

Zelizer, Julian, ed. *The Presidency of George W. Bush: A First Historical Assessment* (2010). Leading historians examine Bush's foreign and domestic politics.

Chapter Review

Review Questions

1. How did his Christian faith shape George W. Bush's domestic agenda?

2. Explain the rationale for tax reform in the early 2000s.

3. How did the Bush administration balance national security concerns and civil liberties?

4. How did the Bush administration build public support for Operation Iraqi Freedom?

5. How did the 2003 War in Iraq differ from the Persian Gulf War in 1991?

6. Why was President Bush unable to privatize Social Security?

7. Evaluate the policy responses to Hurricane Katrina.

8. What caused the collapse of the home mortgage market?

9. How did Barack Obama appeal to the electorate in the election of 2008?

10. Why was bipartisanship so difficult to achieve in the 2009–14 period?

Key Terms

Bush v. Gore p. 302

No Child Left Behind Act p. 304

White House Office of Faith-Based and Community Initiatives p. 304

Economic Growth and Tax Relief Reconciliation Act p. 306

Al Qaeda p. 307

USA PATRIOT Act p. 308

Department of Homeland Security p. 309

Guantánamo Bay p. 309

black sites p. 309

"axis of evil" p. 311

Operation Iraqi Freedom p. 313

Abu Ghraib p. 314

Social Security privatization p. 316

Federal Emergency Management Agency (FEMA) p. 317

Gulf Coast Opportunity Zone p. 318

predatory lending p. 319

foreclosure p. 320

American Recovery and Reinvestment Act p. 324

Obamacare p. 324

Islamic State of Iraq and Syria (ISIS) p. 327

NOTES

PREFACE: "WE ARE STILL IN THE MAKING"

1. Franklin D. Roosevelt: "Radio Address on Brotherhood Day," February 23, 1936, http://bit.ly/1zpxXO6.
2. Saul Bellow, *It All Adds Up: From the Dim Past to the Uncertain Future* (New York: Penguin Books, 1995), 28.
3. Thomas Piketty, *Capital in the Twenty-first Century* (Cambridge, MA: Belknap Press of Harvard University Press, 2014), 316. The exception is the 1920s, when income disparity rose preceding the Great Depression.
4. Robert E. Gallman, "Trends in the Size Distribution of Wealth in the Nineteenth Century: Some Speculations," in Lee Soltow, ed., *Six Papers on the Size Distribution of Wealth and Income* (Washington, DC: National Bureau of Economic Research, 1969), 12; Piketty, *Capital*, 323.
5. Piketty, *Capital*, 11–15. This theory is known as the Kuznets curve, after economist Simon Kuznets who proposed it.
6. Piketty, *Capital*, 323–24.
7. Ibid., 316.
8. "U.S. Properties with Foreclosure Findings," http://bit.ly/1ARn44P.
9. "Remarks by Senator Barack Obama on Martin Luther King, Jr.," April 4, 2008, http://bit.ly/1JJJ8Vb.
10. U.S. Department of Homeland Security, Enforcement Actions, "Aliens Removed or Returned: Fiscal Years 1892 to 2012," http://1.usa.gov/1JJJcnE.
11. Blanche Wiesen Cook, *Eleanor Roosevelt*, vol. 1, *1884–1933* (New York: Penguin, 1993), 338.
12. Center for American Women and Politics, Eagleton Institute of Politics, Rutgers, the State University of New Jersey, "Gender Differences in Voter Turnout," http://bit.ly/1weOJZ9.
13. U.S. Bureau of Labor Statistics, "Women in the Labor Force: A Databook," http://1.usa.gov/1AYtpv7; Claudia Goldin, "The Female Labor Force and American Economic Growth, 1890–1980," http://bit.ly/1sQXwQL.

14. U.S. Bureau of Labor Statistics, "Women in the Labor Force: A Databook," http://1.usa
.gov/1AYtpv7.

CHAPTER 1: A RISING SUPERPOWER

1. Merle Miller, *Plain Speaking: An Oral Biography of Harry S. Truman* (New York: Berkeley, 1974), 33.
2. Joshua B. Freeman, *American Empire: The Rise of a Global Power, The Democratic Revolution at Home, 1945–2000* (New York: Penguin, 2012), 52.
3. Elizabeth Borgwardt, *A New Deal for the World: America's Vision for Human Rights* (Cambridge, MA: Belknap Press, 2005), 122.
4. Harry S. Truman, "First Speech to Congress," April 16, 1945, http://bit.ly/1wzTAZA.
5. Harry S. Truman, "Address to the United Nations Conference in San Francisco," April 25,
1945, http://bit.ly/1wbs9p4.
6. United Nations Charter, Preamble, www.un.org/en/documents/charter/preamble.shtml.
7. Cynthia Soohoo, Catherine Albisa, and Martha F. Davis, eds., *Bringing Human Rights
Home: A History of Human Rights in the United States* (Philadelphia: University of Pennsylvania Press, 2009), 80.
8. Natalie Kaufman, *Human Rights Treaties and the Senate: A History of Opposition* (Chapel
Hill: University of North Carolina Press, 1990), 17.
9. Susan L. Carruthers, " 'Produce More Joppolos': John Hersey's *A Bell for Adano* and
the Making of the 'Good Occupation,' " *Journal of American History* 100 (2014), 1086–
1113.
10. Joint Chiefs of Staff, "Directive to Commander-in-Chief of United States Forces of Occupation Regarding the Military Government in Germany," April 1945, cited in James
Dobbins, et al., *After the War: Nation-Building from FDR to George W. Bush* (Santa Monica: Rand Corporation, 2008), 21–22.
11. "Stalin Sets a Huge Output Near Ours in 5-Year Plan; Expects to Lead in Science," *New
York Times*, February 10, 1946.
12. Deborah Larson, *The Origins of Containment: A Psychological Explanation* (Princeton,
N.J.: Princeton University Press, 1985), 252.
13. Melvyn P. Leffler and David S. Painter, eds., *Origins of the Cold War: An International
History* (New York: Routledge, 1994), 27.
14. Martin J. Medhurst and H. W. Brands, eds., *Critical Reflections on the Cold War: Linking
Rhetoric and History* (College Station: Texas A&M University Press, 2000), 50.
15. George F. Kennan, *The Kennan Diaries*, ed. Frank Costigliola (New York: W. W. Norton,
2014), 105.
16. George F. Kennan, "The Charge in the Soviet Union (Kennan) to the Secretary of State,"
February 22, 1946, http://bit.ly/1OFhztv.
17. "Divorce—the Postwar Wave," *Newsweek*, October 7, 1946.
18. Harry S. Truman, "Radio Address to the American People on Wages and Prices in the
Reconversion Period," October 30, 1945, www.presidency.ucsb.edu/ws/?pid=12391.
19. Olivier Zunz, Leonard Schoppa, and Nobuhiro Hiwatari, eds., *Social Contracts Under
Stress: The Middle Classes of America, Europe, and Japan at the Turn of the Century* (New
York: Russell Sage Foundation, 2002), 136.
20. James T. Sparrow, *Warfare State: World War II Americans and the Age of Big Government*
(New York: Oxford University Press, 2011), 249.
21. Ibid., 250.

22. Nelson Lichtenstein, *State of the Union: A Century of American Labor* (Princeton, NJ: Princeton University Press, 2002), 103.
23. Kimberly Phillips-Fein, "American Counterrevolutionary: Lemuel Ricketts Boulware and General Electric, 1950–1960," in Nelson Lichtenstein, ed., *American Capitalism: Social Thought and Political Economy in the Twentieth Century* (Philadelphia: University of Pennsylvania Press, 2006), 252–53.
24. Melvyn Dubofsky and Foster Rhea Dulles, *Labor in America: A History*, 8th ed. (Wheeling, IL: Harland Davidson, 2010), 322.
25. Ibid., 319.
26. Harry S. Truman, "Radio Address to the American People on the Railroad Strike Emergency," May 24, 1946, www.presidency.ucsb.edu/ws/?pid=12406.
27. *Congressional Record*, 79th Cong., 1st sess. (1945), 12,512.
28. John Patrick Diggins, *The Proud Decades: America in War and Peace, 1941–1960* (New York: W. W. Norton, 1988), 102.
29. T.R.B., "Neanderthal Men," *The New Republic* 117, no. 5 (August 1947): 3.
30. Harry S. Truman, "Annual Message to the Congress on the State of the Union," January 6, 1947, www.presidency.ucsb.edu/ws/?pid=12762.
31. Elizabeth Tandy Shermer, *Sunbelt Capitalism: Phoenix and the Transformation of American Politics* (Philadelphia: University of Pennsylvania Press, 2013), 147.
32. Michelle Brattain, *The Politics of Whiteness: Race, Workers, and Culture in the Modern South* (Athens: University of Georgia Press, 2004), 143.
33. James T. Patterson, *Grand Expectations: The United States, 1945–1974* (New York: Oxford University Press, 1996), 127.
34. Ibid., 128.
35. Stephen E. Ambrose and Douglas G. Brinkley, *Rise to Globalism: American Foreign Policy Since 1938* (New York: Penguin Books, 1997), 81.
36. George Kennan, "The Sources of Soviet Conduct," *Foreign Affairs* 25, no. 4 (July 1947): 566–82.
37. George C. Marshall, "Marshall Plan Speech," address, Harvard University, Cambridge, MA, June 5, 1947.
38. Walter A. McDougall, *Promised Land, Crusader State: The American Encounter with the World Since 1776* (New York: Houghton Mifflin, 1997), 164.
39. Ambrose and Brinkley, *Rise to Globalism*, 91.
40. Freeman, *American Empire*, 52.
41. Henry Luce, "The American Century," *Life* (February 17, 1941), 63.
42. Freeman, *American Empire*, 75.
43. Joseph Crespino, *Strom Thurmond's America* (New York: Hill & Wang, 2012), 71.
44. Geoffrey Kabaservice, *Rule and Ruin: The Downfall of Moderation and the Destruction of the Republican Party, from Eisenhower to the Tea Party* (New York: Oxford University Press, 2012), 8.
45. *To Secure These Rights: The Report of the President's Committee on Civil Rights*, October 1947, http://bit.ly/137GHtW.
46. Harry S. Truman, Executive Order 9980, July 26, 1948, www.trumanlibrary.org/9980a.htm; and Executive Order 9981, July 26, 1948, www.trumanlibrary.org/9981a.htm.
47. Patterson, *Grand Expectations*, 191.
48. Alien Registration Act of 1940, 18 U.S.C § 2683 (1940).
49. Quoted in Thomas Sugrue, *Sweet Land of Liberty: The Forgotten Struggle for Civil Rights in the North* (New York: Random House, 2008), 22.

50. Arthur Schlesinger, *The Vital Center: The Politics of Freedom* (Boston: Houghton Mifflin, 1949), xviii.

51. Stephen Whitfield, *The Culture of the Cold War* (Baltimore: Johns Hopkins University Press, 1991), 172.

52. Greg Mitchell, *Tricky Dick and the Pink Lady: Richard Nixon vs. Helen Gahagan Douglas* (New York: Random House, 1998), 168.

53. Martin Halpern, "'I'm Fighting for Freedom': Coleman Young, HUAC, and the Detroit African American Community," *Journal of American Ethnic History* 17 (Fall 1997): 29.

54. Harry S. Truman, *Memoirs*, vol. 2, *Years of Trial and Hope* (Garden City, NY: Doubleday, 1956), 333.

55. "McCarthy Charges Reds Hold U.S. Jobs," *Wheeling Intelligencer*, February 10, 1950.

56. Thomas Rosteck, *"See It Now" Confronts McCarthyism: Television Documentary and the Politics of Representation* (Tuscaloosa: University of Alabama Press, 1994), 55.

57. "Have You No Sense of Decency?" June 9, 1954, U.S. Senate, Senate History, 1941–63, http://1.usa.gov/1wUhH7w.

58. *Investigation of Communist Activities, New York Area—Part VII (Entertainment), Hearings Before the Committee on Un-American Activities, House of Representatives*, 84th Cong., 1st sess. (August 17 and 18, 1955).

59. Ambrose and Brinkley, *Rise to Globalism*, 128.

CHAPTER 2: POSTWAR PROSPERITY AND ITS DISCONTENTS

1. The account of Friedan draws from Daniel Horowitz, *Betty Friedan and the Making of "The Feminine Mystique": The American Left, the Cold War, and Modern Feminism* (Amherst: University of Massachusetts Press, 1998); and Sylvie Murray, *The Progressive Housewife: Community Activism in Suburban Queens, 1945–1965* (Philadelphia: University of Pennsylvania Press, 2003).

2. Donald Pisani, *From the Family Farm to Agribusiness: The Irrigation Crusade in California and the West* (Berkeley and Los Angeles: University of California Press, 1984), 451.

3. Julia Grant, *Raising Baby by the Book: The Education of American Mothers* (New Haven, CT: Yale University Press, 1998), 222.

4. Ibid.

5. Kevin Kruse, *White Flight: Atlanta and the Making of Modern Conservatism* (Princeton, NJ: Princeton University Press, 2005), 60.

6. Ibid., 61.

7. U.S. Bureau of the Census, *1960 Census of Housing*, vol. 1, *States and Small Areas* (Washington, DC: U.S. Bureau of the Census, 1963), xxxix.

8. Thomas Doherty, *Cold War, Cool Medium: Television, McCarthyism, and American Culture* (New York: Columbia University Press, 2003), 51.

9. Richard Butsch, *The Citizen Audience: Crowds, Publics, and Individuals* (New York: Routledge, 2008), 104.

10. John Reese, "The Air-Conditioning Revolution," *Saturday Evening Post*, July 9, 1960, 100, quoted in Raymond Arsenault, "The End of the Long Hot Summer: The Air Conditioner and Southern Culture," *Journal of Southern History* 50 (1984): 597–628.

11. Elizabeth Tandy Shermer, *Sunbelt Capitalism: Phoenix and the Transformation of American Politics* (Philadelphia: University of Pennsylvania Press, 2013).

12. Christopher W. Wells, *Car Country: An Environmental History* (Seattle: University of Washington Press, 2012), 279.

13. Robert Lifset, ed., *American Energy Policy in the 1970s* (Norman: University of Oklahoma Press, 2014), 165.

14. T.R.B., "Washington Wire," *The New Republic* 127, no. 24 (December 15, 1952): 3.

15. "Stresses 'Business Climate,'" *New York Times*, December 2, 1952, 34.

16. *Hearings Before the Senate Committee on Armed Services on Nominee Designates: Charles E. Wilson, etc.*, 83rd Cong., 1st sess. (1953) [statement of Charles E. Wilson].

17. "Ike vs. Democratic Party," *Life*, October 29, 1956, 130.

18. President Eisenhower to Edgar Eisenhower, November 8, 1954, in *Dwight D. Eisenhower: Papers as President of the United States, 1953–1961*, National Archives, http://research .archives.gov/description/186596.

19. Nelson Lichtenstein, *American Capitalism: Social Thought and Political Economy in the Twentieth Century* (Philadelphia: University of Pennsylvania Press, 2006), 251.

20. Kim Phillips-Fein, *Invisible Hands: The Businessmen's Crusade Against the New Deal* (New York: W. W. Norton, 2010), 99.

21. Kevin Kruse, "For God So Loved the 1 Percent . . . ," *New York Times*, January 18, 2012.

22. U.S. Department of Justice, *Justice and Crime Atlas, 2000* (Washington, D.C.: Justice Research and Statistics Association, 2000), 36–38, www.jrsa.org/projects/Crime_Atlas _2000.pdf.

23. *Juvenile Delinquency (Comic Books): Hearings Before the Subcommittee to Investigate Juvenile Delinquency*, 83rd Cong., 2nd sess. (1954) [statement of Fredric Wertham].

24. *Employment of Homosexuals and Other Sex Perverts in Government*, 81 S. Rep. No. 241, (1950): 4.

25. David Johnson, *The Lavender Scare: The Cold War Persecution of Gays and Lesbians in the Federal Government* (Chicago: University of Chicago Press, 2004), 98.

26. Isabel Wilkerson, *The Warmth of Other Suns: The Epic Story of America's Great Migration* (New York: Random House, 2010), 208.

27. Thomas J. Sugrue, *Sweet Land of Liberty: The Forgotten Struggle for Civil Rights in the North* (New York: Random House, 2008), 32.

28. Ibid., 150.

29. "The First Freedom Ride: Bayard Rustin on His Work with CORE," interview by Ed Edwin, September 9, 1985, http://historymatters.gmu.edu/d/6909/.

30. Claudia Goldin and Lawrence F. Katz, *The Race Between Technology and Education* (Cambridge, MA: Harvard University Press, 2008), esp. 194–246.

31. *Brown v. Board of Education*, 347 U.S. 483 (1954).

32. *The Southern Manifesto: Declaration of Constitutional Principles*, 84th Cong., 2nd sess. (March 12, 1956).

33. Mary Dudziak, *Cold War Civil Rights* (Princeton, N.J.: Princeton University Press, 2000), 130.

34. James Patterson, *Brown v. Board of Education: A Civil Rights Milestone and Its Troubled Legacy* (New York: Oxford University Press, 2001), 60.

35. Dudziak, *Cold War Civil Rights*, 128.

36. Jeff Woods, *Black Struggle, Red Scare: Segregation and Anti-Communism in the South, 1948–1968* (Baton Rouge: Louisiana State University Press, 2004), 69.

37. Andrew Hartman, *Education and the Cold War: The Battle for the American School* (New York: Palgrave Macmillan, 2008), 172.

38. Harvard Sitkoff, *The Struggle for Black Equality, 1954–1992* (New York: Hill & Wang, 1993), 36.

39. Stephen E. Ambrose and Douglas G. Brinkley, *Rise to Globalism: American Foreign Policy Since 1938* (New York: Penguin, 1997), 149.

40. Greg Grandin, *Empire's Workshop: Latin America, the United States, and the Rise of the New Imperialism* (New York: Metropolitan Books, 2006), 45.

CHAPTER 3: A SEASON OF CHANGE

1. John Lewis with Michael D'Orso, *Walking with the Wind: A Memoir of the Movement* (New York: Simon & Schuster, 1998), 127.
2. Ibid., 124.
3. Ibid., 115.
4. C. Wright Mills, "Letter to the New Left," *New Left Review* 1, no. 5 (September–October, 1960).
5. Shaun Casey, *The Making of a Catholic President: Kennedy vs. Nixon, 1960* (New York: Oxford University Press, 2009), 113, 139.
6. John F. Kennedy, "Address to Greater Houston Ministerial Association," September 12, 1960, in James T. Fisher, ed., *Communion of Immigrants: A History of Catholics in America* (New York: Oxford University Press, 2007), 135.
7. John F. Kennedy, "Inaugural Address," January 21, 1961, www.presidency.ucsb.edu/ws/?pid=8032.
8. John F. Kennedy, "Remarks to Members of the White House Conference on National Economic Issues," May 21, 1962, www.presidency.ucsb.edu/ws/?pid=8670.
9. Irving Bernstein, *Promises Kept: John F. Kennedy's New Frontier* (New York: Oxford University Press, 1991), 124.
10. Lewis, *Walking*, 124.
11. Raymond Arsenault, *Freedom Riders: 1961 and the Struggle for Racial Justice* (New York: Oxford University Press, 2006), 164.
12. "Anger that Inflamed Route 40 Yields to Common Sense," *Life*, December 8, 1961, 32.
13. Marc Trachtenberg, *History and Strategy* (Princeton, N.J.: Princeton University Press, 1991), 245–46.
14. John F. Kennedy, "Radio and Television Report to the American People on the Soviet Arms Buildup in Cuba," October 22, 1962, http://bit.ly/1GybLD1.
15. Lewis, *Walking*, 124.
16. Martin Luther King, Jr., "Letter from Birmingham Jail," April 16, 1963, http://stanford.io/1u78SUq.
17. Philip A. Klinkner and Rogers M. Smith, *The Unsteady March: The Rise and Decline of Racial Equality in America* (Chicago: University of Chicago Press, 1999), 267.
18. Thomas J. Sugrue, *Sweet Land of Liberty: The Forgotten Struggle for Civil Rights in the North* (New York: Random House, 2008), 294.
19. George C. Wallace, "Inaugural Address," January 15, 1963, http://1.usa.gov/10z7aPJ.
20. Martin Luther King, Jr., *All Labor Has Dignity*, ed. Michael K. Honey (Boston: Beacon Press, 2011), 79.
21. Martin Luther King, Jr., *A Call to Conscience: The Landmark Speeches of Dr. Martin Luther King, Jr.*, ed. Clayborne Carson and Kris Shephard (New York: Warner Books, 2001), 85.
22. William Jones, *The March on Washington: Jobs, Freedom, and the Forgotten History of Civil Rights* (New York: W. W. Norton, 2013), 193.
23. Eric Sundquist, *King's Dream* (New Haven, CT: Yale University Press, 2009), 46.
24. Sugrue, *Sweet Land of Liberty*, 313–14.
25. Malcolm X, "Message to the Grassroots," in *Malcolm X Speaks: Selected Speeches and Statements*, ed. George Breitman (New York: Grove Press, 1994), 12.
26. Ibid., 9.

27. Thomas Cowger and Sherwin Markman, eds., *Lyndon Johnson Remembered: An Intimate Portrait of a Presidency* (Lanham, MD: Rowman and Littlefield, 2003), 37.

28. Robert Caro, *The Years of Lyndon Johnson*, vol. 2, *Means of Ascent* (New York: Random House, 1990), 344.

29. Civil Rights Act of 1964, http://1.usa.gov/10Fk2nG.

30. "The National Organization for Women's 1966 Statement of Purpose," October 29, 1966, http://now.org/about/history/statement-of-purpose.

31. James Cobb, *The South and America Since World War II* (New York: Oxford University Press, 2012), 89.

32. "Individual Property Owners Are Given Bill of Rights by Realtors," *Washington World* 3 (1963): 25.

33. John Andrew, *The Other Side of the Sixties: Young Americans for Freedom and the Rise of Conservative Politics* (New Brunswick, NJ: Rutgers University Press, 1997), 222.

34. Barry Goldwater, *The Conscience of a Conservative* (Princeton, N.J.: Princeton University Press, 2007), xxii.

35. Ibid., 4.

36. Ibid., 49.

37. Ibid., 10.

38. Nancy MacLean, *Freedom Is Not Enough: The Opening of the American Workplace* (Cambridge, MA: Harvard University Press, 2008), 46.

39. Rick Perlstein, *Before the Storm: Barry Goldwater and the Unmaking of the American Consensus* (New York: Hill & Wang, 2001), 364.

40. MacLean, *Freedom Is Not Enough*, 62.

41. Ed Cray, *Chief Justice: A Biography of Earl Warren* (New York: Simon & Schuster, 1997), 386.

42. Matthew Lassiter and Joseph Crespino, eds., *The Myth of Southern Exceptionalism* (New York: Oxford University Press, 2010), 296.

43. Lucas Powe, Jr., *The Supreme Court and the American Elite, 1789–2008* (Cambridge, MA: Harvard University Press, 2009), 265.

44. Goldwater, *Conscience*, 75.

45. Perlstein, *Before the Storm*, 391.

46. Ibid., 374.

47. Kathleen Hall Jamieson, *Packaging the Presidency: A History and Criticism of Presidential Campaign Advertising* (New York: Oxford University Press, 1984), 220.

48. Richard Hofstadter, "A Long View: Goldwater in History," *New York Review of Books* (October 8, 1964): 20.

49. Rick Perlstein, *Nixonland: The Rise of a President and the Fracturing of America* (New York: Simon & Schuster, 2008), 6.

50. Lyndon B. Johnson, "Annual Message to the Congress on the State of the Union," January 8, 1964, www.presidency.ucsb.edu/ws/?pid=26787.

51. Thomas J. Sugrue, *Origins of the Urban Crisis: Race and Inequality in Postwar Detroit* (Princeton, NJ: Princeton University Press, 2005), 126.

52. Maurice Isserman and Michael Kazin, *America Divided: The Civil War of the 1960s* (New York: Oxford University Press, 2000), 109.

53. John Morton Blum, *Years of Discord: American Politics and Society, 1961–1974* (New York: W. W. Norton, 1991), 178.

54. Lyndon B. Johnson, Annual Message to Congress on the State of the Union, January 8, 1964, www.presidency.ucsb.edu/ws/?pid=26787.

55. Larry Dewitt and Edward Berkowitz, "Health Care," in Mitchell Lerner, ed., *A Companion to Lyndon B. Johnson* (New York: Wiley-Blackwell, 2012), 167.

56. Daniel Béland and Alex Waddan, *The Politics of Policy Change: Welfare, Medicare, and Social Security Reform* (Washington, DC: Georgetown University Press, 2012), 81.

57. William McCord, *Mississippi: The Long Hot Summer* (New York: W. W. Norton, 1965), 18.

58. Fannie Lou Hamer, *Testimony Before the Credentials Committee, Democratic National Convention*, August 22, 1964, transcript and audio, http://bit.ly/1BQRjws.

59. Lewis, *Walking*, 291.

60. Voting Rights Act of 1965, www.ourdocuments.gov/doc.php?flash=true&doc=100.

61. Martin Luther King, Jr., *Why We Can't Wait* (Boston: Beacon Press, 2010), 164.

62. Peniel E. Joseph, *The Black Power Movement: Rethinking the Civil Rights–Black Power Era* (New York: Routledge, 2006), 344.

CHAPTER 4: MAY DAY

1. On Merschel, the narrative draws from Virginia Merschel, interview by Thomas J. Sugrue, October 8, 1996; "Lawrence James Merschel," Vietnam Veterans Memorial Fund, http://bit.ly/LJMerschel; obituary, *Philadelphia Inquirer*, May 4, 1968; and "Merschel, Lawrence James, PFC," http://bit.ly/PFCMerschel.

2. Gabriel Kolko, *Anatomy of a War: Vietnam, the United States, and the Modern Historical Experience* (New York: Pantheon, 1994), 117.

3. David L. DiLeo, *George Ball, Vietnam, and the Rethinking of Containment* (Chapel Hill: University of North Carolina Press, 1991), 52.

4. Ibid., 53.

5. McNamara quoted in Michael H. Hunt, ed., *Crises in U.S. Foreign Policy: An International History Reader* (New Haven, CT: Yale University Press, 1996), 333.

6. Larry Berman, *Planning a Tragedy: The Americanization of the War in Vietnam* (New York: W. W. Norton, 1982), 144.

7. Maurice Isserman and Michael Kazin, *America Divided: The Civil War of the 1960s* (New York: Oxford University Press, 2000), 115.

8. Robert David Johnson, *Ernest Gruening and the American Dissenting Tradition* (Cambridge, MA: Harvard University Press, 1998), 253.

9. Fredrik Logevall, *The Origins of the Vietnam War* (New York: Routledge, 2013), 117.

10. David Levy, *The Debate Over Vietnam* (Baltimore: Johns Hopkins University Press, 1991), 103.

11. Stanley Karnow, *Vietnam, a History* (New York: Penguin, 1997), 361.

12. Kim McQuaid, *The Anxious Years: America in the Vietnam-Watergate Era* (New York: Basic Books, 1989), 73.

13. Michael H. Hunt, *Lyndon Johnson's War: America's Cold War Crusade in Vietnam, 1945–1968* (New York: Hill & Wang, 1996), 105.

14. Ibid., 91.

15. Michael S. Foley, *Confronting the War Machine: Draft Resistance During the Vietnam War* (Chapel Hill: University of North Carolina Press, 2003), 39.

16. Ward Just, "Vietnam Notebook (April 1968)," in Katharine Whittemore, Ellen Rosenbush, and Jim Nelson, eds., *The Sixties: Recollections from the Decade from "Harper's Magazine"* (New York: Franklin Square Press, 1995), 143.

17. DiLeo, *George Ball*, 53.

18. Ibid., 64.

19. David L. Anderson, ed., *The Columbia Guide to the Vietnam War* (New York: Columbia University Press, 2002), 267.

20. Randall B. Woods, *LBJ: Architect of American Ambition* (New York: Free Press, 2006), 677.

21. "Ho Chi Kennedy: An Editorial," *Chicago Tribune*, February 21, 1966.

22. Max Frankel, "Demonstrators Decorous—3 White House Aides Meet with Leaders: Thousands Join Antiwar March," *New York Times*, November 28, 1965.

23. Mary Hershberger, *Traveling to Vietnam: American Peace Activists and the War* (Syracuse, NY: Syracuse University Press, 1998), 16.

24. Shawn Francis Peters, *The Catonsville Nine: A Story of Faith and Resistance in the Vietnam Era* (New York: Oxford University Press, 2012), 35.

25. Michael S. Neiberg, *Making Citizen-Soldiers: ROTC and the Ideology of American Military Service* (Cambridge, MA: Harvard University Press, 2000).

26. Students for a Democratic Society, "Port Huron Statement of the Students for a Democratic Society," 1962, http://bit.ly/1u7a4Hl.

27. Francesca Polletta, *Freedom Is an Endless Meeting: Democracy in American Social Movements* (Chicago: University of Chicago Press, 2002), 205.

28. Todd Gitlin, *The Sixties: Years of Hope, Days of Rage* (New York: Bantam Books, 1989), 427.

29. Jay Sand, "The Radio Waves Unnamable," Senior Honors Thesis, Department of History, University of Pennsylvania, 1994.

30. Paul Krassner, "Revolution for the Hell of It: Reason, Let Us Come Together," *Realist* (August 1967), 20, www.ep.tc/realist/76/20.html.

31. Christian G. Appy, *Working-Class War: American Combat Soldiers and Vietnam* (Chapel Hill: University of North Carolina Press, 1993), 6.

32. Ibid., 42.

33. Simon Hall, *Peace and Freedom: The Civil Rights and Antiwar Movements in the 1960s* (Philadelphia: University of Pennsylvania Press, 2005), 8.

34. David Remnick, *King of the World: Muhammad Ali and the Rise of an American Hero* (New York: Random House, 1998), 267; Fred Shapiro, ed., *The Yale Book of Quotations* (New Haven: Yale University Press, 2006), 14.

35. Martin Luther King, Jr., "Beyond Vietnam," April 4, 1967, http://stanford.io/1tIZogG.

36. "A Tragedy," *Washington Post*, April 6, 1967.

37. Peniel Joseph, *Waiting 'Til the Midnight Hour: A Narrative History of Black Power in America* (New York: Henry Holt, 2006), 193.

38. Stokely Carmichael, "Black Power," October 29, 1966, http://voicesofdemocracy.umd.edu/carmichael-black-power-speech-text.

39. Peniel Joseph, *Dark Days, Bright Nights: From Black Power to Barack Obama* (New York: Basic Books, 2010), 134.

40. Seth Rosenfeld, *Subversives: The FBI's War on Student Radicals, and Reagan's Rise to Power* (New York: Farrar, Straus & Giroux, 2012), 302.

41. "McCarthy Statement on Entering the 1968 Primaries," *New York Times*, December 1, 1967.

42. Lyndon B. Johnson, *Public Papers of the Presidents of the United States: Lyndon B. Johnson*, book 2, *1968–1969* (Washington, DC: Government Printing Office, 1970), 2.

43. *The Viet Cong "Tet" Offensive*, ed. Pham Van Son, trans. J5/JGS Translation Board (Saigon: RVNAF, 1968), 47.

44. Larry Berman, *Lyndon Johnson's War: The Road to Stalemate in Vietnam* (New York: W. W. Norton, 1989), 175.

45. Ibid., 197.

46. Lyndon B. Johnson, *Public Papers of the Presidents of the United States: Lyndon B. Johnson*, book 2, *1968–1969* (Washington, DC: Government Printing Office, 1970), 469–76.

47. Gitlin, *Sixties*, 307.

48. Che Guevara, *Global Justice: Liberation and Socialism*, ed. Ernesto Guevara (New York: Ocean Press, 2002), 62.

49. Christian G. Appy, *Patriots: The Vietnam War Remembered from All Sides* (New York: Penguin, 2003), 425.

CHAPTER 5: WHICH SIDE ARE YOU ON?

1. Material on Carmen Roberts can be found in Carmen Roberts Papers (hereafter CRP), Michigan Historical Collections, Bentley Historical Library, University of Michigan, Ann Arbor.

2. Heather Ann Thompson, *Whose Detroit?: Politics, Labor, and Race in a Modern American City* (Ithaca, NY: Cornell University Press, 2001), 78.

3. Quotes from "Biographical Field Notes," August 15, 1986, CRP, and "Detroit School Board Member Says: 'I Have a Dream Too . . . ,'" *Wisconsin Report* in CRP, Folder: Clippings 1977.

4. Robert F. Kennedy, "Statement on Assassination of Martin Luther King, Jr.," April 4, 1968, http://bit.ly/112NULA.

5. Evan Thomas, *Robert Kennedy: His Life* (New York: Simon & Schuster, 2002), 390.

6. Todd Gitlin, *The Sixties: Years of Hope, Days of Rage* (New York: Bantam Books, 1993), 54.

7. David Farber, *Chicago '68* (Chicago: University of Chicago Press, 1988), 200.

8. Louis Gould, *1968: The Election that Changed America*, 2nd ed. (Chicago: Ivan Dee, 2010), 125.

9. Richard Nixon, "Address Accepting the Presidential Nomination at the Republican National Convention in Miami Beach, Florida," August 8, 1968, www.presidency.ucsb.edu/ws/?pid=25968.

10. Ronald Reagan, "A Time for Choosing," October 27, 1964, http://bit.ly/1zZqB2m.

11. Seth Rosenfield, *Subversives: The FBI's War on Student Radicals, and Reagan's Rise to Power* (New York: Farrar, Straus & Giroux, 2012), 324.

12. Ibid.

13. Marisa Chappell, *The War on Welfare: Family, Poverty, and Politics in Modern America* (Philadelphia: University of Pennsylvania Press, 2010), 66.

14. Max Frankel, "A Team of Moderates," *New York Times*, December 12, 1968.

15. Max Johnson, "Agnew Insults Leaders: Guests Quit Meeting in Bitterness," *Baltimore Afro-American*, April 13, 1968.

16. Rick Perlstein, *Nixonland: The Rise of a President and the Fracturing of America* (New York: Simon & Schuster, 2008), 526.

17. Weathermen—First Communiqué, July 31, 1970, Pacifica Radio/UC Berkeley Social Activism Sound Recording Project, http://bit.ly/1wCco9j.

18. Thomas J. Sugrue, "Affirmative Action from Below: Civil Rights, the Building Trades, and the Politics of Racial Equality in the Urban North, 1945–1969," *Journal of American History* 91, no. 1 (June 2004): 146.

19. Dean J. Kotlowski, *Nixon's Civil Rights: Politics, Principle, and Policy* (Cambridge, MA: Harvard University Press, 2001), 177.

20. Richard Scammon and Ben Wattenberg, *The Real Majority* (New York: Coward-McCann, 1970), 46.

21. "Man and Woman of the Year: The Middle Americans," *Time*, January 5, 1970.

22. Pete Hamill, "The Revolt of the White Lower Middle Class," *New York Magazine*, April 14, 1969. nymag.com/news/features/46801

23. Ibid.

24. Perlstein, *Nixonland*, 495.

25. Ibid., 498.

26. Christopher Bonastia, *Knocking on the Door: The Federal Government's Attempt to Desegregate the Suburbs* (Princeton, NJ: Princeton University Press, 2006), 106.

27. Ibid., 107.

28. Ibid., 130.

29. Quoted in Walter Mondale, "Retreat on Civil Rights," *Congressional Record*, 91st. Cong., 1st sess. (1969), S31810.

30. J. Todd Moye, *Let the People Decide: Black Freedom and White Resistance Movements in Sunflower County Mississippi, 1945–1986* (Chapel Hill: University of North Carolina Press, 2004), 178.

31. George H. Gallup, *The Gallup Poll: Public Opinion, 1935–1971*, 3 vols. (New York: Random House, 1972), 3:2329.

32. Thomas J. Sugrue, *Sweet Land of Liberty: The Forgotten Struggle for Civil Rights in the North* (New York: Random House, 2008), 483.

33. Kotlowski, *Nixon's Civil Rights*, 39.

34. Sugrue, *Sweet Land of Liberty*, 484.

35. Paul R. Dimond, *Beyond Busing: Reflections on Urban Segregation, the Courts, and Equal Opportunity* (Ann Arbor: University of Michigan Press, 1985), 76.

36. Richard Nixon, "Remarks to Reporters About Nominations to the Supreme Court," April 9, 1970, www.presidency.ucsb.edu/ws/?pid=2455.

37. John C. Jeffries, Jr., *Justice Lewis F. Powell, Jr., A Biography* (New York: Scribner, 1994), 238.

38. Richard Kluger, *Simple Justice: The History of Brown v. Board of Education and Black America's Struggle for Equality* (New York: Knopf, 1975), 606.

39. *Milliken v. Bradley* 418 U.S. 717 (1974), at 741–42, 815.

40. Beth L. Bailey, *Sex in the Heartland* (Cambridge, MA: Harvard University Press, 1999), 139.

41. Robin Morgan, "Good-Bye to All That," in Rosalyn Baxandall and Linda Gordon, eds., *Dear Sisters: Dispatches from the Women's Liberation Movement* (New York: Basic Books, 2000), 53.

42. John D'Emilio and Estelle B. Friedman, *Intimate Matters: A History of Sexuality in America*, 2nd ed. (Chicago: University of Chicago Press, 1997), 311.

43. Robert O. Self, *All in the Family: The Realignment of American Democracy Since the 1960s* (New York: Hill & Wang, 2012), 191.

44. Steve Estes, *I Am a Man! Race, Manhood, and the Civil Rights Movement* (Chapel Hill: University of North Carolina Press, 2006), 82–83, 165.

45. Morgan, "Good-Bye to All That," 53.

46. Carol Hanisch, "The Personal Is Political," in Shulamith Firestone and Anne Koedt, eds., *Notes from the Second Year: Women's Liberation* (New York: Radical Feminism, 1970), www.carolhanisch.org/CHwritings/PIP.html.

47. Molly Ginty, "*Our Bodies, Ourselves* Turns 35 Today," *Women's eNews*, May 4, 2004, http://bit.ly/1GyeLPQ.

48. Marc Stein, *Sexual Injustice: Supreme Court Decisions from Griswold to Roe* (Chapel Hill: University of North Carolina Press, 2010), 142.

49. Ibid.

50. Lucian Truscott IV, "Gay Power Comes to Sheridan Square," *Village Voice*, July 2, 1969.

51. Jeffrey O. G. Ogbar, *Black Power: Radical Politics and African American Identity* (Baltimore: Johns Hopkins University Press, 2005), 102.

52. Huey P. Newton, *The Huey P. Newton Reader*, ed. David Hilliard and Donald Weise (New York: Seven Stories Press, 2002), 159.

53. Susan J. Douglas, *Where the Girls Are: Growing Up Female with the Mass Media* (New York: Three Rivers Press, 1995), 162.

54. Dorothy Sue Cobble, *The Other Women's Movement: Workplace Justice and Social Rights in Modern America* (Princeton, NJ: Princeton University Press, 2004), 3.

55. *Equal Rights 1970: Hearings Before the Committee on the Judiciary*, 91st Cong., 2nd sess. (September 1970) [testimony of Myra K. Wolfgang], http://historymatters.gmu.edu/d/7018/.

56. "Equal Rights Amendment Passed by Congress," *New York Times*, March 22, 1972.

57. Donald T. Critchlow, *Phyllis Schlafly and Grassroots Conservatism: A Woman's Crusade* (Princeton, NJ: Princeton University Press, 2005), 121.

58. Ibid., 217.

59. "Housewives Protest 'Equal Rights Bill,'" *Sarasota Herald-Tribune*, April 2, 1972.

60. Carol Frances Cini, "Making Women's Rights Matter: Diverse Activists, California's Commission on the Status of Women, and the Legislative and Social Impact of a Movement, 1962–1976," Ph.D. diss., University of California, Los Angeles, 2007, 437.

61. "Diary of a Glad Housewife," *Detroit Free Press*, February 4, 1974.

62. *Northeast Detroiter*, October 4, 1973.

63. John David Skrentny, *The Minority Rights Revolution* (Cambridge, MA: Harvard University Press, 2009), 318.

64. Kotlowski, *Nixon's Civil Rights*, 234.

65. *Roe v. Wade*, 410 U.S. 113 (1973).

66. David J. Garrow, *Liberty and Sexuality: The Right to Privacy and the Making of Roe v. Wade* (Berkeley: University of California Press, 1994), 483.

67. Jefferson Cowie, *Stayin' Alive: The 1970s and the Last Days of the Working Class* (New York: New Press, 2010), 105.

68. John Morton Blum, *Years of Discord: American Politics and Society, 1961–1974* (New York: W. W. Norton, 1991), 417.

69. "Caught on Tape: The White House Reaction to the Shooting of Alabama Governor and Democratic Presidential Candidate George Wallace," http://nixontapes.org/wallace.html.

70. Perlstein, *Nixonland*, 615.

71. Ibid., 652.

72. Carl Bernstein and Bob Woodward, *All the President's Men* (New York: Simon & Schuster, 1974), 132; also quoted in David von Drehle, "FBI's No. 2 Was Deep Throat," *Washington Post*, June 1, 2005.

73. Bart Barnes, "John Sirica, Watergate Judge, Dies," *Washington Post*, August 15, 1992.

74. Peter Baker, "Newly Released Tapes Show Nixon Maneuvering as Watergate Unfolds," *New York Times*, August 21, 2013.

75. *United States v. Nixon*, 418 U.S. 683 (1974).

CHAPTER 6: A SEASON OF DARKNESS

1. The material in this and the following paragraphs on Ksionska's life history draws from Henry Goldman, "A Way of Life Ends with Fairless Decline," *Philadelphia Inquirer*, April 10, 1983; "Obituary: John F. (Book) Ksionska, Sr.," *Bucks County-Courier Times*,

August 10, 2003; Thomas Dublin and Walter Licht, *The Face of Decline: The Pennsylvania Anthracite Region in the Twentieth Century* (Ithaca, NY: Cornell University Press, 2005).

2. Julian E. Zelizer, *Arsenal of Democracy: The Politics of National Security—From World War II to the War on Terrorism* (New York: Basic Books, 2010), 217,

3. Richard Nixon, "Address to the Nation on the War in Vietnam," November 3, 1969, http://bit.ly/1vab2VI.

4. Gerald S. Strober and Deborah H. Strober, *Nixon: An Oral History of His Presidency* (New York: Harper Perennial, 1996), 178.

5. Eric Pace, "Le Duc Tho, Top Hanoi Aide, Dies at 79," *New York Times*, October 14, 1990.

6. Larry Berman, *No Peace, No Honor: Nixon, Kissinger, and Betrayal in Vietnam* (New York: Free Press, 2001), 172.

7. Geoffrey Kabaservice, *Rule and Ruin: The Downfall of Moderation and the Destruction of the Republican Party, from Eisenhower to the Tea Party* (New York: Oxford University Press, 2012), 174.

8. Henry Kissinger, *White House Years* (New York: Simon & Schuster, 1979), 745.

9. Memorandum of Conversation, Beijing, July 10, 1971, document 140 in *Foreign Relations of the United States, 1969–1976*, vol. 17, *China, 1969–1972*, http://1.usa.gov/1GX NVRh.

10. Kissinger, *White House Years*, 750.

11. H. W. Brands, *American Dreams: The United States Since 1945* (New York: Penguin, 2010), 173.

12. Kabaservice, *Rule and Ruin*, 328.

13. Donald T. Critchlow, *The Conservative Ascendancy: How the GOP Right Made Political History* (Cambridge, MA: Harvard University Press, 2007), 95.

14. Brands, *American Dreams*, 172.

15. Campbell Craig and Fredrik Logevall, *America's Cold War: The Politics of Insecurity* (Cambridge, MA: Harvard University Press, 2009), 281–82.

16. Rick Perlstein, *Nixonland: The Rise of a President and the Fracturing of America* (New York: Simon & Schuster, 2008), 469.

17. Judith Stein, *Pivotal Decade: How the United States Traded Factories for Finance in the Seventies* (New Haven, CT: Yale University Press, 2010), 28.

18. Geir Lundestad, *The United States and Western Europe Since 1945* (New York: Oxford University Press, 2003), 159.

19. Richard Nixon, "Annual Message to the Congress on the State of the Union," January 22, 1971, http://bit.ly/1loEXwi.

20. Jefferson Cowie, *Stayin' Alive: The 1970s and the Last Days of the Working Class* (New York: New Press, 2010), 150.

21. Leonard Silk, *Nixonomics* (New York: Praeger Publishers, 1972), 99.

22. Mark Fiege, *The Republic of Nature: An Environmental History of the United States* (Seattle: University of Washington Press, 2012), 377.

23. Norman Podhoretz, "Now, Instant Zionism," *New York Times*, February 3, 1974.

24. Richard Nixon, "Address to the Nation About Policies to Deal with the Energy Shortages," November 7, 1973, http://bit.ly/1uuJ05e.

25. Chad M. Kimmel, "'No Gas, My Ass!': Marking the End of the Postwar Period in Levittown," in Dianne Harris, ed., *Second Suburb: Levittown, Pennsylvania* (Pittsburgh: University of Pittsburgh Press, 2010), 344.

26. Michael J. Graetz, *The End of Energy: The Unmaking of America's Environment, Security, and Independence* (Cambridge, MA: MIT Press, 2011), 36.

27. Fiege, *Republic of Nature*, 381.

28. Meg Jacobs, "The Conservative Struggle and the Energy Crisis," in Bruce J. Schulman and Julian E. Zelizer, ed., *Rightward Bound: Making America Conservative in the 1970s* (Cambridge, MA: Harvard University Press, 2008), 198.

29. C. W. McCall, "Convoy," *Black Bear Road*, MGM Records, 1975.

30. Gerald R. Ford: "Remarks on Signing a Proclamation Granting Pardon to Richard Nixon," September 8, 1974, http://bit.ly/1vabfZ2.

31. Gerald Ford, "Whip Inflation Now" speech, October 8, 1974, http://bit.ly/1sNYsFk.

32. Alan Greenspan, interview by Richard Norton Smith, December 17, 2008, http://bit.ly/1Br70Lu.

33. Leslie H. Gelb, "Poll Finds U.S. Isolationism on Rise, Hope at Ebb," *New York Times*, June 16, 1974.

34. Marilyn Bender, "The Energy Trauma at General Motors," *New York Times*, March 24, 1974.

35. Alexandra Orchard, "The 1972 Lordstown Strike," *Walter P. Reuther Library* (blog), August 12, 2013, http://reuther.wayne.edu/node/10756.

36. Cowie, *Stayin' Alive*, 48.

37. Judson Gooding, "Blue-Collar Blues in the Assembly Line," *Fortune*, July 1970; Agis Salpukas, "G.M.'s Toughest Division 'Binbuster?'," *New York Times*, April 16, 1972.

38. Jefferson Cowie, *Capital Moves: RCA's Hundred Year Quest for Cheap Labor* (Ithaca, NY: Cornell University Press, 2001), 102.

39. Rachel Carson, *Silent Spring* (Boston: Houghton Mifflin, 1962), 17.

40. Christopher C. Sellers, *Crabgrass Crucible: Suburban Nature and the Rise of Environmentalism in Twentieth Century America* (Chapel Hill: University of North Carolina Press, 2012), 223, 236.

41. Joni Mitchell, "Big Yellow Taxi," *Ladies of the Canyon*, Reprise Records, 1970.

42. Adam Rome, *The Genius of Earth Day: How a 1970 Teach-In Unexpectedly Made the First Green Revolution* (New York: Hill & Wang, 2013), 161.

43. Bruce J. Schulman, *The Seventies: The Great Shift in American Culture, Society, and Politics* (Cambridge, MA: Da Capo, 2002), 30.

44. David Sibley, *Geographies of Exclusion* (New York: Routledge, 1995), 61.

45. "The Crime Wave," *Time*, June 30, 1975.

46. U.S. Department of Justice, FBI, Uniform Crime Reporting Statistics, www.ucrdatatool.gov/index.cfm.

47. Heather Ann Thompson, "Why Mass Incarceration Matters: Rethinking Crisis, Decline, and Transformation in Postwar American History," *Journal of American History* 97 (2010): 708.

48. Ruth Wilson Gilmore, *Golden Gulag: Prisons, Surplus, Crisis, and Opposition in Globalizing California* (Berkeley: University of California Press, 2007), 101.

49. Norman Miller, "The Transformation of Gary Hart," *Wall Street Journal*, October 28, 1974.

50. Laura Kalman, *Right Star Rising: A New Politics, 1974–1980* (New York: W. W. Norton, 2010), 255.

51. Jimmy Carter, "Inaugural Address," January 20, 1977, http://bit.ly/1wAlz7n.

52. Thomas J. Sugrue, "Carter's Urban Policy Crisis," in Gary M. Fink and Hugh Davis Graham, eds., *The Carter Presidency: Policy Choices in the Post–New Deal Era* (Lawrence: University Press of Kansas, 1998), 139–40.

53. U.S. Bureau of Labor Statistics, *Labor Force Statistics from the Current Population Survey, 1947–2014*, http://1.usa.gov/1vdVGis.

54. Melvyn Dubofsky, "Jimmy Carter and the End of the Politics of Productivity," in Fink and Graham, *Carter Presidency*, 99.

55. U.S. Bureau of Labor Statistics, *Labor Force Statistics from the Current Population Survey, 1947–2014*, http://1.usa.gov/1vdVGis.

56. Stephen B. Reed, "One Hundred Years of Price Change: The Consumer Price Index and the American Inflation Experience," *Monthly Labor Review* (April 2014), http://1.usa.gov/1EFOawC.

57. Jimmy Carter, "Airline Industry Regulation Message to the Congress," March 4, 1977, http://bit.ly/1xA5e5H.

58. Phillip J. Cooper, *The War Against Regulation: From Jimmy Carter to George W. Bush* (Lawrence: University Press of Kansas, 2009), 28.

59. Ralph Blumenthal, "Reflections of Alfred Kahn: He Won Some Battles But Lost the War," *New York Times*, November 9, 1980.

60. Jimmy Carter, "Acceptance Speech at the Democratic National Convention," August 14, 1980, http://bit.ly/1uuJnwz.

61. Graetz, *End of Energy*, 140.

62. David Farber, *Taken Hostage: The Iran Hostage Crisis and America's First Encounter with Radical Islam* (Princeton, NJ: Princeton University Press, 2005), 26.

63. Ibid.

64. Kimmel, "No Gas, My Ass," 340.

65. George F. Will, "Levittown Revisited," *Newsweek*, July 9, 1979.

66. Jimmy Carter, "Address to the Nation on Energy and National Goals," July 15, 1979, http://bit.ly/1xA5kdJ.

67. Farber, *Taken Hostage*, 176.

68. Jefferson Cowie, "'Vigorously Left, Right, and Center': The Crosscurrents of Working-Class America in the 1970s," in Beth Bailey and David Farber, eds., *America in the Seventies* (Lawrence: University Press of Kansas, 2004), 76.

69. Camper Van Beethoven, "Ambiguity Song," *Telephone Free Landslide Victory*, I.R.S. Records, 1985.

CHAPTER 7: THE NEW GILDED AGE

1. Material on Dukes comes from Liza Featherstone, *Selling Women Short: The Landmark Battle for Workers' Rights at Wal-Mart* (New York: Basic Books, 2005) and Rick Radin, "Pittsburg Woman Back at Work After Star Turn at Supreme Court," *Contra Costa Times*, April 21, 2011. Material on Wal-Mart comes from Bethany Moreton, *To Serve God and Wal-Mart: The Making of Christian Free Enterprise* (Cambridge, MA: Harvard University Press, 2009); and Nelson Lichtenstein, *The Retail Revolution: How Wal-Mart Created a Brave New World of Business* (New York: Metropolitan Books, 2009).

2. Carter-Reagan Presidential Debate, October 28, 1980, http://bit.ly/1xFtWmi.

3. Ronald Reagan, "Inaugural Address," January 20, 1981, http://bit.ly/1yqtxCD.

4. Ronald Reagan, "Message to the Congress Transmitting the Proposed Package on the Program for Economic Recovery," February 18, 1981, http://bit.ly/16tkEA8.

5. Ronald Reagan, "Remarks to Reporters on Releasing an Audit of the United States Economy," February 12, 1981, www.presidency.ucsb.edu/ws/?pid=43376.

6. Meg Jacobs and Julian Zelizer, *Conservatives In Power: The Reagan Years, 1981–1989* (New York: Bedford Books, 2011), 21.

7. Romain D. Huret, *American Tax Resisters* (Cambridge, MA: Harvard University Press, 2014), 231.

8. Ronald Reagan, "White House Report on the Program for Economic Recovery," February 18, 1981, http://bit.ly/1xYjMLG.

9. William Greider, "The Education of David Stockman," *Atlantic Monthly*, December 1981.

10. Jacob S. Hacker and Paul Pierson, *Winner-Take-All Politics: How Washington Made the Rich Richer and Turned Its Back on the Middle Class* (New York: Simon & Schuster, 2010), 23.

11. Martha Derthick and Steven M. Teles, "Riding the Third Rail: Social Security Reform," in W. Elliott Brownlee and Hugh Davis Graham, eds., *The Reagan Presidency: Pragmatic Conservatism and Its Legacies* (Lawrence: University Press of Kansas, 2003), 194.

12. U.S. Bureau of the Census, Historical Poverty Tables, Table 2, http://1.usa.gov/1xp7RK8.

13. *New York Times*, February 15 and 29, 1976, and December 27, 1983; *Chicago Defender*, November 14 and 30, 1974, and February 19, 1975.

14. *Roger Biles, The Fate of Cities: Urban America and the Federal Government, 1945–2000* (Lawrence: University Press of Kansas, 2011), 285.

15. Joseph A. McCartin, *Collision Course: Ronald Reagan, the Air Traffic Controllers and the Strike that Changed America* (New York: Oxford University Press, 2011), 292.

16. U.S. Bureau of Labor Statistics, *Major Work Stoppages*, 2013, http://1.usa.gov/1xA5uSm.

17. Nelson Lichtenstein, "Wal-Mart, John Tate, and Their Anti-Union America," in Nelson Lichtenstein and Elizabeth Tandy Shermer, eds., *The Right and Labor in America: Politics, Ideology, and Imagination* (Philadelphia: University of Pennsylvania Press, 2012), 263.

18. Robert O. Self, *All in the Family: The Realignment of American Democracy Since the 1960s* (New York: Hill & Wang, 2012), 345–56.

19. John G. Turner, *Bill Bright and the Campus Crusade for Christ* (Chapel Hill: University of North Carolina Press, 2008), 118.

20. Jon Butler, Grant Wacker, and Randall Balmer, *Religion in American Life: A Short History*, 2nd ed. (New York: Oxford University Press, 2011), 394.

21. James T. Patterson, *Restless Giant: The United States from Watergate to Bush v. Gore* (New York: Oxford University Press, 2005), 139.

22. Joseph Crespino, "Civil Rights and the Religious Right," in Bruce J. Schulman and Julian Zelizer, eds., *Rightward Bound: Making America Conservative in the 1970s* (Cambridge, MA: Harvard University Press, 2008), 104.

23. Gary Scott Smith, *Faith and the Presidency from George Washington to George W. Bush* (New York: Oxford University Press, 2006), 345.

24. Self, *All in the Family*, 370.

25. Stanley K. Henshaw and Kathryn Kost, *Trends in the Characteristics of Women Obtaining Abortions, 1974 to 2004* (New York: Guttmacher Institute, 2008), 7.

26. Stephen Waldmann, "Stuart's Table," Belief.net, http://bit.ly/1zpwtQO.

27. Aydin Tözeren, *A New Life: Being a Gay Man in the Era of HIV* (Lanham, MD: University Press of America, 1997), 140–62.

28. Leslie Maitland Werner, "Education Chief Presses AIDS Tests," *New York Times*, May 1, 1987.

29. Philip M. Boffey, "Reagan Names 12 to Panel on AIDS," *New York Times*, July 24, 1987.

30. Sheldon Goldman, *Picking Federal Judges: Lower Court Selection from Roosevelt Through Reagan* (New Haven, CT: Yale University Press, 1997), 348, 353.

31. *Bowers v. Hardwick*, 478 U.S. 186 (1986).

32. John Patrick Diggins, *Ronald Reagan: Fate, Freedom, and the Making of History* (New York: W. W. Norton, 2007), 316.

33. Ronald Reagan, "Remarks at the Annual Convention of the National Association of Evangelicals in Orlando, Florida," March 8, 1983, http://bit.ly/1xYhRGR.

34. All figures from National Research Council, *Funding a Revolution: Government Support for Computing Research* (Washington, DC: National Academies Press, 1999), http://bit.ly/1qJ1PfY.

35. Margaret Pugh O'Mara, *Cities of Knowledge: Cold War Science and the Search for the Next Silicon Valley* (Princeton, NJ: Princeton University Press, 2005).

36. Sean Wilentz, *The Age of Reagan: A History, 1974–2008* (New York: Harper, 2009), 159.

37. Ronald Reagan, "Remarks of Reporters Announcing the Deployment of United States Forces in Beirut, Lebanon," August 20, 1982, http://bit.ly/1wFtDI3.

38. Ronald Reagan, "Radio Address to the Nation on the Budget Deficit, Central America, and Lebanon," February 4, 1984, http://bit.ly/1wgPLsk.

39. Greg Grandin, *Empire's Workshop Latin America, the United States, and the Rise of the New Imperialism* (New York: Macmillan, 2006), 100.

40. Ronald Reagan, "Remarks on Central America and El Salvador at the Annual Meeting of the National Association of Manufacturers," March 10, 1983, http://bit.ly/1BY7vsQ.

41. Ronald Reagan, "Address Before a Joint Session of Congress on Central America," April 27, 1983, http://bit.ly/1wFtNzj.

42. Ronald Reagan, "Address to the Nation on the Iran Arms and Contra Aid Controversy," November 13, 1986, http://bit.ly/1uSRyyB.

43. Ronald Reagan, "Remarks on East-West Relations at the Brandenburg Gate in West Berlin," June 12, 1987, http://bit.ly/1wgPUw1.

44. Julian E. Zelizer, *Arsenal of Democracy: The Politics of National Security from World War II to the War on Terrorism* (New York: Basic Books, 2010), 351.

45. Ibid., 370.

46. U.S. Bureau of Labor Statistics, *Spotlight on Statistics: Fashion*, June 2012, http://1.usa.gov/1ubi6hb.

47. Steve Striffler, *Chicken: The Dangerous Transformation of America's Favorite Food* (New Haven, CT: Yale University Press, 2007), 22.

48. Daniel J. Tichenor, *Dividing Lines: The Politics of Immigration Control in America* (Princeton, NJ: Princeton University Press, 2002), 262.

49. Joseph Rosenbloom, "Victims in the Heartland," *American Prospect*, June 16, 2003.

50. The Third Clinton-Bush-Perot Presidential Debate, October 19, 1992, http://bit.ly/16JUedv.

51. Kenneth S. Baer, *Reinventing Democrats: The Politics of Liberalism from Reagan to Clinton* (Lawrence: University Press of Kansas, 2000), 64.

52. Jon F. Hale, "Making the New Democrats," *Political Science Quarterly* 110 (1995), 217, 220.

53. Baer, *Reinventing Democrats*, 166.

54. Democratic Leadership Council, "The New Orleans Declaration," March 1, 1990, http://bit.ly/1ARCtSC.

55. Hale, "Making the New Democrats," 226.

56. Jacob S. Hacker and Paul Pierson, *Winner-Take-All Politics: How Washington Made the Rich Richer and Turned Its Back on the Middle Class* (New York: Simon & Schuster, 2010), 232.

57. Paul Pierson, "The Deficit and the Politics of Domestic Reform," in Margaret Weir, ed., *The Social Divide: Political Parties and the Future of Activist Government* (Washington, DC: Brookings Institution, 1998), 136.

58. Mark A. Peterson, "The Politics of Health Care Policy," in Weir, *Social Divide*, 183.
59. Ibid., 194.
60. *The Contract with America*, 1994, http://bit.ly/1ulRvzy.
61. Lawrence Mead, *The New Politics of Poverty: The Nonworking Poor in America* (New York: Basic Books, 1992), 15, 57.
62. Michael B. Katz, *The Price of Citizenship: Redefining the American Welfare State* (New York: Metropolitan Books, 2001), 339.
63. Ibid., 339–40.
64. U.S. Census Bureau, *Current Population Reports, P60-213, Money Income in the United States: 2000* (Washington, DC: U.S. Government Printing Office, 2001).
65. Hacker and Pierson, *Winner-Take-All Politics*, 22.
66. Sheldon A. Pollock, *Refinancing America: The Republican Antitax Agenda* (Albany: State University of New York Press, 2003), 141.
67. Dan Roberts, "Wall Street Deregulation Pushed by Clinton Advisors, Documents Reveal," *Guardian*, April 17, 2014, http://bit.ly/1Br5YPH.
68. William J. Clinton, "Remarks on the National Homeownership Strategy," June 5, 1995, http://bit.ly/1xYibpd.
69. Charles A. Kupchan, "Hollow Hegemony or Stable Multipolarity," in G. John Ikenberry, ed., *America Unrivaled: The Future of the Balance of Power* (Ithaca, NY: Cornell University Press, 2002), 83.
70. "The Year 2000: Keeping Watch: With Fears of Terrorism, Precautions Will Continue," *New York Times*, January 2, 2000.
71. William J. Clinton, "The President's Radio Address," January 1, 2000, http://bit.ly/1vdUStU.

CHAPTER 8: UNITED WE STAND, DIVIDED WE FALL

1. This account of Patricia Thompson is drawn from her oral history in Lolla Vollen and Chris Ying, eds., *Voices from the Storm: The People of New Orleans on Hurricane Katrina and Its Aftermath* (San Francisco: McSweeney's Books, 2006).
2. The First Gore-Bush Presidential Debate, October 3, 2000, http://bit.ly/1wegwc3.
3. Kevin M. Kruse, "Compassionate Conservatism: Religion in the Age of George W. Bush," in Julian Zelizer, ed., *The Presidency of George W. Bush: A First Historical Assessment* (Princeton, NJ: Princeton University Press, 2010), 229.
4. George W. Bush, "GOP Nomination Acceptance Address," August 3, 2000, http://bit.ly/1E2RW8b.
5. Robert Johnston, *The Radical Middle Class: Populist Democracy and the Question of Capitalism in Progressive Era Portland, Oregon* (Princeton, NJ: Princeton University Press, 2006), 273.
6. George W. Bush, "Remarks on Signing Executive Orders With Respect to Faith-Based and Community Initiatives," January 29, 2001, http://bit.ly/13wlAC2.
7. Sean Wilentz, *The Age of Reagan: A History, 1974–2008* (New York: Harper Collins, 2008), 438.
8. Stephen P. Miller, *The Age of Evangelicalism: America's Born-Again Years* (New York: Oxford University Press, 2014), 127.
9. George W. Bush, "Address to the Nation on Stem Cell Research," August 9, 2001, http://bit.ly/1x3dEm6.
10. Richard Land, interviewed in "The Jesus Factor," PBS *Frontline*, April 29, 2004, http://to.pbs.org/1wW0gl1.
11. James T. Patterson, "Transformative Economic Policies: Tax Cutting, Stimuli, and Bailouts," in Zelizer, ed., *Presidency of George W. Bush*, 130.

12. *Final Report of the National Commission on Terrorist Attacks Upon the United States*, Executive Summary (Washington, DC: U.S. Government Printing Office, 2004), http://1 .usa.gov/1wBG7kk.

13. Timothy Naftali, "George W. Bush and the 'War on Terror,'" in Zelizer, ed., *Presidency of George W. Bush*, 66.

14. Mary L. Dudziak, "A Sword and a Shield: The Uses of Law in the Bush Administration," in Zelizer, ed., *Presidency of George W. Bush*, 43–44.

15. U.S. Senate, Select Committee on Intelligence, *Committee Study of the CIA's Detention and Interrogation Program, Findings and Conclusions*, December 2014, 2, http://1.usa.gov /13w3hwE.

16. George W. Bush, "Address Before a Joint Session of the Congress on the State of the Union," January 29, 2002, www.presidency.ucsb.edu/ws/?pid=29644.

17. Ibid.

18. George W. Bush, "Commencement Address at the United States Military Academy in West Point, New York," June 1, 2002, www.presidency.ucsb.edu/ws/?pid=62730.

19. Fredrik Logevall, "Anatomy of an Unnecessary War: The Iraq Invasion," in Zelizer, ed., *Presidency of George W. Bush*, 101.

20. Lloyd C. Gardner, *The Long Road to Baghdad: A History of U.S. Foreign Policy from the 1970s to the Present* (New York: New Press, 2008), 141.

21. Bob Woodward, "Cheney Was Unwavering in Desire to Go to War; Tension Between Vice President and Powell Grew Deeper as Both Tried to Guide Bush's Decision," *Washington Post*, April 20, 2004.

22. Logevall, "Anatomy of an Unnecessary War," 109.

23. George W. Bush, "Address to the Nation on Iraq from the *U.S.S. Abraham Lincoln*," May 1, 2003, www.presidency.ucsb.edu/ws/index.php?pid=68675.

24. Amy Belasco, *Troop Levels in the Afghan and Iraq Wars, FY 2001–FY 2012: Cost and Other Potential Issues* (Washington, DC: Congressional Research Service, 2009), figs. 6 and 7.

25. Hedrick Smith, *Who Stole the American Dream?* (New York: Random House, 2011), 357–58.

26. Mark Sandalow, "Bush Claims Mandate, Sets 2nd-Term Goals," *San Francisco Chronicle*, November 5, 2004.

27. Nelson Lichtenstein, "Ideology and Interest on the Social Policy Home Front," in Zelizer, ed., *Presidency of George W. Bush*, 190.

28. Romain Huret, "Explaining the Unexplainable: Hurricane Katrina, FEMA, and the Bush Administration," in Romain Huret and Randy J. Sparks, eds., *Hurricane Katrina in Transatlantic Perspective* (Baton Rouge: Louisiana State University Press, 2014), 39.

29. U.S. Department of Health and Human Services, Office of Human Services Policy, *The Role of Faith Based and Community Organizations in Providing Relief and Recovery Services After Hurricanes Katrina and Rita*, September 2008, http://urbn.is/1x309mB.

30. *A Fresh Start for New Orleans' Children: Improving Education after Katrina: Hearing Before the Subcommittee on Education and Early Childhood Development*, Committee on Health, Education, Labor, and Pensions, U.S. Senate, 109th Cong., 2nd. sess. (July 14, 2006).

31. Louis Hyman, *Borrow: The American Way of Debt* (New York: Vintage Books, 2012), 236.

32. Debbie Gruenstein Bocian, Wei Li, Carolina Reid, and Roberto G. Quercia, *Lost Ground, 2011: Disparities in Mortgage Lending and Foreclosures* (Durham, NC: Center for Responsible Lending, 2011), 8.

33. Sheila Bair, *Bull By the Horns: Fighting to Save Main Street from Wall Street and Wall Street from Itself* (New York: Free Press, 2012).

34. Barack Obama, "Address to the Democratic National Convention," *Washington Post*, July 27, 2004.

35. Michael Cooper, "McCain on U.S. Economy: From 'Strong' to 'Total Crisis' in 36 Hours," *New York Times*, September 17, 2008.

36. The best overviews of Obama's economic policy to date are Ron Suskind, *Confidence Men: Wall Street, Washington, and the Education of a President* (New York: Harper, 2011), and Noam Scheiber, *The Escape Artists: How Obama Fumbled the Recovery* (New York: Simon & Schuster, 2012).

37. Among the overviews of Obama's policy initiatives and the constraints that he faced, the most useful is Theda Skocpol and Lawrence Jacobs, eds., *Reaching for a New Deal: Ambitious Governance, Economic Meltdown, and Polarized Politics in Obama's First Two Years* (New York: Russell Sage Foundation, 2011). On Obama's penchant toward moderation and bipartisanship, see James Kloppenberg, *Reading Obama* (Princeton, NJ: Princeton University Press, 2010).

38. Emanuel Saez, "Striking it Richer: The Evolution of Top Incomes in the United States," University of California, Berkeley, Department of Economics, September 2013, http://bit.ly/13VZUQx.

39. Rakesh Kochhar, Richard Fry, and Paul Taylor, *Twenty-to-One: Wealth Gaps Rise to Record Highs Between Whites, Blacks and Hispanics* (Pew Research Center, Social and Demographic Trends, July 26, 2011), http://pewrsr.ch/13r5FVn.

GLOSSARY

Abu Ghraib A former Iraqi prison used from 2003 to 2006 by the United States for the detention and torture of suspected Iraqi insurgents. These practices became a flashpoint in debates about human rights and international law violations by American troops and contractors during the Iraq War.

affirmative action A controversial program to increase the representation of minorities and women in the workforce, later applied to college admissions. In 1969 the Nixon administration set goals and timetables for the hiring of black and Puerto Rican construction workers on government-funded building sites in Philadelphia; the plan that became a national model for most firms with government contracts.

AIDS Coalition to Unleash Power (ACT UP) An activist group founded in New York City in 1987 that staged mass protests to raise consciousness about the growing AIDS epidemic and to demand that public officials and the medical profession prioritize and fund AIDS research.

Akron v. Akron Center for Reproductive Health (1983) A Supreme Court ruling that struck down the city of Akron's ordinance to regulate abortion by requiring parental consent, requiring doctors to notify their patients that a fetus is a human life from the moment of conception, and establishing a twenty-four-hour waiting period for planned abortions.

Al Qaeda A terrorist organization led by the wealthy Saudi petroleum heir Osama bin Laden. Al Qaeda fought the Soviet Union in Afghanistan with American support in the 1980s. Beginning in the 1990s, it launched terror strikes on targets in the Middle East and Africa and was responsible for attacks on New York's World Trade Center in 1993, on the U.S. embassies in Kenya and Tanzania in 2008, and on the Pentagon and the World Trade Center in September 2001.

American Recovery and Reinvestment Act (2009) Offered over $800 billion in tax breaks, infrastructure improvements, and public education funding to create jobs and reinvigorate the U.S. economy. Signed by President Barack Obama, it was also known as the stimulus package.

Americanization In 1965 President Johnson decided to increase the number of American ground troops in Vietnam, in hopes of achieving a swift victory. By the end of the year, 185,000 Americans had been deployed. Deployments in Vietnam would peak at 535,000 in 1968.

Anti-Ballistic Missile Treaty (1972) An arms control treaty between the United States and the Soviet Union that set a cap on antiballistic missile systems in both countries, in an effort to slow the arms race. The treaty signaled the beginning of détente between the two superpowers.

Army-McCarthy hearings Between April and June 1954, the U.S. Senate held televised hearings investigating charges by Senator Joseph McCarthy (R-WI) that the army harbored Communists. McCarthy emerged from the hearings widely discredited, in part because of the lack of evidence to substantiate his claims, in part because of his combative tone.

Asiatic Squadron On April 30, 1898, Commodore George Dewey led the small U.S. Asiatic Squadron of nine vessels in a surprise attack that defeated the Spanish warships in the Philippines' Manila Bay.

"Axis of Evil" President George W. Bush's term, first used in his 2003 State of the Union address, to describe countries—Iraq, Iran, and North Korea—that were said to support terrorist activities and that sought to acquire nuclear and chemical weapons of mass destruction.

Bay of Pigs invasion (1961) Authorized by President John Kennedy, fourteen hundred Cuban refugees, trained and financed by the CIA, attempted to topple Fidel Castro's Communist government. The Cuban military quickly overwhelmed the anti-Castro insurgents when they landed at the Bay of Pigs.

Black Panthers A political organization launched in 1966 by Oakland activists Bobby Seale and Huey Newton, its name inspired by the crouching black panther symbol of the Lowndes County Alabama Freedom Party. Black activists in cities around the country formed Black Panther parties, calling for black self-determination, race pride, self-defense against police, and economic redistribution.

black sites Secret prisons operated outside the United States by the CIA for the detention, interrogation, and torture of suspected terrorists and enemy combatants. Prisoners could be held indefinitely there, without the protections of American law.

Boland Amendment Passed by Congress in 1982 as an amendment to a defense appropriations bill, it forbade the use of defense funds to assist the anti-communist Contras in Nicaragua. The Reagan administration used a loophole in the amendment to continue to fund covert CIA operations in Nicaragua. In 1984 another version of the amendment forbade the use of CIA funds.

Bowers v. Hardwick **(1986)** A Supreme Court ruling that upheld a Georgia state law banning sodomy, arguing that the Constitution did not protect a fundamental right to engage in same-sex relations.

Bretton Woods Conference Delegates from forty-four allied nations gathered in Bretton Woods, New Hampshire, in 1944 to devise a system to regulate the international monetary and financial system and to provide financing for postwar reconstruction. Bretton Woods created the International Bank for Reconstruction and Development (later known as the World Bank) and the International Monetary Fund.

Brown v. Board of Education of Topeka **(1954)** The landmark Supreme Court ruling that the provision of separate public schools for black and white students was unconstitutional.

Bush v. Gore **(2000)** The Supreme Court decision that ended Florida's court-ordered manual recount of contested ballots in the 2000 presidential election, giving Republican candidate George W. Bush a 327-vote margin in Florida and thus a majority of Electoral College votes.

Civil Rights Act of 1957 Promoted the right of African Americans to vote. The first civil rights legislation passed by Congress since Reconstruction, it was a mostly symbolic gesture. It established the Civil

Rights Commission to investigate discriminatory claims and to recommend reforms, but it provided no mechanism for the enforcement of civil rights.

Civil Rights Act of 1964 Outlawed segregation in public accommodations and schools and prohibited employment discrimination by race, color, sex, religion, or national origin. The most sweeping civil rights legislation since Reconstruction, the act also created the Equal Employment Opportunity Commission, a federal agency, to investigate workplace discrimination and file lawsuits against discriminatory employers.

COINTELPRO An acronym for Counter Intelligence Program. Beginning in the Eisenhower administration. COINTELPRO—directed by the FBI—deployed undercover agents to infiltrate and disrupt left-wing organizations, including civil rights and black power, antiwar, and radical student groups.

Committee to Re-elect the President (CREEP) The fundraising arm of President Nixon's 1972 reelection campaign, CREEP engaged in illegal campaign financing, oversaw efforts to discredit the president's opponents, and supported covert activities, including break-ins at the offices of Nixon's critics.

Common Sense Book of Baby and Child Care, The (1946) A best-selling advice book authored by Dr. Benjamin Spock that overturned traditional standards of strict discipline and parental control. The book sold tens of millions of copies in multiple editions.

Congress of Racial Equality (CORE) A civil rights organization founded in Chicago in 1942 by black and white theology students inspired by Mohandas K. Gandhi's nonviolent civil disobedience efforts in India. CORE challenged segregation in restaurants, swimming pools, buses, and amusement parks and pioneered the sit-in strategy.

Conscience of a Conservative, The (1960) With the publication of this best-selling book, Senator Barry Goldwater (R-AZ) emerged as the leading figure of the political right. Goldwater argued against both New Deal Democrats and moderate Republicans, asserting that social welfare programs sapped individual initiative, that taxes and regulation hindered liberties, and that Cold War foreign policy was insufficiently aggressive.

Conscientious Objection (CO) A provision by which drafted men could qualify for nonmilitary service if they held religious or moral beliefs that prevented them from fighting. During the Vietnam War, more draftees than ever—nearly a half million—petitioned the Selective Service for conscientious objector status. Nearly 170,000 achieved it.

Contract with America (1994) A ten-point document issued by Republicans six weeks before the 1994 congressional election. It called for a constitutional amendment to require a balanced budget and limit taxation, a reduction in business regulations, a limit on welfare benefits, and programs to promote "family values."

Cost-of-living allowance (COLA) During the strike wave of 1945–46, workers demanded that their wages be linked to a cost-of-living index, to protect them from inflation. General Motors and the United Automobile Workers negotiated COLA in their 1946 contract, which became a model for similar agreements in many other industries as well.

Cuban Missile Crisis (1962) A thirteen-day confrontation between the United States and the Soviet Union over Soviet missile sites in Cuba that brought the two superpowers to the brink of war. Secret negotiations between Washington and Moscow resulted in Soviet withdrawal of missiles from Cuba and an American pledge not to invade Cuba and to withdraw its missiles from Turkey.

Democratic Leadership Council (DLC) Founded in 1985, this organization of moderate and conservative Democrats, including Bill Clinton and Al Gore, worked to move their party rightward on issues of civil rights, criminal justice, foreign policy, welfare, and economics. The DLC advocated pro-business policies, including free trade, tax cuts, and government subsidies for high-tech research, and it called for a reduction in welfare spending.

Department of Homeland Security A cabinet-level department created by the Homeland Security Act of 2002 that consolidated antiterrorism and disaster preparedness efforts under a single agency, oversaw increased funding to state and local police departments, enhanced border patrols, made new efforts to prevent cyber terrorism, and enforced strict security at airports and large public events.

Depository Institutions Deregulation and Monetary Control Act (1980) Removed interest-rate ceilings on bank deposits and allowed savings and loan associations and banks to create interest-bearing checking accounts, offer adjustable-rate mortgages, and issue credit cards. This federal financial statute was signed by President Jimmy Carter.

détente A period of improved relations between the United States and the Soviet Union beginning in the Nixon administration and lasting until 1980. The two superpowers negotiated trade agreements, the ABM treaty, and another treaty to limit the number of intercontinental range ballistic missiles (ICBMs) that each country could possess.

Dixie-GOP coalition An alliance of pro-business Republicans and southern Democrats who often voted together in Congress in opposition to civil rights legislation and measures supported by organized labor, from the mid-1940s through the mid-1960s.

Domino Theory The theory that if a country came under Communist control, it would lead to a chain reaction of Communist takeovers in neighboring countries. In Southeast Asia, the United States used the domino theory to justify its involvement in the Vietnam War.

Earth Day (April 22, 1970) About twenty million people around the United States gathered in loosely coordinated protests, parades, teach-ins, and festivals to raise consciousness about environmental issues and to push for greater regulation of air and water pollution and the protection of natural areas and endangered plants and animals.

Economic Growth and Tax Relief Reconciliation Act (2001) President George W. Bush's signature program to reduce taxes, particularly for corporations and high-income taxpayers. The law phased in a dramatic estate tax reduction over a ten-year period. It provided a modest rebate for individual taxpayers, expanded a child credit, and incentivized investments in Individual Retirement Accounts (IRAs).

Economic Research and Action Project (ERAP) A program launched by Students for a Democratic Society in 1963 to create an interracial movement of the poor by organizing against racism and economic exploitation. The main ERAP sites were Chicago and Newark.

Environmental Protection Agency (EPA) A federal agency created by President Nixon in 1970, as part of a wave of environmental reform that included the National Environmental Policy Act (1969), the Clean Air Act (1970), the Clean Water Act (1972), and the Endangered Species Act (1973). The EPA is responsible for drafting and administering environmental regulations.

Equal Rights Amendment (1972) A proposed constitutional amendment that would guarantee equal rights to women. It passed the Senate with overwhelming bipartisan support in 1972, but failed to gain ratification by the necessary thirty-eight states by the 1979 deadline or the 1982 deadline extension.

European Recovery Program (Marshall Plan) Enacted in 1948, the Marshall Plan initially provided $13 billion to finance the reconstruction of western European countries ravaged by the Second World War.

Executive Order 9835 (1947) Issued by President Harry Truman, the order created loyalty review boards to investigate federal employees suspected of disloyalty to the U.S. government. The boards targeted individuals affiliated with groups labeled by the attorney general as "totalitarian, fascistic, communistic, or subversive." During Truman's administration, approximately twelve hundred federal workers lost their jobs because of suspected disloyalty.

Executive Order 9980 (1948) Issued by President Truman, the order banned discrimination by race, color, religion, or national origin in the federal workforce.

Executive Order 9981 (1948) Issued by President Truman, the order desegregated the U.S. military.

Family Assistance Plan (FAP) (1969) A Nixon administration welfare reform proposal to replace Aid to Families with Dependent Children with a guaranteed annual income for poor families of approximately $1,600 for a household of four. It met with opposition from liberals who considered it too stingy and conservatives who saw it as a handout to the undeserving poor.

family wage The concept, endorsed by unionists and by many religious groups, that male workers should be paid enough to support a stay-at-home wife and children.

Federal Emergency Management Agency (FEMA) Created by President Carter in 1979 to manage man-made and natural disasters and to fund disaster relief, FEMA was absorbed into the Department of Homeland Security in 2003. With limited resources and poor management, FEMA was ill equipped to deal with Hurricane Katrina and its aftermath

***Feminine Mystique, The* (1963)** The book widely credited with sparking second-wave feminism in the United States. Author Betty Friedan focused on college-educated women, arguing that they would find fulfillment by engaging in paid labor outside the home.

foreclosure The process by which mortgage lenders repossess and sell a home used as collateral by borrowers who fail to make payments.

Freedom Rides (1961) The Congress of Racial Equality organized interracial teams of activists to travel by bus through the South to challenge segregation on interstate transportation. White officials arrested and jailed many riders; white supremacists often brutally attacked them.

Fulbright Hearings (1966–71) The Senate Foreign Relations Committee, chaired by Senator J. William Fulbright (D-AR), held a series of twenty-two hearings to investigate American policy in Vietnam. Early sessions were televised and helped shift public opinion away from support for the war.

Geneva Accords (1954) An agreement negotiated by France, the People's Republic of China, the Soviet Union, and the United States to end French colonial rule in Indochina. The accords created the independent nations of Laos and Cambodia and temporarily divided Vietnam along the seventeenth parallel until nationwide elections could be held. The United States did not sign the accords and did not support national elections for fear the Communists would win.

***Goldberg v. Kelly* (1970)** A Supreme Court ruling that a state could not terminate welfare benefits without giving the recipient the opportunity for an evidentiary hearing.

Gramm-Leach-Bliley Act (1999) Repealed the 1933 Glass-Steagall Act. Also known as the Financial Services Modernization Act of 1999, this law permitted commercial banks, investment banks, securities firms, and insurance companies to consolidate, and allowed banks to invest in securities. It led to the emergence of loosely regulated megabanks, many of which collapsed during the 2008 economic crisis. The act was signed by President Bill Clinton.

Great Recession (1973–75) A period of major economic stagnation across the United States and Western Europe, characterized by rising unemployment and inflation and a 37 percent decline in the stock market between March and December 1974.

Great Society (1965) Sweeping domestic reforms proposed by President Lyndon Johnson in his State of the Union to address voting rights, poverty, health, education, immigration, and the environment.

Green v. Connally **(1971)** A Supreme Court ruling that religious institutions that discriminated on racial grounds could not claim tax-except status under the Internal Revenue Code.

Guantanamo Bay A detention center at the American naval base at Guantanamo Bay, Cuba, where beginning in 2002 suspected terrorists and war prisoners were held indefinitely and tried by extrajudicial military tribunals. During his 2008 presidential campaign, Senator Barack Obama pledged to close the prison, but as of 2015 it remained open.

Guatemalan coup (1954) In 1951 Guatemala's leftist leader Jacobo Arbenz instituted a sweeping land reform program that included the appropriation of land controlled by United Fruit, an American-based firm. With the authorization of the Eisenhower administration, the CIA backed his overthrow. Arbenz was succeeded by a series of brutal right-wing dictators.

Gulf Coast Opportunity Zone (2005) A program of tax benefits for individuals and businesses in areas affected by Hurricane Katrina, using tax credits to incentivize private rebuilding efforts.

Gulf of Tonkin incident (August 2–4, 1964) In response to an August 2 attack on American ships off the North Vietnamese coast and unsubstantiated claims of another attack on August 4, Congress passed the Tonkin Gulf Resolution, which authorized President Johnson to use military force in Vietnam without a formal declaration of war.

hardhat protests (1970) In the spring of 1970, construction workers in New York City attacked antiwar protesters and sparked a series of protests in Lower Manhattan in favor of the Vietnam War and law and order politics, culminating in a mass march on May 20. President Nixon commended the hardhat protesters for their patriotism.

Hart-Cellar Act (1965) Eliminated nation-specific quotas on immigration that dated to 1924. The act also gave preference to family reunification, skilled workers, and refugees fleeing Communist rule. It placed the first numerical restriction on immigrants from the Western hemisphere.

homophile organizations In response to the government and military investigation of suspected homosexuals, antigay laws, and the censorship of gay and lesbian publications, activists demanded the integration of homosexuals into American life. The most prominent homophile organizations were the Mattachine Society (1951) and the Daughters of Bilitis (1955).

House Un-American Activities Committee (HUAC) Created by legislation in 1938, HUAC investigated dissidents and held hearings in Congress and, later, in cities throughout the United States. After World War II, HUAC focused on left-wing activists and private citizens, public employees, and organizations suspected of having Communist ties.

Hue, Battle of (January 30–February 25, 1968) One of the longest and bloodiest battles of the Vietnam War, it was a struggle for control of the ancient city of Hue that began during the Tet Offensive. The U.S. and South Vietnamese troops took control of the city after twenty-six days of fighting.

Immigration Reform and Control Act (IRCA) (1986) Made it illegal for employers to employ immigrants without the proper identification. The first major revision to immigration law since the 1965 Hart-Cellar Act, IRCA tightened border controls and allowed for the legalization of undocumented immigrants who had resided in the United States before January 1, 1982. The act was signed by President Ronald Reagan.

Inchon, Battle of (1950) In one of the riskiest invasions in modern military history, General Douglas MacArthur commanded an amphibious surprise landing at Inchon Bay that enabled American troops to flank North Korean troops and led to the recapture of Seoul two weeks later.

International Banking Act (1978) Placed domestic and foreign banks under federal banking regulations and allowed foreign-held banks to purchase American banks and compete against American owned banks for customers. The act was signed by President Jimmy Carter.

Interstate Highway Act (1956) Created a nationally funded system of superhighways both to spur economic growth and to allow for the decentralization of military operations to prevent a crippling nuclear attack.

Iran-Contra affair A complex set of transactions, authorized by high-level Reagan administration officials, to fund the Nicaraguan Contras illegally. The United States secretly sold arms to Iran, which in turn pressured Lebanon to release seven American hostages. The proceeds from the arms trade were transferred to intermediaries in Israel and sent to the Contras. The scheme was revealed when a plane delivering arms to the Contras crashed in Nicaragua in October 1986. From 1987 to 1990, an independent prosecutor and Congress investigated the scandal.

Iranian hostage crisis (1979–80) In response to President Carter's decision to allow the exiled Shah of Iran, Mohammad Reza Pahlavi, to receive cancer treatment in the United States, a group of revolutionaries seized the U.S. embassy in Teheran and took fifty-two Americans hostage and held them for 444 days. Carter authorized a rescue mission that disastrously failed and resulted in the death of eight U.S. soldiers. The crisis became a sign of presidential and national impotence.

Islamic State of Iraq and Syria (ISIS) An insurgency that emerged from the sectarian civil wars that destabilized Syria and post-Saddam Hussein Iraq. Beginning in 2014, ISIS forces attacked towns and cities in Iraq, systematically murdering members of ethnic and religious minorities.

Journey of Reconciliation (1947) A protest led by sixteen CORE members, eight black and eight white men, who boarded southbound buses from Washington, D.C., headed into Virginia and North Carolina, and refused to obey Jim Crow rules. Several were arrested and jailed.

juvenile delinquency A term for adolescent disregard of authority figures, resulting in crime, sexual promiscuity, and rebellion. In the mid-1950s Senator Estes Kefauver (D-TN) launched Senate hearings on the topic, including an investigation of the impact of comic books on youth morality.

Laffer Curve A hypothesis that held that tax cuts would bolster productive activity and increase tax revenue. Devised by economist Arthur Laffer, it was the basis of President Reagan's proposed tax reforms. It was disproven when tax cuts worsened federal deficits, but it nonetheless remains an influential argument for tax reduction.

Law Enforcement Assistance Act (LEAA) (1965) Authorized federal grants for to train state and local enforcement personnel and to modernize police equipment. In the first two years, over $300 million was spent on riot preparations.

Levittowns Large-scale, affordable suburban housing developments that opened in New York, Pennsylvania, New Jersey, and elsewhere in the post–World War II years. Builder William Levitt used mass production technology with standardized components to build new houses quickly and cheaply. The original Levittowns were racially segregated.

liberal feminism The effort to achieve formal equality between men and women, including the enforcement of anti-sex-discrimination laws, equal pay for equal work, and affordable child care. Liberal feminists worked to achieve their goals through lobbying, legislation, and litigation. They were especially influential in Kennedy's Presidential Commission on the Status of Women (1961–63) and in the founding of the National Organization of Women (1966–).

"long telegram" (1946) A lengthy telegram sent by George Kennan, the deputy head of mission in Moscow, to the Department of State that asserted that the Soviet Union could not permanently and peacefully coexist with the West and was inherently expansionist. The United States, it argued, must contain Soviet influence in areas of strategic importance. This policy, which became known as containment, became a central U.S. Cold War strategy.

malaise speech (1979) A speech by President Carter in which he described the national crisis as existential rather than political or economic. Carter remarked that the nation faced a "crisis of confidence." It became known as the "malaise speech" even though Carter never used the word in his speech.

March on Washington for Jobs and Freedom (1963) Organized by civil rights, labor, and religious organizations, 250,000 people gathered on the Mall in Washington, D.C., to demand antidiscrimination legislation and economic opportunity for African Americans. In front of the Lincoln Memorial, the Reverend Martin Luther King, Jr., delivered his famous "I Have a Dream Speech."

military-industrial complex President Eisenhower's term for the extensive network of private firms that manufactured weapons, aircraft, ships, vehicles, and other supplies for the American military in a period of increasing defense spending.

***Milliken v. Bradley* (1974)** A narrowly decided Supreme Court decision that struck down a plan for cross-district busing in metropolitan Detroit. Drawing a distinction between de jure segregation (by law) and de facto segregation (in practice), it held that school districts, even if they were racially homogeneous, could be held responsible for racial segregation only if it resulted from intentionally discriminatory policy.

***Miranda v. Arizona* (1966)** A Supreme Court ruling that detained criminal suspects must be informed of their rights to an attorney and against self-incrimination prior to police questioning.

Montgomery Bus Boycott A grassroots challenge to segregated transit in Montgomery, Alabama, that began in late 1955, when activist Rosa Parks refused to give up a bus seat to a white passenger. The boycott, which lasted for nearly a year, launched the civil rights career of the Reverend Martin Luther King, Jr.

My Lai Massacre (1968). In March, Lieutenant William Calley and troops under his command massacred 347 Vietnamese civilians in the village of My Lai. U.S. army officers covered up the massacre for a year until an investigation uncovered the events. Eventually twenty-five army officers were charged with complicity in the massacre and its cover-up, but only Calley was convicted. He served little time for his crimes.

Nation of Islam An African American religious sect founded in the early 1930s that reached over 100,000 members at its height. The Nation and its most prominent ministers, Elijah Muhammad and Malcolm X (who left in 1964), called for black self-determination, separatism, and self-defense while opposing racial integration and nonviolence.

National Association for the Advancement of Colored People (NAACP) Founded in 1909, the NAACP was the nation's largest mass-membership civil rights organization, with hundreds of local branches around the country. The NAACP lobbied for civil rights legislation, sponsored local protests, and engaged in litigation to challenge discrimination and segregation in housing, education, and the workplace.

National Energy Plan (NEP) In 1977, the Carter administration proposed comprehensive legislation to conserve energy, including energy efficiency standards for appliances and cars, the development of alternatives to fossil fuels, taxes on firms that relied on petroleum and natural gas, and the lifting of price ceilings on oil and gas. Amid significant controversy and resistance from Republicans, the NEP passed Congress but without a tax to discourage consumption.

National Liberation Front (NLF) Formed in 1960, the NLF was a coalition of Communists and non-Communists committed to the overthrow of the South Vietnamese government. The NLF worked closely with the North Vietnamese government and built a substantial base of support in much of rural South Vietnam.

National Mobilization Committee to End the Vietnam War (the Mobe) A coalition of anti–Vietnam War organizations that organized large-scale demonstrations, including the 100,000-person March on the Pentagon in October 1967 and mass protests at the Democratic National Convention in Chicago in August 1968.

National Organization for Women (NOW) Founded in 1966, NOW promoted equal rights for women and challenged sex discrimination in all areas of American society, with a special emphasis on the workplace. Betty Friedan was among its founders. NOW pressed for strong enforcement of the anti-sex-discrimination provisions of Title VII of the Civil Rights Act of 1964 and lobbied for the Equal Rights Amendment.

National Security Act (1947) Reorganized U.S. military and intelligence operations by creating the National Military Establishment (renamed the Department of Defense in 1949), under the direction of the new secretary of defense. It created the U.S. Air Force and the Joint Chiefs of Staff to coordinate strategy among the military services. It established the National Security Council to oversee security policy in the executive branch and the Central Intelligence Agency to handle foreign intelligence gathering and analysis.

New Democrats Also called Atari Democrats, these legislators argued that the Democratic Party's future lay in supporting a high-tech economy rather than the declining manufacturing sector. They felt that the party had to distance itself from its previous base of support, including trade unions and racial minorities, to achieve electoral success.

No Child Left Behind Act (2001) Required the expansion of standardized testing to measure educational progress and impose "accountability" on school districts and teachers for their students' academic achievement. This comprehensive education reform plan passed Congress with wide bipartisan support.

North American Free Trade Agreement (NAFTA) Negotiated by President George H. W. Bush, endorsed by President Bill Clinton, and ratified by Congress in 1993, this trade agreement with Canada and Mexico allowed goods to travel across their borders free of tariffs. It spurred rapid industrialization, particularly in Mexico.

Obamacare (2010) The popular name for President Obama's health care reform initiative, the Affordable Care Act. Obamacare mandated that all Americans purchase health insurance or pay a penalty, established state health care exchanges to provide and market private insurance options, allowed young people to remain on their parents' insurances policies until they turned twenty-six, and forbade insurance companies to deny coverage on the basis of preexisting medical conditions. The act passed with no Republican votes and faced legislative and legal challenges for several years afterwards.

oil embargo In response to U.S. and Western European support for Israel in the 1973 Yom Kippur War, the Organization of Petroleum Exporting Countries, dominated by Middle Eastern producers, declared an oil embargo in October 1973. The rise in gas prices and fuel shortages resulted in a global economic recession and profoundly impacted the American economy.

Operation Chaos (1967) Code name for a CIA domestic espionage program that targeted opponents of the Vietnam War.

Operation Desert Storm (1991) In 1991 President George H. W. Bush won authorization from Congress to take military action against Iraq after its 1990 invasion of Kuwait. On January 17, the United States launched Operation Desert Storm with with massive airstrikes, followed by a ground assault that began on February 24. On February 28, after the swift defeat of Iraqi troops, Bush declared a cease-fire and announced the liberation of Kuwait.

Operation Dixie A post–Second World War campaign launched by the Congress of Industrial Organizations in 1946 to unionize black and white workers in the South. Operation Dixie collapsed by the late 1940s in the face of widespread harassment. Southern officials frequently jailed organizers and charged them with subversion.

Operation Iraqi Freedom (2003) The U.S. invasion of Iraq to topple the regime of Saddam Hussein. Beginning on March 19, the United States deployed approximately 140,000 troops and launched airstrikes.

Within five weeks, the Baghdad regime fell, and Hussein went into hiding. He was eventually captured and executed, but Iraq remained unstable, and American troops occupied the country until 2011.

Operation Just Cause (1989) Launched just six weeks after the fall of the Berlin Wall, President George H. W. Bush authorized 28,000 U.S. military personnel to invade Panama to unseat the corrupt dictator General Manuel Noriega, a former American ally turned international drug dealer. Noriega was captured, brought to the United States, and tried and convicted on drug charges.

Operation Rolling Thunder (1965–68) A strategic military bombing campaign against targets in North Vietnam; the longest and most devastating aerial campaign in U.S. history.

Operation Urgent Fury (1983) The American-led invasion of Grenada, a small Caribbean nation, following a military coup that brought a leftist government there to power. The war lasted about seven weeks, resulting in several hundred deaths. While criticized widely abroad, the invasion was popular in the United States.

Organization of the Petroleum Exporting Countries (OPEC) An international organization created in 1960 by Iran, Iraq, Kuwait, Saudi Arabia, and Venezuela to standardize petroleum prices among producers and regulate the supply of petroleum in the global market.

pacification The American military strategy to drive out the Vietcong from South Vietnamese villages, establish anti-Communist local governments, and fund economic development programs, all in an effort to win the "hearts and minds" of the populace.

Peace Corps Created in 1961 by President Kennedy as a method of "soft diplomacy" during the Cold War, this program sent young Americans across the world to work on projects in education, disease eradication, agriculture, and engineering.

Personal Responsibility and Work Opportunity Reconciliation Act (1996) Replaced Aid to Families with Dependent Children (AFDC) with Temporary Assistance for Needy Families (TANF), a time-limited program that required household heads to obtain work in exchange for modest benefits. It also funded state experiments to promote marriage. The act was negotiated by President Bill Clinton and House Speaker Newt Gingrich. After its passage, welfare expenditures plummeted but poverty rates remained steady.

Port Huron Statement (1962) The manifesto of Students for a Democratic Society. It critiqued American economic and military policy, called for racial equality, criticized corporations, challenged postwar conformity, and advocated a broadly inclusive system of "participatory democracy."

predatory lending Loans that may include high fees, exorbitant interest rates, and penalties to discourage refinancing. Many mortgage lenders took advantage of the deregulation of the home financing market in the 1990s to offer predatory loans. They marketed home equity loans and mortgages to high-risk borrowers, often overvaluing their properties to offer higher loans. Many borrowers who took out predatory loans lost their homes or went into bankruptcy when the housing market collapsed beginning in 2006.

Professional Air Traffic Controllers Organization (PATCO) Strike (1981) On August 3, 1981, thirteen thousand PATCO members voted to strike for higher wages, a shorter work week, and better retirement benefits. When they did not appear for work, President Reagan authorized their firing and replacement by nonunion workers.

Project Independence (1973) Launched by President Richard Nixon in response to the oil embargo, this initiative aimed to free the United States from dependence on foreign energy supplies by 1980. Measures included developing alternative energy sources, a national commitment to energy conservation, converting oil power plants to coal, and reducing the speed limit on interstate highways to 55 miles per hour.

Proposition 187 (1994) A successful California ballot initiative that denied welfare, public education, nonemergency health care, and other social services to undocumented immigrants. It was found unconstitutional by a federal court in 1995 but inspired anti-immigration legislation nationwide.

radical feminism In the late 1960s, radical feminists, inspired by left-wing social movements but critical of their male domination, argued that women's subordinate status was rooted in a system of patriarchy and endemic sexism. In contrast to liberal feminists, radical feminists advocated revolutionary challenges to male domination, created separate all-women, nonhierarchical organizations, and emphasized women's sexual independence.

Reaganomics (1981) President Reagan's plan to reinvigorate the economy by cutting taxes, especially on corporations and the wealthy, to reduce domestic spending, and to tighten the money supply. It was premised on the notion that tax cuts would spur economic growth and increase federal revenue, bringing the budget into balance. The combination of higher defense spending and tax reductions substantially increased federal budget deficits.

Rockefeller Republicans Sometimes called Rockefeller-Eisenhower Republicans, these moderate members of the GOP were staunchly pro-business but generally supportive of civil rights, modest economic regulations, and environmentalism. Many joined bipartisan coalitions with Democrats and fought supporters of Barry Goldwater and Ronald Reagan for control of the Republican Party.

Roe v. Wade **(1973)** The Supreme Court ruling that made abortion legal in the United States. It held that during the first trimester, an abortion was a decision for a woman and her doctor, but after the first trimester, a state could restrict abortions.

Shelley v. Kraemer (1948) A Supreme Court ruling that courts could not enforce racially based restrictive covenants—clauses in property titles, deeds, or lease agreements that forbade the occupancy of a house by African Americans, Jews, Asians, and other racial minorities.

Silent Majority. Richard Nixon's phrase to describe white, middle-class Americans disaffected by the civil rights movement, antiwar protests, and the counterculture.

Sipuel v. Regents of the University of Oklahoma (1948) A Supreme Court ruling, in a case brought by the NAACP, overturning an Oklahoma state law that made it a misdemeanor to educate black and white students together. The Court required Oklahoma to provide equal instruction for blacks and whites and to admit qualified black students to its hitherto all-white law school.

Six Day War (1967) A short war between Israel and Egypt, Jordan, and Syria, in which Israel seized and occupied the Sinai Peninsula and Gaza Strip (formerly under Egyptian control), East Jerusalem and the West Bank (from Jordan), and the Golan Heights (from Syria).

Social Security privatization (2005) The Bush administration's effort to replace Social Security with personal investment accounts that would allow Americans to divert payroll taxes to mutual funds, stocks, and bonds. The plan met with fierce, bipartisan resistance and failed.

Southern Christian Leadership Conference (SCLC) An umbrella organization of African American religious leaders who advocated nonviolent resistance to racial inequality. The SCLC was founded by the Reverend Martin Luther King, Jr., and others in 1957.

stagflation An economic condition in which persistent inflation is coupled with stagnant economic growth and high unemployment. It was first named during the 1973–75 recession.

States' Rights Democratic Party A political party, popularly known as the Dixiecrats, composed of southerners who broke from the Democratic Party in 1948 over its civil rights platform. It named Governor Strom Thurmond (D-SC) as a candidate for the presidency in 1948.

Stonewall riots (1969) On June 28, 1969, police raided the Stonewall Inn, a gay bar in New York's Greenwich Village neighborhood, arresting many of its patrons. Afterward thousands of gay men took to the streets protesting and clashing with the police over a three-day period. The protests marked the rise of a new, assertive gay liberation movement.

STOP ERA (1972) The movement to pressure states against the ratification of the Equal Rights Amendment. It was founded by antifeminist Phyllis Schlafly, who argued that the ERA would undermine women's favored positions, take away the protection of men, and force women to fight in wars.

Strategic Defense Initiative (SDI) The Reagan administration's proposed system to repel incoming nuclear missiles. Announced in 1983, it would involve the creation of a "shield" in outer space of X-rays and lasers. Skeptics dubbed it "Star Wars" after the popular science fiction movie. Congress and the first Bush administration cut funds for the expensive but unsuccessful program in the early 1990s, and the Clinton administration dismantled it in 1993.

Strike Wave of 1945–46 A series of massive labor strikes that swept the nation after the Second World War and affected nearly every sector of the U.S. economy. In the year after the war, there were 4,630 work stoppages involving more than five million workers.

Student Non-Violent Coordinating Committee (SNCC). Founded in 1960 with the assistance of longtime civil rights activist Ella Baker, SNCC engaged in community organizing, education, and voter registration campaigns in the rural

South. The target of white reprisals and official indifference, SNCC grew more militant, and in 1966 the organization rejected its commitment to nonviolence and racial integration.

Students for a Democratic Society (SDS) The leading New Left organization, SDS was founded at the University of Michigan in 1960. At its peak, it had about 100,000 members throughout the United States. Decentralized, its chapters fought for freedom of speech and civil rights, worked to mobilize the poor, opposed the Vietnam War, and organized mass protests on hundreds of campuses. By 1969, SDS had spilt into rival factions, including the militant Weather Underground, which advocated armed revolution.

***Swann v. Charlotte-Mecklenburg Board of Education* (1971)** A Supreme Court decision that upheld a district-wide school desegregation program in Charlotte, North Carolina, approving busing to achieve racial balance in public schools.

Taft-Hartley Act (1947) Restricted the activities and power of labor unions. The act gave the president the authority to intervene in strikes to protect national security and allowed states to pass "right to work" laws. It required all union leaders to sign affidavits stating they were not Communist Party members, forbade "secondary strikes," and limited unions' use of the closed shop. President Truman vetoed the act, but the Dixie-GOP coalition overrode his veto 68 to 25 in the Senate and 331 to 83 in the House.

Tet Offensive (1968) With the goal of humiliating the South Vietnamese and the American governments in order to restart negotiations, Vietcong launched surprise attacks on five of the six largest cities in South Vietnam and thirty-six provincial capitals during Tet, the Vietnamese New Year. Among the targets was the U.S. embassy in Saigon. American and South Vietnamese forces quickly repelled most of the attacks, but news coverage of the offensive contributed to declining American support for the war.

Truman Doctrine (1947) Before a joint session of Congress, President Truman established that the United States would provide political, military, and economic assistance to all democratic nations that were under threat from external or internal authoritarian forces.

United Electrical Workers (UE) The largest left-led union in the postwar period, the UE represented workers in major electronics companies including General Electric and Westinghouse. A special target of the House Un-American Activities Committee, its membership plummeted after passage of the Taft-Hartley Act because so many members were suspected to be Communists or would not sign loyalty oaths.

United Farm Workers Originally named the National Farmworkers Association, this organization was founded in California in 1962 by Cesar Chavez and Dolores Huerta to advocate for better wages and working conditions among the mostly Hispanic laborers who harvested fruit and vegetables.

United Nations Chartered in 1945, the UN is an international agency charged with preventing war, protecting human rights and equality, and promoting economic development and social progress. All UN member nations participate in the General Assembly, while the Security Council members include five permanent members (United States, Soviet Union, Britain, France, and China) and six members selected to two-year terms.

USA PATRIOT Act (2001) Expanded the power of intelligence agencies to investigate suspected terrorists, including through the interception of electronic communications by both American citizens and suspected terrorists overseas. Its name is an acronym for the United and Strengthening America by Providing Appropriate Tools Required to Intercept and Obstruct Terrorism Act. It was signed by President Bush shortly after the 9/11 attacks on New York City and the Pentagon.

Viet Cong The guerrilla military force in South Vietnam that emerged in the late 1950s in opposition to the American-backed dictator Ngo Dinh Diem and that led resistance to the South Vietnamese regime and to the United States during the Vietnam War.

Vietnamization President Nixon's plan to gradually reduce American ground troops in Vietnam beginning in 1969 and to shift the burden of the Vietnam War to the army of South Vietnam.

Voting Rights Act (1965) Prohibited racial discrimination in voting. By enforcing voting rights guaranteed by the Fourteenth and Fifteenth Amendments, this federal act enabled the mass enfranchisement of racial minorities, particularly in the South, and dramatically increased the number of African American elected officials.

War on Poverty Announced by President Johnson in January 1964, this series of antipoverty initiatives focused on job training (the Job Corps), education, and community empowerment. The Economic Opportunity Act created the Community Action program, the Elementary and Secondary Education Act (ESEA) provided unprecedented levels of federal funding for public schools, and Medicare and Medicaid provided health insurance to the elderly and poor.

Watergate (1972) Five men with surveillance equipment were arrested outside the office of DNC chairman Lawrence O'Brien in Washington's Watergate Hotel. A subsequent investigation of the break-in by Bob Woodward and Carl Bernstein, reporters for the *Washington Post*, revealed this and other illegal activities of the Nixon reelection campaign, leading to the impeachment and resignation of the president in 1974.

Watergate babies Moderate Democrats, among them Senator Gary Hart (D-CO), who successfully challenged Republicans on an anticorruption platform during the 1974 midterm elections, after President Richard Nixon resigned.

Weather Underground A small revolutionary group that split off from Students for a Democratic Society, formed secret cells, and used violence, including planting bombs at the Pentagon, police stations, and other high-profile targets, to gain the public's attention and spur a mass uprising that would destabilize the United States. In March 1970 three members of the Weather Underground accidently blew up a Greenwich Village townhouse while creating a bomb.

Whip Inflation Now (WIN) (1974) President Gerald Ford's attempt to control inflation through a grassroots effort involving voluntary anti-inflationary initiatives.

White House Office of Faith-Based and Community Initiatives. Created by President George W. Bush by executive order in January 2001, this office oversaw one of the administration's signature initiatives: channeling funds to churches and religious nonprofits to deliver social services and promote pro-marriage and family preservation programs.

Yippies Members of the loosely organized Youth International Party, a group of counterculturalists founded by Abbie Hoffman. Yippies staged theatrical protests in New York and San Francisco, celebrating nonconformity and sexual freedom and challenging Wall Street brokers, the police, and the military.

Yom Kippur War (1973) A three-week war that began on the Jewish holiday of Yom Kippur, when Egyptian and Syrian forces, with support from other Arab nations, attacked Israel to regain territory lost in 1967. With substantial support from the United States, Israel turned back the attacks. The war inflamed tensions between the United States and the So-

Glossary   **G15**

viet Union and further destabilized the Middle East.

Young Americans for Freedom (YAF) Founded after a 1960 gathering at conservative journalist William F. Buckley, Jr.'s family estate in Connecticut, YAF mobilized college students around the principles of economic liberty, anti-Communism, and traditional morality. By the end of the 1960s, YAF had about 70,000 members.

APPENDIX

THE DECLARATION OF INDEPENDENCE (1776)

When in the course of human events, it becomes necessary for one people to dissolve the political bands which have connected them with another, and to assume among the Powers of the earth, the separate and equal station to which the Laws of Nature and of Nature's God entitle them, a decent respect to the opinions of mankind requires that they should declare the causes which impel them to the separation.

We hold these truths to be self-evident, that all men are created equal, that they are endowed by their Creator with certain unalienable rights, that among these are Life, Liberty, and the pursuit of Happiness. That to secure these rights, Governments are instituted among Men, deriving their just powers from the consent of the governed. That whenever any Form of Government becomes destructive of these ends, it is the Right of the People to alter or to abolish it, and to institute new Government, laying its foundation on such principles and organizing its powers in such form, as to them shall seem most likely to effect their Safety and Happiness. Prudence, indeed, will dictate that Governments long established should not be changed for light and transient causes; and accordingly all experience hath shown, that mankind are more disposed to suffer, while evils are sufferable, than to right themselves by abolishing the forms to which they are accustomed. But when a long train of abuses and usurpations, pursuing invariably the same Object evinces a design to reduce them under absolute Despotism, it is their right, it is their duty, to throw off such Government, and to provide new Guards for their future security.—Such has been the patient sufferance of these Colonies; and such is now the necessity which constrains them to alter their former Systems of Government. The history of the present King of Great Britain is a history of repeated injuries and usurpations, all having in direct object the establishment of an absolute Tyranny over these States. To prove this, let Facts be submitted to a candid world.

He has refused his Assent to Laws, the most wholesome and necessary for the public good.

He has forbidden his Governors to pass Laws of immediate and pressing importance, unless suspended in their operation till his Assent should be obtained; and when so suspended, he has utterly neglected to attend to them.

He has refused to pass other Laws for the accommodation of large districts of people, unless those people would relinquish the right of Representation in the Legislature, a right inestimable to them and formidable to tyrants only.

He has called together legislative bodies at places unusual, uncomfortable, and distant from the depository of their public Records, for the sole purpose of fatiguing them into compliance with his measures.

He has dissolved Representative Houses repeatedly, for opposing with manly firmness his invasions on the rights of the people.

He has refused for a long time, after such dissolutions, to cause others to be elected; whereby the Legislative powers, incapable of Annihilation, have returned to the People at large for their exercise; the State remaining in the mean time exposed to all dangers of invasion from without, and convulsions within.

He has endeavoured to prevent the population of these States; for that purpose obstructing the Laws of Naturalization of Foreigners; refusing to pass others to encourage their migrations hither, and raising the conditions of new Appropriations of Lands.

He has obstructed the Administration of Justice, by refusing his Assent to Laws for establishing Judiciary powers.

He has made Judges dependent on his Will alone, for the tenure of their offices, and the amount and payment of their salaries.

He has erected a multitude of New Offices, and sent hither swarms of Officers to harass our People, and eat out their substance.

He has kept among us, in times of peace, Standing Armies without the Consent of our legislatures.

He has affected to render the Military independent of and superior to the Civil Power.

He has combined with others to subject us to a jurisdiction foreign to our constitution, and unacknowledged by our laws; giving his Assent to their Acts of pretended Legislation:

For quartering large bodies of armed troops among us:

For protecting them, by a mock Trial, from Punishment for any Murders which they should commit on the Inhabitants of these States:

For cutting off our Trade with all parts of the world:

For imposing taxes on us without our Consent:

For depriving us of many cases, of the benefits of Trial by jury:

For transporting us beyond Seas to be tried for pretended offences:

For abolishing the free System of English Laws in a neighbouring Province, establishing therein an Arbitrary government, and enlarging its Boundaries so as to render it at once an example and fit instrument for introducing the same absolute rule into these Colonies:

For taking away our Charters, abolishing our most valuable Laws, and altering fundamentally the Forms of our Governments:

For suspending our own Legislatures, and declaring themselves invested with Power to legislate for us in all cases whatsoever.

He has abdicated Government here, by declaring us out of his Protection and waging War against us.

He has plundered our seas, ravaged our Coasts, burnt our towns, and destroyed the lives of our people.

He is at this time transporting large armies of foreign mercenaries to compleat the works of death, desolation, and tyranny, already begun with circumstances of Cruelty & perfidy scarcely paralleled in the most barbarous ages, and totally unworthy the Head of a civilized nation.

He has constrained our fellow Citizens taken Captive on the high Seas to bear Arms against their Country, to become the executioners of their friends and Brethren, or to fall themselves by their Hands.

He has excited domestic insurrections amongst us, and has endeavoured to bring on the inhabitants of our frontiers, the merciless Indian Savages, whose known rule of warfare, is an undistinguished destruction of all ages, sexes, and conditions.

In every stage of these Oppressions We have Petitioned for Redress in the most humble terms: Our repeated Petitions have been answered only by repeated injury. A Prince, whose character is thus marked by every act which may define a Tyrant, is unfit to be the ruler of a free people.

Nor have We been wanting in attention to our British brethren. We have warned them from time to time of attempts by their legislature to extend an unwarrantable jurisdiction over us. We have reminded them of the circumstances of our emigration and settlement here. We have appealed to their native justice and magnanimity, and we have conjured them by the ties of our common kindred to disavow these usurpations, which, would inevitably interrupt our connections and correspondence. They too must have been deaf to the voice of justice and of consanguinity. We must, therefore, acquiesce in the necessity, which denounces our Separation, and hold them, as we hold the rest of mankind, Enemies in War, in Peace Friends.

WE, THEREFORE, the Representatives of the UNITED STATES OF AMERICA, in General Congress, Assembled, appealing to the Supreme Judge of the world for the rectitude of our intentions, do, in the Name, and by Authority of the good People of these Colonies, solemnly publish and declare, That these United Colonies are, and of Right ought to be FREE AND INDEPENDENT STATES; that they are Absolved from all Allegiance to the British Crown, and that all political connection between them and the State of Great Britain, is and ought to be totally dissolved; and that as Free and Independent States, they have full Power to levy War, conclude Peace, contract Alliances, establish Commerce, and to do all other Acts and Things which Independent States may of right do. And for the support of this Declaration, with a firm reliance on the Protection of Divine Providence, we mutually pledge to each other our Lives, our Fortunes, and our sacred Honor.

The foregoing Declaration was, by order of Congress, engrossed, and signed by the following members:

John Hancock

NEW HAMPSHIRE
Josiah Bartlett
William Whipple
Matthew Thornton

MASSACHUSETTS BAY
Samuel Adams
John Adams
Robert Treat Paine
Elbridge Gerry

RHODE ISLAND
Stephen Hopkins
William Ellery

CONNECTICUT
Roger Sherman
Samuel Huntington
William Williams
Oliver Wolcott

NEW YORK
William Floyd
Philip Livingston
Francis Lewis
Lewis Morris

NEW JERSEY
Richard Stockton
John Witherspoon
Francis Hopkinson
John Hart
Abraham Clark

PENNSYLVANIA
Robert Morris
Benjamin Rush
Benjamin Franklin
John Morton
George Clymer
James Smith
George Taylor
James Wilson
George Ross

DELAWARE
Caesar Rodney
George Read
Thomas M'Kean

MARYLAND
Samuel Chase
William Paca
Thomas Stone
Charles Carroll, of Carrollton

VIRGINIA
George Wythe
Richard Henry Lee
Thomas Jefferson
Benjamin Harrison
Thomas Nelson, Jr.
Francis Lightfoot Lee
Carter Braxton

NORTH CAROLINA
William Hooper
Joseph Hewes
John Penn

SOUTH CAROLINA
Edward Rutledge
Thomas Heyward, Jr.
Thomas Lynch, Jr.
Arthur Middleton

GEORGIA
Button Gwinnett
Lyman Hall
George Walton

Resolved, That copies of the Declaration be sent to the several assemblies, conventions, and committees, or councils of safety, and to the several commanding officers of the continental troops; that it be proclaimed in each of the United States, at the head of the army.

THE CONSTITUTION OF THE UNITED STATES (1787)

We the People of the United States, in order to form a more perfect Union, establish Justice, insure domestic Tranquility, provide for the common defence, promote the general Welfare, and secure the Blessings of Liberty to ourselves and our Posterity, do ordain and establish this Constitution for the United States of America.

ARTICLE. I.

SECTION. 1. All legislative Powers herein granted shall be vested in a Congress of the United States, which shall consist of a Senate and House of Representatives.

SECTION. 2. The House of Representatives shall be composed of Members chosen every second Year by the People of the several States, and the Electors in each State shall have the Qualifications requisite for Electors of the most numerous Branch of the State Legislature.

No Person shall be a Representative who shall not have attained to the Age of twenty five Years, and been seven Years a Citizen of the United States, and who shall not, when elected, be an Inhabitant of that State in which he shall be chosen.

Representatives and direct Taxes shall be apportioned among the several States which may be included within this Union, according to their respective Numbers, which shall be determined by adding to the whole Number of free Persons, including those bound to Service for a Term of Years, and excluding Indians not taxed, three fifths of all other Persons. The actual Enumeration shall be made within three Years after the first Meeting of the Congress of the United States, and within every subsequent Term of ten Years, in such Manner as they shall by Law direct. The Number of Representatives shall not exceed one for every thirty Thousand, but each State shall have at Least one Representative; and until such enumeration shall be made, the State of New Hampshire shall be entitled to chuse three, Massachusetts eight, Rhode-Island and Providence Plantations one, Connecticut five, New York six, New Jersey four, Pennsylvania eight, Delaware one, Maryland six, Virginia ten, North Carolina five, South Carolina five, and Georgia three.

When vacancies happen in the Representation from any state, the Executive Authority thereof shall issue Writs of Election to fill such Vacancies.

The House of Representatives shall chuse their Speaker and other Officers; and shall have the sole Power of Impeachment.

SECTION. 3. The Senate of the United States shall be composed of two Senators from each State, chosen by the legislature thereof, for six Years; and each Senator shall have one Vote.

Immediately after they shall be assembled in Consequence of the first Election, they shall be divided as equally as may be into three Classes. The Seats of the Senators of the first Class shall be vacated at the Expiration of the second Year, of the second Class at the Expiration of the fourth Year, and of the third Class at the Expiration of the sixth Year, so that one third may be chosen every second Year; and if Vacancies happen by Resignation, or otherwise, during the Recess of the Legislature of any State, the Executive thereof may make temporary Appointments until the next Meeting of the Legislature, which shall then fill such Vacancies.

No Person shall be a Senator who shall not have attained to the Age of thirty Years, and been nine Years a Citizen of the United States, and who shall not, when elected, be an Inhabitant of that State for which he shall be chosen.

The Vice President of the United States shall be President of the Senate, but shall have no Vote, unless they be equally divided.

The Senate shall chuse their other Officers, and also a President pro tempore, in the Absence of the Vice President, or when he shall exercise the Office of President of the United States.

The Senate shall have the sole Power to try all Impeachments. When sitting for that Purpose, they shall be on Oath or Affirmation. When the President of the United States is tried, the Chief Justice shall preside: And no Person shall be convicted without the Concurrence of two thirds of the Members present.

Judgment in Cases of Impeachment shall not extend further than to removal from Office, and disqualification to hold and enjoy any Office of honor, Trust or Profit under the United States: but the Party convicted shall nevertheless be liable and subject to Indictment, Trial, Judgment and Punishment, according to Law.

SECTION. 4. The Times, Places and Manner of holding Elections for Senators and Representatives, shall be prescribed in each State by the Legislature thereof; but the Congress may at any time by Law make or alter such Regulations, except as to the Places of chusing Senators.

The Congress shall assemble at least once in every Year, and such Meeting shall be on the first Monday in December, unless they shall by Law appoint a different Day.

SECTION. 5. Each House shall be the Judge of the Elections, Returns and Qualifications of its own Members, and a Majority of each shall constitute a Quorum to do Business; but a smaller Number may adjourn from day to day, and may be authorized to compel the Attendance of absent Members, in such Manner, and under such Penalties as each House may provide.

Each House may determine the Rules of its Proceedings, punish its Members for disorderly Behaviour, and, with the Concurrence of two thirds, expel a Member.

Each House shall keep a Journal of its Proceedings, and from time to time publish the same, excepting such Parts as may in their Judgment require Secrecy; and the Yeas and Nays of the Members of either House on any question shall, at the Desire of one fifth of those Present, be entered on the Journal.

Neither House, during the Session of Congress, shall, without the Consent of the other, adjourn for more than three days, not to any other Place than that in which the two Houses shall be sitting.

SECTION. 6. The Senators and Representatives shall receive a Compensation for their Services, to be ascertained by Law, and paid out of the Treasury of the United States. They shall in all Cases, except Treason, Felony and Breach of the Peace, be privileged from Arrest during their Attendance at the Session of their respective Houses, and in going to and returning from the same; and for any Speech or Debate in either House, they shall not be questioned in any other Place.

No Senator or Representative shall, during the Time for which he was elected, be appointed to any civil Office under the Authority of the United States, which shall have been created, or the Emoluments whereof shall have been encreased during such time; and no Person holding any Office under the United States, shall be a Member of either House during his Continuance in Office.

SECTION. 7. All Bills for raising Revenue shall originate in the House of Representatives; but the Senate may propose or concur with Amendments as on other Bills.

Every Bill which shall have passed the House of Representatives and the Senate shall, before it become a Law, be presented to the President of the United States; If he approve he shall sign it, but if not he shall return it, with his Objections to that House in which it shall have originated, who shall enter the Objections at large on their Journal, and proceed to reconsider it. If after such Reconsideration two thirds of that House shall agree to pass the Bill, it shall be sent, together with the Objections, to the other House, by which it shall likewise be reconsidered, and if approved by two thirds of that House, it shall become a Law. But in all such Cases the Votes of both Houses shall be determined by Yeas and Nays, and the Names of the Persons voting for and against the Bill shall be entered on the Journal of each House respectively. If any Bill shall not be returned by the President within ten Days (Sundays excepted) after it shall have been presented to him, the Same shall be a Law, in like Manner as if he had signed it, unless the Congress by their Adjournment prevent its Return, in which Case it shall not be a Law.

Every Order, Resolution, or Vote to which the Concurrence of the Senate and House of Representatives may be necessary (except on a question of Adjournment) shall be presented to the President of the United States; and before the Same shall take Effect, shall be approved by him, or being disapproved by him, shall be repassed by two thirds of the Senate and House of Representatives, according to the Rules and Limitations prescribed in the Case of a Bill.

SECTION. 8. The Congress shall have Power To lay and collect Taxes, Duties, Imposts and Excises, to pay the Debts and provide for the common Defence and general Welfare of the United States; but all Duties, Imposts and Excises shall be uniform throughout the United States;

To borrow Money on the credit of the United States;

To regulate Commerce with foreign Nations, and among the several States, and with the Indian Tribes;

To establish an uniform Rule of Naturalization, and uniform Laws on the subject of Bankruptcies throughout the United States;

To coin Money, regulate the Value thereof, and of foreign Coin, and fix the Standard of Weights and Measures;

To provide for the Punishment of counterfeiting the Securities and current Coin of the United States;

To establish Post Offices and Post Roads;

To promote the Progress of Science and useful Arts, by securing for limited Times to Authors and Inventors the exclusive Right to their respective Writings and Discoveries;

To constitute Tribunals inferior to the supreme Court;

To define and punish Piracies and Felonies committed on the high Seas, and Offences against the Law of Nations;

To declare War, grant Letters of Marque and Reprisal, and make Rules concerning Captures on Land and Water;

To raise and support Armies, but no Appropriation of Money to that Use shall be for a longer Term than two Years;

To provide and maintain a Navy;

To make Rules for the Government and Regulation of the land and naval Forces;

To provide for calling forth the Militia to execute the Laws of the Union, suppress Insurrections and repel Invasions;

To provide for organizing, arming, and disciplining, the Militia, and for governing such Part of them as may be employed in the Service of the United States, reserving to the States respectively, the Appointment of the Officers, and the Authority of training the Militia according to the discipline prescribed by Congress;

To exercise exclusive Legislation in all Cases whatsoever, over such District (not exceeding ten Miles square) as may, by Cession of Particular States, and the Acceptance of

Congress, become the Seat of the Government of the United States, and to exercise like Authority over all Places purchased by the Consent of the Legislature of the State in which the Same shall be, for the Erection of Forts, Magazines, Arsenals, dock-Yards, and other needful Buildings;—And

To make all Laws which shall be necessary and proper for carrying into Execution the foregoing Powers, and all other Powers vested by this Constitution in the Government of the United States, or in any Department or Officer thereof.

SECTION. 9. The Migration or Importation of such Persons as any of the States now existing shall think proper to admit, shall not be prohibited by the Congress prior to the Year one thousand eight hundred and eight, but a Tax or duty may be imposed on such Importation, not exceeding ten dollars for each Person.

The Privilege of the Writ of Habeas Corpus shall not be suspended, unless when in Cases of Rebellion or Invasion the public Safety may require it.

No Bill of Attainder or ex post facto Law shall be passed.

No Capitation, or other direct, Tax shall be laid, unless in Proportion to the Census or Enumeration herein before directed to be taken.

No Tax or Duty shall be laid on Articles exported from any State.

No Preference shall be given by any Regulation of Commerce or Revenue to the Ports of one State over those of another: nor shall Vessels bound to, or from, one State, be obliged to enter, clear, or pay Duties in another.

No Money shall be drawn from the Treasury, but in Consequence of Appropriations made by Law; and a regular Statement and Account of the Receipts and Expenditures of all public Money shall be published from time to time.

No Title of Nobility shall be granted by the United States: And no Person holding any Office of Profit or Trust under them, shall, without the Consent of the Congress, accept of any present, Emolument, Office, or Title, of any kind whatever, from any King, Prince, or foreign State.

SECTION. 10. No State shall enter into any Treaty, Alliance, or Confederation; grant Letters of Marque and Reprisal; coin Money; emit Bills of Credit; make any Thing but gold and silver Coin a Tender in Payment of Debts; pass any Bill of Attainder, ex post facto Law, or Law impairing the Obligation of Contracts, or grant any Title of Nobility.

No State shall, without the Consent of the Congress, lay any Imposts or Duties on Imports or Exports, except what may be absolutely necessary for executing its inspection Laws: and the net Produce of all Duties and Imposts, laid by any State on Imports or Exports, shall be for the Use of the Treasury of the United States; and all such Laws shall be subject to the Revision and Controul of the Congress.

No State shall, without the Consent of Congress, lay any Duty of Tonnage, keep Troops, or Ships of War in time of Peace, enter into any Agreement or Compact with another State, or with a foreign Power, or engage in War, unless actually invaded, or in such imminent Danger as will not admit of delay.

ARTICLE. II.

SECTION. 1. The executive Power shall be vested in a President of the United States of America. He shall hold his Office during the term of four Years, and, together with the Vice President, chosen for the same Term, be elected, as follows:

Each State shall appoint, in such Manner as the Legislature thereof may direct, a Number of Electors, equal to the whole Number of Senators and Representatives to which the

State may be entitled in the Congress: but no Senator or Representative, or Person holding an Office of Trust or Profit under the United States, shall be appointed an Elector.

The Electors shall meet in their respective States, and vote by Ballot for two Persons, of whom one at least shall not be an Inhabitant of the same State with themselves. And they shall make a List of all the Persons voted for, and of the Number of Votes for each; which List they shall sign and certify, and transmit sealed to the Seat of the Government of the United States, directed to the President of the Senate. The President of the Senate shall, in the Presence of the Senate and House of Representatives, open all the Certificates, and the Votes shall then be counted. The Person having the greatest Number of Votes shall be the President, if such Number be a Majority of the whole Number of Electors appointed; and if there be more than one who have such Majority, and have an equal Number of Votes, then the House of Representatives shall immediately chuse by Ballot one of them for President; and if no Person have a Majority, then from the five highest on the List the said House shall in like Manner chuse the President. But in chusing the President, the Votes shall be taken by States, the Representation from each State having one Vote; A quorum for this Purpose shall consist of a Member or Members from two thirds of the States, and a Majority of all the States shall be necessary to a Choice. In every Case, after the Choice of the President, the Person having the greatest Number of Votes of the Electors shall be the Vice President. But if there should remain two or more who have equal Votes, the Senate shall chuse from them by Ballot the Vice President.

The Congress may determine the Time of chusing the Electors, and the Day on which they shall give their Votes; which Day shall be the same throughout the United States.

No Person except a natural born Citizen, or a Citizen of the United States, at the time of the Adoption of this Constitution, shall be eligible to the Office of President; neither shall any Person be eligible to that Office who shall not have attained to the Age of thirty five Years, and been fourteen Years a Resident within the United States.

In Case of the Removal of the President from Office, or of his Death, Resignation, or Inability to discharge the Powers and Duties of the said Office, the Same shall devolve on the Vice President, and the Congress may by Law provide for the Case of Removal, Death, Resignation or Inability, both of the President and Vice President, declaring what Officer shall then act as President, and such Officer shall act accordingly, until the Disability be removed, or a President shall be elected.

The President shall, at stated Times, receive for his Services, a Compensation, which shall neither be encreased or diminished during the Period for which he shall have been elected, and he shall not receive within that Period any other Emolument from the United States, or any of them.

Before he enters on the Execution of his Office, he shall take the following Oath or Affirmation:—"I do solemnly swear (or affirm) that I will faithfully execute the Office of President of the United States, and will to the best of my Ability, preserve, protect and defend the Constitution of the United States."

SECTION. 2. The President shall be Commander in Chief of the Army and Navy of the United States, and of the Militia of the several States, when called into the actual Service of the United States; he may require the Opinion, in writing, of the principal Officer in each of the executive Departments, upon any Subject relating to the Duties of their respective Offices, and he shall have Power to grant Reprieves and Pardons for Offences against the United States, except in Cases of Impeachment.

He shall have Power, by and with the Advice and Consent of the Senate, to make Treaties, provided two thirds of the Senators present concur; and he shall nominate, and by and with the Advice and Consent of the Senate, shall appoint Ambassadors, other public Ministers and Consuls, Judges of the supreme Court, and all other Officers of the United States, whose Appointments are not herein otherwise provided for, and which shall be established by Law; but the Congress may by Law vest the Appointment of such inferior Officers, as they think proper, in the President alone, in the Courts of Law, or in the Heads of Departments.

The President shall have Power to fill up all Vacancies that may happen during the Recess of the Senate, by granting Commissions which shall expire at the End of their next Session.

SECTION. 3. He shall from time to time give to the Congress Information of the State of the Union, and recommend to their Consideration such Measures as he shall judge necessary and expedient; he may, on extraordinary Occasions, convene both Houses, or either of them, and in Case of Disagreement between them, with Respect to the Time of Adjournment, he may adjourn them to such Time as he shall think proper; he shall receive Ambassadors and other public Ministers; he shall take Care that the Laws be faithfully executed, and shall Commission all the Officers of the United States.

SECTION. 4. The President, Vice President and all civil Officers of the United States, shall be removed from Office on Impeachment for, and Conviction of, Treason, Bribery, or other high Crimes and Misdemeanors.

ARTICLE. III.

SECTION. 1. The judicial Power of the United States, shall be vested in one supreme Court, and in such inferior Courts as the Congress may from time to time ordain and establish. The Judges, both of the supreme and inferior Courts, shall hold their Offices during good Behavior, and shall, at stated Times, receive for their Services, a Compensation, which shall not be diminished during their Continuance in Office.

SECTION. 2. The judicial Power shall extend to all Cases, in Law and Equity, arising under this Constitution, the Laws of the United States, and Treaties made, or which shall be made, under their Authority;—to all Cases affecting Ambassadors, other public Ministers and Consuls;—to all Cases of admiralty and maritime Jurisdiction;—the Controversies to which the United States shall be a Party;—to Controversies between two or more States;—between a State and Citizens of another State;—between Citizens of different States;—between Citizens of the same State claiming Lands under Grants of different States, and between a State, or the Citizens thereof, and foreign States, Citizens or Subjects.

In all cases affecting Ambassadors, other public Ministers and Consuls, and those in which a State shall be Party, the supreme Court shall have original Jurisdiction. In all the other Cases before mentioned, the supreme Court shall have appellate Jurisdiction, both as to Law and Fact, with such Exceptions, and under such Regulations as the Congress shall make.

The Trial of all Crimes, except in Cases of Impeachment, shall be by Jury; and such Trial shall be held in the State where the said Crimes shall have been committed; but when not committed within any State, the Trial shall be at such Place or Places as the Congress may by Law have directed.

SECTION. 3. Treason against the United States, shall consist only in levying War against them, or in adhering to their Enemies, giving them Aid and Comfort. No Person shall be convicted of Treason unless on the Testimony of two Witnesses to the same overt Act, or on Confession in open Court.

The Congress shall have Power to declare the Punishment of Treason, but no Attainder of Treason shall work Corruption of Blood, or Forfeiture except during the Life of the Person attainted.

ARTICLE. IV.

SECTION. 1. Full Faith and Credit shall be given in each State to the public Acts, Records, and judicial Proceedings of every other State. And the Congress may by general Laws prescribe the Manner in which such Acts, Records and Proceedings shall be proved, and the Effect thereof.

SECTION. 2. The Citizens of each State shall be entitled to all Privileges and Immunities of Citizens in the several States.

A Person charged in any State with Treason, Felony, or other Crime, who shall flee from Justice, and be found in another State, shall on Demand of the executive Authority of the State from which he fled, be delivered up, to be removed to the State having Jurisdiction of the Crime.

No Person held to Service or Labour in one State, under the Laws thereof, escaping into another, shall, in Consequence of any Law or Regulation therein, be discharged from such Service or Labour, but shall be delivered up on Claim of the Party to whom such Service or Labour may be due.

SECTION. 3. New States may be admitted by the Congress into this Union; but no new State shall be formed or erected within the Jurisdiction of any other State; nor any State be formed by the Junction of two or more States, or Parts of States, without the consent of the Legislatures of the States concerned as well as of the Congress.

The Congress shall have Power to dispose of and make all needful Rules and Regulations respecting the Territory or other Property belonging to the United States; and nothing in this Constitution shall be so construed as to Prejudice any Claims of the United States, or of any particular States.

SECTION. 4. The United States shall guarantee to every State in this Union a Republican Form of Government, and shall protect each of them against Invasion; and on Application of the Legislature, or of the Executive (when the Legislature cannot be convened) against domestic Violence.

ARTICLE. V.

The Congress, whenever two thirds of both Houses shall deem it necessary, shall propose Amendments to this Constitution, or, on the Application of the Legislatures of two thirds of the several States, shall call a Convention for proposing Amendments, which, in either Case, shall be valid to all Intents and Purposes, as Part of this Constitution, when ratified by the Legislatures of three fourths of the several States, or by Conventions in three fourths thereof, as the one or the other Mode of Ratification may be proposed by the Congress; Provided that no Amendment which may be made prior to the Year One thousand eight hundred and eight shall in any Manner affect the first and fourth Clauses in the Ninth Section of the first Article; and that no State, without its Consent, shall be deprived of its equal Suffrage in the Senate.

ARTICLE. VI.

All Debts contracted and Engagements entered into, before the Adoption of this Constitution, shall be as valid against the United States under this Constitution, as under the Confederation.

This Constitution, and the Laws of the United States which shall be made in Pursuance thereof; and all Treaties made, or which shall be made, under the Authority of the United States, shall be the supreme Law of the Land; and the Judges in every State shall be bound thereby, any Thing in the Constitution or Laws of any State to the Contrary notwithstanding.

The Senators and Representatives before mentioned, and the Members of the several State Legislatures, and all executive and judicial Officers, both of the United States and of the several States, shall be bound by Oath or Affirmation, to support this Constitution; but no religious Test shall ever be required as a Qualification to any Office or public Trust under the United States.

ARTICLE. VII.

The Ratification of the Conventions of nine States, shall be sufficient for the Establishment of this Constitution between the States so ratifying the Same.

Done in Convention by the Unanimous Consent of the States present the Seventeenth Day of September in the Year of our Lord one thousand seven hundred and Eighty seven and of the Independence of the United States of America the Twelfth. In witness thereof We have hereunto subscribed our Names,

Go. *WASHINGTON*—Presd^t.
and deputy from Virginia

NEW HAMPSHIRE
John Langdon
Nicholas Gilman

MASSACHUSETTS
Nathaniel Gorham
Rufus King

CONNECTICUT
Wm Sam^1 Johnson
Roger Sherman

NEW YORK
Alexander Hamilton

NEW JERSEY
Wil: Livingston
David A. Brearley
Wm Paterson
Jona: Dayton

PENNSYLVANIA
B Franklin
Thomas Mifflin
Robt Morris
Geo. Clymer
Thos FitzSimons
Jared Ingersoll
James Wilson
Gouv Morris

DELAWARE
Geo: Read
Gunning Bedford jun
John Dickinson
Richard Bassett
Jaco: Broom

MARYLAND
James McHenry
Dan of St Thos Jenifer
Dan^1 Carroll

VIRGINIA
John Blair—
James Madison Jr.

NORTH CAROLINA
Wm Blount
Richd Dobbs Spaight
Hu Williamson

SOUTH CAROLINA
J. Rutledge
Charles Cotesworth
* Pinckney*
Charles Pinckney
Pierce Butler

GEORGIA
William Few
Abr Baldwin

AMENDMENTS TO THE CONSTITUTION

Articles in addition to, and Amendment of the Constitution of the United States of America, proposed by Congress, and ratified by the Legislatures of the several States, pursuant to the fifth Article of the original Constitution.

AMENDMENT I.*

Congress shall make no law respecting an establishment of religion, or prohibiting the free exercise thereof; or abridging the freedom of speech, or of the press; or the right of the people peaceably to assemble, and to petition the Government for a redress of grievances.

AMENDMENT II.

A well regulated Militia, being necessary to the security of a free State, the right of the people to keep and bear Arms, shall not be infringed.

AMENDMENT III.

No Soldier shall, in time of peace be quartered in any house, without the consent of the Owner, nor in time of war, but in a manner to be prescribed by law.

AMENDMENT IV.

The right of the people to be secure in their persons, houses, papers, and effects, against un-reasonable searches and seizures, shall not be violated, and no Warrants shall issue, but upon probable cause, supported by Oath or affirmation, and particularly describing the place to be searched, and the persons or things to be seized.

AMENDMENT V.

No person shall be held to answer for a capital, or otherwise infamous crime, unless on a presentment or indictment of a Grand Jury, except in cases arising in the land or naval forces, or in the Militia, when in actual service in time of War or public danger; nor shall any person be subject for the same offence to be twice put in jeopardy of life or limb; nor shall be compelled in any criminal case to be a witness against himself, nor be deprived of life, liberty, or property, without due process of law; nor shall private property be taken for public use, without just compensation.

AMENDMENT VI.

In all criminal prosecutions, the accused shall enjoy the right to a speedy and public trial, by an impartial jury of the State and district wherein the crime shall have been committed, which district shall have been previously ascertained by law, and to be informed of the nature and cause of the accusation; to be confronted with the witnesses against him; to have compulsory process for obtaining witnesses in his favor, and to have the Assistance of Counsel for his defence.

AMENDMENT VII.

In Suits at common law, where the value in controversy shall exceed twenty dollars, the right of trial by jury shall be preserved, and no fact tried by a jury, shall be otherwise re-examined in any Court of the United States, than according to the rules of the common law.

*The first ten Amendments (the Bill of Rights) were ratified in 1791.

AMENDMENT VIII.

Excessive bail shall not be required, nor excessive fines imposed, nor cruel and unusual punishments inflicted.

AMENDMENT IX.

The enumeration in the Constitution, of certain rights, shall not be construed to deny or disparage others retained by the people.

AMENDMENT X.

The powers not delegated to the United States by the Constitution, nor prohibited by it to the States, are reserved to the States respectively, or to the people.

AMENDMENT XI.

The Judicial power of the United States shall not be construed to extend to any suit in law or equity, commenced or prosecuted against one of the United States by Citizens of another State, or by Citizens or Subjects of any Foreign State. [January 8, 1798]

AMENDMENT XII.

The Electors shall meet in their respective states, and vote by ballot for President and Vice-President, one of whom, at least, shall not be an inhabitant of the same state with themselves; they shall name in their ballots the person voted for as President, and in distinct ballots the person voted for as Vice-President, and they shall make distinct lists of all persons voted for as President, and of all persons voted for as Vice President, and of the number of votes for each, which lists they shall sign and certify, and transmit sealed to the seat of the government of the United States, directed to the President of the Senate;—The President of the Senate shall, in the presence of the Senate and House of Representatives, open all the certificates and the votes shall then be counted;—The person having the greatest number of votes for President, shall be the President, if such number be a majority of the whole number of Electors appointed; and if no person have such majority, then from the persons having the highest numbers not exceeding three on the list of those voted for as President, the House of Representatives shall choose immediately, by ballot, the President. But in choosing the President, the votes shall be taken by states, the representation from each state having one vote; a quorum for this purpose shall consist of a member or members from two-thirds of the states, and a majority of all the states shall be necessary to a choice. And if the House of Representatives shall not choose a President whenever the right of choice shall devolve upon them, before the fourth day of March next following, then the Vice-President shall act as President, as in the case of the death or other constitutional disability of the President.—The person having the greatest number of votes as Vice-President, shall be the Vice-President, if such number be a majority of the whole number of Electors appointed, and if no person have a majority, then from the two highest numbers on the list, the Senate shall choose the Vice-President; a quorum for the purpose shall consist of two-thirds of the whole number of Senators, and a majority of the whole number shall be necessary to a choice. But no person constitutionally ineligible to the office of President shall be eligible to that of Vice-President of the United States. [September 25, 1804]

AMENDMENT XIII.

SECTION. 1. Neither slavery nor involuntary servitude, except as a punishment for crime whereof the party shall have been duly convicted, shall exist within the United States, or any place subject to their jurisdiction.

SECTION. 2. Congress shall have power to enforce this article by appropriate legislation. [December 18, 1865]

AMENDMENT XIV.

SECTION. 1. All persons born or naturalized in the United States, and subject to the jurisdiction thereof, are citizens of the United States and of the State wherein they reside. No State shall make or enforce any law which shall abridge the privileges or immunities of citizens of the United States; nor shall any State deprive any person of life, liberty, or property, without due process of law; nor deny to any person within its jurisdiction the equal protection of the laws.

SECTION. 2. Representatives shall be apportioned among the several States according to their respective numbers, counting the whole number of persons in each State, excluding Indians not taxed. But when the right to vote at any election for the choice of electors for President and Vice President of the United States, Representatives in Congress, the Executive and Judicial officers of a State, or the members of the Legislature thereof, is denied to any of the male inhabitants of such State, being twenty-one years of age, and citizens of the United States, or in any way abridged, except for participation in rebellion, or other crime, the basis of representation therein shall be reduced in the proportion which the number of such male citizens shall bear to the whole number of male citizens twenty-one years of age in such State.

SECTION. 3. No person shall be a Senator or Representative in Congress, or elector of President and Vice President, or hold any office, civil or military, under the United States, or under any State, who, having previously taken an oath, as a member of Congress, or as an officer of the United States, or as a member of any State legislature, or as an executive or judicial officer of any State, to support the Constitution of the United States, shall have engaged in insurrection or rebellion against the same, or given aid or comfort to the enemies thereof. But Congress may by a vote of two-thirds of each House, remove such disability.

SECTION. 4. The validity of the public debt of the United States, authorized by law, including debts incurred for payment of pensions and bounties for services in suppressing insurrection or rebellion, shall not be questioned. But neither the United States nor any State shall assume or pay any debt or obligation incurred in aid of insurrection or rebellion against the United States, or any claim for the loss or emancipation of any slave; but all such debts, obligations and claims shall be held illegal and void.

SECTION. 5. The Congress shall have power to enforce, by appropriate legislation, the provisions of this article. [July 28, 1868]

AMENDMENT XV.

SECTION. 1. The right of citizens of the United States to vote shall not be denied or abridged by the United States or by any State on account of race, color, or previous condition of servitude—

SECTION. 2. The Congress shall have power to enforce this article by appropriate legislation. [March 30, 1870]

AMENDMENT XVI.

The Congress shall have power to lay and collect taxes on incomes, from whatever source derived, without apportionment among the several States, and without regard to any census or enumeration. [February 25, 1913]

AMENDMENT XVII.

The Senate of the United States shall be composed of two senators from each State, elected by the people thereof, for six years; and each Senator shall have one vote. The electors in each State shall have the qualifications requisite for electors of the most numerous branch of the State legislatures.

When vacancies happen in the representation of any State in the Senate, the executive authority of such State shall issue writs of election to fill such vacancies: *Provided*, That the legislature of any State may empower the executive thereof to make temporary appointments until the people fill the vacancies by election as the legislature may direct.

This amendment shall not be so construed as to affect the election or term of any senator chosen before it becomes valid as part of the Constitution. [May 31, 1913]

AMENDMENT XVIII.

After one year from the ratification of this article, the manufacture, sale, or transportation of intoxicating liquors within, the importation thereof into, or the exportation thereof from the United States and all territory subject to the jurisdiction thereof for beverage purposes is hereby prohibited.

The Congress and the several States shall have concurrent power to enforce this article by appropriate legislation.

This article shall be inoperative unless it shall have been ratified as an amendment to the Constitution by the legislatures of the several States, as provided in the Constitution, within seven years from the date of the submission thereof to the States by Congress. [January 29, 1919]

AMENDMENT XIX.

The right of citizens of the United States to vote shall not be denied or abridged by the United States or by any State on account of sex.

The Congress shall have power by appropriate legislation to enforce the provisions of this article. [August 26, 1920]

AMENDMENT XX.

SECTION. 1. The terms of the President and Vice-President shall end at noon on the twentieth day of January, and the terms of Senators and Representatives at noon on the third day of January, of the years in which such terms would have ended if this article had not been ratified; and the terms of their successors shall then begin.

SECTION. 2. The Congress shall assemble at least once in every year, and such meeting shall begin at noon on the third day of January, unless they shall by law appoint a different day.

SECTION. 3. If, at the time fixed for the beginning of the term of the President, the President-elect shall have died, the Vice-President-elect shall become President. If a President shall not have been chosen before the time fixed for the beginning of his term, or if the President-elect shall have failed to qualify, then the Vice-President-elect shall act as President until a President shall have qualified; and the Congress may by law provide for the case wherein neither a President-elect nor a Vice-President-elect shall have qualified, declaring who shall then act as President, or the manner in which one who is to act shall be selected, and such person shall act accordingly until a President or Vice-President shall have qualified.

SECTION. 4. The Congress may by law provide for the case of the death of any of the persons from whom the House of Representatives may choose a President whenever the right of choice shall have devolved upon them, and for the case of the death of any of the persons from whom the Senate may choose a Vice-President whenever the right of choice shall have devolved upon them.

SECTION. 5. Sections 1 and 2 shall take effect on the 15th day of October following the ratification of this article.

SECTION. 6. This article shall be inoperative unless it shall have been ratified as an amendment to the Constitution by the legislatures of three-fourths of the several States within seven years from the date of its submission. [February 6, 1933]

AMENDMENT XXI.

SECTION. 1. The eighteenth article of amendment to the Constitution of the United States is hereby repealed.

SECTION. 2. The transportation or importation into any State, Territory or possession of the United States for delivery or use therein of intoxicating liquors, in violation of the laws thereof, is hereby prohibited.

SECTION. 3. This article shall be inoperative unless it shall have been ratified as an amendment to the Constitution by convention in the several States, as provided in the Constitution, within seven years from the date of the submission thereof to the States by the Congress. [December 5, 1933]

AMENDMENT XXII.

SECTION. 1. No person shall be elected to the office of the President more than twice, and no person who has held the office of President, or acted as President, for more than two years of a term to which some other person was elected President shall be elected to the office of the President more than once. But this Article shall not apply to any person holding the office of President when this Article was proposed by the Congress, and shall not prevent any person who may be holding the office of President, or acting as President, during the term within which this Article becomes operative from holding the office of President or acting as President during the remainder of such term.

SECTION. 2. This article shall be inoperative unless it shall have been ratified as an amendment to the Constitution by the legislatures of three-fourths of the several States within seven years from the date of its submission to the States by the Congress. [February 27, 1951]

AMENDMENT XXIII.

SECTION. 1. The District constituting the seat of government of the United States shall appoint in such manner as the Congress may direct:

A number of electors of President and Vice-President equal to the whole number of Senators and Representatives in Congress to which the District would be entitled if it were a State, but in no event more than the least populous State; they shall be in addition to those appointed by the States, but they shall be considered, for the purposes of the election of President and Vice-President, to be electors appointed by a State; and they shall meet in the District and perform such duties as provided by the twelfth article of amendment.

SECTION. 2. The Congress shall have the power to enforce this article by appropriate legislation. [March 29, 1961]

AMENDMENT XXIV.

SECTION. 1. The right of citizens of the United States to vote in any primary or other election for President or Vice President, for electors for President or Vice President, or for Senator or

Representative in Congress, shall not be denied or abridged by the United States or any State by reason of failure to pay any poll tax or other tax.

SECTION. 2. The Congress shall have power to enforce this article by appropriate legislation. [January 23, 1964]

AMENDMENT XXV.

SECTION. 1. In case of the removal of the President from office or of his death or resignation, the Vice President shall become President.

SECTION. 2. Whenever there is a vacancy in the office of Vice President, the President shall nominate a Vice President who shall take office upon confirmation by a majority vote of both Houses of Congress.

SECTION. 3. Whenever the President transmits to the President pro tempore of the Senate and the Speaker of the House of Representatives his written declaration that he is unable to discharge the powers and duties of his office, and until he transmits to them a written declaration to the contrary, such powers and duties shall be discharged by the Vice President as Acting President.

SECTION. 4. Whenever the Vice President and a majority of either the principal officers of the executive departments or of such other body as Congress may by law provide, transmit to the President pro tempore of the Senate and the Speaker of the House of Representatives their written declaration that the President is unable to discharge the powers and duties of his office, the Vice President shall immediately assume the powers and duties of the office as Acting President.

Thereafter, when the President transmits to the President pro tempore of the Senate and the Speaker of the House of Representatives his written declaration that no inability exists, he shall resume the powers and duties of his office unless the Vice President and a majority of either the principal officers of the executive departments or of such other body as Congress may by law provide, transmit within four days to the President pro tempore of the Senate and the Speaker of the House of Representatives their written declaration that the President is unable to discharge the powers and duties of his office. Thereupon Congress shall decide the issue, assembling within forty-eight hours for that purpose if not in session. If the Congress, within twenty-one days after receipt of the latter written declaration, or, if Congress is not in session, within twenty-one days after Congress is required to assemble, determines by two-thirds vote of both Houses that the President is unable to discharge the powers and duties of his office, the Vice-President shall continue to discharge the same as Acting President; other-wise, the President shall resume the powers and duties of his office. [February 10, 1967]

AMENDMENT XXVI.

SECTION. 1. The right of citizens of the United States, who are eighteen years of age or older, to vote shall not be denied or abridged by the United States or by any State on account of age.

SECTION. 2. The Congress shall have power to enforce this article by appropriate legislation. [June 30, 1971]

AMENDMENT XXVII.

No law, varying the compensation for the services of the Senators and Representatives shall take effect, until an election of Representatives shall have intervened. [May 8, 1992]

PRESIDENTIAL ELECTIONS, 1884–2012

Year	Number of States	Candidates	Parties	Popular Vote	% of Popular Vote	Electoral Vote	% Voter Participation
1884	38	**GROVER CLEVELAND**	DEMOCRAT	4,879,507	48.5	219	77.5
		James G. Blaine	Republican	4,850,293	48.2	182	
		Benjamin F. Butler	Greenback-Labor	175,370	1.8		
		John P. St. John	Prohibition	150,369	1.5		
1888	38	**BENJAMIN HARRISON**	REPUBLICAN	5,447,129	47.9	233	79.3
		Grover Cleveland	Democrat	5,537,857	48.6	168	
		Clinton B. Fisk	Prohibition	249,506	2.2		
		Anson J. Streeter	Union Labor	146,935	1.3		
1892	44	**GROVER CLEVELAND**	DEMOCRAT	5,555,426	46.1	277	74.7
		Benjamin Harrison	Republican	5,182,690	43.0	145	
		James B. Weaver	People's	1,029,846	8.5	22	
		John Bidwell	Prohibition	264,133	2.2		
1896	45	**WILLIAM McKINLEY**	REPUBLICAN	7,102,246	51.0	271	79.3
		William J. Bryan	Democrat	6,492,559	47.0	176	
1900	45	**WILLIAM McKINLEY**	REPUBLICAN	7,218,491	52.0	292	73.2
		William J. Bryan	Democrat	6,356,734	46.0	155	
		John C. Wooley	Prohibition	208,914	1.5		
1904	45	**THEODORE ROOSEVELT**	REPUBLICAN	7,628,461	56.4	336	65.2
		Alton B. Parker	Democrat	5,084,223	37.6	140	
		Eugene V. Debs	Socialist	402,283	3.0		
		Silas C. Swallow	Prohibition	258,536	1.9		
1908	46	**WILLIAM H. TAFT**	REPUBLICAN	7,675,320	52.0	321	65.4
		William J. Bryan	Democrat	6,412,294	43.4	162	
		Eugene V. Debs	Socialist	420,793	2.8		
		Eugene W. Chafin	Prohibition	253,840	1.7		

Year	Number of States	Candidates	Parties	Popular Vote	% of Popular Vote	Electoral Vote	% Voter Participation
1912	48	**WOODROW WILSON**	DEMOCRAT	6,296,547	41.9	435	58.8
		Theodore Roosevelt	Progressive	4,118,571	27.4	88	
		William H. Taft	Republican	3,486,720	23.2	8	
		Eugene V. Debs	Socialist	900,672	6.0		
		Eugene W. Chafin	Prohibition	206,275	1.4		
1916	48	**WOODROW WILSON**	DEMOCRAT	9,127,695	49.4	277	61.6
		Charles E. Hughes	Republican	8,533,507	46.2	254	
		A. L. Benson	Socialist	585,113	3.2		
		J. Frank Hanly	Prohibition	220,506	1.2		
1920	48	**WARREN G. HARDING**	REPUBLICAN	16,153,115	60.6	404	49.2
		James M. Cox	Democrat	9,133,092	34.3	127	
		Eugene V. Debs	Socialist	915,490	3.4		
		P. P. Christensen	Farmer-Labor	265,229	1.0		
1924	48	**CALVIN COOLIDGE**	REPUBLICAN	15,719,921	54.0	382	48.9
		John W. Davis	Democrat	8,386,704	29.0	136	
		Robert M. La Follette	Progressive	4,832,532	16.5	13	
1928	48	**HERBERT C. HOOVER**	REPUBLICAN	21,437,277	58.2	444	56.9
		Alfred E. Smith	Democrat	15,007,698	40.9	87	
1932	48	**FRANKLIN D. ROOSEVELT**	DEMOCRAT	22,829,501	57.7	472	56.9
		Herbert C. Hoover	Republican	15,760,684	39.8	59	
		Norman Thomas	Socialist	884,649	2.2		
1936	48	**FRANKLIN D. ROOSEVELT**	DEMOCRAT	27,757,333	60.8	523	61.0
		Alfred M. Landon	Republican	16,684,231	36.6	8	
		William Lemke	Union	892,267	2.0		
1940	48	**FRANKLIN D. ROOSEVELT**	DEMOCRAT	27,313,041	54.9	449	62.5
		Wendell L. Willkie	Republican	22,348,480	44.9	82	
1944	48	**FRANKLIN D. ROOSEVELT**	DEMOCRAT	25,612,610	53.5	432	55.9
		Thomas E. Dewey	Republican	22,017,617	46.0	99	

Year	Number of States	Candidates	Parties	Popular Vote	% of Popular Vote	Electoral Vote	% Voter Participation
1948	48	**HARRY S. TRUMAN**	DEMOCRAT	24,179,345	49.7	303	53.0
		Thomas E. Dewey	Republican	21,991,291	45.3	189	
		J. Strom Thurmond	States' Rights	1,176,125	2.4	39	
		Henry A. Wallace	Progressive	1,157,326	2.4		
1952	48	**DWIGHT D. EISENHOWER**	REPUBLICAN	33,936,234	55.1	442	63.3
		Adlai E. Stevenson	Democrat	27,314,992	44.4	89	
1956	48	**DWIGHT D. EISENHOWER**	REPUBLICAN	35,590,472	57.6	457	60.6
		Adlai E. Stevenson	Democrat	26,022,752	42.1	73	
1960	50	**JOHN F. KENNEDY**	DEMOCRAT	34,226,731	49.7	303	62.8
		Richard M. Nixon	Republican	34,108,157	49.6	219	
1964	50	**LYNDON B. JOHNSON**	DEMOCRAT	43,129,566	61.0	486	61.9
		Barry M. Goldwater	Republican	27,178,188	38.4	52	
1968	50	**RICHARD M. NIXON**	REPUBLICAN	31,785,480	43.2	301	60.9
		Hubert H. Humphrey	Democrat	31,275,166	42.6	191	
		George C. Wallace	American Independent	9,906,473	12.9	46	
1972	50	**RICHARD M. NIXON**	REPUBLICAN	47,169,911	60.7	520	55.2
		George S. McGovern	Democrat	29,170,383	37.5	17	
		John G. Schmitz	American Independent	1,099,482	1.4		
1976	50	**JIMMY CARTER**	DEMOCRAT	40,830,763	50.0	297	53.5
		Gerald R. Ford	Republican	39,147,793	48.0	240	
1980	50	**RONALD REAGAN**	REPUBLICAN	43,904,153	50.9	489	52.6
		Jimmy Carter	Democrat	35,483,883	41.1	49	
		John B. Anderson	Independent	5,720,060	6.6		
		Ed Clark	Libertarian	921,299	1.1		
1984	50	**RONALD REAGAN**	REPUBLICAN	54,455,075	58.8	525	53.1
		Walter F. Mondale	Democrat	37,577,185	40.5	13	
1988	50	**GEORGE H. BUSH**	REPUBLICAN	48,886,097	53.4	426	50.1
		Michael Dukakis	Democrat	41,809,074	45.6	111	

Year	Number of States	Candidates	Parties	Popular Vote	% of Popular Vote	Electoral Vote	% Voter Participation
1992	50	**BILL CLINTON**	DEMOCRAT	44,909,326	42.9	370	55.0
		George H. Bush	Republican	39,103,882	37.4	168	
		H. Ross Perot	Independent	19,741,657	18.9		
1996	50	**BILL CLINTON**	DEMOCRAT	47,402,357	49.2	379	49.0
		Bob Dole	Republican	39,198,755	40.7	159	
		H. Ross Perot	Reform Party	8,085,402	8.4		
2000	50	**GEORGE W. BUSH**	REPUBLICAN	50,455,156	47.9	271	50.4
		Albert Gore	Democrat	50,992,335	48.4	266	
		Ralph Nader	Green Party	2,882,738	2.7		
2004	50	**GEORGE W. BUSH**	REPUBLICAN	62,040,610	50.7	286	56.2
		John F. Kerry	Democrat	59,028,111	48.3	251	
2008	50	**BARACK H. OBAMA**	DEMOCRAT	66,882,230	52.9	365	56.8
		John S. McCain	Republican	58,343,671	45.7	173	
2012	50	**BARACK H. OBAMA**	DEMOCRAT	62,611,250	51.1	332	53.6
		W. Mitt Romney	Republican	59,134,475	47.2	206	

Candidates receiving less than 1 percent of the popular vote have been omitted. Thus, the percentage of popular vote given for any election year may not total 100 percent. Before the passage of the Twelfth Amendment in 1804, the electoral college voted for two presidential candidates; the runner-up became vice president.

ADMISSION OF STATES, 1889–1959

ORDER OF ADMISSION	STATE	DATE OF ADMISSION
39	North Dakota	November 2, 1889
40	South Dakota	November 2, 1889
41	Montana	November 8, 1889
42	Washington	November 11, 1889
43	Idaho	July 3, 1890
44	Wyoming	July 10, 1890
45	Utah	January 4, 1896
46	Oklahoma	November 16, 1907
47	New Mexico	January 6, 1912
48	Arizona	February 14, 1912
49	Alaska	January 3, 1959
50	Hawaii	August 21, 1959

POPULATION OF THE UNITED STATES, 1890–2010

YEAR	NUMBER OF STATES	POPULATION	% INCREASE	POPULATION PER SQUARE MILE
1890	44	62,947,714	25.5	21.1
1900	45	75,994,575	20.7	25.6
1910	46	91,972,266	21.0	31.0
1920	48	105,710,620	14.9	35.6
1930	48	122,775,046	16.1	41.2
1940	48	131,669,275	7.2	44.2
1950	48	150,697,361	14.5	50.7
1960	50	179,323,175	19.0	50.6
1970	50	203,235,298	13.3	57.5
1980	50	226,504,825	11.4	64.0
1985	50	237,839,000	5.0	67.2
1990	50	250,122,000	5.2	70.6
1995	50	263,411,707	5.3	74.4
2000	50	281,421,906	6.8	77.0
2005	50	296,410,404	5.3	81.7
2010	50	308,745,538	4.2	87.4

Unemployment Rate, 1890–2013

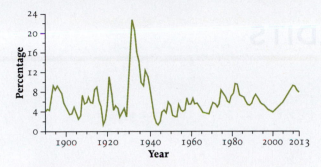

Union Membership as a Percentage of Nonagricultural Employment, 1880–2012

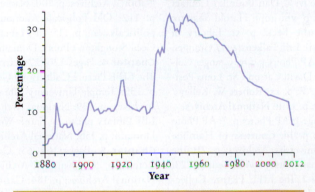

CREDITS

PHOTOGRAPHS

Preface: Page iv: © Dan Budnik / Contact Press Images; p. viii (top): Harold Shapiro; (bottom): Laurie Beck; p. xi: Library of Congress; p. xii: Erik Falkensteen / Granger, NYC; p. xiii: AP Photo; p. xiv: Granger Collection; p. xv: David Carson / St. Louis Post-Dispatch via AP; p. xx: Robert W. Kelley / Getty Images; p. xxiii: National Archives.

Chapter 1: Page 1: AP Photo; p. 7: AP Photo / Pool / Life; p. 14: Courtesy of Hamline University, University Archives; p. 21: The Harry S. Truman Library and Museum; p. 23: Francis Miller / The LIFE Picture Collection / Getty Images; p. 32: The Harry S. Truman Library and Museum; p. 36: National Archives.

Chapter 2: Pages 42–43: J. R. Eyerman / The LIFE Picture Collection / Getty Images; p. 45: Smith College Archives; p. 53: National Archives; p. 61: Courtesy Lemuel R. Boulware papers, Kislak Center for Special Collections, Rare Books and Manuscripts, University of Pennsylvania; p. 63: Nina Leen / ime Life Pictures/Getty Images; p. 78: Temple University Libraries, Special Collections Research Center.

Chapter 3: Pages 84–85: Robert W. Kelley / Getty Images; p. 94: Bettmann / Corbis; p. 97:

National Archives; p. 100: National Archives; p. 112: Old Politicals Auctions, www.old politicals.com; p. 115: LBJ Library photo by Cecil Stoughton / Public Domain.

Chapter 4: Pages 126–27: Larry Burrows / The LIFE Picture Collection / Getty Images; p. 135: Temple University Libraries, Urban Archives; p. 139: National Archives; p. 141: LBJ Library photo by Frank Wolfe / Public Domain; p. 156: National Archives.

Chapter 5: Pages 164–65: Granger Collection; p. 173: National Archives; p. 180: National Archives; p. 184: Carmen Roberts papers, Folder Photos; Bentley Historical Library, University of Michigan; p. 187: Photo: © Bettye Lane / Schlesinger Library on the History of Women in America, Radcliffe Institute; p. 191: Library of Congress.

Chapter 6: Pages 204–05: © Lisa Kahane, NYC, All Rights Reserved; p. 211: National Archives; p. 219: EPA / National Archives; p. 221: AP Photo; p. 224: Walter P. Reuther Library, Wayne State University; p. 226: EPA / National Archives; p. 229: Bettmann / Corbis.

Chapter 7: Pages 244–45: National Archives; p. 247: AP Photo / Ben Margot; p. 261: Reuters / Corbis; p. 271: Courtesy

Ronald Reagan Library; p. 275: George Bush Presidential Library and Museum; p. 279: National Archives / K. A. Sevie.

Chapter 8: Pages 296–97: David Carson / St. Louis Post-Dispatch via AP; p. 299: Jason Reed / Reuters / Corbis; p. 313: National Archives; p. 315: National Archives / TSGT Jerry Morrison, Jr., USAF; p. 318: AP Photo / Eric Gay; p. 321: AP Photo / Ben Margot; p. 330: Jonathan Ernst / Reuters / Landov.

TEXT

Robert Carter: "Boys Going Nowhere," by Robert Carter, from *The New Republic*, Vol. 74, March 8, 1933, 92–95. © 1933 *The New Republic*. All rights reserved. Used by permission and protected by the Copyright Laws of the United States. The printing, copying, redistribution, or retransmission of this Content without express written permission is prohibited. www.newrepublic.com

Chuck Collins: "The 99 Percent Spring," by Chuck Collins. Inequality.org, April 3, 2012. Content Licensed under CC by 3.0.

William Galston and Elaine Ciulla Kamarck: Excerpts from *The Politics of Evasion: Democrats and the Presidency* (Washington, DC: Progressive Policy Institute, 1989). Reprinted by permission of the Progressive Policy Institute.

Ed Gillespie and Bob Schellhas (eds.): Excerpt from *Contract with America: The Bold Plan by Rep. Newt Gingrich, Rep. Dick Armey and the House Republicans to Change the Nation* (New York: Times Books, 1994). Copyright © 1994 by the Republican National Committee. Reprinted by permission of the Republican National Committee.

Pete Hamill: "The Revolt of the White Lower Middle Class," by Pete Hamill. Originally published in *New York Magazine*, April 14, 1969. Reprinted by permission of International Creative Management.

Harry Henderson: "The Mass Produced Suburbs," by Harry Henderson. Copyright © 1953 *Harper's Magazine*. All rights reserved. Reproduced from the November issue by special permission.

Langston Hughes: "Jim Crow's Last Stand" from *The Collected Poems of Langston Hughes* by Langston Hughes, edited by Arnold Rampersad with David Roessel, Associate Editor. Copyright © 1994 by the Estate of Langston Hughes. Used by permission of Alfred A. Knopf, an imprint of the Knopf Doubleday Publishing Group, a division of Penguin Random House LLC. All rights reserved. Additional rights by permission of Harold Ober Associates Incorporated.

Joseph S. Kalinowski: "Politics and Policy— The Truth about Income Inequality," by Joseph S. Kalinowski. *Tea Party Tribune*, October 4, 2012. Reprinted by permission of the *Tea Party Tribune*.

League of Women Voters of California: Excerpts from "Yes ERA! Equal Rights Action Kit," February 1974, are reprinted by permission of the League of Women Voters of California.

Edward Levinson: "Labor on the March," by Edward Levinson. Copyright © 1937 *Harper's Magazine*. All rights reserved. Reproduced from the May issue by special permission.

John Lewis: Excerpts from speech written for the March on Washington, August 28, 1963, by John Lewis. Reprinted by permission of John Lewis.

Alain Locke: "Negro Youth Speaks," reprinted with the permission of Scribner, a Division of Simon & Schuster, Inc., from *The New Negro* by Alain Locke. Copyright © 1925 by Albert & Charles Boni, Inc. All rights reserved.

The New York Times: "Our Peaceful Revolution," from *The New York Times*, January 20, 1924. © 1924 *The New York Times*. All rights reserved. Used by permission and protected by the Copyright Laws of the United States. The printing, copying, redistribution, or retransmission of this Content without express written permission is prohibited.

The New York Times: "Levittown Incident," from *The New York Times*, August 26, 1957. © 1957 *The New York Times*. All rights reserved. Used by permission and protected by the Copyright Laws of the United States. The printing, copying, redistribution, or retrans-

Paul Potter: Excerpts from "Naming the System," speech delivered by Paul Potter, April 17, 1965. Reprinted by permission of the Estate of Paul Potter.

A. Philip Randolph: Excerpts from "Call to Negro America to March on Washington for Jobs and Equal Participation in National Defense," *Black Worker* 14, May 1941. Reprinted by permission of the A. Phillip Randolph Institute.

Phyllis Schlafly: "What's Wrong with Equal Rights for Women?" *Phyllis Schlafly Report* 5, no. 7 (February 1972). Reprinted by permission of Phyllis Schlafly.

Studs Terkel: Interview with Gary Bryner, President GM Local 1114, Lordstown GM Plant, from Studs Terkel, *Working* (New York: Avon Books, 1975), pp. 256–65. Reprinted by permission of International Creative Management.

INDEX